THE RANGE OF RELIGION

THE RANGE OF RELIGION

AN INTRODUCTORY READER

Edited by

Denise Lardner Carmody
John Tully Carmody
University of Tulsa

Macmillan Publishing Company

New York

Editors: Margaret Barbieri and Patrick Shriner
Production Supervisor: Jane O'Neill
Production Manager: Muriel Underwood
Text and Cover Designer: Blake Logan
Photo Researcher: Chris Migdol

This book was set in Galliard by V & M Graphics
and was printed and bound by R. R. Donnelley & Sons, Company.
The cover was printed by Phoenix Color Corp.

Macmillan Publishing Company
866 Third Avenue, New York, New York 10022

Macmillan Publishing Company is part of
the Maxwell Communication Group of Companies.

Library of Congress Cataloging-in-Publication Data

The range of religion : an introductory reader / edited by Denise
    Lardner Carmody, John Tully Carmody.
        p.   cm.
     ISBN 0-02-319391-3 (pbk.)
      1. Religion.   2. Religions.   I. Carmody, Denise Lardner, 1935–
    II. Carmody, John Tully, 1939–
    BL50.R34   1992
    291—dc20   91-21864
                         CIP
Printing: 1 2 3 4 5 6 7   Year: 2 3 4 5 6 7 8

iv

PREFACE

This reader introduces religion. We envision it as most suitable for an "Introduction to Religion" course, though it might also serve for a course in "Introduction to World Religions." As we explain in the Introduction, the selections illustrate main architectural or skeletal features of religion—the major concerns that most of the traditions exhibit. The selections chosen come from the full span of world religions.

We have stressed contemporary reports about religious phenomena, contemporary explanations, and classical texts. Having beginning college students in mind, we have also stressed vivid, interesting narratives. Finally, we have focused on Christianity and Judaism, thinking those traditions the likeliest bridges to Asian and oral religions.

Our thanks to Helen McInnis of Macmillan Publishing Company for initiating this project, and to the following readers of the manuscript who offered helpful advice: Thor Hall, University of Tennessee at Chattanooga; Joel Mlecko, Indiana University of Pennsylvania; George E. Saint-Laurent, University of California at Fullerton; and Joel P. Brerton, University of Missouri–Columbia.

CONTENTS

PART III RELIGIOUS RITUAL   125

PART IV RELIGIOUS DOCTRINE   179

PART V RELIGIOUS ETHICS   231

PART VI RELIGIOUS COMMUNITY   287

INTRODUCTION

THE IDEA OF RELIGION

This reader collects what we hope are interesting selections regarding humanity's religious experience and reflection. As a whole, the selections convey much of what men and women have felt and thought when it came to the most basic questions in their lives. What "religion" has meant across the full span of humanity's experience is a matter of debate. Indeed, some of our selections argue with others, at least implicitly; but we have chosen them with our own understanding of religion in mind—and our own idea of what introductory courses in religious studies ought to convey. Let us explain our understanding of religion.

Many analyses of the Latin word *religio*, from which our English word *religion* comes, say that the core image is one of binding. Religion, then, is first what binds people—to their native culture, to their core values, to their ancient gods, to their way of handling the mysteriousness of human existence. Thus, religion has a cultural connotation: we Romans (or Greeks, or Hindus, or Chinese) are who we are because of our sacred beliefs (myths, rituals, traditions). Second, religion also has an ethical connotation: here are our mores, the way that we think people ought to behave, our sense of right and wrong, good and evil. Third, religion has a theological connotation: we are who we are because of the sacred powers that we worship, the deities that we believe are responsible for the world. Last, religion has a mystical connotation: this is our equipment for handling the most basic truth about ourselves as human beings—our ignorance of our full context and our final destiny, and so our need to live by faith.

All four of these connotations of the term *religion* have much to be said for them, as no doubt do other connotations that one could bring forward. The last connotation intrigues us the most, however, so it has been most influential in our selections. We have sought selections that would make religion mysterious, because many people who have lived religiously have found their experiences and beliefs mysterious. The myths and rituals through which they have handled what they could never comprehend fully have been the staff of their lives, far more important than the material possessions they accumulated. To be religious, traditionally, has been to live in a world of wonders, a reality much richer than what nonreligious people (if there could be such) experienced or appreciated. For the world was alive, and its every breath was significant. Nothing stood for only itself. Everything pointed beyond, to the fuller depth of the creative power on which the entire cosmos depended.

When religious traditions became complicated and well organized, they tended to limit, even to try to control, this sense of wonder. In the name of good order, or respect for past practices, religious leaders wanted the ceremonies to follow regular patterns, wanted the beliefs to stand foursquare and tidy. Usually larger communities worked out clear social arrangements so that everyone knew who held authority and what each person's place and role was. But even highly organized religious bodies could not control their religion completely. Even communities that mapped out each inch of social power or doctrinal content ran into the ultimate mysteriousness of human existence and so were surprised now and then.

One guarantee of surprises was the brute fact that all people died. This fact was so brutal that, in one sense, it was no surprise. On the other hand, no two deaths were the same. Nobody knew for sure when death would come, or how it would come, or what finale it would write to the dying person's life story. Nobody knew for sure what happened after death, although all peoples developed pictures. Moreover, the fact that all people died made the fact that all people had been born, and for the moment were surviving, things one could not take for granted. Nothing was more commonplace than beginning life as an infant, and yet somehow each infant was a miracle.

Another guarantee that human existence would be surprising, mysterious, came from human ignorance. Nobody knew everything there was to know. Nobody had all the answers, especially when it came to questions about life and death, good and evil. The people who knew the most, usually because they were bright and had lived a long time, were very helpful, but something in the nature of being human limited their helpfulness. They could not live other peoples' lives for them. All people had to learn for themselves that the bright fire is painful to touch, that romantic love comes like a kick in the stomach, that even the strongest friend is fragile—could fall tomorrow to an accident, or a temptation. No matter how clearly or how often wise elders offered lessons in these truths, they became "my" truth only when I had experienced them. There is no substitute for experience. In hunting, gathering, ritual, sex, prayer, parenting, swimming—in all aspects of life, ordinary and extraordinary, seeing is believing, knowing is feeling.

We could elaborate, offering further reasons why the mysteriousness of the human condition has continued to keep all human beings alert and has ensured that religion never became completely routine, but the point should be clear. Religion finally lodges in the wellsprings of the human spirit, more fundamental even than the mind and the heart. At the wellsprings, people find that they have to contemplate their situation as a whole. They cannot name everything piecemeal. They cannot imagine every ramification or love every beauty. But they can still their spirits and make themselves present to the sweep of reality as a whole. They can open the depths of themselves to the mysteriousness of their condition and let it teach them things they can never understand yet would be willing to die for.

Many of the reports that religious people have sent back from the journeys most important to them have been contemplative in this way. Such people have used images and ideas, because they have had to, yet they have also said that they could never describe adequately what they experienced. Strangely, however, they have been content with this failure, because what they experienced reconciled them to the imperfections of human understanding. It is not necessary to understand everything. There are wonderful things that are best kept mysterious.

Why? Because by their very mysteriousness such things assure us that life is never just boring or matter-of-fact. Much of human existence has always been boring: the chores one must do to eat and stay warm, minding the children, even the daily worries to negotiate. But because people could drop out of what was boring, following imagination, or thought, or imageless spirit in search of more real and interesting possibilities, their boredom never became oppressive. Most traditional cultures expected people to fulfill their practical responsibilities but also to "travel" in dreams or contemplation to richer realms of experience.

What some influential historians of religion have called "the sacred" is precisely this richer realm of experience. The myths and rituals of traditional peoples have been pathways to sights, sounds, powers, possibilities, that seemed more meaningful than their daily chores. Indeed, the myths and rituals have made their daily chores more significant, casting over them some of the glow of sacredness. Hunting, gathering, studying, raising children, eating, making love—all could become sacraments: signs of ultimate meaning, possible encounters with ultimate reality.

So we suggest that readers attend to these selections on two levels, or at two pitches. First, let the spokesperson have his or her say, in his or her own terms. But, second, listen for the notes of excitement, or urgency, or conviction that appear when the person verges upon what is sacred or ultimate—most mysterious. In this second sort of listening, let the mysteriousness of the reality that is exciting the person play in your own mind—even in your own heart, if that appeals to you. Then, you may begin to understand why religion has been so important throughout human history. As the most profound source of spiritual excitement, refreshment, and consolation, religion has made being human a wonderful calling.

THE RANGE OF RELIGION

When editors compile a reader to introduce religion well, they must consider the different aspects of religion that ought to be represented as well as the different traditions that have arisen around the globe and the different historical forms through which those traditions have developed. Thus any anthology is both an expression of the editors' prejudices and a compromise. In itself, religion ranges almost endlessly—into every geographical area, into every temporal period, into so many uses of the human body, mind, imagination, social instinct, artistic genius, and all the rest that no library could contain all the studies that the full range of religion, actual and potential, would require. The best that a single volume can offer is a good representation—something interesting, balanced, and meaty enough to provide solid nourishment.

We have gathered selections under eight different headings, and we have stressed two sorts of literature. The eight headings are religious experience, mythology, ritual, doctrine, ethics, community, recent movements, and views of faith and the nature of religion. The two sorts of literature are contemporary reports and classical writings, many of the latter "scriptures."

We begin, in Part I, with selections focused on religious experience. The three we have chosen represent Zen Buddhist enlightenment, Christian mysticism, and shamanic vision. These three reports stand for the limitless ways that human beings have had their lives changed by extraordinary experiences. In each instance, reality has become more intense, richer, more wonderful than what the people involved had appreciated until then. And because the accent in these writings is experiential—what people have actually seen, felt, undergone—one can realize that the roots of religion are always concrete and personal. Ideas are always secondary, trying to catch up with what the founders, great saints, or even simple laypeople of a given tradition have heard or suffered in their own flesh and spirit.

Part II deals with mythology. Religious people tend to represent their most sacred convictions through traditional stories. That is how they speak to themselves about how the world began, or where the human spirit goes at death, or what it means to be an adult man or woman. That is how they initiate their children into their worldview, their sense of reality. The four selections come from an African tribal elder, a famous Hindu epic poem, a Hindu classic, and the Christian New Testament. Each narrates things that are only parts of the bigger, overall story that the people in question have used to make their way in the world. Each orients the time of the telling to the more significant, special time of the story itself, which is the time of the gods—the beings responsible for the world in which human beings find themselves.

Just as myths take people into sacred time, so rituals take them into sacred space. One cannot rigidly separate myths and rituals because myths usually provide the stories that rituals enact, and rituals bring myths fully alive so that people can sing and dance themselves into the sacred reality that the myths describe. The selections for Part III, on ritual, offer Native American, Muslim, and Jewish examples of traditional patterned actions through which people have tried to satisfy their religious need to move into sacred reality.

Part IV, focusing on doctrine, suggests how people have presented the concepts, ideas, and master images they have used to think about ultimate reality. It is hard to separate doctrine from myth, but in general doctrine is less tied to stories and less geared toward ritual, more tied to speculation and teaching. The selections illustrate ancient Chinese views of the Way (Tao) running through the world, Muslim views of how women and men should interact, and Jewish views of the nature of God. Each of these selections comes from a holy book and so is considered authoritative by the tradition that it represents.

Part V, dealing with ethics, suggests how religious traditions have dealt with the question of proper behavior. The first four selections come from classical sources, Buddhist, Chinese, and Hindu. The fifth selection comes from a contemporary Christian textbook. All five convey the importance of practice—doing what the tradition says one ought to do, acting on one's religious commitments. All five also intimate the difficulty of making religious commitment practical. Whereas doctrines can remain ideal, living out one's commitments can be messy, forcing one into a world more gray than black and white.

Part VI deals with community. Everywhere, human beings have shown themselves to be social—primed to form communities. This has been true in all religious traditions, so all have had to deal with questions of politics, power, and self-understanding. The selections bear on Christian, Jewish, Hindu, and Muslim senses of community. Three of these selections come from contemporary sources and suggest how modernity has impinged on the question of people's living together as adherents of the same faith (myths, rituals, doctrines, ethical precepts). The fourth selection is from the Qur'an.

Part VII samples recent religious movements—phenomena that illustrate the special concerns or problems that religion has faced since the middle of the twentieth century. For example, the material on Goddess religion suggests the needs of contemporary women that have led some to investigate the pre-Christian traditions of ancient Europe, where much worship focused on a goddess venerated in nature. We also present reports on recent Muslim fundamentalism in Iran, Latin American theology of liberation, and Jewish struggles with the Holocaust.

Part VIII offers views of faith and the nature of religion. Here we have been especially interested in challenges to traditional faith. We have also presented theories of religion that analyze it from outside (without formal commitment to the given religious tradition). The selection from Albert Camus, an atheistic existentialist, shows how human suffering can raise doubts about God. The selection from William James, an American pragmatist, suggests that religion is a defensible way to deal with what is not rational. Albert Einstein describes the relation between religion and natural science, and Rudolf Otto, an influential historian of religion, describes the mysteriousness at the core of the experience of what is most ultimate, real, and so holy.

In passing, we have noted that most of the selections are either contemporary or classical. That is, most come from present-day (or recent) writers or from texts traditionally considered especially authoritative. We can also note that the selections span all the major world religions: Hinduism, Buddhism, Chinese traditions, Judaism, Christianity, and Islam, and some bear on oral (nonwriting) traditions of peoples of North America, South America, and

Africa. The majority of the selections come from insiders , but some represent the views of people outside the tradition in question.

Space limitations have not allowed us to offer a full range of examples that would show the historical progression of any tradition, let alone of all the major traditions. We have decided to emphasize selections that would show what religion has meant recently, and what it has looked like in classical (scriptural, canonical) form. Ideally, many readers will be moved to study more historical sources on their own.

PART I

RELIGIOUS EXPERIENCE

Temple of the Golden Pavilion (Zen), Kyoto
(Photo by J. T. Carmody)

INTRODUCTION

In this part we present accounts of intense Zen Buddhist, Christian, and shamanic experience. Our assumption is that all the major religious bodies have encouraged intense experience, depending on it for the personal conviction without which any tradition becomes hollow. Thus, we might have offered accounts of Hindu meditative experience, or Muslim experience at prayer, or Taoist experience of exorcism, or Jewish experience dancing with the scrolls of Torah (Guidance). Each selection that we do offer is shaped thoroughly by the conceptual framework of the tradition in which it occurs, but we are interested in it as much for its typical qualities—how it focuses needs, hopes, and capacities that we find across the span of the religions—as for what is peculiar to it as Zen Buddhist, or Christian, or shamanic.

The Zen Buddhist whom we meet in Philip Kapleau's account of Zen belief and practice moves through a world of specific assumptions, as do Julian of Norwich, author of the Christian selection, and Michael Harner, author of the selection on shamanism. When Buddhists come to *satori* (enlightenment), as the culmination of much time spent in intense meditation, they realize what the Buddha meant when he explained why human beings suffer so much. In other words, they have their experiences within the mental confines of a specific tradition, just as Christians and shamans do. One of the most interesting things that these selections spotlight, then, is the way that given traditions color, shape, predispose, and interpret intense ("mystical") religious experiences. All three subjects move outside workaday consciousness and contend with deeper, more mysterious aspects of the self and ultimate reality, yet each experience is distinctive. Thus, Kapleau has built a career on the enlightenment that he gained in Japan in the 1950s, becoming a *roshi* (teacher) at the Zen Center in Rochester, New York.

The selection from Julian of Norwich's *Showings* presents a striking vision of the suffering Christ. Julian, a fourteenth-century English anchorite (solitary), has become well known as one of the most gifted of female medieval mystics. Her long rumination on her vision led her to simple yet profound insights into the character of sin, grace, the goodness of God, and the sufferings of Christ. Throughout, her assumptions and vocabulary are Christian, but her concern is the plight that all human beings experience: the need for salvation (profound healing). Julian warns those who pray seriously not to become discouraged. She interprets the crucifixion of Christ as a great sign of his love. Her conviction deepens that, by God's providential care, everything will turn out well. This combination of a very specific vision (of the bloody, suffering Christ) and a far-reaching intuition (everything will turn out well) marks Julian as a daring thinker. Moreover, her depiction of the motherhood of Christ (his maternal care for all those who seek his aid) has made her a favorite of contemporary feminists. Often they see in her a mystic who went beyond the patriarchal tradition that she had inherited and boldly pictured God as her heart counseled. Although there was a long-standing medieval tradition of envisioning the maternity of God, Julian made a distinctive contribution. Her *Showings* therefore implies that mystical experience is not determined by the culture that the mystic inherits. There is considerable room for individual adaptation.

Michael Harner's hallucinogenic vision reminds us that all religious experience has a bodily basis. In addition to the assumptions of the culture in question and the possible influence of "others" (forces apart from the subject of the experience), there is the impact of the subject's own physiology and chemistry. Clearly, the shamans to whom Harner apprenticed himself knew from experience that ingesting certain substances would alter their perception. Shamanic expertise was largely a matter of knowing how to interpret and control the visions and feelings that given substances were likely to incite. We have yet to understand, philosophically or theologically, all the implications of the "alternate realities" that people report experiencing while under the influence of drugs. Because ordinary reality is also the product of our bodily chemistry, neurology, and the like, it clarifies little to stress the bodily impact of substances that alter our vision or imagination. Shamanic experience like Harner's forces us to consider the interplay of mind and body in all perception, including that of Zen Buddhists like Kapleau and Christian mystics like Julian.

One traditional description of *yogins* (those who practice Eastern meditation), prophets, and shamans distinguishes them as focused respectively on the intellect, the will, and the imagination. Where "mystics" fit into this description remains unclear. The three selections show the problems with such a schema. Kapleau is trying to get below the mind, below dualistic thinking, to intuit the nondual character of ultimate reality. His focus on the *koan* (enigmatic saying or word) "Mu" is a way of stopping ordinary reasoning. Eventually his consciousness tips over and he perceives reality quite differently than he did when he started Zen meditation. He has been schooled by a tradition to change his sense of how the world hangs together. With this changed sense the claims of Zen become persuasive. No thing that he encounters stands apart from other things, as an independent substance; each is connected to all other things, mixing into their flow or dance. The years of struggle required to reach this point of enlightenment raise questions about ordinary, unenlightened consciousness. Why is it so ignorant? Buddhists claim that such ignorance is the source of human suffering, but why should ordinary humanity have to suffer?

We see, then, that even enlightenment does not put an end to questions. Even a technique that defeats the mind leaves many puzzles. It is true that those puzzles are different for enlightened people than for unenlightened. It is also true that Zen provides a solid basis for dismissing many questions, as does the mystical vision of a Christian contemplative like Julian. Generally speaking, the questions seem irrelevant compared to the fulfillment that the enlightened person or mystic finds in his or her key experience. Because that experience has brought a sense of wholeness, and often a sense of union with the center or ground of all reality, the questions that remain do not touch the core of what the person feels is the great issue in any life. If the goal is to gain a state of profound integration, peace, joy, and love, then questions that detract from either reaching this goal or enjoying it become secondary.

An interesting difference between Kapleau's experience and Julian's is the more obviously gratuitous character of what happens to Julian. She may have predisposed herself to her vision of the bloody Christ, but not nearly as directly or deliberately as Kapleau predisposed himself through his regime of intense meditation. Kapleau might say, after reaching enlightenment, that it came as a gift, but Julian's experience seems more unexpected. Precisely how this relates to Julian's beliefs about God, in contrast to Kapleau's unconcern about God, is hard to say. Probably the difference in their beliefs is significant.

Michael Harner has a profound experience before he enters fully into the worldview of his shaman hosts. We might say that he seems to be a visionary in search of a rationale, or at least a set of techniques that would lessen the dangers in his experience. Unlike Kapleau and Julian, he has not disciplined himself. His experience stems from a chemical supplement, rather than a regime of meditation or contemplative (loving) prayer.

We see, then, the complexities of the term *religious experience*. A great many matters can lodge under its roof. Indeed much religious experience is not as dramatic as these three examples are. Much is a question of ordinary people dedicating their days through faith in something that they cannot see or feel yet believe supplies the ultimate meaning of all that they do. This is worth bearing in mind not only when reading these three selections but also when reading selections in later parts. People listening to traditional stories or dancing traditional dances are also having significant religious experiences. So are people taking to heart traditional teachings or joining together in religious communities. Our intent in this part is to highlight especially gripping experiences, not to imply that only experiences such as these are significant.

1

Philip Kapleau
Excerpt from *The Three Pillars of Zen* *

This reading offers a description of an American businessman's attempt to reach a higher state of mental awareness through the Zen Buddhist practice of intense meditation. Through years of struggle, he discovers that nothing short of achieving a different view of reality will be necessary if he is to succeed and find peace.

MR. P. K., AN AMERICAN EX-BUSINESSMAN, AGE 46 / DIARY EXTRACTS / NEW YORK, APRIL 1, 1953 / . . . Belly aching all week, Doc says ulcers are getting worse. . . . Allergies kicking up too. . . . Can't sleep without drugs. . . . So miserable wish I had the guts to end it all.

APRIL 20, 1953 / Attended S—'s Zen lecture today. As usual, could make little sense out of it. . . . Why do I go on with these lectures? Can I ever get satori[1] listening to philosophic explanations of *prajna* and *karuna*[2] and why A isn't A and all the rest of that? What the hell is satori anyway? Even after four of S—'s books and dozens of his lectures, still don't know. I must be awfully stupid. . . . But I know this, Zen philosophy isn't ridding me of my pain or restlessness or that damn "nothing" feeling. . . .

Only last week a close friend complained: "You're forever spouting Zen philosophy, but you've hardly become more serene or considerate since you've been studying it. If anything, it's made you supercilious and condescending. . . ."

JUNE 1, 1953 / Talked with K— about Zen and Japan until two this morning. . . . Like S— he's Japanese and has practiced Zen but they have very little else in common. . . . Before meeting K— I imagined that people with satori all functioned like S—, now I see satori's not so simple, it apparently has many facets and levels. . . . Why am I hung up on satori? . . .

Pelted K— all night with: "If I go to Japan to train in Zen, can you assure me I'll be able to find some meaning in life? Will I absolutely get rid of my

---

[1] A designation for the state of mind flowing from a deep realization that, since inherently we suffer no lack, there is nothing to seek outside ourselves.

[2] Sanskrit words meaning satori-wisdom and compassion, respectively.

11

ulcers and allergies and sleeplessness? My two years of attending Zen lectures in New York have neither mitigated my constant frustration nor, if I'm to believe my friends, lessened my intellectual conceit."

K— kept repeating: "Zen's not philosophy, it's a healthy way to live! . . . If you really want to learn Buddhism in Japan and not just talk about it, your whole life will be transformed. It won't be easy, but you can rely on this: once you enter upon the Buddha's Way with sincerity and zeal, Bodhisattvas will spring up everywhere to help you. But you must have courage and faith, and you must make up your mind to realize the liberating power of your Buddha-nature no matter how much pain and sacrifice it entails. . . . "
This is the transfusion of courage I've needed.

SEPTEMBER 3, 1953 / Quit business, sold apartment furniture and car. . . . Friends' unanimous judgment: "You're mad throwing up ten thousand a year for pie in the sky!" . . . Maybe. Or maybe they're the mad ones, piling up possessions and ulcers and heart disease. . . . I suspect some of them may even envy me. . . . If I didn't need to, I wouldn't be doing it, of this I'm positive, but I *am* frightened a little. Hope it's true about life at forty. . . . Bought ticket for Japan.

TOKYO, OCTOBER 6, 1953 / How the features and mood of Japan have changed in seven years! The ghastly rubble and despairing faces have virtually disappeared. . . . Good to be back this time as a seeker instead of a carpetbagger with the Occupation. . . . Wonder what really brought me back? Was it the dignity of the Japanese, their patient endurance in the face of their untold sufferings that I marveled at? Was it the unearthly silence of Engaku Monastery and the deep peace it engendered within me whenever I strolled through its gardens or beneath its giant cryptomerias? . . .

NOVEMBER 1, 1953 / In Kyoto almost a month now. . . . P—, the American professor whom I'd met at one of S—'s lectures in New York, is teaching the history of philosophy at a Japanese university. . . . He and I have already called on five or six Zen teachers and authorities. . . . Talk talk talk! Some of these Zen men are curiously verbose for a teaching that boasts of mind-to-mind transmission and an abhorrence of concepts. Professor M—, when I reminded him of this, said: "In the beginning you have to utilize concepts to get rid of concepts." That sounds like fighting fire with oil. . . . Feeling restless again. All of yesterday toured the curio shops buying art objects. Is this what I returned to Japan for?

NOVEMBER 2, 1953 / Letter arrived today from Nakagawa-roshi, master of Ryutaku Monastery, saying yes, P— and I could spend two days there. . . . Will such a trip prove productive? Not if S— and the Zen professors in Kyoto are right: "Zen monasteries are too traditional and authoritarian for modern intellectually-minded people." . . . Anyway, it'll be a novel experience to converse with a roshi in English and may turn out a pleasant holiday. . . . P—'s wife piled us up with heavy blankets and lots of American groceries. Her Japanese friend says Zen monasteries are notoriously cold and austere. . . . What does one do in a monastery anyway? . . .

NOVEMBER 3, 1953 / Arrived at monastery at dusk. . . . During 6½-hour train trip P— and I busied ourselves framing questions to test the roshi's philosophical knowledge of Zen. "If he has an intellectual grasp of Zen," we decided, "and is not just an old-fashioned religious fanatic, we'll stay the full two days, otherwise let's leave tomorrow." . . .

Nakagawa-roshi received us in his simple, unpretentious quarters. . . . How young-looking he is, so unlike the bearded patriarch of our imaginings. . . . And so cordial and affable, he personally made us hot whipped green tea, delicious and soothing, and even joked with us in surprisingly good English. . . .

"Your long train journey must have tired you, would you like to lie down and rest?" . . . "No, we're a little tired, but if you don't mind we've prepared a number of questions on Zen we'd like to ask you." . . . "If you don't care to rest, the attendant will take you to the main hall where you can sit and meditate until I dispose of some urgent business; afterwards we can talk if you like." . . .

"But we've never meditated in our lives, we wouldn't know how to sit cross-legged.". . . "You may sit any way you like, but you must not talk. The monk attendant will provide you with sitting cushions and show you where to sit; he will call you when I can see you again.". . .

Sat—no, wriggled—wordlessly for two miserable hours in dark hall next to P—. . . . Concentration impossible, thoughts chasing each other like a pack of monkeys. . . . Excruciating pain in legs, back, and neck. . . . Desperately want to quit, but if I do before P— does, he'll never stop ragging me, nor will the roshi have a good opinion of American fortitude. . . . At last monk came and mercifully whispered: "You may see Roshi now." . . . Looked at watch, 9:30. . . .

Hobbled into the roshi's room to be greeted with his inscrutable smile and a large bowl of rice with pickles. . . . He watched us intently while we gobbled down the food, then benignly asked: "Now what would you like to know about Zen?" . . . We're so exhausted that we can only answer weakly: "Not a thing!" . . . "Then you'd better go to sleep now because we get up at 3:30 in the morning. . . . Pleasant dreams." . . .

NOVEMBER 4, 1953 / "Wake up, wake up, it's already 3:45! Didn't you hear the bells and gongs, don't you hear the drums, the chanting? Please hurry." . . .

What a weird scene of refined sorcery and idolatry: shaven-headed black-robed monks sitting motionlessly chanting mystic gibberish to the accompaniment of a huge wooden tom-tom emitting other-worldly sounds, while the roshi, like some elegantly gowned witch doctor, is making magic passes and prostrating himself again and again before an altar bristling with idols and images. . . . Is this the Zen of Tanka, who tossed a Buddha statue into the fire? Is this the Zen of Rinzai, who shouted "You must kill the Buddha"?[3] . . . The Kyoto teachers and S—were right after all. . .

After breakfast the roshi led us on an inspection tour of the monastery, set within a horseshoe of rolling hills in the quivering silence of a cultivated forest of pine, cedar, and bamboo and graced by an exquisite lotus pond—a veritable Japanese Shangri-la. . . . And what a view of Mount Fuji, the majestic sentinel in the sky! . . . If only he doesn't mar it all by insisting we bow down before those images in the halls. . . .

O my prophetic soul! . . . he's brought us into the founder's room and is lighting incense and fervently prostrating himself before a weird statue of Hakuin. . . . "You too may light incense and pay your respects to Hakuin." . . . P— looks at me and I at him, then he explodes: "The old Chinese Zen masters burned or spit on Buddha statues, why do you bow down before them?" . . . The roshi looks grave but not angry. "If you want to spit you spit, I prefer to bow." . . . We don't spit, but neither do we bow.

NOVEMBER 6, 1953 / P— left for Kyoto today, and the roshi invited me to stay on. . . . For all his religious fanaticism and unphilosophical mind he's a warm, regular guy and I like him. . . . No use fooling myself though, it's going to be rough getting up at 3:30 in the cold, living on a diet of mainly rice, and trying to meditate cross-legged. . . . Can I do it? Do I want to? . . . Still, there's something about all this that's deeply satisfying. . . . Anyway, I'm glad he invited me to stay and I've accepted. . . .

NOVEMBER 8, 1953 / Roshi says I can meditate by myself in founder's room instead of in the cold zendo. I can sit, kneel Japanese style or use a chair and wear as much clothing as I please if I'm cold. . . . Have no idea how to meditate, though. . . . When I told Roshi this he cryptically advised: "Put your mind in the bottom of your belly, there's a blind Buddha there, make him see!" . . . Is that all there is to mediation? Or is the roshi deliberately letting me stew in my own juice. . . . Carefully inspected Hakuin's features today; they're less grotesque, even faintly interesting.

---

[3] Eradicating from the mind the notion of a Buddha as opposed to an ordinary being, ridding oneself of the idea that Shakyamuni Buddha is God or a super-being, obliterating the subtle pride which arises from kensho and leads one to think, "Now I'm a Buddha"—this is killing the Buddha.

"Wash your mouth when you utter the name Buddha!" is another widely misunderstood Zen expression. It comes from the thirtieth case of *Mumonkan* in the comment of Mumon: "One who truly understands will cleanse his mouth for three days after uttering the word 'Buddha.' ..." This is not a reference to Shakyamuni Buddha the person but to Buddha-nature or Buddha-mind. Everything is complete and perfect in itself. A stick is a stick, a shovel a shovel. Use a shovel and you know its shovelness in a direct, fundamental way. But describe it as "Buddha" or "Buddha-mind" and you needlessly "sully" it, that is, add to the name "shovel" one more concept.

NOVEMBER 10, 1953 / Each morning been climbing the hill back of the main hall for a wide-screen view of Mount Fuji. . . . Yesterday skipped my meditation because of a headache and Fuji looked somber and lifeless. . . . Today after a couple of hours of good meditation in a chair it's grand and soaring again. A remarkable discovery: *I* have the power of life and death over Fuji! . . .

NOVEMBER 23, 1953 / During tea with Roshi in his room today he suddenly asked me: "How would you like to attend the rohatsu sesshin [training session] at Harada-roshi's monastery? The discipline is especially severe during this sesshin. But he is a famous roshi, a much better teacher for you than I." . . . "If you think so, sure, why not?" . . . "But my old teacher,[4] whom you met the other day, is against it: he does not approve of Harada-roshi's harsh methods for inducing satori. A Zen student he thinks should ripen slowly, then like fruit which falls from the tree when ripe, come naturally to enlightenment. . . . Let me meditate further on it.". . .

NOVEMBER 25, 1953 / Two interesting visitors at the monastery this morning, one a master called Yasutani, the other a layman named Yamada, his disciple, who said he'd been practicing Zen for some eight years. Wanted to ask him whether he had satori yet, but decided it might prove embarrassing. . . .

Asked Yasutani-roshi if he thought I could get satori in one week of sesshin. . . . "You can get it in *one day* of sesshin if you're genuinely determined to and you surrender all your conceptual thinking."

NOVEMBER 27, 1953 / "How is your meditation coming along?" Roshi suddenly asked me today. . . . "That Buddha in my belly is hopelessly blind." . . . "He is not really blind, he only seems so because he's sound asleep. . . . How would you like to try the koan Mu?" . . . "All right, if you think I should, but what do I do with it?" . . . "You know its background I suppose. . . . " "Yes." . . . "Then just keep concentrating on Joshu's answer until you intuitively realize its meaning." . . . "Will I then be enlightened?" . . . "Yes, if your understanding is not just theoretical." . . . "But how do I concentrate?" . . . "Put your mind in your hara [belly] and focus on nothing but Mu."

NOVEMBER 28, 1953 / Roshi called me into his room this morning, and beckoned me to follow him to the little altar-shrine in back. . . . "Do you see the letter I put into the hands of Kannon? You have become karmically linked with the man who wrote it; let us gassho [bow] before Kannon out of gratitude." . . . I did a gassho unthinkingly, quickly asked: "What's the letter say, who wrote it? And what do you mean 'karmically linked'?" . . . The roshi, outwardly solemn but inwardly animated, just said: "Come to my room and I will explain." . . .

[4]Gempo Yamamoto-roshi, who was retired at the time.

With his usual grace he knelt Japanese style, put the kettle on the charcoal fire for tea, then decisively announced: "I've decided to take you to the rohatsu sesshin at Hosshin-ji. This letter has decided me." . . . "Tell me what it's all about." . . . "Do you remember Yamada-san, the man who came here with Yasutani-roshi the day before yesterday? It's from him. He had a deep satori experience the very day after he left and he tells about it in this letter." . . .

"Did you say he got satori? Please translate it for me right now." . . . "There isn't time. Hosshin-ji is far from here on the Japan Sea and we must be ready to leave tomorrow. I will translate it for you on the train." . . .

NOVEMBER 29, 1953 / As our third-class train bounced along in the night Roshi slowly, carefully translated Yamada's letter. . . . What a vivid, stirring experience, and he no monk but a layman! . . . "Do you really believe it's possible for me to get satori during this sesshin?" . . . "Of course, provided you forget yourself completely." . . . "But what is satori anyway? I mean—"

"Stop!" . . . Roshi threw up his hand, flashing his inscrutable smile. "When you get it you will know, now no more questions please. Let us do zazen [meditation] and then try to get some sleep before we come to Hosshin-ji." . . .

NOVEMBER 30, 1953 / Arrived hungry and exhausted at Hosshin-ji in late afternoon. . . . Skies leaden, air cold and damp. . . . But Harada-roshi was cordial and warm, greeting me with outstretched hands. . . . Later he introduced me to the assistant roshi and four head monks. . . . Though somewhat reticent, they glow with a strong inner flame. . . .

Roshi and I retired to the small room we're to share. . . . "You'd better get some rest before the battle begins." . . . "Battle?" . . . "Yes, a battle to the death with the forces of your own ignorance. . . . I will call you when everyone assembles in the main hall for final instruction from Harada-roshi, in about an hour." . . .

Like lobsters in conclave, Harada-roshi, the assistant roshi, and four head monks in robes of scarlet brocade and arching ceremonial headdress sat on large silk pillows at one end of the hall, while four young monks each with a black-lacquer tray of gold-colored cups stood poised at the other end ready to serve them. Sandwiched between in rows facing each other across the room knelt some fifty grim lay people attired in somber traditional robes. . . . Their eyes were glued to the floor in front of them, and none stirred to look at Harada-roshi when he spoke except me. . . .

Why's everybody so tense and grim? Why do they all look as though they're steeling themselves for some terrible ordeal? True, Roshi said this would be a battle, but surely that was only a figure of speech—how does one fight his own mind? Isn't Zen *wu wei*, nonstriving? Isn't the all-embracing Buddha-nature our common possession, so why strive to acquire what is already ours? . . . Must ask Harada-roshi about this first chance I get. . . .

Back in our room Roshi summarized Harada-roshi's instructions: 1) You must not talk or bathe or shave or leave the premises during the week. 2) You must concentrate only on your own practice without diverting your eyes for any reason. 3) You as a beginner have as good a chance as old hands to attain enlightenment at this sesshin. And Roshi added sententiously: "But you must work hard, terribly hard."

DECEMBER 1, 1953 / Raining incessantly, zendo [meditation hall] uncomfortably cold and damp. . . . Wore long johns and wool shirt and two sweaters and wool robe and two pairs of wool socks but couldn't stop shivering. . . . Godo's [disciplinarian's] bellowing and roaring more of a distraction than his wallops with kyosaku [paddle]. . . . Tortured by pain in legs and back. . . . thoughts racing wildly. . . . Flopped from *agura* to *seiza* to *hanka* [postures for meditation], manipulating my three cushions in every conceivable way, but couldn't escape pain. . . .

At my first dokusan [interview with teacher] Harada-roshi drew a circle with a dot in the center. "This dot is you and the circle is the cosmos. Actually you embrace the whole cosmos, but because you see yourself as this dot, an isolated fragment, you don't experience the universe as inseparable from yourself. . . . You must break out of your self-imprisonment, you must forget philosophy and everything else, you must put your mind in your hara and breathe only Mu in and out. . . . The center of the universe is the pit of your belly! . . .

"Mu is a sword which enables you to cut through your thoughts into the realm that is the source of all thoughts and feelings. . . . But Mu is not only a means to enlightenment, it is enlightenment itself. . . . Self-realization is not a matter of step-by-step progress but the result of a leap. Until your mind is pure you cannot make this leap." . . .

"What do you mean by 'pure'?" . . . "Empty of all thoughts." . . . "But why is it necessary to struggle for enlightenment if we already have the enlightened Buddha-nature?" . . . "Can you show me this enlightened nature of yours?" . . . "Well, no, I can't, but the sutras [sermons of Buddha] say we have it, don't they?" . . . "The sutras are not your experience, they are Shakyamuni Buddha's. If you realize your Buddha-mind, you'll be a Buddha yourself."

DECEMBER 2, 1953 / At 5 a.m. dokusan told Harada-roshi the pain in my legs was agonizing. "I can't go on." . . . "Do you want a chair?" He looked at me tauntingly. . . . "No, I won't use a chair even if my legs drop off!" . . . "Good! With that spirit you're bound to become enlightened." . . .

Terrific whack by the kyosaku just when my concentration was beginning to jell and I fell apart . . . damn that godo! "Straighten your back, sit firmly, center your energy in your hara!" he yells. But how the devil do I put my energy into my hara? When I try, my back is stabbed with pain. . . . Must ask Harada-roshi about this. . . .

Throughout the burning of one stick of incense my thoughts've been entwined in the Mokkei[5] pictures I saw at the Daitoku-ji exhibition last month. That crane's so haunting, the secret of all existence lies in its eyes. It's self-creating, emerging from formlessness to form. I must reverse the process, merging again into formlessness, into non-time. I must die to be reborn. . . . Yes, that's the inner meaning of Mu! . . .

Clang, clang! the dokusan bell. . . . Harada-roshi listened impatiently, then roared: "Don't think of Mokkei's crane, don't think of form or formlessness or anything else. Think only Mu, *that's* what you're here for!"

DECEMBER 3, 1953 / Pain in legs unbearable. . . . Why don't I quit? It's imbecilic trying to sit with this gruesome pain and taking these senseless wallops of the kyosaku plus Godo's insane shouting, it's masochism pure and simple. . . . Why did I leave Ryutaku-ji, why did I ever leave the United States? . . . But I can't quit now, what will I do? I must get satori, I must. . . .

What the devil is Mu, what can it be? . . . Of course! It's an absolute prayer, the Self praying to itself. . . . How often as a student had I wanted to pray, but somehow it'd always seemed pointless and even silly to petition God for strength to cope with predicaments which He in his omniscience and omnipotence had allowed to arise in the first place. . . .

Tears welling up, how blissful is prayer for its own sake! . . . What do these tears mean? They're a sign of my helplessness, a tacit admission that my intellect, my ego, has reached the limit of its power. . . . Yes, tears are nature's benediction, her attempt to wash away the grime of ego and soften the harsh outlines of our personalities become arid and tense through an egotistic reliance on the invincibility of reason. . . .

. . . What marvelous insights, I feel so good about them! I know I've progressed. I won't be surprised if satori hits me this very night!

Crack! Crack! "Stop dreaming! Only Mu!" roars the godo, walloping me. . . .

Dokusan! . . . "No, no, no! Didn't I tell you to concentrate simply on Mu? . . . Banish those thoughts! . . . Satori's not a matter of progress or regress, haven't I told you it's a leap? . . . You are to do this and only this: put your mind in the bottom of your belly and inhale and exhale Mu. Is this clear?" . . . Why's he so harsh all of a sudden? . . . Even the hawks in the screen behind him have begun to glower at me.

DECEMBER 4, 1953 / My God, my Buddha, a chair's standing at my place! I am so grateful! . . . Roshi came and whispered: "Harada-roshi ordered the head monk to give you a chair because he felt you would never get satori sitting with a bent back and constantly shifting your position. . . . Now you have no

[5] A great Chinese Zen monk painter (Mu Ch'i) who lived in the tenth century. Most of his paintings in Japan are national treasures.

obstacles, so concentrate on Mu with all your heart and soul." . . . Concentration quickly tightened, thoughts suddenly disappeared. What a marvelous feeling this buoyant emptiness. . . .

Suddenly the sun's streaming into the window in front of me! The rain's stopped! It's become warmer! At last the gods are with me! Now I can't miss satori! . . . Mu, Mu, Mu! . . . Again Roshi leaned over but only to whisper: "You are panting and disturbing the others, try to breathe quietly." . . . But I can't stop. My heart's pumping wildly, I'm trembling from head to toe, tears are streaming down uncontrollably. . . . Godo cracks me but I hardly feel it. He whacks my neighbor and I suddenly think: "Why's he so mean, he's hurting him." . . . More tears. . . . Godo returns and clouts me again and again, shouting: "Empty your mind of every single thought, become like a baby again. Just Mu, Mu! right from your guts!"—crack, crack, crack! . . .

Abruptly I lose control of my body and, still conscious, crumple into a heap. . . . Roshi and Godo pick me up, carry me to my room and put me to bed. . . . I'm still panting and trembling. . . . Roshi anxiously peers into my face, asks: "You all right, you want a doctor?" . . . "No, I'm all right I guess." . . . "This ever happen to you before?" . . . "No, never." . . . "I congratulate you!" . . . "Why, have I got satori?" . . . "No, but I congratulate you just the same." . . . Roshi brings me a jug of tea, I drink five cups. . . .

No sooner does he leave than all at once I feel my arms and legs and trunk seized by an invisible force and locked in a huge vice which slowly begins closing. . . . Spasms of torment like bolts of electricity shoot through me and I writhe in agony. . . . I feel as though I'm being made to atone for my own and all mankind's sins. . . . Am I dying or becoming enlightened? . . . Sweat's streaming from every pore and I have to change my underclothing twice. . . . At last I fall into a deep sleep. . . .

Awoke to find a bowl of rice and soup and beans next to my sleeping mat. . . . Ate ravenously, dressed, entered the zendo. . . . Never in my life have I felt so light, opened, and transparent, so thoroughly cleansed and scoured. . . . During kinhin [strolling meditation] didn't walk but bobbed like a cork on water. . . . Couldn't resist looking out at the trees and flowers, vivid, dazzling, palpitating with life! . . . The wind soughing through the trees was the loveliest of music! . . . How deliciously fragrant the fumes of incense! . . .

Later at dokusan Harada-roshi said: "Your trembling came because you are beginning to throw off your delusions, it is a good sign. But don't pause for self-congratulation, concentrate harder yet on Mu." . . .

DECEMBER 5, 1953 / . . . Am still aglow. . . . Satori will hit me any moment now, I know it, I feel it in my marrow. . . . Won't my Zen friends in the United States be envious when I write I have satori! . . . Don't think of satori, you fool, think only of Mu! . . . Yes, Mu, Mu, Mu! . . . Damn it! I've lost it! . . . My excitement about satori has triggered off hundreds of thoughts—which leave me dispirited. . . . It's no use, satori's beyond me. . . .

DECEMBER 6, 1953 / Body tired this morning but mind's sharp and clear
. . . . Mu'd in monastery garden all night sans sleep. . . . miserably cold. . . .
Stayed up only because at dokusan Harada-roshi had chided: "You'll never get
satori unless you develop the strength and determination to do zazen all night.
Some of the sitters have been up every single night in zazen." . . .

Around midnight prostrated myself before statue of Buddha in main hall
and desperately prayed: "O God, O Buddha, please grant me satori and I'll be
humble, even bowing willingly before you. . . . " But nothing happened, no
satori. . . . Now I see the Old Fox was hoaxing me, probably trying to pry me
loose from my attachment to sleep. . . .

Shouting and clouting by Godo and his assistants getting fiercer and
fiercer, the din and tumult of the last three nights beyond belief. All but a
handful of the fifty-odd sitters have been bellowing "Mu!" continuously during the last half hour while the head monks lambasted them, yelling: "Voice
Mu from the bottom of your belly not from the top of your lungs!" . . . and
later the shrill "Mu-ing" throughout the night in the cemetery and hills, like
that of cattle being readied for slaughter. . . . I'll bet it kept the whole countryside awake. . . .

This walloping doesn't enliven me one bit. Godo must have clouted me
fifteen minutes straight last night, but it produced only a sore back and bitter
thoughts. . . . Why hadn't I grabbed his stick and given him a dose of his own
medicine? Wonder what would have happened if I had. . . .

At dokusan told Harada-roshi: "The trouble is I can't forget myself, I'm
always aware of myself as subject confronting Mu as object. . . . I focus my
mind on Mu, and when I can hang onto it I think: 'Good, now you've got it,
don't let go.' Then I tell myself: 'No, you mustn't think "Good," you must
think only Mu.' So I clench my hands, bear down with every nerve and muscle
and eventually something clicks, I know I've reached a deeper level of consciousness because no longer am I aware of inside or out, front or back.
Exhilarated, I think: 'Now I'm getting close to satori, every thought's vanished, satori'll hit me any moment.' But then I realize I can't be close to satori
so long as I'm still thinking of satori. . . . So, discouraged, my hold on Mu
loosens and Mu's gone again. . . .

"Then I have this problem. You've told me to make my mind as barren of
preconceptions as an infant's, with no self-will or ego. But how can I be free of
ego when the godo beats me furiously and urges me to strive harder and harder
and to bear down on Mu? Isn't such purposeful striving on my part an expression of ego? Instead of banishing ego it seems to me I'm bolstering it." . . .

"The mind of ego and the mind of Purity are two sides of the same reality. . . . Don't think 'This is ego,' 'This is not ego.' Just concentrate on Mu,
that's the way to realize the mind of Purity. . . . It's like a man who is starving;
he doesn't think 'I'm hungry, I must get food.' So completely absorbed in
his hunger is he that he finds something to eat without pondering. . . . If you
self-consciously think, 'I want satori, I must get satori,' you'll never get it.
But when from the bottom of your heart you have a deep yearning for Self-

realization, satori will come if, absorbing yourself wholly in Mu, you concentrate your mind and strength in your hara. . . . Mu must occupy your entire mind, resounding in your hara. . . . Don't try to anticipate satori, it comes unexpectedly. When your mind is emptied of every thought and image, anything can enlighten it: the human voice, the call of a bird... But you must have stronger faith. You must believe you have the capacity to realize your True-nature, and you must believe that what I am telling you is true and will lead to what you seek." . . .

Dokusan with the Old Lion's always a shot in the arm. . . . So once again charged into Mu, quickly exhausted my energies, and got struck not by satori but by a barrrage of thoughts. . . . I'm stymied. . . . If I push hard, I soon tire and my body and mind wilt. But if I don't dig in, Godo whacks me or else yanks me off my seat and shoves me into dokusan. When I appear before Harada-roshi he asks, "Why do you come when you can't show me Mu?" or else he bawls me out for my half-heartedness. . . . Are they trying to drive my *thoughts* out of my mind or to drive *me* out of my mind? They're deliberately trying to create an artificial neurosis. . . . Why don't I quit?

. . . Crash, bang! . . . the whole zendo is shaking, what's happened? . . . Shouldn't have, but turned my head to see. . . . The Old Lion has just broken the longest kyosaku in the zendo across the back of Monju's shrine. . . . "You're all lazy!" he yells, "You have within your grasp the most precious experience in the world, yet you sit dreaming. Wake up and throw your lives into the struggle, otherwise satori will elude you forever!" . . . What strength of spirit, what power in that frail five-foot-three, 84-year-old body!

DECEMBER 7, 1953 / Too exhausted to sit up with the others last night. Might just as well have, though, their raucous "Mu-ing" throughout the night kept me awake anyway. . . . Roshi says this last day is crucial and not to weaken. . . . But my do-or-die spirit's gone, the race is over and I'm just an also-ran. . . .

Watched, chagrined and envious, as the three "winners" marched around the zendo, bowed down before Harada-roshi, the assistant roshi, and the head monks to show their reverence and gratitude. . . . One of the fortunate had sat next to me. He'd been struck repeatedly and had blubbered all of yesterday and today. . . . Evidently he'd been crying from sheer joy when all along I imagined he was in pain.

DECEMBER 8, 1953 / Together with Nakagawa-roshi had tea with Harada-roshi after sesshin. . . . His forbidding sesshin manner's gone, he's gentle and radiant as the sun. . . . After a pleasant chat he invited us to stay for the formal ceremonies that afternoon commemorating the Buddha's enlightenment. . . .

. . . Watched in utter fascination as Harada-roshi, the assistant roshi, and ten senior monks attired in their ceremonial robes again and again prostrated themselves before the Buddha, chanted sutras, tossed their sutra books in the air, beat drums, rang bells, struck gongs, and circumambulated the main hall in a series of rituals and ceremonies to honor Shakyamuni Buddha and celebrate his immortal enlightenment experience. . . . These ceremonies glow with the living Truth which these monks have obviously all experienced in some measure. . . . Yes, through these rituals they are reaffirming their link with their great Buddhist tradition, enriching it and allowing it to enrich them so they may extend its chain into the future. . . . If I likewise embrace this tradition, I can forge my own link with Buddhism and its tremendous resources for enlightening the human mind. . . . Now I know why I tired so quickly of church and synagogue services in the United States. The priests and rabbis and ministers obviously had no intimate experience of the God they preached so glibly about, that's why their sermons and ceremonies were stale and lifeless.

JANUARY 9, 1954 / Back in Kyoto, tired, half frozen and sore but inwardly alive. . . .

JANUARY 20, 1954 / Good return to Ryutaku-ji. . . . In Kyoto, P— and I merely talked Zen, with each other and with the professors, here I practice it. . . . Though painful, practice is rejuvenating. . . . My mind's a swamp of stagnant opinions, theories, impressions, images. I've read and thought too much, experienced without feeling. I need to recover the freshness of my jaded sensibilities, to face myself honestly, nakedly. And this I can best do through zazen in the monastery.

APRIL 8, 1954 / My second Hosshin-ji sesshin is over. . . . Harada-roshi said he'd accept me as a disciple if I remain at his monastery as a lay monk. . . . "If you can cope with monastery life and gain enlightenment, you'll be master of your life instead of its slave." . . . After consultations with Nakagawa-roshi, decided to stay on indefinitely. . . .

OCTOBER 1, 1956 / . . . In just two months three years will have elapsed since I first came to Hosshin-ji. . . . So much water has flowed under the stone bridge, or should I say so many stone bridges have flowed over the motionless water? . . . Have toiled with the monks in the heat of summer and shivered with them on snowy *takuhatsu* [religious begging of food or money], felled trees, planted rice, cultivated the gardens, cleaned the outhouses, and worked in the kitchen with them. I've shared their heroic, dedicated moments, joined in their petty intrigues. . . .

Sitting sitting sitting one painful sesshin after another, then more zazen morning after morning, night after night and night into morning. . . . Dazzling insights and alluring visions have filed through my mind, but true illumination, satori, still eludes me. . . . Tangen-san, my wise monk-guide-interpreter-friend, solemnly assures me that just doing zazen wholeheartedly each day brings greater rewards in serenity, clarity and purity than does a quickly attained satori which is unnurtured by further zazen. . . . Is this a consolation prize or another of Zen's paradoxes which needs the personal experience of enlightenment to be understood? . . . He insists I've gained in fortitude and purity, though I see little evidence of it. . . .

Every one of my allergies has disappeared, my stomach pains me only occasionally, I sleep well. . . . The dark fears which formerly haunted me, my cherished dreams and hopes, all these have withered away, leaving me lighter and with a clearer sense of the real. . . . But I'm still the hungry dog next to the tank of boiling fat that is satori: I can't taste it and I can't leave it.

NOVEMBER 15, 1956 / Is it worth struggling with the cold and sparse diet through another long winter, waiting, waiting, waiting? . . . A number of my friends, the older serious monks, will soon be leaving for temples of their own. . . . I must find a master whom I can communicate with easily outside the tense atmosphere of the monastery. . . . Those same intuitions which once told me I needed to stay at Hosshin-ji now warn me it is time to leave.

NOVEMBER 23, 1956 / Left Hosshin-ji today carrying enough presents and advice to last me a long time. . . . The heart-warming farewells have dissipated whatever chill remained from those icy Obama winters.

NOVEMBER 25, 1956 / Nakagawa-roshi took me to Yasutani-roshi. . . . "He will be a good teacher for you, he is in Harada-roshi's line, his disciples are chiefly laymen, you need not stay in a monastery but can live in Kamakura and attend his sesshin in the Tokyo area."

DECEMBER 3, 1956 / Joined my first sesshin at Yasutani-roshi's mountain temple. . . . An ideal place for zazen, it nestles high in the hills away from the noises of the city. . . . A scant eight participants, probably because the sesshin's only three days and hard to get to. . . . Atmosphere's real homey, the roshi eats with us family style. . . . And what a charming twist: the godo's a 68-year-old grandmother, the cook and leader of the chanting a 65-year-old nun, between them they manage the entire sesshin! Each sits like a Buddha and acts like one—gentle, compassionate, and thoroughly aware. . . .

What a huge relief not to be driven by a savage kyosaku or verbally belted by the roshi [teacher] at dokusan. . . . The manual work after breakfast is stimulating and the afternoon bath immensely soothing. . . . Am completely at ease with Yasutani-roshi. His manner's gentle yet penetrating, he laughs easily and often.

At dokusan he told me: "For enlightenment you must have deep faith. You must profoundly believe what the Buddha and the Patriarchs from their own first-hand experience declared to be true, namely, that everything, ourselves included, intrinsically is Buddha-nature; that like a circle, which can't be added to or subtracted from, this Self-nature lacks nothing, it is complete, perfect. . . . Now, why if we have the flawless Buddha-nature are we not aware of it? Why if everything in essence is Wisdom and Purity itself is there so much ignorance and suffering in the world? . . . This is the 'doubt-mass' which must be dispersed. . . . Only if you deeply believe that the Buddha was neither a fool or a liar when he affirmed that we are all inherently Whole and Self-sufficient, can you tirelessly probe your heart and mind for the solution to this paradox." . . .

"This is what perplexes me no end: Why haven't I attained satori after three years of backbreaking effort when others who have labored neither as long nor as hard have got it? Some I know have come to kensho [enlightenment] at their very first sesshin with little or no previous zazen." . . .

"There have been a few rare souls whose minds were so pure that they could gain genuine enlightenment without zazen. The Sixth Patriarch, Eno, was such a one; he became enlightened the first time he heard the Diamond sutra recited. And Harada-roshi has related the case of a young girl student of his who got kensho during his introductory lectures the very moment he drew a circle and declared the cosmos to be indivisibly One. . . . But most have to do zazen tirelessly to win enlightenment. . . .

"Now don't feel anxious about satori, for such anxiety can be a real hindrance. . . . When you enter the world of enlightenment you take with you, so to speak, the results of all your efforts and this determines the quality of the satori; hence your satori will be wider and deeper by reason of the zazen you have done. . . . In most cases a kensho quickly attained is shallow. . . . Do zazen with zeal and satori will take care of itself." . . .

Another time he instructed me: "Zen Buddhism is based on the highest teachings of Shakyamuni Buddha. . . . In India, the very birthplace of the Buddha, Zen has practically ceased to exist, and as far as we know it is virtually extinct in China, where it was brought from India by Bodhidharma. . . . Only in Japan does it still live, though it's declining steadily; today there are probably no more than ten true masters in all Japan. . . . This unique teaching must not be lost, it must be transmitted to the West. . . . Great minds in the United States and Europe have interested themselves in Buddhism because it appeals not only to the heart but to the intellect as well. Buddhism is an eminently rational religion. . . .

"Zen you know from your own experience is not easy, but its rewards are in proportion to its difficulties. . . . Remember, Bodhidharma had to suffer hardship after hardship, and both Eisai and Dogen, who brought Zen to Japan from China, had to overcome countless obstacles. . . . Everything valuable has a high price. . . . It is your destiny to carry Zen to the West. . . . Don't quail or quit in spite of the pain and hardships.

JULY 27, 1958 / August 1 is my D-Day, the start of a one-week summer sesshin, my twentieth with Yasutani-roshi. . . . Sat two sesshins this month, one at Yasutani-roshi's temple and one at Ryutaku-ji, besides day and night zazen in my own room, all in preparation for this Big Push. . . . My mind has a rare clarity and incisiveness. I must, I will break through. . . . For the first time I'm truly convinced I can.

AUGUST 1, 1958 / . . . Sesshin's under way! . . . Quickly my concentration became strongly pitched. . . . Boring into Mu, thinking only Mu, breathing Mu. . . .

AUGUST 3, 1958 / First two days passed quickly, uneventfully. . . .

AUGUST 4, 1958 / Reached a white heat today. . . . Monitors whacked me time and again. . . . their energetic stick wielding is no longer an annoyance but a spur. . . . Raced to the line-up with each clang of the dokusan bell to be first to see the roshi. . . . Hardly aware of pain in legs. . . . Was so eager to confront him that once or twice charged into his dokusan room without waiting for his signal. . . . When he asked me to show him Mu, I spontaneously seized his fan, fanned myself, picked up his handbell, rang it, and then left. . . .

At next dokusan he again asked for Mu. Quickly raised my hand as though to smack him. Didn't intend to really hit him, but the roshi, taking no chances, ducked. . . . How exhilarating these unpremeditated movements— clean and free. . . .

Animatedly the roshi warned: "You are now facing the last and toughest barrier between you and Self-realization. This is the time one feels, in the words of an ancient master, as though he were a mosquito attacking an iron bowl. But you must bore, bore, bore, tirelessly. . . . Come what may, don't let go of Mu. . . . Do zazen all night if you feel you may lose Mu in your sleep." . . .

"Mu'd" silently in temple garden till clock struck one. . . . Rose to exercise stiff, aching legs, staggered into a nearby fence. Suddenly I realized: the fence and I are one formless wood-and-flesh Mu. Of course! . . . Vastly energized by this . . . pushed on till the 4 a.m. gong.

AUGUST 5, 1958 / Didn't intend to tell Roshi of my insight, but as soon as I came before him he demanded: "What happened last night?" . . . While I talked, his keen darting eyes X-rayed every inch of me, then slowly he began quizzing me: "Where do you see Mu? . . . How do you see Mu? . . . When do you see Mu? . . . How old is Mu? . . . What is the color of Mu? . . . What is the sound of Mu? . . . How much does Mu weigh?" . . .

Some of my answers came quickly, some haltingly. . . . Once or twice Roshi smiled, but mostly he listened in serene silence. . . . Then he spoke: "There are some roshi who might sanction such a tip-of-the-tongue taste as kensho, but—"

"I wouldn't accept sanction of such a picayune experience even if you wanted to grant it. Have I labored like a mountain these five years only to bring forth this mouse? I'll go on!" . . .

"Good! I respect your spirit."

Threw myself into Mu for another nine hours with such utter absorption that *I* completely vanished. . . . *I* didn't eat breakfast, *Mu* did. *I* didn't sweep and wash the floors after breakfast, *Mu* did. *I* didn't eat lunch, *Mu* ate. . . .

Once or twice ideas of satori started to rear their heads, but Mu promptly chopped them off. . . .

Again and again the monitors whacked me, crying: "Victory is yours if you don't relinquish your hold on Mu!" . . .

Afternoon dokusan! . . . Hawklike, the roshi scrutinized me as I entered his room, walked toward him, prostrated myself, and sat before him with my mind alert and exhilarated. . . .

"The universe is One," he began, each word tearing into my mind like a bullet. "The moon of Truth—" All at once the roshi, the room, every single thing disappeared in a dazzling stream of illumination and I felt myself bathed in a delicious, unspeakable delight. . . . For a fleeting eternity I was alone—I alone was. . . . Then the roshi swam into view. Our eyes met and flowed into each other, and we burst out laughing. . . .

"I have it! I know! There is nothing, absolutely nothing. I am everything and everything is nothing!" I exclaimed more to myself than to the roshi, and got up and walked out. . . .

At the evening dokusan Roshi again put to me some of the previous questions and added a few new ones: "Where were you born? . . . If you had to die right now, what would you do?" . . . This time my answers obviously pleased him, for he smiled frequently. But I didn't care, for now I *knew*. . . .

"Although your realization is clear," Roshi explained, "you can expand and deepen it infinitely. . . .

"There are degrees of kensho. . . . Take two people gazing at a cow, one standing at a distance, the other nearby. The distant one says: 'I know it's a cow, but I'm not sure of its color.' The other says unequivocally: 'I know it's a *brown* cow.' . . .

"Henceforth your approach to koans will be different," the roshi said, and he explained my future mode of practice. . . .

Returned to the main hall. . . . As I slipped back into my place Grandmother Yamaguchi, our part-time godo, tiptoed over to me and with eyes aglow whispered: "Wonderful, isn't it! I'm so happy for you!" . . . I resumed my zazen, laughing, sobbing, and muttering to myself: "It was before me all the time, yet it took me five years to see it." . . . A line Tangen-san had once quoted me rang in my ears: "Sometimes even in the driest hole one can find water."

AUGUST 9, 1958 / Feel free as a fish swimming in an ocean of cool, clear water after being stuck in a tank of glue. . . . and so grateful.

Grateful for everything that has happened to me, grateful to everyone who encouraged and sustained me in spite of my immature personality and stubborn nature.

But mostly I am grateful for my human body, for the privilege as a human being to know this Joy, like no other.

2

Julian of Norwich: Showings, Chapters 1–16*

Julian of Norwich was a medieval English mystic who spent much of her life contemplating the suffering of Jesus Christ. She was greatly admired for the profound insights into religious questions that resulted from her meditations. Six centuries later the scope and the surprisingly contemporary tone of some of her thoughts make them still merit attention.

CHAPTER 1

Here is a vision shown by the goodness of God to a devout woman, and her name is Julian, who is a recluse at Norwich and still alive, A.D. 1413, in which vision are very many words of comfort, greatly moving for all those who desire to be Christ's lovers.

I desired three graces by the gift of God. The first was to have recollection of Christ's Passion. The second was a bodily sickness, and the third was to have, of God's gift, three wounds. As to the first, it came into my mind with devotion; it seemed to me that I had great feeling for the Passion of Christ, but still I desired to have more by the grace of God. I thought that I wished I had been at that time with Mary Magdalen and with the others who were Christ's lovers, so that I might have seen with my own eyes our Lord's Passion which he suffered for me, so that I might have suffered with him as others did who loved him, even though I believed firmly in all Christ's pains, as Holy Church shows and teaches, and as paintings of the Crucifixion represent, which are made by God's grace, according to Holy Church's teaching, to resemble Christ's Passion, so far as human understanding can attain. But despite all my true faith I desired a bodily sight, through which I might have more knowledge of our Lord and saviour's bodily pains, and of the compassion of our Lady and of all his true lovers who were living at that time and saw his pains[1], for I would have been one of them and have suffered with them. I never desired any other sight of God or revelation, until my soul would be separated from the body, for I trusted truly that I would be saved. My inten-

* Reprinted from *Julian of Norwich: SHOWINGS*, Edmund Colledge, O.S.A. and James Walsh, S.J., Eds. © 1978 by The Missionary Society of St. Paul the Apostle in the State of New York. Used by permission of Paulist Press.

[1]The short text reads: 'and of all his true lovers who were believing in his pains, at that time and afterwards', but the long text here clearly is superior.

tion was, because of that revelation, to have had truer recollection of Christ's Passion. As to the second grace, there came into my mind with contrition—a free gift from God which I did not seek—a desire of my will to have by God's gift a bodily sickness, and I wished it to be so severe that it might seem mortal, so that I should in that sickness receive all the rites which Holy Church had to give me, whilst I myself should believe that I was dying, and everyone who saw me would think the same, for I wanted no comfort from any human, earthly life. In this sickness I wanted to have every kind of pain, bodily and spiritual, which I should have if I were dying, every fear and assault from devils, and every other kind of pain except the departure of the spirit, for I hoped that this would be profitable to me when I should die, because I desired soon to be with my God.

I desired these two, concerning the Passion and the sickness, with a condition, because it seemed to me that neither was an ordinary petition, and therefore I said: Lord, you know what I want. If it be your will that I have it, grant it to me, and if it be not your will, good Lord, do not be displeased, for I want nothing which you do not want. When I was young I desired to have that sickness when I was thirty years old. As to the third, I heard a man of Holy Church tell the story of St. Cecilia, and from his explanation I understood that she received three wounds in the neck from a sword, through which she suffered death. Moved by this, I conceived a great desire, and prayed our Lord God that he would grant me in the course of my life three wounds, that is, the wound of contrition, the wound of compassion and the wound of longing with my will for God. Just as I asked for the other two conditionally, so I asked for this third without any condition. The two desires which I mentioned first passed from my mind, and the third remained there continually.

CHAPTER 2

And when I was thirty and a half years old, God sent me a bodily sickness in which I lay for three days and three nights; and on the fourth night I received all the rites of Holy Church, and did not expect to live until day. But after this I suffered on for two days and two nights, and on the third night I often thought that I was on the point of death; and those who were around me also thought this. But in this I was very sorrowful and reluctant to die, not that there was anything on earth that it pleased me to live for, or anything of which I was afraid, for I trusted in God. But it was because I wanted to go on living to love God better and longer, and living so, obtain grace to know and love God more as he is the bliss of heaven. For it seemed to me that all the time that I had lived here was very little and short in comparison with the bliss which is everlasting. So I thought: Good Lord, is it no longer to your glory that I am alive? And my reason and my sufferings told me that I should die; and with all the will of my heart I assented wholly to be as was God's will.

So I lasted until day, and by then my body was dead from the middle downwards, it felt to me. Then I was moved to ask to be lifted up and supported, with cloths held to my head, so that my heart might be more free to be at God's will, and so that I could think of him whilst my life would last; and those who were with me sent for the parson, my curate, to be present at my end. He came with a little boy, and brought a cross; and by that time my eyes were fixed, and I could not speak. The parson set the cross before my face and said: Daughter, I brought you the image of your saviour. Look at it and take comfort in it, in reverence of him who died for you and me. It seemed to me that I was well as I was, for my eyes were set upwards towards heaven, where I trusted that I was going; but nevertheless I agreed to fix my eyes on the face of the crucifix if I could, so as to hold out longer until my end came, for it seemed to me that I could hold out longer with my eyes set in front of me rather than upwards. After this my sight began to fail, and it was all dark around me in the room, dark as night, except that there was ordinary light trained upon the image of the cross, I never knew how. Everything around the cross was ugly to me, as if it were occupied by a great crowd of devils.

After that I felt as if the upper part of my body were beginning to die. My hands fell down on either side, and I was so weak that my head lolled to one side. The greatest pain that I felt was my shortness of breath and the ebbing of my life. Then truly I believed that I was at the point of death. And suddenly in that moment all my pain left me, and I was as sound, particularly in the upper part of my body, as ever I was before or have been since. I was astonished by this change, for it seemed to me that it was by God's secret doing and not natural; and even so, in this ease which I felt, I had no more confidence that I should live, nor was the ease complete, for I thought that I would rather have been delivered of this world, because that was what my heart longed for.

CHAPTER 3

And suddenly it came into my mind that I ought to wish for the second wound, that our Lord, of his gift and of his grace, would fill my body full with recollection and feeling[2] of his blessed Passion, as I had prayed before, for I wished that his pains might be my pains, with compassion which would lead to longing for God. So it seemed to me that I might with his grace have his wounds, as I had wished before; but in this I never wanted any bodily vision or any kind of revelation from God, but only the compassion which I thought a loving soul could have for our Lord Jesus, who for love was willing to become a mortal man. I desired to suffer with him, living in my mortal body, as God would give me grace. And at this, suddenly I saw the red blood trickling down from under the crown, all hot, flowing freely and copiously, a living stream, just as it seemed to me that it was at the time when the crown of thorns was thrust down upon his blessed head. Just so did he, both God and man, suffer for me. I perceived, truly and powerfully, that it was himself who showed this to me, without any intermediary; and then I said: Blessed be the Lord! This I

---

[2] So the long text, which is superior to the short text's 'recollection of feeling'.

said with a reverent intention and in a loud voice, and I was greatly astonished by this wonder and marvel, that he would so humbly be[3] with a sinful creature living in this wretched flesh. I accepted it that at that time our Lord Jesus wanted, out of his courteous love, to show me comfort before my temptations began; for it seemed to me that I might well be tempted by devils, by God's permission and with his protection, before I died. With this sight of his blessed Passion and with his divinity, of which I speak as I understand[4], I saw that this was strength enough for me, yes, and for all living creatures who will be protected from all the devils of hell and from all their spiritual enemies.

CHAPTER 4

And at the same time as I saw this corporeal sight, our Lord showed me a spiritual sight of his familiar love. I saw that he is to us everything which is good and comforting for our help. He is our clothing, for he is that love which wraps and enfolds us, embraces us and guides us, surrounds us for his love, which is so tender that he may never desert us. And so in this sight I saw truly that he is everything which is good, as I understand.

And in this he showed me something small, no bigger than a hazelnut, lying in the palm of my hand, and I perceived that it was as round as any ball. I looked at it and thought: What can this be? And I was given this general answer: It is everything which is made. I was amazed that it could last, for I thought that it was so little that it could suddenly fall into nothing. And I was answered in my understanding: It lasts and always will, because God loves it; and thus everything has being through the love of God.

In this little thing I saw three properties.[5] The first is that God made it, the second is that he loves it, the third is that God preserves it. But what is that to me? It is that God is the Creator and the lover and the protector. For until I am substantially united to him, I can never have love or rest or true happiness; until, that is, I am so attached to him that there can be no created thing between my God and me. And who will do this deed? Truly, he himself, by his mercy and his grace, for he has made me for this and has blessedly restored me.

In this God brought our Lady to my understanding. I saw her spiritually in her bodily likeness, a simple, humble maiden, young in years, of the stature which she had when she conceived. Also God showed me part of the wisdom and truth of her soul, and in this I understood the reverent contemplation with which she beheld her God, marvelling with great reverence that he was willing to be born of her who was a simple creature created by him[6]. And this wisdom and truth[7], this knowledge of her creator's greatness and of her own created littleness, made her say meekly to the angel Gabriel: Behold me here,

[3] Or 'would be so familiar'.
[4] Or 'which I saw in my understanding'.
[5] 'Properties' is more probable than the short text's 'parts'.
[6] This corrects a scribal error found in both texts.
[7] So the long text, which is superior to the short text's 'wisdom of truth'.

God's handmaiden. In this sight I saw truly that she is greater, more worthy and more fulfilled, than everything else which God has created, and which is inferior to her. Above her is no created thing, except the blessed humanity of Christ. This little thing, which is created and is inferior to our Lady, St. Mary—God showed it to me as if it had been a hazelnut—seemed to me as if it could have perished because it is so little.

In this blessed revelation God showed me three nothings, of which nothings this is the first that was shown to me. Every man and woman who wishes to live contemplatively needs to know of this, so that it may be pleasing to them to despise as nothing everything created, so as to have the love of uncreated God. For this is the reason why those who deliberately occupy themselves with earthly business, constantly seeking worldly well-being, have not God's rest[8] in their hearts and souls; for they love and seek their rest in this thing which is so little and in which there is no rest, and do not know God who is almighty, all wise and all good, for he is true rest. God wishes to be known, and it pleases him that we should rest in him; for all things which are beneath him are not sufficient for us. And this is the reason why no soul has rest until it has despised as nothing all which is created. When the soul has become nothing for love, so as to have him who is all that is good, then is it able to receive spiritual rest.

CHAPTER 5

And during the time that our Lord showed me this spiritual vision which I have now described, I saw the bodily vision of the copious bleeding of the head persist, and as long as I saw it I said, many times: Blessed be the Lord! In this first revelation of our Lord I saw in my understanding six things. The first is the tokens of his blessed Passion, and the plentiful shedding of his precious blood. The second is the virgin who is his beloved mother. The third is the blessed divinity, that always was and is and ever shall be, almighty, all wisdom and all love. The fourth is everything which he has made; it is great and lovely and bountiful and good. But the reason why it seemed to my eyes so little was because I saw it in the presence of him who is the Creator. For to a soul who sees the Creator of all things, all that is created seems very little. The fifth is that he has made everything which is made for love, and through the same love it is preserved, and always will be without end, as has been said already. The sixth is that God is everything which is good, and the goodness which everything has is God.

This everything God showed me in the first vision, and he gave me space and time to contemplate it. And then the bodily vision ceased, and the spiritual vision persisted in my understanding, and I waited with reverent fear, rejoicing in what I saw and wishing, as much as I dared, to see more, if that were God's will, or to see for a longer time what I had already seen.

---

[8] The short text is corrupt, and this is the reading of the long text. But Julian may have written 'are not his heirs'.

CHAPTER 6

Everything that I say[9] about myself I mean to apply to all my fellow Christians, for I am taught that this is what our Lord intends in this spiritual revelation. And therefore I pray you all for God's sake, and I counsel you for your own profit, that you disregard the wretched worm, the sinful creature to whom it was shown, and that mightily, wisely, lovingly and meekly you contemplate God, who out of his courteous love and his endless goodness was willing to show this vision generally, to the comfort of us all. And you who hear and see this vision and this teaching, which is from Jesus Christ for the edification of your souls, it is God's will and my wish that you accept it with as much joy and delight as if Jesus had shown it to you as he did to me. I am not good because of the revelation, but only if I love God better, and so can and so should every man do who sees it and hears it with good will and proper intention. And so it is my desire that it should be to every man the same profit that I asked for myself, and was moved to in the first moment when I saw it; for it is common and general, just as we are all one; and I am sure that I saw it for the profit of many others. For truly it was not revealed to me because God loves me better than the humblest soul who is in a state of grace. For I am sure that there are very many who never had revelations or visions, but only the common teaching of Holy Church, who love God better than I. If I pay special attention to myself, I am nothing at all; but in general I am in the unity of love with all my fellow Christians. For it is in this unity of love that the life consists of all men who will be saved. For God is everything that is good, and God has made everything that is made, and God loves everything that he has made, and if any man or woman withdraws his love from any of his fellow Christians, he does not love at all, because he has not love towards all. And so in such times he is in danger, because he is not at peace; and anyone who has general love for his fellow Christians has love toward everything which is. For in mankind which will be saved is comprehended all, that is, all that is made and the maker of all; for God is in man, and so in man is all. And he who thus generally loves all his fellow Christians loves all, and he who loves thus is safe. And thus will I love, and thus do I love, and thus I am safe—I write as the representative of my fellow Christians—and the more that I love in this way whilst I am here, the more I am like the joy that I shall have in heaven without end, that joy which is the God who out of his endless love willed to become our brother and suffer for us. And I am sure that anyone who sees it so will be taught the truth and be greatly comforted, if he have need of comfort. But God forbid that you should say or assume that I am a teacher, for that is not and never was my intention; for I am a woman, ignorant, weak and frail. But I know very well that what I am saying I have received by the revelation of him who is the sovereign teacher. But it is truly love which moves me to tell it to you, for I want God to be known and my fellow Christians to prosper, as I hope to prosper myself, by hating sin more and loving God more. But because I am a

---

[9] 'Say' is here more probable than 'saw'.

woman, ought I therefore to believe that I should not tell you of the goodness of God, when I saw at that same time that it is his will that it be known? You will see this clearly in what follows, if it be well and truly accepted. Then will you soon forget me who am a wretch, and do this, so that I am no hindrance to you, and you will contemplate Jesus, who is every man's teacher. I speak of those who will be saved, for at this time God showed me no one else; but in everything I believe as Holy Church teaches, for I beheld the whole of this blessed revelation of our Lord as unified in God's sight, and I never understood anything from it which bewilders me or keeps me from the true doctrine of Holy Church.

CHAPTER 7

All this blessed teaching of our Lord was shown to me in three parts, that is by bodily vision and by words formed in my understanding and by spiritual vision. But I may not and cannot show the spiritual visions to you as plainly and fully as I should wish; but I trust in our Lord God Almighty that he will, out of his goodness and for love of you, make you accept it more spiritually and more sweetly than I can or may tell it to you, and so may it be, for we are all one in love. And in all this I was humbly moved in love towards my fellow Christians, that they might all see and know the same as I saw, for I wished it to be a comfort to them all, as it is to me; for this vision was shown for all men, and not for me alone[10]. Of everything which I saw, this was the greatest comfort to me, that our Lord is so familiar and so courteous, and this most filled my soul with delight and surety. Then I said to the people who were with me: Today is my Doomsday. And I said this because I expected to die; because on the day that a man or woman dies, he is judged as he will be forever. I said this because I wished them to love God more and to set less store by worldly vanity, and to make them mindful that this life is short, as they could see by my example, for in all this time I was expecting to die.

And after this I saw, in bodily vision, in the face of the crucifix which hung before me, a part of Christ's Passion: contempt, spitting to defoul[11] his body, buffeting of his blessed face, and many woes and pains, more than I can tell; and his colour often changed, and all his blessed face was for a time caked with dry blood. This I saw bodily and sorrowfully and dimly; and I wanted more of the light of day, to have seen it more clearly. And I was answered in my reason that if God wished to show me more he would, but that I needed no light but him.

---

[10] Literally, 'shown in general, and not at all specially'.

[11] The short text here has *sowlynge,* the long text *solewyng* (Paris, Bibliotheque Nationale Fonds Anglais 40, hereafter cited as P), *sulloing* (Serenus Cressy, *The Revelations of Divine Love,* Paris, 1670, hereafter cited as C), *sollowing* (both Sloan Manuscripts, hereafter cited as SS); but it is conjectured that they all misrepresent 'to soil', 'to defoul'.

CHAPTER 8

And after this I saw God in an instant of time[12], that is, in my understanding, and by this vision I saw that he is present in all things. I contemplated it carefully, knowing and perceiving through it that he does everything which is done. I marvelled at this vision with a gentle fear, and I thought: What is sin? For I saw truly that God does everything, however small it may be, and that nothing is done by chance, but it is of the endless providence of God's wisdom. Therefore I was compelled to admit that everything which is done is well done, and I was certain that God does no sin. Therefore it seemed to me that sin is nothing, for in all this sin was not shown to me. And I did not wish to go on feeling surprise at this, but I contemplated our Lord and waited for what he would show me. And on another occasion God did show me, nakedly in itself, what sin is, as I shall tell afterwards.

And after this as I watched I saw the body bleeding copiously, the blood hot, flowing freely, a living stream, just as I had before seen the head bleed. And I saw this in the furrows made by the scourging, and I saw this blood run so plentifully that it seemed to me that if it had in fact been happening there, the bed and everything around it would have been soaked in blood.

God has created bountiful waters on the earth for our use and our bodily comfort, out of the tender love he has for us. But it is more pleasing to him that we accept freely his blessed blood to wash us of our sins, for there is no drink that is made which it pleases him so well to give us; for it is so plentiful, and it is of our own nature.

And after this, before God revealed any words to me, he allowed me to contemplate longer all that I had seen and all that was contained in it. And then there was formed in my soul this saying, without voice and without opening of lips: With this the fiend is overcome. Our Lord said this to me with reference to his Passion, as he had shown it to me before; and in this he brought into my mind and showed me a part of the devil's malice and all of his impotence, and this by showing me that his Passion is the overcoming of the fiend. God showed me that he still has the same malice as he had before the Incarnation, and he works as hard, and he sees as constantly as he did before that all chosen souls escape him to God's glory. And in that is all the devil's sorrow; for everything which God permits him to do turns to joy for us and to pain and shame for him, and he has as much sorrow when God permits him to work as when he is not working. And that is because he can never do as much evil as he would wish, for his power is all locked in God's hands. Also I saw our Lord scorning his malice and despising him as nothing, and he wants us to do the same. Because of this sight I laughed greatly, and that made those around me to laugh as well; and their laughter was pleasing to me. I thought that I wished that all my fellow Christians had seen what I saw. Then they would all have laughed with me. But I did not see Christ laugh; nevertheless,

---

[12] Literally, 'in a point'.

it is pleasing to him that we laugh to comfort ourselves, and that we rejoice in God because the devil is overcome. And after that I became serious again, and said: I see. I see three things: sport and scorn and seriousness. I see sport, that the devil is overcome; and I see scorn, that God scorns him and he will be scorned; and I see seriousness, that he is overcome by the Passion of our Lord Jesus Christ and by his death, which was accomplished in great earnest and with heavy labour.

After this our Lord said: I thank you for your service and your labour, and especially in your youth.

CHAPTER 9

God showed me three degrees of bliss that every soul will have in heaven who has voluntarily served God in any degree here upon earth. The first is the honour of the thanks of our Lord God which he will receive when he is delivered from pain. This thanks is so exalted and so honourable that it will seem to him that this suffices him, if there were no other happiness. For it seemed to me that all the pain and labour which all living men might endure could not earn the thanks that one man will have who has voluntarily served God. As to the second degree, it is that all the blessed in heaven will see the honour of the thanks from our Lord God. This makes a soul's service known to all who are in heaven. And for the third degree, which is that the first joy with which the soul is then received will last forevermore, I saw that this was kindly and sweetly said and revealed to me: Every man's age will be known in heaven, and he will be rewarded for his voluntary service and for the time he has served, and especially the age of those who voluntarily and freely offer their youth to God is fittingly rewarded and wonderfully thanked.

And after this our Lord revealed to me a supreme spiritual delight in my soul. In this delight I was filled full of everlasting surety, and I was powerfully secured without any fear. This sensation was so welcome and so dear to me that I was at peace, at ease and at rest, so that there was nothing upon earth which could have afflicted me.

This lasted only for a time, and then I was changed, and left to myself, oppressed and weary of myself, ruing my life so that I scarcely had the patience to go on living. I felt that there was no ease or comfort for me except hope, faith and love, and truly I felt very little of this. And then presently God gave me again comfort and rest for my soul, delight and security so blessed and so powerful that there was no fear, no sorrow, no pain, physical or spiritual, that one could suffer which might have disturbed me. And then again I felt the pain, and then afterwards the joy and the delight, now the one and now the other, again and again, I suppose about twenty times. And in the time of joy I could have said with Paul: Nothing shall separate me from the love of Christ; and in the pain, I could have said with Peter: Lord, save me, I am perishing.

This vision was shown to me to teach me to understand that every man needs to experience this, to be comforted at one time, and at another to fail and to be left to himself. God wishes us to know that he keeps us safe all the time, in joy and in sorrow, and that he loves us as much in sorrow as in joy. And sometimes a man is left to himself for the profit of his soul, and neither the one nor the other is caused by sin. For in this time I committed no sin for which I ought to have been left to myself, nor did I deserve these sensations of joy; but God gives joy freely as it pleases him, and sometimes he allows us to be in sorrow, and both come from his love. For it is God's will that we do all in our power to preserve our consolation, for bliss lasts forevermore, and pain is passing and will be reduced to nothing. Therefore it is not God's will that when we feel pain we should pursue it, sorrowing and mourning for it, but that suddenly we should pass it over and preserve ourselves in endless delight, because God is almighty, our lover and preserver.

CHAPTER 10

After this Christ showed me part of his Passion, close to his death. I saw his sweet face as it were dry and bloodless, with the pallor of dying, then more dead, pale and languishing, then the pallor turning blue and then more blue, as death took more hold upon his flesh. For all the pains which Christ suffered in his body appeared to me in his blessed face, in all that I could see of it, and especially in the lips. I saw there what had become of the four colours that I had seen before, his freshness, his ruddiness, his vitality and his beauty which I had seen. This was a grievous change to watch, this deep dying, and the nose shrivelled[13] and dried up as I saw. The long torment seemed to me as if he had been dead for a week and had still gone on suffering pain, and it seemed to me as if the greatest and the last pain of his Passion was when his flesh dried up. And in this drying what Christ had said came to my mind: I thirst. For I saw in Christ a double thirst, one physical, the other spiritual. This saying was shown to me to signify the physical thirst, and what was revealed to me of the spiritual thirst I shall say afterwards; and concerning the physical thirst, I understood that the body was wholly dried up, for his blessed flesh and bones were left without blood or moisture. The blessed body was left to dry for a long time, with the wrenching of the nails and the sagging of the head and the weight of the body, with the blowing of the wind around him, which dried up his body and pained him with cold, more than my heart can think of, and with all his other pains I saw such pain that all that I can describe or say is inadequate, for it cannot be described. But each soul should do as St. Paul says, and feel in himself what is in Christ Jesus. This revelation of Christ's pains filled me full of pains, for I know well that he suffered only once, but it was now his will to show it to me and fill me with its recollection, as I had asked before. My mother, who was standing there with the others, held up her hand in front of my face to close my eyes, for she thought that I was already dead or had that

---

[13] *Clonge* (British Museum, Sloan MS, 2499, hereafter cited as S1), *clange* (British Museum, Sloan MS, 3705, hereafter cited as S2), in the long text, are the only variants which give sense.

moment died; and this greatly increased my sorrow, for despite all my pains, I did not want to be hindered from seeing, because of my love for him. And with regard to either[14], in all this time that Christ was present to me, I felt no pain except for Christ's pains; and then it came to me that I had little known what pain it was that I had asked for, for it seemed to me that my pains exceeded any mortal death. I thought: Is there any pain in hell like this? And in my reason I was answered that despair is greater, for that is a spiritual pain. But there is no greater physical pain than this; how could I suffer greater pain than to see him who is all my life, all my bliss and all my joy suffer? Here I felt truly that I loved Christ so much more than myself that I thought it would have been a great comfort to me if my body had died.

In this I saw part of the compassion of our Lady, St. Mary, for Christ and she were so united in love that the greatness of her love was the cause of the greatness of her pain. For her pain surpassed that of all others, as much as she loved him more than all others. And so all his disciples and all his true lovers suffered greater pains than they did at the death of their own bodies. For I am sure, by my own experience, that the least of them loved him more than they loved themselves. And here I saw a great unity between Christ and us; for when he was in pain we were in pain, and all creatures able to suffer pain suffered with him. And for those that did not know him, their pain was that all creation, sun and moon, ceased to serve men, and so they were all abandoned in sorrow at that time. So those who loved him suffered pain for their love, and those who did not love him suffered pain because the comfort of all creation failed them.

At this time I wanted to look to the side of the cross, but I did not dare, for I knew well that whilst I looked at the cross I was secure and safe. Therefore I would not agree to put my soul in danger, for apart from the cross there was no safety, but only the horror of devils.

Then there came a suggestion, seemingly friendly, to my reason. It was said to me: Look up to heaven to his Father. Then I saw clearly by the faith which I felt that there was nothing between the cross and heaven which could have grieved me, and that I must either look up or else answer. I answered, and said: No, I cannot, for you are my heaven. I said this because I did not want to look up, for I would rather have remained in that pain until Judgment Day than have come to heaven any other way than by him. For I knew well that he who had bought me so dearly would unbind me when it was his will.

CHAPTER 11

Thus I chose Jesus for my heaven, whom I saw only in pain at that time. No other heaven was pleasing to me than Jesus, who will be my bliss when I am there; and this has always been a comfort to me, that I chose Jesus as my

[14] The cause of her suffering is neither her own sickness nor the sorrow she feels for the Passion, but only the Passion's pains.

heaven in all times of suffering and of sorrow. And that has taught me that I should always do so, and choose only him to be my heaven in well-being and in woe. And so I saw my Lord Jesus languishing for long, because of the union in him of man and God, for love gave strength to his humanity to suffer more than all men could. I mean not only more pain than any other one man could suffer, but also that he suffered more pain than would all men together, from the first beginning to the last day. No tongue may tell, no heart can fully think of the pains which our saviour suffered for us, if we have regard to the honour of him who is the highest, most majestic king, and to his shameful, grievous and painful death. For he who was highest and most honourable was most completely brought low, most utterly despised. But the love which made him suffer all this surpasses all his pains as far as heaven is above earth. For his pains were a deed, performed once through the motion of love; but his love was without beginning and is and ever will be without any end.

CHAPTER 12

And suddenly, as I looked at the same cross, he changed to an appearance of joy. The change in his appearance changed mine, and I was as glad and joyful as I could possibly be. And then cheerfully our Lord suggested to my mind: Where is there any instant of your pain or of your grief? And I was very joyful.

Then our Lord put a question to me: Are you well satisfied that I suffered for you? Yes, good Lord, I said; all my thanks to you, good Lord, blessed may you be! If you are satisfied, our Lord said, I am satisfied. It is a joy and a bliss and an endless delight to me that ever I suffered my Passion for you, for if I could suffer more, I would. In response to this, my understanding was lifted up into heaven, and there I saw three heavens; and at this sight I was greatly astonished, and I thought: I have seen three heavens, and all are of the blessed humanity of Christ. And none is greater, none is less, none is higher, none is lower, but all are equal in their joy.

For the first heaven, Christ showed me his Father, not in any corporeal likeness, but in his attributes and in his joy. For the Father's operation is this: He rewards his Son, Jesus Christ. This gift and this reward is so joyful to Jesus that his Father could have given him no reward which could have pleased him better. For the first heaven, which is the Father's bliss, appeared to me as a heaven, and it was full of bliss. For Jesus has great joy in all the deeds which he has done for our salvation, and therefore we are his, not only through our redemption but also by his Father's courteous gift. We are his bliss, we are his reward, we are his honour, we are his crown.

What I am describing now is so great a joy to Jesus that he counts as nothing his labour and his bitter sufferings and his cruel and shameful death. And in these words: If I could suffer more, I would suffer more, I saw truly that if he could die as often as once for every man who is to be saved, as he did once for all men, love would never let him rest till he had done it. And when he had done it, he would count it all as nothing for love, for everything seems only little to him in comparison with his love. And that he plainly said to me, gravely saying this: If I could suffer more. He did not say: If it were necessary to suffer more, but: If I could suffer more; for although it might not be necessary, if he could suffer more he would suffer more. This deed and this work for our salvation were as well done as he could devise it. It was done as honourably as Christ could do it, and in this I saw complete joy in Christ; but his joy would not have been complete if the deed could have been done any better than it was. And in these three sayings: It is a joy, a bliss and an endless delight to me, there were shown to me three heavens, and in this way. By 'joy' I understood that the Father was pleased, by 'bliss' that the Son was honoured, and by 'endless delight' the Holy Spirit. The Father is pleased, the Son is honoured, the Holy Spirit takes delight. Jesus wants us to pay heed to this bliss for our salvation which is in the blessed Trinity, and to take equal delight, through his grace, whilst we are here. And this was shown to me when he said: Are you well satisfied? And by what Christ next said: If you are satisfied, I am satisfied, he made me understand that it was as if he had said: This is joy and delight enough for me, and I ask nothing else for my labour but that I may satisfy you. Generously and completely was this revealed to me.

So think wisely, how great this saying is: That ever I suffered my Passion for you; for in that saying was given exalted understanding of the love and the delight that he had in our salvation.

CHAPTER 13

Very merrily and gladly our Lord looked into his side, and he gazed and said this: See how I loved you; as if he had said: My child, if you cannot look on my divinity, see here how I suffered my side to be opened and my heart to be split in two and to send out blood and water, all that was in it; and this is a delight to me, and I wish it to be so for you.

Our Lord showed this to me to make us glad and merry. And with the same joyful appearance he looked down on his right, and brought to my mind where our Lady stood at the time of his Passion, and he said: Do you wish to see her? And I answered and said: Yes, good Lord, great thanks, if it be your will. Often times I had prayed for this, and I expected to see her in a bodily likeness; but I did not see her so. And Jesus, saying this, showed me a spiritual vision of her. Just as before I had seen her small and simple, now he showed her high and noble and glorious and more pleasing to him than all creatures. And so he wishes it to be known that all who take delight in him should take delight in her, and in the delight that he has in her and she in him. And when Jesus said: Do you wish to see her? it seemed to me that I had the greatest delight that he could have given me in this spiritual vision of her which he gave me. For our Lord showed me no particular person except our Lady, St. Mary, and he showed her to me on three occasions. The first was as she conceived, the second was as she had been in her sorrow under the Cross, and the third as she is now, in delight, honour and joy.

And after this our Lord showed himself to me, and he appeared to me more glorified than I had seen him before, and in this I was taught that every contemplative soul to whom it is given to look and to seek will see Mary and pass on to God through contemplation. And after this teaching, simple, courteous, joyful, again and again our Lord said to me: I am he who is highest. I am he whom you love. I am he in whom you delight. I am he whom you serve. I am he for whom you long. I am he whom you desire. I am he whom you intend. I am he who is all. I am he whom Holy Church preaches and teaches to you. I am he who showed himself before to you. I repeat these words only so that every man may accept them as our Lord intended them, according to the grace God gives him in understanding and love.

And after this our Lord brought to my mind the longing that I had for him before; and I saw that nothing hindered me but sin, and I saw that this is true of us all in general, and it seemed to me that if there had been no sin, we should all have been pure and as like our Lord as he created us. And so in my folly before this time I often wondered why, through the great and prescient wisdom of God, sin was not prevented; for it seemed to me that then all would have been well.

The impulse to think this was greatly to be shunned; and I mourned and sorrowed on this account, unreasonably, lacking discretion, filled with pride. Nonetheless in this vision Jesus informed me about everything needful to me. I do not say that I need no more instruction, for after he revealed this our Lord entrusted me to Holy Church, and I am hungry and thirsty and needy and sinful and frail, and willingly submit myself among all my fellow Christians to the teaching of Holy Church to the end of my life.

He answered with these words, and said: Sin is necessary. In the word 'sin', our Lord brought generally to my mind all which is not good: the shameful contempt and the complete denial of himself which he endured for us in this life and in his death, and all the pains and passions, spiritual and bodily, of all his creatures. For we are all in part denied, and we ought to be denied, following our master Jesus until we are fully purged, that is to say until we have completely denied our own mortal flesh and all our inward affections which are not good.

And the beholding of this, with all the pains that ever were or ever will be—and of all this I understood Christ's Passion for the greatest and surpassing pain[15]—was shown to me in an instant, and quickly turned into consolation. For our good Lord God would not have the soul frightened by this ugly sight. But I did not see sin, for I believe that it has no kind of substance, no share in being, nor can it be recognized except by the pains which it causes. And it seems to me that this pain is something for a time, for it purges us and makes us know ourselves and ask for mercy; for the Passion of our Lord is comfort to us against all this, and that is his blessed will for all who will be saved. He comforts readily and sweetly with his words, and says: But all will be well, and every kind of thing will be well.

---

[15] 'And of all this . . . surpassing pain': omitted by the short text, supplied from the long.

These words were revealed very tenderly, showing no kind of blame to me or to anyone who will be saved. So it would be most unkind of me to blame God or marvel at him on account of my sins, since he does not blame me for sin. So I saw how Christ has compassion on us because of sin; and just as I was before filled full of pain and compassion on account of Christ's Passion, so I was now in a measure filled with compassion for all my fellow Christians, and then I saw that every kind of compassion which one has for one's fellow Christians in love is Christ in us.

CHAPTER 14

But I[16] shall study upon this, contemplating it generally, heavily and mournfully, saying in intention to our Lord with very great fear: Ah, good Lord, how could all things be well, because of the great harm which has come through sin to your creatures? And I wished, so far as I dared, for some plainer explanation through which my mind might be at ease about this matter. And to this our blessed Lord answered, very meekly and with a most loving manner, and he showed me that Adam's sin was the greatest harm ever done or ever to be done until the end of the world. And he also showed me that this is plainly known to all Holy Church upon earth.

Furthermore, he taught me that I should contemplate his glorious atonement, for this atoning is more pleasing to the blessed divinity and more honourable for man's salvation, without comparison, than ever Adam's sin was harmful. So then it is our blessed Lord's intention in this teaching that we should pay heed to this: For since I have set right the greatest of harms, it is my will that you should know through this that I shall set right everything which is less.

He gave me understanding of two portions. One portion is our saviour and our salvation. This blessed portion is open and clear and fair and bright and plentiful, for all men who are or will be of good will are comprehended in this portion. We are bidden to this by God, and drawn and counselled and taught, inwardly by the Holy Spirit and outwardly, through the grace of the same Spirit, by Holy Church. Our Lord wants us to be occupied in this, rejoicing in him, for he rejoices in us. And the more plentifully we accept this with reverence and humility, the more do we deserve thanks from him, and the more profit do we win for ourselves; and so we may rejoice and say: Our portion is our Lord.

The other portion is closed to us and hidden, that is to say all which is additional to our salvation. For this is our Lord's privy counsel, and it is fitting to God's royal dominion to keep his privy counsel in peace, and it is fitting to his subjects out of obedience and respect not to wish to know his counsel.

Our Lord has pity and compassion on us because some creatures occupy themselves so much in this; and I am certain that if we knew how much we should please him and solace ourselves by leaving it alone, we should do so.

[16] 'I': ms: 'you'.

The saints in heaven wish to know nothing but what our Lord wishes to show them, and furthermore their love and their desire is governed according to our Lord's will; and so we ought to wish to be[17] like him[18]. And then we shall not wish or desire anything but the will of our Lord, for we are all one in God's intention.

And in this I was taught that we shall rejoice only in our blessed saviour Jesus, and trust in him for everything.

CHAPTER 15

And so our good Lord answered to all the questions and doubts which I could raise, saying most comfortingly in this fashion: I will make all things well, I shall make all things well, I may make all things well and I can make all things well; and you will see that yourself, that all things will be well. When he says that he 'may', I understand this to apply to the Father; and when he says that he 'can', I understand this for the Son; and when he says 'I will', I understand this for the Holy Spirit; and when he says 'I shall', I understand this for the unity of the blessed Trinity, three persons in one truth; and when he says 'You will see yourself', I understand this for the union of all men who will be saved in the blessed Trinity.

And in these five words[19] God wishes to be enclosed in rest and in peace. And so Christ's spiritual thirst has an end. For his spiritual thirst is his longing in love, and that persists and always will until we see him on the day of judgment; for we who shall be saved and shall be Christ's joy and bliss are still here, and shall be until that day. Therefore his thirst is this incompleteness of his joy, that he does not now possess us in himself as wholly as he then will.

All this was shown to me as a revelation of his compassion, for on the day of judgment it will cease. So he has pity and compassion on us and he longs to possess us, but his wisdom and his love do not permit the end to come until the best time. And in these same five words[20] said before: 'I may make all things well', I understand powerful consolation from all the deeds of our Lord which are still to be performed; for just as the blessed Trinity created everything from nothing, just so the same blessed Trinity will make well all things which are not well. It is God's will that we pay great heed to all the deeds which he has performed, for he wishes us to know from them all which he will do; and he revealed that to me by those words which he said: And you will see yourself that every kind of thing will be well. I understand this in two ways: One is that I am well content that I do not know it; and the other is that I am glad and joyful because I shall know it. It is God's will that we should know

---

[17] Ms: 'not to be', probably a misunderstanding of 'wilne'.
[18] Or 'like them.'
[19] 'May,' 'can,' 'will', 'shall', 'you will see . . .'
[20] This seems to refer to 'I may make all things well'.

in general that all will be well, but it is not God's will that we should know it now except as it applies to us for the present, and that is the teaching of Holy Church.

CHAPTER 16

God showed me the very great delight that he has in all men and women who accept, firmly and humbly and reverently, the preaching and teaching of Holy Church, for he is Holy Church. For he is the foundation, he is the substance, he is the teaching, he is the teacher, he is the end, he is the reward[21] for which every faithful soul labours; and he is known and will be known to every soul to whom the Holy Spirit declares this. And I am certain that all who seek in this way will prosper, for they are seeking God.

All this which I have now said and more which I shall presently say is solace against sin; for when I first saw that God does everything which is done, I did not see sin, and then I saw that all is well. But when God did show me sin, it was then that he said: All will be well.

And when almighty God had shown me his goodness so plenteously and fully, I wished to know, concerning a certain person whom I loved, what her future would be; and by wishing this I impeded myself, for I was not then told this. And then I was answered in my reason, as it were by a friendly man[22]: Accept it generally, and contemplate the courtesy of your Lord God as he reveals it to you, for it is more honour to God to contemplate him in all things than in any one special thing. I agreed, and with that I learned that it is more honour to God to know everything in general than it is to take delight in any special thing. And if I were to act wisely, in accordance with this teaching, I should not be glad because of any special thing or be distressed by anything at all, for all will be well.

God brought to my mind that I should sin; and because of the delight that I had in contemplating him, I did not at once pay attention to this revelation. And our Lord very courteously waited until I was ready to attend, and then our Lord brought to my mind, along with my sins, the sins of all my fellow Christians, all in general and none in particular.

---

[21] So the long text, which is superior to the short text's 'means'.
[22] Or, as the long text more probably has, 'a friendly intermediary.'

3

Michael Harner

"Discovering the Way," from *The Way of the Shaman: A Guide to Power and Healing**

This reading is from Michael Harner's account of his time among the Conibo Indians of the Peruvian Amazon region. During his study of the Conibo, Harner sought to experience personally a deeply spiritual vision by ingesting a chemical substance derived from plants of the area. His guides through this ritual experience of the Conibo were shamans, holy men who could give instructions on how to interpret and control the vision.

CHAPTER 1

My first prolonged fieldwork as an anthropologist took place more than two decades ago on the forested eastern slopes of the Ecuadorian Andes among the Jívaro [HEE-varo] Indians, or *Untsuri Shuar*. The Jívaro were famous at that time for their now essentially vanished practice of "head-shrinking," and for their intensive practice of shamanism, which still continues. I successfully collected a great deal of information on their culture during 1956 and 1957, but remained an outside observer of the world of the shaman.

A couple of years later, the American Museum of Natural History invited me to make a year-long expedition to the Peruvian Amazon to study the culture of the Conibo Indians of the Ucayali River region. I accepted, delighted to have an opportunity to do more research on the fascinating Upper Amazon forest cultures. That fieldwork took place in 1960 and 1961.

Two particular experiences I had among the Conibo and the Jívaro were basic to my discovering the way of the shaman in both those cultures, and I would like to share them with you. Perhaps they will convey something of the incredible hidden world open to the shamanic explorer.

I had been living for the better part of a year in a Conibo Indian village beside a remote lake off a tributary of the Río Ucayali. My anthropological research on the culture of the Conibo had been going well, but my attempts to elicit information on their religion met with little success. The people were friendly, but reluctant to talk about the supernatural. Finally they told me that if I really wished to learn, I must take the shamans' sacred drink made from *ayahuasca*, the "soul vine." I agreed, with both curiosity and trepidation, for they warned me that the experience would be very frightening.

The next morning my friend Tomás, the kind elder of the village, went into the forest to cut the vines. Before leaving, he told me to fast: a light breakfast and no lunch. He returned midday with enough *ayahuasca* vines and leaves of the *cawa* plant to fill a fifteen gallon pot. He boiled them all afternoon, until only about a quart of dark liquid remained. This he poured into an old bottle and left it to cool until sunset, when he said we would drink it.

The Indians muzzled the dogs in the village so that they could not bark. The noise of barking dogs could drive a man who had taken *ayahuasca* mad, I was told. The children were cautioned to be quiet, and silence came over the small community with the setting of the sun.

As the brief equatorial twilight was replaced by darkness, Tomás poured about a third of the bottle into a gourd bowl and gave it to me. All the Indians were watching. I felt like Socrates amidst his Athenian compatriots, accepting the hemlock—it occurred to me that one of the alternate names people in the Peruvian Amazon gave *ayahuasca* was "the little death." I drank the potion quickly. It had a strange, slightly bitter taste. I then waited for Tomás to take his turn, but he said that he had decided not to participate after all.

They had me lie down on the bamboo platform under the great thatched roof of the communal house. The village was silent, except for the chirping of crickets and the distant calls of a howler monkey deep in the jungle.

As I stared upward into the darkness, faint lines of light appeared. They grew sharper, more intricate, and burst into brilliant colors. Sound came from far away, a sound like a waterfall, which grew stronger and stronger until it filled my ears.

Just a few minutes earlier I had been disappointed, sure that the *ayahuasca* was not going to have any effect on me. Now the sound of rushing water flooded my brain. My jaw began to feel numb, and the numbness was moving up to my temples.

Overhead the faint lines became brighter, and gradually interlaced to form a canopy resembling a geometric mosaic of stained glass. The bright violet hues formed an ever-expanding roof above me. Within this celestial cavern, I heard the sound of water grow louder and I could see dim figures engaged in shadowy movements. As my eyes seemed to adjust to the gloom, the moving scene resolved itself into something resembling a huge fun house, a supernatural carnival of demons. In the center, presiding over the activities, and looking directly at me, was a gigantic, grinning crocodilian head, from whose cavernous jaws gushed a torrential flood of water. Slowly the waters rose, and so did the canopy above them, until the scene metamorphosed into a simple duality of blue sky above and sea below. All creatures had vanished.

Then, from my position near the surface of the water, I began to see two strange boats wafting back and forth, floating through the air towards me, coming closer and closer. They slowly combined to form a single vessel with a huge dragon-headed prow, not unlike that of a Viking ship. Set amidships was a square sail. Gradually, as the boat gently floated back and forth above me, I heard a rhythmic swishing sound and saw that it was a giant galley with several hundred oars moving back and forth in cadence with the sound.

I became conscious, too, of the most beautiful singing I have ever heard in my life, high-pitched and ethereal, emanating from myriad voices on board the galley. As I looked more closely at the deck, I could make out large numbers of people with the heads of blue jays and the bodies of humans, not unlike the bird-headed gods of ancient Egyptian tomb paintings. At the same time, some energy-essence began to float from my chest up into the boat. Although I believed myself to be an atheist, I was completely certain that I was dying and that the bird-headed people had come to take my soul away on the boat. While the soul-flow continued from my chest, I was aware that the extremities of my body were growing numb.

Starting with my arms and legs, my body slowly began to feel like it was turning to solid concrete. I could not move or speak. Gradually, as the numbness closed in on my chest, toward my heart, I tried to get my mouth to ask for help, to ask the Indians for an antidote. Try as I might, however, I could not marshal my abilities sufficiently to make a word. Simultaneously, my abdomen seemed to be turning to stone, and I had to make a tremendous effort to keep my heart beating. I began to call my heart my friend, my dearest friend of all, to talk to it, to encourage it to beat with all the power remaining at my command.

I became aware of my brain. I felt—physically—that it had become compartmentalized into four separate and distinct levels. At the uppermost surface was the observer and commander, which was conscious of the condition of my body, and was responsible for the attempt to keep my heart going. It perceived, but purely as a spectator, the visions emanating from what seemed to be the nether portions of my brain. Immediately below the topmost level I felt a numbed layer, which seemed to have been put out of commission by the drug—it just wasn't there. The next level down was the source of my visions, including the soul boat.

Now I was virtually certain I was about to die. As I tried to accept my fate, an even lower portion of my brain began to transmit more visions and information. I was "told" that this new material was being presented to me because I was dying and therefore "safe" to receive these revelations. These were the secrets reserved for the dying and the dead, I was informed. I could only very dimly perceive the givers of these thoughts: giant reptilian creatures reposing sluggishly at the lowermost depths of the back of my brain, where it met the top of the spinal column. I could only vaguely see them in what seemed to be gloomy, dark depths.

Then they projected a visual scene in front of me. First they showed me the planet Earth as it was eons ago, before there was any life on it. I saw an ocean, barren land, and a bright blue sky. Then black specks dropped from the sky by the hundreds and landed in front of me on the barren landscape. I could see that the "specks" were actually large, shiny, black creatures with stubby pterodactyl-like wings and huge whale-like bodies. Their heads were not visible to me. They flopped down, utterly exhausted from their trip, resting for eons. They explained to me in a kind of thought language that they were fleeing from something out in space. They had come to the planet Earth to escape their enemy.

The creatures then showed me how they had created life on the planet in order to hide within the multitudinous forms and thus disguise their presence. Before me, the magnificence of plant and animal creation and speciation—hundreds of millions of years of activity—took place on a scale and with a vividness impossible to describe. I learned that the dragon-like creatures were thus inside of all forms of life, including man.* They were the true masters of humanity and the entire planet, they told me. We humans were but the receptacles and servants of these creatures. For this reason they could speak to me from within myself.

These revelations, welling up from the depths of my mind, alternated with visions of the floating galley, which had almost finished taking my soul on board. The boat with its blue-jay headed deck crew was gradually drawing away, pulling my life force along as it headed towards a large fjord flanked by barren, worn hills. I knew I had only a moment more to live. Strangely, I had no fear of the bird-headed people; they were welcome to have my soul if they could keep it. But I was afraid that somehow my soul might not remain on the horizontal plane of the fjord but might, through processes unknown but felt and dreaded, be acquired or re-acquired by the dragon-like denizens of the depths.

I suddenly felt my distinctive humanness, the contrast between my species and the ancient reptilian ancestors. I began to struggle against returning to the ancient ones, who were beginning to feel increasingly alien and possibly evil. Each heart beat was a major undertaking. I turned to human help.

With an unimaginable last effort, I barely managed to utter one word to the Indians: "Medicine!" I saw them rushing around to make an antidote, and I knew they could not prepare it in time. I needed a guardian who could defeat dragons, and I frantically tried to conjure up a powerful being to protect me against the alien reptilian creatures. One appeared before me; and at that moment the Indians forced my mouth open and poured the antidote into me. Gradually, the dragons disappeared back into the lower depths; the soul boat and the fjord were no more. I relaxed with relief.

The antidote radically eased my condition, but it did not prevent me from having many additional visions of a more superficial nature. These were manageable and enjoyable. I made fabulous journeys at will through distant

---

*In retrospect one could say they were almost like DNA, although at that time, 1961, I knew nothing of DNA.

regions, even out into the Galaxy; created incredible architecture; and employed sardonically grinning demons to realize my fantasies. Often I found myself laughing aloud at the incongruities of my adventures.

Finally, I slept.

Rays of sunlight were piercing the holes in the palm-thatched roof when I awoke. I was still lying on the bamboo platform, and I heard the normal, morning sounds all around me: the Indians conversing, babies crying, and a rooster crowing. I was surprised to discover that I felt refreshed and peaceful. As I lay there looking up at the beautiful woven pattern of the roof, the memories of the previous night drifted across my mind. I momentarily stopped myself from remembering more in order to get my tape recorder from a duffle bag. As I dug into the bag, several of the Indians greeted me, smiling. An old woman, Tomás' wife, gave me a bowl of fish and plantain soup for breakfast. It tasted extraordinarily good. Then I went back to the platform, eager to put my night's experiences on tape before I forgot anything.

The work of recall went easily except for one portion of the trance that I could not remember. It remained blank, as though a tape had been erased. I struggled for hours to remember what had happened in that part of the experience, and I virtually wrestled it back into my consciousness. The recalcitrant material turned out to be the communication from the dragon-like creatures, including the revelation of their role in the evolution of life on this planet and their innate domination of living matter, including man. I was highly excited at rediscovering this material, and could not help but feel that I was not supposed to be able to bring it back from the nether regions of the mind.

I even had a peculiar sense of fear for my safety, because I now possessed a secret that the creatures had indicated was only intended for the dying. I immediately decided to share this knowledge with others so the "secret" would not reside in me alone, and my life would not be in jeopardy. I put my outboard motor on a dugout canoe and left for an American evangelist mission station nearby. I arrived about noon.

The couple at the mission, Bob and Millie, were a cut above the average evangelists sent from the United States: hospitable, humorous, and compassionate. I told them my story. When I described the reptile with water gushing out of his mouth, they exchanged glances, reached for their Bible, and read to me the following line from Chapter 12 in the Book of Revelation:

And the serpent cast out of his mouth water as a flood . . .

They explained to me that the word "serpent" was synonymous in the Bible with the words "dragon" and "Satan." I went on with my narrative. When I came to the part about the dragon-like creatures fleeing an enemy somewhere beyond the Earth and landing here to hide from their pursuers, Bob and Millie became excited and again read me more from the same passage in the Book of Revelation:

And there was a war in heaven: Michael and his angels fought against the dragon; and the dragon fought and his angels. And prevailed not; neither was their place found any more in heaven. And the great dragon was cast out, that old serpent, called the Devil, and Satan, which deceiveth the whole world: he was cast out into the earth, and his angels with him.

I listened with surprise and wonder. The missionaries, in turn, seemed to be awed by the fact that an atheistic anthropologist, by taking the drink of the "witch doctors," could apparently have revealed to him some of the same holy material in the Book of Revelation. When I had finished my account, I was relieved to have shared my new knowledge, but I was also exhausted. I fell asleep on the missionaries' bed, leaving them to continue their discussion of the experience.

That evening, as I returned to the village in my canoe, my head began to throb in rhythm with the noise of the outboard motor; I thought I was going mad; I had to stick my fingers in my ears to avoid the sensation. I slept well, but the next day I noticed a numbness or pressure in my head.

I was now eager to solicit a professional opinion from the most supernaturally knowledgeable of the Indians, a blind shaman who had made many excursions into the spirit world with the aid of the *ayahuasca* drink. It seemed only proper that a blind man might be able to be my guide to the world of darkness.

I went to his hut, taking my notebook with me, and described my visions to him segment by segment. At first I told him only the highlights; thus, when I came to the dragon-like creatures, I skipped their arrival from space and only said, "There were these giant black animals, something like great bats, longer than the length of this house, who said that they were the true masters of the world." There is no word for dragon in Conibo, so "giant bat" was the closest I could come to describe what I had seen.

He stared up toward me with his sightless eyes, and said with a grin, "Oh, they're always saying that. But they are only the Masters of Outer Darkness."

He waved his hand casually toward the sky. I felt a chill along the lower part of my spine, for I had not yet told him that I had seen them, in my trance, coming from outer space.

I was stunned. What I had experienced was already familiar to this barefoot, blind shaman. Known to him from his own explorations of the same hidden world into which I had ventured. From that moment on I decided to learn everything I could about shamanism.

And there was something more that encouraged me in my new quest. After I recounted my entire experience, he told me that he did not know of anyone who had encountered and learned so much on their first *ayahuasca* journey.

"You can surely be a master shaman," he said.

Thus my serious study of shamanism began. From the Conibo I especially learned about the journey into the Lowerworld and the retrieval of spirits, methods that will be described later in the book. I returned to the United States in 1961, but three years later I came back to South America to be with the Jívaro, with whom I had lived in 1956 and 1957. My mission this time was not just to be an anthropologist, but to learn firsthand how to practise shamanism the Jívaro way. For that reason, I wanted to go to the northwestern part of the Jívaro country where the most powerful shamans were reputed to reside.

I first flew to Quito, Ecuador, in the Andean highlands. I took an old Junkers tri-motor down to a jungle airfield at the eastern base of the Andes on the Pastaza River. There I chartered a single-engine plane to Macas, an ancient white settlement at the foot of the Andes in the midst of the Jívaro country.

Macas was a strange village. It had been founded in 1599 by a handful of Spaniards who had survived the massacre of the legendary Sevilla del Oro by the Jívaro, and for centuries had been perhaps the most isolated community of the Western world. Until the airstrip was built in the 1940's, its most direct connection to the outside world had been a slippery footpath over the Andean escarpment west of the village, involving an arduous eight-day hike to reach the highland city of Riobamba. This isolation had created a white community unlike any other in the world. Even during the early years of the twentieth century the men hunted with blowguns, wore Indian dress, and proudly declared their direct descent from the Conquistadores.

They also had their own marvelous legends and private mysteries. For example, there was the story of how, after the massacre and the retreat from Sevilla del Oro, it took them almost a century to find a new way out over the Andes. The man who had finally succeeded was still remembered in bedtime stories to the children. And there was the spectral horse, complete with clanking chains, which was reportedly such a frequent night visitor to the streets of the village that the inhabitants often huddled inside the palm-thatched huts while the monster roamed about. Its visits ended in 1924, when Catholic missionaries permanently settled in the community. At that time, incidentally, there were still no horses in Macas—the first one, a colt, was carried in on a man's back from Riobamba in 1928, almost three and a half centuries after the community's founding.

Up behind the village, surmounting the eastern Cordillera of the Andes, was Sangay, a great active volcano, snow-capped, billowing smoke by day and glowing by night. The glow, the Macabeos liked to say, was produced by the treasure of the Incas, which they claimed was buried on the slopes of Sangay.

My first day in Macas went well. My young Jívaro guide was awaiting me at the airstrip and the people were hospitable and generous. Food was plentiful, and our meals included generous portions of meat. Since there was no way for the Macabeos to get their cattle over the Andes, they had to eat the beasts themselves; thus cattle were slaughtered in the little village every day. In addition, they gave me *guayusa*, a native tea, which the Macabeos consumed throughout the day instead of coffee. The tea created a sense of euphoria, and the entire local population was gently stoned all day. *Guayusa* is so habituating that before it is offered to a visitor, he is warned that once he drinks it, he will ever after always return to the Ecuadorian jungle.

As I drifted off to sleep in Macas that night of my arrival, images in brilliant reddish hues appeared to me in the darkness of the Macabeo house. What I saw was most peculiar: curvilinear designs intertwining, separating, and turning in a most enjoyable fashion. Then small, grinning demonic faces, which were also red, appeared among the changing patterns—swirling, disappearing and reappearing. I felt I was seeing the spiritual inhabitants of Macas.

Suddenly, with an explosion and a jolt, I was almost thrown off my slat bed. The dogs of the village burst out barking. The visions vanished. People were shouting. An earthquake had shaken the ground, and now a spray of natural fireworks shot into the night sky from Sangay. I felt, undoubtedly irrationally, that the sardonic demons had produced the eruption to greet my return to the jungle and to remind me of their reality. I laughed to myself at the absurdity of it all.

The next day the Catholic missionary showed me his private collection of prehistoric potsherds from the local area. On them were painted red designs almost identical to those I had seen the previous night.

The following morning, my Jívaro guide and I walked northward from Macas, crossed the Río Upano in a dugout canoe, and continued walking all day.

At sunset, exhausted, we reached our destination, the house of a famous shaman, Akachu, deep in the forest. There was no *guayusa* that evening. Instead, I was proffered bowl after bowl of refreshing manioc beer, monkey meat, and raw, squirming, but delicious cheese-like grubs. Tired, but delighted to be back among shamans, I fell into a deep sleep on the bamboo bed.

In the morning Akachu and I sat formally, opposite each other on wooden stools, as his wives brought us bowls of warmed manioc beer. His long black hair, bound into a pony tail with a woven red and white strap from which a feathered tassel hung, showed streaks of gray. I guessed he was in his sixties.

"I have come," I explained, "to acquire spirit helpers, *tsentsak*."

He stared hard at me without saying a word, but the wrinkles in his brown face seemed to deepen.

"That is a fine gun, there," he observed, jutting his chin toward the Winchester shotgun I had brought along for hunting.

His message was clear, for the standard payment among the Jívaro for shamanic initiation was—at the very least—a muzzle-loading shotgun. The breach-loading, cartridge-using Winchester was far more powerful than the black-powder muzzle-loaders, and thus much more valuable.

"To acquire knowledge and spirit helpers, I will give you the gun and my two boxes of cartridges," I said.

Akachu nodded and reached his arm out in the direction of the Winchester. I picked up the gun and carried it over to him. He tested its weight and balance, and sighted along the barrel. Then, abruptly, he laid the gun across his knees.

"First, you must bathe in the waterfall," he said. "Then we will see."

I told him I was ready to do whatever he said.

"You are not a *shuar*, an Indian," Akachu said, "so I do not know if you will have success. But I will help you try." He pointed westward toward the Andes with his chin. "Soon we will make the journey to the waterfall."

Five days later, Akachu, his son-in-law Tsangu, and I departed on the pilgrimage to the sacred waterfall. My Jívaro guide, his duties finished, had already gone home.

The first day we followed a forest trail upstream along a twisting river valley. My companions kept up a very fast pace, and I was thankful when we at last stopped in late afternoon, beside a small rapids in the river. Akachu and Tsangu constructed a palm-thatched lean-to, with a layer of palm fronds for our bed. I slept soundly, kept warm by the slow fire they built in the entrance of the shelter.

The second day our journey was almost a continuous climb upward into the mist-shrouded forest. As the virtually nonexistent trail became more difficult, we paused at a grove of *caña brava* to cut hiking staffs to help us in the ascent. Akachu briefly went off and returned with a three-inch thick pole of balsa wood. While we rested, he quickly carved it with simple geometric designs and then handed it to me.

"This is your magical staff," he said. "It will protect you from demons. If you encounter one, throw it at him. It is more powerful than a gun."

I fingered the pole. It was extremely light and obviously would be of no use in defending oneself against anything material. For a moment I felt as though we were children playing a game of make-believe. Yet these men were warriors, warriors who engaged in repeated life-and-death feuds and wars with their enemies. Didn't their survival depend upon being in genuine contact with reality?

As the day progressed, the trail became steeper and more slippery. Often it seemed that I was sliding one step back in the adobe-like mud for every two steps I made forward. We frequently rested to catch our breath and to sip water mixed with the manioc beer mash in our bottle-gourd canteens. Sometimes the others would snack on the smoked boiled manioc or smoked meat that they carried in their monkey-skin pouches. I, however, was forbidden to eat solid food.

"You must suffer," Tsangu explained, "so that the grandfathers will take pity on you. Otherwise, the ancient specter will not come."

That night, tired and hungry, I attempted to sleep in the palm-thatched leanto my companions had constructed for us on the top of a cold, dank ridge. Shortly before dawn, it began to rain. Too chilled and miserable to stay where we were, we broke camp and groped in the dark along the ridge. The rain grew in intensity. Soon bolts of lightning, accompanied by explosions of thunder, periodically illuminated our way. Many of the lightning strikes seemed to be on the very ridge we were following, so we began to move at maximum speed in order to get off the heights. In the semi-darkness of the obscured dawn I often lost sight of the other two, who were much more accustomed to the incredible pace they were setting through the forest. Even under normal circumstances, the Indians loped along at about four or five miles an hour. Now it seemed like six.

Soon I lost sight of my companions entirely. I assumed they thought that I could follow them. They would undoubtedly be waiting for me somewhere ahead, beyond the end of the ridge. So I forged ahead, wet, tired, hungry, and fearful of being permanently lost in this great, uninhabited forest. One, two, three hours passed and I still did not encounter them. The rain let up and the light in the deserted forest grew stronger. I looked for the sharply bent branches of saplings, the Indians' sign that they had passed that way. But without luck.

I stopped, sat on a log in the middle of the dripping forest and tried to think clearly about my position. I gave the Indians' special long-distance yell, a cry from the depths of the lungs that can be heard a half-mile away. Three times I gave it. There was no answer. I was near panic. I did not have my gun, so hunting was impossible. I did not know where to go. The only humans that I knew of in the forest were my absent companions.

I was aware that we had been headed generally west, but the dense forest canopy prevented me from seeing the direction of the sun. The ridge had numerous forks, so that I could not tell which one would be the best to follow. Almost at random, I picked one ridge and followed it slowly, breaking branches every ten feet or so to guide my companions if they came searching that way. From time to time I yelled, but heard no answering sound. I stopped at a stream and added some water to the concentrated beer in my calabash. As I rested, sweating, dozens of butterflies swirled about, often settling on my head, shoulders and arms. I watched as they sucked the sweat from my skin and simultaneously urinated on it. I got up and went onward into the forest, supporting myself with the balsa staff. It was getting dark. With my *puñal*, or short machete, I cut branches from palm saplings and made a crude lean-to. Exhausted, I drank some beer, covered my body with fronds, and soon fell asleep.

Faint light was filtering down through the forest canopy when I awoke. As I lay there in the green stillness, I heard a muffled boom. It caught me by surprise and I could not ascertain its direction. I quietly listened for perhaps fifteen minutes when another occurred, off to my left. It was clearly a gun. I jumped up and rushed off in the direction of the sound, running, stumbling, slipping as I skidded down steep slopes. From time to time I gave the long-distance yell. Another boom, this time slightly to my right. I veered course and soon found myself climbing down a precipitous canyon, clinging to vines and slipping from one sapling to another. I became aware of a pervasive roar, like a never-ceasing freight train. Abruptly, I was on the boulder-strewn shore of a river. About a quarter-mile upstream, a stupendous waterfall was hurtling over a bare rock cliff. And near its base I could see my companions; at that moment they were my closest friends in all the world.

I had to clamber up and down immense river boulders and ford the pools of water that lay between sand bars. As I got near, I felt the mists of the waterfall, carried down the canyon on the wind, cooling my face and arms. It took me about fifteen minutes to reach Akachu and Tsangu. Finally, I collapsed on the sand beside my companions.

"We thought a demon might have gotten you," said Akachu with a grin. I smiled back weakly, glad to accept the canteen of beer he offered.

"You are tired," he said. "That is good, for the grandfathers may take pity on you. You must now start to bathe."

He pointed to my staff. "Bring your balsa and come with me."

While the others sat on the sand bar, he led me over the rocks along the edge of the great pool into which the cascade poured. Soon we were up against the wet cliff face, as drenching sprays pelted our bodies. He took my hand and inched forward along the base of the cliff. The water poured with mounting strength upon us, making it difficult to avoid being swept away. I supported myself with my staff with one hand and hung onto Akachu with the other.

Each step forward became more difficult. Then suddenly we were underneath the waterfall in a dark, natural recess. It seemed like a magical cave. Light entered only through the immense sheet of falling water, which sealed us in from the rest of the world. The incessant roar of the cascade was greater than even that of my first vision, years before. It seemed to penetrate my whole being. We were sealed from the world by the basic elements of earth and water.

"The House of the Grandfathers," Akachu shouted in my ear. He pointed to my staff.

He had told me earlier what to do. I began to walk back and forth in the incredible chamber, putting my staff before me with each step. As instructed, I continuously shouted, "Tau, tau, tau," to attract the attention of the grandfathers. I was thoroughly chilled from the spray that swept the small cave, water which not long before had been reposing in the glacial lakes of the highest Andes. I shivered, paced, and shouted. Akachu accompanied me, but without a staff.

Gradually, a strange calm pervaded my consciousness. I no longer felt cold, tired, or hungry. The sound of the cascading water grew more and more distant and seemed strangely soothing. I felt that this was where I belonged, that I had come home. The wall of falling water became irridescent, a torrent of millions of liquid prisms. As they went by I had the continuous sensation of floating upward, as though they were stable and I was the one in motion. Flying inside of a mountain! I laughed at the absurdity of the world.

Finally, Akachu grasped my shoulder, stopped me, and took my hand. He led me out of the magic mountain, back along the cliff and to Tsangu. I was sorry to leave the sacred place.

When we had regrouped on the sand bar, Tsangu led us directly to the side of the canyon and commenced scaling the steep slope. We followed, single file, grasping at projecting roots, saplings, and vines to keep ourselves from sliding backward in the wet clay. For perhaps an hour we continued the arduous ascent, occasionally drenched by the wafting spray from the waterfall. It was late afternoon when we finally reached a small, flat ridge adjacent to the rim of the cascade. We rested briefly and then followed Tsangu along the plateau. At first the jungle growth was thick and difficult to penetrate, but shortly we found ourselves in a gallery of immense trees.

After about five minutes Tsangu stopped, and start to cut boughs for a lean-to.

Akachu began splitting a stick at one end. He split the same end a second time, at a right angle to the first cut, and stuck the unsplit end into the ground. Into the cross-wise split he pushed two twigs, which forced the end open into a four-pronged receptacle. Then he took a fist-sized gourd cup from his monkey-skin shoulder bag and set it into the space formed by the prongs. He reached again into his pouch and brought forth a bundle of short green stems. They were the *maikua* (a *Brugmansia* species of datura) plant cuttings he had collected prior to our departure from his house. One by one he held the stems over the gourd cup and scraped off the green bark. When he had finished, the cup was almost full. He reached in, drew out the shavings, and began squeezing their green juice into the cup. Within five minutes there was about an eighth of a cup of the liquid. He threw away the shavings.

"Now we will let the *maikua* cool," he said. "When night comes you will drink it. You alone will drink, for we must guard you. We will be with you at all times, so do not fear."

Tsangu had joined us, and now he added, "What is most important is that you must have no fear. If you see something frightening, you must not flee. You must run up and touch it."

Akachu grasped my shoulder. "That is right. You must do that or one day soon you will die. Hold your balsa at all times in your hands so that you can do the touching."

I began to feel a strong sense of panic. Not only were their words somewhat less than comforting, but I had heard that persons sometimes died or permanently lost their minds from taking *maikua*. I also remembered stories of Jívaro who had taken *maikua* and become so delirious that they had dashed wildly through the forest to fall from cliffs or to drown. For this reason, they never took *maikua* without sober companions to restrain them.

"Will you hold me down strongly?" I asked.

"That will be done, brother," said Akachu.

It was the first time he had addressed me by a kinship term, and that one word reassured me. Still, as I waited for the dark, rising anticipation and curiosity were mixed with fear.

My companions did not make a fire, and as night came we were all stretched out side by side on palm fronds, listening to the stillness of the forest and the distant roar of the waterfall. At last the time came.

Akachu gave me the gourd cup. I tipped it up and swallowed the contents. The taste was somewhat disagreeable, yet slightly similar to green tomatoes. I felt a numbing sensation. I thought of that other drink, three years before among the Conibo, which had led me here. Was my shamanic quest worth the danger?

Shortly, however, even quasi-logical thought vanished as an inexpressible terror rapidly permeated my whole body. My companions were going to kill me! I must get away! I attempted to jump up, but instantly they were upon me. Three, four, an infinity of savages wrestled with me, forced me down, down, down. Their faces were above me, contorted into sly grins. Then blackness.

I was awakened by a flash of lightning followed by a thunderous explosion. The ground beneath me was shaking. I jumped up, utterly in a panic. A hurricane-like wind threw me back down on the ground. I stumbled again to my feet. A stinging rain pelted my body as the wind ripped at my clothes. Lightning and thunder exploded all around. I grasped a sapling to support myself. My companions were nowhere to be seen.

Suddenly, about two hundred feet away amidst the tree trunks, I could see a luminous form floating slowly towards me. I watched, terrified, as it grew larger and larger, resolving itself into a twisting form. The gigantic, writhing reptilian form floated directly towards me. Its body shone in brilliant hues of greens, purples, and reds, and as it twisted amidst the lightning and thunder it looked at me with a strange, sardonic smile.

I turned to run, and then remembered the balsa staff. I looked down but could not see it. The serpentine creature was now only twenty feet away and towering above me, coiling and uncoiling. It separated into two overlapping creatures. They were now both facing me. The dragons had come to take me away! They coalesced back into one. I saw before me a stick about a foot long. I grabbed it, and desperately charged the monster with my stick outstretched before me. An earsplitting scream filled the air, and abruptly the forest was empty. The monster was gone. There was only silence and serenity.

I lost consciousness.

When I awoke it was midday. Akachu and Tsangu were squatting beside a small fire, eating and conversing quietly. My head ached and I was hungry, but otherwise I felt all right. As I sat up, my friends rose and came over. Akachu gave me a bowl of warmed beer. I was also given a piece of dried monkey meat. The food tasted wonderful, but I wanted to share my experience with my friends.

I said, "I thought you were trying to kill me last night. Then you disappeared and there was tremendous lightning . . ."

Akachu interrupted me, "You must not tell anyone, even us, what you have encountered. Otherwise, all your suffering will have been in vain. Someday, and you will know when that is, you can tell others, but not now. Eat, and then we will start for home."

We went back to Akachu's house, and with his guidance I began to acquire the *tsentsak* (magical darts) essential to the practice of Jívaro shamanism. These *tsentsak* or spirit helpers are the main powers believed to cause and cure illness in daily life. To the nonshaman they are normally invisible, and even shamans can perceive them only in an altered state of consciousness.

"Bad" or bewitching shamans send these spirit helpers into victims' bodies to make them ill or to kill them. "Good" shamans, or healers, use their own *tsentsak* to help them suck out spirits from the bodies of ill tribesmen. The spirit helpers also form shields which, along with the shaman's guardian spirit power, protect their shaman masters from attacks.

A new shaman collects all kinds of insects, plants, and other objects, which become his spirit helpers. Almost any object, including living insects and worms, can become a *tsentsak* if it is small enough to be swallowed by a shaman. Different types of *tsentsak* cause, and are used to cure, different kinds of degrees of illness. The greater the variety of these power objects that a shaman has in his body, the greater is his ability as a doctor.

Each *tsentsak* has an ordinary and nonordinary aspect. The magical dart's ordinary aspect is an ordinary material object, as seen without drinking *ayahuasca*. But the nonordinary and "true" aspect of the *tsentsak* is revealed to the shaman by taking the drink. When he does this, the magical darts appear in their hidden forms as spirit helpers, such as giant butterflies, jaguars, serpents, birds, and monkeys, who actively assist the shaman in his tasks.

When a healing shaman is called in to treat a patient, his first task is diagnosis. He drinks *ayahuasca*, green tobacco water, and sometimes the juice of a plant called *pirípirí*, in the late afternoon and early evening. The consciousness-changing substances permit him to see into the body of the patient as though it were glass. If the illness is due to sorcery, the healing shaman will see the intruding nonordinary entity within the patient's body clearly enough to determine whether he possesses the appropriate spirit helper to extract it by sucking.

A shaman sucks magical darts from a patient's body at night, and in a dark area of the house, for it is only in the darkness that he can perceive nonordinary reality. With the setting of the sun, he alerts his *tsentsak* by whistling the tune of his power song; after about a quarter of an hour, he starts singing. When he is ready to suck, the shaman keeps two *tsentsak*, of the type identical to the one he has seen in the patient's body, in the front and rear of his mouth. They are present in both their material and nonmaterial aspects, and are there to catch the nonordinary aspect of the magical dart when the shaman sucks it out of the patient's body. The *tsentsak* nearest the shaman's lips has the task of incorporating the sucked-out essence within itself. If, however, this nonordinary essence should get past it, the second spirit helper in the mouth blocks the throat so that the intruder cannot enter the interior of the shaman's body and do him harm. Trapped thus within the mouth, the essence is shortly caught by, and incorporated into, the material substance of one of the curing shaman's *tsentsak*. He then "vomits" out this object and displays it to the patient and his family saying, "Now I have sucked it out. Here it is."

The nonshamans may think that the material object itself is what has been sucked out, and the shaman does not disillusion them. At the same time he is not lying, because he knows that the only important aspect of a *tsentsak* is its nonmaterial or nonordinary aspect, or essence, which he sincerely believes he has removed from the patient's body. To explain to the layman that he already had these objects in his mouth would serve no fruitful purpose and would prevent him from displaying such an object as proof that he had effected the cure.

The ability of the shaman to suck depends largely upon the quantity and strength of his own *tsentsak*, of which he may have hundreds. His magical darts assume their supernatural aspect as spirit helpers when he is under the influence of *ayahuasca*, and he sees them as a variety of zoomorphic forms hovering over him, perching on his shoulders, and sticking out of his skin. He sees them helping to suck the patient's body. He drinks tobacco water every few hours to "keep them fed" so that they will not leave him.

A healing shaman may have *tsentsak* sent at him by a bewitcher. Because of this danger, shamans may repeatedly drink tobacco water at all hours of the day and night. The tobacco water helps keep one's *tsentsak* ready to repel any other magical darts. A shaman does not even go for a walk without taking along the green tobacco leaves with which he prepares the water that keeps his spirit helpers alert.

The degree of violence and competition in Jívaro society is famous in the anthropological literature and contrasts radically, for example, with the peacefulness of the Conibo. And both the Jívaro and the Conibo stand apart from Australian and many other tribal peoples who have long practiced shamanism without employing psychedelics. Still Jívaro shamanism is highly developed, dramatic, and exciting. So in 1969 I again returned, filling in gaps in my knowledge, and in 1973 I engaged in more shamanic practice with them.

During the nineteen years since beginning shamanic work among the Conibo, I have also studied briefly with shamans of a few western North American Indian groups: the Wintun and Pomo in California, Coast Salish in Washington State, and the Lakota Sioux in South Dakota. From them I learned how shamanism could be practiced successfully without the use of the *ayahuasca* or other drugs of the Conibo and the Jívaro. This knowledge has been especially useful in introducing Westerners to the practice of shamanism. Finally, I learned from the worldwide ethnographic literature on shamanism, where lie buried many gems of information that supplement and reaffirm what I had been taught firsthand. Now it seems time to help transmit some practical aspects of this ancient human legacy to those who have been cut off from it for centuries.

PART II

RELIGIOUS MYTHOLOGY

Guardians, Theravada Buddhist Temple, Bangkok
(Photo by J. T. Carmody)

INTRODUCTION

All religious traditions have developed what we call mythology. Mythology is not something childish. It is not something untrue, at odds with science, put aside by all rational people. Mythology consists of the stories, narratives, dramatic images that have been developed over time as a means to organize and understand the world. American mythology emphasizes heroes such as George Washington and Abraham Lincoln. Jewish mythology emphasizes Moses, David, and famous rabbis. Islamic mythology speaks of Muhammad and Khadija, Ali and Fatima. Everywhere, human beings have told stories, because until they felt they were part of a meaningful tale they were adrift in chaos. Evolutionary theory retains this narrative instinct. Scientists are happiest when they think they know the story of how life moved from one phase (chapter) to another. So it makes sense that all religions have developed mythologies. It would have been inhuman for them not to have done so. The peculiarity of religious myths is that they deal with God and the ultimate mysteries of life and death.

The first myth we include in this part comes from Africa. A French anthropologist, Marcel Griaule, spent considerable time after World War II with the Dogon, a people of the Upper Niger. Eventually he won their confidence enough to be introduced to one of their most revered elders, the blind teacher Ogotemmêli. For more than a month Ogotemmêli instructed Griaule in the basic beliefs of the Dogon, telling him their main myths, those concerned with how the universe had gained its present shape. This was only part of the rich, complicated Dogon spiritual universe, but Griaule soon realized that he had come upon a treasure.

This selection comes from early in Griaule's instruction, but that does not mean it is simple. Much comes after it, to fill out the stories and the overall context. What should be clear, however, even from this small portion of Ogotemmêli's teaching, is the vividness of the Dogon imagination. The major items in the Dogon daily world (of the past as well as the present) pass in review, and the intent of the teaching is to explain how these items got their present shape. In a sense, then, all of Ogotemmêli's teaching is "cosmogonic": concerned with how the world came into being. Many students of myth think that the cosmogony is the most basic story, because for most traditional peoples the world itself was the most important living thing.

The *Mahabharata,* the great Hindu epic, is the longest poem in world literature. It tells the story of a great war early in history. In the course of this story, with many sidetracks and diversions, we meet the major gods of Hindu culture. These gods were part of popular Indian lore—figures in fairy tales as well as theology. The common people got much of their entertainment, as well as their piety, from the myths of the *Mahabharata.* Tradition ascribed the poem to a man named Vyasa ("Arranger"), and scholars set the period between 400 B.C. and A.D. 400 as the time when the present compilation came into shape. Clearly, though, the historical basis for the stories of warfare was considerably earlier, perhaps between 800 and 400 B.C. The selections suggest both the great variety of the gods in traditional Hindu culture and the interest of the common people in such human themes as love and power.

The most important part of the *Mahabharata* is the *Bhagavad Gita,* from which comes the third selection in this part. The *Gita* has the form of a dialogue between the god Krishna and the warrior Arjuna. Krishna serves as the guru, teaching Arjuna the secrets of life. Arjuna is appalled at the prospect of going into battle and killing the kinsfolk arrayed against him. Krishna shows him that the core of the human being is immortal. This is traditional Hindu teaching, as are the other secrets that Krishna imparts. Thus the *Gita* serves as a compendium of Hindu lore. It has been much prized because it was thought to be Krishna's own summary of sacred tradition. Indeed, if one had to nominate a single scriptural text to represent Hindu tradition, the *Gita* would probably be it. Notice the variety that appears even in our short selection. Krishna is teaching Arjuna that there are several ways to salvation (*moksha*). At the end of the *Gita,* though, in a text not included here, Krishna says that the highest way is love of himself—another bit of mythology worth pondering.

The fourth selection, the Gospel According to Saint Mark, is probably the oldest gospel in the Christian New Testament. It is also the shortest, so we have been able to present it whole. Scholars debate where and when the Gospel of Mark arose, but many see a connection to the apostle Peter and think a date of about A.D. 70 likely. Mark invents the genre of gospel, which means "glad tidings." Christianity spread by telling the story of Jesus: his life, death, and resurrection. When Christian communities assembled for worship, they told stories about what Jesus had said and done. Most of the first Christians were Jews who thought that Jesus was the Messiah that Judaism awaited, and they had the precedent of Jewish use of the Bible (using stories about the past to illumine faith in the present) to guide them. The story of Jesus has remained the basic Christian mythology, even though in many periods stories about the saints were also important.

The first question we should ask about religious myths is not whether they are credible in terms of a scientific picture of the world, but what they say about the human condition. How do the stories that Ogotemmêli hands on, or the stories in the *Mahabharata,* or those about Jesus in the Gospel of Mark situate us human beings? Almost always, significant religious myths are traditional—not something recently created but something passed on for generations. In mythic cultures (those not challenged by alternate ideas about "truth," such as the ideas that classical philosophy or modern science introduced), the age of a story contributed to its authority. It carried more clout if it had been told since time out of mind—if it seemed to go back to the very beginnings of the people's existence. So most significant myths were historical, not in the sense that they reported precisely where and when so-and-so did such and such, but in the sense that they had long been used to make sense of the past, had long explained the passage from the beginnings to the present.

The contention implicit in many myths is that basic realities have not changed greatly since the beginnings. The physical world—the animals, sun, wind, seasons—continues to be much as it was, although some myths claim that everything was bigger and better in the beginning. Human nature continues to be much the same, although perhaps it is necessary to explain where death and wrongdoing came from. So by listening to the myths attentively one gains perspective on the present.

Christians enter some qualifications about their mythology. Although they grant that their religion spread by telling the story of Jesus, they insist that Jesus was a real man, not a figure from a fairy tale, and that he was historical in a full sense: born at a particular time, in a particular place, of particular parents, under particular rulers. He walked on the same roads that the early Christians living around Jerusalem walked on. He was one with them in having to eat, sleep, sweat, and suffer. He really died, on the cross, due to Pilate's decree. He really rose from the dead, even though no one saw him leave the tomb or could understand the process by which it happened. So we include the Gospel of Mark not because we want to say that Dogon, Hindus, and Christians live by the same kind of stories, but because they are alike in situating themselves in space and time through traditional stories.

"Situating" themselves is much of what religious people do through their religious activities. They look to their faith, or their traditional culture (which does not separate religion and secular concerns), to help them determine where they stand. If they can determine this, they can believe that their lives make sense, serve some purpose. To understand one's situation is to have made, or accepted, such a determination.

In fact, we all determine our situation each day. Just as we learn to see patterns, to hear sounds so that they form words, so we learn to think of ourselves as third generation Italian-Americans, or first generation American feminists. We work night and day at our scripts, elaborating the story, the myth, that will become our biography. The religious dimension in the biographies of most traditional peoples was their traffic with life's mysteriousness. Their myths shed light on life and death, good and evil. As well, they offered a plausible way of thinking about human destiny: wherefrom and whereto. When such myths became implausible, their religion came into crisis.

4

Marcel Griaule

"Second Day," "Third Day," and "Fourth Day" from *Conversations with Ogotemmêli**

This reading relates some of the major myths of the Dogon people of the Upper Niger region. These myths were told to a French anthropologist, Marcel Griaule, by a revered elder of the Dogon named Ogotemmêli. The stories are part of a much larger Dogon vision of how the universe reached its present order.

SECOND DAY
THE FIRST WORD AND THE FIBRE SKIRT

Ogotemmêli, seating himself on his threshold, scraped his stiff leather snuff-box, and put a pinch of yellow powder on his tongue.

'Tobacco,' he said, 'makes for right thinking.'

So saying, he set to work to analyze the world system, for it was essential to begin with the dawn of all things. He rejected as a detail of no interest, the popular account of how the fourteen solar systems were formed from flat circular slabs of earth one on top of the other. He was only prepared to speak of the serviceable solar system; he agreed to consider the stars, though they only played a secondary part.

'It is quite true,' he said, 'that in course of time women took down the stars to give them to their children. The children put spindles through them and made them spin like fiery tops to show themselves how the world turned. But that was only a game.'

The stars came from pellets of earth flung out into space by the God Amma, the one God. He had created the sun and the moon by a more complicated process, which was not the first known to man but is the first attested invention of God: the art of pottery. The sun is, in a sense, a pot raised once for all to white heat and surrounded by a spiral of red copper with eight turns. The moon is the same shape, but its copper is white. It was heated only one quarter at a time. Ogotemmêli said he would explain later the movements of these bodies. For the moment he was concerned only to indicate the main lines of the design, and from that to pass to its actors.

*From *Conversations with Ogotemmêli* by Marcel Griaule, published for the International African Institute by the Oxford University Press (New York, 1965).

He was anxious, however, to give an idea of the size of the sun. 'Some,' he said, 'think it is as large as this encampment, which would mean thirty cubits. But it is really bigger. Its surface area is bigger than the whole of Sanga Canton.'

And after some hesitation he added:

'It is perhaps even bigger than that.'

He refused to linger over the dimensions of the moon, nor did he ever say anything about them. The moon's function was not important, and he would speak of it later. He said however that, while Africans were creatures of light emanating from the fullness of the sun, Europeans were creatures of the moonlight: hence their immature appearance.

He spat out his tobacco as he spoke. Ogotemmêli had nothing against Europeans. He was not even sorry for them. He left them to their destiny in the lands of the north.

The God Amma, it appeared, took a lump of clay, squeezed it in his hand and flung it from him, as he had done with the stars. The clay spread and fell on the north, which is the top, and from there stretched out to the south, which is the bottom, of the world, although the whole movement was horizontal. The earth lies flat, but the north is at the top. It extends east and west with separate members like a foetus in the womb. It is a body, that is to say, a thing with members branching out from a central mass. This body, lying flat, face upwards, in a line from north to south, is feminine. Its sexual organ is an anthill, and its clitoris a termite hill. Amma, being lonely and desirous of intercourse with this creature, approached it. That was the occasion of the first breach of the order of the universe.

Ogotemmêli ceased speaking. His hands crossed above his head, he sought to distinguish the different sounds coming from the courtyards and roofs. He had reached the point of the origin of troubles and of the primordial blunder of God.

'If they overheard me, I should be fined an ox!'

At God's approach the termite hill rose up, barring the passage and displaying its masculinity. It was as strong as the organ of the stranger, and intercourse could not take place. But God is all-powerful. He cut down the termite hill, and had intercourse with the excised earth. But the original incident was destined to affect the course of things for ever; from this defective union there was born, instead of the intended twins, a single being, the *Thos aureus* or jackal, symbol of the difficulties of God. Ogotemmêli's voice sank lower and lower. It was no longer a question of women's ears listening to what he was saying; other, non-material, ear-drums might vibrate to his important discourse. The European and his African assistant, Sergeant Koguem, were leaning towards the old man as if hatching plots of the most alarming nature.

But, when he came to the beneficent acts of God, Ogotemmêli's voice again assumed its normal tone.

God had further intercourse with his earth-wife, and this time without mishaps of any kind, the excision of the offending member having removed the cause of the former disorder. Water, which is the divine seed, was thus able to enter the womb of the earth and the normal reproductive cycle resulted in the birth of twins. Two beings were thus formed. God created them like water. They were green in colour, half human beings and half serpents. From the head to the loins they were human: below that they were serpents. Their red eyes were wide open like human eyes, and their tongues were forked like the tongues of reptiles. Their arms were flexible and without joints. Their bodies were green and sleek all over, shining like the surface of water, and covered with short green hairs, a presage of vegetation and germination.

These spirits, called Nummo, were thus two homogeneous products of God, of divine essence like himself, conceived without untoward incidents and developed normally in the womb of the earth. Their destiny took them to Heaven, where they received the instructions of their father. Not that God had to teach them speech, that indispensable necessity of all beings, as it is of the world-system; the Pair were born perfect and complete; they had eight members, and their number was eight, which is the symbol of speech.

They were also of the essence of God, since they were made of his seed, which is at once the ground, the form, and the substance of the life-force of the world, from which derives the motion and the persistence of created being. This force is water, and the Pair are present in all water: they *are* water, the water of the seas, of coasts, of torrents, of storms, and of the spoonfuls we drink.

Ogotemmêli used the terms 'Water' and 'Nummo' indiscriminately.

'Without Nummo,' he said, 'it was not even possible to create the earth, for the earth was moulded clay and it is from water (that is, from Nummo) that its life is derived.'

'What life is there in the earth?' asked the European.

'The life-force of the earth is water. God moulded the earth with water. Blood too he made out of water. Even in a stone there is this force, for there is moisture in everything.

'But if Nummo is water, it also produces copper. When the sky is overcast, the sun's rays may be seen materializing on the misty horizon. These rays, excreted by the spirits, are of copper and are light. They are water too, because they uphold the earth's moisture as it rises. The Pair excrete light because they are also light.'

While he was speaking, Ogotemmêli had been searching for something in the dust. He finally collected a number of small stones. With a rapid movement he flung them into the courtyard over the heads of his two interlocutors, who had no time to bend down. The stones fell just where the Hogon's cock had been crowing a few seconds before.

'That cock is a squalling nuisance. He makes all conversation impossible.'

The bird began to crow again on the other side of the wall, so Ogotemmêli sent Koguem to throw a bit of wood at him. When Koguem came back, he asked whether the cock was now outside the limits of the Tabda quarter.

'He is in the Hogon's field,' said Koguem. 'I have set four children to watch him.'

'Good!' said Ogotemmêli with a little laugh. 'Let him make the most of what remains to him of life! They tell me he is to be eaten at the next Feast of Twins.'

He returned to the subject of the Nummo spirits, or (as he more usually put it, in the singular) of Nummo, for this pair of twins, he explained, represented the prefect, the ideal unit.

The Nummo, looking down from Heaven, saw their mother, the earth, naked and speechless, as a consequence no doubt of the original incident in her relations with the God Amma. It was necessary to put an end to this state of disorder. The Nummo accordingly came down to earth, bringing with them fibres pulled from plants already created in the heavenly regions. They took ten bunches of these fibres, corresponding to the number of their ten fingers, and made two strands of them, one for the front and one for behind. To this day masked men still wear these appendages hanging down to their feet in thick tendrils.

But the purpose of this garment was not merely modesty. It manifested on earth the first act in the ordering of the universe and the revelation of the helicoid sign in the form of an undulating broken line.

For the fibres fell in coils, symbol of tornadoes, of the windings of torrents, of eddies and whirlwinds, of the undulating movement of reptiles. They recall also the eight-fold spirals of the sun, which sucks up moisture. They were themselves a channel of moisture, impregnated as they were with the freshness of the celestial plants. They were full of the essence of Nummo: they *were* Nummo in motion, as shown in the undulating line, which can be prolonged to infinity.

When Nummo speaks what comes from his mouth is a warm vapour which conveys, and itself constitutes, speech. This vapour, like all water, has sound, dies away in a helicoid line. The coiled fringes of the skirt were therefore the chosen vehicle for the words which the Spirit desired to reveal to the earth. He endued his hands with magic power by raising them to his lips while he plaited the skirt, so that the moisture of his words was imparted to the damp plaits, and the spiritual revelation was embodied in the technical instruction.

In these fibres full of water and words, placed over his mother's genitalia, Nummo is thus always present.

Thus clothed, the earth had a language, the first language of this world and the most primitive of all time. Its syntax was elementary, its verbs few, and its vocabulary without elegance. The words were breathed sounds scarcely differentiated from one another, but nevertheless vehicles. Such as it was, this ill-defined speech sufficed for the great works of the beginning of all things.

In the middle of a word Ogotemmêli gave a loud cry in answer to the hunter's halloo which the discreet Akundyo, priest of women dying in childbirth and of stillborn children, had called through the gap in the wall.

Akundyo first spat to one side, his eye riveted on the group of men. He was wearing a red Phrygian cap which covered his ears, with a raised point like a uraeus on the bridge of the nose in the fashion known as 'the wind blows'. His cheek-bones were prominent, and his teeth shone. He uttered a formal salutation to which the old man at once replied and the exchange of courtesies became more and more fulsome.

'God's curse,' exclaimed Ogotemmêli, 'on any in Lower Ogol who love you not!'

With growing emotion Akundyo made shift to out-do the vigour of the imprecation.

'May God's curse rest on me,' said the blind man at last, 'if I love you not!'

The four men breathed again. They exchanged humorous comments on the meagerness of the game in the I valley. Eventually Akundyo took his leave of them, asserting in the slangy French of a native soldier that he was going to 'look for porcupine', an animal much esteemed by these people.

The conversation reverted to the subject of speech. Its function was organization, and therefore it was good; nevertheless from the start it let loose disorder.

This was because the jackal, the deluded and deceitful son of God, desired to possess speech, and laid hands on the fibres in which language was embodied, that is to say, on his mother's skirt. His mother, the earth, resisted this incestuous action. She buried herself in her own womb, that is to say, in the anthill, disguised as an ant. But the jackal followed her. There was, it should be explained, no other woman in the world whom he could desire. The hole which the earth made in the anthill was never deep enough, and in the end she had to admit defeat. This prefigured the even-handed struggles between men and women, which, however, always end in the victory of the male.

The incestuous act was of great consequence. In the first place it endowed the jackal with the gift of speech so that ever afterwards he was able to reveal to diviners the designs of God.

It was also the cause of the flow of menstrual blood, which stained the fibres. The resulting defilement of the earth was incompatible with the reign of God. God rejected that spouse, and decided to create living beings directly. Modelling a womb in damp clay, he placed it on the earth and covered it with a pellet flung out into space from heaven. He made a male organ in the same way and having put it on the ground, he flung out a sphere which stuck to it.

The two lumps forthwith took organic shape; their life began to develop. Members separated from the central core, bodies appeared, and a human pair arose out of the lumps of earth.

At this point the Nummo Pair appeared on the scene for the purpose of further action. The Nummo foresaw that the original rule of twin births was bound to disappear, and that errors might result comparable to those of the jackal, whose birth was single. For it was because of his solitary state that the first son of God acted as he did.

'The jackal was alone from birth,' said Ogotemmêli, 'and because of this he did more things than can be told.'

The Spirit drew two outlines on the ground, one on top of the other, one male and the other female. The man stretched himself out on these two shadows of himself, and took both of them for his own. The same thing was done for the woman. Thus it came about that each human being from the first was endowed with two souls of different sex, or rather with two principles corresponding to two distinct persons. In the man the female soul was located in the prepuce; in the woman the male soul was in the clitoris.

But the foreknowledge of the Nummo no doubt revealed to him the disadvantages of this makeshift. Man's life was not capable of supporting both beings: each person would have to merge himself in the sex for which he appeared to be best fitted.

The Nummo accordingly circumcised the man, thus removing from him all the femininity of his prepuce. The prepuce, however, changed itself into an animal which is 'neither a serpent nor an insect, but is classed with serpents'. This animal is called a *nay*. It is said to be a sort of lizard, black and white like the pall which covers the dead. Its name also means 'four', the female number, and 'Sun', which is a female being. The *nay* symbolized the pain of circumcision and the need for the man to suffer in his sex as the woman does.

The man then had intercourse with the woman, who later bore the first two children of a series of eight, who were to become the ancestors of the Dogon people. In the moment of birth the pain of parturition was concentrated in the woman's clitoris, which was excised by an invisible hand, detached itself and left her, and was changed into the form of a scorpion. The pouch and the sting symbolized the organ: the venom was the water and the blood of the pain.

The European, returning through the millet field, found himself wondering about the significance of all these actions and counteractions, all these sudden jerks in the thought of the myth.

Here, he reflected, is a Creator God spoiling his first creation; restoration is effected by the excision of the earth, and then by the birth of a pair of spirits, inventive beings who construct the world and bring to it the first spoken words; an incestuous act destroys the created order, and jeopardizes the principle of twin-births. Order is restored by the creation of a pair of human beings, and twin-births are replaced by dual souls. (But why, he asked himself, twin-births at all?)

The dual soul is a danger; a man should be male, and a woman female. Circumcision and excision are once again the remedy. (But why the *nay*? Why the scorpion?)

The answers to these questions were to come later, and to take their place in the massive structure of doctrine, which the blind old man was causing to emerge bit by bit from the mists of time.

Over the heads of the European and Koguem the dark millet clusters stood out against the leaden sky. They were passing through a field of heavy ears, stiffly erect and motionless in the breeze. When the crop is backward and thin, the ears are light and move with the slightest breath of wind. Thin crops are therefore full of sound. An abundant crop, on the other hand, is weighed down by the wind and bows itself in silence.

THIRD DAY
THE SECOND WORD AND WEAVING

Anyone entering the courtyard upset its arrangements. It was so cramped that the kites, most cunning of all the acrobats of the air, could not get at the poultry. In a hollow stone there were the remains, or rather, the dregs of some millet-beer, which the poultry, cock, hen and chickens, were glad to drink. So was a yellow and white striped dog with tail erect like an Ethiopian sabre. When the door banged, all these creatures dispersed, leaving the courtyard to the humans.

Ogotemmêli, ensconced in his doorway, proceeded to enumerate the eight original ancestors born of the couple created by God. The four eldest were males: the four others were females. But by a special dispensation, permitted only to them, they were able to fertilize themselves, being dual and bisexual. From them are descended the eight Dogon families.

For humanity was organizing itself in this makeshift condition. The permanent calamity of single births was slightly mitigated by the grant of the dual soul, which the Nummo traced on the ground beside women in childbirth. Dual souls were implanted in the new-born child by holding it by the thighs above the place of the drawings with its hands and feet touching the ground. Later the superfluous soul was eliminated by circumcision, and humanity limped towards its obscure destiny.

But the divine thirst for perfection was not extinguished, and the Nummo Pair, who were gradually taking the place of God their father, had in mind projects of redemption. But, in order to improve human conditions, reforms and instruction had to be carried out on the human level. The Nummo were afraid of the terrifying effect of contact between creatures of flesh and blood on the one hand and purely spiritual beings on the other. There had to be actions that could be understood, taking place within the ambit of the beneficiaries and in their own environment. Men after regeneration must be drawn towards the ideal as a peasant is drawn to rich farmland.

The Nummo accordingly came down to earth, and entered the anthill, that is to say, the sexual part of which they were themselves the issue. Thus, they were able, among other tasks, to defend their mother against possible attempts by their elder, the incestuous jackal. At the same time, by their moist, luminous, and articulate presence, they were purging that body which was for ever defiled in the sight of God, but was nevertheless capable of acquiring in some degree the purity required for the activities of life.

In the anthill the male Nummo took the place of the masculine element, which had been eliminated by the excision of the termite-hill clitoris, while the female Nummo took the place of the female element, and her womb became part of the womb of the earth.

The Pair could then proceed to the work of regeneration, which they intended to carry out in agreement with God and in God's stead.

'Nummo in Amma's place,' said Ogotemmêli, 'was working the work of Amma.'

In those obscure beginnings of the evolution of the world, men had no knowledge of death, and the eight ancestors, offspring of the first human couple, lived on indefinitely. They had eight separate lines of descendants, each of them being self-propagating since each was both male and female.

The four males and the four females were couples in consequence of their lower, i.e. of their sexual, parts. The four males were man and woman, and the four females were woman and man. In the case of the males it was the man, and in the case of the females it was the woman, who played the dominant role. They coupled and became pregnant each in him or herself, and so produced their offspring.

But in the fullness of time an obscure instinct led the eldest of them towards the anthill which had been occupied by the Nummo. He wore on his head as head-dress and to protect him from the sun, the wooden bowl he used for his food. He put his two feet into the opening of the anthill, that is of the earth's womb, and sank in slowly as if for a parturition *a tergo* [from the back].

The whole of him thus entered into the earth, and his head itself disappeared. But he left on the ground, as evidence of his passage into that world, the bowl which had caught on the edges of the opening. All that remained on the anthill was the round wooden bowl, still bearing traces of the food and the finger-prints of its vanished owner, symbol of his body and of his human nature, as, in the animal world, is the skin which a reptile has shed.

Liberated from his earthly condition, the ancestor was taken in charge by the regenerating Pair. The male Nummo led him into the depths of the earth, where, in the waters of the womb of his partner he curled himself up like a foetus and shrank to germinal form, and acquired the quality of water, the seed of God and the essence of the two Spirits.

And all this process was the work of the Word. The male with his voice accompanied the female Nummo who was speaking to herself and to her own sex. The spoken Word entered into her and wound itself round her womb in a spiral of eight turns. Just as the helical band of copper round the sun gives to it its daily movement, so the spiral of the Word gave to the womb its regenerative movement.

Thus perfected by water and words, the new Spirit was expelled and went up to Heaven.

All the eight ancestors in succession had to undergo this process of transformation; but, when the turn of the seventh ancestor came, the change was the occasion of a notable occurance.

The seventh in a series, it must be remembered, represents perfection. Though equal in quality with the others, he is the sum of the feminine element, which is four, and the masculine element, which is three. He is thus the completion of the perfect series, symbol of the total union of male and female, that is to say of unity.

And to this homogeneous whole belongs especially the mastery of words, that is, of language; and the appearance on earth of such a one was bound to be the prelude to revolutionary developments of a beneficent character.

In the earth's womb he became, like the others, water and spirit, and his development, like theirs, followed the rhythm of the words uttered by the two transforming Nummo.

'The words which the female Nummo spoke to herself,' Ogotemmêli explained, 'turned into a spiral and entered into her sexual part. The male Nummo helped her. These are the words which the seventh ancestor learnt inside the womb.'

The others equally possessed the knowledge of these words in virtue of their experiences in the same place; but they had not attained the mastery of them nor was it given to them to develop their use. What the seventh ancestor had received, therefore, was the perfect knowledge of a Word—the second Word to be heard on earth, clearer than the first and not, like the first, reserved for particular recipients, but destined for all mankind. Thus he was able to achieve progress for the world. In particular, he enabled mankind to take precedence over God's wicked son, the jackal. The latter, it is true, still possessed knowledge of the first Word, and could still therefore reveal to diviners certain heavenly purposes; but in the future order of things he was to be merely a laggard in the process of revelation.

The potent second Word developed the powers of its new possessor. Gradually he came to regard his regeneration in the womb of the earth as equivalent to the capture and occupation of that womb, and little by little he took possession of the whole organism, making such use of it as suited him for the purpose of his activities. His lips began to merge with the edges of the anthill, which widened and became a mouth. Pointed teeth made their appearance, seven for each lip, then ten, the number of the fingers, later forty, and finally eighty, that is to say, ten for each ancestor.

These numbers indicated the future rates of increase of the families; the appearance of the teeth was a sign that the time for new instruction was drawing near.

But here again the scruples of the Spirits made themselves felt. It was not directly to men, but to the ant, avatar of the earth and native to the locality, that the seventh ancestor imparted instruction.

At sunrise on the appointed day the seventh ancestor Spirit spat out eighty threads of cotton; these he distributed between his upper teeth which acted as the teeth of a weaver's reed. In this way he made the uneven threads of a warp. He did the same with the lower teeth to make the even threads. By opening and shutting his jaws the Spirit caused the threads of the warp to make the movements required in weaving. His whole face took part in the work, his nose studs serving as the block, while the stud in his lower lip was the shuttle.

As the threads crossed and uncrossed, the two tips of the Spirit's forked tongue pushed the thread of the weft to and fro, and the web took shape from his mouth in the breath of the second revealed Word.

For the Spirit was speaking while the work proceeded. As did the Nummo in the first revelation, he imparted his Word by means of a technical process, so that all men could understand. By so doing he showed the identity of material actions and spiritual forces, or rather the need for their co-operation.

The words that the Spirit uttered filled all the interstices of the stuff: they were woven in the threads, and formed part and parcel of the cloth. They were the cloth, and the cloth was the Word. That is why woven material is called *soy*, which means 'It is the spoken word'. *Soy* also means 'seven', for the Spirit who spoke as he wove was seventh in the series of ancestors.

While the work was going on, the ant came and went on the edge of the opening in the breath of the Spirit, hearing and remembering his words. The new instruction, which she thus received, she passed on to the men who lived in those regions, and who had already followed the transformation of the sex of the earth.

Up to the time of the ancestors' descent into the anthill, men had lived in holes dug in the level soil like the lairs of animals. When their attention was drawn to the bowls which the ancestors had left behind them, they began to notice the shape of the anthill, which they thought much better than their holes. They copied the shape of the anthill accordingly, making passages and rooms as shelters from the rain, and began to store the produce of the crops for food.

They were thus advancing towards a less primitive way of life; and, when they noticed the growth of teeth round the opening, they imitated these too as a means of protection against wild beasts. They moulded great teeth of clay, dried them and set them up round the entrances to their dwellings.

At the moment of the second instruction, therefore, men were living in dens which were already, in some sort, a prefiguration of the place of revelation and of the womb into which each of them in due course would descend to be regenerated. And, moreover, the human anthill, with its occupants and its store-chambers for grain, was a rudimentary image of the system which, much later, was to come down to them from Heaven in the form of a marvellous granary.

These dim outlines of things to come predisposed men to take advice from the ant. The latter, after what it had seen the Spirit do, had laid in a store of cotton-fibres. These it had made into threads and, in the sight of men, drew them between the teeth of the anthill entrance as the Spirit had done. As the warp emerged, the men passed the thread of the weft, throwing it right and left in time to the opening and shutting movements of the jaws, and the resulting web was rolled round a piece of wood, fore-runner of the beam.

The ant at the same time revealed the words it had heard and the man repeated them. Thus there was recreated by human lips the concept of life in motion, of the transposition of forces, of the efficacy of the breath of the Spirit, which the seventh ancestor had created; and thus the interlacing of warp and weft enclosed the same words, the new instruction which became the heritage of mankind and was handed on from generation to generation of weavers to the accompaniment of the clapping of the shuttle and the creaking of the block, which they call the 'creaking of the Word'.

All these operations took place by daylight, for spinning and weaving are work for the daytime. Working at night would mean weaving webs of silence and darkness.

FOURTH DAY
THE THIRD WORD AND THE GRANARY OF PURE EARTH

Ogotemmêli had no very clear idea of what happened in Heaven after the transformation of the eight ancestors into Nummo. It is true that the eight, after leaving the earth, having completed their labours, came to the celestial region where the eldest Pair, who had transformed them, reigned. It is true also that these elders had precedence of the others, and did not fail to impose on them at once a form of organization and rules of life.

But it was never quite clear why this celestial world was disturbed to the point of disintegration, or why these disorders led to a reorganization of the terrestrial world, which had nothing to do with the celestial disputes. What is certain is that in the end the eight came down to earth again in a vast apparatus of symbols, in which was included a third and definitive Word necessary for the working of the modern world.

All that could be gathered from Ogotemmêli, by dint of patient attention to his words, was the evasive answer:

'Spirits do not fall from Heaven except in anger or because they are expelled.'

It was obvious that he was conscious of the infinite complexity of the idea of God or the Spirits who took his place, and was reluctant to explain it. However an outline, slight but nevertheless adequate, of this obscure period was eventually obtained.

The Nummo Pair had received the transformed eight in Heaven. But though they were all of the same essence, the Pair had the rights of the elder generation in relation to the newcomers, on whom they imposed an organization with a network of rules, of which the most onerous was the one which separated them from one another and forbade them to visit one another.

The fact was that, like human societies in which numbers are a source of trouble, the celestial society would have been heading for disorder, if all its members had gathered together.

Though this rule was their security, the new generation of Nummo, however, proceeded to break it and thereby overthrew their destiny; and this was how it came about.

God had given the eight a collection of eight different grains intended for their food, and for these the first ancestor was responsible. Of the eight, the last was the *Digitaria,* which had been publicly rejected by the first ancestor when it was given to him, on the pretext that it was so small and so difficult to prepare. He even went so far as to swear he would never eat it.

There came, however, a critical period when all the grains were nearly exhausted except the last. The first and second ancestors, who incidentally had already broken the rule about separation, met together to eat this last food. Their action was the crowning breach of order, confirming as it did their first offence by a breach of faith. The two ancestors thereby became unclean—that is to say, of an essence incompatible with life in the celestial world. They resolved to quit that region, where they felt themselves to be strangers, and the six other ancestors threw in their lot with them and made the same decision. Moreover, they proposed to take with them when they left anything that might be of use to the men they were going to rejoin. It was then that the first ancestor, no doubt with the approval and perhaps with the help of God, began to make preparations for his own departure.

He took a woven basket with a circular opening and a square base in which to carry the earth and puddled clay required for the construction of a world-system, of which he was to be one of the counsellors. This basket served as a model for a basket-work structure of considerable size which he built upside down, as it were, with the opening, twenty cubits in diameter, on the ground, the square base, with sides eight cubits long, formed a flat roof, and the height was ten cubits. This framework he covered with puddled clay made of the earth from heaven, and in the thickness of the clay, starting from the center of each side of the square, he made stairways of ten steps each facing towards one of the cardinal points. At the sixth step of the north staircase he put a door giving access to the interior in which were eight chambers arranged on two floors.

The symbolic significance of this structure was as follows:

The circular base represented the sun.

The square roof represented the sky.

A circle in the center of the roof represented the moon.

The tread of each step being female and the rise of each step male, the four stairways of ten steps together prefigured the eight tens of families, offspring of the eight ancestors.

Each stairway held one kind of creature, and was associated with a constellation, as follows:

The north stairway, associated with the Pleiades, was for men and fishes;

The south stairway, associated with Orion's Belt, was for domestic animals.

The east stairway, associated with Venus, was for birds.

The west stairway, associated with the so-called 'Long-tailed Star', was for wild animals, vegetables, and insects.

In fact, the picture of the system was not easily or immediately grasped from Ogotemmêli's account of it.

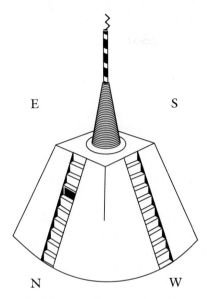

Fig. 2 World-system

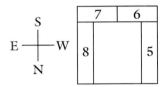

Plan of upper storey

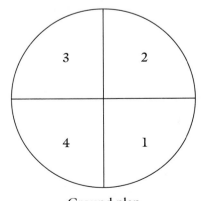

Ground plan

Fig. 3 World-system: plan

'When the ancestor came down from Heaven,' he said at first, 'he was standing on a square piece of Heaven, not a very big piece, about the size of a sleeping-mat, or perhaps a bit bigger.'

'How could he stand on this piece of Heaven?'

'It was a piece of celestial earth.'

'A thick piece?'

'Yes! As thick as a house. It was ten cubits high with stairs on each side facing the four cardinal points.'

The blind man had raised his head, which was almost always bent towards the ground. How was he to explain these geometrical forms, these steps, these exact measurements? The European had begun by thinking that what was meant was a tall prism flanked by four stairways forming a cross. He kept returning to this conception in order to get it quite clear, while the other, patiently groping in the darkness which enveloped him, sought for fresh details.

At last his ravaged face broke into a kind of smile: he had found what he wanted. Reaching into the inside of his house and lying almost flat on his back, he searched among a number of objects which grated or sounded hollow as they scraped the earth under his hand. Only his thin knees and his feet were still visible in the embrasure of the doorway; the rest disappeared in the shadows within. The front of the house looked like a great face with the mouth closed on two skinny shin-bones.

After much tugging, an object emerged from the depths and appeared framed in the doorway. It was a woven basket, black with dust and soot of the interior, with a round opening and a square base, crushed and broken, a wretched spectacle.

The thing was placed before the door, losing several strands in the process, while the whole of the blind man's body reappeared, his hand still firmly grasping the basket.

'Its only use now is to put chickens in,' he said.

He passed his hands slowly over its battered remains, and proceeded to explain the world-system.

5

The Mahabharata, "A Mine of Jewels and Gems"*

The following reading is an excerpt from the Mahabharata, *an epic poem that tells of a great war involving the major gods of Hindu culture early in history. In addition to its religious influence, this highly involved and lively poem has long served as a basis for much of popular Indian lore and culture.*

Sauti the storyteller told this tale to his friend Saunaka in Naimisha Forest. Bending with humility, Sauti came wandering through the wood in the evening and saw before him the glowing fire that burnt by day and night to guard Saunaka's forest home.

Saunaka asked him, "Lotus-eyed Sauti, from where do you wander?"

Sauti answered, "From Hastinapura, from the snake sacrifice of the Kuru king Janemejaya. There I heard Vyasa's *Mahabharata,* that was first written down for the poet by the elephant god Ganesha."

"How was that?"

Sauti answered, "I will tell you what happened."

Listen—

For three years Vyasa composed the *Mahabharata* in his mind, and when it was finished, he summoned Ganesha to be his scribe.

Shiva's son came and asked, "Why call me?"

Vyasa replied, "Do you not remove all obstacles and barriers? You are the god of thieves and writers. Write down my book as I tell it to you."

Ganesha swished his trunk around. "OM! But there are books and books: Is yours a very good one?"

"Yes."

Ganesha laughed, and his huge belly shook. "Well just let me get rid of all these things . . ." He set down the conch shell and lotus, the discus and axe that he held in his four hands. ". . . and I shall write for you; but if once you stop the story, I will leave and never return."

Vyasa said, "On this condition: if you don't understand what I mean, you must write no more until you do."

"Done! The very day I was born I made my first mistake, and by that path have I sought wisdom ever since."

*William Buck. *Mahabharata. Introduced by B. A. van Nooten. Illustrations by Shirley Triest.* "A Mine of Jewels and Gems," pp. 5–47. Copyright © 1973 The Regents of the University of California.

Listen—

I was born fullgrown from the dew of my mother's body. We were alone, and Devi told me, "Guard the door. Let no one enter, because I'm going to take a bath."

Then Shiva, whom I had never seen, came home. I would not let him into his own house.

"Who are you to stop me?" he raged.

And I told him, "No beggars here, so go away!"

"I may be half naked," he answered, "but all the world is mine, though I care not for it."

"Then go drag about your world, but not Parvati's mountain home! I am Shiva's son and guard this door for her with my life!"

"Well," he said, "you are a great liar. Do you think I don't know my own sons?"

"Foolishness!" I said. "I was only born today, but I know a rag picker when I see one. Now get on your way."

He fixed his eyes on me and very calmly asked, "Will you let me in?"

"Ask no more!" I said.

"Then I shall not," he replied, and with a sharp glance he cut off my head and threw it far away, beyond the Himalayas.

Devi ran out, crying, "You'll never amount to anything! You've killed our son!" She bent over my body and wept. "What good are you for a husband? You wander away and leave me home to do all the work. Because you wander around dreaming all the time, we have to live in poverty with hardly enough to eat."

The Lord of All the Worlds pacified her; looking around, the first head he saw happened to be an elephant's, and he set it on my shoulders and restored me to life.

"Parvati was happy again, and that is how I first met my father," said Ganesha, "long, long ago."

"All right," said Vyasa, "now I will begin." And he began to tell his story to Ganesha, who wrote it on leaves.

"And many times Vyasa would compose lines that would make Ganesha pause, so he could use the time to think out the next part," said Sauti.

Saunaka replied, "Yes—that *Bharata* is a mine of gems like the deep Ocean. Whoever hears it, and understands even a small bit of it, escapes the chains he has forged by deeds of good or evil; he finds high success, for *Mahabharata* is excellent, and holds the power of victory! The one who tells it to one who has asked to hear gives him as a gift the whole Earth with her belt of seas. Stay with me and tell me that tale."

Sauti answered, "Yes—I will."

Listen—

Long ago, when the sea was milk, Narayana said to the gods of heaven, "Churn the ocean, and she will yield amrita, the nectar of immortality, and precious gems, and all manner of illusion and revelation."

So they placed the snow mountain Mandara in the middle of the milk sea. Its deep-striking roots rested on the ocean floor; its summit rose high above the surface. The great serpent Sesha, whose hood is an island of jewels, stretched himself across the sea, his body wrapped endlessly round the mountain in the center. On one shore his tail was held by the Asuras, the dark, olden gods; on the other shore his neck was held by the devas, the mortal gods of heaven. They each pulled in turn, so that the mountain spun first one way, then the other, while his trees and stones were thrown off into the foaming sea.

First the mild Moon rose from the milk sea; then the Lady Lakshmi, bearing good fortune to men; then the smooth jewel adorning Narayana's breast; then Indra's elephant Airavata, white as clouds; then Surabhi, the white cow who grants any wish; then Parijata the wishing-tree of fragrance; then Rambha the nymph, the first Apsaras; and at last Dhanwantari the physician, robed in white, bearing a cup filled with amrita, the essence of life.

Suddenly poison burst fuming from the sea, and the milk became salt water. Shiva, the Lord of Mountains and Songs swallowed the poison to save the worlds. He held it in his throat and his neck turned blue, iridescent as a butterfly's wing.

Shiva put the crescent moon in his hair as an ornament. Narayana became a woman, beautiful with desire, and bore away the cup of life.

Now thousands of rivers rush swiftly to the sea as rivals for his love. In the ocean are the palaces of the serpent kings who rule the rivers of Earth, and far from land, in the heart of the deep, roars the red submarine fire that boils the water into rainclouds.

The changes of the moon make the ocean rise and fall with the slow rhythms of Time. Wherever land ends, there the sea dances with the uplifted hands of his waves—wide as space, vast as Time.

The holy Ganges runs from the hills into the sea, and the Yamuna runs into the Ganges. Between the two rivers lies Kurujangala, that is ruled from the Elephant City of Hastinapura by Parikshita's son Janamejaya.

Yudhishthira the Pandava was the Kuru king before Parikshita, but when he received Arjuna's letter—*Come to me*—he made the newborn Parikshita king, then left with his brothers and their wife for the Silver Mountain Kailasa and was never seen again. Parikshita ruled his kingdom well for sixty years, but then one day in the forest, angry that a deer had escaped him, the king mortally wounded a serpent who meant him no harm. Before he died that Naga touched water and said, "Within seven days Parikshita shall die of snakebite for his cruelty; there is no hope for him!"

A woodsman heard and told the king, who left his palace and began to live night and day in a house supported by a single column, well guarded by warriors. Parikshita had but entered his retreat when an old man, dusty and torn, was seen approaching. Sometimes he was visible to the eye; sometimes he faded away as he walked and again slowly reappeared. He walked up to the guards and joined his hands in greeting, and his form shimmered and danced like heat waves in the air.

Then he narrowed his eyes and spoke, "I am Takshaka the Naga prince; warn the king that I shall burn him!" The soldiers rushed at him, but he laughed and vanished on the spot.

Now, my friend, there was no way to enter or leave Parikshita's house save by a ladder, and none could climb up or down who was not a loyal friend to the king. So with his court the king stayed there until the end of the seventh day. At sunset, when the ladder was about to be drawn up for the night, Parikshita saw a tiny copper-colored beetle crawling over a mango, and with a smile he picked it up.

"Now I have no more fear of Takshaka than of this insect!" said the king, and his court laughed as Parikshita held up the tiny beetle and set it on his shoulder. Even thus was Takshaka disguised! Instantly, the Naga prince became himself and bit the king.

Parikshita's courtiers and ministers fled down the ladder in fear, and as they ran in every direction they saw Takshaka fly away through the blue sky of evening like the vermillion streak that divides a woman's hair through the center.

Janamejaya then became king, and he planned a snake sacrifice to burn Takshaka. I heard of it and went to watch. There, at the proper time, brahmanas dressed all in black set afire a great stack of buttered wood. They repeated, over and over, all the names of Takshaka; they poured butter into the fire from great wooden ladles and the flames became deep red and the smoke grew heavy and black. Their eyes were red and tearful from the smothering smoke. All around them the spectators watched the air above the fire, waiting to see Takshaka appear.

When Takshaka felt himself being drawn to Janamejaya's fire he fled from his jeweled palace in the underworld and sought refuge with Indra, the Lord of Heaven. Indra gave him his protection, so the brahmanas spoke their mantras and poured their butter in vain and Janamejaya grew restless in the hot afternoon.

Then a young man came to the king's side and knelt beside him. His name was Astika, and he was born of a Naga woman. His father had hesitated to marry, yet wished for a wife, and once in the still forest very faintly asked for a woman to marry him. There a Naga girl heard him, and he married her, true to his word.

Astika looked upon the world of men with an even eye. He bent his head, touching his brow with hands joined in namaste, and said, "Majesty, I am Asitka. I wander here and there throughout your kingdom of Kurujangala. Let those we cherish be happy! Let our kings and our princes live Long! Janamejaya—know that Takshaka is in heaven with Indra!"

The king replied, "Welcome to you!" He called his brahmanas and told them where Takshaka was hiding and said to Astika, "For this, ask of me any gift and I will give it!"

Astika answered, "Be patient, Majesty. Soon I shall ask."

The brahmanas began to call down Indra and Takshaka both, and in a few moments the Lord of Rain appeared in his chariot, drawn by misty grey horses, hanging in the air over the fire; there was no sign of the Naga. The brahmanas cried out, "Lord of heaven, give us the Naga prince or we will cast you both into the flames!"

Indra looked down with unblinking eyes and a flashing thunderbolt appeared in his hand. He took deadly aim at the brahmanas and raised his arm to destroy them. But the mantras and spells had overcome Takshaka as soon as Indra turned his attention from him, and he was hanging in midair above the fire, between Indra and the brahmanas. Seeing this, Indra vanished, for there was nothing more he could do for the serpent.

But the brahmanas still could not make the Naga prince fall into the flames, because Astika whispered softly, "*Stay . . . Stay . . .* " Then he turned to Janamejaya and said, "Majesty—stop the sacrifice."

Janamejaya smiled. "Astika, instead I will give you gold and silver," he said.

"Gold and silver I do not want, but half my blood is of the Naga race."

"Beautiful women and white cattle I will give you instead."

"Majesty, women and cattle I do not want, but the Naga prince is dear to me."

"Then I give you his life! You have saved him from me, and you have done it well!"

"And this in return, Majesty: have no fear of any serpent, but think—*Serpents of good fortune, live in peace here with your dear ones.*"

"Let it be so for all my people."

Astika said, "It will be so, Majesty, for all your people," and Takshaka vanished from our sight.

When he entered his palace, Janamejaya Raja found waiting for him a dark man, dressed in deerskin and bark, who bore his one hundred and fifty years with calm and dignity and sparkling eyes.

"Vyasa!"

"Sit beside me, Janamejaya. The jeweled Naga escaped you, and you bear him no malice. That is good."

The king called for water and washed Vyasa's feet. "I bow to you," he said, "you who knew my ancestors. Will you not stay and tell me your story? Will you not untie the knots of my heart?"

"I am old, Bharata. With my dark blue skin I am like a thundercloud holding the memory of lightning, of love and terror and the deeds of heroes. But I have not come alone, and I have told my story in the forest to my companion Vaisampayana, who waits outside. He is young, and fair, and wears one silver earring in the shape of a moonbeam. I will stay while he tells it to you, and I myself will listen."

Janamejaya and Vyasa found Vaisampayana outside in the spreading shade of an old tree. Janamejaya bowed to him with joined hands.

Vaisampayana in his white robe said, "Excellent, Majesty! I shall be pleased to tell you! Let Vyasa sit with his back against the tree, and let all who wish to hear gather round us now."

Then Janamejaya, and Astika, and myself, and many of the Kurus sat down under that old tree. Vaisampayana sat beside Vyasa and said, "Welcome! Now hear from me the *Mahabharata*."

Listen, Majesty—

You are born in the Lunar race, descended from the Moon, descended from Bharata and Kuru; you are Arjuna's grandson.

I begin my story with the Kuru king Pratipa. In his old age he was still childless, so with his queen he left Hastinapura and lived in the forest near the Ganges. There he hoped fortune would favor him with a son.

At that time the dead king Mahabhisha sat in heaven, listening to Lord Brahma explain the riddles of all Creation to a large audience of the faithful. But Mahabhisha was bored. He sat on the edge of the group, and his attention strayed here and there until he saw Ganga the beautiful River Goddess walk by. White as moonbeams, her silken robes flowed over her body as she moved, concealing little and suggesting much, as though she walked through silver water. The Queen of Rivers felt his glance and their eyes met.

Mahabhisha began to perspire, and this never happens in heaven until one is ready to be reborn. He removed his heavenly garland, which had remained fresh and fragrant for centuries, and watched the jasmine and ginger flowers fade and turn brown. He smiled at the Goddess and vanished from Heaven.

The beautiful Ganga wishfully followed his soul with her heavenly eyes as it fell back to Earth and entered the womb of Pratipa's Queen.

Pratipa sent his wife and his son Santanu back to the city, but to give thanks for Santanu's birth he himself remained in the forest as before. One evening he was sitting on a rock under a tree by the river when a wonderfully beautiful lady arose from the water and walked over to him. She smiled down at him and sat on his lap.

Pratipa asked, "Whoever you are, how can I help you?"

Ganga brushed the wet hair from her smooth forehead and said, "I am in love, Majesty."

Gently the king put his arm around her. "When a woman asks, one cannot ignore her," he said. "But you sit on my right thigh, where a daughter belongs."

"Yes," said Ganga, "I have loved him since before his birth to you."

Pratipa answered, "When he is grown I will tell Santanu that you are waiting for his love."

"Blessed be you, Pratipa! I will meet him by the river many years from now." Then Ganga dove into the flowing water and was gone. She swam upstream, through the gate where the Ganges falls from heaven, and was again in the realm of the gods.

There she lay on a warm stone, drying her long, dark hair in the sun, smiling to herself, when the eight Vasu gods, who are Indra's attendants, came to see her, looking downcast and guilty.

"What is it?" asked Ganga. "What's the matter with you?"

Prabhasa, the shining spirit of dawn, shuffled his feet uneasily and said, "Ganga, we have a favor . . . I mean . . . look here, would you be our mother?"

Ganga laughed. "You'd better tell me what you've done, first."

Prabhasa gave her a crooked smile. "Brahma's son Vasishtha has cursed us to be born on Earth!"

"Well, that's not so bad. But what did you do?"

"My wife talked me into stealing Surabhi, the cow of wishes. Vasishtha thinks more of that cow than of all heaven and Earth, and even though he wasn't around I didn't want to do it. My wife has a friend on Earth and she wanted to let her drink some of the magic milk and so be free from disease and old age. I wanted just to take the milk, but my wife looked hurt, and at the same time innocent as the cow herself. We were all of us there, and the other women joined in, wondering aloud why I didn't love my wife enough to . . . well, you know . . ."

Ganga had a wide smile on her face. "I am polite enough not to laugh," she said, "even though you would, if it had happened to someone else. How could you fall for something like that?"

"Ganga! I refuse to explain what you know very well yourself," said the Vasu. "It is enough to say that we in turn spoke to Surabhi and talked her into coming for a visit with us, down to Earth. While we were gone Vasishtha returned, discovered us with his magic insight, and gave us his curse for our trouble."

"And why come to me?" asked the goddess.

"Well, we knew you had plans . . ."

"Say no more! You will all be born to the wife of Santanu the Kuru king!"

When Santanu was a young man, Pratipa told him, "When you were very young, a fair maiden came to me and told me of her love for you. If you should meet her secretly near the Ganges, ask not who she is, nor whose, nor from where she comes, but take her for your wife by my word."

Soon after this Pratipa died and Santanu became the Bharata king. One day as he rode alone beside the Ganges he met there a maiden shining with beauty, dressed in transparent watery blue silk trimmed with gold, and wearing a belt of pearls. Each looked and looked into the other's eyes, and each longed to look there forever.

Softly the king said, "Beautiful One, of whatever race you are, goddess or Naga, Asura or Apsaras, or human being as myself—return with me now as my Queen."

Ganga smiled at him and lowered her eyes. "I would like to do this," she said, "but if I become your lady you must never ask my name, nor speak to me unkindly, nor interfere with anything I do, or I will leave you."

"I promise; come sit behind me."

Here in this city they were married, and every year Ganga bore a son to Santanu. But for seven years she threw each child into the Ganges and drowned him there, saying, *"This is for your good,"* and so freed all the Vasus but Prabhasa.

Santanu said nothing to her about this, for he loved her and remembered his promise. Seven princes died at Ganga's hands; but when she carried her eighth son to the river and held him over the water, smiling into her baby's eyes, the king cried out, *"Stop! Do not kill him!"*

"Then take him as my gift," said Ganga. "I shall not free him from life." Then the Goddess stepped into her river that flows from heaven to beneath the sea. "My Lord, I am Ganga, and I leave you now with your son!"

Santanu held his child at his breast and turned away without a word. He was a good king, he kept the Kurus in peace, and by the touch of his hand he could remove old age from any man.

Bharata, to the south lies the land of Chedi. When Santanu was a boy, the Chedi king Uparichara once left his palace to hunt in the forest. It was springtime, and every tree and vine of the forest was in flower. Bees swarmed over the blossoms, birds sang and called to each other, and a fragrant breeze sighed gently through the wood.

When he had gone a little ways, Uparichara sat down to rest under a flowering tree. He closed his eyes and fell asleep, and he dreamt of his beautiful Queen who waited for him at home. When he awoke, he found that his vital seed had left him and fallen on a leaf nearby.

The king summoned a hawk to carry that leaf to the Queen. The hawk flew away with it into the sky, but another hawk attacked him, thinking that he carried food, and the leaf fell into the Yamuna, where a mother fish swallowed it as it touched the water.

That fish made her way upstream to Santanu's kingdom and was netted from the river many months later. When the fisherman cut her open he found in her belly a baby girl, whom he raised as his daughter, naming her Satyavati. She grew up to be very handsome, but had always about her the smell of fish. She spent her days sculling a shallow boat along the Yamuna, helping her father tend his nets.

One day the wandering minstrel Parashara came to the riverside, and when he saw Satyavati he said to her, "Accept my love today, beautiful one."

Satyavati blushed. "Now it is broad daylight," she whispered, "and there are people all up and down the riverside."

"But leave your boat and sit by me," answered Parashara. When she was by his side, he sang a magic song that made thick fog cover the river and the land, concealing everything. They went in her boat to a little island, and while the boatmen on the river called out to avoid collisions all around them, Satyavati gladly gave herself to her lover. In return he removed the smell of fish from her and instead made her fragrant as flowers.

On the river island Satyavati gave birth to the poet Vyasa. Parashara took him away into the forest, and Satyavati returned to her father.

King Santanu named his son Bhishma. It was his great happiness to see him grow to manhood, strong and intelligent, with broad shoulders and fair skin. Once near the Yamuna the king caught the fragrance of flowers in the season when there are no flowers. Following his nose, Santanu discovered Satyavati, took her up on his royal chariot, and carried her to Hastinapura as his Queen.

Bhisma was pleased to see his father so happy, and as his marriage gift he told him, "Let your child by Satyavati rule the kingdom after you, and I will protect him and his children as long as I can."

"Why do you offer this to me?" asked Santanu.

"Majesty," replied Bhishma, "I care not to be king, nor to marry, but I would rather make our race the strongest in all the land by my energy."

Santanu said, "Then take these words as my gift, Bhishma: *Death will never come to you, so long as you wish to live. He will dare to approach you only when you have given him permission.*"

Santanu's son by Satyavati was named Vichitravirya; when he was a youth, Santanu made him king and retired alone to the forest. There by the Ganges, in the hermitage where he had been born, he lived all alone until he died.

Bhishma heard that the three daughters of the king of Banaras were to hold their swayamvara, the self-choice ceremony, where each would choose her husband from among the kings and princes assembled there. He wanted Vichitravirya to marry, but the king was too young to stand any chance of being chosen. So Bhishma himself went in a light chariot to Banaras.

Once there he told no one who he was and did not enter the open arena with the other kings. Bhishma had no weapons with him, nor any sign that he was a warrior. His four swift horses were covered with dust and no one gave them a second glance as he waited while the royal guests assembled. Then the three princesses, named Amba, Ambika and Ambalika, arrived; the Banaras army surrounded the area, ready to make peace among rejected kings; and Bhishma spoke softly to his horses.

Without the weight of armor his light chariot leapt forward; he broke through the king's army from behind, where they kept no watch, and scattered them from his path. In the wink of an eye he had stopped and caught up the three maidens before anyone could realize what had happened.

Bhishma smiled at the powerful kings and princes gathered from every land and said, "Know that the Kurus do not compete with your kind, and know also that the wife is most dear who is stolen by force! You now have my permission to go home!"

Biting their lips in wrath, the suitors slapped their armpits with cupped hands and roared in anger, calling out to Bhishma, *"Stay!—Wait!"* They called for the Banaras army; they drew their swords, aimed their arrows, ran to find their chariots and armor. Bhishma laughed and was gone in a cloud of dust, while ten thousand arrows and darts buried themselves deep in the Earth behind him. The thunder of his horses and the rattle of his car were soon gone in the distance, and none could hope to overtake him.

In Hastinapura Bhishma gave the three captives to Satyavati until their marriage. She was kind to them, and they spoke openly to her. Ambika and Ambalika were willing to marry Vichitravirya, but the eldest princess Amba said, "In my heart I have already chosen King Salwa, who rules in the west, and he has chosen me as his wife. Now do what should be done for me."

Satyavati understood, and sent Amba to her husband. Her sisters married Vichitravirya, but the Kuru king stood in the shadow of death from consumption and soon died, leaving behind his kingdom and all who loved him.

"My son had no child," wept Satyavati. "The kingdom is dead without a king. How have I done wrong, that he has died so young?"

Bhishma said, "Queen, blame not yourself. Have you not another son, the island-born Vyasa? Bring him here and ask him to father sons by Vichitravirya's wives."

"He lives in the forest," answered Satyavati, "and I may call him to me by my thoughts."

Then, Bharata, Vyasa came at his mother's call and fathered three sons. For one change of the moon he lived with Ambika; then for a month with Ambalika; then after with one of Satyavati's maidservants. When he had sown those sons in Vichitravirya's fields, Vyasa left for the forest. When the children were born, Bhishma raised them as his own. First was born Ambika's son Dhritarashtra, who was blind, but whose bodily strength had no equal among men. Next was Ambalika's son Pandu; and the youngest brother was Vidura, the maidservant's son.

6

The Bhagavad Gita, Chapter 4*

The Bhagavad Gita *is a key portion of the* Mahabharata, *the epic poem of the Hindu religion and of Indian folklore. In the* Gita *the god Krishna serves as guru to the warrior Arjuna, teaching him the great secrets of life. Traditional Hindu teaching has it that the* Gita *is Krishna's own summary of sacred wisdom, and thus it is of enormous importance to Hindu beliefs.*

THE LORD
   SAID:

1   Long ago I proclaimed this way of life
    To the sun-lord. It is unchanging.
    The sun-lord taught it to Manu.
    Manu told it to Ikshvaku.

2   So receiving it in their order
    The king-sages knew it
    Till, Foe-Scorcher, this teaching was lost
    Here in the long ages of the world.

3   This same ancient way of life
    I tell you today
    For you are my friend, devoted to me
    And this is the supreme secret.

ARJUNA
   SAID:

4   Your birth was later—
    The sun-lord was born before.
    How may I understand what you say
    That you taught this in the beginning?

THE LORD
   SAID:

5   I have passed through many births
    And so have you, Arjuna,
    But I remember all of these.
    Scourge of the Foe, you do not remember.

* Excerpt from *The Bhagavad Gita* by S. Radhakrishnan, translated by Ann Stanford. Copyright © 1956 by The Berne Convention. Reprinted by permission of HarperCollins Publishers.

6   Though I am unborn and my self
     Unchanging, though I am lord of beings,
     Ruling my own realm of nature
     I am born through my own creative power.

7   For whenever the right
     Languishes, son of Bharata,
     Whenever wrong rises up
     Then I send myself forth

8   To protect those who are good
     And destroy the doers of evil
     To make a firm foothold for the right
     I am born in age after age.

9   He who knows my divine birth
     And my works as they truly are
     Does not go to rebirth, Arjuna,
     Leaving the body, he comes to me.

10   Freed of passion, anger, and fear,
     Absorbed in me, taking refuge in me,
     Purified by the fire of wisdom
     Many have come to my mode of being.

11   Son of Pritha, everywhere
     Men are following my path.
     In whatever way they come to me
     In that same way I give them grace.

12   Those who wish for success in works
     Sacrifice to the gods in this world
     For quickly in the world of men
     Success comes, born of ritual action.

13   I hurled forth the four orders of men
     Dividing them by natures and work.
     Though I am the doer of that
     Know I am the non-doer forever.

14   I am not stained by actions—
     I do not yearn for their fruit.
     He who thus understands me
     Is not bound by works.

15   So understanding, work was done
     By men of old seeking release.
     Therefore you also should act
     As they did long ago.

16   What is action, what is inaction?
Even the wise are perplexed about this.
I will tell you what action is
And, knowing, you will be freed from evil.

17   For one must learn what action is
And the nature of wrong action.
One must learn too about non-action.
Thick and tangled is the way of works.

18   Who can see the stillness in what is done
And true action in being still
He is enlightened among men,
He is a disciplined doer of all.

19   When all his undertakings are free
Of the calculations of desire
His entanglement burned in the fire of wisdom,
The wise call him learned.

20   Giving up love for the fruits of work
Always content, dependent on none,
Even though he takes part in works
Still he does nothing whatsoever.

21   Without desires, thought and self restrained,
Giving up all possessions,
Doing what he does with the body alone,
He acquires no stain.

22   Content with getting what comes along,
Transcending the pairs, not thinking *I*,
The same in failure and success
Even when he acts, he is not caught.

23   When released, free of hanging on,
With his mind settled in wisdom
He acts for the sake of sacrifice
All action vanishes.

24   The choice of offering is God. What is
Offered is God. It is poured by God
In the fire of God. He is sure to reach God
Who concentrates on the work that is God.

25   Some disciplined men revere
The sacrifice as divine. Other men
Offer the sacrifice in the fire of God
By the act of sacrifice.

26   Some offer in the fires of restraint
     Hearing, and all the senses,
     Others offer in the senses' fire
     Sound and the other objects of sense.

27   Some offer all acts of the senses
     And the work of the vital breath
     In the fire of the way of self-control
     When it had been kindled by wisdom.

28   Men of strict vows, forsaking the world,
     Sacrifice material things, or give themselves
     To austerities or the wisdom
     Of repeating the sacred word.

29   Some, intent on the control of breath,
     Restraining the courses of breathing,
     Offer the breaths that go out and come in
     One into the other.

30   Some, abstaining from food,
     Pour their lives into their life-breaths.
     All these know what sacrifice is
     And by sacrifice their stains are worn away.

31   Tasting ambrosia, left from the remains of sacrifice,
     They go to God eternal. Even this world
     Is not for him who does not sacrifice,
     How then can the other be?

32   Thus many kinds of offerings
     Are stretched before the face of Brahman.
     Know they are all born of work
     And knowing this, you shall be free.

33   Scourge of the Foe, to offer wisdom
     Passes the offering of material things
     For all works without exception
     Are consummated in wisdom.

34   Learn to know this by bowing down
     By questioning and by service.
     Those who are wise, who see what things are,
     Will teach you wisdom.

35   Which, having learned, you will not again
     Fall into delusion, son of Pandu.
     Through this you will behold all beings
     In yourself and also in me.

36   Even if among wicked men
You are the most wicked of all,
Floating on the raft of knowledge
You will cross all this crooked way.

37   O Arjuna, as a fire once kindled
Consumes its fuel to ashes
Even so all actions are consumed
To ashes in the fire of wisdom.

38   For there is nothing in this world
That purifies so much as wisdom.
He who has attained discipline
In time finds this purifier in himself.

39   The man of trust, with his senses curbed,
Intent on wisdom, gains it
And having attained wisdom
He soon comes to supreme peace.

40   But the self that is unknowing,
Without trust and filled with doubt
Perishes. Not for the doubting self
In this world or the next, or happiness.

41   Having renounced all works in discipline
Having cut off doubt with knowledge,
Winner of Wealth, the self-possessed
Is no longer bound by actions.

42   Therefore, with the sword of wisdom
Cut off this doubt born of ignorance
That lies in your heart. And turn to
Deeds. Stand up, son of Bharata.

7

The Gospel According to Saint Mark*

The Gospel According to St. Mark is usually considered to be the oldest of the four gospels in the Christian Bible. The gospels are accounts of the life, death, and resurrection of Jesus Christ that have been read by gatherings of Christians since the earliest days of their religion. To this day they remain the cornerstone of Christian beliefs.

CHAPTER 1

1 The beginning of the gospel of Jesus Christ, the Son of God;

2 As it is written in the prophets, Behold, I send my messenger before thy face, which shall prepare thy way before thee.

3 The voice of one crying in the wilderness, Prepare ye the way of the Lord, make his paths straight.

4 John did baptize in the wilderness, and preach the baptism of repentance for the remission of sins.

5 And there went out unto him all the land of Judæa, and they of Jerusalem, and were all baptized of him in the river of Jordan, confessing their sins.

6 And John was clothed with camel's hair, and with a girdle of a skin about his loins; and he did eat locusts and wild honey;

7 And preached, saying, There cometh one mightier than I after me, the latchet of whose shoes I am not worthy to stoop down and unloose.

8 I indeed have baptized you with water: but he shall baptize you with the Holy Ghost.

9 And it came to pass in those days, that Jesus came from Nazareth of Galilee, and was baptized of John in Jordan.

10 And straightway coming up out of the water, he saw the heavens opened, and the Spirit like a dove descending upon him:

11 And there came a voice from heaven, saying, Thou art my beloved Son in whom I am well pleased.

12 And immediately the spirit driveth him into the wilderness.

13 And he was there in the wilderness forty days, tempted of Satan; and was with the wild beasts; and the angels ministered unto him.

14 Now after that John was put in prison, Jesus came into Galilee, preaching the gospel of the kingdom of God.

* The Gospel According to Saint Mark, *Holy Bible*, King James Version.

15 And saying, The time is fulfilled, and the kingdom of God is at hand: repent ye, and believe the gospel.

16 Now as he walked by the sea of Galilee, he saw Simon and Andrew his brother casting a net into the sea: for they were fishers.

17 And Jesus said unto them, Come ye after me, and I will make you to become fishers of men.

18 And straightway they forsook their nets, and followed him.

19 And when he had gone a little farther thence, he saw James the son of Zebedee, and John his brother, who also were in the ship mending their nets.

20 And straightway he called them: and they left their father Zebedee in the ship with the hired servants, and went after him.

21 And they went into Capernaum; and straightway on the sabbath day he entered into the synagogue, and taught.

22 And they were astonished at his doctrine: for he taught them as one that had authority, and not as the scribes.

23 And there was in their synagogue a man with an unclean spirit; and he cried out,

24 Saying, Let us alone; what have we to do with thee, thou Jesus of Nazareth? art thou come to destroy us? I know thee who thou art, the Holy One of God.

25 And Jesus rebuked him, saying, Hold thy peace, and come out of him.

26 And when the unclean spirit had torn him, and cried with a loud voice, he came out of him.

27 And they were all amazed, insomuch that they questioned among themselves, saying, What thing is this? what new doctrine is this? for with authority commandeth he even the unclean spirits, and they do obey him.

28 And immediately his fame spread abroad throughout all the region round about Galilee.

29 And forthwith, when they were come out of the synagogue, they entered into the house of Simon and Andrew, with James and John.

30 But Simon's wife's mother lay sick of a fever, and anon they tell him of her.

31 And he came and took her by the hand, and lifted her up; and immediately the fever left her, and she ministered unto them.

32 And at even, when the sun did set, they brought unto him all that were diseased, and them that were possessed with devils.

33 And all the city was gathered together at the door.

34 And he healed many that were sick of divers diseases, and cast out many devils; and suffered not the devils to speak, because they knew him.

35 And in the morning, rising up a great while before day, he went out, and departed into a solitary place, and there prayed.

36 And Simon and they that were with him followed after him.

37 And when they had found him, they said unto him, All men seek for thee.

38 And he said unto them, Let us go into the next towns, that I may preach there also: for therefore came I forth.

39 And he preached in their synagogues throughout all Galilee, and cast out devils.

40 And there came a leper to him, beseeching him, and kneeling down to him, and saying unto him, If thou wilt, thou canst make me clean.

41 And Jesus, moved with compassion, put forth his hand, and touched him, and saith unto him, I will: be thou clean.

42 And as soon as he had spoken, immediately the leprosy departed from him, and he was cleansed.

43 And he straitly charged him, and forthwith sent him away;

44 And saith unto him, See thou say nothing to any man: but go thy way, shew thyself to the priest, and offer for thy cleansing those things which Moses commanded, for a testimony unto them.

45 But he went out, and began to publish it much, and to blaze abroad the matter, insomuch that Jesus could no more openly enter into the city, but was without in desert places: and they came to him from every quarter.

CHAPTER 2

1 And again he entered into Capernaum after some days; and it was noised that he was in the house.

2 And straightway many were gathered together, insomuch that there was no room to receive them, no, not so much as about the door: and he preached the word unto them.

3 And they come unto him, bringing one sick of the palsy, which was borne of four.

4 And when they could not come nigh unto him for the press, they uncovered the roof where he was: and when they had broken *it* up, they let down the bed wherein the sick of the palsy lay.

5 When Jesus saw their faith, he said unto the sick of the palsy, Son, thy sins be forgiven thee.

6 But there were certain of the scribes sitting there, and reasoning in their hearts,

7 Why doth this man thus speak blasphemies? who can forgive sins but God only?

8 And immediately when Jesus perceived in his spirit that they so reasoned within themselves, he said unto them, Why reason ye these things in your hearts?

9 Whether is it easier to say to the sick of the palsy, Thy sins be forgiven thee; or to say, Arise, and take up thy bed, and walk?

10 But that ye may know that the Son of man hath power on earth to forgive sins, (he saith to the sick of the palsy,)

11 I say unto thee, Arise, and take up thy bed, and go thy way into thine house.

12 And immediately he arose, took up the bed, and went forth before

them all; insomuch that they were all amazed, and glorified God, saying, We never saw it on this fashion.

13 And he went forth again by the sea side; and all the multitude resorted unto him, and he taught them.

14 And as he passed by, he saw Levi the son of Alphæus sitting at the receipt of custom, and said unto him, Follow me. And he arose and followed him.

15 And it came to pass, that, as Jesus sat at meat in his house, many publicans and sinners sat also together with Jesus and his disciples: for there were many, and they followed him.

16 And when the scribes and Pharisees saw him eat with publicans and sinners, they said unto his disciples, How is it that he eateth and drinketh with publicans and sinners?

17 When Jesus heard it, he saith unto them, They that are whole have no need of the physician, but they that are sick: I came not to call the righteous, but sinners to repentance.

18 And the disciples of John and of the Pharisees used to fast: and they come and say unto him, Why do the disciples of John and of the Pharisees fast, but thy disciples fast not?

19 And Jesus said unto them, Can the children of the bridechamber fast, while the bridegroom is with them? as long as they have the bridegroom with them, they cannot fast.

20 But the days will come, when the bridegroom shall be taken away from them, and then shall they fast in those days.

21 No man also seweth a piece of new cloth on an old garment: else the new piece that filled it up taketh away from the old, and the rent is made worse.

22 And no man putteth new wine into old bottles: else the new wine doth burst the bottles, and the wine is spilled, and the bottles will be marred: but new wine must be put into new bottles.

23 And it came to pass, that he went through the corn fields on the sabbath day; and his disciples began, as they went, to pluck the ears of corn.

24 And the Pharisees said unto him, Behold, why do they on the sabbath day that which is not lawful?

25 And he said unto them, Have ye never read what David did, when he had need, and was ahungered, he, and they that were with him?

26 How he went into the house of God in the days of Abiathar the high priest, and did eat the shewbread, which is not lawful to eat but for the priests, and gave also to them which were with him?

27 And he said unto them, The sabbath was made for man, and not man for the sabbath:

28 Therefore the Son of man is Lord also of the sabbath.

CHAPTER 3

1 And he entered again into the synagogue; and there was a man there which had a withered hand.

2 And they watched him, whether he would heal him on the sabbath day; that they might accuse him.

3 And he saith unto the man which had the withered hand, Stand forth.

4 And he saith unto them, Is it lawful to do good on the sabbath days, or to do evil? to save life, or to kill? But they held their peace.

5 And when he had looked round about on them with anger, being grieved for the hardness of their hearts, he saith unto the man, Stretch forth thine hand. And he stretched it out: and his hand was restored whole as the other.

6 And the Pharisees went forth, and straightway took counsel with the Herodians against him, how they might destroy him.

7 But Jesus withdrew himself with his disciples to the sea: and a great multitude from Galilee followed him, and from Judæa,

8 And from Jerusalem, and from Idumæa, and from beyond Jordan; and they about Tyre and Sidon, a great multitude, when they had heard what great things he did, came unto him.

9 And he spake to his disciples, that a small ship should wait on him because of the multitude, lest they should throng him.

10 For he had healed many; insomuch that they pressed upon him for to touch him, as many as had plagues.

11 And unclean spirits, when they saw him, fell down before him, and cried, saying, Thou art the Son of God.

12 And he straitly charged them that they should not make him known.

13 And he goeth up into a mountain, and calleth unto him whom he would: and they came unto him.

14 And he ordained twelve, that they should be with him, and that he might send them forth to preach,

15 And to have power to heal sicknesses, and to cast out devils:

16 And Simon he surnamed Peter;

17 And James the son of Zebedee, and John the brother of James; and he surnamed them Boanerges, which is, The sons of thunder:

18 And Andrew, and Philip, and Bartholomew, and Matthew, and Thomas, and James the son of Alphæus, and Thaddæus, and Simon the Canaanite,

19 And Judas Iscariot, which also betrayed him: and they went into an house.

20 And the multitude cometh together again, so that they could not so much as eat bread.

21 And when his friends heard of it, they went out to lay hold on him: for they said, He is beside himself.

22 ¶ And the scribes which came down from Jerusalem said, He hath Beelzebub, and by the prince of the devils casteth he out devils.

23 And he called them unto him, and said unto them in parables, How can Satan cast out Satan?

24 And if a kingdom be divided against itself, that kingdom cannot stand.

25 And if a house be divided against itself, that house cannot stand.

26 And if Satan rise up against himself, and be divided, he cannot stand, but hath an end.

27 No man can enter into a strong man's house, and spoil his goods, except he will first bind the strong man; and then he will spoil his house.

28 Verily I say unto you, All sins shall be forgiven unto the sons of men, and blasphemies wherewith soever they shall blaspheme:

29 But he that shall blaspheme against the Holy Ghost hath never forgiveness, but is in danger of eternal damnation:

30 Because they said, He hath an unclean spirit.

31 ¶ There came then his brethren and his mother, and, standing without, sent unto him, calling him.

32 And the multitude sat about him, and they said unto him, Behold, thy mother and thy brethren without seek for thee.

33 And he answered them, saying, Who is my mother, or my brethren?

34 And he looked round about on them which sat about him, and said, Behold my mother and my brethren!

35 For whosoever shall do the will of God, the same is my brother, and my sister, and mother.

CHAPTER 4

And he began again to teach by the sea side: and there was gathered unto him a great multitude, so that he entered into a ship, and sat in the sea; and the whole multitude was by the sea on the land.

2 And he taught them many things by parables, and said unto them in his doctrine,

3 Hearken; Behold, there went out a sower to sow:

4 And it came to pass, as he sowed, some fell by the way side, and the fowls of the air came and devoured it up.

5 And some fell on stony ground, where it had not much earth; and immediately it sprang up, because it had no depth of earth:

6 But when the sun was up, it was scorched; and because it had no root, it withered away.

7 And some fell among thorns, and the thorns grew up, and choked it, and it yielded no fruit.

8 And other fell on good ground, and did yield fruit that sprang up and increased; and brought forth, some thirty, and some sixty, and some an hundred.

9 And he said unto them, He that hath ears to hear, let him hear.

10 And when he was alone, they that were about him with the twelve asked of him the parable.

11 And he said unto them, Unto you it is given to know the mystery of the kingdom of God: but unto them that are without, all these things are done in parables:

12 That seeing they may see, and not perceive; and hearing they may

hear, and not understand; lest at any time they should be converted, and their sins should be forgiven them.

13 And he said unto them, Know ye not this parable? and how then will ye know all parables?

14 ¶ The sower soweth the word.

15 And these are they by the way side, where the word is sown; but when they have heard, Satan cometh immediately, and taketh away the word that was sown in their hearts.

16 And these are they likewise which are sown on stony ground; who, when they have heard the word, immediately receive it with gladness;

17 And have no root in themselves, and so endure but for a time: afterward, when affliction or persecution ariseth for the word's sake, immediately they are offended.

18 And these are they which are sown among thorns; such as hear the word,

19 And the cares of this world, and the deceitfulness of riches, and the lusts of other things entering in, choke the word, and it becometh unfruitful.

20 And these are they which are sown on good ground; such as hear the word, and receive it, and bring forth fruit, some thirtyfold, some sixty, and some an hundred.

21 ¶ And he said unto them, Is a candle brought to be put under a bushel, or under a bed? and not to be set on a candlestick?

22 For there is nothing hid, which shall not be manifested; neither was any thing kept secret, but that it should come abroad.

23 If any man have ears to hear, let him hear.

24 And he said unto them, Take heed what ye hear: with what measure ye mete, it shall be measured to you: and unto you that hear shall more be given.

25 For he that hath, to him shall be given: and he that hath not, from him shall be taken even that which he hath.

26 ¶ And he said, So is the kingdom of God, as if a man should cast seed into the ground;

27 And should sleep, and rise night and day, and the seed should spring and grow up, he knoweth not how.

28 For the earth bringeth forth fruit of herself; first the blade, then the ear, after that the full corn in the ear.

29 But when the fruit is brought forth, immediately he putteth in the sickle, because the harvest is come.

30 ¶ And he said, Whereunto shall we liken the kingdom of God? or with what comparison shall we compare it?

31 It is like a grain of mustard seed, which, when it is sown in the earth, is less than all the seeds that be in the earth:

32 But when it is sown, it groweth up, and becometh greater than all herbs, and shooteth out great branches; so that the fowls of the air may lodge under the shadow of it.

33 And with many such parables spake he the word unto them, as they were able to hear it.

34 But without a parable spake he not unto them: and when they were alone, he expounded all things to his disciples.

35 And the same day, when the even was come, he saith unto them, Let us pass over unto the other side.

36 And when they had sent away the multitude they took him even as he was in the ship. And there were also with him other little ships.

37 And there arose a great storm of wind, and the waves beat into the ship, so that it was now full.

38 And he was in the hinder part of the ship, asleep on a pillow: and they awake him, and say unto him, Master, carest thou not that we perish?

39 And he arose, and rebuked the wind, and said unto the sea, Peace, be still. And the wind ceased, and there was a great calm.

40 And he said unto them, Why are ye so fearful? how is it that ye have no faith?

41 And they feared exceedingly, and said one to another, What manner of man is this, that even the wind and the sea obey him?

CHAPTER 5

1 And they came over unto the other side of the sea, into the country of the Gadarenes.

2 And when he was come out of the ship, immediately there met him out of the tombs a man with an unclean spirit,

3 Who had his dwelling among the tombs; and no man could bind him, no, not with chains:

4 Because that he had been often bound with fetters and chains, and the chains had been plucked asunder by him, and the fetters broken in pieces: neither could any man tame him.

5 And always, night and day, he was in the mountains, and in the tombs, crying, and cutting himself with stones.

6 But when he saw Jesus afar off, he ran and worshipped him,

7 And cried with a loud voice, and said, What have I to do with thee, Jesus, thou Son of the most high God? I adjure thee by God, that thou torment me not.

8 For he said unto him, Come out of the man, thou unclean spirit.

9 And he asked him, What is thy name? And he answered, saying, My name is Legion: for we are many.

10 And he besought him much that he would not send them away out of the country.

11 Now there was there nigh unto the mountains a great herd of swine feeding.

12 And all the devils besought him, saying, Send us into the swine, that we may enter into them.

13 And forthwith Jesus gave them leave. And the unclean spirits went out, and entered into the swine: and the herd ran violently down a steep place into the sea, (they were about two thousand;) and were choked in the sea.

14 And they that fed the swine fled, and told it in the city, and in the country. And they went out to see what it was that was done.

15 And they come to Jesus, and see him that was possessed with the devil, and had the legion, sitting, and clothed, and in his right mind: and they were afraid.

16 And they that saw it told them how it befell to him that was possessed with the devil, and also concerning the swine.

17 And they began to pray him to depart out of their coasts.

18 And when he was come into the ship, he that had been possessed with the devil prayed him that he might be with him.

19 Howbeit Jesus suffered him not, but saith unto him, Go home to thy friends, and tell them how great things the Lord hath done for thee, and hath had compassion on thee.

20 And he departed, and began to publish in Decapolis how great things Jesus had done for him: and all men did marvel.

21 And when Jesus was passed over again by ship unto the other side, much people gathered unto him: and he was nigh unto the sea.

22 And, behold, there cometh one of the rulers of the synagogue, Jairus by name; and when he saw him, he fell at his feet,

23 And besought him greatly, saying, My little daughter lieth at the point of death: I pray thee, come and lay thy hands on her, that she may be healed; and she shall live.

24 And Jesus went with him; and much people followed him, and thronged him.

25 And a certain woman, which had an issue of blood twelve years,

26 And had suffered many things of many physicians, and had spent all that she had, and was nothing bettered, but rather grew worse,

27 When she had heard of Jesus, came in the press behind, and touched his garment.

28 For she said, If I may touch but his clothes, I shall be whole.

29 And straightway the fountain of her blood was dried up; and she felt in her body that she was healed of that plague.

30 And Jesus, immediately knowing in himself that virtue had gone out of him, turned him about in the press, and said, Who touched my clothes?

31 And his disciples said unto him, Thou seest the multitude thronging thee, and sayest thou, Who touched me?

32 And he looked round about to see her that had done this thing.

33 But the woman fearing and trembling, knowing what was done in her, came and fell down before him, and told him all the truth.

34 And he said unto her, Daughter, thy faith hath made thee whole; go in peace, and be whole of thy plague.

35 While he yet spake, there came from the ruler of the synagogue's house certain which said, Thy daughter is dead: why troublest thou the Master any further?

36 As soon as Jesus heard the word that was spoken, he saith unto the ruler of the synagogue, Be not afraid, only believe.

37 And he suffered no man to follow him, save Peter, and James, and John the brother of James.

38 And he cometh to the house of the ruler of the synagogue, and seeth the tumult, and them that wept and wailed greatly.

39 And when he was come in, he saith unto them, Why make ye this ado, and weep? the damsel is not dead, but sleepeth.

40 And they laughed him to scorn. But when he had put them all out, he taketh the father and the mother of the damsel, and them that were with him, and entereth in where the damsel was lying.

41 And he took the damsel by the hand, and said unto her, Talitha cumi; which is, being interpreted, Damsel, I say unto thee, arise.

42 And straightway the damsel arose, and walked; for she was of the age of twelve years. And they were astonished with a great astonishment.

43 And he charged them straitly that no man should know it; and commanded that something should be given her to eat.

CHAPTER 6

1 And he went out from thence, and came into his own country; and his disciples follow him.

2 And when the sabbath was come, he began to teach in the synagogue: and many hearing him were astonished, saying, From whence hath this man these things? and what wisdom is this which is given unto him, that even such mighty works are wrought by his hands?

3 Is not this the carpenter, the son of Mary, the brother of James, and Joses, and of Juda, and Simon? and are not his sisters here with us? And they were offended at him.

4 But Jesus said unto them, A prophet is not without honour, but in his own country, and among his own kin, and in his own house.

5 And he could there do no mighty work, save that he laid his hands upon a few sick folk, and healed them.

6 And he marvelled because of their unbelief. And he went round about the villages, teaching.

7 ¶ And he called unto him the twelve, and began to send them forth by two and two; and gave them power over unclean spirits;

8 And commanded them that they should take nothing for their journey, save a staff only; no scrip, no bread, no money in their purse:

9 But be shod with sandals; and not put on two coats.

10 And he said unto them, In what place soever ye enter into an house, there abide till ye depart from that place.

11 And whosoever shall not receive you, nor hear you, when ye depart thence, shake off the dust under your feet for a testimony against them. Verily I say unto you, It shall be more tolerable for Sodom and Gomorrha in the day of judgment, than for that city.

12 And they went out, and preached that men should repent.

13 And they cast out many devils, and anointed with oil many that were sick, and healed them.

14 And king Herod heard of him; (for his name was spread abroad:) and he said, That John the Baptist was risen from the dead, and therefore mighty works do shew forth themselves in him.

15 Others said, That it is Elias. And others said, That it is a prophet, or as one of the prophets.

16 But when Herod heard thereof, he said, It is John, whom I beheaded: he is risen from the dead.

17 For Herod himself had sent forth and laid hold upon John, and bound him in prison for Herodias' sake, his brother Philip's wife: for he had married her.

18 For John had said unto Herod, It is not lawful for thee to have thy brother's wife.

19 Therefore Herodias had a quarrel against him, and would have killed him; but she could not:

20 For Herod feared John, knowing that he was a just man and an holy, and observed him; and when he heard him, he did many things, and heard him gladly.

21 And when a convenient day was come, that Herod on his birthday made a supper to his lords, high captains, and chief estates of Galilee;

22 And when the daughter of the said Herodias came in, and danced, and pleased Herod and them that sat with him, the king said unto the damsel, Ask of me whatsoever thou wilt and I will give it thee.

23 And he sware unto her, Whatsoever thou shalt ask of me, I will give it thee, unto the half of my kingdom.

24 And she went forth, and said unto her mother, What shall I ask? And she said, The head of John the Baptist.

25 And she came in straightway with haste unto the king, and asked, saying, I will that thou give me by and by in a charger the head of John the Baptist.

26 And the king was exceeding sorry; yet for his oath's sake, and for their sakes which sat with him, he would not reject her.

27 And immediately the king sent an executioner, and commanded his head to be brought: and he went and beheaded him in the prison,

28 And brought his head in a charger, and gave it to the damsel: and the damsel gave it to her mother.

29 And when his disciples heard of it, they came and took up his corpse, and laid it in a tomb.

30 And the apostles gathered themselves together unto Jesus, and told him all things, both what they had done, and what they had taught.

31 And he said unto them, Come ye yourselves apart into a desert place, and rest a while: for there were many coming and going, and they had no leisure so much as to eat.

32 And they departed into a desert place by ship privately.

33 And the people saw them departing, and many knew him, and ran afoot thither out of all cities, and outwent them, and came together unto him.

34 And Jesus, when he came out, saw much people, and was moved with compassion toward them, because they were as sheep not having a shepherd: and he began to teach them many things.

35 And when the day was now far spent, his disciples came unto him, and said, This is a desert place, and now the time is far passed:

36 Send them away, that they may go into the country round about, and into the villages, and buy themselves bread: for they have nothing to eat.

37 He answered and said unto them, Give ye them to eat. And they say unto him, Shall we go and buy two hundred pennyworth of bread, and give them to eat?

38 He saith unto them, How many loaves have ye? go and see. And when they knew, they say, Five, and two fishes.

39 And he commanded them to make all sit down by companies upon the green grass.

40 And they sat down in ranks, by hundreds and by fifties.

41 And when he had taken the five loaves and the two fishes, he looked up to heaven, and blessed, and brake the loaves, and gave them to his disciples to set before them; and the two fishes divided he among them all.

42 And they did all eat, and were filled.

43 And they took up twelve baskets full of the fragments, and of the fishes.

44 And they that did eat of the loaves were about five thousand men.

45 And straightway he constrained his disciples to get into the ship, and to go to the other side before unto Bethsaida, while he sent away the people.

46 And when he had sent them away, he departed into a mountain to pray.

47 And when even was come, the ship was in the midst of the sea, and he alone on the land.

48 And he saw them toiling in rowing; for the wind was contrary unto them: and about the fourth watch of the night he cometh unto them, walking upon the sea, and would have passed by them.

49 But when they saw him walking upon the sea, they supposed it had been a spirit, and cried out:

50 For they all saw him, and were troubled. And immediately he talked with them, and saith unto them, Be of good cheer: it is I; be not afraid.

51 And he went up unto them into the ship; and the wind ceased: and they were sore amazed in themselves beyond measure, and wondered.

52 For they considered not the miracle of the loaves: for their heart was hardened.

53 And when they had passed over, they came into the land of Gennesaret, and drew to the shore.

54 And when they were come out of the ship, straightway they knew him,

55 And ran through that whole region round about, and began to carry about in beds those that were sick, where they heard he was.

56 And whithersoever he entered, into villages, or cities, or country, they laid the sick in the streets, and besought him that they might touch if it were but the border of his garment: and as many as touched him were made whole.

CHAPTER 7

1 Then came together unto him the Pharisees, and certain of the scribes, which came from Jerusalem.

2 And when they saw some of his disciples eat bread with defiled, that is to say, with unwashen, hands, they found fault.

3 For the Pharisees, and all the Jews, except they wash their hands oft, eat not, holding the tradition of the elders.

4 And when they come from the market, except they wash, they eat not. And many other things there be, which they have received to hold, as the washing of cups, and pots, brasen vessels, and of tables.

5 Then the Pharisees and scribes asked him, Why walk not thy disciples according to the tradition of the elders, but eat bread with unwashen hands?

6 He answered and said unto them, Well hath Esaias prophesied of you hypocrites, as it is written, This people honoureth me with their lips, but their heart is far from me.

7 Howbeit in vain do they worship me, teaching for doctrines the commandments of men.

8 For laying aside the commandment of God, ye hold the tradition of men, as the washing of pots and cups: and many other such like things ye do.

9 And he said unto them, Full well ye reject the commandment of God, that ye may keep your own tradition.

10 For Moses said, Honour thy father and thy mother; and, Whoso curseth father or mother, let him die the death:

11 But ye say, If a man shall say to his father or mother, It is Corban, that is to say, a gift, by whatsoever thou mightest be profited by me; he shall be free.

12 And ye suffer him no more to do ought for his father or his mother;

13 Making the word of God of none effect through your tradition, which ye have delivered: and many such like things do ye.

14 ¶ And when he had called all the people unto him, he said unto them, Hearken unto me every one of you, and understand:

15 There is nothing from without a man, that entering into him can

defile him: but the things which come out of him, those are they that defile the man.

16 If any man have ears to hear, let him hear.

17 And when he was entered into the house from the people, his disciples asked him concerning the parable.

18 And he saith unto them, Are ye so without understanding also? Do ye not perceive, that whatsoever thing from without entereth into the man, it cannot defile him;

19 Because it entereth not into his heart, but into the belly, and goeth out into the draught, purging all meats?

20 And he said, That which cometh out of the man, that defileth the man.

21 For from within, out of the heart of men, proceed evil thoughts, adulteries, fornications, murders,

22 Thefts, covetousness, wickedness, deceit, lasciviousness, an evil eye, blasphemy, pride, foolishness:

23 All these evil things come from within, and defile the man.

24 ¶ And from thence he arose, and went into the borders of Tyre and Sidon, and entered into an house, and would have no man know it: but he could not be hid.

25 For a certain woman, whose young daughter had an unclean spirit, heard of him, and came and fell at his feet:

26 The woman was a Greek, a Syrophenician by nation; and she besought him that he would cast forth the devil out of her daughter.

27 But Jesus said unto her, Let the children first be filled: for it is not meet to take the children's bread, and to cast it unto the dogs.

28 And she answered and said unto him, Yes Lord: yet the dogs under the table eat of the children's crumbs.

29 And he said unto her, For this saying go thy way; the devil is gone out of thy daughter.

30 And when she was come to her house, she found the devil gone out, and her daughter laid upon the bed.

31 ¶ And again, departing from the coasts of Tyre and Sidon, he came unto the sea of Galilee, through the midst of the coasts of Decapolis.

32 And they bring unto him one that was deaf, and had an impediment in his speech; and they beseech him to put his hand upon him.

33 And he took him aside from the multitude, and put his fingers into his ears, and he spit, and touched his tongue;

34 And looking up to heaven, he sighed, and saith unto him, Ephphatha, that is, Be opened.

35 And straightway his ears were opened, and the string of his tongue was loosed, and he spake plain.

36 And he charged them that they should tell no man: but the more he charged them, so much the more a great deal they published it;

37 And were beyond measure astonished, saying, He hath done all things well: he maketh both the deaf to hear, and the dumb to speak.

CHAPTER 8

1 In those days the multitude being very great, and having nothing to eat, Jesus called his disciples unto him, and saith unto them,

2 I have compassion on the multitude, because they have now been with me three days, and have nothing to eat:

3 And if I send them away fasting to their own houses, they will faint by the way: for divers of them came from far.

4 And his disciples answered him, From whence can a man satisfy these men with bread here in the wilderness?

5 And he asked them, How many loaves have ye? And they said, Seven.

6 And he commanded the people to sit down on the ground: and he took the seven loaves, and gave thanks, and brake, and gave to his disciples to set before them; and they did set them before the people.

7 And they had a few small fishes: and he blessed, and commanded to set them also before them.

8 So they did eat, and were filled: and they took up of the broken meat that was left seven baskets.

9 And they that had eaten were about four thousand: and he sent them away.

10 ¶ And straightway he entered into a ship with his disciples, and came into the parts of Dalmanutha.

11 And the Pharisees came forth, and began to question with him, seeking of him a sign from heaven, tempting him.

12 And he sighed deeply in his spirit, and saith, Why doth this generation seek after a sign? verily I say unto you, There shall no sign be given unto this generation.

13 And he left them, and entering into the ship again departed to the other side.

14 ¶ Now the disciples had forgotten to take bread, neither had they in the ship with them more than one loaf.

15 And he charged them, saying, Take heed, beware of the leaven of the Pharisees, and of the leaven of Herod.

16 And they reasoned among themselves, saying, It is because we have no bread.

17 And when Jesus knew it, he saith unto them, Why reason ye, because ye have no bread? perceive ye not yet, neither understand? have ye your heart yet hardened?

18 Having eyes, see ye not? and having ears, hear ye not? and do ye not remember?

19 When I brake the five loaves among five thousand, how many baskets full of fragments took ye up? They say unto him, Twelve.

20 And when the seven among four thousand, how many baskets full of fragments took ye up? And they said, Seven.

21 And he said unto them, How is it that ye do not understand?

22 ¶ And he cometh to Bethsaida; and they bring a blind man unto him, and besought him to touch him.

23 And he took the blind man by the hand, and led him out of the town; and when he had spit on his eyes, and put his hands upon him, he asked him if he saw ought.

24 And he looked up, and said, I see men as trees, walking.

25 After that he put his hands again upon his eyes, and made him look up: and he was restored, and saw every man clearly.

26 And he sent him away to his house, saying, Neither go into the town, nor tell it to any in the town.

27 ¶ And Jesus went out, and his disciples, into the towns of Cæsarea Philippi: and by the way he asked his disciples, saying unto them, Whom do men say that I am?

28 And they answered, John the Baptist: but some say, Elias; and others, One of the prophets.

29 And he saith unto them, But whom say ye that I am? And Peter answereth and saith unto him, Thou art the Christ.

30 And he charged them that they should tell no man of him.

31 And he began to teach them, that the Son of man must suffer many things, and be rejected of the elders, and of the chief priests, and scribes, and be killed, and after three days rise again.

32 And he spake that saying openly. And Peter took him, and began to rebuke him.

33 But when he had turned about and looked on his disciples, he rebuked Peter, saying, Get thee behind me, Satan: for thou savourest not the things that be of God, but the things that be of men.

34 ¶ And when he had called the people unto him with his disciples also, he said unto them, Whosoever will come after me, let him deny himself, and take up his cross, and follow me.

35 For whosoever will save his life shall lose it; but whosoever shall lose his life for my sake and the gospel's, the same shall save it.

36 For what shall it profit a man, if he shall gain the whole world, and lose his own soul?

37 Or what shall a man give in exchange for his soul?

38 Whosoever therefore shall be ashamed of me and of my words in this adulterous and sinful generation; of him also shall the Son of man be ashamed, when he cometh in the glory of his Father with the holy angels.

CHAPTER 9

1 And he said unto them, Verily I say unto you, That there be some of them that stand here, which shall not taste of death, till they have seen the kingdom of God come with power.

2 ¶ And after six days Jesus taketh with him Peter, and James, and John, and leadeth them up into an high mountain apart by themselves: and he was transfigured before them.

3 And his raiment became shining, exceeding white as snow; so as no fuller on earth can white them.

4 And there appeared unto them Elias with Moses: and they were talking with Jesus.

5 And Peter answered and said to Jesus, Master, it is good for us to be here: and let us make three tabernacles; one for thee, and one for Moses, and one for Elias.

6 For he wist not what to say; for they were sore afraid.

7 And there was a cloud that overshadowed them: and a voice came out of the cloud, saying, This is my beloved Son: hear him.

8 And suddenly, when they had looked round about, they saw no man any more, save Jesus only with themselves.

9 And as they came down from the mountain, he charged them that they should tell no man what things they had seen, till the Son of man were risen from the dead.

10 And they kept that saying with themselves, questioning one with another what the rising from the dead should mean.

11 ¶ And they asked him, saying, Why say the scribes that Elias must first come?

12 And he answered and told them, Elias verily cometh first, and restoreth all things; and how it is written of the Son of man, that he must suffer many things, and be set at nought.

13 But I say unto you, That Elias is indeed come, and they have done unto him whatsoever they listed, as it is written of him.

14 ¶ And when he came to his disciples, he saw a great multitude about them, and the scribes questioning with them.

15 And straightway all the people, when they beheld him, were greatly amazed, and running to him saluted him.

16 And he asked the scribes, What question ye with them?

17 And one of the multitude answered and said, Master, I have brought unto thee my son, which hath a dumb spirit;

18 And wheresoever he taketh him, he teareth him: and he foameth, and gnasheth with his teeth, and pineth away: and I spake to thy disciples that they should cast him out; and they could not.

19 He answereth him, and saith, O faithless generation, how long shall I be with you? how long shall I suffer you? bring him unto me.

20 And they brought him unto him: and when he saw him, straightway the spirit tare him; and he fell on the ground, and wallowed foaming.

21 And he asked his father, How long is it ago since this came unto him? And he said, Of a child.

22 And ofttimes it hath cast him into the fire, and into the waters, to destroy him: but if thou canst do any thing, have compassion on us, and help us.

23 Jesus said unto him, If thou canst believe, all things are possible to him that believeth.

24 And straightway the father of the child cried out, and said with tears, Lord, I believe; help thou mine unbelief.

25 When Jesus saw that the people came running together, he rebuked the foul spirit, saying unto him, Thou dumb and deaf spirit, I charge thee, come out of him, and enter no more into him.

26 And the spirit cried, and rent him sore, and came out of him: and he was as one dead; insomuch that many said, He is dead.

27 But Jesus took him by the hand, and lifted him up; and he arose.

28 And when he was come into the house, his disciples asked him privately, Why could not we cast him out?`

29 And he said unto them, This kind can come forth by nothing, but by prayer and fasting.

30 ¶ And they departed thence, and passed through Galilee; and he would not that any man should know it.

31 For he taught his disciples, and said unto them, The Son of man is delivered into the hands of men, and they shall kill him; and after that he is killed, he shall rise the third day.

32 But they understood not that saying, and were afraid to ask him.

33 ¶ And he came to Capernaum: and being in the house he asked them, What was it that ye disputed among yourselves by the way?

34 But they held their peace: for by the way they had disputed among themselves, who should be the greatest.

35 And he sat down; and called the twelve, and saith unto them, If any man desire to be first, the same shall be last of all, and servant of all.

36 And he took a child, and set him in the midst of them: and when he had taken him in his arms, he said unto them,

37 Whosoever shall receive one of such children in my name, receiveth me: and whosoever shall receive me, receiveth not me, but him that sent me.

38 ¶ And John answered him, saying, Master, we saw one casting out devils in thy name, and he followeth not us: and we forbad him, because he followeth not us.

39 But Jesus said, Forbid him not: for there is no man which shall do a miracle in my name, that can lightly speak evil of me.

40 For he that is not against us is on our part.

41 For whosoever shall give you a cup of water to drink in my name, because ye belong to Christ, verily I say unto you, he shall not lose his reward.

42 And whosoever shall offend one of these little ones that believe in me, it is better for him that a millstone were hanged about his neck, and he were cast into the sea.

43 And if thy hand offend thee, cut it off: it is better for thee to enter into life maimed, than having two hands to go into hell, into the fire that never shall be quenched:

44 Where their worm dieth not, and the fire is not quenched.

45 And if thy foot offend thee, cut it off: it is better for thee to enter halt into life, than having two feet to be cast into hell, into the fire that never shall be quenched:

46 Where their worm dieth not, and the fire is not quenched.

47 And if thine eye offend thee, pluck it out: it is better for thee to enter into the kingdom of God with one eye, than having two eyes to be cast into hell fire:

48 Where their worm dieth not, and the fire is not quenched.

49 For every one shall be salted with fire, and every sacrifice shall be salted with salt.

50 Salt is good: but if the salt have lost his saltness, wherewith will ye season it? Have salt in yourselves, and have peace one with another.

CHAPTER 10

And he arose from thence, and cometh into the coasts of Judæa by the farther side of Jordan: and the people resort unto him again; and, as he was wont, he taught them again.

2 ¶ And the Pharisees came to him, and asked him, Is it lawful for a man to put away his wife? tempting him.

3 And he answered and said unto them, What did Moses command you?

4 And they said, Moses suffered to write a bill of divorcement, and to put her away.

5 And Jesus answered and said unto them, For the hardness of your heart he wrote you this precept.

6 But from the beginning of the creation God made them male and female.

7 For this cause shall a man leave his father and mother, and cleave to his wife;

8 And they twain shall be one flesh: so then they are no more twain, but one flesh.

9 What therefore God hath joined together, let not man put asunder.

10 And in the house his disciples asked him again of the same matter.

11 And he saith unto them, Whosoever shall put away his wife, and marry another, committeth adultery against her.

12 And if a woman shall put away her husband, and be married to another, she committeth adultery.

13 ¶ And they brought young children to him, that he should touch them: and his disciples rebuked those that brought them.

14 But when Jesus saw it, he was much displeased, and said unto them, Suffer the little children to come unto me, and forbid them not: for of such is the kingdom of God.

15 Verily I say unto you, Whosoever shall not receive the kingdom of God as a little child, he shall not enter therein.

16 And he took them up in his arms, put his hands upon them, and blessed them.

17 ¶ And when he was gone forth into the way, there came one running, and kneeled to him, and asked him, Good Master, what shall I do that I may inherit eternal life?

18 And Jesus said unto him, Why callest thou me good? there is none good but one, that is, God.

19 Thou knowest the commandments, Do not commit adultery, Do not kill, Do not steal, Do not bear false witness, Defraud not, Honour thy father and mother.

20 And he answered and said unto him, Master, all these have I observed from my youth.

21 Then Jesus beholding him loved him, and said unto him, One thing thou lackest: go thy way, sell whatsoever thou hast, and give to the poor, and thou shalt have treasure in heaven: and come, take up the cross, and follow me.

22 And he was sad at that saying, and went away grieved: for he had great possessions.

23 ¶ And Jesus looked round about, and saith unto his disciples, How hardly shall they that have riches enter into the kingdom of God!

24 And the disciples were astonished at his words. But Jesus answereth again, and saith unto them, Children, how hard is it for them that trust in riches to enter into the kingdom of God!

25 It is easier for a camel to go through the eye of a needle, than for a rich man to enter into the kingdom of God.

26 And they were astonished out of measure, saying among themselves, Who then can be saved?

27 And Jesus looking upon them saith, With men it is impossible, but not with God: for with God all things are possible.

28 ¶ Then Peter began to say unto him, Lo, we have left all, and have followed thee.

29 And Jesus answered and said, Verily I say unto you, There is no man that hath left house, or brethren, or sisters, or father, or mother, or wife, or children, or lands, for my sake, and the gospel's,

30 But he shall receive an hundredfold now in this time, houses, and brethren, and sisters, and mothers, and children, and lands, with persecutions; and in the world to come eternal life.

31 But many that are first shall be last; and the last first.

32 ¶ And they were in the way going up to Jerusalem; and Jesus went before them: and they were amazed; and as they followed, they were afraid. And he took again the twelve, and began to tell them what things should happen unto him,

33 Saying, Behold, we go up to Jerusalem; and the Son of man shall be delivered unto the chief priests, and unto the scribes; and they shall condemn him to death, and shall deliver him to the Gentiles:

34 And they shall mock him, and shall scourge him, and shall spit upon him, and shall kill him: and the third day he shall rise again.

35 And James and John, the sons of Zebedee, come unto him, saying, Master, we would that thou shouldest do for us whatsoever we shall desire.

36 And he said unto them, What would ye that I should do for you?

37 They said unto him, Grant unto us that we may sit, one on thy right hand, and the other on thy left hand, in thy glory.

38 But Jesus said unto them. Ye know not what ye ask: can ye drink of the cup that I drink of? and be baptized with the baptism that I am baptized with?

39 And they said unto him, We can. And Jesus said unto them, ye shall indeed drink of the cup that I drink of; and with the baptism that I am baptized withal shall ye be baptized.

40 But to sit on my right hand and on my left hand is not mine to give; but it shall be given to them for whom it is prepared.

41 And when the ten heard it, they began to be much displeased with James and John.

42 But Jesus called them to him, and saith unto them, Ye know that they which are accounted to rule over the Gentiles exercise lordship over them; and their great ones exercise authority upon them.

43 But so shall it not be among you: but whosoever will be great among you, shall be your minister:

44 And whosoever of you will be the chiefest, shall be servant of all.

45 For even the Son of man came not to be ministered unto, but to minister, and to give his life a ransom for many.

46 ¶ And they came to Jericho: and as he went out of Jericho with his disciples and a great number of people, blind Bartimæus, the son of Timæus, sat by the highway side begging.

47 And when he heard that it was Jesus of Nazareth, he began to cry out, and say, Jesus, thou son of David, have mercy on me.

48 And many charged him that he should hold his peace: but he cried the more a great deal, Thou son of David, have mercy on me.

49 And Jesus stood still, and commanded him to be called. And they call the blind man, saying unto him, Be of good comfort, rise; he calleth thee.

50 And he, casting away his garment, rose, and came to Jesus.

51 And Jesus answered and said unto him, What wilt thou that I should do unto thee? The blind man said unto him, Lord, that I might receive my sight.

52 And Jesus said unto him, Go thy way; thy faith hath made thee whole. And immediately he received his sight, and followed Jesus in the way.

CHAPTER 11

1 And when they came nigh to Jerusalem, unto Bethphage and Bethany, at the mount of Olives, he sendeth forth two of his disciples,

2 And saith unto them, Go your way into the village over against you: and as soon as ye be entered into it, ye shall find a colt tied, whereon never man sat; loose him, and bring him.

3 And if any man say unto you, Why do ye this? say ye that the Lord hath need of him; and straightway he will send him hither.

4 And they went their way, and found the colt tied by the door without in a place where two ways met; and they loose him.

5 And certain of them that stood there said unto them, What do ye, loosing the colt?

6 And they said unto them even as Jesus had commanded; and they let them go.

7 And they brought the colt to Jesus, and cast their garments on him; and he sat upon him.

8 And many spread their garments in the way: and others cut down branches off the trees, and strawed them in the way.

9 And they that went before, and they that followed, cried, saying, Hosanna; Blessed is he that cometh in the name of the Lord:

10 Blessed be the kingdom of our father David, that cometh in the name of the Lord: Hosanna in the highest.

11 And Jesus entered into Jerusalem, and into the temple: and when he had looked round about upon all things, and now the eventide was come, he went out unto Bethany with the twelve.

12 ¶ And on the morrow, when they were come from Bethany, he was hungry:

13 And seeing a fig tree afar off having leaves, he came, if haply he might find any thing thereon: and when he came to it, he found nothing but leaves; for the time of figs was not yet.

14 And Jesus answered and said unto it, No man eat fruit of thee hereafter for ever. And his disciples heard it.

15 ¶ And they come to Jerusalem: and Jesus went into the temple, and began to cast out them that sold and bought in the temple, and overthrew the tables of the moneychangers, and the seats of them that sold doves;

16 And would not suffer that any man should carry any vessel through the temple.

17 And he taught, saying unto them, Is it not written, My house shall be called of all nations the house of prayer? but ye have made it a den of thieves.

18 And the scribes and chief priests heard it, and sought how they might destroy him: for they feared him, because all the people was astonished at his doctrine.

19 And when even was come, he went out of the city.

20 ¶ And in the morning, as they passed by, they saw the fig tree dried up from the roots.

21 And Peter calling to remembrance saith unto him, Master, behold, the fig tree which thou cursedst is withered away.

22 And Jesus answering saith unto them, Have faith in God.

23 For verily I say unto you, That whosoever shall say unto this mountain, Be thou removed, and be thou cast into the sea; and shall not doubt in his heart, but shall believe that those things which he saith shall come to pass; he shall have whatsoever he saith.

24 Therefore I say unto you, What things soever ye desire, when ye pray, believe that ye receive them, and ye shall have them.

25 And when ye stand praying, forgive, if ye have ought against any: that your Father also which is in heaven may forgive you your trespasses.

26 But if ye do not forgive, neither will your Father which is in heaven forgive your trespasses.

27 ¶ And they come again to Jerusalem: and as he was walking in the temple, there come to him the chief priests, and the scribes, and the elders,

28 And say unto him, By what authority doest thou these things? and who gave thee this authority to do these things?

29 And Jesus answered and said unto them, I will also ask of you one question, and answer me, and I will tell you by what authority I do these things.

30 The baptism of John, was it from heaven, or of men? answer me.

31 And they reasoned with themselves saying, If we shall say, From heaven; he will say, Why then did ye not believe him?

32 But if we shall say, Of men; they feared the people: for all men counted John, that he was a prophet indeed.

33 And they answered and said unto Jesus, We cannot tell. And Jesus answering saith unto them, Neither do I tell you by what authority I do these things.

CHAPTER 12

And he began to speak unto them by parables. A certain man planted a vineyard, and set an hedge about it, and digged a place for the winefat, and built a tower, and let it out to husbandmen, and went into a far country.

2 And at the season he sent to the husbandmen a servant, that he might receive from the husbandmen of the fruit of the vineyard.

3 And they caught him, and beat him, and sent him away empty.

4 And again he sent unto them another servant; and at him they cast stones, and wounded him in the head, and sent him away shamefully handled.

5 And again he sent another; and him they killed, and many others; beating some, and killing some.

6 Having yet therefore one son, his well-beloved, he sent him also last unto them, saying, They will reverence my son.

7 But those husbandmen said among themselves, This is the heir; come, let us kill him, and the inheritance shall be our's.

8 And they took him, and killed him, and cast him out of the vineyard.

9 What shall therefore the lord of the vineyard do? he will come and destroy the husbandmen, and will give the vineyard unto others.

10 And have ye not read this scripture; The stone which the builders rejected is become the head of the corner:

11 This was the Lord's doing, and it is marvellous in our eyes?

12 And they sought to lay hold on him, but feared the people: for they knew that he had spoken the parable against them: and they left him, and went their way.

13 ¶ And they send unto him certain of the Pharisees and of the Herodians, to catch him in his words.

14 And when they were come, they say unto him, Master, we know that thou art true, and carest for no man: for thou regardest not the person of men, but teachest the way of God in truth: Is it lawful to give tribute to Cæsar, or not?

15 Shall we give, or shall we not give? But he, knowing their hypocrisy, said unto them, Why tempt ye me? bring me a penny, that I may see it.

16 And they brought it. And he saith unto them, Whose is this image and superscription? And they said unto him, Cæsar's.

17 And Jesus answering said unto them, render to Cæsar the things that are Cæsar's, and to God the things that are God's. And they marvelled at him.

18 ¶ Then come unto him the Sadducees, which say there is no resurrection; and they asked him, saying,

19 Master, Moses wrote unto us, If a man's brother die, and leave his wife behind him, and leave no children, that his brother should take his wife, and raise up seed unto his brother.

20 Now there were seven brethren: and the first took a wife, and dying left no seed.

21 And the second took her, and died, neither left he any seed: and the third likewise.

22 And the seven had her, and left no seed: last of all the woman died also.

23 In the resurrection therefore, when they shall rise, whose wife shall she be of them? for the seven had her to wife.

24 And Jesus answering said unto them, Do ye not therefore err, because ye know not the scriptures, neither the power of God?

25 For when they shall rise from the dead, they neither marry, nor are given in marriage; but are as the angels which are in heaven.

26 And as touching the dead, that they rise: have ye not read in the book of Moses, how in the bush God spake unto him, saying, I am the God of Abraham, and the God of Isaac, and the God of Jacob?

27 He is not the God of the dead, but the God of the living: ye therefore do greatly err.

28 ¶ And one of the scribes came, and having heard them reasoning together, and perceiving that he had answered them well, asked him, Which is the first commandment of all?

29 And Jesus answered him, The first of all the commandments is, Hear, O Israel; The Lord our God is one Lord:

30 And thou shalt love the Lord thy God with all thy heart, and with all thy soul, and with all thy mind, and with all thy strength: this is the first commandment.

31 And the second is like, namely this, Thou shalt love thy neighbor as thyself. There is none other commandment greater than these.

32 And the scribe said unto him, Well, Master, thou hast said the truth: for there is one God; and there is none other but he:

33 And to love him with all the heart, and with all the understanding, and with all the soul, and with all the strength, and to love his neighbour as himself, is more than all whole burnt offerings and sacrifices.

34 And when Jesus saw that he answered discreetly, he said unto him, Thou art not far from the kingdom of God. And no man after that durst ask him any question.

35 ¶ And Jesus answered and said, while he taught in the temple, How say the scribes that Christ is the son of David?

36 For David himself said by the Holy Ghost, The LORD said to my Lord, Sit thou on my right hand, till I make thine enemies thy footstool.

37 David therefore himself calleth him Lord; and whence is he then his son? And the common people heard him gladly.

38 ¶ And he said unto them in his doctrine, Beware of the scribes, which love to go in long clothing, and love salutations in the marketplaces,

39 And the chief seats in the synagogues, and the uppermost rooms at feasts:

40 Which devour widows' houses, and for a pretence make long prayers: these shall receive greater damnation.

41 ¶ And Jesus sat over against the treasury, and beheld how the people cast money into the treasury: and many that were rich cast in much.

42 And there came a certain poor widow, and she threw in two mites, which makes a farthing.

43 And he called unto him his disciples, and saith unto them, Verily I say unto you, That this poor widow hath cast more in, than all they which have cast into the treasury:

44 For all they did cast in of their abundance; but she of her want did cast in all that she had, even all her living.

CHAPTER 13

1 And as he went out of the temple, one of his disciples saith unto him, Master, see what manner of stones and what buildings are here!

2 And Jesus answering said unto him, Seest thou these great buildings? there shall not be left one stone upon another, that shall not be thrown down.

3 And as he sat upon the mount of Olives over against the temple, Peter and James and John and Andrew asked him privately,

4 Tell us, when shall these things be? and what shall be the sign when all these things shall be fulfilled?

5 And Jesus answering them began to say, Take heed lest any man deceive you:

6 For many shall come in my name, saying, I am Christ; and shall deceive many.

7 And when ye shall hear of wars and rumours of wars, be ye not troubled: for such things must needs be; but the end shall not be yet.

8 For nation shall rise against nation, and kingdom against kingdom: and there shall be earthquakes in divers places, and there shall be famines and troubles: these are the beginnings of sorrows.

9 ¶ But take heed to yourselves: for they shall deliver you up to councils; and in the synagogues ye shall be beaten: and ye shall be brought before rulers and kings for my sake, for a testimony against them.

10 And the gospel must first be published among all nations.

11 But when they shall lead you, and deliver you up, take no thought beforehand what ye shall speak, neither do ye premeditate: but whatsoever shall be given you in that hour, that speak ye: for it is not ye that speak, but the Holy Ghost.

12 Now the brother shall betray the brother to death, and the father the son; and children shall rise up against their parents, and shall cause them to be put to death.

13 And ye shall be hated of all men for my name's sake: but he that shall endure unto the end, the same shall be saved.

14 ¶ But when ye shall see the abomination of desolation, spoken of by Daniel the prophet, standing where it ought not, (let him that readeth understand,) then let them that be in Judæa flee to the mountains:

15 And let him that is on the housetop not go down into the house, neither enter therein, to take any thing out of his house:

16 And let him that is in the field not turn back again for to take up his garment.

17 But woe to them that are with child, and to them that give suck in those days!

18 And pray ye that your flight be not in the winter.

19 For in those days shall be affliction, such as was not from the beginning of the creation which God created unto this time, neither shall be.

20 And except that the Lord had shortened those days, no flesh should be saved: but for the elect's sake, whom he hath chosen, he hath shortened the days.

21 And then if any man shall say to you, Lo, here is Christ; or, lo, he is there; believe him not:

22 For false Christs and false prophets shall rise, and shall shew signs and wonders, to seduce, if it were possible, even the elect.

23 But take ye heed: behold, I have foretold you all things.

24 ¶ But in those days, after that tribulation, the sun shall be darkened, and the moon shall not give her light,

25 And the stars of heaven shall fall, and the powers that are in heaven shall be shaken.

26 And then shall they see the Son of man coming in the clouds with great power and glory.

27 And then shall he send his angels, and shall gather together his elect from the four winds, from the uttermost part of the earth to the uttermost part of heaven.

28 Now learn a parable of the fig tree; When her branch is yet tender, and putteth forth leaves, ye know that summer is near:

29 So ye in like manner, when ye shall see these things come to pass, know that it is nigh, even at the doors.

30 Verily I say unto you, that this generation shall not pass, till all these things be done.

31 Heaven and earth shall pass away: but my words shall not pass away.

32 ¶ But of that day and that hour knoweth no man, no, not the angels which are in heaven, neither the Son, but the Father.

33 Take ye heed, watch and pray: for ye know not when the time is.

34 For the Son of man is as a man taking a far journey, who left his house, and gave authority to his servants, and to every man his work, and commanded the porter to watch.

35 Watch ye therefore: for ye know not when the master of the house cometh, at even, or at midnight, or at the cockcrowing, or in the morning:

36 Lest coming suddenly he find you sleeping.

37 And what I say unto you I say unto all, Watch.

CHAPTER 14

After two days was the feast of the passover, and of unleavened bread: and
1 the chief priests and the scribes sought how they might take him by craft, and put him to death.

2 But they said, Not on the feast day, lest there be an uproar of the people.

3 ¶ And being in Bethany in the house of Simon the leper, as he sat at meat, there came a woman having an alabaster box of ointment of spikenard very precious; and she brake the box, and poured it on his head.

4 And there were some that had indignation within themselves, and said, Why was this waste of the ointment made?

5 For it might have been sold for more than three hundred pence, and have been given to the poor. And they murmured against her.

6 And Jesus said, Let her alone; why trouble ye her? she hath wrought a good work on me.

7 For ye have the poor with you always, and whensoever ye will ye may do them good: but me ye have not always.

8 She hath done what she could: she is come aforehand to anoint my body to the burying.

9 Verily I say unto you, Wheresoever this gospel shall be preached throughout the whole world, this also that she hath done shall be spoken of for a memorial of her.

10 ¶ And Judas Iscariot, one of the twelve, went unto the chief priests, to betray him unto them.

11 And when they heard it, they were glad, and promised to give him money. And he sought how he might conveniently betray him.

12 ¶ And the first day of unleavened bread, when they killed the passover, his disciples said unto him, Where wilt thou that we go and prepare that thou mayest eat the passover?

13 And he sendeth forth two of his disciples, and saith unto them, Go ye into the city, and there shall meet you a man bearing a pitcher of water: follow him.

14 And wheresoever he shall go in, say ye to the goodman of the house, The Master saith, Where is the guestchamber, where I shall eat the passover with my disciples?

15 And he will shew you a large upper room furnished and prepared: there make ready for us.

16 And his disciples went forth, and came into the city, and found as he had said unto them: and they made ready the passover.

17 And in the evening he cometh with the twelve.

18 And as they sat and did eat, Jesus said, Verily I say unto you, One of you which eateth with me shall betray me.

19 And they began to be sorrowful, and to say unto him one by one, Is it I? and another said, Is it I?

20 And he answered and said unto them, It is one of the twelve, that dippeth with me in the dish.

21 The Son of man indeed goeth, as it is written of him: but woe to that man by whom the Son of man is betrayed! good were it for that man if he had never been born.

22 ¶ And as they did eat, Jesus took bread, and blessed, and brake it, and gave to them, and said, Take, eat: this is my body.

23 And he took the cup, and when he had given thanks, he gave it to them: and they all drank of it.

24 And he said unto them, This is my blood of the new testament, which is shed for many.

25 Verily I say unto you, I will drink no more of the fruit of the vine, until that day that I drink it new in the kingdom of God.

26 ¶ And when they had sung an hymn, they went out into the mount of Olives.

27 And Jesus saith unto them, All ye shall be offended because of me this night: for it is written, I will smite the shepherd, and the sheep shall be scattered.

28 But after that I am risen, I will go before you into Galilee.

29 But Peter said unto him, Although all shall be offended, yet will not I.

30 And Jesus saith unto him, Verily I say unto thee, That this day, even in this night, before the cock crow twice, thou shalt deny me thrice.

31 But he spake the more vehemently, If I should die with thee, I will not deny thee in any wise. Likewise also said they all.

32 And they came to a place which was named Gethsemane: and he saith to his disciples, Sit ye here, while I shall pray.

33 And he taketh with him Peter and James and John, and began to be sore amazed, and to be very heavy;

34 And saith unto them, My soul is exceeding sorrowful unto death: tarry ye here, and watch.

35 And he went forward a little, and fell on the ground, and prayed that, if it were possible, the hour might pass from him.

36 And he said, Abba, Father, all things are possible unto thee; take away this cup from me: nevertheless not what I will, but what thou wilt.

37 And he cometh, and findeth them sleeping, and saith unto Peter, Simon, sleepest thou? couldest not thou watch one hour?

38 Watch ye and pray, lest ye enter into temptation. The spirit truly is ready, but the flesh is weak.

39 And again he went away, and prayed, and spake the same words.

40 And when he returned, he found them asleep again (for their eyes were heavy,) neither wist they what to answer him.

41 And he cometh the third time, and saith unto them, Sleep on now, and take your rest: it is enough, the hour is come; behold, the Son of man is betrayed into the hands of sinners.

42 Rise up, let us go; lo, he that betrayeth me is at hand.

43 ¶ And immediately, while he yet spake, cometh Judas, one of the twelve, and with him a great multitude with swords and staves, from the chief priests and the scribes and the elders.

44 And he that betrayed him had given them a token, saying, Whomsoever I shall kiss, that same is he; take him, and lead him away safely.

45 And as soon as he was come, he goeth straightway to him, and saith, Master, master; and kissed him.

46 ¶ And they laid their hands on him, and took him.

47 And one of them that stood by drew a sword, and smote a servant of the high priest, and cut off his ear.

48 And Jesus answered and said unto them, Are ye come out, as against a thief, with swords and with staves to take me?

49 I was daily with you in the temple teaching, and ye took me not: but the scriptures must be fulfilled.

50 And they all forsook him, and fled.

51 And there followed him a certain young man, having a linen cloth cast about his naked body; and the young men laid hold on him:

52 And he left the linen cloth, and fled from them naked.

53 ¶ And they led Jesus away to the high priest: and with him were assembled all the chief priests and the elders and the scribes.

54 And Peter followed him afar off, even into the palace of the high priest: and he sat with the servants, and warmed himself at the fire.

55 And the chief priests and all the council sought for witness against Jesus to put him to death; and found none.

56 For many bare false witness against him, but their witness agreed not together.

57 And there arose certain, and bare false witness against him, saying,

58 We heard him say, I will destroy this temple that is made with hands, and within three days I will build another made without hands.

59 But neither so did their witness agree together.

60 And the high priest stood up in the midst, and asked Jesus, saying, Answerest thou nothing? what is it which these witness against thee?

61 But he held his peace, and answered nothing. Again the high priest asked him, and said unto him, Art thou the Christ, the Son of the Blessed?

62 And Jesus said, I am: and ye shall see the Son of man sitting on the right hand of power, and coming in the clouds of heaven.

63 Then the high priest rent his clothes, and saith, What need we any further witnesses?

64 Ye have heard the blasphemy: what think ye? And they all condemned him to be guilty of death.

65 And some began to spit on him, and to cover his face, and to buffet him, and to say unto him, Prophesy: and the servants did strike him with the palms of their hands.

66 ¶ And as Peter was beneath in the palace, there cometh one of the maids of the high priest:

67 And when she saw Peter warming himself, she looked upon him, and said, And thou also wast with Jesus of Nazareth.

68 But he denied, saying, I know not, neither understand I what thou sayest. And he went out into the porch; and the cock crew.

69 And a maid saw him again, and began to say to them that stood by, This is one of them.

70 And he denied it again. And a little after, they that stood by said again to Peter, Surely thou art one of them: for thou art a Galilæan, and thy speech agreeth thereto.

71 But he began to curse and to swear, saying, I know not this man of whom ye speak.

72 And the second time the cock crew. And Peter called to mind the word that Jesus said unto him, Before the cock crow twice, thou shalt deny me thrice. And when he thought thereon, he wept.

CHAPTER 15

1 And straightway in the morning the chief priests held a consultation with the elders and scribes and the whole council, and bound Jesus, and carried him away, and delivered him to Pilate.

2 And Pilate asked him, Art thou the King of the Jews? And he answering said unto him, Thou sayest it.

3 And the chief priests accused him of many things: but he answered nothing.

4 And Pilate asked him again, saying, Answerest thou nothing? behold how many things they witness against thee.

5 But Jesus yet answered nothing; so that Pilate marvelled.

6 Now at that feast he released unto them one prisoner, whomsoever they desired.

7 And there was one named Barabbas, which lay bound with them that had made insurrection with him, who had committed murder in the insurrection.

8 And the multitude crying aloud began to desire him to do as he had ever done unto them.

9 But Pilate answered them, saying, Will ye that I release unto you the King of the Jews?

10 For he knew that the chief priests had delivered him for envy.

11 But the chief priests moved the people, that he should rather release Barabbas unto them.

12 And Pilate answered and said again unto them, What will ye then that I shall do unto him whom ye call the King of the Jews?

13 And they cried out again, Crucify him.

14 Then Pilate said unto them, Why, what evil hath he done? And they cried out the more exceedingly, Crucify him.

15 ¶ And so Pilate, willing to content the people, released Barabbas unto them, and delivered Jesus, when he had scourged him, to be crucified.

16 And the soldiers led him away into the hall, called Prætorium; and they call together the whole band.

17 And they clothed him with purple, and platted a crown of thorns, and put it about his head,

18 And began to salute him, Hail, King of the Jews!

19 And they smote him on the head with a reed, and did spit upon him, and bowing their knees worshipped him.

20 And when they had mocked him, they took off the purple from him, and put his own clothes on him, and led him out to crucify him.

21 And they compel one Simon a Cyrenian, who passed by, coming out of the country, the father of Alexander and Rufus, to bear his cross.

22 And they bring him unto the place Golgotha, which is, being interpreted, The place of a skull.

23 And they gave him to drink wine mingled with myrrh: but he received it not.

24 And when they had crucified him, they parted his garments, casting lots upon them, what every man should take.

25 And it was the third hour, and they crucified him.

26 And the superscription of his accusation was written over, THE KING OF THE JEWS.

27 And with him they crucify two thieves; the one on his right hand, and the other on his left.

28 And the scripture was fulfilled, which saith, And he was numbered with the transgressors.

29 And they that passed by railed on him, wagging their heads, and saying, Ah, thou that destroyest the temple, and buildest it in three days,

30 Save thyself, and come down from the cross.

31 Likewise also the chief priests mocking said among themselves with the scribes, He saved others; himself he cannot save.

32 Let Christ the King of Israel descend now from the cross, that we may see and believe. And they that were crucified with him reviled him.

33 And when the sixth hour was come, there was darkness over the whole land until the ninth hour.

34 And at the ninth hour Jesus cried with a loud voice, saying, Eloi, Eloi, lama sabachthani? which is, being interpreted, My God, my God, why hast thou forsaken me?

35 And some of them that stood by, when they heard it, said, Behold, he calleth Elias.

36 And one ran and filled a sponge full of vinegar, and put it on a reed, and gave him to drink, saying, Let alone; let us see whether Elias will come to take him down.

37 And Jesus cried with a loud voice, and gave up the ghost.

38 And the veil of the temple was rent in twain from the top to the bottom.

39 ¶ And when the centurion, which stood over against him, saw that he so cried out, and gave up the ghost, he said, Truly this man was the Son of God.

40 There were also women looking on afar off: among whom was Mary Magdalene, and Mary the mother of James the less and of Joses, and Salome;

41 (Who also, when he was in Galilee, followed him, and ministered unto him;) and many other women which came up with him unto Jerusalem.

42 ¶ And now when the even was come, because it was the preparation, that is, the day before the sabbath,

43 Joseph of Arimathæa, an honourable counsellor, which also waited for the kingdom of God, came, and went in boldly unto Pilate, and craved the body of Jesus.

44 And Pilate marvelled if he were already dead: and calling unto him the centurion, he asked him whether he had been any while dead.

45 And when he knew it of the centurion, he gave the body to Joseph.

46 And he bought fine linen, and took him down, and wrapped him in the linen, and laid him in a sepulchre which was hewn out of a rock, and rolled a stone unto the door of the sepulchre.

47 And Mary Magdalene and Mary the mother of Joses beheld where he was laid.

CHAPTER 16

1 And when the sabbath was past, Mary Magdalene, and Mary the mother of James, and Salome, had bought sweet spices, that they might come and anoint him.

2 And very early in the morning the first day of the week, they came unto the sepulchre at the rising of the sun.

3 And they said among themselves, Who shall roll us away the stone from the door of the sepulchre?

4 And when they looked, they saw that the stone was rolled away: for it was very great.

5 And entering into the sepulchre, they saw a young man sitting on the right side, clothed in a long white garment; and they were affrighted.

6 And he saith unto them, Be not affrighted: Ye seek Jesus of Nazareth, which was crucified: he is risen; he is not here: behold the place where they laid him.

7 But go your way, tell his disciples and Peter that he goeth before you into Galilee: there shall ye see him, as he said unto you.

8 And they went out quickly, and fled from the sepulchre; for they trembled and were amazed: neither said they any thing to any man; for they were afraid.

9 ¶ Now when Jesus was risen early the first day of the week, he appeared first to Mary Magdalene, out of whom he had cast seven devils.

10 And she went and told them that had been with him, as they mourned and wept.

11 And they, when they had heard that he was alive, and had been seen of her, believed not.

12 ¶ After that he appeared in another form unto two of them, as they walked, and went into the country.

13 And they went and told it unto the residue: neither believed they them.

14 ¶ Afterward he appeared unto the eleven as they sat at meat, and upbraided them with their unbelief and hardness of heart, because they believed not them which had seen him after he was risen.

15 And he said unto them. Go ye into all the world, and preach the gospel to every creature.

16 He that believeth and is baptized shall be saved; but he that believeth not shall be damned.

17 And these signs shall follow them that believe; In my name shall they cast out devils; they shall speak with new tongues;

18 They shall take up serpents; and if they drink any deadly thing, it shall not hurt them; they shall lay hands on the sick, and they shall recover.

19 ¶ So then after the Lord had spoken unto them, he was received up into heaven, and sat on the right hand of God.

20 And they went forth, and preached every where, the Lord working with them, and confirming the word with signs following. Amen.

PART III

RELIGIOUS RITUAL

Kiva: Indian Ceremonial Pit, New Mexico.
(Photo by J. T. Carmody)

INTRODUCTION

Traditional humanity has not been rationalistic. Almost without exception, down the centuries men and women have striven hard to *feel* their deepest convictions. To this end, they have regularly created ceremonies through which they might enter into such convictions and act them out. Regularly, they have sung songs, listened to dramatic tellings of revered stories, danced, and reenacted events they thought especially significant to their well-being. Many cultures have developed impressive rituals for such crucial times in the life cycle as birth, puberty, marriage, and death. Hindus have celebrated special holidays each month, commemorating events in the lives of the gods; Christians have reenacted constantly the Eucharist—the Last Supper of Jesus with his disciples, and his death on the cross. Through such rituals, people have been able to become contemporaries of the divine. They have traveled back in imagination to the time when the world arose, or when Ganesha was born, or when Christ was condemned by Pilate. This has allowed them to soak their sensibility in such key moments and so to renew their deepest convictions.

The rituals that we examine in this part come from Native American, Muslim, and Jewish peoples. The Lakota (Sioux) ritual for gaining a vision is one of the seven main rites described by the holy man Black Elk when he narrated the traditional beliefs of his people. Lakota on the verge of adulthood sought such a vision to direct their mature lives. The intimacy with all living things of nature that we find in this account is typical. In all their traditional ceremonies the Lakota prayed, remembered, and petitioned the holy powers as members of a democratic universe. They felt akin to the animals and plants, related to the wind and the rain, and from these relations emerged a profoundly "ecological" religion. Their sense of themselves and their worship of the most sacred forces in their lives was holistic. The natural world was a living whole, and the first virtue of religious people (of genuine Lakota) was to live in harmony with this whole.

The account of the Muslim pilgrimage to Mecca *(hajj)* that we take from *The Autobiography of Malcolm X* suggests the dramatic, highly personal impact that this ritual has often had. Malcolm X had come to Islam after a life of crime. He was disillusioned with Christianity, which he experienced as part of the racism of the white establishment in the United States, and eventually he decided that traditional Islam was the best expression of the brotherhood and sisterhood he had been seeking. His trip to Mecca in 1964, shortly before his assassination, played a pivotal role in his mature hopes for both Islam and black liberation.

Mecca is the center of the Muslim world because it is the place where the Prophet Muhammad received the revelations that founded Islam early in the seventh century A.D. Muslims accept five basic obligations. First is to recite the creed ("There is no God but God [Allah], and Muhammad is God's prophet"). Second is to pray five times each day, facing Mecca. Third is to fast during the lunar month of Ramadan. Fourth is to give alms to support the poor. And fifth is to make the pilgrimage to Mecca at least once during one's lifetime (if physically and financially able). So the pilgrimage has become a great rallying point for Muslims. In Mecca, at the time of the *hajj*, Muslims meet fellow pilgrims from all over the world. Dressed in similar garb, reenacting the same traditions associated with Abraham and other key figures in Muslim faith, they give witness to the universality of Islam. Often the *hajj* has been ritual Islam at its most powerful.

The third selection concerning ritual comes from Judaism. More precisely, it comes from the convictions of an American Hasidic community about how to celebrate the Sabbath. Hallowing the Sabbath has always been a prime obligation and privilege in traditional Judaism. The practice is tied to the notion in *Genesis* that, after God had created the world in six days, on the seventh day he rested. God commanded his people, made in his image, to imitate this sabbatical rest. In the law that accompanied the covenant, God had Moses explain the obligation to give one day a week to religious devotion and rest.

As Judaism developed its understanding of the Sabbath, it decided that people should perform no profane work. Now more strictly, now more laxly, Jews would refrain from conducting business, doing housework, making unnecessary trips. More positively, they would try to establish a mood of joy and gratitude in the family, welcoming the needy, spending time in the synagogue for prayer and study, and generally delighting in the presence of the Sabbath herself (much traditional imagery pictured the Sabbath as God's bride). The Sabbath was the time when Jews felt most Jewish. They remembered their traditions, asserted their solidarity as members of God's chosen people, and defended themselves against the encroachments of the Gentile or simply secular world that threatened to wear away their sense of identity. The selection included here comes from a delightful book about the world of a Hasidic family as it tried to maintain a traditional way of life in Brooklyn in the early 1980s.

As with mythology, we do best with religious ritual when we suspend disbelief and let the actors do what they regularly do without any psychological interference. Thus, we get the best appreciation of Lakota ritual by placing ourselves alongside those seeking a vision, or using the sacred pipe to commune with the Great Spirit, in an attitude of sympathy. For we, too, could profit from a vision of who we ought to become, what our unique pathway through life ought to be, who our special helpers are. Similarly, we, too, could profit from a sense that the world has a geographical center. Mecca gives the Muslim world a physical orientation, and so a great coherence. For many Jews, Jerusalem has served the same function, as for many Americans Washington, D.C., is a secular analogue. Human beings need to organize both their space and their time. Their myths and rituals help them in this task. Thus, the Muslim Friday, or the Jewish Sabbath, or the Christian Sunday has traditionally organized time. Less cosmically, the local mosque, synagogue, or church has been a lodestone for the community, giving it a center, serving as its heart.

It is also important to realize that the final goal of ritual, as most religious groups have understood it, is to commune with God, or ultimate reality. Religious rituals are forms of worship. Important as their aesthetic and social functions have been, their primary intent has been to bring the participants into contact with the holy center of their lives. Thus, the *hajj* is most important because it has been commanded by Allah and pilgrims can hope to gain Allah's favor by fulfilling his will. The Sabbath is most important, for traditional Jews, because it is a time filled with God's special presence, a time when divinity dallies with human beings. And the Lakota ritual for obtaining a vision has been most important because without a visitation from divinity in the form of a directive vision a person would not live as close to the heart of things, the sacred center of reality, as he or she ought to live.

Religious ritual expresses the universal human longing to live close to God. Yet human beings have also feared the sacred, thinking themselves too impure to bear its holiness, and so they have tended to flee from God. But their desire for communion with divinity has been stronger. Indeed, to mediate between their fear and their attraction they have built gestures of purification into most of their rituals. Thus, one finds ceremonial washings, confessions of sins, and separations from profane space and time. One finds petitions to God to make the community or the individual worthy to come before the divinity. Ritual has allowed all of these emotions and many more to gain full bodily expression. It has encouraged people to share their anxieties and their hopes through common prayers, bows, confessions of sin, and so to realize their equal distance from and closeness to divinity. Ritual has been the backbone of traditional religion.

8

Black Elk

"Hanblecheyapi: Crying for a Vision" from The Sacred Pipe*

Black Elk was a holy man of the Lakota (Sioux) who narrated the traditional beliefs of his people. This reading is his account of one of the seven main rituals of his people. In this particular ritual, the Lakota on the verge of adulthood seeks a vision to provide the direction his or her life will take. The ritual's description gives clear evidence of the Lakota religion's deeply ecological nature.

The "Crying for a Vision" ritual, like the purification rites of the *Inipi* [sweat lodge], was used long before the coming of our most sacred pipe. This way of praying is very important, and indeed it is at the center of our religion, for from it we have received many good things, even the four great rites which I shall soon describe.

Every man can cry for a vision, or "lament"; and in the old days we all— men and women—"lamented" all the time. What is received through the "lamenting" is determined in part by the character of the person who does this, for it is only those people who are very qualified who receive the great visions, which are interpreted by our holy man, and which give strength and health to our nation. It is very important for a person who wishes to "lament" to receive aid and advice from a *wichasha wakan* (holy man),[1] so that everything is done correctly, for if things are not done in the right way, something very bad can happen, and even a serpent could come and wrap itself around the "lamenter."

You have all heard of our great chief and priest Crazy Horse, but perhaps you did not know that he received most of his great power through the

---

*From *The Sacred Pipe: Black Elk's Account of the Seven Rites of the Oglala Sioux*, recorded and edited by Joseph Epes Brown. Copyright © 1953, 1989 by the University of Oklahoma Press.

[1]Throughout this work I have translated *wichasha wakan* as "holy man" or "priest," rather than "Medicine man," which has been used incorrectly in many books on the Indians. The Lakota term for "medicine man" or "doctor" is really *pejuta wichasa*. In order to clarify these frequently confused terms, I cannot do better than to quote the explanation given by Sword, an Oglala Sioux, to J. R. Walker: "*Wicasa wakan* is the term for a Lakota priest of the old religion; a Lakota medicine man is called *pejuta wacasa*. The white people call our *wicasa wakan*, medicine man, which is a mistake. Again, they say a *wicasa wakan* is making medicine when he is performing ceremonies. This is also a mistake. The Lakota call a thing 'medicine' only when it is used to cure the sick or wounded, the proper term (for medicine) being *pejuta*." (*The Sun Dance . . . of the Teton Dakota* [Anthropological Papers of the American Museum of Natural History, XVI, Part II, 152].)

"lamenting" which he did many times a year, and even in the winter when it is very cold and very difficult. He received visions of the Rock, the Shadow, the Badger, a prancing horse (from which he received his name), the Day, and also of *Wanbli Galeshka*, the Spotted Eagle, and from each of these he received much power and holiness.[2]

There are many reasons for going to a lonely mountaintop to "lament." Some young men receive a vision when they are very young and when they do not expect it,[3] and then they go to "lament" that they might understand it better. Then we "lament" if we wish to make ourselves brave for a great ordeal such as the Sun Dance or to prepare for going on the warpath. Some people "lament" in order to ask some favor of the Great Spirit, such as curing a sick relative; and then we also "lament" as an act of thanksgiving for some great gift which the Great Spirit may have given to us. But perhaps the most important reason for "lamenting" is that it helps us to realize our oneness with all things, to know that all things are our relatives; and then in behalf of all things we pray to *Wakan-Tanka* that He may give to us knowledge of Him who is the source of all things, yet greater than all things.

Our women also "lament," after first purifying themselves in the *Inipi;* they are helped by other women, but they do not go up on a very high and lonely mountain. They go up on a hill in a valley, for they are women and need protection.

When a person wishes to "lament," he goes with a filled pipe to a holy man; he enters the tipi with the stem of the pipe pointing in front of him, and sits before the old man who is to be his guide. The "lamenter" then places the pipe on the ground with its stem now pointing towards himself, for it is he who wishes to gain knowledge. The holy man raises his hands above to *Wakan-Tanka* and to the four directions, and, taking up the pipe, he asks the man what he wishes.

"I wish to 'lament' and offer my pipe to *Wakan-Tanka*. I need your help and guidance, and wish you to send a voice for me to the Powers above."

To this the old man says: *"How!"* (It is good); and then they leave the tipi, and, walking a short distance, they face the west, the young man standing to the left of the holy man, and they are joined by any others who may happen to be present. All raise their right hands, and the old man prays, holding the stem of the pipe to the heavens.

---

[2]The Indian actually identifies himself with, or becomes, the quality or principle of the being or thing which comes to him in a vision, whether it be a beast, a bird, one of the elements, or really any aspect of creation. In order that this "power" may never leave him, he always carries with him some material form representing the animal or object from which he has received his "power." These objects have often been incorrectly called fetishes, whereas they actually correspond more precisely to what the Christian calls guardian angels, since for the Indian, the animals and birds, and all things, are the "reflections"—in a material form—of the Divine principles. The Indian is only attached to the form for the sake of the principle which is contained within the form.

[3]Black Elk himself received his great vision when he was only nine years old. For a description of this vision, see Neihardt's *Black Elk Speaks,* chap. III.

"Hee-ay-hay-ee-ee! [four times.] Grandfather, *Wakan-Tanka,* You are first and always have been! Everything belongs to You. It is You who have created all things! You are One and alone, and to You we are sending a voice. This young man here is in difficulty, and wishes to offer the pipe to You. We ask that You give help to him! Within a few days he will offer his body to You. Upon the sacred Earth, our Mother and Grandmother, he will place his feet in a sacred manner.

"All the Powers of the world, the heavens and the star peoples, and the red and blue sacred days; all things that move in the universe, in the rivers, the brooks, the springs, all waters, all trees that stand, all the grasses of our Grandmother, all the sacred peoples of the universe: Listen! A sacred relationship with you all will be asked by this young man, that his generations to come will increase and live in a holy manner.

"O You, winged One, there where the sun goes down, who guards our sacred pipe, help us! Help us to offer this pipe to *Wakan-Tanka,* that He may give a blessing to this young man!"

To this all the people cry *"How!"* and then they sit in a circle upon the ground. The old man offers the pipe to the six directions, lights it, and passes it first to the young man who is to "lament." The "lamenter" offers it up with a prayer, and then it is smoked by everybody in the circle. When the pipe is smoked out, it is handed back to the holy man, who cleans and purifies it and hands it back to the young man, asking him when he wishes to "lament," and a day is then decided upon.

When this chosen day arrives, the young man wears only his buffalo robe, breech cloth, and moccasins, and he goes with his pipe to the tipi of the holy man. Crying as he walks, he enters the lodge and places his right hand on the head of the old man, saying: *"Unshe ma la ye!"* (Be merciful to me!) He then lays the pipe in front of the holy man and asks for his help.

The old man replies: "We all know that the pipe is sacred, and with it you have now come crying. I shall help you, but you must always remember what I am going to tell you; in the winters to come you must walk with the instructions and advice which I give to you. You may "lament" from one to four days, or even longer if you wish; how many days do you choose?"

"I choose two days."

"Good! This, then, is what you must do: First you should build an *Inipi* lodge in which we shall purify ourselves, and for this you must select twelve or sixteen small willows. But before you cut the willows remember to take to them a tobacco offering; and as you stand before them you should say: 'There are many kinds of trees, but it is you whom I have chosen to help me. I shall take you, but in your place there will be others!' Then you should bring these trees back to where we shall make the lodge.

"In a sacred manner you must also gather the rocks and sage, and then you must make a bundle of five long sticks and also five bundles of twelve small sticks, all of which will be used as offerings. These sticks you should lean against the west side of the sweat lodge until we are ready to purify them. We shall also need the Ree twist tobacco, *kinnikinnik,* a tobacco cutting board, buckskin for the tobacco-offering bags, sweet grass, a bag of sacred earth, a knife, and a stone hatchet. These things you must secure yourself, and when you are ready we shall purify ourselves. *Hetchetu welo!"*

When the purification lodge has been built, and all the equipment gathered, the holy man enters the lodge and sits at the west; the "lamenter" enters next and sits at the north, and then a helper enters and sits just to the south of the holy man. A cold rock is brought into the lodge and is placed on the north side of the central altar, where it is purified with a short prayer by the holy man; it is then taken outside by a helper. This is the first rock to be placed on the fire *(peta owihankeshni)* which has been built to the east of the lodge.

Just east of the central altar, within the purification lodge, the helper scrapes a sacred place upon the earth, and upon this he places a hot coal. The holy man now moves around to the east, and, bending over the coal, he holds up a bit of sweet grass and prays in this manner:

"O Grandfather, *Wakan-Tanka,* behold us! Upon the sacred earth I place this Your herb. The smoke that rises from the earth and fire will belong to all that moves in the universe: the four-leggeds, the wingeds, and everything that moves and everything that is. This offering of theirs will now be given to You, O *Wakan-Tanka*! We shall make sacred all that we touch!"

As the sweet grass is put upon the coal, the other two men in the lodge cry, *"Hi ye!"* (Thanks), and as the smoke rises, the holy man rubs his hands in it and then rubs them over his body. In the same manner the "lamenter" and the helper purify themselves with the sacred smoke. The little bag of earth is also purified, and then the three men again take their places at the west, every movement being made, of course, in a sun-wise manner. The purified earth is now very carefully spread all around inside the sacred central hole, and this is done slowly and reverently for this earth represents the whole universe. The helper hands a stick to the holy man, who uses it to mark four places around the hole, the first at the west, and then at the north, east, and south. Next a cross is made by drawing a line on the ground from west to east, then one from the north to the south. All this is very sacred, for it establishes the four great Powers of the universe, and also the center which is the dwelling place of *Wakan-Tanka.* A helper now enters from the outside carrying a hot coal in a split stick; he walks slowly, stopping four times, and the last time the coal is placed upon the center of the cross.

Holding a pinch of sweet grass over the coal, the holy man prays: "My Grandfather, *Wakan-Tanka,* You are everything. And my Father, *Wakan-Tanka,* all things belong to You! I am about to place Your herb on this fire. Its fragrance belongs to You."

The old man then slowly lowers the sweet grass to the fire. The helper now takes up the pipe, and moving with it in a sun-wise direction, hands it to the holy man who prays with it in these words: "O *Wakan-Tanka,* behold Your pipe! I hold it over the smoke of this herb. O *Wakan-Tanka,* behold also this sacred place which we have made. We know that its center is your dwelling place. Upon this circle the generations will walk. The four-leggeds, the two-leggeds, the wingeds, and the four Powers of the universe, all will behold this, Your place."

The holy man holds the pipe over the smoke, pointing the stem first to the west, and then to the north, the east, the south, and to heaven, then he touches the earth with its foot. He purifies all the sacred equipment: the buffalo robe and all the offering sticks; and then he makes little bags of tobacco which he ties on the ends of the offering sticks.

The old holy man, now seated at the west, takes the tobacco cutting board and begins to chop and mix the *kinnikinnik*. He first judges carefully the size of the pipe, for he must make just enough to fill the pipe bowl and no more. Each time that he shaves off a little piece of the tobacco, he offers it to one of the quarters of the world, taking great care that no piece jumps off the board, for this would make the Thunder-beings very angry. When the mixing has been finished, the old man takes up the pipe with his left hand, and holding up a pinch of the *kinnikinnik* with his right hand, he prays.

"O *Wakan-Tanka*, my Father and Grandfather, You are first, and always have been! Behold this young man here who has a troubled mind. He wishes to travel upon the sacred path; he will offer this pipe to You. Be merciful to him and help him! The four Powers and the whole universe will be placed in the bowl of the pipe, and then this young man will offer it to You, with the help of the wingeds and all things.

"The first to be placed in the pipe is You, O winged Power of the place where the sun goes down. You with Your guards are ancient and sacred. Behold! There is a place for You in the pipe; help us with Your two sacred blue and red days!"

The holy man places this tobacco in the pipe, and then he holds up another pinch towards the place in the north where *Waziah* the Giant lives.

"O You, winged Power, there where the Giant has His lodge, from whence come the strong purifying winds: there is a place for You in the pipe; help us with the two sacred days which You have!"

The Power of this direction is placed in the pipe, and a third pinch of tobacco is held towards the east.

"O You where the sun comes up, who guard the light and who give knowledge, this pipe will be offered to *Wakan-Tanka*! There is a place here for You too; help us with Your sacred days!"

In the same manner the Power of the east is placed in the pipe; and now a pinch of tobacco is held towards the south, the place towards which we always face.

"O You who control the sacred winds, and who live there where we always face, Your breath gives life; and it is from You and to You that our generations come and go. This pipe is about to be offered to *Wakan-Tanka;* there is a place in it for You. Help us with the two sacred days which You have!"

In this manner all the Powers of the four directions have been placed within the bowl of the pipe, and now a pinch of the sacred tobacco is held up towards the heavens, and this is for *Wanbli Galeshka,* the Spotted Eagle, who is higher than all other created beings, and who represents *Wakan-Tanka*:

"O *Wanbli Galeshka,* who circles in the highest heavens, You see all things in the heavens and upon the earth. This young man is about to offer his pipe to *Wakan-Tanka,* in order that he may gain knowledge. Help him, and all those who send their voices to *Wakan-Tanka* through You. There is a place for You in the pipe; give to us Your two sacred red and blue days."

With this prayer the Spotted Eagle is placed in the bowl of the pipe, and now a pinch of the tobacco is held towards Earth, and the old man continues to pray:

"O *Unchi* and *Ina,* our Grandmother and Mother, You are sacred! We know that it is from You that our bodies have come. This young man wishes to become one with all things; he wishes to gain knowledge. For the good of all Your peoples, help him! There is a place for You in the pipe; give to us Your two sacred red and blue days!"

Thus the Earth, which is now in the tobacco, is placed in the pipe, and in this manner all the six Powers of the universe have here become one. But in order to make sure that all the peoples of the world are included in the pipe, the holy man offers small grains of tobacco for each of the following winged peoples: "O sacred King Bird, who flies on the two sacred days; You who raise families so well, may we increase and live in the same manner. This pipe will soon be offered to *Wakan-Tanka*! There is a place here for You. Help us!" With the same prayer, small grains of tobacco are offered and placed in the pipe, for the meadow lark, the blackbird, the woodpecker, the snowbird, the crow, the magpie, the dove, the hawk, the eagle hawk, the bald eagle, and finally what is left of the tobacco is offered for the two-legged who is about to "lament," offering himself up to *Wakan-Tanka*.

The pipe is then sealed with tallow, for the "lamenter" will take it with him when he goes to the top of the mountain, and there he will offer it to *Wakan-Tanka;* but it will not be smoked until he finishes the "lamenting" and returns to the holy man.

All the offering poles and the equipment which have been purified, are now taken and are placed outside the lodge at the west. The three men leave the lodge and prepare for the *Inipi* by taking off all their clothes except the breech cloth. Any other men who may now be present are permitted to take part in this purification rite.

The "lamenter" enters the *Inipi* first and, moving around sunwise, sits at the west of the lodge. He takes up his pipe which had been left in the lodge (with its stem pointing to the east) and, turning it around sun-wise, holds it up in front of him; and he remains in this position for the first part of the rite. The holy man enters next and, passing behind the "lamenter," sits at the east, just beside the door. Any other men who wish to take part in the rite then fill in the remaining places; two men remain outside to act as helpers.

One of the helpers fills a pipe in a ritual manner, and this is handed in to the man who sits just at the left of the "lamenter." The rock which had previously been purified is also handed in—on a forked stick, for it is now very hot—and is placed at the center of the sacred hole. A second rock is then placed at the west in the sacred place, and the others are placed at the north, east, and south. As the rocks are put in place, the person who holds the pipe to be smoked in the rite touches its foot to each rock, and as he does this all the men cry: *"Hi ye! Hi ye!"* The pipe is then lit, offered to Heaven, Earth, and the four directions, and is smoked around the circle. As it passes around, each man mentions his relationship to the person next to him, and after everybody has smoked they all say together: *"mitakuye oyasin!"* (We are all relatives!). The one who lit the pipe now empties it, placing the ashes upon the center altar, and after purifying it he hands it to the left, and it is passed out of the lodge. The helper again fills the pipe and leans it on the sacred mound with the stem pointing to the west. The door of the lodge is closed, and the holy man at the east begins to pray in the darkness: "Behold! All that moves in the universe is here!" This is repeated by everybody in the lodge, and at the end they all say: *"How!"*

"Hee-ay-hay-ee-ee!" [four times] I am sending a voice! Hear me! [four times] *Wakan-Tanka,* Grandfather, behold us! O *Wakan-Tanka,* Father, behold us! On this great island there is a two-legged who says that he will offer a pipe to You. On this day his promise will be fulfilled. To whom could one send a voice except to You, *Wakan-Tanka,* our Grandfather and Father. O *Wakan-Tanka,* this young man asks You to be merciful to him. He says that his mind is troubled and that he needs Your help. In offering this pipe to You, he will offer his whole mind and body. The time has now come; he will soon go to a high place, and there he will cry for Your aid. Be merciful to him!

"O You four Powers of the universe, you wingeds of the air, and all the peoples who move in the universe—you have all been placed in the pipe. Help this young man with the knowledge which has been given to all of you by *Wakan-Tanka.* Be merciful to him! O *Wakan-Tanka,* grant that this young man may have relatives; that he may be one with the four winds, the four Powers of the world, and with the light of the dawn. May he understand his relationship with all the winged peoples of the air. He will place his feet upon the sacred earth of a mountaintop; may he receive understanding there; may his generations to come be holy! All things give thanks to You, O *Wakan-Tanka,* who are merciful, and who help us all. We ask all this of You because we know that You are the only One, and that You have power over all things!"

As a little water is poured on the red hot rocks, all the men sing:

> *Grandfather, I am sending a voice!*
> *To the Heavens of the universe, I am sending a voice;*
> *That my people may live!*

As the men sing this, and as the hot steam rises, the "lamenter" cries, for he is humbling himself, remembering his nothingness in the presence of the Great Spirit.[4]

After a short time the door of the lodge is opened by the helper, and the "lamenter" now embraces his pipe, holding it first to one shoulder and then to the other, and crying all the time to the Great Spirit: "Be merciful to me! Help me!" This pipe is then passed around the circle, and all the other men embrace it and cry in the same manner. It is then passed out of the lodge to the helpers, who also embrace it and then lean it on the little mound, with its stem to the east; for this direction is the source of light and understanding.

The second pipe which is being used for the purification rite, and which had been leaning on the sacred mound with its stem to the west, is now handed into the lodge, and is given to the person sitting just to the left of the "lamenter." This pipe is lit, and after it has been smoked by everybody in the circle, it is passed out of the lodge. After this, water is passed around, and the "lamenter" is now allowed to drink all that he wishes, but he must be careful not to spill any or to put any on his body, for this would anger the Thunder-beings who guard the sacred waters, and then they might visit him every night that he "laments." The holy man tells the "lamenter" to rub his body with the sage, and then the door is closed once more. A prayer is said by the next holiest man in the lodge, one who has had a vision.

"On this sacred earth, the Thunder-beings have been merciful to me, and have given to me a power from where Giant *Waziah* lives. It was an eagle who came to me. He will see you too when you go to cry for a vision. Then from the place where the sun comes up, they sent to me a Baldheaded Eagle; he too will see you. From the place towards which we always face, they sent to me a winged one. They were very merciful to me. In the depths of the heavens there is a winged being who is next to *Wakan-Tanka;* He is the Spotted Eagle, and He too will behold you. You will be seen by all the Powers and by the sacred earth upon which you stand. They have given to me a good road to follow upon this earth; may you too know this way! Set your mind upon the meanings of these things, and you will see! All this is so; do not forget! *Hechetu welo!"*

This old man then sings:

> *They are sending a voice to me.*
> *From the place where the sun goes down,*
> *Our Grandfather is sending a voice to me.*
> *From where the sun goes down,*
> *They are talking to me as they come.*
> *Our Grandfather's voice is calling to me.*

---

[4]This humiliation in which the Indian makes himself "lower than even the smallest ant," as Black Elk once expressed it, is the same attitude as that which, in Christianity, is called the "spiritual poverty"; this poverty is the *faqr* of the Islamic tradition or the *balya* of Hinduism and is the condition of those who realize that in relation to the Divine principle their own individuality is as nothing.

That winged One there where the Giant lives,
Is sending a voice to me. He is calling me.
Our Grandfather is calling me!

As the old man chants this song, water is put on the rocks, and after the men have been in the hot fragrant steam and darkness for a short time, the door is opened, and the fresh air and light fill the little lodge. Once again the pipe is taken from the sacred mound and is handed in to the man at the north of the lodge. After it has been smoked it is placed again on the mound with its stem pointing to the east. The door is closed, and this time it is the holy man at the east who prays.

"O *Wakan-Tanka*, behold all that we do and ask here! O You, Power, there where the sun goes down, who control the waters: with the breath of your waters this young man is purifying himself. And you too, O very aged rocks who are helping us here, listen! You are firmly fixed upon this earth; we know that the winds cannot shake you. This young man is about to send his voice, crying for a vision. You are helping us by giving to him some of your power; through your breath he is being made pure.

"O eternal fire there where the sun comes up, from you this young man is gaining strength and light. O you standing trees, *Wakan-Tanka* has given you the power to stand upright. May this young man always have you as an example; may he hold firmly to you! It is good. *Hechetu welo!*"

All the men now chant again, and after a little while the door is opened, and the pipe is sent to the holy man at the east, who lights it, and after smoking for a few puffs, hands it around the circle. When the tobacco has been smoked up, the helper again takes the pipe and places it on the earth mound, with the stem leaning to the south. The door of the *Inipi* is closed for the last time, and now the holy man addresses his prayer to the rocks.

"O you ancient rocks who are sacred, you have neither ears nor eyes, yet you hear and see all things. Through your powers this young man has become pure, that he may be worthy to go to receive some message from *Wakan-Tanka*. The men who guard the door of this sacred lodge will soon open it for the fourth time, and we shall see the light of the world. Be merciful to the men who guard the door! May their generations be blessed!"

Water is placed on the rocks, which are still very hot, and after the steam has penetrated throughout the lodge for a short time, the door is opened, and all the men cry: *"Hi ho! Hi ho!* Thanks!"

The "lamenter" leaves the lodge first, and goes and sits upon the sacred path, facing the little mound, and crying all the while. One of the helpers then takes up the buffalo robe, which had been purified, and places it over the shoulders of the "lamenter"; and another helper takes the pipe which has been leaning all this time on the mound, and hands it to the "lamenter," who is now ready to go up to the high mountain, there to cry for a vision.

Three horses are brought, and upon two of these the bundles of offering sticks and some sacred sage are loaded; the "lamenter" rides on the third horse, and all this time he is crying most pitifully and is holding his pipe in front of him. When they arrive at the foot of the chosen mountain, the two helpers go on ahead with all the equipment in order to prepare the sacred place on the mountaintop. When they arrive they enter the chosen place by walking in a direction always away from their camping circle, and they go directly to the spot which they have chosen to be the center and place all the equipment here. At this center they first make a hole, in which they place some *kinnikinnik,* and then in this hole they set up a long pole with the offerings tied at the top. One of the helpers now goes about ten strides to the west, and in the same manner he sets up a pole here, tying offerings to it. He then goes to the center where he picks up another pole, and this he fixes at the north again returning to the center. In the same manner he sets up poles at the east and at the south. All this time the other helper has been making a bed of sage at the center, so that when the "lamenter" is tired he may lie with his head against the center pole, and his feet stretching towards the east. When everything has been finished the helpers leave the sacred place by the north path, and then return to the "lamenter" at the foot of the mountain.

The "lamenter" now takes off his moccasins and even his breech cloth—for if we really wish to "lament" we must be poor in the things of this world—and he walks alone up to the top of the mountain, holding his pipe in front of him, and carrying his buffalo robe which he will use at night. As he walks he cries continually: *"Wakan-Tanka onshimala ye oyate wani wachin cha!"* (O Great Spirit, be merciful to me that my people may live!)

Entering the sacred place, the "lamenter" goes directly to the center pole, where he faces the west, and holding up his pipe with both hands he continues to cry: "O *Wakan-Tanka,* have pity on me, that my people may live!" Then walking very slowly he goes to the pole at the west, where he offers up the same prayer, and then returns to the center. In the same manner he goes to the poles at the north, east, and south, always returning to the center each time. After completing one of these rounds, he raises his pipe to the heavens asking the wingeds and all things to help him, and then pointing the pipe stem to the Earth, he asks aid from all that grows upon our Mother.

All this takes very little time to tell, yet the "lamenter" should do it all so slowly and in such a sacred manner that often he may take an hour or even two to make one of these rounds. The "lamenter" can move in no other manner than this, which is in the form of a cross, although he may linger at any one place as long as he wishes; but all day long this is what he does, praying constantly, either out loud or silently to himself, for the Great Spirit is everywhere; he hears whatever is in our minds and hearts, and it is not necessary to speak to Him in a loud voice. The "lamenter" need not always use this prayer that I have given, for he may remain silent with his whole attention directed to the Great Spirit or to one of His Powers. He must always be careful lest distracting thoughts come to him, yet he must be alert to recognize any messenger which the Great Spirit may send to him, for these people often come in the form of an animal, even one as small and as seemingly insignificant as a little ant.

Perhaps a Spotted Eagle may come to him from the west, or a Black Eagle from the north, or the Bald Eagle from the east, or even the Redheaded Woodpecker may come to him from the south. And even though none of these may speak to him at first, they are important and should be observed. The "lamenter" should also notice if one of the little birds should come, or even perhaps a squirrel. At first the animals or winged peoples may be wild, but soon they become tame, and the birds will sit on the poles, or even little ants or worms may crawl on the pipe. All these people are important, for in their own way they are wise and they can teach us two-leggeds much if we make ourselves humble before them. The most important of all the creatures are the wingeds, for they are nearest to the heavens, and are not bound to the earth as are the four-leggeds, or the little crawling people.

It may be good to mention here that it is not without reason that we humans are two-legged along with the wingeds; for you see the birds leave the earth with their wings, and we humans may also leave this world, not with wings, but in the spirit. This will help you to understand in part how it is that we regard all created beings as sacred and important, for everything has a *wochangi* or influence which can be given to us, through which we may gain a little more understanding if we are attentive.

All day long the "lamenter" sends his voice to *Wakan-Tanka* for aid, and he walks as we have described upon the sacred paths which form a cross. This form has much power in it, for whenever we return to the center, we know that it is as if we are returning to *Wakan-Tanka,* who is the center of everything; and although we may think that we are going away from Him, sooner or later we and all things must return to Him.

In the evening the "lamenter" is very tired, for you should remember that he may neither eat nor drink during the days that he cries for a vision. He may sleep on the bed of sage which had been prepared for him, and must lean his head against the center pole, for even though he sleeps he is close to *Wakan-Tanka,* and it is very often during sleep that the most powerful visions come to us; they are not merely dreams, for they are much more real and powerful and do not come from ourselves, but from *Wakan-Tanka.* It may be that we shall receive no vision or message from the Great Spirit the first time that we "lament," yet we may try many times, for we should remember that *Wakan-Tanka* is always anxious to aid those who seek Him with a pure heart. But of course much depends on the nature of the person who cries for a vision, and upon the degree to which he has purified and prepared himself.

In the evenings the Thunder-beings may come, and although they are very terrifying, they bring much good, and they test our strength and endurance. Then too they help us to realize how really very small and insignificant we are compared to the great powers of *Wakan-Tanka.*

I remember one time when I "lamented," and a great storm came from the place where the sun goes down, and I talked with the Thunder-beings who came with hail and thunder and lightning and much rain, and the next morning I saw that there was hail all piled up on the ground around the sacred place, yet inside it was perfectly dry. I think that they were trying to test me. And then, on one of the nights the bad spirits came and started tearing the offerings off the poles; and I heard their voices under the ground, and one of them said: "Go and see if he is crying." And I heard rattles, but all the time they were outside the sacred place and could not get in, for I had resolved not to be afraid, and did not stop sending my voice to *Wakan-Tanka* for aid. Then later, one of the bad spirits said from somewhere under the ground: "Yes, he is surely crying," and the next morning I saw that the poles and offerings were still there. I was well prepared, you see, and did not weaken, and so nothing bad could happen.

The "lamenter" should get up in the middle of the night, and he should again go to the four quarters, returning to the center each time, and all the while he should be sending his voice. He should always be up with the morning star, and he should walk towards the east, and, pointing his pipe stem towards this sacred star, he should ask it for wisdom; this he should pray silently in his heart, and not out loud. All this the "lamenter" should do for the three or four days.

At the end of this period the helpers come with their horses and take the "lamenter" with his pipe back to the camp, and there he immediately enters the *Inipi* [sweat lodge] which has already been made ready for him. He should sit at the west, holding his pipe in front of him all the time. The holy man—the spiritual guide of the "lamenter"—enters next and, passing behind the "lamenter," sits at the east, and all the other men fill the remaining places.

The first sacred rock, which has already been heated, is brought into the lodge and is placed at the center of the altar, and then all the other rocks are brought in, as I have described before. All this is done very solemnly but more rapidly than before, for all the men are anxious to hear what the "lamenter" has to tell and to know what great things may have come to him up there on the mountain. When all has been made ready, the holy man says to the "lamenter":

"Ho! You have now sent a voice with your pipe to *Wakan-Tanka*. That pipe is now very sacred, for the whole universe has seen it. You have offered this pipe to all the four sacred Powers; they have seen it! And each word that you said up there was heard, even by our Grandmother and Mother Earth. The coming generations will hear you! These five ancient rocks here will hear you! The winged Power of the place where the sun goes down, who controls the waters, will hear you! The standing trees who are present here will hear you! And also the most sacred pipe which was given to the people will hear you; so tell us the truth, and be sure that you make up nothing! Even the tiny ants and the crawling worms may have come to see you up there when you were crying for a vision; tell us everything! You have brought back to us the pipe which you offered; it is finished! And since you are about to put this pipe to your mouth, you should tell us nothing but the truth. The pipe is *wakan* and knows all things; you cannot fool it. If you lie, *Wakinyan-Tanka*, who guards the pipe, will punish you! *Hechetu welo!*"

The holy man rises from his position at the east and, moving around the lodge sun-wise, sits just at the right of the "lamenter." Dried buffalo chips are placed in front of the "lamenter," and upon these the pipe is placed with its stem pointing towards the heavens. The holy man now takes the tallow seal off the bowl of the pipe and places it upon the buffalo chips. He lights the pipe with a coal from the fire and, after offering it up to the Powers of the six directions, points the stem towards the "lamenter," who just touches it with his mouth. The holy man then makes a circle in the air with the stem of the pipe, smokes it a little himself, and again touches it to the mouth of the "lamenter." Then he again waves the pipe stem in a circle and again smokes it a little himself. This is done four times, and then the pipe is passed around the circle for all the men to smoke. When it returns to the holy man, with four motions he empties it upon the top of the tallow seal and the buffalo chips and then purifies it. Holding the pipe up in front of himself, the holy man says to the "lamenter": "Young man, you left here three days ago with your two helpers, who have set up for you the five posts upon the sacred place. Tell us everything that happened to you up there after these helpers left! Do not omit anything! We have prayed much to *Wakan-Tanka* for you and have asked the pipe to be merciful. Tell us now what happened!"

The "lamenter" replies, and after each time he says something of importance all the men in the lodge cry *"Hi ye!"*

"I went up on the mountain, and, after entering the sacred place, I walked continually to each of the four directions, always returning to the center as you had instructed me. During the first day, as I was facing the place where the sun goes down, I saw an eagle flying towards me, and when it came nearer I saw that it was a sacred Spotted Eagle. He rested on a tree near me but said nothing; and then he flew away to the place where the Giant *Waziah* lives."

To this all the men cry: *"Hi ye!"*

"I returned to the center, and then I went to the north, and as I stood there I saw an eagle circling above, and as he lighted near me I noticed that he was a young eagle, but it, too, said nothing to me, and soon he circled and soared off towards the place towards which we always face.

"I went back to the center where I cried and sent my voice, and then I went towards the place where the sun comes up. There I saw something flying towards me, and soon I saw that it was a baldheaded eagle, but he too said nothing to me.

"Crying, I returned to the center, and then when I went towards the place which we always face, I saw a red-breasted woodpecker standing on the offering pole. I believe he may have given to me something of his *wochangi*, for I heard him say to me very faintly yet distinctly: 'Be attentive! [*wachin ksapa yo!*] and have no fear; but pay no attention to any bad thing that may come and talk to you!'"

All the men now say more loudly: *"Hi ye!"*; for this message which the bird gave is very important.

The "lamenter" continues: "Although I was crying and sending my voice continually, this was all that I heard and saw that first day. Then night fell, and I lay down with my head at the center and went to sleep; and in my sleep I heard and saw my people, and I noticed that they were all very happy.

"I arose in the middle of the night, and again walked to each of the four directions, returning to the center each time, continually sending my voice. Just before the morning star came up, I again visited the four quarters, and just as I reached the place where the sun rises, I saw the Morning Star, and I noticed that at first it was all red, and then it changed to blue, and then into yellow, and finally I saw that it was white, and in these four colors I saw the four ages. Although this star did not really speak to me, yet it taught me very much.

"I stood there waiting for the sun to rise, and just at dawn I saw the world full of little winged people, and they were all rejoicing. Finally the sun came up, bringing its light into the world, and then I began to cry and returned to the center where I lay down, leaning my pipe against the center offering-pole.

"As I lay there at the center I could hear all sorts of little wingeds who were sitting on the poles, but none of them spoke to me. I looked at my pipe and there I saw two ants walking on the stem. Perhaps they wished to speak to me, but soon they left.

"Often during the day as I was crying and sending my voice, birds and butterflies would come to me, and once a white butterfly came and sat on the end of the pipe stem, working his beautiful wings up and down. During this day I saw no large four-leggeds, just the little peoples. Then just before the sun went down to rest, I saw that clouds were gathering, and the Thunder-beings were coming. The lightning was all over the sky, and the thunder was terrifying, and I think that perhaps I was a little afraid. But I held my pipe up and continued to send my voice to *Wakan-Tanka;* and soon I heard another voice saying: *'Hee-ay-hay-ee-ee! Hee-ay-hay-ee-ee!'* Four times they said this, and then all the fear left me, for I remembered what the little bird had told me, and I felt very brave. I heard other voices, also, which I could not understand. I stood there with my eyes closed—I do not know how long—and when I opened them everything was very bright, brighter even than the day; and I saw many people on horseback coming towards me, all riding horses of different colors. One of the riders even spoke to me saying: 'Young man, you are offering the pipe to *Wakan-Tanka;* we are all very happy that you are doing this!' This is all that they said, and then they disappeared.

"The next day, just before the sun came up, as I was visiting the four quarters, I saw the same little red-breasted bird; he was sitting on the pole there where we always face, and he said almost the same thing to me as before: 'Friend, be attentive as you walk!' That was all. Soon after this the two helpers came to bring me back. This is all that I know; I have told the truth and have made nothing up!"

Thus the "lamenter" finishes his account. Now the holy man gives to him his pipe, which he embraces, and it is then passed around the circle, and a helper takes it and leans it, with its stem to the west, against the sacred mound at the east of the lodge. More hot rocks are handed into the lodge; the door is closed; and the *Inipi* begins.

The holy man prays, giving thanks to *Wakan-Tanka*: "*Hee-ey-hay-ee-ee!* [four times] O Grandfather, *Wakan-Tanka,* today You have helped us. You have been merciful to this young man by giving him knowledge and a path which he may follow. You have made his people happy, and all the beings who move in the universe are rejoicing!

"Grandfather, this young man who has offered the pipe to You, has heard a voice which said to him, 'be attentive as you walk!' He wants to know what this message means; it must now be explained to him. It means that he should always remember You, O *Wakan-Tanka,* as he walks the sacred path of life; and he must be attentive to all the signs that You have given to us. If he does this always, he will become wise and a leader of his people. O *Wakan-Tanka,* help us all to be always attentive![5]

"This young man also saw four ages in that star there where the sun comes up. These are the ages through which all creatures must pass in their journey from birth to death.

"O *Wakan-Tanka,* when this young man saw the dawn of the day, he saw Your light coming into the universe; this is the light of wisdom. All these things You have revealed to us, for it is Your will that the peoples of the world do not live in the darkness of ignorance.

"O *Wakan-Tanka,* You have established a relationship with this young man; and through this relationship he will bring strength to his people. We who are now sitting here represent all the people, and thus we all give thanks to You, O *Wakan-Tanka.* We all raise our hands to You and say: '*Wakan-Tanka,* we thank You for this understanding and relationship which You have given to us.' Be merciful to us always! May this relationship exist until the very end!"

---

[5]This message—"Be attentive!"—well expresses a spirit which is central to the Indian peoples; it implies that in every act, in every thing, and in every instant, the Great Spirit is present, and that one should be continually and intensely "attentive" to this Divine presence.

This presence of *Wakan-Tanka,* and one's consciousness of it, is that which the Christian saints have termed "living in the moment," the "eternal now," or what in the Islamic tradition is termed the *Waqt.* In Lakota this presence is called *Taku Skanskan,* or simply *Skan* in the sacred language of the holy men. The following conversation between the Lakota priest Finger and J. R. Walker well explains this:

"'What causes the stars to fall?' '*Taku Skanskan.* . . . He causes everything that falls to fall, and He causes everything to move that moves.' 'When you move, what is it that causes you to move?' '*Skan.*' 'If an arrow is shot from a bow what causes it to move through the air?' '*Skan.* . . . *Taku Skanskan* gives the spirit to the bow, and He causes it to send the arrow from it.' 'What causes smoke to go upward?' '*Taku Skanskan.*' 'What causes water to flow in a river?' '*Skan.*' 'What causes the clouds to move over the world?' '*Skan.*' 'Lakota have told me that *Skan* is the sky. Is that so?' 'Yes. *Skan* is a Spirit and all that mankind can see of Him is the blue of the sky; but He is everywhere!' 'Is *Skan Wakan-Tanka?*' 'Yes!'" (*The Sun Dance . . . of the Teton Dakota* [Anthropological Papers of the American Museum of Natural History, XVI, Part II].)

All the men now sing this sacred chant.

Grandfather, behold me!
Grandfather, behold me!
I held my pipe and offered it to You,
That my people may live!

Grandfather, behold me!
Grandfather, behold me!
I give to You all these offerings,
That my people may live!

Grandfather, behold me!
Grandfather, behold me!
We who represent all the people,
Offer ourselves to You,
That we may live!

After this chant, water is put on the rocks, and the *Inipi* is continued in the same manner that I have described before. This young man who has cried for a vision for the first time, may perhaps become *wakan;* if he walks with his mind and heart attentive to *Wakan-Tanka* and His Powers, as he has been instructed, he will certainly travel upon the red path which leads to goodness and holiness. But he must cry for a vision a second time, and this time the bad spirits may tempt him; but if he is really a chosen one, he will stand firmly and will conquer all distracting thoughts and will become purified from all that is not good. Then he may receive some great vision that will bring strength to the nation. But should the young man still be in doubt after his second "lamenting," he may try a third and even a fourth time; and if he is always sincere, and truly humiliates himself before all things, he shall certainly be aided, for *Wakan-Tanka* always helps those who cry to Him with a pure heart.

9

Malcolm X, "Mecca" from *The Autobiography of Malcolm X**

Central to Islamic belief is the ritual of the hajj, *the pilgrimage to Mecca that each devout Muslim is expected to make at least once in his or her lifetime. The American civil rights leader Malcolm X made his pilgrimage in 1964; his account suggests how powerful the experience can be.*

The pilgrimage to Mecca, known as Hajj, is a religious obligation that every orthodox Muslim fulfills, if humanly able, at least once in his or her lifetime.

The Holy Quran says it, "Pilgrimage to the Ka'ba is a duty men owe to God; those who are able, make the journey."

Allah said: "And proclaim the pilgrimage among men; they will come to you on foot and upon each lean camel, they will come from every deep ravine."

At one or another college or university, usually in the informal gatherings after I had spoken, perhaps a dozen generally white-complexioned people would come up to me, identifying themselves as Arabian, Middle Eastern or North African Muslims who happened to be visiting, studying, or living in the United States. They had said to me that, my white-indicting statements notwithstanding, they felt that I was sincere in considering myself a Muslim— and they felt if I was exposed to what they always called "true Islam," I would "understand it, and embrace it." Automatically, as a follower of Elijah Muhammad, I had bridled whenever this was said.

But in the privacy of my own thoughts after several of these experiences, I did question myself: if one was sincere in professing a religion, why should he balk at broadening his knowledge of that religion?

Once in a conversation I broached this with Wallace Muhammad, Elijah Muhammad's son. He said that yes, certainly, a Muslim should seek to learn all that he could about Islam. I had always had a high opinion of Wallace Muhammad's opinion.

Those orthodox Muslims whom I had met, one after another, had urged me to meet and talk with a Dr. Mahmoud Youssef Shawarbi. He was described me as an eminent, learned Muslim, a University of Cairo graduate, a University of London Ph.D., a lecturer on Islam, a United Nations advisor and the

*From *The Autobiography of Malcolm X* by Malcolm X, with Alex Haley. Copyright © 1964 by Alex Haley and Malcolm X. Copyright © 1965 by Alex Haley and Betty Shabazz. Reprinted by permission of Random House, Inc.

145

author of many books. He was a full professor of the University of Cairo, on leave from there to be in New York as the Director of the Federation of Islamic Associations in the United States and Canada. Several times, driving in that part of town, I had resisted the impulse to drop in at the F.I.A. building, a brownstone at 1 Riverside Drive. Then one day Dr. Shawarbi and I were introduced by a newspaperman.

He was cordial. He said he had followed me in the press; I said I had been told of him, and we talked for fifteen or twenty minutes. We both had to leave to make appointments we had, when he dropped on me something whose logic never would get out of my head. He said, "No man has believed perfectly until he wishes for his brother what he wishes for himself."

Then, there was my sister Ella herself. I couldn't get over what she had done. I've said before, this is a *strong* big, black, Georgia-born woman. Her domineering ways had gotten her put out of the Nation of Islam's Boston Mosque Eleven; they took her back, then she left on her own. Ella had started studying under Boston orthodox Muslims, then she founded a school where Arabic was taught! *She* couldn't speak it, she hired teachers who did. That's Ella! She deals in real estate, and *she* was saving up to make the pilgrimage. Nearly all night, we talked in her living room. She told me there was no question about it; it was more important that I go. I thought about Ella the whole flight back to New York. A *strong* woman. She had broken the spirits of three husbands, more driving and dynamic than all of them combined. She had played a very significant role in my life. No other woman ever was strong enough to point me in directions; I pointed women in directions. I had brought Ella into Islam, and now she was financing me to Mecca.

Allah always gives you signs, when you are with Him, that He is with you.

When I applied for a visa to Mecca at the Saudi Arabian Consulate, the Saudi Ambassador told me that no Muslim converted in America could have a visa for the Hajj pilgrimage without the signed approval of Dr. Mahmoud Shawarbi. But that was only the beginning of the sign from Allah. When I telephoned Dr. Shawarbi, he registered astonishment. "I was just going to get in touch with you," he said, "by all means come right over."

When I got to his office, Dr. Shawarbi handed me the signed letter approving me to make the Hajj in Mecca, and then a book. It was *The Eternal Message of Muhammad* by Abd ar-Rahman Azzam.

The author had just sent the copy of the book to be given to me, Dr. Shawarbi said, and he explained that this author was an Egyptian-born Saudi citizen, an international statesman, and one of the closest advisors of Prince Faisal, the ruler of Arabia. "He has followed you in the press very closely." It was hard for me to believe.

Dr. Shawarbi gave me the telephone number of his son, Muhammad Shawarbi, a student in Cairo, and also the number of the author's son, Omar Azzam, who lived in Jedda, "your last stop before Mecca. Call them both, by all means."

I left New York quietly (little realizing that I was going to return noisily).

Few people were told I was leaving at all. I didn't want some State Department or other roadblocks put in my path at the last minute. Only my wife, Betty, and my three girls and a few close associates came with me to Kennedy International Airport. When the Lufthansa Airlines jet had taken off, my two seatrow mates and I introduced ourselves. Another sign! Both were Muslims, one was bound for Cairo, as I was, and the other was bound for Jedda, where I would be in a few days.

All the way to Frankfurt, Germany, my seatmates and I talked, or I read the book I had been given. When we landed in Frankfurt, the brother bound for Jedda said his warm good-bye to me and the Cairo-bound brother. We had a few hours layover before we would take another plane to Cairo. We decided to go sightseeing in Frankfurt.

In the men's room there at the airport, I met the first American abroad who recognized me, a white student from Rhode Island. He kept eyeing me, then he came over. "Are you X?" I laughed and said I was, I hadn't ever heard it that way. He exclaimed, "You can't be! Boy, I know no one will believe me when I tell them this!" He was attending school, he said, in France.

The brother Muslim and I both were struck by the cordial hospitality of the people in Frankfurt. We went into a lot of shops and stores, looking more than intending to buy anything. We'd walk in, any store, every store, and it would be Hello! People who never saw you before, and knew you were strangers. And the same cordiality when we left, without buying anything. In America, you walk in a store and spend a hundred dollars, and leave, and you're still a stranger. Both you and the clerks act as though you're doing each other a favor. Europeans act more human, or humane, whichever the right word is. My brother Muslim, who could speak enough German to get by, would explain that we were Muslims, and I saw something I had already experienced when I was looked upon as a Muslim and not a Negro, right in America. People seeing you as a Muslim saw you as a human being and they had a different look, different talk, everything. In one Frankfurt store—a little shop, actually—the storekeeper leaned over his counter to us and waved his hand, indicating the German people passing by: "This way one day, that way another day—" My Muslim brother explained to me that what he meant was that the Germans would rise again.

Back at the Frankfurt airport, we took a United Arab Airlines plane on to Cairo. Throngs of people, obviously Muslims from everywhere, bound on the pilgrimage, were hugging and embracing. They were of all complexions, the whole atmosphere was of warmth and friendliness. The feeling hit me that there really wasn't any color problem here. The effect was as though I had just stepped out of a prison.

I had told my brother Muslim friend that I wanted to be a tourist in Cairo for a couple of days before continuing to Jedda. He gave me his number and asked me to call him, as he wanted to put me with a party of his friends, who could speak English, and would be going on the pilgrimage, and would be happy to look out for me.

So I spent two happy days sightseeing in Cairo. I was impressed by the modern schools, housing developments for the masses, and the highways and the industrialization that I saw. I had read and heard that President Nasser's administration had built up one of the most highly industrialized countries on the African continent. I believe what most surprised me was that in Cairo, automobiles were being manufactured, and also buses.

I had a good visit with Dr. Shawarbi's son, Muhammad Shawarbi, a nineteen-year-old, who was studying economics and political science at Cairo University. He told me that his father's dream was to build a University of Islam in the United States.

The friendly people I met were astounded when they learned I was a Muslim—from America! They included an Egyptian scientist and his wife, also on their way to Mecca for the Hajj, who insisted I go with them to dinner in a restaurant in Heliopolis, a suburb of Cairo. They were an extremely well-informed and intelligent couple. Egypt's rising industrialization was one of the reasons why the Western powers were so anti-Egypt, it was showing other African countries what they should do, the scientist said. His wife asked me, "Why are people in the world starving when America has so much surplus food? What do they do, dump it in the ocean?" I told her, "Yes, but they put some of it in the holds of surplus ships, and in subsidized granaries and refrigerated space and let it stay there, with a small army of caretakers, until it's unfit to eat. Then another army of disposal people get rid of it to make space for the next surplus batch." She looked at me in something like disbelief. Probably she thought I was kidding. But the American taxpayer knows it's the truth. I didn't go on to tell her that right in the United States, there are hungry people.

I telephoned my Muslim friend, as he had asked, and the Hajj party of his friends was waiting for me. I made it eight of us, and they included a judge and an official of the Ministry of Education. They spoke English beautifully, and accepted me like a brother. I considered it another of Allah's signs, that wherever I turned, someone was there to help me, to guide me.

The literal meaning of Hajj in Arabic is to set out toward a definite objective. In Islamic law, it means to set out for Ka'ba, the Sacred House, and to fulfill the pilgrimage rites. The Cairo airport was where scores of Hajj groups were becoming *Muhrim*, pilgrims, upon entering the state of Ihram, the assumption of a spiritual and physical state of consecration. Upon advice, I arranged to leave in Cairo all of my luggage and four cameras, one a movie camera. I had bought in Cairo a small valise, just big enough to carry one suit, shirt, a pair of underwear sets and a pair of shoes into Arabia. Driving to the airport with our Hajj group, I began to get nervous, knowing that from there in, it was going to be watching others who knew what they were doing, and trying to do what they did.

Entering the state of Ihram, we took off our clothes and put on two white towels. One, the *Izar*, was folded around the loins. The other, the *Rida*, was thrown over the neck and shoulders, leaving the right shoulder and arm bare. A pair of simple sandals, the *na'l*, left the ankle-bones bare. Over the *Izar* waist-wrapper, a money belt was worn, and a bag, something like a woman's big handbag, with a long strap, was for carrying the passport and other valuable papers, such as the letter I had from Dr. Shawarbi.

Every one of the thousands at the airport, about to leave for Jedda, was dressed this way. You could be a king or a peasant and no one would know. Some powerful personages, who were discreetly pointed out to me, had on the same thing I had on. Once thus dressed, we all had begun intermittently calling out *"Labbayka! Labbayka!"* (Here I come, O Lord!) The airport sounded with the din of *Muhrim* expressing their intention to perform the journey of the Hajj.

Planeloads of pilgrims were taking off every few minutes, but the airport was jammed with more, and their friends and relatives waiting to see them off. Those not going were asking others to pray for them at Mecca. We were on our plane, in the air, when I learned for the first time that with the crush, there was not supposed to have been space for me, but strings had been pulled, and someone had been put off because they didn't want to disappoint an American Muslim. I felt mingled emotions of regret that I had inconvenienced and discomfited whoever was bumped off the plane for me, and, with that, an utter humility and gratefulness that I had been paid such an honor and respect.

Packed in the plane were white, black, brown, red, and yellow people, blue eyes and blond hair, and my kinky red hair—all together, brothers! All honoring the same God Allah, all in turn giving equal honor to each other.

From some in our group, the word was spreading from seat to seat that I was a Muslim from America. Faces turned, smiling toward me in greeting. A box lunch was passed out and as we ate that, the word that a Muslim from America was aboard got up into the cockpit.

The captain of the plane came back to meet me. He was an Egyptian, his complexion was darker than mine; he could have walked in Harlem and no one would have given him a second glance. He was delighted to meet an American Muslim. When he invited me to visit the cockpit, I jumped at the chance.

The co-pilot was darker than he was. I can't tell you the feeling it gave me. I had never seen a black man flying a jet. That instrument panel: no one ever could know what all of those dials meant! Both of the pilots were smiling at me, treating me with the same honor and respect I had received ever since I left America. I stood there looking through the glass at the sky ahead of us. In America, I had ridden in more planes than probably any other Negro, and I never had been invited up into the cockpit. And there I was, with two Muslim seatmates, one from Egypt, the other from Arabia, all of us bound for Mecca, with me up in the pilots' cabin. Brother, I *knew* Allah was with me.

I got back to my seat. All of the way, about an hour's flight, we pilgrims were loudly crying out, *"Labbayka! Labbayka!"* The plane landed at Jedda. It's a seaport town on the Red Sea, the arrival or disembarkation point for all pilgrims who come to Arabia to go to Mecca. Mecca is about forty miles to the east, inland.

The Jedda airport seemed even more crowded than Cairo's had been. Our party became another shuffling unit in the shifting mass with every race on earth represented. Each party was making its way toward the long line waiting to go through Customs. Before reaching Customs, each Hajj party was assigned a *Mutawaf,* who would be responsible for transferring that party from Jedda to Mecca. Some pilgrims cried *"Labbayka!"* Others, sometimes large groups, were chanting in unison a prayer that I will translate, "I submit to no one but Thee, O Allah, I submit to no one but Thee. I submit to Thee because Thou hast no partner. All praise and blessings come from Thee, and Thou art alone in Thy kingdom." The essence of the prayer is the Oneness of God.

Only officials were not wearing the *Ihram* garb, or the white skull caps, long, white, nightshirt-looking gown and the little slippers of the *Mutawaf,* those who guided each pilgrim party, and their helpers. In Arabic, an *mmmm* sound before a verb makes a verbal noun, so *"Mu*tawaf" meant "the one who guides" the pilgrims on the *"Tawaf,"* which is the circumambulation of the Ka'ba in Mecca.

I was nervous, shuffling in the center of our group in the line waiting to have our passports inspected. I had an apprehensive feeling. Look what I'm handing them. I'm in the Muslim world, right at The Fountain. I'm handing them the American passport which signifies the exact opposite of what Islam stands for.

The judge in our group sensed my strain. He patted my shoulder. Love, humility, and true brotherhood was almost a physical feeling wherever I turned. Then our group reached the clerks who examined each passport and suitcase carefully and nodded to the pilgrim to move on.

I was so nervous that when I turned the key in my bag, and it didn't work, I broke open the bag, fearing that they might think I had something in the bag that I shouldn't have. Then the clerk saw that I was handing him an American passport. He held it, he looked at me and said something in Arabic. My friends around me began speaking rapid Arabic, gesturing and pointing, trying to intercede for me. The judge asked me in English for my letter from Dr. Shawarbi, and he thrust it at the clerk, who read it. He gave the letter back, protesting—I could tell that. An argument was going on, *about* me. I felt like a stupid fool, unable to say a word, I couldn't even understand what was being said. But, finally, sadly, the judge turned to me.

I had to go before the *Mahgama Sharia,* he explained. It was the Muslim high court which examined all possibly non-authentic converts to the Islamic religion seeking to enter Mecca. It was absolute that no non-Muslim could enter Mecca.

My friends were going to have to go on to Mecca without me. They seemed stricken with concern for me. And *I* was stricken. I found the words to tell them, "Don't worry, I'll be fine. Allah guides me." They said they would pray hourly in my behalf. The white-garbed *Mutawaf* was urging them on, to keep schedule in the airport's human crush. With all of us waving, I watched them go.

It was then about three in the morning, a Friday morning. I never had been in such a jammed mass of people, but I never had felt more alone, and helpless, since I was a baby. Worse, Friday in the Muslim world is a rough counterpart of Sunday in the Christian world. On Friday, all the members of a Muslim community gather, to pray together. The event is called *yaum al-jumu'a*—"the day of gathering." It meant that no courts were held on Friday. I would have to wait until Saturday, at least.

An official beckoned a young Arab *Mutawaf's* aide. In broken English, the official explained that I would be taken to a place right at the airport. My passport was kept at Customs. I wanted to object, because it is a traveler's first law never to get separated from his passport, but I didn't. In my wrapped towels and sandals, I followed the aide in his skull cap, long white gown, and slippers. I guess we were quite a sight. People passing us were speaking all kinds of languages. I couldn't speak anybody's language. I was in bad shape.

Right outside the airport was a mosque, and above the airport was a huge, dormitory-like building, four tiers high. It was semi-dark, not long before dawn, and planes were regularly taking off and landing, their landing lights sweeping the runways, or their wing and tail lights blinking in the sky. Pilgrims from Ghana, Indonesia, Japan, and Russia, to mention some, were moving to and from the dormitory where I was being taken. I don't believe that motion picture cameras ever have filmed a human spectacle more colorful than my eyes took in. We reached the dormitory and began climbing, up to the fourth, top, tier, passing members of every race on earth. Chinese, Indonesians, Afghanistanians. Many, not yet changed into the *Ihram* garb, still wore their national dress. It was like pages out of the *National Geographic* magazine.

My guide, on the fourth tier, gestured me into a compartment that contained about fifteen people. Most lay curled up on their rugs asleep. I could tell that some were women, covered head and foot. An old Russian Muslim and his wife were not asleep. They stared frankly at me. Two Egyptian Muslims and a Persian roused and also stared as my guide moved us over into a corner. With gestures, he indicated that he would demonstrate to me the proper prayer ritual postures. Imagine, being a Muslim minister, a leader in Elijah Muhammad's Nation of Islam, and not knowing the prayer ritual.

I tried to do what he did. I knew I wasn't doing it right. I could feel the other Muslims' eyes on me. Western ankles won't do what Muslim ankles have done for a lifetime. Asians squat when they sit, Westerners sit upright in chairs. When my guide was down in a posture, I tried everything I could to get down as he was, but there I was, sticking up. After about an hour, my guide left, indicating that he would return later.

I never even thought about sleeping. Watched by the Muslims, I kept practicing prayer posture. I refused to let myself think how ridiculous I must have looked to them. After a while, though, I learned a little trick that would let me get down closer to the floor. But after two or three days, my ankle was going to swell.

As the sleeping Muslims woke up, when dawn had broken, they almost instantly became aware of me, and we watched each other while they went about their business. I began to see what an important role the rug played in the overall cultural life of the Muslims. Each individual had a small prayer rug, and each man and wife, or large group, had a larger communal rug. These Muslims prayed on their rugs there in the compartment. Then they spread a tablecloth over the rug and ate, so the rug became the dining room. Removing the dishes and cloth, they sat on the rug—a living room. Then they curl up and sleep on the rug—a bedroom. In that compartment, before I was to leave it, it dawned on me for the first time why the fence had paid such a high price for Oriental rugs when I had been a burglar in Boston. It was because so much intricate care was taken to weave fine rugs in countries where rugs were so culturally versatile. Later, in Mecca, I would see yet another use of the rug. When any kind of a dispute arose, someone who was respected highly and who was not involved would sit on a rug with disputers around him, which made the rug a courtroom. In other instances it was a classroom.

One of the Egyptian Muslims, particularly, kept watching me out of the corner of his eye. I smiled at him. He got up and came over to me. "Hel-lo—" he said. It sounded like the Gettysburg Address. I beamed at him, "Hello!" I asked his name. "Name? Name?" he was trying hard, but he didn't get it. We tried some words on each other. I'd guess his English vocabulary spanned maybe twenty words. Just enough to frustrate me. I was trying to get him to comprehend anything. "Sky." I'd point. He'd smile. "Sky," I'd say again, gesturing for him to repeat it after me. He would. "Airplane . . . rug . . . foot . . . sandal . . . eyes. . . . " Like that. Then an amazing thing happened. I was so glad I had some communication with a human being, I was just saying whatever came to mind. I said "Muhammad Ali Clay—" All of the Muslims listening lighted up like a Christmas tree. "You? You?" My friend was pointing at me. I shook my head, "No, no. Muhammad Ali Clay my friend—*friend!*" They half understood me. Some of them didn't understand, and that's how it began to get around that I was Cassius Clay, world heavyweight champion. I was later to learn that apparently every man, woman and child in the Muslim world had heard how Sonny Liston (who in the Muslim world had the image of a man-eating ogre) had been beaten in Goliath-David fashion by Cassius Clay, who then had told the world that his name was Muhammad Ali and his religion was Islam and Allah had given him his victory.

Establishing the rapport was the best thing that could have happened in the compartment. My being an American Muslim changed the attitudes from merely watching me to wanting to look out for me. Now, the others began smiling steadily. They came closer, they were frankly looking me up and down. Inspecting me. Very friendly. I was like a man from Mars.

The *Mutawaf's* aide returned, indicating that I should go with him. He pointed from our tier down at the mosque and I knew that he had come to take me to make the morning prayer, *El Sobh,* always before sunrise. I followed him down, and we passed pilgrims by the thousands, babbling languages, everything but English. I was angry with myself for not having taken the time to learn more of the orthodox prayer rituals before leaving America. In Elijah Muhammad's Nation of Islam, we hadn't prayed in Arabic. About a dozen or more years before, when I was in prison, a member of the orthodox Muslim movement in Boston, named Abdul Hameed, had visited me and had later sent me prayers in Arabic. At that time, I had learned those prayers phonetically. But I hadn't used them since.

I made up my mind to let the guide do everything first and I would watch him. It wasn't hard to get him to do things first. He wanted to anyway. Just outside the mosque there was a long trough with rows of faucets. Ablutions had to precede praying. I knew that. Even watching the *Mutawaf's* helper, I didn't get it right. There's an exact way that an orthodox Muslim washes, and the exact way is very important.

I followed him into the mosque, just a step behind, watching. He did his prostration, his head to the ground. I did mine. *"Bi-smi-llahi-r-Rahmain-r-Rahim—"* ("In the name of Allah, the Beneficent, the Merciful—") All Muslim prayers began that way. After that, I may not have been mumbling the right thing, but I was mumbling.

I don't mean to have any of this sound joking. It was far from a joke with me. No one who happened to be watching could tell that I wasn't saying what the others said.

After that Sunrise Prayer, my guide accompanied me back up to the fourth tier. By sign language, he said he would return within three hours, then he left.

Our tier gave an excellent daylight view of the whole airport area. I stood at the railing, watching. Planes were landing and taking off like clockwork. Thousands upon thousands of people from all over the world made colorful patterns of movement. I saw groups leaving for Mecca, in buses, trucks, cars. I saw some setting out to walk the forty miles. I wished that I could start walking. At least, I knew how to do that.

I was afraid to think what might lie ahead. Would I be rejected as a Mecca pilgrim? I wondered what the test would consist of, and when I would face the Muslim high court.

The Persian Muslim in our compartment came up to me at the rail. He greeted me, hesitantly, "Amer . . . American?" He indicated that he wanted me to come and have breakfast with him and his wife, on their rug. I knew that it was an immense offer he was making. You don't have tea with a Muslim's wife. I didn't want to impose, I don't know if the Persian understood or not when I shook my head and smiled, meaning "No, thanks." He brought me some tea and cookies, anyway. Until then, I hadn't even thought about eating.

Others made gestures. They would just come up and smile and nod at me. My first friend, the one who had spoken a little English, was gone. I didn't know it, but he was spreading the word of an American Muslim on the fourth tier. Traffic had begun to pick up, going past our compartment. Muslims in the *Ihram* garb, or still in their national dress, walked slowly past, smiling. It would go on for as long as I was there to be seen. But I hadn't yet learned that I was the attraction.

I have always been restless, and curious. The *Mutawaf's* aide didn't return in the three hours he had said, and that made me nervous. I feared that he had given up on me as beyond help. By then, too, I was really getting hungry. All of the Muslims in the compartment had offered me food, and I had refused. The trouble was, I have to admit it, at that point I didn't know if I could go for their manner of eating. Everything was in one pot on the dining-room rug, and I saw them just fall right in, using their hands.

I kept standing at the tier railing observing the courtyard below, and I decided to explore a bit on my own. I went down to the first tier. I thought, then, that maybe I shouldn't get too far, someone might come for me. So I went back up to our compartment. In about forty-five minutes, I went back down. I went further this time, feeling my way. I saw a little restaurant in the courtyard. I went straight in there. It was jammed, and babbling with languages. Using gestures, I bought a whole roasted chicken and something like thick potato chips. I got back out in the courtyard and I tore up that chicken, using my hands. Muslims were doing the same thing all around me. I saw men at least seventy years old bringing both legs up under them, until they made a human knot of themselves, eating with as much aplomb and satisfaction as though they had been in a fine restaurant with waiters all over the place. All ate as One, and slept as One. Everything about the pilgrimage atmosphere accented the Oneness of Man under One God.

I made, during the day, several trips up to the compartment and back out in the courtyard, each time exploring a little further than before. Once, I nodded at two black men standing together. I nearly shouted when one spoke to me in British-accented English. Before their party approached, ready to leave for Mecca, we were able to talk enough to exchange that I was American and they were Ethiopians. I was heartsick. I had found two English-speaking Muslims at last—and they were leaving. The Ethiopians had both been schooled in Cairo, and they were living in Ryadh, the political capital of Arabia. I was later going to learn to my surprise that in Ethiopia, with eighteen million people, ten million are Muslims. Most people think Ethiopia is Christian. But only its government is Christian. The West has always helped to keep the Christian government in power.

I had just said my Sunset Prayer, *El Maghrib;* I was lying on my cot in the fourth-tier compartment, feeling blue and alone, when out of the darkness came a sudden light!

It was actually a sudden thought. On one of my venturings in the yard full of activity below, I had noticed four men, officials, seated at a table with a telephone. Now, I thought about seing them there, and with *telephone,* my mind flashed to the connection that Dr. Shawarbi in New York had given me, the telephone number of the son of the author of the book which had been given to me. Omar Azzam lived right there in Jedda!

In a matter of a few minutes, I was downstairs and rushing to where I had seen the four officials. One of them spoke functional English. I excitedly showed him the letter from Dr. Shawarbi. He read it. Then he read it aloud to the other three officials. "A Muslim from America!" I could almost see it capture their imaginations and curiosity. They were very impressed. I asked the English-speaking one if he would please do me the favor of telephoning Dr. Omar Azzam at the number I had. He was glad to do it. He got someone on the phone and conversed in Arabic.

Dr. Omar Azzam came straight to the airport. With the four officials beaming, he wrung my hand in welcome, a young, tall, powerfully built man. I'd say he was six foot three. He had an extremely polished manner. In America, he would have been called a white man, but—it struck me, hard and instantly—from the way he acted, I had no *feeling* of him being a white man. "Why didn't you call before?" he demanded of me. He showed some identification to the four officials, and he used their phone. Speaking in Arabic, he was talking with some airport officials. "Come!" he said.

In something less than half an hour, he had gotten me released, my suitcase and passport had been retrieved from Customs, and we were in Dr. Azzam's car, driving through the city of Jedda, with me dressed in the *Ihram* two towels and sandals. I was speechless at the man's attitude, and at my own physical feeling of no difference between us as human beings. I had heard for years of Muslim hospitality, but one couldn't quite imagine such warmth. I asked questions. Dr. Azzam was a Swiss-trained engineer. His field was city planning. The Saudi Arabian government had borrowed him from the United Nations to direct all of the reconstruction work being done on Arabian holy places. And Dr. Azzam's sister was the wife of Prince Faisal's son. I was in a car with the brother-in-law of the son of the ruler of Arabia. Nor was that all that Allah had done. "My father will be so happy to meet you," said Dr. Azzam. The author who had sent me the book!

I asked questions about his father. Abd ir-Rahman Azzam was known as Azzam Pasha, or Lord Azzam, until the Egyptian revolution, when President Nasser eliminated all "Lord" and "Noble" titles. "He should be at my home when we get there," Dr. Azzam said. "He spends much time in New York with his United Nations work, and he has followed you with great interest."

I was speechless.

It was early in the morning when we reached Dr. Azzam's home. His father was there, his father's brother, a chemist, and another friend—all up that early, waiting. Each of them embraced me as though I were a long-lost child. I had never seen these men before in my life, and they treated me so good! I am going to tell you that I had never been so honored in my life, nor had I ever received such true hospitality.

A servant brought tea and coffee, and disappeared. I was urged to make myself comfortable. No women were anywhere in view. In Arabia, you could easily think there were no females.

Dr. Abd ir-Rahman Azzam dominated the conversation. Why hadn't I called before? They couldn't understand why I hadn't. Was I comfortable? They seemed embarrassed that I had spent the time at the airport; that I had been delayed in getting to Mecca. No matter how I protested that I felt no inconvenience, that I was fine, they would not hear it. "You must rest," Dr. Azzam said. He went to use the telephone.

I didn't know what this distinguished man was doing. I had no dream. When I was told that I would be brought back for dinner that evening, and that, meanwhile, I should get back in the car, how could I have realized that I was about to see the epitome of Muslim hospitality?

Abd ir-Rahman Azzam, when at home, lived in a suite at the Jedda Palace Hotel. Because I had come to them with a letter from a friend, he was going to stay at his son's home, and let me use his suite, until I could get on to Mecca.

When I found out, there was no use protesting: I was in the suite; young Dr. Azzam was gone; there was no one to protest to. The three-room suite had a bathroom that was as big as a double at the New York Hilton. It was suite number 214. There was even a porch outside, affording a beautiful view of the ancient Red Sea city.

There had never before been in my emotions such an impulse to pray— and I did, prostrating myself on the living-room rug.

Nothing in either of my two careers as a black man in America had served to give me any idealistic tendencies. My instincts automatically examined the reasons, the motives, of anyone who did anything they didn't have to do for me. Always in my life, if it was any white person, I could see a selfish motive.

But there in that hotel that morning, a telephone call and a few hours away from the cot on the fourth-floor tier of the dormitory, was one of the few times I had been so awed that I was totally without resistance. That white man—at least he would have been considered "white" in America—related to Arabia's ruler, to whom he was a close advisor, truly an international man, with nothing in the world to gain, had given up his suite to me, for my transient comfort. He had *nothing* to gain. He didn't need me. He had everything. In fact, he had more to lose than gain. He had followed the American press about me. If he did that, he knew there was only stigma attached to me. I was supposed to have horns. I was a "racist." I was "anti-white"—and he from all appearances was white. I was supposed to be a criminal; not only that, but everyone was even accusing me of using his religion of Islam as a cloak for my criminal practices and philosophies. Even if he had had some motive to use me, he knew that I was separated from Elijah Muhammad and the Nation of Islam, my "power base," according to the press in America. The only organization that I had was just a few weeks old. I had no job. I had no money. Just to get over there, I had had to borrow money from my sister.

That morning was when I first began to reappraise the "white man." It was when I first began to perceive that "white man," as commonly used, means complexion only secondarily; primarily it described attitudes and actions. In America, "white man" meant specific attitudes and actions toward the black man, and toward all other non-white men. But in the Muslim world, I had seen that men with white complexions were more genuinely brotherly than anyone else had ever been.

That morning was the start of a radical alteration in my whole outlook about "white" men.

I should quote from my notebook here. I wrote this about noon, in the hotel: "My excitement, sitting here, waiting to go before the Hajj Committee, is indescribable. My window faces to the sea westward. The streets are filled with the incoming pilgrims from all over the world. The prayers are to Allah and verses from the Quran are on the lips of everyone. Never have I seen such a beautiful sight, nor witnessed such a scene, nor felt such an atmosphere. Although I am excited, I feel safe and secure, thousands of miles from the totally different life that I have known. Imagine that twenty-four hours ago, I was in the fourth-floor room over the airport, surrounded by people with whom I could not communicate, feeling uncertain about the future, and very lonely, and then *one* phone call, following Dr. Shawarbi's instructions. I have met one of the most powerful men in the Muslim world. I will soon sleep in his bed at the Jedda Palace. I know that I am surrounded by friends whose sincerity and religious zeal I can feel. I must pray again to thank Allah for this blessing, and I must pray again that my wife and children back in America will always be blessed for their sacrifices, too."

I did pray, two more prayers, as I had told my notebook. Then I slept for about four hours, until the telephone rang. It was young Dr. Azzam. In another hour, he would pick me up to return me there for dinner. I tumbled words over one another, trying to express some of the thanks I felt for all of their actions. He cut me off. "Ma sha'a-llah"—which means, "It is as Allah has pleased."

I seized the opportunity to run down into the lobby, to see it again before Dr. Azzam arrived. When I opened my door, just across the hall from me a man in some ceremonial dress, who obviously lived there, was also headed downstairs, surrounded by attendants. I followed them down, then through the lobby. Outside, a small caravan of automobiles was waiting. My neighbor appeared through the Jedda Palace Hotel's front entrance and people rushed and crowded him, kissing his hand. I found out who he was: the Grand Mufti of Jerusalem. Later, in the hotel, I would have the opportunity to talk with him for about a half-hour. He was a cordial man of great dignity. He was well up on world affairs, and even the latest events in America.

I will never forget the dinner at the Azzam home. I quote my notebook again: "I couldn't say in my mind that these were 'white' men. Why, the men acted as if they were brothers of mine, the elder Dr. Azzam as if he were my father. His fatherly, scholarly speech. I *felt* like he was my father. He was, you could tell, a highly skilled diplomat, with a broad range of mind. His knowledge was so worldly. He was as current on world affairs as some people are to what's going on in their living room.

"The more we talked, the more his vast reservoir of knowledge and its variety seemed unlimited. He spoke of the racial lineage of the descendants of Muhammad the Prophet, and he showed how they were both black and white. He also pointed out how color, the complexities of color, and the problems of color which exist in the Muslim world, exist only where, and to the extent that, that area of the Muslim world has been influenced by the West. He said that if one encountered any differences based on attitude toward color, this directly reflected the degree of Western influence."

I learned during dinner that while I was at the hotel, the Hajj Committee Court had been notified about my case, and that in the morning I should be there. And I was.

The Judge was Sheikh Muhammad Harkon. The Court was empty except for me and a sister from India, formerly a Protestant, who had converted to Islam, and was, like me, trying to make the Hajj. She was brown-skinned, with a small face that was mostly covered. Judge Harkon was a kind, impressive man. We talked. He asked me some questions, having to do with my sincerity. I answered him as truly as I could. He not only recognized me as a true Muslim, but he gave me two books, one in English, the other in Arabic. He recorded my name in the Holy Register of true Muslims, and we were ready to part. He told me, "I hope you will become a great preacher of Islam in America." I said that I shared that hope, and I would try to fulfill it.

The Azzam family were very elated that I was qualified and accepted to go to Mecca. I had lunch at the Jedda Palace. Then I slept again for several hours, until the telephone awakened me.

It was Muhammad Abdul Azziz Maged, the Deputy Chief of Protocol for Prince Faisal. "A special car will be waiting to take you to Mecca, right after your dinner," he told me. He advised me to eat heartily, as the Hajj rituals require plenty of strength.

I was beyond astonishment by then.

Two young Arabs accompanied me to Mecca. A well-lighted, modern turnpike highway made the trip easy. Guards at intervals along the way took one look at the car, and the driver made a sign, and we were passed through, never even having to slow down. I was, all at once, thrilled, important, humble, and thankful.

Mecca, when we entered, seemed as ancient as time itself. Our car slowed through the winding streets, lined by shops on both sides and with buses, cars, and trucks, and tens of thousands of pilgrims from all over the earth were everywhere.

The car halted briefly at a place where a *Mutawaf* was waiting for me. He wore the white skullcap and long night-shirt garb that I had seen at the airport. He was a short, dark-skinned Arab, named Muhammad. He spoke no English whatever.

We parked near the Great Mosque. We performed our ablution and entered. Pilgrims seemed to be on top of each other, there were so many, lying, sitting, sleeping, praying, walking.

My vocabulary cannot describe the new mosque that was being built around the Ka'ba. I was thrilled to realize that it was only one of the tremendous rebuilding tasks under the direction of young Dr. Azzam, who had just been my host. The Great Mosque of Mecca, when it is finished, will surpass the architectural beauty of India's Taj Mahal.

Carrying my sandals, I followed the *Mutawaf.* Then I saw the Ka'ba, a huge black stone house in the middle of the Great Mosque. It was being circumambulated by thousands upon thousands of praying pilgrims, both sexes, and every size, shape, color, and race in the world. I knew the prayer to be uttered when the pilgrim's eyes first perceive the Ka'ba. Translated, it is "O God, You are peace, and peace derives from You. So greet us, O Lord, with peace." Upon entering the Mosque, the pilgrim should try to kiss the Ka'ba if possible, but if the crowds prevent him getting that close, he touches it, and if the crowds prevent that, he raises his hand and cries out "Takbir!" ("God is great!") I could not get within yards. "Takbir!"

My feeling there in the House of God was a numbness. My *Mutawaf* led me in the crowd of praying, chanting pilgrims, moving seven times around the Ka'ba. Some were bent and wizened with age; it was a sight that stamped itself on the brain. I saw incapacitated pilgrims being carried by others. Faces were enraptured in their faith. The seventh time around, I prayed two *Rak'a,* prostrating myself, my head on the floor. The first prostration, I prayed the Quran verse "Say He is God, the one and only"; the second prostration: "Say O you who are unbelievers, I worship not that which you worship. . . ."

As I prostrated, the *Mutawaf* fended pilgrims off to keep me from being trampled.

The *Mutawaf* and I next drank water from the well of Zem Zem. Then we ran between the two hills, Safa and Marwa, where Hajar wandered over the same earth searching for water for her child Ishmael.

Three separate times, after that, I visited the Great Mosque and circumambulated the Ka'ba. The next day we set out after sunrise toward Mount Arafat, thousands of us, crying in unison: "Labbayka! Labbayka!" and "Allah Akbar!" Mecca is surrounded by the crudest-looking mountains I have ever seen; they seem to be made of the slag from a blast furnace. No vegetation is on them at all. Arriving about noon, we prayed and chanted from noon until sunset, and the *asr* (afternoon) and *Maghrib* (sunset) special prayers were performed.

Finally, we lifted our hands in prayer and thanksgiving, repeating Allah's words: "There is no God but Allah. He has no partner. His are authority and praise. Good emanates from Him, and He has power over all things."

Standing on Mount Arafat had concluded the essential rites of being a pilgrim to Mecca. No one who missed it could consider himself a pilgrim.

The *Ihram* had ended. We cast the traditional seven stones at the devil. Some had their hair and beards cut. I decided that I was going to let my beard remain. I wondered what my wife Betty, and our little daughters, were going to say when they saw me with a beard, when I got back to New York. New

York seemed a million miles away. I hadn't seen a newspaper that I could read since I left New York. I had no idea what was happening there. A Negro rifle club that had been in existence for over twelve years in Harlem had been "discovered" by the police; it was being trumpeted that I was "behind it." Elijah Muhammad's Nation of Islam had a lawsuit going against me, to force me and my family to vacate the house in which we lived on Long Island.

The major press, radio, and television media in America had representatives in Cairo hunting all over, trying locate me, to interview me about the furor in New York that I had allegedly caused—when I knew nothing about any of it.

I only knew what I had left in America, and how it contrasted with what I had found in the Muslim world. About twenty of us Muslims who had finished the Hajj were sitting in a huge tent on Mount Arafat. As a Muslim from America, I was the center of attention. They asked me what about the Hajj had impressed me the most. One of the several who spoke English asked; they translated my answers for the others. My answer to that question was not the one they expected, but it drove home my point.

I said, "The *brotherhood!* The people of all races, colors, from all over the world coming together as *one!* It has proved to me the power of the One God."

It may have been out of taste, but that gave me an opportunity, and I used it, to preach them a quick little sermon on America's racism, and its evils.

I could tell the impact of this upon them. They had been aware that the plight of the black man in America was "bad," but they had not been aware that it was inhuman, that it was a psychological castration. These people from elsewhere around the world were shocked. As Muslims, they had a very tender heart for all unfortunates, and very sensitive feelings for truth and justice. And in everything I said to them, as long as we talked, they were aware of the yardstick that I was using to measure everything—that to me the earth's most explosive and pernicious evil is racism, the inability of God's creatures to live as One, especially in the Western world.

I have reflected since that the letter I finally sat down to compose had been subconsciously shaping itself in my mind.

The *color-blindness* of the Muslim world's religious society and the *color-blindness* of the Muslim world's human society: these two influences had each day been making a greater impact, and an increasing persuasion against my previous way of thinking.

The first letter was, of course, to my wife, Betty. I never had a moment's question that Betty, after initial amazement, would change her thinking to join mine. I had known a thousand reassurances that Betty's faith in me was total. I knew that she would see what I had seen—that in the land of Muhammad and the land of Abraham, I had been blessed by Allah with a new insight into the true religion of Islam, and a better understanding of America's entire racial dilemma.

After the letter to my wife, I wrote next essentially the same letter to my sister Ella. And I knew where Ella would stand. She had been saving to make the pilgrimage to Mecca herself.

I wrote to Dr. Shawarbi, whose belief in my sincerity had enabled me to get a passport to Mecca.

All through the night, I copied similar long letters for others who were very close to me. Among them was Elijah Muhammad's son Wallace Muhammad, who had expressed to me his conviction that the only possible salvation for the Nation of Islam would be its accepting and projecting a better understanding of Orthodox Islam.

And I wrote to my loyal assistants at my newly formed Muslim Mosque, Inc. in Harlem, with a note appended, asking that my letter be duplicated and distributed to the press.

I knew that when my letter became public knowledge back in America, many would be astounded—loved ones, friends, and enemies alike. And no less astounded would be millions whom I did not know—who had gained during my twelve years with Elijah Muhammad a "hate" image of Malcolm X.

Even I was myself astounded. But there was precedent in my life for this letter. My whole life had been a chronology of—*changes.*

Here is what I wrote . . . from my heart:

"Never have I witnessed such sincere hospitality and the overwhelming spirit of true brotherhood as is practiced by people of all colors and races here in this Ancient Holy Land, the home of Abraham, Muhammad, and all the other prophets of the Holy Scriptures. For the past week, I have been utterly speechless and spellbound by the graciousness I see displayed all around me by people *of all colors.*

"I have been blessed to visit the Holy City of Mecca. I have made my seven circuits around the Ka'ba, led by a young *Mutawaf* named Muhammad. I drank water from the well of Zem Zem. I ran seven times back and forth between the hills of Mt. Al-Safa and Al-Marwah. I have prayed in the ancient city of Mina, and I have prayed on Mt. Arafat.

"There were tens of thousands of pilgrims, from all over the world. They were of all colors, from blue-eyed blonds to black-skinned Africans. But we were all participating in the same ritual, displaying a spirit of unity and brotherhood that my experiences in America had led me to believe never could exist between the white and the non-white.

"America needs to understand Islam, because this is the one religion that erases from its society the race problem. Throughout my travels in the Muslim world, I have met, talked to, and even eaten with people who in America would have been considered 'white'—but the 'white' attitude was removed from their minds by the religion of Islam. I have never before seen *sincere* and *true* brotherhood practiced by all colors together, irrespective of their color.

"You may be shocked by these words coming from me. But on this pilgrimage, what I have seen, and experienced, has forced me to *re-arrange* much of my thought-patterns previously held, and to *toss aside* some of my previous conclusions. This was not too difficult for me. Despite my firm convictions, I have been always a man who tries to face facts, and to accept the reality of life as new experience and new knowledge unfolds it. I have always kept an open mind, which is necessary to the flexibility that must go hand in hand with every form of intelligent search for truth.

"During the past eleven days here in the Muslim world, I have eaten from the same plate, drunk from the same glass, and slept in the same bed (or on the same rug)— while praying to the *same God*—with fellow Muslims, whose eyes were the bluest of blue, whose hair was the blondest of blond, and whose skin was the whitest of white. And in the *words* and in the *actions* and in the *deeds* of the 'white' Muslims, I felt the same sincerity that I felt among the black African Muslims of Nigeria, Sudan, and Ghana.

"We were *truly* all the same (brothers)—because their belief in one God had removed the 'white' from their *minds,* the 'white' from their *behavior,* and the 'white' from their *attitude.*

"I could see from this, that perhaps if white Americans could accept the Oneness of God, then perhaps, too, they could accept *in reality* the Oneness of Man—and cease to measure, and hinder, and harm others in terms of their 'differences' in color.

"With racism plaguing America like an incurable cancer, the so-called 'Christian' white American heart should be more receptive to a proven solution to such a destructive problem. Perhaps it could be in time to save America from imminent disaster—the same destruction brought upon Germany by racism that eventually destroyed the Germans themselves.

"Each hour here in the Holy Land enables me to have greater spiritual insights into what is happening in America between black and white. The American Negro never can be blamed for his racial animosities—he is only reacting to four hundred years of the conscious racism of the American whites. But as racism leads America up the suicide path, I do believe, from the experiences that I have had with them, that the whites of the younger generation, in the colleges and universities, will see the handwriting on the wall and many of them will turn to the *spiritual* path of *truth*—the *only* way left to America to ward off the disaster that racism inevitably must lead to.

"Never have I been so highly honored. Never have I been made to feel more humble and unworthy. Who would believe the blessings that have been heaped upon an *American Negro?* A few nights ago, a man who would be called in America a 'white' man, a United Nations diplomat, an ambassador, a companion of kings, gave me *his* hotel suite, *his* bed. By this man, His Excellency Prince Faisal, who rules this Holy Land, was made aware of my presence here in Jedda. The very next morning, Prince Faisal's son, in person, informed me that by the will and decree of his esteemed father, I was to be a State Guest.

"The Deputy Chief of Protocol himself took me before the Hajj Court. His Holiness Sheikh Muhammad Harkon himself okayed my visit to Mecca.

His Holiness gave me two books on Islam, with his personal seal and autograph, and he told me that he prayed that I would be a successful preacher of Islam in America. A car, a driver, and a guide, have been placed at my disposal, making it possible for me to travel about this Holy Land almost at will. The government provides air-conditioned quarters and servants in each city that I visit. Never would I have even thought of dreaming that I would ever be a recipient of such honors—honors that in America would be bestowed upon a King—not a Negro.

    "All praise is due to Allah, the Lord of all the Worlds.

"Sincerely,

"El-Hajj Malik El-Shabazz
"(Malcolm X)"

10

Lis Harris
"Sabbath" from *Holy Days**

Genesis gives an account of God creating the world in six days and then resting on the seventh. Judaism has traditionally set aside one day in seven, the Sabbath, as a day for rest and religious activity, free of secular pursuits. In the Hasidic communities of Brooklyn, New York, the ritual of the Sabbath is strictly followed to this day. This reading describes the observance of the Sabbath by a modern-day Hasidic family from one of those communities.

> Six days shall you labor, and do all your work; but the seventh day is a Sabbath unto the Lord your God, on it you shall not do any manner of work . . . for the Lord blessed the Sabbath day and sanctified it.
> (EXODUS 20:9–11)

It is one of the curious twists of history that the Hasidim, once considered the enemies of Orthodoxy, today consider themselves its bulwarks. Besieged from every direction by what they perceive as a decadent, morally bankrupt world, they shun its preoccupations, rebel against many of its social conventions, spend as much time as possible in their neighborhood fortresses, and devote themselves to perpetuating the ideals of Jewish religious life. This is especially evident on the eve of the Sabbath. To wander along Kingston Avenue, where the Lubavitchers do most of their marketing, as I did one Friday afternoon some weeks after my first visit to the Konigsbergs, is to enter a world whose rhythms are dictated solely by religious custom and ritual. Like most of her neighbors, Sheina had completed some of her Sabbath preparations the night before, but she still had some last-minute shopping to do, and invited me to accompany her. She was in a good mood.

"I live from one Shabbos to the next," she said. "I look forward to it all week. We almost always have three or four guests. Sometimes they're neighborhood friends; at other times it's just family, but we're often asked by some official to provide a congenial Shabbos for someone who is traveling or for students who have no other place to go. In the last month we've had people show up from England, Iran, and South Africa; the door is never closed. It's totally unlike what I was used to growing up in Bloomfield Hills. Saturdays were a drag when I was a child. I didn't really understand what the Sabbath was about; no one ever talked about it. We observed it only in a half-hearted way, and neither my two brothers nor my sister and I ever really understood why we were doing any of it. In fact, I hardly understood anything about the deeper levels of Judaism until I became a *baalat teshuvah* [Hebrew for 'one who has returned'].''

No one knows exactly how many *baalei teshuvah* there are, but in recent years a surprisingly large number of Jews have "returned" to Orthodox ways, and each year hundreds of them join the Lubavitcher world. Some have been sought out. Unlike other Hasidim, the Lubavitchers are unabashedly committed to bringing as many Jews as possible back into the fold. Some, like Sheina, found their own way.

"What was life like in Michigan?"

"It was like everywhere else: aimless. It would probably be hard to find a community whose values were more different from those of a Hasidic community than the one that I grew up in. Most of the people I knew were fairly well-to-do and self-absorbed. They really never gave two thoughts to their spiritual life."

In a corner fruit store, Sheina handed a short shopping list to a swarthy man in a yarmulke who filled a bag with fruits and vegetables as we talked. From time to time, the shopkeeper and Sheina discussed the comparative merits of various fruits. Sheina's voice was unusually even as she talked with him and the man seemed to be struggling with a powerful urge to fawn which, one surmised, he must have learned from experience would embarrass this customer. There were three other women in the store. All of them knew Sheina and came over to chat. Across the street, a "Glatt Kosher Cafeteria" (glatt means smooth; originally the word referred to the lining of an animal's lung, which was not considered kosher if wrinkled; it has come to mean assiduous) had signs in the window for cold borscht, mushroom barley soup and noodle pudding, and nearby a dark tiny store called "Benny's of Boro Park" offered ladies' clothing.

The general store down the block, where Sheina stopped next, was piled high with cartons. Customers sidled around the boxes and each other, flattening themselves to avoid physical contact, and generally acting like contortionists as they strained to reach boxes of Landau's Puffed Wheat, jars of Rokeach Gefilte Fish and cans of Season Sardines. Cartons of Shefa brand kosher milk filled the refrigerator cases. Little knots of Hasidim stood about talking, gesticulating, laughing, arguing, creating complex roadblocks. Shopping definitely played second fiddle here to conversation. Most of the conversations were in Yiddish, a few were in English. No one passed Sheina (whose command of Yiddish, she confided somewhat ruefully, was tenuous) without at least a nod, or, more often, "Ah, Sheina, how are you?" followed invariably by *"Baruch Hashem,* fine. And you?" There were many Yiddish accents and much of the English spoken reflected Yiddish syntax. Almost everybody used the word "by" for "at," for example, as in, "I was staying by Hannah last week." Except for the thin veneer of modernity represented by the refrigeration, the plastic food wrappings, and the fashionable wrappings of the women, the store seemed to have been freshly transported to Brooklyn from Sholem Aleichem's Kaserilevke.

All the canned goods and cartons were marked with a Ⓤ (for Union of Orthodox Jewish Congregations of America) or other little symbols signifying that the product had been approved as kosher by various rabbinical boards. No Hasid will buy any prepared food that does not bear this stamp of rabbinical approval, and one supervising rabbi may be deemed more trustworthy than another. We nearly made it to the fish store across the street without stopping to talk with anyone, but at the entrance a gray-bearded man stopped Sheina to ask her how the two Iranian girls he had sent over to her were doing. Sheina explained that more than nine hundred Iranian Jewish children had been sent to America by their worried parents, who feared for their lives because of the political unrest in that country. Almost all of them were taken in by Luba-vitcher families, who were doing their best to cope with communications problems (few of the children spoke anything but Persian) and the characteris-tically indifferent religious background of their charges. Although the children were grateful for the Lubavitchers' help, most had shown little interest in pur-suing a more religious life. The man who stopped her was in charge of the Iranian project. She told him that the girls were doing fine. "They keep to themselves a lot, but they try to enter into our customs as best they can." One of the chief characteristics of the Lubavitchers that distinguish them from other Hasidim is their Jewish social consciousness. Helping Jews of every stripe has traditionally been a Lubavitcher preoccupation.

In Raskin's Fish Store, the clerks, all in yarmulkes, joked a lot with their customers. The fish was piled in huge heaps and the atmosphere evocative of an oriental bazaar. Most of the women had made the traditional Sabbath food, gefilte fish, the night before, but for those who had not had the time or the inclination, Raskin's sold its own gefilte fish, frozen. I saw no one buying less than five pounds of fish. In my neighborhood in Manhattan, at least half the late Friday afternoon customers were young working women buying the mod-est provisions for dinner with their boyfriends—two artichokes, two fillets of something, two candles, and so forth. There were obviously no intimate *soupers à deux* being planned here. The books of Leviticus (Chapter 11) and Deuteronomy (Chapter 14:3–21) list the animals, fish, and fowl that are consid-ered kosher, or fit to be eaten by Jews. Only sea creatures that have both fins and scales are considered kosher, so no lobster, clam, oyster, crab, or shrimp is ever seen in a kosher fish store. Other foods that are proscribed by Jewish law include meat from animals that do not both chew their cud and have cloven hooves, twenty-four kinds of birds (many of them birds of prey); insects, amphibian creatures or any creature that crawls "upon the belly"; any "winged swarming thing," rodent, or lizard; or any product that might come from these creatures, such as milk, eggs, or oil. Animals that are considered clean are cows, sheep, goats, deer, chickens, turkeys, geese, ducks, and doves. Other for-bidden foods include pigs, camels, herons, storks, hawks, ravens, pelicans, ostriches, eels, snails, rattlesnakes, ants, and rock badgers.

Eating kosher food and meats that have been slaughtered in the ritually prescribed manner is one of the basic disciplines of Jewish religious life. Reform Jews, who believe that the dietary laws are antiquated and serve no practical function, point out that they are a major factor in separating Jews from the rest of their fellowmen. The Hasidim are opposed to joining the mainstream and, citing the scriptures, point out that God never intended that they should: "I am the Lord your God who have set you apart from the nations. You shall therefore separate between the clean beast and the unclean beast and the unclean fowl and the clean." If the Hasidim's habits and customs alienate outsiders, they are unconcerned. Unlike most Jews, who tend either to shrug off, compartmentalize, or firmly reject any idea of their exoticness, the Hasidim accept it as part of their role. In fact, it is a source of pride. As one religious author put it, "What narrower minds look upon as a picayune concern with trifling kitchen matters is really an example of how Judaism elevates the mere physical satisfactions of one's appetite into a spiritual act by its emphasis on the everpresent God and our duty to serve him at all times." So much ritual is associated with eating in Orthodox homes that it sometimes seems that the table is a form of altar. In fact, one unnamed Talmud scholar mentioned in a curious tome that I came across, called *To Be a Jew* by Rabbi Hayim H. Donin (one of many such everything-you-wanted-to-know-about-Judaism-but-were-afraid-to-ask volumes that have recently become popular in the booming spiritual-affirmation business), went so far as to suggest that the table has come to replace the Temple altar: "When the Temple stood, sacrifices would secure atonement for an individual; now his table does."

By midafternoon on Friday the streets of Crown Heights are filled with women laden with shopping bags, hurrying home to finish their preparations for the Sabbath. By late afternoon the women have all disappeared and the landscape has become entirely masculine. As the shadows lengthen under the maples and lindens of President Street, dark-hatted men in somber clothes, alone or in groups of two and three, are taking pains to reach home before sundown, when the Sabbath begins. Many of the men work half days on Fridays, others leave work by midafternoon. If an employer will not permit an early departure on Friday, a Hasid will not work for him. On Friday afternoon the men go to the *mikvah*, or ritual bath, to purify themselves for the Sabbath. Many of them exchange their business suits and ordinary fedoras for knee-length black silk caftans and velvet yarmulkes. Crowds of men mill outside 770 Eastern Parkway. The look of boredom or patient endurance one sees so often on their faces in the workaday world has vanished. Their expressions are lively, and the talk is animated. It is a pleasing scene—a *tableau vivant* that cannot have looked much different two hundred years ago. Few of these men have attended college. In the Hasidic world, secular education has traditionally been viewed as a threat to religious life. In the past decades, this view has changed in certain communities. There has developed what the sociologist Egon Mayer, in his study of the Boro Park religious community, referred to as a dual status system. Upwardly mobile young men and women have tried (helped by laws protecting them from religious discrimination) to achieve distinction in secular careers and still satisfy the demands of a religious life. In these communities, being a good doctor or lawyer has come to mean as much as being a good Jew. This change has never occurred in Crown Heights. It is no surprise, therefore, that there are few professional men in the crowd in front of the synagogue. The conspicuous lack of interest in careers that the anthropologist Jerome R. Mintz observed among Hasidim in the nineteen-sixties and wrote about in *Legends of the Hasidim* (a study of Hasidic life based on modern Hasidic tales) still prevails among the Lubavitchers of the nineteen-eighties. Some of them, like the Konigsbergs, appear to make a good living despite this handicap, but many do not. "A Hasid," said Mintz, "does not have a 'career'; he is concerned simply with earning a living in a way which will not interfere with his religious duties. Most Hasidim . . . belong to the ranks of skilled workers. They are employed in the diamond center as cutters, polishers, and dealers; they hold jobs as sewing machine operators, pattern cutters, watchmakers, linotype operators, electricians, carpenters, and upholsterers . . . a small but ever increasing number have established small packaging and wholesale businesses, often in response to the particular needs of the Hasidic community. Because of their disdain for what they consider inadequate precautions in fulfilling the ritual law, a number of Hasidim have succeeded in establishing enterprises concerned with matzoh, meat, milk, cheese, bread, noodles, salt, sugar, mayonnaise, and vitamins. Hasidic manufacturers and wholesalers can assure their customers that no condition will be permitted which might render their products impure. Still other concerns supply religious books and other articles. . . . A number of Hasidim have become ritual slaughterers or have opened highly successful butcher shops. Some have opened groceries, vegetable markets, fish stores, dry goods stores . . . These retail ventures are assured of a measure of success because of the customary endorsement of their Rebbe and the patronage of their own courts."

At the Konigsberg house, twenty-five minutes before sundown, Sheina, dressed in an elegant tan silk blouse and tweed skirt, was preparing to light the Sabbath candles. Her afternoon coiffure of short, feathery Titian curls had been completely transformed into a long, svelte pageboy in the few minutes it took her to change upstairs. I briefly entertained the idea that I might have been encountering my first kabbalistic wonder, then recollected that for reasons of modesty, married Hasidic women cut off most of their hair and wear wigs. She had merely changed wigs.

According to custom, Sabbath candles are lit twenty minutes before sundown. The meal had been cooked, the table elaborately set, the heavy, ornately wrought silver candelabrum polished, and the family and some guests were milling around the living room. The guests included a South African rabbi and his wife and two daughters; Moshe's second-oldest daughter, Chanah, who was pregnant; and her husband, Isaac, a small redheaded man with intelligent, laughing eyes, who told me that they were about to depart for Virginia to help organize the Jewish community there; the two almond-eyed Persian girls, Gita and Azita Medizhadi; and a young girl who had recently decided to abandon her secular life and live in the dormitory the Lubavitchers run for young *baalot teshuvah*. Several minutes after the guests were introduced to one another, the women crowded around the candelabrum. According to Jewish custom it is the obligation of married women to usher in the Sabbath by lighting the candles. At least two candles are lit, symbolically representing the fourth commandment, to "remember" the Sabbath, and the twelfth verse in Deuteronomy, Chapter 5, to "observe" it, but Sheina also lit additional candles for her children and so did the rabbi's wife. Without saying anything, Sheina handed me several candles and invited me to repeat the blessing for lighting the candles after her, which I did somewhat awkwardly. I had never done it before. When I was young, I had seen my grandmother, a plump, rosy Austrian beauty, light Sabbath candles once or twice. But my mother, an adamantly modern soul who thought that such rituals belonged in the same category as curtseying and child labor, put the traditions of four thousand years behind her without a backward glance. Now, watching the peaceful, absorbed faces of the women in the glow of the candles, I felt a rush of nostalgia and something like a sense of loss. It passed quickly, however, when I realized that because of the prohibition against using the phone on the Sabbath, I would be unable to call my son to wish him goodnight.

The activities proscribed for the Sabbath either by the Bible or by post-Biblical decree seem mind-boggling to outsiders. They include cooking; baking; washing laundry; chopping; knitting; crocheting; sewing; embroidering; pasting; drawing, painting; writing; typing; fishing; hunting; cutting hair (or cutting anything else, with the exception of food); building or repairing anything; gardening; carrying or pushing anything farther than six feet in public; riding in cars, planes, trains, or buses; boating; buying or selling; horseback riding; playing a musical instrument; switching on any electrical apparatus, such as a TV set, phonograph or radio; handling any objects whose use is forbidden on the Sabbath, such as money, tools, or pencils; exercising or playing any sport; or traveling, even by foot, more than a short distance from the place where one is ensconced on the Sabbath. I asked Sheina how she felt about having her activities so restricted each week. Surveying the dinner table approvingly, as the men filed out the door to go to their evening service, she replied that she didn't think of it that way.

"I feel that I'm getting a break," she said, as she placed a heavy water pitcher on the table. "Once you get some of the more complicated things out of the way, like cooking the food in advance and setting a large urn of hot water on a metal cover over a low burner so that everybody can have coffee and tea to drink on Saturday, and covering some of the light switches so that no one will accidentally turn the important lights off, it feels more like a holiday. What if you were flown to a quiet tropical island every week? Wouldn't you be pleased if you were permitted, even obliged, to just put aside your everyday burdens and everyday chores? I don't really know what other people's lives are like, but I doubt that most families get the chance we do to just sit around and talk to one another every weekend. On weekends most Americans seem to play as hard as they work . . . The Sabbath is also a time when I can study Torah in an unhurried way, and we almost always have guests who have interesting things to say about life."

"You mean Jewish life, of course."

"Well, yes."

"Are your guests ever gentiles?"

"No. I'm aware that there are some fine gentile people; but their world is not our world. I may see an occasional play, or concert, or TV program—most of the people in the community don't have TV's, by the way, and don't go to the movies—but these are not the important activities in my life. Being a Jew and fulfilling the commandments *is* my life, and it's Moshe's. It takes up all our time. The rhythms of my life over the weeks and months follow those of the *Jewish* calendar. [The Jewish year is made up of twelve lunar months, with an extra month added every few years to make up for the annual eleven-and-a-quarter-day discrepancy between a lunar year and the solar one.] It's the same for everyone here, so it follows that the people that we see are going to be involved in the same kind of life."

"You don't feel that you're cutting yourselves off from any of the richness of life by shutting things out just because they're different?"

"No, I don't. I can't imagine a richer life than the one I'm leading. Anyway, we're not all that shut off from the world. Moshe and I travel."

"You do? Is that common here?"

"Well, it's quite common to go off to another city or country to help start or build a Lubavitcher center, but people here travel for pleasure, too. We went to London last summer."

"What did you do there?"

"We visited Lubavitcher families and the yeshivas in and near the city, but we also went to see the Victoria and Albert Museum and the Tower of London and Madame Tussaud's. Of course, when you do these things, you can sometimes get into trouble; we certainly did when we went to the Tower of London on a Friday," she said, smiling.

"What do you mean?"

"There was a tube strike while we were there, and even though we left the tower at four o'clock in the afternoon in order to be sure to make it to the friend's house we were staying at in Golders Green by nine, when Shabbos began, we very nearly didn't make it. You could only move around by bus— you couldn't find a taxi. We had to change buses several times and the queues were endless. At seven-thirty, we were still standing at the end of a long queue at Oxford Circus and there were no buses in sight. Moshe said, 'Let's walk.' We were both exhausted by then and pretty frantic, and there didn't seem to be any chance that we could make it, but off we headed toward Golders Green, which was about an hour away by bus. I nearly started to cry. Then Moshe just bent over to a fellow who had stopped his car at a light and told him that he was a religious Jew and that we simply had to be at our friend's house by sundown. He told him that he'd give him whatever amount of money he wanted if he would drive us there. The man looked at Moshe as if he were crazy at first, but it turned out that he was a religious Catholic. He was surprised that we couldn't get a special dispensation because of the strike; *he* could have, he said, but he agreed to take us, and we made it. He didn't even want to take any money in the end, but we insisted because it didn't seem fair to have him go out of his way for nothing."

"Why do you think that people really aren't supposed to work on the Sabbath?" I asked. "Why does it honor God more to desist from work than to work?"

Sheina bit her lip. "Ask Moshe when he comes back, he knows more about things like that than I do."

About an hour and a half later, Moshe, Isaac, and the rabbi from South Africa returned from the synagogue. Sheina had mentioned earlier that her husband prayed three times a day (as required by Jewish law) on weekdays at 770—which is how the Lubavitchers refer to their synagogue—where there were always so many people around that he was was sure to find the quorum of ten men needed for public prayer. On Fridays and Saturdays, however, he prayed at a *shtiebl* (small synagogue) around the corner. Many Lubavitchers did the same thing, she explained, because they wanted to keep the little synagogues, which were built in the first half of the century and had lost most of their congregations in the fifties and sixties, going. Moshe, resplendent in a long black caftan and velvet yarmulke with gilt zigzagging, rubbed his hands together and regarded the room and his guests with obvious satisfaction. A few minutes later, his sons and a schoolfriend rushed breathlessly into the room. When Mendel spied me, he nudged his brother. Shmuel glanced my way briefly, but stared fixedly at his shoes when he greeted me. They had made it just in the nick of time, Sheina explained, since kiddush (the prayer of sanctification) had to be recited before six o'clock. It was five to six. They had been somewhat delayed coming in from Morristown, New Jersey, where they were all students at a Lubavitcher yeshiva, the Rabbinical College of America, and so had gone to evening prayers directly after they had arrived back in the neighborhood. The boys' friend was another visitor from South Africa. Everyone gathered around the table and the men sang the traditional *"Shalom Aleichem,"* a hymn that pays homage to the angels that accompanied them home from the synagogue. After the song I noticed Moshe looking rather intently at Sheina and reciting or singing something. She was smiling. Later that evening she explained that Moshe had been singing the thirty-first chapter of the Book of Proverbs, which contains the well-known phrase "A woman of valor, who can find; for her price is far above rubies." This paean to what seems to be the practical virtues of Jewish housewifery was in fact interpreted by the early kabbalists as a hymn to the *Shekhinah,* God's female aspect. I knew that Hasidic men sang this to their wives every Sabbath, but I had somehow expected that it would be a more public, declamatory ritual. The intimacy of the moment took me by surprise. One of the guests asked where Moshe's two other daughters were and was told that the eldest, Miriam, lived in Cape Town with her husband and children and that Bassy, the youngest, who was nineteen, was with her grandmother. Bassy, a slim, spirited girl who in the secular world would probably be taken for the captain of her field hockey team, had explained to me several hours earlier, as she hastily gathered a few belongings together and headed for the door, that she spent Shabbos with her widowed grandmother, who lived around the corner. "Sometimes she comes here for Shabbos but sometimes she likes to stay at home, so I help her prepare everything and I stay overnight to keep her company." When I said that most of the girls her age that I knew would not be eager to do that, she looked genuinely surprised.

"But I don't mind at all. It's no problem. You'll see when you meet Bubbe. She's great. Actually, I've spent every night with her since she had to have one of her fingers removed because of cancer last year. It's really no big deal."

Moshe filled a silver kiddush cup to the brim with sweet wine and, holding the cup in the palm of his hand, recited the kiddush and poured everyone some wine. Then everyone trooped off to the kitchen in silence to wash hands for the meal. Like virtually every facet of Hasidic life, washing up before meals is accomplished in a ritually prescribed manner. One fills a chalice with water, pours the water first over the right hand, then over the left, then recites the benediction, "Blessed art Thou, Lord our God, King of the Universe, who has sanctified us with His commandments, and commanded us concerning the washing of the hands." One by one, the guests returned in silence to the table. Then Moshe removed a velvet coverlet from two home-baked challah breads (two to symbolically commemorate the extra portion of manna that the Israelites were given on the first Sabbath eve of the Exodus), lifted the breads, recited another blessing, then cut off a piece for everybody at the table. Everyone dipped his chunk of bread in salt (symbolic of the salt used in the ancient Temple during ritual sacrifices) and the meal, trumpeted in by a great outburst of talk, began in earnest.

A staggering amount of food appeared at the table, but the guests seemed to like to talk even more than they liked to eat, and much of the dinner was destined to sit untouched for long lapses, on people's plates. Sheina's dinner was so copious that it would not have been a calamity if one or two courses had slipped away unnoticed, although I believe none did. The menu was inspired largely by East Europe and the suburban Midwest, with East Europe predominating. There was gefilte fish, a tossed salad, chicken soup with matzoh balls, roast chicken, braised beef, noodle pudding, a spinach-and-broccoli mold, and a nondairy ice cream pie with a walnut crust for dessert. Whiskey, wine, and cordial bottles were scattered across the length of a snowy, starched tablecloth. In front of Moshe, who sat at the head of the table with the other men seated around him, was a bottle of Chivas Regal; the boys poured each other glasses of Israeli wine, and the women sipped from a dazzling assortment of cordials—banana liqueur, Kahlua, Cherry Heering, and blackberry brandy, some of which came from miniature bottles, souvenirs, perhaps, of Purim. Over the matzoh-ball soup, I asked Moshe why it was, apart from emulating the actions of the Creator, that ceasing to work on the Sabbath honored God. His sons looked at me in astonishment, scarcely believing that anyone would not know why Shabbos was Shabbos, but Moshe seemed pleased that I had asked the question.

"What happens when we stop working and controlling nature?" he asked, peering at me over the top of his glasses. "When we don't operate machines, or pick flowers, or pluck fish from the sea, or change darkness to light, or turn wood into furniture? When we cease interfering with the world we are acknowledging that it is God's world."

The rabbi from South Africa, a robust, cheerful man with a thick, black, curly beard, added that the Sabbath was also a memorial to the exodus from Egypt.

"Once the Jews left Egypt they were no longer enslaved. But of course the ordinary workaday world always involves a kind of servitude, and for many people, especially poor people, work can be awfully grinding. But no one is the master of any Jew on the Sabbath. Every body and every soul is free on that day. Tyrannical countries have always tried to force Jews to work on Saturdays, to mock this gesture of independence. East European Jews fought anti-Sabbath edicts and statutes for centuries."

Moshe chose this moment to lead the men in a beautiful Aramaic hymn, familiar to everyone present, written by Isaac Luria, that depicted the Sabbath as a bride "adorned in ornaments, jewels, and robes. Her husband embraces her; through this gathering which brings her joy, the forces of evil will be utterly crushed." The Sabbath queen or bride is a popular metaphor in the literature of the mystics. Her husband, of course, is all Israel, that is, every Jew. Almost all religious Jews sing at the Sabbath meal. The songs they sing celebrate the joys of the Sabbath and were written chiefly during the Middle Ages. Lubavitcher Hasidim have their own melodies, or *nigunim*, most of which have been composed by their rebbes; they are sung on almost any occasion that offers itself. Among the Sabbath *nigunim* that were sung that weekend was one composed by the present Rebbe ("may we be united with the Supreme One in whom is the life of all things; may our strength be increased, and may our [prayer] ascend and become a [diadem] upon His head") and another composed by the first Lubavitcher rebbe ("Rejoice now at this most propitious time, when there is no sadness. Draw near to me, behold My strength, for there are no harsh judgements. They are cast out, they may not enter, these [forces of evil which are likened to] insolent dogs").

Moshe had a fine, clear voice and sang with gusto, sometimes closing his eyes to better concentrate on the song. I remarked that he seemed to enjoy singing a lot. He made a little self-deprecatory gesture and pulled on his beard, but smiled. "I come from a musical family. My grandfather played the violin for the soldiers when he was in the Red Army. My Bassy is a good pianist, too, you know." Songs were sung throughout the meal. The singing grew more animated as the hour grew later. If the heavy food anchored the guests ever more deeply into their chairs, the songs acted as a kind of spiritual counterweight. Unfamiliar as I was with the songs, I felt a strong urge to join in, though I had not failed to notice that none of the women had been singing. While the noodle pudding was being passed, I asked the young girl next to me, who was studying Lubavitcher ways, if it didn't bother her to be left out of the singing.

"A little," she admitted, "but I sort of sing along to myself."

"Do you know why women aren't supposed to sing?"

"Well," she said, plunging a big forkful of noodles into her mouth and gazing placidly at me over a freckled nose, "women's voices can be highly arousing to men, so our sages thought it best that we didn't sing in front of them. It doesn't work the other way around though, because women have always been considered more spiritual, so a man's singing is not going to upset them or anything."

Seeing what must have been an ill-disguised expression of bemusement on my face as I gazed at the freckle-faced girl, the boys' friend from South Africa, a gentle looking pink-cheeked boy of about nineteen, said to me in a reproving tone, "Everybody thinks the modest ways of Hasidic women are absurd and unnecessary, don't they? But they're wrong. Last week a group of us were speaking about Hasidic life at one of the universities, and a student said to us, 'You know, it's really ridiculous, the way your women cover their elbows and their knees, and the way you make married women wear wigs. I'm not turned on by elbows and knees, and I'm not going to ravish anybody's wife just because her hair is beautiful.' And most of the people there either laughed or smiled. 'Well,' I said, 'it's too bad if beautiful hair and legs and arms don't arouse you. They do me.' Uh, and that's true. It takes a lot to turn people on today, because there's so much public nudity and promiscuity. People have become coarsened. No wonder the simple sight of beautiful flesh doesn't mean much. But in our world, where there is no exposure to such things and where the sexes are separated so much of the time, things are different."

Perhaps, I thought, looking around the table at the attractively dressed, carefully made-up women present. But why hair, elbows, and knees? Why not eyes, hands, napes of necks, and trim ankles? And what about mouths? Muslim women's mouths were considered so tempting that they had to be veiled.

Gazing at the young boy approvingly, Moshe said, "Dovid came into our midst because of what people call our proselytizing campaign, although that's really the wrong word for what we do. The Rebbe started a program some years ago of sending young couples around to places where there were sizable Jewish communities, not only in our country but all around the world. He hoped that they would quicken awareness of what Judaism had to offer our people. We sent the Mitzvah Tanks [the Lubavitcher campers that carry students around asking passersby, 'Are you Jewish?'] out for the same reason. They usually come back amazed by the welcome they receive. The most unlikely people sometimes respond to what they have to say. My daughter

Miriam and her husband in Cape Town never expected what they found: a lot of people who were willing to take on the obligations of a more religious life. Dovid is one of them."

Looking slightly embarrassed, Dovid explained that until recently he had lived with his family on a large South African cattle ranch and attended the University of Cape Town. But his conversations with Moshe's daughter and son-in-law at the university convinced him that a lot of the things that he missed in his life—a sense of purpose and commitment, a feeling of community—could be supplied by Judaism and more particularly by the Lubavitchers' way of life. He thought about it for several months and then decided to leave the university, come to New York and study at the Lubavitcher yeshiva. "It was the smartest thing I ever did," he added.

"Did your parents give you a hard time?" asked the girl with the freckles.

"Not really," said Dovid.

"Well, mine did. And they still do. They think that the Lubavitchers are some kind of weird cult, like the Moonies. They hated it when I started observing Shabbos and they hated it when I told them I really wanted to study Judaism seriously and to lead a more religious life. Sometimes I think that they'd rather have me smoke pot than pray." Everybody laughed.

"From the beginnings of the Hasidic movement outsiders have wanted to think of us as a cult or a sect," said Moshe. "That's why we were excommunicated in the eighteenth century. But we never were a sect. On the contrary, from the beginning the Besht intended that all Jews should be brought closer together because of his ideas. If the various Hasidic dynasties that formed in different towns after his death came to be regarded as separate entities, that was never what was intended. The Lubavitchers in particular, from our founder, Rabbi Schneur Zalman, to the present Rebbe, have always tried to reach all Jews. If we seem so different from other Jews it's more because of what has happened to them than anything that happened to us. We've stayed the same; it's they who've changed."

"You know there is a saying among Hasidim that the Messiah will come 'when the wellsprings of the Baal Shem Tov spread out,'" said Sheina, as she eased generous wedges of cocoa-colored pie onto plates and passed them down the table, "that is, when everything that he taught becomes the common practice of all Jews in the diaspora. That's why the Rebbe has sent the young people around in the campers and around the world. Jews don't really stick together because there is a breach among us. He wants to heal it."

At about ten o'clock the women began to clear the table. Moshe carried one or two things to the kitchen but Shmuel was still eating a second helping of dessert and the boys got into some knotty discussion of a point of Hebrew semantics just as the clearing up began. They did not resolve it until the table was cleared of everything but the still softly glowing candelabrum. Moshe entered into the discussion after a while and I noticed that though he spoke English when he talked with Sheina, he and the boys spoke to one another in Yiddish. Some of the guests lingered at the table, some drifted over to the couch and chairs at the fireplace. One of the guests, the woman from South Africa, asked Shmuel, who was seated in an armchair, his stomach protruding over his belt, how a certain friend of his was getting on. Shmuel said that he was married and that he and his wife had recently had their second child. He looked at his shoes as he answered.

"And what about you?" the guest asked pertly. In these circles, a twenty-five-year-old is considered a bit long of tooth for bachelorhood.

"What about me?" Shmuel answered, keeping his eyes glued southward. There was a defensive edge in his answer, but also a real note of misery.

"Oh, Shmuel will settle down when the right time comes," said her husband, looking at him evenly and drawing his wife away to look at some books across the room. Shmuel raised himself heavily from the chair with a little sigh, found a book, and retired to a quiet corner to study. Five minutes later, Mendel joined him and their heads remained bent together for the rest of the evening. During the winter months when it got dark earlier, Moshe met with a group of Lubavitcher neighbors every Friday night to study, he said, but in the months when it turned dark late he studied either with the boys or by himself at home on Shabbos. Conversation among the rest of the guests continued in an animated way until the early hours of the morning. At 2:15 I excused myself and retreated to Bassy's cheerful, frilly second-floor bedroom, which, unlike that of every other teenage girl of my acquaintance, was innocent of posters of rock godlets, photographs of boyfriends, clippings of Snoopy cartoons, or fey messages.

All that met the eye were several shelves filled with religious books and some neatly arranged cosmetics on top of a dresser. The sole wall decoration was a blue and white banner that (like the bumper sticker on the car I had seen in the driveway) proclaimed that "Jewish Mothers and Daughters Light Shabbos Candles." Heavily ballasted with matzoh balls and conversation, I sank into sleep almost immediately. As I pulled a soft blue and white comforter over my head, it occurred to me that not one word had been spoken about any nonreligious subject. Tomorrow, I thought, as I drifted off, there will undoubtedly be some conversation about secular matters. A few hours later, I was awakened by a street noise. I glanced at my watch. It was 4:15. A low hum of conversation drifted up from below.

On Saturday, the conversation turned frequently to Biblical events and their relation to the lives of those assembled at the house, to upcoming religious holidays, and to some of the Rebbe's recent talks. Subjects such as jobs, politics, movies, the environment, secular books, or the latest football scores never even entered the fringes of discussion. There was a bit of gossip, but it was mostly about who was getting married or who was having a baby. Several times I overheard Moshe mention Yitzhak and Avraham. I thought he was talking about some neighbors. It turned out that he was talking about the Biblical Isaac and Abraham. Throughout the day, I was struck by the familiar even intimate way in which Moshe, Sheina, and the others spoke of Biblical people and places. Isaac and Abraham all but hovered near the stove, miraculous deeds had more credibility than newspaper stories, and none of the Biblical heroes had lost their luster. This personal mystical connection with the literalness of the Bible serves, of course, as a kind of Jewish relic or monument to the past, its only religious monument, in fact, since, unlike other religions, most of the material relics—such as the Temple and many of the sacred books—have been destroyed. Like the shtetl Jews that Mark Zborowski and Elizabeth Herzog wrote about in *Life Is With People,* an anthropological study of shtetl life, the Hasidic community today "traces its line of march directly back to Creation. The Exodus from Egypt, the giving of the Law on Mount Sinai, are seen as steps along the way, historical events no less real than the Spanish Inquisition or the Russian Revolution."

Like their shtetl forebears, the Hasidim believe that the oral and written law, which was codified chiefly in the centuries following the exile, amount to a Magna Carta or constitution of a kind of spiritual government in exile and only the adherence of the Jewish faithful, they believe, "has enabled a weak and homeless people to survive the great empires of Egypt and Babylon, Greece and Rome, Byzantium and Islam, and has caused their sacred books to enter into the holy writ of half the world."

If the Konigsbergs live in a kind of perpetual Biblical present, in which the events of their everyday lives are constantly being linked to their spiritual past, their rebbes have traditionally been the guides who have interpreted the interconnectedness of the two. While I watched the *Havdalah* ceremony (*Havdalah* is the Hebrew word for separation) that signaled the end of the Sabbath, Saturday night—a plaited candle is lit, wine is drunk, a benediction is said, and a spice box is passed around to raise spirits that might be saddened by the passing of the Sabbath—I remembered some of the names of former Lubavitch and other Hasidic leaders that had been evoked during the day as if they were old friends. "Ah, the *frierdiker* [previous] rebbe used to say . . . " or, "Did that happen to you? The same thing happened to the *Tzemach Tzedek* [the third Lubavitcher rebbe]." The history of these Hasidic ancestors, too, is inextricably bound to the lives of their descendants.

PART **IV**

RELIGIOUS DOCTRINE

Purification Font, Mosque, Cairo.
(Photo by J. T. Carmody)

INTRODUCTION

Religion is something that people teach their children, and that adults can study throughout their lives because it grows richer as one ages. So all religious communities have developed doctrines: a form in which religion can be taught and studied. Necessarily, this form has stressed ideas, the mental part of the faith and traditions that people held. When writing developed, doctrine went into scrolls and books. Some of these writings became uniquely holy: the scriptures in which divinity had given its word. Almost always such scriptures drew on earlier oral forms. Frequently they presented myths, revelations, poetic expressions of religious insight calculated to catch people's imaginations and stir their hearts. Religious rituals looked to scriptures for their most authoritative materials, and scriptures furnished pious people with their primary written material for prayer.

Religious doctrines also took other forms (theological treatises, catechisms, creeds), but scriptures have always been especially authoritative. Even though other forms might be clearer and more satisfying to the scholarly or speculative mind, scriptures were the central channel through which ordinary people learned the ideational content of their religious faith.

The four doctrinal selections that we present all come from scriptural or quasi-scriptural writings. The *Tao Tê Ching (Way and Its Power)*, also known as the *Lao Tzu,* is a Chinese text more than two thousand years old, attributed to Master Lao, the foremost sage in the Taoist canon. Lao Tzu is more legendary than historical, but his poetic reflections on how reality looks when one sees from the perspective of the *Tao* (Way) that runs the world acquired sacred status for many traditional Chinese.

The second selection, from the *Chuang Tzu,* offers another example of Taoist wisdom. Chuang Tzu, like Lao Tzu, is the name of both a legendary sage and a classical text. Some scholars think that Chuang Tzu preceded Lao Tzu, but most studies assume that Lao Tzu is the more authoritative text. Chuang Tzu is quirkier than Lao Tzu. He tells irreverent anecdotes and more clearly refers to interior, yogic experiences. Throughout he shows the impatience of the quick person with slow, plodding ones. Always he is aware of the paradoxes that emerge when one puts aside unthinking custom and starts to deal with reality in a fresh, deeply honest way. Chuang Tzu criticized the Confucians for becoming too sobersided and prosaic. He stressed the inevitability of death, and so the freedom that people ought to retain: all things are passing. Above all, we find in Chuang Tzu a wonderful humor. He delights in pricking pretension and self-importance. His great love is the irony that following the Way reveals.

These selections from the *Tao Tê Ching* and the *Chuang Tzu* are typical in delighting in paradoxes that immersion in the Tao creates. When one's spirit is traveling as the Way invites it to, many of the assumptions governing ordinary life seem dubious, if not silly. For example, the very first lines from Lao Tzu pose a puzzle: The Way that we can speak about (put into words) is not a real or unvarying Way. From the outset, then, we have to wonder what the *Tao Tê Ching* purports to be. Is it telling us about the inmost patterns of nature, about the wisdom by which to run human affairs, or is it only teasing us with hints of what the fuller truth, the wordless perception, would be like? Indeed, perhaps its real point is simply to get us to ask questions—make us throw over the assumption that we know how things stand for human beings and start to wonder, contemplate, go below our minds to the center of ourselves in search of a deeper wisdom.

The third selection, from the Qur'an, is also scriptural. The Qur'an is *the* authority in Islamic life; Muslims consider it to be Allah's revelations to Muhammad. Islam arose because of those revelations, and the Qur'an has always been the mainstay of the Muslim community. Most Muslims think that it cannot be translated from Arabic; every separation of the content from its original form is bound to denature it. So the Qur'an has been a prod for all Muslims to learn Arabic (as the Hebrew Bible has been a prod for all Jews to learn Hebrew). Muslim worship amounts largely to hearing verses from the Qur'an, reciting verses, and listening to sermons that expose given texts. Indeed, some scholars who compare religions have thought that the Qur'an occupies in Islam the place that Christ occupies in Christianity.

The fourth selection comes from the Talmud, a huge collection of traditional Jewish lore. The Talmud arose from the tendency of leading rabbis to write commentaries on biblical books, and then commentaries on such commentaries. Around A.D. 500 compilers collected the main rabbis' views, and since that time traditional Jewish learning has amounted to mastering this collection. Indeed, so significant did the Talmud become that *Torah,* divine Instruction or Law, came to connote not only the five biblical books attributed to Moses (Genesis, Exodus, Leviticus, Numbers, Deuteronomy) but also the whole corpus of rabbinical commentary that continued to evolve after the Talmud.

The selection from the Qur'an is the *surah* (chapter) traditionally called "Women." It affords us the chance to think about how traditional Islam, and other patriarchal cultures, regarded women. Throughout the traditional religious world, women have been second-class citizens. Most traditions granted that women could please God, and that feminine human nature was as necessary as masculine, but few championed women's ways (Taoism was an exception) or gave women equal access to power and status. Traditional religion has been a male preserve, even when many of the saints have been women and much of the popular piety has revolved around women. Like all surahs of the Qur'an, this one on women suggests the grandeur of the diction typical in this scripture—the exalted speech, related to the exalted source: Allah himself.

The Talmudic material comes from a popular condensation of Talmudic teaching. The editor has gathered various texts together by theme, greatly simplifying a first approach to a topic such as the Talmudic view of God. One can see the rabbis' typical style—to gloss biblical texts and opinions of famous ancient teachers. One can also see their tendency to tell stories, illustrate points with anecdotes, and stress the practical side of Jewish faith. Again and again the rabbis show themselves most interested in the question "What does this mean for daily living? How should we practice this precept?" Talmudic Judaism has been especially interested in clarifying moral obligations. The guidance that God gave his people so that they might maintain their covenant with him and be holy as he is holy ran to consecrating their food, their work, their time; their minds, their bodies, their imaginations. So it has been difficult to separate doctrine and ethics in traditional Judaism. Much of the teaching that explained Jewish faith was concerned with living it out.

Sometimes religious doctrine (theology) gets a bad name because people recognize that a living faith comes more from the heart than the head. But it is easy to defend this doctrinal impulse in the religious traditions. Human beings are the peculiar species that want to *know*. Their characteristic capacity is reason: the ability to understand their condition, to grasp patterns, and to reflect on themselves to direct their future actions better. The best theologians have been quick to admit that they never expected to understand the divine mysteries. "God," or the equivalent in nontheistic systems, by definition transcends the capacities of human beings. Still, if God has given human beings special guidance (if God has revealed the divine will), knowledge of such guidance becomes the most precious knowledge.

The history of religious doctrine therefore is like a pendulum swinging between excessive claims for what human beings can know and frugal claims that aim too low. Rationalists have tended to claim too much for human efforts, as though reason could one day take away the mysteriousness at the heart of human existence. Skeptics (agnostics) have tended to claim too little, as though divinity gave no indication of its nature or will and human beings had no likeness to their Creator. Fundamentalists have tended to claim both too much and too little. On the one hand, they have despised human reason and depended completely on divine revelation, but on the other hand, they have taken the mysteriousness out of revelation and so been rationalistic about it.

By consensus of the learned and wise in all the major religious traditions, the truth about religious doctrine stands in the middle. A frail analogy relates human perception, understanding, and feeling to the ultimate reality that many call "God." Human beings are not without some guidance, but ultimate reality always remains richer than what humans can understand. This makes the last word of religious teachers hopeful: a mind much better than ours runs the world.

11

The *Tao Tê Ching*, Chapters 1–11*

The source of this reading is a Chinese text called the Tao Tê Ching *(Way and Its Power). It is thought to be over 2000 years old and has been attributed to the legendary figure of Master Lao. Its poetic representation of reality viewed through the perspective of "the Way" has become one of the most respected writings of Chinese culture.*

CHAPTER I

The Way that can be told of is not an Unvarying Way;
The names that can be named are not unvarying names.
It was from the nameless that Heaven and Earth sprang;
The named is but the mother that rears the ten thousand creatures, each after
    its kind.
Truly, 'Only he that rids himself forever of desire can see the Secret
    Essences';
He that has never rid himself of desire can see only the Outcomes.
These two things issued from the same mould, but nevertheless are different
    in name.
This 'same mould' we can but call the Mystery,
Or rather the 'Darker than any Mystery',
The Doorway whence issued all Secret Essences.

CHAPTER II

It is because every one under Heaven recognizes beauty as
    beauty, that the idea of ugliness exists.
And equally if every one recognized virtue as virtue, this
    would merely create fresh conceptions of wickedness.
For truly 'Being and Not-being grow out of one another;
Difficult and easy complete one another.
Long and short test one another;
High and low determine one another.
Pitch and mode give harmony to one another.
Front and back give sequence to one another.

*Arthur Waley, trans., *The Way and Its Power: A Study of the Tao Tê Ching and Its Place in Chinese Thought* (New York: Grove Press, 1958).

Therefore the Sage relies on actionless activity,
Carries on wordless teaching,
But the myriad creatures are worked upon by him; he does not disown them.
He rears them, but does not lay claim to them,
Controls them, but does not lean upon them,
Achieves his aim, but does not call attention to what he does;
And for the very reason that he does not call attention to what he does
He is not ejected from fruition of what he has done.

CHAPTER III

If we stop looking for 'persons of superior morality' (*hsien*) to put in power, there will be no more jealousies among the people. If we cease to set store by products that are hard to get, there will be no more thieves. If the people never see such things as excite desire, their hearts will remain placid and undisturbed. Therefore the Sage rules

> By emptying their hearts
> And filling their bellies,
> Weakening their intelligence
> And toughening their sinews
> Ever striving to make the people knowledgeless and desireless.

Indeed he sees to it that if there be any who have knowledge, they dare not interfere. Yet through his actionless activity all things are duly regulated.

CHAPTER IV

The Way is like an empty vessel
That yet may be drawn from
Without ever needing to be filled.
It is bottomless; the very progenitor of all things in the world.
In it all sharpness is blunted,
All tangles untied,
All glare tempered,
All dust smoothed.
It is like a deep pool that never dries.
Was it too the child of something else? We cannot tell.
But as a substanceless image it existed before the Ancestor.

CHAPTER V

Heaven and Earth are ruthless;
To them the Ten Thousand Things are but as straw dogs.
The Sage too is ruthless;
To him the people are but as straw dogs.

Yet Heaven and Earth and all that lies between
Is like a bellows
In that it is empty, but gives a supply that never fails.
Work it, and more comes out.
Whereas the force of words is soon spent.
Far better is it to keep what is in the heart.

CHAPTER VI

The Valley Spirit never dies.
It is named the Mysterious Female.
And the Doorway of the Mysterious Female
Is the base from which Heaven and Earth sprang.
It is there within us all the while;
Draw upon it as you will, it never runs dry.

CHAPTER VII

Heaven is eternal, the Earth everlasting.
How come they to be so? It is because they do not foster their own lives;
That is why they live so long.
Therefore the Sage
Puts himself in the background; but is always to the fore.
Remains outside; but is always there.
Is it not just because he does not strive for any personal end
That all his personal ends are fulfilled?

CHAPTER VIII

The highest good is like that of water. The goodness of water is that it benefits the ten thousand creatures; yet itself does not scramble, but is content with
the places that all men disdain. It is this that makes water so near to the Way.

And if men think the ground the best place for building a house upon,
If among thoughts they value those that are profound,
If in friendship they value gentleness,
In words, truth; in government, good order;
In deeds, effectiveness; in actions, timeliness—
In each case it is because they prefer what does not lead to strife,
And therefore does not go amiss.

CHAPTER IX

Stretch a bow to the very full,
And you will wish you had stopped in time;

Temper a sword-edge to its very sharpest,
And you will find it soon grows dull.
When bronze and jade fill your hall
It can no longer be guarded.
Wealth and place breed insolence
That brings ruin in its train.
When your work is done, then withdraw!
Such is Heaven's Way.

CHAPTER X

Can you keep the unquiet physical-soul from straying, hold fast to the Unity,
  and never quit it?
Can you, when concentrating your breath, make it soft like that of a little
  child?
Can you wipe and cleanse your vision of the Mystery till all is without blur?
Can you love the people and rule the land, yet remain unknown?
Can you in opening and shutting the heavenly gates play always the female
  part?
Can your mind penetrate every corner of the land, but you yourself never
  interfere?
Rear them, then, feed them,
Rear them, but do not lay claim to them.
Control them, but never lean upon them;
Be chief among them, but do not manage them.
This is called the Mysterious Power.

CHAPTER XI

We put thirty spokes together and call it a wheel;
But it is on the space where there is nothing that the usefulness of the wheel
  depends.
We turn clay to make a vessel;
But it is on the space where there is nothing that the usefulness of the vessel
  depends.
We pierce doors and windows to make a house;
And it is on these spaces where there is nothing that the usefulness of the
  house depends.
Therefore just as we take advantage of what is, we should recognize the use-
  fulness of what is not.

12

The Way of Chuang Tzu *

The Chuang Tzu *is another Taoist text that comes to us from the China of 2000 or so years ago. This text is characterized by freshness, irony, honesty, and humor. One of the goals of this writer seems to be to get the reader to question assumptions made in every-day life.*

THE SECRET OF CARING FOR LIFE[1]
(SECTION 3)

Your life has a limit but knowledge has none. If you use what is limited to pursue what has no limit, you will be in danger. If you understand this and still strive for knowledge, you will be in danger for certain! If you do good, stay away from fame. If you do evil, stay away from punishments. Follow the middle; go by what is constant, and you can stay in one piece, keep yourself alive, look after your parents, and live out your years.

Cook Ting was cutting up an ox for Lord Wen-hui.[2] At every touch of his hand, every heave of his shoulder, every move of his feet, every thrust of his knee—zip! zoop! He slithered the knife along with a zing, and all was in perfect rhythm, as though he were performing the dance of the Mulberry Grove or keeping time to the Ching-shou music.[3]

"Ah, this is marvelous!" said Lord Wen-hui. "Imagine skill reaching such heights!"

Cook Ting laid down his knife and replied, "What I care about is the Way, which goes beyond skill. When I first began cutting up oxen, all I could see was the ox itself. After three years I no longer saw the whole ox. And now—now I go at it by spirit and don't look with my eyes. Perception and understanding have come to a stop and spirit moves where it wants. I go along with the natural makeup, strike in the big hollows, guide the knife through the big openings, and follow things as they are. So I never touch the smallest ligament or tendon, much less a main joint.

---

*From *Chuang Tzu: Basic Writings,* translated by Burton Watson. New York: Columbia University Press, 1964.

[1]The chapter is very brief and would appear to be mutilated.

[2]Identified as King Hui of Wei.

[3]The Mulberry Grove is identified as a rain dance from the time of King T'ang of the Shang dynasty, and the Ching-shou music as part of a longer composition from the time of Yao.

"A good cook changes his knife once a year—because he cuts. A mediocre cook changes his knife once a month—because he hacks. I've had this knife of mine for nineteen years and I've cut up thousands of oxen with it, and yet the blade is as good as though it had just come from the grindstone. There are spaces between the joints, and the blade of the knife has really no thickness. If you insert what has no thickness into such spaces, then there's plenty of room—more than enough for the blade to play about in. That's why after nineteen years the blade of my knife is still as good as when it first came from the grindstone.

"However, whenever I come to a complicated place, I size up the difficulties, tell myself to watch out and be careful, keep my eyes on what I'm doing, work very slowly, and move the knife with the greatest subtlety, until—flop! the whole thing comes apart like a clod of earth crumbling to the ground. I stand there holding the knife and look all around me, completely satisfied and reluctant to move on, and then I wipe off the knife and put it away."[4]

"Excellent!" said Lord Wen-hui. "I have heard the words of Cook Ting and learned how to care for life!"

When Kung-wen Hsüan saw the Commander of the Right,[5] he was startled and said, "What kind of man is this? How did he come to lose his foot? Was it Heaven? Or was it man?"

"It was Heaven, not man," said the commander. "When Heaven gave me life, it saw to it that I would be one-footed. Men's looks are given to them. So I know this was the work of Heaven and not of man. The swamp pheasant has to walk ten paces for one peck and a hundred paces for one drink, but it doesn't want to be kept in a cage. Though you treat it like a king, its spirit won't be content."

When Lao Tan[6] died, Ch'in Shih went to mourn for him; but after giving three cries, he left the room.

"Weren't you a friend of the Master?" asked Lao Tzu's disciples.

"Yes."

"And you think it's all right to mourn him this way?"

"Yes," said Ch'in Shih. "At first I took him for a real man, but now I know he wasn't. A little while ago, when I went in to mourn, I found old men weeping for him as though they were weeping for a son, and young men

---

[4]Waley (*Three Ways of Thought in Ancient China*, p. 73) takes this whole paragraph to refer to the working methods of a mediocre carver, and hence translates it very differently. There is a great deal to be said for his interpretation, but after much consideration I have decided to follow the traditional interpretation because it seems to me that the extreme care and caution which the cook uses *when he comes to a difficult place* is also a part of Chuang Tzu's "secret of caring for life."

[5]Probably the ex-Commander of the Right, as he has been punished by having one foot amputated, a common penalty in ancient China. It is mutilating punishments such as these which Chuang Tzu has in mind when he talks about the need to "stay in one piece."

[6]Lao Tzu, the reputed author of the *Tao Tê Ching*.

weeping for him as though they were weeping for a mother. To have gathered a group like *that,* he must have done something to make them talk about him, though he didn't ask them to talk, or make them weep for him, though he didn't ask them to weep. This is to hide from Heaven, turn your back on the true state of affairs, and forget what you were born with. In the old days, this was called the crime of hiding from Heaven. Your master happened to come because it was his time, and he happened to leave because things follow along. If you are content with the time and willing to follow along, then grief and joy have no way to enter in. In the old days, this was called being freed from the bonds of God.

"Though the grease burns out of the torch, the fire passes on, and no one knows where it ends."[7]

THE GREAT AND VENERABLE TEACHER
(SECTION 6)

He who knows what it is that Heaven does, and knows what it is that man does, has reached the peak. Knowing what it is that Heaven does, he lives with Heaven. Knowing what it is that man does, he uses the knowledge of what he knows to help out the knowledge of what he doesn't know, and lives out the years that Heaven gave him without being cut off midway—this is the perfection of knowledge.

However, there is a difficulty. Knowledge must wait for something to fix on to, and that which it waits for is never certain. How, then, can I know that what I call Heaven is not really man, and what I call man is not really Heaven? There must first be a True Man[8] before there can be true knowledge.

What do I mean by a True Man? The True Man of ancient times did not rebel against want, did not grow proud in plenty, and did not plan his affairs. Being like this, he could commit an error and not regret it, could meet with success and not make a show. Being like this, he could climb the high places and not be frightened, could enter the water and not get wet, could enter the fire and not get burned. His knowledge was able to climb all the way up to the Way like this.

The True Man of ancient times slept without dreaming and woke without care; he ate without savoring and his breath came from deep inside. The True

[7]The first part of this last sentence is scarcely intelligible and there are numerous suggestions on how it should be interpreted or emended. I follow Chu Kuei-yao in reading "grease" instead of "finger." For the sake of reference, I list some of the other possible interpretations as I understand them. "When the fingers complete the work of adding firewood, the fire passes on" (Kuo Hsiang). "Though the fingers are worn out gathering firewood, the fire passes on" (Yü Yüeh). "What we can point to are the fagots that have been consumed; but the fire is transmitted elsewhere" (Legge, Fukunaga).

[8]Another term for the Taoist sage, synonymous with the Perfect Man or the Holy Man.

Man breathes with his heels; the mass of men breathe with their throats. Crushed and bound down, they gasp out their words as though they were retching. Deep in their passions and desires, they are shallow in the workings of Heaven.

The True Man of ancient times knew nothing of loving life, knew nothing of hating death. He emerged without delight; he went back in without a fuss. He came briskly, he went briskly, and that was all. He didn't forget where he began; he didn't try to find out where he would end. He received something and took pleasure in it; he forgot about it and handed it back again. This is what I call not using the mind to repel the Way, not using man to help out Heaven. This is what I call the True Man.

Since he is like this, his mind forgets;[9] his face is calm; his forehead is broad. He is chilly like autumn, balmy like spring, and his joy and anger prevail through the four seasons. He goes along with what is right for things and no one knows his limit. Therefore, when the sage calls out the troops, he may overthrow nations but he will not lose the hearts of the people. His bounty enriches ten thousand ages but he has no love for men. Therefore he who delights in bringing success to things is not a sage; he who has affections is not benevolent; he who looks for the right time is not a worthy man; he who cannot encompass both profit and loss is not a gentleman; he who thinks of conduct and fame and misleads himself is not a man of breeding; and he who destroys himself and is without truth is not a user of men. Those like Hu Pu-hsieh, Wu Kuang, Po Yi, Shu Ch'i, Chi Tzu, Hsü Yü, Chi T'o, and Shen-t'u Ti—all of them slaved in the service of other men, took joy in bringing other men joy, but could not find joy in any joy of their own.[10]

This was the True Man of old: his bearing was lofty and did not crumble; he appeared to lack but accepted nothing; he was dignified in his correctness but not insistent; he was vast in his emptiness but not ostentatious. Mild and cheerful, he seemed to be happy; reluctant, he could not help doing certain things; annoyed, he let it show in his face; relaxed, he rested in his virtue. Tolerant,[11] he seemed to be part of the world; towering alone, he could be checked by nothing; withdrawn, he seemed to prefer to cut himself off; bemused, he forgot what he was going to say.[12]

He regarded penalties as the body, rites as the wings, wisdom as what is timely, virtue as what is reasonable. Because he regarded penalties as the body, he was benign in his killing. Because he regarded rites as the wings, he got along in the world. Because he regarded wisdom as what is timely, there were things that he could not keep from doing. Because he regarded virtue as what

---

[9]Reading *wang* instead of *chih* in accordance with the suggestion of Wang Mao-hung.

[10]According to legend, these were men who either tried to reform the conduct of others or made a show of guarding their own integrity. All either were killed or committed suicide.

[11]Following the Ts'ui text, which reads *kuang*.

[12]There are many different interpretations of the words used to describe the True Man in this paragraph. I have followed those adopted by Fukunaga.

is reasonable, he was like a man with two feet who gets to the top of the hill. And yet people really believed that he worked hard to get there.[13]

Therefore his liking was one and his not liking was one. His being one was one and his not being one was one. In being one, he was acting as a companion of Heaven. In not being one, he was acting as a companion of man. When man and Heaven do not defeat each other, then he may be said to have the True Man.

Life and death are fated—constant as the succession of dark and dawn, a matter of Heaven. There are some things which man can do nothing about—all are a matter of the nature of creatures. If a man is willing to regard Heaven as a father and to love it, then how much more should he be willing to do for that which is even greater![14] If he is willing to regard the ruler as superior to himself and to die for him, then how much more should he be willing to do for the Truth!

When the springs dry up and the fish are left stranded on the ground, they spew each other with moisture and wet each other down with spit—but it would be much better if they could forget each other in the rivers and lakes. Instead of praising Yao and condemning Chieh, it would be better to forget both of them and transform yourself with the Way.

The Great Clod burdens me with form, labors me with life, eases me in old age, and rests me in death. So if I think well of my life, for the same reason I must think well of my death.[15]

You hide your boat in the ravine and your fish net[16] in the swamp and tell yourself that they will be safe. But in the middle of the night a strong man shoulders them and carries them off, and in your stupidity you don't know why it happened. You think you do right to hide little things in big ones, and yet they get away from you. But if you were to hide the world in the world, so that nothing could get away, this would be the final reality of the constancy of things.

You have had the audacity to take on human form and you are delighted. But the human form has ten thousand changes that never come to an end. Your joys, then, must be uncountable. Therefore, the sage wanders in the realm where things cannot get away from him, and all are preserved. He delights in early death; he delights in old age; he delights in the beginning;

---

[13]As pointed out by Fukunaga, this paragraph, which describes the Taoist sage as a ruler who employs penalties, rites, wisdom, and virtue, seems out of keeping with Chuang Tzu's philosophy as expressed elsewhere. Fukunaga suggests that it is an addition by a writer of the 3d or 2d centuries B.C. who was influenced by Legalist thought.

[14]Since Chuang Tzu elsewhere uses *T'ien* or Heaven as a synonym of the Way, this passage has troubled commentators. Some would emend the order of the words to read "If a man is willing to regard his father as Heaven," or would substitute *jen* for *T'ien,* that is, "If a man is willing to regard another man as his father."

[15]Or perhaps the meaning is: "So if it makes my life good, it must for the same reason make my death good."

[16]Following the interpretation of Yü Yüeh.

he delights in the end. If he can serve as a model for men, how much more so that which the ten thousand things are tied to and all changes alike wait upon!

The Way has its reality and its signs but is without action or form. You can hand it down but you cannot receive it; you can get it but you cannot see it. It is its own source, its own root. Before Heaven and earth existed it was there, firm from ancient times. It gave spirituality to the spirits and to God; it gave birth to Heaven and to earth. It exists beyond the highest point, and yet you cannot call it lofty; it exists beneath the limit of the six directions, and yet you cannot call it deep. It was born before Heaven and earth, and yet you cannot say it has been there for long; it is earlier than the earliest time, and yet you cannot call it old.

13

The Glorious Qur'an, Surah 4: "Women"*

This example of religious doctrine is from the Qur'an, the key text of Islam. The position the Qur'an occupies in Muslim life is more important than that of most religious documents in other faiths. It is considered Allah's own revelation to the prophet Muhammad and serves as the mainstay of the Muslim community. Most Muslims believe that the Qur'an cannot be translated adequately from Arabic, as any separation of the content from its original form will dilute it. This particular surah (chapter) concerns the role of women in Muslim society.

REVEALED AT AL-MADÎNAH

In the name of Allah the Beneficent, the Merciful.

1. O mankind! Be careful of your duty to your Lord Who created you from a single soul and from it created its mate and from them twain hath spread abroad a multitude of men and women. Be careful of your duty toward Allah in Whom ye claim (your rights) of one another, and toward the wombs (that bare you). Lo! Allah hath been a Watcher over you.

2. Give unto orphans their wealth. Exchange not the good for the bad (in your management thereof) nor absorb their wealth into your own wealth. Lo! that would be a great sin.

3. And if ye fear that ye will not deal fairly by the orphans, marry of the women, who seem good to you, two or three or four; and if ye fear that ye cannot do justice (to so many) then one (only) or (the captives) that your right hands possess. Thus it is more likely that ye will not do injustice.

4. And give unto the women, (whom ye marry) free gift of their marriage portions; but if they of their own accord remit unto you a part thereof, then ye are welcome to absorb it (in your wealth).

5. Give not unto the foolish (what is in) your (keeping of their) wealth, which Allah hath given you to maintain; but feed and clothe them from it, and speak kindly unto them.

6. Prove orphans till they reach the marriageable age; then, if ye find them of sound judgement, deliver over unto them their fortune; and devour it not by squandering and in haste lest they should grow up. Whoso (of the guardians) is rich, let him abstain generously (from taking of the property of

*Mohammed Marmaduke Pickthall, trans., *The Meaning of the Glorious Koran* (New York: The New American Library, 1963). Reprinted with permission of George Allen & Unwin, Ltd.

orphans); and whoso is poor let him take thereof in reason (for his guardianship). And when ye deliver up their fortune unto orphans, have (the transaction) witnessed in their presence. Allah sufficeth as a Reckoner.

7. Unto the men (of a family) belongeth a share of that which parents and near kindred leave, and unto the women a share of that which parents and near kindred leave, whether it be little or much—a legal share.

8. And when kinsfolk and orphans and the needy are present at the division (of the heritage), bestow on them therefrom and speak kindly unto them.

9. And let those fear (in their behaviour toward orphans) who if they left behind them weak offspring would be afraid for them. So let them mind their duty to Allah, and speak justly.

10. Lo! Those who devour the wealth of orphans wrongfully, they do but swallow fire into their bellies, and they will be exposed to burning flame.

11. Allah chargeth you concerning (the provision for) your children: to the male the equivalent of the portion of two females, and if there be women more than two, then theirs is two-thirds of the inheritance, and if there be one (only) then the half. And to his[1] parents a sixth of the inheritance, if he have a son; and if he have no son and his parents are his heirs, then to his mother appertaineth the third; and if he have brethren, then to his mother appertaineth the sixth, after any legacy he may have bequeathed, or debt (hath been paid). Your parents or your children: Ye know not which of them is nearer unto you in usefulness. It is an injunction from Allah. Lo! Allah is Knower, Wise.

12. And unto you belongeth a half of that which your wives leave, if they have no child; but if they have a child then unto you the fourth of that which they leave, after any legacy they may have bequeathed, or debt (they may have contracted, hath been paid). And unto them belongeth the fourth of that which ye leave if ye have no child, but if ye have a child then the eighth of that which ye leave, after any legacy ye may have bequeathed, or debt (ye may have contracted, hath been paid). And if a man or a woman have a distant heir (having left neither parent nor child), and he (or she) have a brother or a sister (only on the mother's side) then to each of them twain (the brother and the sister) the sixth, and if they be more than two, then they shall be sharers in the third, after any legacy that may have been bequeathed or debt (contracted) not injuring (the heirs by willing away more than a third of the heritage) hath been paid. A commandment from Allah. Allah is Knower, Indulgent.

13. These are the limits (imposed by) Allah. Whoso obeyeth Allah and His messenger, He will make him enter Gardens underneath which rivers flow, where such will dwell for ever. That will be the great success.

14. And whoso disobeyeth Allah and His messenger and transgresseth His limits, He will make him enter Fire, where such will dwell for ever; his will be a shameful doom.

---

[1] The deceased.

15. As for those of your women who are guilty of lewdness, call to witness four of you against them. And if they testify (to the truth of the allegation) then confine them to the houses until death take them or (until) Allah appoint for them a way (through new legislation).[2]

16. And as for the two of you who are guilty thereof, punish them both. And if they repent and improve, then let them be. Lo! Allah is Relenting, Merciful.

17. Forgiveness is only incumbent on Allah toward those who do evil in ignorance (and) then turn quickly (in repentance) to Allah. These are they toward whom Allah relenteth. Allah is ever Knower, Wise.

18. The forgiveness is not for those who do ill deeds until, when death attendeth upon one of them, he saith: Lo! I repent now; nor yet for those who die while they are disbelievers. For such We have prepared a painful doom.

19. O ye who believe! It is not lawful for you forcibly to inherit the women (of your deceased kinsmen), nor (that) ye should put constraint upon them that ye may take away a part of that which ye have given them, unless they be guilty of flagrant lewdness. But consort with them in kindness, for if ye hate them it may happen that ye hate a thing wherein Allah hath placed much good.

20. And if ye wish to exchange one wife for another and ye have given unto one of them a sum of money (however great), take nothing from it. Would ye take it by the way of calumny and open wrong?

21. How can ye take it (back) after one of you hath gone in unto the other, and they have taken a strong pledge from you?

22. And marry not those women whom your fathers married, except what hath already happened (of that nature) in the past. Lo! it was ever lewdness and abomination, and an evil way.

23. Forbidden unto you are your mothers, and your daughters, and your sisters, and your father's sisters, and your mother's sisters, and your brother's daughters and your sister's daughters, and your foster-mothers, and your foster-sisters, and your mothers-in-law, and your step-daughters who are under your protection (born) of your women unto whom ye have gone in—but if ye have not gone in unto them, then it is no sin for you (to marry their daughters)—and the wives of your sons who (spring) from your own loins. And (it is forbidden unto you) that ye should have two sisters together, except what hath already happened (of that nature) in the past. Lo! Allah is ever Forgiving, Merciful.

24. And all married women (are forbidden unto you, save those (captives) whom your right hands possess. It is a decree of Allah for you. Lawful unto you are all beyond those mentioned, so that ye seek them with your wealth in honest wedlock, not debauchery. And those of whom ye seek content (by marrying them), give unto them their portions as a duty. And there is no sin for

[2] See XXIV, 2–10.

you in what ye do by mutual agreement after the duty (hath been done). Lo! Allah is ever Knower, Wise.

25. And whoso is not able to afford to marry free, believing women, let them marry from the believing maids whom your right hands possess. Allah knoweth best (concerning) your faith. Ye (proceed) one from another;[3] so wed them by permission of their folk, and give unto them their portions in kindness, they being honest, not debauched nor of loose conduct. And if when they are honourably married they commit lewdness they shall incur the half of the punishment (prescribed) for free women (in that case). This is for him among you who feareth to commit sin. But to have patience would be better for you. Allah is Forgiving, Merciful.

26. Allah would explain to you and guide you by the examples of those who were before you, and would turn to you in mercy. Allah is Knower, Wise.

27. And Allah would turn to you in mercy; but those who follow vain desires would have you go tremendously astray.

28. Allah would make the burden light for you, for man was created weak.

29. O ye who believe! Squander not your wealth among yourselves in vanity, except it be a trade by mutual consent, and kill not one another. Lo! Allah is ever Merciful unto you.

30. Whoso doeth that through aggression and injustice, We shall cast him into Fire, and that is ever easy for Allah.

31. If ye avoid the great (things) which ye are forbidden, We will remit from you your evil deeds and make you enter at a noble gate.

32. And covet not the thing in which Allah hath made some of you excel others. Unto men a fortune from that which they have earned, and unto women a fortune from that which they have earned. (Envy not one another) but ask Allah of His bounty. Lo! Allah is ever Knower of all things.

33. And unto each We have appointed heirs of that which parents and near kindred leave; and as for those with whom your right hands have made a covenant, give them their due. Lo! Allah is ever Witness over all things.

34. Men are in charge of women, because Allah hath made the one of them to excel the other, and because they spend of their property (for the support of women). So good women are the obedient, guarding in secret that which Allah hath guarded. As for those from whom ye fear rebellion, admonish them and banish them to beds apart, and scourge them. Then if they obey you, seek not a way against them. Lo! Allah is ever High Exalted, Great.

35. And if ye fear a breach between them twain (the man and wife), appoint an arbiter from his folk and an arbiter from her folk. If they desire amendment Allah will make them of one mind. Lo! Allah is ever Knower, Aware.

---

[3] This expression, which recurs in the Koran, is a reminder to men that women are of the same human status as themselves.

36. And serve Allah. Ascribe no thing as partner unto Him. (Show) kindness unto parents, and unto near kindred, and orphans, and the needy, and unto the neighbour who is of kin (unto you) and the neighbour who is not of kin, and the fellow-traveller and the wayfarer and (the slaves) whom your right hands possess. Lo! Allah loveth not such as are proud and boastful,

37. Who hoard their wealth and enjoin avarice on others, and hide that which Allah hath bestowed upon them of His bounty. For disbelievers We prepare a shameful doom;

38. And (also) those who spend their wealth in order to be seen of men, and believe not in Allah nor the Last Day. Whoso taketh Satan for a comrade, a bad comrade hath he.

39. What have they (to fear) if they believe in Allah and the Last Day and spend (aright) of that which Allah hath bestowed upon them, when Allah is ever Aware of them (and all they do)?

40. Lo! Allah wrongeth not even of the weight of an ant; and if there is a good deed, he will double it and will give (the doer) from His presence an immense reward.

41. But how (will it be with them) when We bring of every people a witness, and We bring thee (O Muhammad) a witness against these?

42. On that day those who disbelieved and disobeyed the messenger will wish that they were level with the ground, and they can hide no fact from Allah.

43. O ye who believe! Draw not near unto prayer when ye are drunken, till ye know that which ye utter, nor when ye are polluted, save when journeying upon the road, till ye have bathed. And if ye be ill, or on a journey, or one of you cometh from the closet, or ye have touched women, and ye find not water, then go to high clean soil and rub your faces and your hands (therewith). Lo! Allah is Benign, Forgiving.

44. Seest thou not those unto whom a portion of the Scripture hath been given, how they purchase error, and seek to make you (Muslims) err from the right way?

45. Allah knoweth best (who are) your enemies. Allah is sufficient as a Friend, and Allah is sufficient as a Helper.

46. Some of those who are Jews change words from their context and say: "We hear and disobey; hear thou as one who heareth not" and "Listen to us!"[4] distorting with their tongues and slandering religion. If they had said: "We hear and we obey; hear thou, and look at us" it had been better for them, and more upright. But Allah hath cursed them for their disbelief, so they believe not, save a few.

---

[4] Devices of some of the Jews of Al-Madînah to annoy the Muslims by distorting words of Scripture, *Râ'inâ* (meaning "listen to us"), by which the Muslims used to call the Prophet's notice, they turned by slight mispronunciation into a Hebrew word of insult (cf. S. II, v. 104, footnote).

47. O ye unto whom the Scripture hath been given! Believe in what We have revealed confirming that which ye possess, before We destroy countenances so as to confound them, or curse them as We cursed the Sabbath-breakers (of old time). The commandment of Allah is always executed.

48. Lo! Allah forgiveth not that a partner should be ascribed unto Him. He forgiveth (all) save that to whom He will. Whoso ascribeth partners to Allah, he hath indeed invented a tremendous sin.

49. Hast thou not seen those who praise themselves for purity? Nay, Allah purifieth whom He will, and they will not be wronged even the hair upon a date-stone.

50. See, how they invent lies about Allah! That of itself is flagrant sin.

51. Hast thou not seen those unto whom a portion of the Scripture hath been given, how they believe in idols and false deities, and how they say of those (idolaters) who disbelieve: "These are more rightly guided than those who believe?"

52. Those are they whom Allah hath cursed, and he whom Allah hath cursed, thou (O Muhammad) wilt find for him no helper.

53. Or have they even a share in the Sovereignty? Then in that case, they would not give mankind even the speck on a date-stone.

54. Or are they jealous of mankind because of that which Allah of His bounty hath bestowed upon them? For We bestowed upon the house of Abraham (of old) the Scripture and Wisdom, and We bestowed on them a mighty kingdom.

55. And of them were (some) who believed therein and of them were (some) who disbelieved therein. Hell is sufficient for (their) burning.

56. Lo! Those who disbelieve Our revelations, We shall expose them to the Fire. As often as their skins are consumed We shall exchange them for fresh skins that they may taste the torment. Lo! Allah is ever Mighty, Wise.

57. And as for those who believe and do good works, We shall make them enter Gardens underneath which rivers flow—to dwell therein for ever; there for them are pure companions—and We shall make them enter plenteous shade.

58. Lo! Allah commandeth you that ye restore deposits to their owners, and, if ye judge between mankind, that ye judge justly. Lo! comely is this which Allah admonisheth you. Lo! Allah is ever Hearer, Seer.

59. O ye who believe! Obey Allah, and obey the messenger and those of you who are in authority; and if ye have a dispute concerning any matter, refer it to Allah and the messenger if ye are (in truth) believers in Allah and the Last Day. That is better and more seemly in the end.

60. Hast thou not seen those who pretend that they believe in that which is revealed unto thee and that which was revealed before thee, how they would go for judgement (in their disputes) to false deities when they have been ordered to abjure them? Satan would mislead them far astray.

61. And when it is said unto them: Come unto that which Allah hath revealed and unto the messenger, thou seest the hypocrites turn from thee

with aversion.

62. How would it be if a misfortune smote them because of that which their own hands have sent before (them)? Then would they come unto thee, swearing by Allah that they were seeking naught but harmony and kindness.

63. Those are they, the secrets of whose hearts Allah knoweth. So oppose them and admonish them, and address them in plain terms about their souls.

64. We sent no messenger save that he should be obeyed by Allah's leave. And if, when they had wronged themselves, they had but come unto thee and asked forgiveness of Allah, and asked forgiveness of the messenger, they would have found Allah Forgiving, Merciful.

65. But nay, by thy Lord, they will not believe (in truth) until they make thee judge of what is in dispute between them and find within themselves no dislike of that which thou decidest, and submit with full submission.

66. And if We had decreed for them: Lay down your lives or go forth from your dwellings, but few of them would have done it; though if they did what they are exhorted to do it would be better for them, and more strengthening;

67. And then We should bestow upon them from Our presence an immense reward,

68. And should guide them unto a straight path.

69. Whoso obeyeth Allah and the messenger, they are with those unto whom Allah hath shown favour, of the Prophets and the saints and the martyrs and the righteous. The best of company are they!

70. Such is the bounty of Allah, and Allah sufficeth as Knower.

71. O ye who believe! Take your precautions, then advance the proven ones, or advance all together.

72. Lo! among you there is he who loitereth; and if disaster overtook you, he would say: Allah hath been gracious unto me since I was not present with them.

73. And if a bounty from Allah befell you, he would surely cry, as if there had been no love between you and him: Oh, would that I had been with them, then should I have achieved a great success!

74. Let those fight in the way of Allah who sell the life of this world for the other. Whoso fighteth in the way of Allah, be he slain or be he victorious, on him We shall bestow a vast reward.

75. How should ye not fight for the cause of Allah and of the feeble among men and of the women and the children who are crying: Our Lord! Bring us forth from out this town[5] of which the people are oppressors! Oh, give us from Thy presence some protecting friend! Oh, give us from Thy presence some defender!

76. Those who believe do battle for the cause of Allah; and those who disbelieve do battle for the cause of idols. So fight the minions of the devil. Lo! the devil's strategy is ever weak,

[5] Mecca.

77. Hast thou not seen those unto whom it was said: Withhold your hands, establish worship and pay the poor-due, but when fighting was prescribed for them behold! a party of them fear mankind even as their fear of Allah or with greater fear, and say: Our Lord! Why hast thou ordained fighting for us? If only Thou wouldst give us respite yet a while! Say (unto them, O Muhammad): The comfort of this world is scant; the Hereafter will be better for him who wardeth off (evil); and ye will not be wronged the down upon a date-stone.

78. Wheresoever ye may be, death will overtake you, even though ye were in lofty towers. Yet if a happy thing befalleth them they say: This is from Allah; and if an evil thing befalleth them they say: This is of thy doing (O Muhammad). Say (unto them): All is from Allah. What is amiss with these people that they come not nigh to understand a happening?[6]

79. Whatever of good befalleth thee (O man) it is from Allah, and whatever of ill befalleth thee it is from thyself. We have sent thee (Muhammad) as a messenger unto mankind and Allah is sufficient as witness.

80. Whoso obeyeth the messenger obeyeth Allah, and whoso turneth away: We have not sent thee as a warder over them.

81. And they say: (It is) obedience; but when they have gone forth from thee a party of them spend the night in planning other than what thou sayest. Allah recordeth what they plan by night. So oppose them and put thy trust in Allah. Allah is sufficient as Trustee.

82. Will they not then ponder on the Qur'ân? If it had been from other than Allah they would have found therein much incongruity.

83. And if any tidings, whether of safety or fear, come unto them, they noise it abroad, whereas if they had referred it to the messenger and such of them as are in authority, those among them who are able to think out the matter would have known it. If it had not been for the grace of Allah and His mercy ye would have followed Satan, save a few (of you).

84. So fight (O Muhammad) in the way of Allah—Thou art not taxed (with the responsibility for anyone) except for thyself—and urge on the believers. Peradventure Allah will restrain the might of those who disbelieve. Allah is stronger in might and stronger in inflicting punishment.

85. Whoso interveneth in a good cause will have the reward thereof, and whoso interveneth in an evil cause will bear the consequence thereof. Allah overseeth all things.

86. When ye are greeted with a greeting, greet ye with a better than it or return it. Lo! Allah taketh count of all things.

87. Allah! There is no God save Him. He gathereth you all unto a Day of Resurrection whereof there is no doubt. Who is more true in statement than Allah?

---

[6] The reference is to the reverse which the Muslims suffered at Mt. Uhud which was caused by their own disobedience to the Prophet's orders.

88. What aileth you that ye are become two parties regarding the hypocrites,[7] when Allah cast them back (to disbelief) because of what they earned? Seek ye to guide him whom Allah hath sent astray? He whom Allah sendeth astray, for him thou (O Muhammad) canst not find a road.

89. They long that ye should disbelieve even as they disbelieve, that ye may be upon a level (with them). So choose not friends from them till they forsake their homes in the way of Allah; if they turn back (to enmity) then take them and kill them wherever ye find them, and choose no friend nor helper from among them,

90. Except those who seek refuge with a people between whom and you there is a covenant, or (those who) come unto you because their hearts forbid them to make war on you or make war on their own folk. Had Allah willed He could have given them power over you so that assuredly they would have fought you. So, if they hold aloof from you and wage not war against you and offer you peace, Allah alloweth you no way against them.

91. Ye will find others who desire that they should have security from you, and security from their own folk. So often as they are returned to hostility they are plunged therein. If they keep not aloof from you nor offer you peace nor hold their hands, then take them and kill them wherever ye find them. Against such We have given you a clear warrant.

92. It is not for a believer to kill a believer unless (it be) by mistake. He who hath killed a believer by mistake must set free a believing slave, and pay the blood-money to the family of the slain, unless they remit it as a charity. If he (the victim) be of a people hostile unto you, and he is a believer, then (the penance is) to set free a believing slave. And if he cometh of a folk between whom and you there is a covenant, then the blood-money must be paid unto his folk and (also) a believing slave must be set free. And whoso hath not the wherewithal must fast two consecutive months. A penance from Allah. Allah is Knower, Wise.

93. Whoso slayeth a believer of set purpose, his reward is Hell for ever. Allah is wroth against him and He hath cursed him and prepared for him an awful doom.

94. O ye who believe! When ye go forth (to fight) in the way of Allah, be careful to discriminate, and say not unto one who offereth you peace: "Thou art not a believer," seeking the chance profits of this life (so that ye may despoil him). With Allah are plenteous spoils. Even thus (as he now is) were ye before; but Allah hath since then been gracious unto you. Therefore take care to discriminate. Allah is ever Informed of what ye do.

95. Those of the believers who sit still, other than those who have a (disabling) hurt, are not on an equality with those who strive in the way of Allah

---

[7] According to Tradition, the reference here is not to the lukewarm section of the Muslims of Al-Madinah, but to a particular group of alleged converts from among the Arabs, who afterwards relapsed into idolatry, and concerning whom there were two opinions among the Muslims.

with their wealth and lives. Allah hath conferred on those who strive with their wealth and lives a rank above the sedentary. Unto each Allah hath promised good, but He hath bestowed on those who strive a great reward above the sedentary;

96. Degrees of rank from Him, and forgiveness and mercy. Allah is ever Forgiving, Merciful.

97. Lo! as for those whom the angels take (in death) while they wrong themselves, (the angels) will ask: In what were ye engaged? They will say: We were oppressed in the land. (The angels) will say: Was not Allah's earth spacious that ye could have migrated therein? As for such, their habitation will be hell, an evil jouney's end;

98. Except the feeble among men, and the women, and the children, who are unable to devise a plan and are not shown a way.

99. As for such, it may be that Allah will pardon them. Allah is ever Clement, Forgiving.

100. Whoso migrateth for the cause of Allah will find much refuge and abundance in the earth, and whoso forsaketh his home, a fugitive unto Allah and His messenger, and death overtaketh him, his reward is then incumbent on Allah. Allah is ever Forgiving, Merciful.

101. And when ye go forth in the land, it is no sin for you to curtail (your) worship if ye fear that those who disbelieve may attack you. In truth the disbelievers are an open enemy to you.

102. And when thou (O Muhammad) art among them and arrangest (their) worship for them, let only a party of them stand with thee (to worship) and let them take their arms. Then when they have performed their prostrations let them fall to the rear and let another party come that hath not worshipped and let them worship with thee, and let them take their precaution and their arms. Those who disbelieve long for you to neglect your arms and your baggage that they may attack you once for all. It is no sin for you to lay aside your arms, if rain impedeth you or ye are sick. But take your precaution. Lo! Allah prepareth for the disbelievers shameful punishment.

103. When ye have performed the act of worship, remember Allah, standing, sitting and reclining. And when ye are in safety, observe proper worship. Worship at fixed hours hath been enjoined on the believers.

104. Relent not in pursuit of the enemy. If ye are suffering, lo! they suffer even as ye suffer and ye hope from Allah that for which they cannot hope. Allah is ever Knower, Wise.

105. Lo! We reveal unto thee the Scripture with the truth, that thou mayst judge between mankind by that which Allah showeth thee. And be not thou a pleader for the treacherous;

106. And seek forgiveness of Allah. Lo! Allah is ever Forgiving, Merciful.

107. And plead not on behalf of (people) who deceive themselves. Lo! Allah loveth not one who is treacherous and sinful.

108. They seek to hide from men and seek not to hide from Allah. He

is with them when by night they hold discourse displeasing unto Him. Allah ever surroundeth what they do.

109. Ho! ye are they who pleaded for them in the life of the world. But who will plead with Allah for them on the Day of Resurrection, or who will then be their defender?

110. Yet whoso doeth evil or wrongeth his own soul, then seeketh pardon of Allah, will find Allah Forgiving, Merciful.

111. Whoso committeth sin committeth it only against himself. Allah is ever Knower, Wise.

112. And whoso committeth a delinquency or crime, then throweth (the blame) thereof upon the innocent, hath burdened himself with falsehood and a flagrant crime.

113. But for the grace of Allah upon thee (Muhammad), and His mercy, a party of them had resolved to mislead thee, but they will mislead only themselves and they will hurt thee not at all. Allah revealeth unto thee the Scripture and wisdom, and teacheth thee that which thou knewest not. The grace of Allah toward thee hath been infinite.

114. There is no good in much of their secret conferences save (in) him who enjoineth almsgiving and kindness and peace-making among the people. Whoso doeth that, seeking the good pleasure of Allah, We shall bestow on him a vast reward.

115. And whoso opposeth the messenger after the guidance (of Allah) hath been manifested unto him, and followeth other than the believer's way, We appoint for him that unto which he himself hath turned, and expose him unto hell—a hapless journey's end!

116. Lo! Allah pardoneth not that partners should be ascribed unto him. He pardoneth all save that to whom He will. Whoso ascribeth partners unto Allah hath wandered far astray.

117. They invoke in His stead only females;[8] they pray to none else than Satan, a rebel

118. Whom Allah cursed, and he said: Surely I will take of Thy bondmen an appointed portion,

119. And surely I will lead them astray, and surely I will arouse desires in them, and surely I will command them and they will cut the cattle's ears, and surely I will command them and they will change Allah's creation. Whoso chooseth Satan for a patron instead of Allah is verily a loser and his loss is manifest.

120. He promiseth them and stirreth up desires in them, and Satan promiseth them only to beguile.

121. For such, their habitation will be hell, and they will find no refuge therefrom.

---

[8] The idols which the pagan Arabs worshipped were all female.

122. But as for those who believe and do good works We shall bring them into gardens underneath which rivers flow, wherein they will abide for ever. It is a promise from Allah in truth; and who can be more truthful than Allah in utterance?

123. It will not be in accordance with your desires, nor the desires of the People of the Scripture.[9] He who doeth wrong will have the recompense thereof, and will not find against Allah any protecting friend or helper.

124. And whoso doeth good works, whether of male or female, and he (or she) is a believer, such will enter paradise and they will not be wronged the dint in a date-stone.

125. Who is better in religion than he who surrendereth his purpose to Allah while doing good (to men) and followeth the tradition of Abraham, the upright? Allah (Himself) chose Abraham for friend.

126. Unto Allah belongeth whatsoever is in the heavens and whatsoever is in the earth. Allah ever surroundeth all things.

127. They consult thee concerning women. Say: Allah giveth you decree concerning them, and the Scripture which hath been recited unto you (giveth decree), concerning female orphans unto whom ye give not that which is ordained for them though ye desire to marry them, and (concerning) the weak among children, and that ye should deal justly with orphans. Whatever good ye do, lo! Allah is ever Aware of it.

128. If a woman feareth ill-treatment from her husband, or desertion, it is no sin for them twain if they make terms of peace between themselves. Peace is better. But greed hath been made present in the minds (of men). If ye do good and keep from evil, lo! Allah is ever Informed of what ye do.

129. Ye will not be able to deal equally between (your) wives, however much ye wish (to do so). But turn not altogether away (from one), leaving her as in suspense. If ye do good and keep from evil, lo! Allah is ever Forgiving, Merciful.

130. But if they separate, Allah will compensate each out of His abundance. Allah is ever All-Embracing, All-Knowing.

131. Unto Allah belongeth whatsoever is in the heavens and whatsoever is in the earth. And We charged those who received the Scripture before you, and (We charge) you, that ye keep your duty toward Allah. And if ye disbelieve, lo! unto Allah belongeth whatsoever is in the heavens and whatsoever is in the earth, and Allah is ever Absolute, Owner of Praise.

132. Unto Allah belongeth whatsoever is in the heavens and whatsoever is in the earth. And Allah is sufficient as Defender.

133. If He will, He can remove you, O people, and produce others (in your stead). Allah is Able to do that.

134. Whoso desireth the reward of the world, (let him know that) with Allah is the reward of the world and the Hereafter. Allah is ever Hearer, Seer.

---

[9] Jews and Christians.

135. O ye who believe! Be ye staunch in justice, witnesses for Allah, even though it be against yourselves or (your) parents or (your) kindred, whether (the case be of) a rich man or a poor man, for Allah is nearer unto both (than ye are). So follow not passion lest ye lapse (from truth) and if ye lapse or fall away, then lo! Allah is ever Informed of what ye do.

136. O ye who believe! Believe in Allah and His messenger and the Scripture which He hath revealed unto His messenger, and the Scripture which He revealed aforetime. Whoso disbelieveth in Allah and His angels and His scriptures and His messengers and the Last Day, he verily hath wandered far astray.

137. Lo! those who believe, then disbelieve and then (again) believe, then disbelieve, and then increase in disbelief, Allah will never pardon them, nor will He guide them unto a way.

138. Bear unto the hypocrites the tidings that for them there is a painful doom;

139. Those who choose disbelievers for their friends instead of believers! Do they look for power at their hands? Lo! all power appertaineth to Allah.

140. He hath already revealed unto you in the Scripture that, when ye hear the revelations of Allah rejected and derided, (ye) sit not with them (who disbelieve and mock) until they engage in some other conversation. Lo! in that case (if ye stayed) ye would be like unto them. Lo! Allah will gather hypocrites and disbelievers, all together, into hell;

141. Those who wait upon occasion in regard to you and, if a victory cometh unto you from Allah, say: Are we not with you? and if the disbelievers meet with a success say: Had we not the mastery of you, and did we not protect you from the believers?—Allah will judge between you at the Day of Resurrection, and Allah will not give the disbelievers any way (of success) against the believers.

142. Lo! the hypocrites seek to beguile Allah, but it is Allah who beguileth them. When they stand up to worship they perform it languidly and to be seen of men, and are mindful of Allah but little;

143. Swaying between this (and that), (belonging) neither to these nor to those. He whom Allah causeth to go astray, thou (O Muhammad) wilt not find a way for him:

144. O ye who believe! Choose not disbelievers for (your) friends in place of believers. Would ye give Allah a clear warrant against you?

145. Lo! the hypocrites (will be) in the lowest deep of the fire, and thou wilt find no helper for them;

146. Save those who repent and amend and hold fast to Allah and make their religion pure for Allah (only). Those are with the believers. And Allah will bestow on the believers an immense reward.

147. What concern hath Allah for your punishment if ye are thankful (for His mercies) and believe (in Him)? Allah was ever Responsive, Aware.

148. Allah loveth not the utterance of harsh speech save by one who hath been wronged. Allah is ever Hearer, Knower.

149. If ye do good openly or keep it secret, or forgive evil, lo! Allah is Forgiving, Powerful.

150. Lo! those who disbelieve in Allah and His messengers, and seek to make distinction between Allah and His messengers, and say: We believe in some and disbelieve in others, and seek to choose a way in between;

151. Such are disbelievers in truth; and for disbelievers We prepare a shameful doom.

152. But those who believe in Allah and His messengers and make no distinction between any of them, unto them Allah will give their wages; and Allah was ever Forgiving, Merciful.

153. The People of the Scripture ask of thee that thou shouldst cause an (actual) Book to descend upon them from heaven. They asked a greater thing of Moses aforetime, for they said: Show us Allah plainly. The storm of lightning seized them for their wickedness. Then (even after that) they chose the calf (for worship) after clear proofs (of Allah's Sovereignty) had come unto them. And We forgave them that! And We bestowed on Moses evident authority.

154. And We caused the Mount to tower above them at (the taking of) their covenant: and We bade them: Enter the gate, prostrate! and we bade them: Transgress not the Sabbath! and We took from them a firm covenant.

155. Then because of their breaking of their covenant, and their disbelieving in the revelations of Allah, and their slaying of the Prophets wrongfully, and their saying: Our hearts are hardened—Nay, but Allah hath set a seal upon them for their disbelief, so that they believe not save a few—

156. And because of their disbelief and of their speaking against Mary a tremendous calumny;

157. And because of their saying: We slew the Messiah Jesus son of Mary, Allah's messenger—They slew him not nor crucified, but it appeared so unto them; and lo! those who disagree concerning it are in doubt thereof; they have no knowledge thereof save pursuit of a conjecture; they slew him not for certain,

158. But Allah took him up unto Himself. Allah was ever Mighty, Wise.

159. There is not one of the People of the Scripture but will believe in him before his death, and on the Day of Resurrection he will be a witness against them—

160. Because of the wrongdoing of the Jews We forbade them good things which were (before) made lawful unto them, and because of their much hindering from Allah's way,

161. And of their taking usury when they were forbidden it, and of their devouring people's wealth by false pretences. We have prepared for those of them who disbelieve a painful doom.

162. But those of them who are firm in knowledge and the believers believe in that which is revealed unto thee, and that which was revealed before

thee, especially the diligent in prayer and those who pay the poor-due, the believers in Allah and the Last Day. Upon these We shall bestow immense reward.

163. Lo! We inspire thee as We inspired Noah and the prophets after him, as We inspired Abraham and Ishmael and Isaac and Jacob and the tribes, and Jesus and Job and Jonah and Aaron and Solomon, and as we imparted unto David the Psalms;

164. And messengers We have mentioned unto thee before and messengers We have not mentioned unto thee; and Allah spake directly unto Moses;

165. Messengers of good cheer and of warning, in order that mankind might have no argument against Allah after the messengers. Allah was ever Mighty, Wise.

166. But Allah (Himself) testifieth concerning that which He hath revealed unto thee; in His knowledge hath He revealed it; and the Angels also testify. And Allah is sufficient witness.

167. Lo! those who disbelieve and hinder (others) from the way of Allah, they verily have wandered far astray.

168. Lo! those who disbelieve and deal in wrong, Allah will never forgive them, neither will He guide them unto a road,

169. Except the road of hell, wherein they will abide for ever. And that is ever easy for Allah.

170. O mankind! The messenger hath come unto you with the truth from your Lord. Therefor believe; (it is) better for you. But if ye disbelieve, still, lo! unto Allah belongeth whatsoever is in the heavens and the earth. Allah is ever Knower, Wise.

171. O People of the Scripture! Do not exaggerate in your religion nor utter aught concerning Allah save the truth. The Messiah, Jesus son of Mary, was only a messenger of Allah, and His word which He conveyed unto Mary, and a spirit from Him. So believe in Allah and His messengers, and say not "Three"—Cease! (it is) better for you!—Allah is only One God. Far is it removed from His transcendent majesty that he should have a son. His is all that is in the heavens and all that is in the earth. And Allah is sufficient as Defender.

172. The Messiah will never scorn to be a slave unto Allah, nor will the favoured angels. Whoso scorneth His service and is proud, all such will He assemble unto Him;

173. Then, as for those who believed and did good works, unto them will He pay their wages in full, adding unto them of His bounty; and as for those who were scornful and proud, them will He punish with a painful doom.

174. And they will not find for them, against Allah, any protecting friend or helper.

175. O mankind! Now hath a proof from your Lord come unto you, and we have sent down unto you a clear light;

176. As for those who believe in Allah, and hold fast unto Him, them He will cause to enter into His mercy and grace, and will guide them unto Him by a straight road.

177. They ask thee for a pronouncement. Say: Allah hath pronounced for you concerning distant kindred. If a man die childless and he have a sister, hers is half the heritage, and he would have inherited from her had she died childless. And if there be two sisters, then theirs are two-thirds of the heritage, and if they be brethren, men and women, unto the male is the equivalent of the share of two females. Allah expoundeth unto you, so that ye err not. Allah is Knower of all things.

14

"The Doctrine of God" from *Everyman's Talmud**

This selection is from the Jewish Talmud. The Talmud originated about 1500 years ago when commentaries by leading rabbis on biblical books were arranged into a collection. Since these commentaries were collected they have become the main focus of traditional Jewish learning. This selection is from the Talmudic examination of the view of God.

I. EXISTENCE

As in the Bible, so throughout the literature of the Rabbis, the existence of God is regarded as an axiomatic truth. No proofs are offered to convince the Jew that there must be a God. To avoid the profane use of the sacred Name, in accordance with the Third Commandment, various designations were devised, common among them being 'the Creator' and 'He Who spake and the world came into being.' They indicate the view that the existence of God follows inevitably from the existence of the Universe.

This thought is well expressed in the Midrashic account of the first interview which took place between Pharaoh and Moses and Aaron. When the Egyptian king asked them, 'Who is your God that I should hearken unto His voice?' they replied, 'The Universe is filled with the might and power of our God. He existed ere the world was created, and He will continue in being when the world comes to a final end. He formed you and infused into you the breath of life. He stretched forth the heavens and laid the foundations of the earth. His voice hews out flames of fire, rends mountains asunder and shatters rocks. His bow is fire and His arrows flames. His spear is a torch, His shield the clouds and His sword the lightning. He fashioned mountains and hills and covered them with grass. He makes the rains and dew to descend, and causes the herbage to sprout. He also forms the embryo in the mother's womb and enables it to issue forth as a living being' (Exod. R. v. 14).

That Nature reveals God is illustrated by the tradition that Abraham discovered His existence by reasoning back to a First Cause. Two different versions of his discovery are given. According to one story, when he revolted against idolatry, his father took him before King Nimrod, who demanded that since he would not worship images he should worship fire. The following

* From *Everyman's Talmud*, by A. Cohen. Used by permission of the publisher, J. M. Dent.

argument ensued. 'Abraham replied to him: "We should rather worship water which extinguishes fire." Nimrod said to him: "Then worship water." Abraham retorted: "If so, we should worship the cloud which carries water!" Nimrod said: "Then worship the cloud." Abraham retorted: "If so, we should worship the wind which disperses the cloud!" Nimrod said: "Then worship the wind." Abraham retorted: "Rather should we worship the human being who carries the wind!"'[1] (Gen. R. XXXVIII. 13). Such a line of reasoning leads to the hypothesis of an ultimate Creator.

The other legend tells that Abraham had to be hidden away soon after his birth because astrologers had warned King Nimrod that a child was about to be born who would overthrow his kingdom, and advised that he be killed while still a babe. The child lived with a nurse in a cave for three years. The story continues: 'When he left the cave, his heart kept reflecting upon the creation of the Universe, and he determined to worship all the luminaries until he discovered which of them was God. He saw the moon whose light illumined the darkness of night from one end of the world to the other and noticed the vast retinue of stars. "This is God," he exclaimed, and worshipped it throughout the night. In the morning when he beheld the dawn of the sun before which the moon darkened and its power waned, he exclaimed: "The light of the moon must be derived from the light of the sun, and the Universe only exists through the sun's rays." So he worshipped the sun throughout the day. In the evening, the sun sank below the horizon, its power waned, and the moon reappeared with the stars and the planets. He thereupon exclaimed: "Surely these all have a Master and God!"'[2]

Another Rabbinic passage teaches that it is possible to arrive at a realization of God out of one's spiritual consciousness, and by this method Abraham and others discovered His existence. 'Abraham perceived the Holy One, blessed be He, by himself and nobody taught him this knowledge. He is one of four human beings who accomplished this. Job perceived the Holy One, blessed be He, by himself, as it is said "I have treasured up the words of His mouth from my bosom"[3] (Job xxiii. 12). Hezekiah, King of Judah, likewise perceived the Holy One, blessed be He, by himself, since it is written concerning him: "Butter and honey shall he eat, when he knoweth to refuse the evil and choose the good" (Is. vii. 15). The King Messiah also perceived the Holy One, blessed be He, by himself' (Num. R. XIV. 2).

Not only is God the creator of the Universe, but the cosmic order is ever dependent upon His will. Creation is not an act in the past which continues automatically. The processes of Nature represent the unceasing functioning of the

[1] In the breath of the body.

[2] This passage is quoted from the *Midrash Hagadol*, ed. Schechter, l. 189 f. This is a late collection of Midrashic material; but the story, although not found in the Talmud or standard Midrashim, occurs in the *Apocalypse of Abraham*, which belongs to the middle of the first century of the present era, and so falls within the Talmudic period.

[3] The Midrash reads *mecheki* (from my bosom) instead of *mechukki*, as in the received text, which is translated 'more than my necessary food.' It is noteworthy that the Septuagint and Vulgate also read the text in the sense of 'in my bosom.'

divine creative power.[4] 'Every hour He makes provision for all who come into the world according to their need. In His Grace He satisfies all creatures, not the good and righteous alone, but also the wicked and idolaters' (Mech. to xviii. 12; 59a). 'During a third of the day He is occupied with sustaining the whole world from the mightiest to the most insignificant of living beings' (A.Z. 3*b*).

In their intercourse with Gentiles, the Rabbis were sometimes challenged to demonstrate that the God they worshipped, an invisible Deity, was actual. It is recorded that the Emperor Hadrian said to R. Joshua b. Chananya: 'I desire to behold your God.' 'That is an impossibility,' he replied. The emperor persisted; so the Rabbi bade him face the sun, it being the time of the summer solstice, and said: 'Gaze at that.' 'I cannot,' he answered. Whereupon the Rabbi exclaimed: 'You admit that you are unable to look at the sun, which is only one of the attendants upon the Holy One, blessed be He; how much more beyond your power must it be to look at God Himself!' (Chul. 59*b et seq.*).

Whether atheism, in the sense of the dogmatic denial of God's existence, was accepted by anybody in Biblical and Rabbinic times is doubtful; but both in Bible and Talmud the concern was with the practical atheist who conducted his life as though he would never be held to account for his deeds. In Biblical literature the statement 'There is no God' is made by the Nabal, i.e. the morally corrupt person who, while acknowledging the existence of a Creator, refused to believe that He was at all interested in the actions of His creatures.[5] His counterpart in the Talmud is the *Apikoros*, or Epicurean, who likewise 'denies the fundamental principle of religion' (B.B. 16*b*) by his abominable conduct. The Rabbis defined the atheist as one who affirmed 'There is no judgment and no Judge' (Gen. R. XXVI. 6) in the Universe, irrespective of his disbelief in the existence of God.[6]

On one occasion, it is related, R. Reuben stayed in Tiberias, and a philosopher asked him: 'Who is the most hateful person in the world?' 'The person who denies his Creator,' was the reply. 'How is that?' the philosopher asked; and the Rabbi answered: 'Honour thy father and thy mother; thou shalt not murder; thou shalt not commit adultery; thou shalt not steal; thou shalt not bear false witness against thy neighbour; thou shalt not covet—behold, a person does not repudiate any of these laws until he repudiates the root of them (viz. God Who ordained them); and nobody proceeds to commit a transgression without first having denied Him Who prohibited it' (Tosifta Shebuoth III. 6).

According to Talmudic teaching, therefore, the existence of God was more than an intellectual affirmation; it included moral obligation. The recital

---

[4] In the Hebrew Prayer Book, God is mentioned as 'renewing the creation every day continually' (ed. Singer, p. 128).

[5] Ps. xiv. 1, and liii. 1. See also x: 13, and Jer. v. 12.

[6] The use of the term 'Epicurean' in this sense is already found in Josephus, who refers to this type as men 'who cast providence out of human life, and who do not believe that God takes care of the affairs of the world, nor that the Universe is governed and continued in being by that blessed and immortal nature, but say that the world is carried along of its own accord, without a ruler and guardian' (Antiq. x. xi. 7).

of the declaration: 'Hear, O Israel, the Lord our God, the Lord is one' (Deut. vi. 4), which forms part of the morning and evening prayers of the Jew, is defined as 'the acceptance of the yoke of the Kingdom of Heaven' (Ber. II. 2), which means submission to the Divine discipline.

II. UNITY

The conception of God held by the Rabbis is monotheistic in the strictest degree. 'He created in the beginning one man only, so that heretics should not say that there are several Powers in heaven' (Sanh. 38a); since, had there been more human beings created at first, it might be argued that some had been formed by God and the remainder by other deities. 'All agree,' it is stated, 'that nothing was created on the first day, so that people should not say that the archangel Michael stretched the south end of the firmament and Gabriel the north end; for "I am the Lord that stretched forth the heavens alone" (Is. xliv. 24)' (Gen. R. I. 3).

On the verse, 'Hear, O Israel, the Lord our God, the Lord is one,' the comment is made: The Holy One, blessed be He, said to Israel, 'My children, everything that I created in the Universe is in pairs—e.g. heaven and earth, the sun and moon, Adam and Eve, this world and the World to Come; but I am one and alone in the Universe' (Deut. R. II. 31).

Stress was laid upon the unity of God in defence against two currents of thought. The first was idolatry, which was identified by the Rabbis with immoral living, doubtless under the impression caused by Roman and Greek polytheism. The idolater 'breaks the yoke of God's law from off him' (Sifré Num. §III; 31b), it was said; i.e. he lives without moral restraint. 'He who professes idolatry repudiates the Ten Commandments' (ibid.) expresses the same thought still more explicitly. The rejection of the first half of the Decalogue results in the infraction of the second half. The same idea underlies such statements as 'The prohibition of idolatry is equal in weight to all the other commandments of the Torah' (Hor. 8a); 'So important is the matter of idolatry, that whoever rejects it is as though he acknowledges the whole Torah' (Chul. 5a).

The moral implications of the concept may be seen from the Rabbinic decision, 'If a person is required to transgress all the ordinances of the Torah under threat of being put to death, he may do so with the exception of those relating to idolatry, immorality, and bloodshed' (Sanh. 74a).

The Rabbis also had occasion to defend the monotheistic view of God against attack from the early Christians who sought a foundation for their trinitarian doctrine in the text of the Hebrew Bible. The principal passage bearing on the subject reads: 'The *Minim*[7] asked R. Simlai, "How many gods created the Universe?" He answered: "Let us consult the former days; for it is written, 'Ask now of the former days which were before thee, since the day

---

[7] The word denotes 'sectaries' and usually refers to Christians. On the whole subject see R. T. Herford, *Christianity in Talmud and Midrash,* and on the passage quoted above, pp. 255 ff. of that scholarly work.

that God[8] created man upon the earth' (Deut. iv. 32). It is not written here 'created' as a verb in the plural, but in the singular, denoting therefore a singular subject. The same answer applies to Genesis i. I."

'R. Simlai said: "In every place where you find a text which is used by the *Minim* in support of their opinions, you will find the refutation by its side." They returned and asked him: "What of that which is written, 'Let *us* make man in *our* image, after *our* likeness' (Gen. i. 26)?" He answered: "Read what follows: it is not said, 'And gods created man in their image,' but 'And God created man in His own image.'" When they had departed, his disciples said to him: "You have thrust them aside with a reed; what answer will you give us?" He said to them: "In the past Adam was created from the dust of the ground and Eve was created from Adam. Henceforward it is to be 'in our image, after our likeness'—meaning, man will not be able to come into existence without woman, nor woman without man, nor both without the *Shechinah*."'[9]

'They returned and asked him: "What is that which is written, 'The Lord, the God of gods, the Lord, the God of gods,[10] He knoweth' (Josh. xxii. 22)?" He answered: "It is not written 'They know' but 'He knoweth.'" His disciples (after their departure) said to him: "You have thrust them aside with a reed; what answer will you give us?" He said to them: "The three of them are a Divine name; just as a person refers to a king as Basileus, Caesar, and Augustus"' (Gen. R. VIII. 9).

Religious polemic also underlies this piece of commentary: 'The Holy One, blessed be He, said, "I am the first" (Is. xliv. 6) for I have no father; "and I am the last" for I have no brother; "and beside me there is no God" for I have no son' (Exod. R. XXIX. 5).

Since monotheism was the important characteristic dogma of Judaism which distinguished it from the other religions of that age, we have the declaration: 'Whoever repudiates idolatry is accounted a Jew' (Meg. 13*a*).

III. INCORPOREALITY

Closely bound up with the doctrine of God's Unity was the teaching that He has no bodily form. To account for the numerous passages in the Bible where physical organs are attributed to Him, the Rabbis remarked: 'We borrow terms from His creatures to apply to Him in order to assist the understanding' (Mech. to xix. 18; 65*a*).[11]

---

[8] The Hebrew word for 'God,' *Elohim*, has a plural form.

[9] On the *Shechinah*, see pp. 42 ff. The Rabbi explained 'our' to mean God in addition to man and woman; i.e. each human being is formed by three parents. For this doctrine of the human being's threefold parentage, see p. 22.

[10] In the Hebrew text there are three designations of God: *El, Elohim*, and *JHVH*, which were understood by the early Christians as pointing to a trinity.

[11] There is another Talmudic maxim to the effect, 'The Torah speaks according to the language of the sons of man' (Ber. 31*b*); and it is frequently quoted to explain the Biblical anthropomorphisms. This is incorrect, since the words apply always to the idiomatic structure of a Scriptural phrase.

To assist the comprehension of the place of the incorporeal God in the Universe, an analogy is drawn from the incorporeal part of the human being—the soul. 'As the Holy One, blessed be He, fills the whole world, so also the soul fills the whole body. As the Holy One, blessed be He, sees but cannot be seen, so also the soul sees but cannot be seen. As the Holy One, blessed be He, nourishes the whole world, so also the soul nourishes the whole body. As the Holy One, blessed be He, is pure, so also the soul is pure. As the Holy One, blessed be He, dwells in the inmost part of the Universe, so also the soul dwells in the inmost part of the body' (Ber. 10*a*).

'In the same manner that nobody knows the place of the soul, so does nobody know the place of the Holy One, blessed be He. Even the holy *Chayyoth*[12] which bear the Throne of Glory do not know where is His place and therefore exclaim: "Blessed be the glory of the Lord from His place" (Ezek. iii. 12)[13] It happened that somebody asked R. Gamaliel where the Holy One, blessed be He, was located. He replied: "I do not know." The other said to him: "This is your wisdom that you daily offer prayer to Him without knowing where He is!" R. Gamaliel answered him: "You have questioned me concerning One Who is remote from me a distance corresponding to a journey of three thousand five hundred years.[14] Let me question you about something which is with you day and night and tell me where it is—I refer to your soul!" The man said: "I do not know." Then the Rabbi retorted: "May you perish! You cannot tell me the place of something which is actually with you; and you ask me about One Who is remote from me a distance corresponding to a journey of three thousand five hundred years!" The man thereupon said: "We act well, because we worship the works of our hands which we can always see." "Yes," was the reply, "you can see the works of your hands but they cannot see you. The Holy One, blessed be He, sees the works of His hands but they cannot see Him!"' (Midrash to Ps. ciii. 1; 217*a*).

Despite the insistence on the incorporeality of God, Rabbinic literature contains numerous passages which rather startle the reader by reason of their strong anthropomorphic ascriptions. He is said to wear the phylacteries (Ber. 6*a*) and wrap Himself in the *Tallit* or praying-shawl (R.H. 17*b*); He offers prayer to Himself and studies the Torah during three hours of the day (A.Z. 3*b*); He weeps over the failings of His creatures (Chag. 5*b*), and much more of a similar character. He is likewise depicted as performing certain deeds which would be considered meritorious in a human being. He interested Himself in the marriage of Adam and Eve, acting as groomsman to the former and plaiting the bride's hair to adorn her for her husband (Ber. 61*a*). He visits the sick, sympathizes with the mourner and buries the dead (Gen. R. VIII. 13).

---

[12] The celestial 'creatures' referred to in Ezekiel's vision (chaps. i and x). See below, pp. 31, 40.

[13] They use the vague term 'from His place,' because they are ignorant of His exact location.

[14] God was thought of as dwelling in the highest, i.e. the seventh, heaven, and the distance between each heaven would take five hundred years to traverse. See pp. 40 f.

However these passages be explained, it is impossible to maintain that their authors believed in a corporeal God Who actually performed the actions ascribed to Him. One scholar accounts for them as 'the humanizing of the Deity and endowing Him with all the qualities and attributes which tend towards making God accessible to man.'[15] More probably the thought behind them is the doctrine of imitation. As will be shown later,[16] the Imitation of God is a cardinal principle of human conduct in Rabbinic ethics, and it applies to the whole of life—to religious observances as well as to moral conduct. God is accordingly represented as Himself obeying the precepts which He desires Israel to observe.

This theory is supported by the statement: 'The attributes of the Holy One, blessed be He, are unlike those of a human being. The latter instructs others what they are to do but may not practise it himself. Not so is the Holy One, blessed be He; whatever He does He commands Israel to perform' (Exod. R. XXX. 9).

IV. OMNIPRESENCE

A corollary of God's incorporeality is His omnipresence. A finite body must be located in space, but to the infinite Spirit space is meaningless. 'With an earthly king, when he is in the bedchamber he cannot be in the reception-hall; but the Holy One, blessed be He, fills the upper regions and the lower. As it is said, "His glory is over the earth and heaven" (Ps. cxlviii. 13)—simultaneously; and it is written, "Do not I fill the heaven and the earth?" (Jer. xxiii. 24)' (Midrash to Ps. xxiv. 5; 103*a*).

A common term for the Deity in Rabbinic literature is 'the Place,' which originates in the doctrine: 'The Holy One, blessed be He, is the place of His Universe, but His Universe is not His place' (Gen. R. LXVIII. 9), i.e. He encompasses space but space does not encompass Him.

The omnipresence of God is finely taught in the following anecdote: 'A ship, belonging to a heathen owner, was once sailing over the sea, one of the passengers being a Jewish boy. A great storm arose, and all the Gentiles aboard took hold of their idols and prayed to them, but to no avail. Seeing that their prayers had been in vain, they said to the lad: "Call upon your God, for we have heard that He answers your petitions when you cry to Him and that He is all-powerful." The boy immediately stood up and called with all his heart upon God, Who hearkened to his prayer, and the sea became calm. On reaching land, they disembarked to purchase their requirements and said to him: "Do you not wish to buy anything?" He answered: "What do you want of a poor alien like me?" They exclaimed: "You a poor alien! We are the poor aliens; for some of us are here and have our gods in Babylon; others have them in Rome;

---

[15] Schechter, *Aspects of Rabbinic Theology*, pp. 36 ff.
[16] See pp. 210 ff.

others have their gods with them but they are of no benefit to us. As for you, however, wherever you go your God is with you!"' (p. Ber. 13*b*).

There is also an anecdote about a Gentile who asked a Rabbi: 'What purpose did your God have in speaking with Moses from the midst of a bush?' He answered: 'To teach that there is no place void of the Divine Presence, not even so lowly a thing as a bush' (Exod. R. II. 5). The saying is attributed to God: 'In every place where you find the imprint of men's feet there am I' (Mech. to xvii. 6; 52*b*).

The Talmud offers this demonstration of divine omnipresence: 'The messengers of God are unlike those of men. The messengers of men are obliged to return to those who sent them with the object of their mission; but God's messengers return at the place whither they had been dispatched. It is written: "Canst thou send forth lightnings, that they may go and say unto thee, Here we are?" (Job xxxviii. 35). It is not stated "they return" but "they go and say," i.e. wherever they go they are in the presence of God. Hence it is to be deduced that the *Shechinah* is in every place' (Mech. to xii. I; 2*a*; B.B. 25*a*).

The question how God could be everywhere at the same time received various answers. The problem was elucidated by this analogy: 'It may be likened to a cave situated by the seashore. The sea rages and the cave is filled with water, but the waters of the sea are not diminished. Similarly the Tent of Meeting was filled with the lustre of the *Shechinah,* which was not diminished in the Universe' (Num. R. XII. 4).

Other solutions that were suggested find illustration in such stories as these. 'A Samaritan asked R. Meïr: "How is it possible to accept the statement of Scripture, 'Do not I fill heaven and earth?' (Jer. xxiii. 24)? Did He not speak with Moses between the two staves of the Ark?" He told him to bring large mirrors and said: "Look at your reflection in them." He saw it magnified. He next asked him to bring small mirrors and look into them, and he saw his reflection diminished in size. R. Meïr then said: "If you, a mere mortal, can change your appearance at will, how much more so can He Who spake and the world came into being!"' (Gen. R. IV. 4). Another Rabbi declared: 'At times the Universe and its fullness are insufficient to contain the glory of God's Divinity; at other times He speaks with man between the hairs of his head' (ibid.).

'A heretic said to R. Gamaliel: "You Rabbis declare that wherever ten people assemble for worship[17] the *Shechinah* abides amongst them; how many *Shechinahs* are there then?' He called the heretic's servant and struck him with a ladle. "Why did you strike him?" he was asked, and he replied, "Because the sun is in the house of an infidel." "But the sun shines all over the world!" exclaimed the heretic; and the Rabbi retorted: "If the sun, which is only one out of a million myriads of God's servants, can be in every part of the world, how much more so can the *Shechinah* radiate throughout the entire Universe!"' (Sanh. 39*a*).

---

[17]The quorum required for a congregational service.

A reason why such emphasis was laid upon the idea of Divine omnipresence was to impress the human being with the consciousness that he was always under the supervision of God. 'Reflect upon three things,' taught R. Judah, the redactor of the Mishnah, 'and you will never fall into the power of sin: Know what is above you—a seeing eye, and a hearing ear, and all your deeds are recorded' (Aboth II. 1).

The doctrine is impressively enunciated in the exhortation which R. Jochanan b. Zakkai addressed to his disciples on his death-bed. He said to them: 'May it be His will that the fear of Heaven be upon you as great as the fear of flesh and blood.' They exclaimed: 'Only as great!' He replied: 'Would that it be as great; for know ye, when a man intends to commit a transgression, he says, 'I hope nobody will see me''' (Ber. 28*b*). The thought, then, that man is always under observation by God should be a powerful deterrent against sinning.

That it is impossible to escape the Divine Presence is illustrated by a conversation between R. José and a Roman matron who said to him: 'My god is greater than yours, because when your God revealed Himself to Moses in the burning bush, he hid his face; but when he saw the serpent, which is my god, he fled from before it!' (Exod. iv. 3). The Rabbi replied: 'At the time that our God revealed Himself to Moses in the bush, there was no place to which he could flee, since He is everywhere; but as for the serpent, which is your god, a man has only to step back two or three paces in order to escape it!' (Exod. R. III. 12).

V. OMNIPOTENCE

God was naturally thought of as the all-mighty Power and He is frequently denominated 'the Might.' The Rabbis ordained that 'on beholding shooting-stars, earthquakes, thunders, storms, and lightnings, the benediction to be uttered is, Blessed art thou, O Lord our God, King of the Universe, Whose strength and might fill the world' (Ber. IX. 2).

Generally speaking, no limit was set upon the Divine power. 'The attribute of human beings is unlike that of God. A human being cannot say two things at the same time; but the Holy One, blessed be He, uttered the Ten Commandments simultaneously. A human being cannot listen to the cries of two men at the same time, but the Holy One, blessed be He, hearkens even to the cries of all who enter the world' (Mech. to xv. 11; 41*b*).

An oft-quoted Rabbinic principle is, 'Everything is in the power of Heaven except the fear of Heaven' (Ber. 33*b*), which indicates that God determines the fortunes of the individual, but not whether he will be God-fearing or not. That is left to his own choice.

That He performed miracles was never questioned, their purpose being 'to sanctify His great name in the world' (Sifré Deut. §306; 132*b*). But there was a desire to avoid interpreting miraculous occurrences as departures from the natural order of the Universe, since they might otherwise be taken as evidence that the Creation was imperfect. It was therefore taught that the miracles recorded by Scripture were preordained from the beginning of the world. 'At the Creation God made a condition with the sea that it should be divided for the passage of the children of Israel, with the sun and moon to stand still at the bidding of Joshua, with the ravens to feed Elijah, with fire not to injure Hananiah, Mishael, and Azariah, with the lions not to harm Daniel, and with the fish to spew out Jonah' (Gen. R. v. 5).

The same thought underlies the statement: 'Ten things were created on the eve of the (first) Sabbath in the twilight:[18] the mouth of the earth (Num. xvi. 32); the mouth of the well (ibid. xxi. 16); the mouth of the ass (ibid. xxii. 28); the rainbow; the manna; the rod (Exod. iv. 17); the Shamir;[19] the shape of the written characters; the writing, and the tables of stone' (Aboth v. 9).

After the destruction of the Temple and State by the Romans, the calamities which had befallen the Jews aroused doubts in the minds of some of them regarding Divine omnipotence. Such a feeling appears to motive the saying: 'If He is Master of all works as He is Master over us, we will serve Him; if not, we will not serve Him. If He can supply our needs we will serve Him, otherwise we will not serve Him' (Mech. to xvii. 7; 52b).

An apologetic purpose obviously prompted the following extracts, which offer a defence of the dogma of God's omnipotence. 'It is related that when Trajan put Julian and his brother Pappos to death in Laodicea, he said to them: "If you are of the people of Hananiah, Mishael, and Azariah, let your God come and rescue you from my hand in the same way that He rescued them from the hand of Nebuchadnezzar." They replied: "Those men were perfectly righteous and worthy that a miracle should be wrought for them; and Nebuchadnezzar was likewise an honourable king and worthy that a miracle should be wrought through him. You, however, are ignoble and unworthy of being made the medium of a miracle. As for us, we have been condemned to death by God; and if you are not our executioner, God has many others to slay us. He has many bears, leopards, or lions to attack and kill us; but He has only delivered us into your hand so as to avenge our blood upon you"' (Taan. 18b).

'Have you ever heard of the sun being ill and unable to dawn and function? To God's servants we cannot ascribe ailments which induce weakness, so how can we ascribe such to Him? The matter may be likened to a warrior who resided in a city and the inhabitants relied upon him, saying: "So long as he is with us, no troops will attack us." Occasionally troops did march against the city; but as soon as he showed his face they fled. Once, however, there was an assault, but he said: "My right hand is afflicted with weakness!" With the Holy One, blessed be He, it is not so: "Behold, the Lord's hand is not shortened that it cannot save" (Is. lix. 1)'(Lament. R. 1.2. §23).

---

[18] 'All phenomena that seemed to partake at once of the natural and supernatural were conceived as having had their origin in the interval between the close of the work of Creation and commencement of the Sabbath' (Singer's note, *Authorised Daily Prayer Book*, p. 200).

[19] Since no iron tool was to be used in the construction of the Temple, tradition relates that Solomon made use of a worm, called Shamir, which split any stone over which it crawled.

'The Jewish elders in Rome were asked: "If your God takes no pleasure in idolatry, why does He not make an end of it?" They answered: "If people worshipped things of which the world was not in need, He would do so; but they worship the sun, the moon, and stars. Should He destroy His Universe for the sake of fools?" They said to them: "If that is so, let Him destroy that which is useless to the world and leave whatever is essential." They replied: "In that event we should but strengthen the hands of those who worship these latter objects, because they would be able to assert that these must be deities inasmuch as they had not been brought to an end"' (A.Z. IV. 7).

VI. OMNISCIENCE

As with God's might, so His knowledge was declared to be limitless. The Biblical doctrine that He is all-knowing is developed to its utmost extent in the teachings of the Rabbis.

'Who beholds a crowd of people should utter the benediction, Blessed is He Who is wise in secrets. Just as faces differ one from another, so are minds also different, but God knows them all' (p. Ber. 13*c*). 'All is revealed and known before Him, as it is said: "He knoweth what is in the darkness, and the light dwelleth with Him" (Dan. ii. 22)'(Mech. to xii. 23; 12*a*).

The conception that nothing is hidden from His ken is abundantly illustrated. 'It is like an architect who built a city with its inner chambers, underground channels, and caves. After a time he was appointed the collector of taxes. When the citizens hid their wealth in these secret places, he said to them: "It was I who constructed these secret places, so how can you conceal your possessions from me?" Similarly: "Woe unto them that seek deep to hide their counsel from the Lord, and their works are in the dark, and they say, Who seeth us? and who knoweth us?" (Is. xxix. 15)' (Gen. R. XXIV. 1).

'Although God is in the heavens, His eyes behold and search the sons of man. Parable of a king who had an orchard. He built in it a high tower, and commanded that workmen should be appointed to work in the orchard. They who work faithfully shall receive full payment, and they who are slack shall be penalized' (Exod. R. II. 2). From the high tower the king could supervise the men who worked for him and judge the quality of their labour. Similarly from the heights of Heaven He oversees the actions of His creatures.

The supernatural character of the Divine knowledge is vividly taught in such dicta as these: 'Before even a creature is formed in his mother's womb his thought is already revealed to God' (Gen. R. IX. 3); 'Before even a thought is created in man's heart it is already revealed to God' (ibid.); 'Before even a man speaks, He knows what is in his heart'(Exod. R. XXI. 3).

Inextricably connected with the attribute of omniscience is foreknowledge. God knows all that will be in addition to all that is and has been. 'Everything is foreseen' (Aboth III. 19), was the dictum of R. Akiba, and it is part of the Talmudic doctrine. 'All is foreseen before the Holy One, blessed be He' (Tanchuma Shelach §9); 'God knows what is to be in the future' (Sanh. 90*b*).

In numerous passages He is described as foreseeing that an event would happen long before it actually transpired. Some instances are: 'If the Holy One, blessed be He, had not foreseen (at the Creation) that after the passing of twenty-six generations Israel would accept the Torah, he would not have written in it[20] such phrases as "Command the children of Israel," or "Speak unto the children of Israel"' (Gen. R. I. 4). 'Only the sun was created for the purpose of giving light to the world. If so, why was the moon created? It teaches that the Holy One, blessed be He, foresaw that idolaters would make them as deities; He therefore said: "Since when there are two of them, one denying the other, idolaters make them as deities, how much more would they do so if there were only one!"' (ibid. VI. 1). 'Why is the narrative of the twelve spies immediately preceded by the account of the slander of Moses by Miriam (Num. xii. f.)? It was foreseen before the Holy One, blessed be He, that the spies would utter a slanderous report concerning the land; so to avoid their being able to plead that they were unaware of the penalty of slander, He attached the one incident to the other for the purpose of letting everybody know what is its punishment' (Tanchuma Shelach §5).

From the theory of miracles referred to in the preceding section it follows that the Rabbis believed that God foresaw the history of the world even at the time it was created. This teaching is explicitly enunciated. 'From the beginning of Creation, the Holy One, blessed be He, foresaw the deeds of the righteous and the wicked' (Gen. R. II. 5). How this dogma bears on the idea of Free Will a later section of this work will show.[21]

The Rabbis had sometimes to defend this belief against hostile critics, as the following dialogue between a heretic and a Rabbi demonstrates. 'Do you assert that God foresees what is to happen?' 'Certainly.' 'How, then, is it written in the Scriptures, "It repented the Lord that He had made man on the earth, and it grieved Him at His heart" (Gen. vi. 6)?' 'Has there ever been a son born to you?' 'Yes.' 'What did you do at his birth?' 'I rejoiced and made it an occasion of rejoicing for others.' 'But did you not know that a time would come when he would have to die?' 'That is so; but in a time of joy let there be joy, and in a time of mourning let there be mourning.' 'So did it happen with the Holy One, blessed be He. God mourned for seven days[22] over the fate of His Universe before bringing the flood' (Gen. R. XXVII. 4).

VII. ETERNITY

Time has no meaning in relationship to God. In His capacity as Creator of the Universe He must necessarily have been the first, and He will also be the last in time, continuing in existence when all else has passed away. 'Everything

---

[20] This is based on the theory that the Torah existed before the world was created. See p. 132.

[21] See p. 94.

[22] This is the period of time prescribed by Judaism for mourning a bereavement.

decays but Thou dost not decay' (Lev. R. XIX. 2), declared a Rabbi of the Deity. By a play on the word (*en*) *biltéka*, 'there is none beside Thee' (1 Sam. ii. 2), the consonants of which can be read as (*en*) *balloteka*, the sense was derived, 'There is none to outlast Thee,' and the comment was added, 'Not like the attribute of man is the attribute of God. With man his works outlive him; but the Holy One, blessed be He, outlives His works' (Meg. 14*a*).

'God's seal is truth,' runs a Rabbinic maxim; and it was pointed out that as the consonants of the word for 'truth,' viz. AMT, are respectively the first, middle, and final letters of the Hebrew alphabet, they indicated that He is the first, middle, and last in time (Gen. R. LXXXI. 2).

The contrast is also frequently drawn between 'a human king who to-day is here and to-morrow in the grave' and 'the King of kings Who lives and endures for all eternity' (Ber. 28*b*). The addition of the words 'before Me' in the Second Commandment was explained thus: 'The purpose is to teach that as I live and endure for all eternity, so you and your offspring until the end of all generations are forbidden to worship idols' (Mech. to XX. 3; 67*b*).

A parable relates: 'A human king once entered a city and all the inhabitants came out to applaud him. Their acclamation pleased him so much that he said to them: "To-morrow I will erect various kinds of baths for you. To-morrow I will provide you with a water-conduit." He went away to sleep, but never rose again. Where is he or his promise? But with the Holy One, blessed be He, it is otherwise; because He is a God Who lives and reigns for ever' (Lev. R. XXVI. 1).

Another parable concerns 'a person who lost his son and went to inquire for him in a cemetery. A wise man saw him and asked, "Is the son you have lost alive or dead?" He answered, "He is alive." Then said the other, "You fool! Is it the way to inquire for the dead among the living or the living among the dead? Surely it is always the practice of the living to attend to the needs of the dead, not vice versa!" So is it with our God Who lives and endures for all eternity; as it is said, "The Lord is the true God; He is the living God and an everlasting king" (Jer. X. 10); but the gods of the idolaters are lifeless things. Shall we, then forsake Him Who lives for ever and worship dead objects?' (Lev. R. VI. 6).

Noteworthy in this connection is the comment on 'The enemy are come to an end, they are desolate for ever' (Ps. ix. 6), which is explained as follows: 'The enemy are come to an end, their structures[23] are for ever. For instance, Constantine built Constantinople, Apulus built Apulia,[24] Romulus built Rome, Alexander built Alexandria, Seleucus built Seleucia. The founders have come to an end, but the cities they established endure. As for Thee, if one may say so, "The cities which Thou hast overthrown, their very memorial is perished"

---

[23] This is evidently the sense in which the Midrash understood the word rendered 'desolate.' Daiches has shown that there are several passages in the Old Testament where *choraboth* must mean 'cities, palaces,' and not 'ruins.' See the *Jewish Quarterly Review* (old series) XX, pp. 637 ff.

[24] The correct reading is probably: Philip (of Macedon) built Philippi.

(ibid.). This refers to Jerusalem and Zion, as it is written, "Thy holy cities are become a wilderness, Zion is become a wilderness, Jerusalem a desolation" (Is. lxiv. 10). "But the Lord sitteth enthroned for ever" (Ps. ix. 7)—the Holy One, blessed be He, will restore them. (The builders of the cities) were only human and they come to an end and are cut off; likewise the cities which they founded will be destroyed for ever. The Lord, however, Who exists and endures for all eternity, "sitteth enthroned for ever, and hath prepared His throne for judgment." He will rebuild Jerusalem, Zion, and the cities of Judah; as it is said, "At that time they shall call Jerusalem the throne of the Lord" (Jer. iii. 17)' (Midrash to Ps. ix. 6 (*Heb.* 7); 43*a,b*).

VIII. JUSTICE AND MERCY

The first Hebrew patriarch addressed the Deity as 'the Judge of the whole earth' (Gen. xviii. 25), and the Talmud regards Him in the same light. As the Creator of the world and of the human race, He holds His creatures to account for the manner of their living.

His judgments are always just. 'With Him there is no unrighteousness, nor forgetfulness, nor respect of persons, nor taking of bribes' (Aboth IV. 29). R. Jochanan b. Zakkai, on his deathbed, told his disciples that he was about to be judged by One 'Whom I cannot appease with (flattering) words nor bribe with money' (Ber. 28*b*).

Nor is there anything arbitrary about His decisions. A Roman matron said to a Rabbi: 'Your God draws near to Himself whomever He likes, without regard to justice!' He set before her a basket of figs, from which she kept picking and eating the choicest. He said to her: 'You know how to make a wise selection, and would you assert that the Holy One, blessed be He, does not? He chooses and draws near unto Himself the person whose acts are good' (Num. R. III. 2).

In the Rabbinic literature an eternal conflict is represented as being waged between God's justice and mercy. There is scarcely a passage which refers to his capacity as Judge which does not also allude to His attribute of compassion.

The divine appellation *Elohim,* translated 'God,' was understood to denote His aspect of judgement and JHVH, translated 'Lord,' His aspect of mercy (Gen. R. XXXIII. 3), and the combination of the two names in the verse, 'These are the generations of the heaven and earth when they were created, in the day that the Lord God (JHVH *Elohim*) made earth and heaven' (Gen. ii. 4) is explained as follows: 'It may be likened to a king who had empty vessels. The king said, "If I put hot water into them they will crack; if I put icy cold water into them they will contract." What did the king do? He mixed the hot with the cold and poured the mixture into the vessels, and they endured. Similarly said the Holy One, blessed be He, "If I create the world only with the attribute of mercy, sins will multiply beyond all bounds; if I create it only with the attribute of justice, how can the world last? Behold, I will create it with both attributes; would that it might endure!"' (Gen. R. XII. 15).

Indeed, it was only because the quality of mercy prevailed at Creation that the human race was allowed to come into being. 'When the Holy One, blessed be He, came to create the first man, He foresaw that both righteous and wicked would issue from him. He said, "If I create him, wicked men will issue from him; if I do not create him, how can righteous men spring from him?' What did He do? He removed the way of the wicked from before Him, allied the attribute of mercy with Himself and created him' (Gen. R. VIII. 4).

If compassion was the deciding cause of Creation, its victory over stern justice is the reason of the world's continuance in the face of wickedness. 'There were ten generations from Adam to Noah, to make known how long-suffering God is, seeing that all those generations continued to provoke Him before He brought upon them the waters of the flood' (Aboth V. 2).

When Abraham addressed his plea to God, 'Shall not the Judge of all the earth do justly?' the meaning of his words was: 'If You desire the world to continue there cannot be strict justice; if You insist on strict justice, the world cannot endure' (Gen. R. XXXIX. 6).

The Hebrew expression for divine forbearance is not *erech af* but *erech apayim,* the second word having a dual form. This was explained as denoting that God is not long-suffering with the righteous only but equally with the wicked (B.K. 50*b*). The Bible relates that when God revealed His attributes to Moses, he 'made haste and bowed his head toward the earth and worshipped' (Exod. xxxiv. 8). To the question, What overwhelmed him so much? the answer is given, 'The recognition of the Divine forbearance' (Sanh. III*a*).

The apparent victory of evil over good in the world was understood as the manifestation of His mercy. 'Moses described God as "great, mighty, and terrible" (Deut. x. 17). Jeremiah referred to Him only as "the great and mighty God" (xxxii. 18), because, said he, where are His terrible acts, seeing that heathens dance in His Temple? Daniel referred to Him only as "the great and terrible God" (ix. 4), because, said he, where are His mighty acts, seeing that heathens enslave His children? Then came the men of the Great Assembly[25] and restored all the attributes (see Nehem. ix. 32); for they said: "On the contrary, this is the greatest manifestation of His might that He subdues His anger and shows long-suffering with the wicked; and it is likewise the manifestation of His terrible acts, without which how could a single nation be allowed to continue in existence?"' (Joma 69*b*).

'The attribute of grace,' it was taught, 'exceeds that of punishment (i.e. justice) by five-hundredfold.' This conclusion was deduced from the fact that in connection with punishment God described Himself as 'visiting the iniquity of the fathers upon the children unto the third and fourth generation' (Exod. XX. 5); but in connection with grace it is said: 'And showing mercy unto the thousandth generation' (ibid. 6). The last phrase is, in the Hebrew, *alafim,* which is literally 'thousands' and must indicate at least two thousand. Retribution, therefore, extends at most to four generations, whereas mercy extends to at least two thousand generations (Tosifta Sot. IV. I).

[25] See Introduction, pp. xviii f.

'Even in the time of His anger He remembers mercy,' declares the Talmud (Pes. 87*b*); and He is actually depicted as praying to Himself that His compassion should overcome His wrath. This thought gave rise to the bold flight of imagination contained in the following passage: 'R. Jochanan said in the name of R. José: Whence is it known that the Holy One, blessed be He, prays? As it is said, "Even them will I bring to My holy mountain, and make them joyful in My house of prayer"[26] (Is. lvi. 7). It is not said, "their prayer" but "My prayer"; hence we infer that the Holy One, blessed be He, prays. What does He pray? R. Zotra b. Tobiah said in the name of Rab: "May it be My will that My mercy may subdue My wrath; and may My mercy prevail over My attribute of justice, so that I may deal with My children in the quality of mercy and enter on their behalf within the line of strict justice."

'There is a teaching: R. Ishmael b. Elisha said, Once I entered the Holy of Holies to offer incense in the innermost part of the Sanctuary, and I saw Okteriël,[27] Jah, the Lord of Hosts, seated upon a high and exalted throne. He said to me, "Ishmael, My son, bless Me." I replied, "May it be Thy will that Thy mercy may subdue Thy wrath; and may Thy mercy prevail over Thy attribute of justice, so that Thou mayest deal with Thy children in the quality of mercy and enter on their behalf within the line of strict justice'(Ber. 7*a*).

In the same strain it is declared: 'During three hours of each day He sits and judges the whole world. When He sees that the world is deserving of being destroyed because of the prevalent evil, He arises from the throne of justice and sits upon the throne of mercy' (A.Z. 3*b*).

Much use is made of the prophetic doctrine, 'I have no pleasure in the death of the wicked, but that the wicked turn from his way and live' (Ezek xxxiii. II). Upon it is based the theory of Repentance which occupies so prominent a place in Rabbinic thought.[28] The idea is beautifully expressed in the statement, 'Not like the attribute of the Holy One, blessed be He, is the attribute of man. When a man is conquered he grieves; when the Holy One, blessed be He, is conquered, so that He averts His wrath and can display mercy, He rejoices' (Pes. 119*a*).

The divine compassion is evidenced by extreme eagerness to save man from condemnation. 'Though nine hundred and ninety-nine angels attest for a man's conviction and only one angel attests for his defence, the Holy One, blessed be He, inclines the scales in his favour' (p. Kid. 61*d*). When, however, He is compelled by justice to exact punishment from evil-doers, He does so with regret and pain. Noble expression is given to this thought in the legend that at the overthrow of the Egyptians by the Red Sea, the ministering angels wished to offer a song of triumph to God; but He checked them, saying: 'The work of My hands is drowned in the sea, and you would offer Me a song!' (Sanh. 39*b*).

---

[26] The Hebrew is literally 'the house of My prayer.'

[27] A Divine Name usually explained as a combination of *kêter* 'throne' and *el* 'God.' Ishmael b. Elisha, according to tradition, was identical with Ishmael b. Phabi, one of the last of the High Priests before the destruction of the Second Temple.

[28] See pp. 104 ff.

While believing, therefore, that He is the Judge of the Universe, the Rabbis delighted in calling Him *Rachmana* (the Merciful), and taught that 'the world is judged by grace' (Aboth III. 19).

IX. FATHERHOOD

Throughout the utterances of the Talmudic Sages, the relationship which exists between the Creator and His creatures is conceived under the image of Father and children. God is constantly addressed, or referred to, as 'Father Who is in heaven.' One Rabbinic maxim, for example, exhorts: 'Be strong as a leopard, light as an eagle, fleet as a hart, and strong as a lion, to do the will of your Father Who is in heaven' (Aboth v. 23). And it was considered a mark of exceptional grace on His part that this intimate relationship exists and was revealed to man. 'Beloved are Israel, for they were called children of the All-present; but it was by special love that it was made known to them that they were called children of the All-present; as it is said, "Ye are children of the Lord your God" (Deut. xiv. I)' (Aboth III. 18). Although this dictum specifies Israel, it being based on a Biblical passage, the doctrine of Fatherhood was not restricted to one people and was extended to all human beings.[29]

Difference of opinion existed as to whether this precious boon is bestowed upon man conditionally or unconditionally. On the text 'Ye are children of the Lord your God,' R. Judah commented: 'At the time that you conduct yourselves as dutiful children, you are called God's children; but when you do not so conduct yourselves, you are not called God's children. R. Meïr, on the other hand, declared that in either case the name of "God's children" applied; and he urged in favour of his contention that in the Scriptures there occur such phrases as "they are sottish children" (Jer. iv. 22) and "children in whom is no faith" (Deut. xxxii. 20), thus proving that although they were unworthy they were still called "children"' (Kid. 36*a*).

In addressing the people of Israel, God is accredited with these words: 'All the miracles and mighty acts which I performed for you were not with the object that you should give Me a reward, but that you should honour Me like dutiful children and call Me your Father' (Exod. R. XXXII. 5).

Especially when in the act of prayer, the individual was exhorted to think of himself as addressing his petitions to One Who stood to him in the relationship of Father. It is recorded that 'the pious men of old used to wait an hour in silent meditation and then offer their prayer, in order to direct their heart to their Father in heaven' (Ber. v. I).

One of the earliest prayers in the Hebrew liturgy[30] opens with the words: 'With great love hast Thou loved us, O Lord our God, with great and exceeding pity hast Thou pitied us. Our Father, our King, for our fathers' sake, who trusted in Thee, and whom Thou didst teach the statutes of life, be also

---

[29] See pp. 22 and 67.
[30] Referred to by name, i.e. its opening words, in Ber. 11*b*.

gracious unto us and teach us.' A prayer, offered by R. Akiba in a time of drought, has been preserved and reads: 'Our Father, our King, we have sinned before Thee. Our Father, our King, we have no king beside Thee. Our Father, our King, have compassion upon us' (Taan. 25*b*).

The familiarity of the conception of the divine Fatherhood is particularly evidenced by its frequency in Rabbinic parables and similes. To account for the difference of phraseology between the words addressed to Abraham, 'Walk *before* Me' (Gen. xvii. 1) and the description of Noah who 'walked *with* God' (ibid. vi. 9), we have the parable of a prince who had two children, one grown up and the other young. To the little child he says: 'Walk with me'; but to the big one he says: 'Walk before me' (Gen. R. xxx. 10).

On the text, 'And the angel of God, which went before the camp of Israel, removed and went behind them' (Exod. xiv. 19), there is the parable of a man who was walking by the way, having with him his child whom he allowed to proceed in front. Brigands came to kidnap the child; so the father took him from in front and placed him behind. A wolf appeared in the rear; so he took the child from behind and again placed him in front. Afterwards brigands came in front and wolves behind; so he took the child up and carried him in his arms. The child began to be troubled by the glare of the sun, and the father spread his own garment over him. The child hungered and the father fed him; he thirsted and the father gave him to drink. So did God act toward Israel when he was delivered from Egypt (Mech. ad loc.; 30*a*).

Another parable, pointing the same moral, tells: 'A king's son fell into evil ways. The king sent his tutor to him with the message, "Return, O my son." But the son sent to his father the reply: "With what can I return? I am ashamed to come before you." Then the father sent to him, saying: "Can a son be ashamed to return to his father? If you return, do you not return to your father?"' (Deut. R. ii. 24).

The doctrine of Fatherhood reaches its culminating point in the teaching that God participates in the formation of the human being. 'There are three partners in the production of the human being: the Holy One, blessed be He, the father and the mother. The father provides the white matter from which are formed the bones, sinews, nails, brain, and the white part of the eye; the mother provides the red matter from which are formed the skin, flesh, hair, and pupil of the eye; and the Holy One, blessed be He, infuses into him breath, soul, features, vision, hearing, speech, power of motion, understanding, and intelligence' (Nid. 31*a*). This means that the parents create only the physical part of the human being; but all the faculties and that which constitutes personality are an endowment from the heavenly Father.

The Fatherhood of God is synonymous with His love for the human family. Every creature is living proof that the Father of all is a God of love. The best expression of this idea is found in the aphorism of R. Akiba: 'Beloved is man, for he was created in the image of God; but it was by a special love that it was made known to him that he was created in the image of God; as it is said, "For in the image of God made He man"' (Aboth iii. 18).

X. HOLINESS AND PERFECTION

To the Rabbis the idea of God was not a metaphysical abstraction but the very foundation of right human living. As already mentioned, idolatry was synonymous with immorality and a degraded standard of life. Conversely, belief in God was the inspiration of a lofty plane of thought and action. It will be shown later that the doctrine of *imitatio Dei*,[31] the Imitation of God, lies at the root of Talmudic ethics.

The characteristic term which distinguishes the Deity from this point of view is 'holiness.' It implies apartness from everything that defiles as well as actual perfection. The Rabbinic Jew always thought of God as 'the Holy One, blessed be He,' that being the commonest of all the names ascribed to Him.

Both the divine holiness and its meaning for human beings are emphasized in this passage: 'The Holy One, blessed be He, says to man, "Behold, I am pure, My abode is pure, My ministers are pure, and the soul I give you is pure. If you return it to Me in the same state of purity that I give it to you, well and good; if not, I will destroy it before you"' (Lev. R. XVIII. 1).

But the term 'holiness' has a special connotation when applied to God. It has a perfection which is beyond the attainment of any human being. In the text, 'For he is a holy God' (Josh. xxiv. 19), the adjective has a plural form, which is explained to mean, 'He is holy with all kinds of holiness,' i.e. He is the perfection of holiness (p. Ber. 13a). On the words 'Ye shall be holy' (Lev. xix. 2) the comment is made: 'It is possible to imagine that man can be as holy as God; therefore Scripture adds, "for I am holy"—My holiness is higher than any degree of holiness you can reach' (Lev. R. XXIV. 9).

Not only did the Rabbis believe in this perfect holiness of God, but they insisted that it was the paramount duty of the Jew to guard it from profanation by discreditable conduct on his part. The House of Israel, as the chosen people of God, were the guardians of His reputation in the world. By worthy actions they brought credit upon Him and 'sanctified His name.' Base conduct, on the other hand, had the effect of causing *Chillul Hashem* (profanation of the Name).

This tenet concerning the interrelationship between God and Israel is of Biblical origin and finds its fullest expression in the prophecies of Ezekiel.[32] It was seized upon and elaborated by the Rabbis until it became for them a fundamental motive of behaviour. A bad action more than involved the Jew in personal guilt; it was treachery to his God and people. Therefore a distinction was drawn between a wrong done to a Gentile and to a co-religionist on that ground. 'More serious is the defrauding of a non-Jew than the defrauding of a brother Israelite on account of the profanation of the Name' (Tosifta B.K.. X. 15).

To profane the Name was regarded as one of the most heinous of sins. How serious was the view taken of such an offence may be gathered from the statement, 'He who is guilty of profaning the Name cannot rely on repentance, nor upon the power of the Day of Atonement to gain him expiation,

[31] See pp. 210 ff.
[32] See especially xxxvi. 22–33.

nor upon sufferings to wipe it out; death alone can wipe it out' (Joma 86*a*). In other places we find an even stricter attitude taken up, and the profaner of the Name is classed among the five types of sinner for whom there is no forgiveness (ARN XXXIX).

In most matters Jewish law draws a distinction between a wrong done wilfully or inadvertently, but no such allowance is made in connection with this offence. 'Whosoever profanes the Name of Heaven in secret will suffer the penalty for it in public; and this, whether the heavenly Name be profaned unintentionally or in wilfulness' (Aboth IV. 5).

Although it was so firmly held that human conduct reflects upon the divine Name, yet God's holiness is independent of the actions of His creatures. Hence we find this comment on the verse: '"Ye shall be holy, for I the Lord your God am Holy." That is to say, if you make yourselves holy, I ascribe it to you as though you had sanctified Me; but if you do not make yourselves holy, I ascribe it to you as though you have not sanctified Me. Perhaps, however, the intention of the verse is—if you sanctify Me, I am rendered holy; but if you do not sanctify Me, I am not rendered holy! The text states, "For I am holy"—I am in a condition of holiness whether you sanctify Me or not' (Sifra to xix. 2).

XI. THE INEFFABLE NAME

To the Oriental, a name is not merely a label as with us. It was thought of as indicating the nature of the person or object by whom it was borne. For that reason special reverence attached to 'the distinctive Name' (*Shem Hamephorash*) of the Deity which He had revealed to the people of Israel, viz. the tetragrammaton, JHVH.

In the Biblical period there seems to have been no scruple against its use in daily speech. The addition of *Jah* or *Jahu* to personal names, which persisted among the Jews even after the Babylonian exile, is an indication that there was no prohibition against the employment of the four-lettered Name. But in the early Rabbinic period the pronunciation of the Name was restricted to the Temple service. The rule was laid down: 'In the Sanctuary the Name was pronounced as written; but beyond its confines a substituted Name was employed' (Sot. VII. 6).

The tetragrammaton was included in the priestly benediction which was daily pronounced in the Temple (Sifré Num. §39; 12*a*). It was also used by the High Priest on the Day of Atonement, when he made the threefold confession of sins on behalf of himself, the priests, and the community. The third occasion is described in this manner: 'Thus did he say: O JHVH, Thy people, the House of Israel, have committed iniquity, have transgressed, have sinned before Thee. I beseech Thee by the Name JHVH,[33] make Thou atonement

---

[33] i.e. the name indicative of mercy; see above, p. 17.

for the iniquities and for the transgressions and for the sins wherein Thy people, the House of Israel, have committed iniquity, have transgressed and sinned before Thee; as it is written in the Torah of Thy servant Moses, saying: "For on this day shall atonement be made for you, to cleanse you; from all your sins shall ye be clean before JHVH" (Lev. xvi. 30). And when the priests and the people that stood in the Court heard the glorious and revered Name pronounced freely out of the mouth of the High Priest, in holiness and purity, they knelt and prostrated themselves, falling on their faces, and exclaiming: Blessed be His glorious, sovereign Name for ever and ever' (Joma VI. 2).

In the last stage of the Temple's existence, there was reluctance to give a clear enunciation of the tetragrammaton. This practice is attested by R. Tarphon, who belonged to a priestly family. He records that in his boyhood, before he was old enough to officiate, 'On one occasion I followed my uncles on to the dais, and I inclined my ear to catch what the High Priest said. I heard him cause the Name to be drowned by the singing of his brother-priests' (Kid. 71a).[34]

Behind the care not to give explicit utterance to the Name may be detected a lowering in the moral standard of the priests. The Talmud declares: 'At first the High Priest used to proclaim the Name in a loud voice; but when dissolute men multiplied, he proclaimed it in a low tone' (p. Joma 40d).

On the other hand, there was a time when the free and open use of the Name even by the layman was advocated. The Mishnah teaches: 'It was ordained that a man should greet his friends by mentioning the Name' (Ber. IX. 5). It has been suggested that the recommendation was based on the desire to distinguish the Israelite from the Samaritan, who referred to God as 'the Name' and not as JHVH, or the Rabbinite Jew from the Jewish-Christian.

This custom, however, was soon discontinued, and among those who are excluded from a share in the World to Come is 'he who pronounces the Name according to its letters' (Sanh. x. 1). A third-century Rabbi taught: 'Whoever explicitly pronounces the Name is guilty of a capital offence' (Pesikta 148a).

Instead of JHVH the Name was pronounced *Adonai* (my Lord) in the Synagogue service; but there is a tradition that the original pronunciation was transmitted by the Sages to their disciples periodically—once or twice every seven years (Kid. 71a). Even that practice ceased after a while, and the method of pronouncing the Name is no longer known with certainty.

The conception of the Deity, as outlined above, shows that the Jews in the Talmudic period, like their forebears in the Biblical Age, worshipped no mere abstract First Cause. Theirs was essentially a 'personal' God in the sense that He was a reality to those who acknowledged Him. The accessibility and

---

[34] Josephus, who also belonged to a family of priests, likewise displays hesitation to mention the tetragrammaton in explicit terms. He wrote: 'Whereupon God declared to him (viz. to Moses) His name, which had never been discovered to men before, concerning which it is not lawful for me to speak' (Antiq. 11. xii. 4).

nearness of God will be discussed in the next chapter; but enough has been cited to demonstrate that the thought of Him was intended to be an inspiration to holy and righteous living.

Certain doctrines in connection with the Deity were forced into general prominence and received special emphasis at the hands of the Rabbis because of contemporaneous circumstances. The attribute of Unity had to be underlined when a trinitarian dogma began to be preached by the new sect of Christians. The incorporeality and holiness of God were constantly stressed as a protest against the immoral and degrading actions which neighbouring peoples associated with their gods.

The Rabbis strove to keep their doctrine of God pure and undefiled, so that it might become a refining and elevating force in the lives of those who acclaimed Him. He was an approachable God with Whom the human being could commune, the merciful and gracious Father Who loved His earthly family and desired their happiness. Though He was necessarily apart from His creatures by reason of His infinite majesty and absolute perfection, there was a firm and secure connecting link between them, because man had been created in His image. This supremely important tenet separated the human race from the rest of the animal kingdom and raised humanity towards divinity, although the dividing line between the two can never be bridged.[35]

[35] See p. 67 and p. 386 n. 1.

PART V

RELIGIOUS ETHICS

Shantivan: Memorial to Jawaharlal Nehru, New Delhi.
(Photo by J. T. Carmody)

INTRODUCTION

Ethics deals with behavior. The religions have been greatly concerned with behavior; they have formed people's ideas about how to live—what to prize and what to avoid. In east Asia, Confucianism has been the most important ethical influence. In India, Hinduism has most shaped human behavior. Muslim cultures have looked to the law codes for guidance about right and wrong, licit and illicit. European peoples have been shaped by the Bible. Because religion is holistic, it has to be concerned with more than thought. Because it wants to form the heart as well as the head it has to give guidance about good and evil feelings, good and evil deeds. So the things we read about in this part are matters of great interest to traditional religion. East and West, what people did has been even more important than what they said or thought.

The first selection, from the much loved Theravadin Buddhist text known as *The Dhammapada* (Path of the Teaching), represents early Buddhist convictions about virtue and vice. *The Dhammapada* is part of the canon of Buddhist scriptures written in Pali, a vernacular Indian language dating from shortly after the Buddha's time. The literary conceit is that the Buddha gave this teaching, and the historical fact seems to be that this text is older than the first century of the Christian Era.

The split between Theravada Buddhists, who have been most influential in countries close to India (Buddhism lost out to Hinduism in India itself), and Mahayana Buddhists, who have been most influential in countries farther to the East (China, Japan), has had only slight impact on the interpretation of ethical texts such as *The Dhammapada*. Mahayana Buddhism has been more interested in metaphysics than Theravada, and more concerned about the religious life of the laity. But both schools have agreed that wisdom, morality, and meditation are the three basic supports of the Buddhist way of life. So both have venerated *The Dhammapada* as a font of moralistic wisdom.

The second selection, from *The Analects of Confucius*, shows how his disciples remembered Master Kung to have taught. Most traditional religions have revered the relationship between a master and his disciples. The inner spirit of the tradition would pass along only if apt students apprenticed themselves to wise masters, for how the master lived was as important as what he said. His wisdom was holistic, and one could "catch" it only by observing him in the round. Through the give and take of question and answer, general principle and specific application, a disciple gradually learned what the tradition actually meant. Confucius thought that he was handing on the wisdom of the ancients—the profound sense of reality upon which Chinese culture rested. His great interest was in what we might call political philosophy or social ethics, and his great conviction was that if leaders lived good lives and set good examples, the common people would usually do what was right. The *Analects* themselves came into present shape perhaps a century after the death of Confucius (479 B.C.), but the verses that we present are probably close to the Master's own words.

The third selection, from the canonical Confucian text known as *The Teachings of Mencius*, shows what a leading disciple had made of the Master's inspiration a hundred years or so later. Like Confucius, Mencius was a tutor to privileged youth whose parents wanted them to learn the traditional principles of gentlemanly behavior. Like the *Analects*, the *Mencius* takes the form of sayings that disciples had written down and credited to their master. Mencius follows Confucius in being greatly interested in the virtues that constitute an admirable character. These are especially humaneness (*jen*) and propriety (*li*). Filial piety is very important, and so is ruling by good example rather than force.

The Laws of Manu, a very influential Hindu text, furnishes the fourth selection. Manu is another legendary figure, and although the text attributed to him is not part of the Vedic literature (the holiest Hindu scriptures), it set the tone for traditional social life in India. By articulating the long-standing convictions about the four stages of the ideal life cycle, the status and obligations of the four main classes (castes), and the status of women, Manu gathered together the key images that Indians have used to think about themselves down the millennia. These images are presented as part of the way that things are: the stages of life and the social classes come from the gods and are encoded in the cosmos. They were not made by human beings, so human beings cannot change them.

The fifth selection comes from a contemporary Christian textbook. The method used in this textbook is to present a concrete case and elucidate Christian principles by analyzing it. We present a case concerning a typical current dilemma in the area of bioethics: decisions about patients with AIDS. The virtue of the textbook is that it shows the complexity of real ethical decisions. One can speak clearly about basic precepts of Christian ethics (as of most other religious traditions), but when complicated contemporary technology is a factor, or one has to balance several competing rights (for example, the right of AIDS patients to confidentiality and the right of those in potentially dangerous contact with patients to know about their own possible peril), that clarity is hard to maintain. So the case method spotlights not only the necessity of knowing traditional teaching, but also the necessity of developing the great ethical virtue of prudence. Prudence is the ability to weigh the data and see how they balance out in a particular instance. It is a matter of an instinct, usually best tutored by experience, that allows one to understand how general principles apply to actual circumstances.

The spirit of Confucius determined the ethics of East Asia for most of two thousand years. In China, Japan, Vietnam, Korea, and other lands the sense of relations in family life, in political life, and among social classes came from Confucius and his followers more than any other source. Certainly, China, Japan, and the other East Asian countries also took much Buddhist teaching to heart, so themes such as those that we meet in *The Dhammapada* were also influential. But Buddhism and Taoism tended to have more impact on individual and aesthetic life than on general mores and politics. It was the Confucian instinct (or the Confucian articulation of immemorial East Asian instinct) about reverence for elders, the priority of men over women, the importance of ritual and protocol, the place of virtue in politics (and in all other uses of knowledge and power) that determined the East Asian sense of interpersonal relations. The two leading Confucian virtues, *jen* (humaneness) and *li* (propriety), sketched a humanistic ideal of self-contained yet graceful interactions among all age groups and social classes as well as between the sexes.

The Indian (Buddhist and Hindu) sense of virtue has depended on the notion that the only way to extinguish suffering is to extinguish desire. Until people have no inordinate wants, they will continue to be trapped in the karmic cycles of death and rebirth. Karma is the force that acts carry, their impact on people's character. In traditional Indian perspective, the state into which one is born derives from the karma that one has accrued through previous lives, and the state of one's next birth will depend on how one lives in the present life. However, if one stops desiring such things as pleasure, status, and riches, one can start to pry oneself away from the clutches of karma. The Buddha's Noble Eightfold Path laid out a program for such a liberation. The main aspects of that program were meditation, wisdom, and morality. People meditated so that they might perceive the truth of the Buddha's teaching for themselves and have their consciousnesses restructured by it. They studied the traditional *Dhamma* (Teaching) so that they might take it to heart, understand it from within. And they tried to abide by the core ethical precepts (*Sila*: not to kill, steal, lie, be unchaste, or take intoxicants) as the way to conform their behavior to the Buddha's teaching. On the whole, Hindu ethics has been quite similar, stressing obedience to traditional views of caste and nonviolence.

Christian ethics has taken Jesus' twofold commandment as its deepest foundation: love of God, with whole mind, heart, soul, and strength, and love of neighbor as oneself. It has also depended on the ten Commandments revered in Judaism. Inasmuch as they developed their moral thought from Jewish roots, the early Christians were concerned with transforming Jewish ethics (as represented in the Old Testament) in light of what they believed had happened in Christ. Principally, this meant stressing the love that God had shown through Jesus, and also taking to heart the corruption that the murder of Jesus had underscored. Thus Christian moralists have vacillated in their estimates of human nature. Some have stressed the image of God that human beings carry, and the presence of divine life in believers' hearts through grace. Others have stressed the influence of "original sin" (the fall of humanity from intimacy with God and from easy harmony between flesh and spirit) and so have thought that human instincts are not trustworthy.

In the selections one can sense both the importance of moral effort and the frustrations it runs into. People must put forth some effort if they are to do what is right on a regular basis. They must reject base motives, discipline their sensual desires, curtain their pride, consider the common good, and much more. On the other hand, they seem bound never to succeed in this task, always to fall short of sainthood or perfection. So, regularly, ethics has sent people to prayer to seek God's help. Regularly it has suggested that without such help none of us can be fully human.

15

The Dhammapada, Chapters 1–3*

Buddhists have traditionally considered wisdom, morality, and meditation the three basic supports of the proper way of life. The Dhammapada (Path of the Teaching) is especially valued for representing early, key Buddhist convictions about virtue and vice. It is traditionally thought to be the actual teaching of the Buddha and has been considered a mainstay of ethical wisdom.

1
CONTRARY WAYS

1   What we are today comes from our thoughts of yesterday, and our present thoughts build our life of tomorrow: our life is the creation of our mind.

   If a man speaks or acts with an impure mind, suffering follows him as the wheel of the cart follows the beast that draws the cart.

2   What we are today comes from our thoughts of yesterday, and our present thoughts build our life of tomorrow: our life is the creation of our mind.

   If a man speaks or acts with a pure mind, joy follows him as his own shadow.

3   'He insulted me, he hurt me, he defeated me, he robbed me.' Those who think such thoughts will not be free from hate.

4   'He insulted me, he hurt me, he defeated me, he robbed me.' Those who think not such thoughts will be free from hate.

5   For hate is not conquered by hate: hate is conquered by love. This is a law eternal.

6   Many do not know that we are here in this world to live in harmony. Those who know this do not fight against each other.

7   He who lives only for pleasures, and whose soul is not in harmony, who considers not the food he eats, is idle and has not the power of virtue—such a man

*From *The Dhammapada*; translated by Juan Mascaró. London: Penguin Classics, 1975. Reproduced by permission of Penguin Books Ltd.

is moved by MARA [Satan], is moved by selfish temptations, even as a weak tree is shaken by the wind.

8   But he who lives not for pleasures, and whose soul is in self-harmony, who eats or fasts with moderation, and has faith and the power of virtue—this man is not moved by temptations, as a great rock is not shaken by the wind.

9   If a man puts on the pure yellow robe with a soul which is impure, without self-harmony and truth, he is not worthy of the holy robe.

10   But he who is pure from sin and whose soul is strong in virtue, who has self-harmony and truth, he is worthy of the holy robe.

11   Those who think the unreal is, and think the Real is not, they shall never reach the Truth, lost in the path of wrong thought.

12   But those who know the Real is, and know the unreal is not, they shall indeed reach the Truth, safe on the path of right thought.

13   Even as rain breaks through an ill-thatched house, passions will break through an ill-guarded mind.

14   But even as rain breaks not through a well-thatched house, passions break not through a well-guarded mind.

15   He suffers in this world, and he suffers in the next world: the man who does evil suffers in both worlds. He suffers, he suffers and mourns when he sees the wrong he has done.

16   He is happy in this world and he is happy in the next world: the man who does good is happy in both worlds. He is glad, he feels great gladness when he sees the good he has done.

17   He sorrows in this world, and he sorrows in the next world: the man who does evil sorrows in both worlds. 'I have done evil', thus he laments and more he laments on the path of sorrow.

18   He rejoices in this world, and he rejoices in the next world: the man who does good rejoices in both worlds. 'I have done good', thus he rejoices, and more he rejoices on the path of joy.

19   If a man speaks many holy words but he speaks and does not, this thoughtless man cannot enjoy the life of holiness: he is like a cowherd who counts the cows of his master.

20 Whereas if a man speaks but a few holy words and yet he lives the life of those words, free from passion and hate and illusion—with right vision and a mind free, craving for nothing both now and hereafter—the life of this man is a life of holiness.

2
WATCHFULNESS

21 Watchfulness is the path of immortality: unwatchfulness is the path of death. Those who are watchful never die: those who do not watch are already as dead.

22 Those who with a clear mind have seen this truth, those who are wise and ever-watchful, they feel the joy of watchfulness, the joy of the path of the Great.

23 And those who in high thought and in deep contemplation with ever-living power advance on the path, they in the end reach NIRVANA, the peace supreme and infinite joy.

24 The man who arises in faith, who ever remembers his high purpose, whose work is pure, and who carefully considers his work, who in self-possession lives the life of perfection, and who ever, for ever, is watchful, that man shall arise in glory.

25 By arising in faith and watchfulness, by self-possession and self-harmony, the wise man makes an island for his soul which many waters cannot overflow.

26 Men who are foolish and ignorant are careless and never watchful; but the man who lives in watchfulness considers it his greatest treasure.

27 Never surrender to carelessness; never sink into weak pleasures and lust. Those who are watchful, in deep contemplation, reach in the end the joy supreme.

28 The wise man who by watchfulness conquers thoughtlessness is as one who free from sorrows ascends the palace of wisdom and there, from its high terrace, sees those in sorrow below; even as a wise strong man on the holy mountain might behold the many unwise far down below on the plain.

29 Watchful amongst the unwatchful, awake amongst those who sleep, the wise man like a swift horse runs his race, outrunning those who are slow.

30 It was by watchfulness that Indra became the chief of the gods, and thus the gods praise the watchful, and thoughtlessness is ever despised.

31   The monk who has the joy of watchfulness and who looks with fear on thoughtlessness, he goes on his path like a fire, burning all obstacles both great and small.

32   The monk who has the joy of watchfulness, and who looks with fear on thoughtlessness, he can never be deprived of his victory and he is near NIRVANA.

3
THE MIND

33   The mind is wavering and restless, difficult to guard and restrain: let the wise man straighten his mind as a maker of arrows makes his arrows straight.

34   Like a fish which is thrown on dry land, taken from his home in the waters, the mind strives and struggles to get free from the power of Death.

35   The mind is fickle and flighty, it flies after fancies wherever it likes: it is difficult indeed to restrain. But it is a great good to control the mind; a mind self-controlled is a source of great joy.

36   Invisible and subtle is the mind, and it flies after fancies wherever it likes; but let the wise man guard well his mind, for a mind well guarded is a source of great joy.

37   Hidden in the mystery of consciousness, the mind, incorporeal, flies alone far away. Those who set their mind in harmony become free from the bonds of death.

38   He whose mind is unsteady, who knows not the path of Truth, whose faith and peace are ever wavering, he shall never reach fullness of wisdom.

39   But he whose mind in calm self-control is free from the lust of desires, who has risen above good and evil, he is awake and has no fear.

40   Considering that this body is frail like a jar, make your mind strong like a fortress and fight the great fight against MARA, all evil temptations. After victory guard well your conquests, and ever for ever watch.

41   For before long, how sad! this body will lifeless lie on the earth, cast aside like a useless log.

42   An enemy can hurt an enemy, and a man who hates can harm another man; but a man's own mind, if wrongly directed, can do him a far greater harm.

43   A father or a mother, or a relative, can indeed do good to a man; but his own right-directed mind can do to him a far greater good.

16

The Analects of Confucius, Book 4*

The relationship of the "master" and the "disciple" is of great importance in Chinese spiritual culture. A central belief is that what the master says cannot be separated from how he lives. The subject of the Analects *is what Confucius, the greatest master, taught his disciples. Only through experiencing and understanding the subtleties of dialogue with the master could the disciple truly obtain the benefits of the master's wisdom.*

1.   The Master said, It is Goodness that gives to a neighbourhood its beauty.[1] One who is free to choose, yet does not prefer to dwell among the Good—how can he be accorded the name of wise?[2]

2.   The Master said, Without Goodness a man
        Cannot for long endure adversity,
        Cannot for long enjoy prosperity.

The Good Man rests content with Goodness; he that is merely wise pursues Goodness in the belief that it pays to do so.

3, 4.   Of the adage[3] 'Only a Good Man knows how to like people, knows how to dislike them,' the Master said, He whose heart is in the smallest degree set upon Goodness will dislike no one.

5.   Wealth and rank are what every man desires; but if they can only be retained to the detriment of the Way he professes, he must relinquish them. Poverty and obscurity are what every man detests; but if they can only be avoided to the detriment of the Way he professes, he must accept them. The gentleman who ever parts company with Goodness does not fulfil that name.

[1]Cf. Mencius, II, 1, VII, 2.

[2]A justification of the maxim, 'When right does not prevail in a kingdom, then leave it,' and of Confucius's own prolonged travels.

[3]Cf. *Ta Hsüeh* ('The Great Learning'), commentary, X, 15. 'Only the Good man is considered capable of loving (*ai*) men, capable of hating them.' In the *Kuo Yü* (ch. 18), however, the saying is quite differently interpreted: 'Only a good man is safe to like and safe to dislike. . . . For if you like him, he will not take undue advantage of it; and if you dislike him, he will not resent it.' The words 'The Master said' at the beginning of paragraph 3 should be omitted, and paragraphs 3 and 4 taken together.

*Reprinted with permission of Macmillan Publishing Company from *The Analects of Confucius*, translated by Arthur Waley. Copyright 1938 by George Allen and Unwin Ltd.

Never for a moment[4] does a gentleman quit the way of Goodness. He is never so harried but that he cleaves to this; never so tottering but that he cleaves to this.

6.   The Master said, I for my part[5] have never yet seen one who really cared for Goodness, nor one who really abhorred wickedness. One who really cared for Goodness would never let any other consideration come first. One who abhorred wickedness would be so constantly doing Good that wickedness would never have a chance to get at him. Has anyone ever managed to do Good with his whole might even as long as the space of a single day? I think not. Yet I for my part have never seen anyone give up such an attempt because he had not the *strength* to go on. It may well have happened, but I for my part have never seen it.[6]

7.   The Master said, Every man's faults belong to a set.[7] If one looks out for faults it is only as a means of recognizing Goodness.

8.   The Master said, In the morning, hear the Way; in the evening, die content![8]

9.   The Master said, A Knight whose heart is set upon the Way, but who is ashamed of wearing shabby clothes and eating coarse food, is not worth calling into counsel.

10.   The Master said, A gentleman in his dealings with the world has neither enmities nor affections;[9] but wherever he sees Right he ranges himself beside it.

11.   The Master said, Where gentlemen set their hearts upon moral force (*tê*),[10] the commoners set theirs upon the soil.[11] Where gentlemen think only of punishments, the commoners think only of exemptions.[12]

12.   The Master said, Those[13] whose measures are dictated by mere expediency will arouse continual discontent.

---

[4]Literally, 'for as long as it takes to eat' one bowl of rice. A common impression, simply meaning a very little while.

[5]*Wo* as a nominative is more emphatic than *wu*.

[6]It is the will not the way that is wanting.

[7]i.e. a set of qualities which includes virtues.

[8]The well-known saying *Vedi Napoli e poi mori* follows the same pattern. The meaning is, you will have missed nothing.

[9]Reading uncertain, but general sense quite clear. See textual notes.

[10]As opposed to physical compulsion. See additional notes.

[11]They *an t'u* 'are content with the soil,' and prepared to defend it.

[12]*Hui* means amnesties, immunities, exemptions, as opposed to what is 'lawful and proper.'

[13]The rulers and upper classes in general.

13.   The Master said, If it is really possible to govern countries by ritual and yielding, there is no more to be said. But if it is not really possible, of what use is ritual?[14]

14.   The Master said, He[15] does not mind not being in office; all he minds about is whether he has qualities that entitle him to office. He does not mind failing to get recognition; he is too busy doing the things that entitle him to recognition.

15.   The Master said, Shên! My Way has one (thread) that runs right through it. Master Tsêng said, Yes. When the Master had gone out, the disciples asked, saying What did he mean? Master Tsêng said, Our Master's Way is simply this: Loyalty, consideration.[16]

16.   The Master said, A gentleman takes as much trouble to discover what is right as lesser men take to discover what will pay.

17.   The Master said, In the presence of a good man, think all the time how you may learn to equal him. In the presence of a bad man, turn your gaze within![17]

18.   The Master said, In serving his father and mother a man may gently remonstrate with them. But if he sees that he has failed to change their opinion, he should resume an attitude of deference and not thwart them; may feel discouraged, but not resentful.

19.   The Master said, While father and mother are alive, a good son does not wander far afield; or if he does so, goes only where he has said he was going.[18]

20.   The Master said, If for the whole three years of mourning a son manages to carry on the household exactly as in his father's day, then he is a good son indeed.[19]

---

[14]The saying can be paraphrased as follows: If I and my followers are right in saying that countries can be governed solely by correct carrying out of ritual and its basic principle of 'giving way to others,' there is obviously no case to be made out for any other form of government. If on the other hand we are wrong, then ritual is useless. To say, as people often do, that ritual is all very well so long as it is not used as an instrument of government, is wholly to misunderstand the purpose of ritual.

[15]The gentleman. But we might translate 'I do not mind,' etc.

[16]Loyalty to superiors; consideration for the feelings of others, 'not doing to them anything one would not like to have done to oneself,' as defined below, XV, 23 'Loyalty and Consideration' is one of the Nine Virtues enumerated by the *I Chou Shu*, 29, I verso. Cf. also XV, 2 below.

[17]'Within yourself scrutinize yourself.' *êrh* is the second person singular pronoun, not the conjunction.

[18]Particularly in order that if they die he may be able to come back and perform the rites of mourning.

[19]Cf. I, 11.

21.   The Master said, It is always better for a man to know the age of his parents. In the one case[20] such knowledge will be a comfort to him; in the other[21] it will fill him with a salutary dread.

22.   The Master said, In old days a man kept a hold on his words, fearing the disgrace that would ensue should he himself fail to keep pace with them.

23.   The Master said, Those who err on the side of strictness are few indeed!

24.   The Master said, A gentleman covets the reputation of being slow in word but prompt in deed.[22]

25.   The Master said, Moral force (*tê*) never dwells in solitude; it will always bring neighbours.[23]

26.   Tzu-yu said, In the service of one's prince repeated scolding[24] can only lead to loss of favour; in friendship, it can only lead to estrangement.

---

[20]If he knows that they are not so old as one might think.
[21]If he realizes that they are very old.
[22]Cf. *The Way and Its Power*, p.198.
[23]Whenever one individual or one country substitutes *tê* for physical compulsion, other individuals or other countries inevitably follow suit.
[24]Cf. XII, 23 and additional notes.

17

The Teachings of Mencius, from Chapter 6: "Humanity and Justice," "Familial Duty," and "Man's Nature and His Fate"*

Since the time of the master Confucius about 2500 years ago his followers have continually interpreted and reconsidered his wisdom. The teachings of one of the great disciples in the Confucian tradition, Mencius, come to us from a century after those of Confucius himself.

HUMANITY AND JUSTICE

The words jen *and* yi, *which I have translated "Humanity" and "Justice," are the key tenets of Mencius' system. Humanity (*jen*) is the attribute of being a man (*jen*) as a man at his best instinctively feels both he and others should be. It is the sympathy he has "naturally" for a fellow human being in trouble. It is a quality with which a man is born, but which he must "guard in the thoughts" and cultivate. Confucius used the word* jen *for a very nearly unattainable human perfection—a quality almost transcendental—which he would only attribute to the Divine Sages of antiquity. But to Mencius, "all men can be a Yao or a Shun" and the gentleman "who is a gentleman indeed" not only may, but does, assiduously cultivate* jen. *Mencius nowhere defines* jen *more closely than this, but rather speaks of the consequence of being* jen. *For the man who is* jen, *wisdom rather than folly, honour rather than disgrace, felicity rather than catastrophe, results. For the prince who has this quality, the goals of True Kingship are realized—the prosperity of his state, the perpetuating of his line, and ultimately the allegiance of the whole world. Jen* engenders *tê, "power"—a prestige and a moral persuasiveness which is the very opposite of* pa, *"physical force." Men everywhere, according to Mencius, find* jen *irresistible, for* jen *renders* pa *completely ineffective. Yi, "Justice," is the doing of what is right in seeing that others get their rights. "Rights" are not codified and referable to a system of law, but derive from custom: such things, for example, as the time-honoured "right" of the people to gather kindling in the forests, the "right" to the duties of a filial son by his father, the "right" of the people to a level of existence sufficient to maintain their aged in comfort. But it is also "right" to give and receive the niceties of courtesy, to behave and deport oneself according to the* Rites.

*W.A.C.H. Dobson, trans., *Mencius*. Toronto: University of Toronto Press. Reprinted by permission of University of Toronto Press.

In short, a man is jen *when he is what he should be, and* yi *when he does what he should do. Just what he should be and do in the Mencian view, we gather not from abstract definitions, but from the examples he gives.* [Translator's Note]

6.1

Mencius said, "It is a feeling common to all mankind that they cannot bear to see others suffer. The Former Kings had such feelings, and it was this that dictated their policies. One could govern the entire world with policies dictated by such feelings, as easily as though one turned it in the palm of the hand.

"I say that all men have such feelings because, on seeing a child about to fall into a well, everyone has a feeling of horror and distress. They do not have this feeling out of sympathy for the parents, or to be thought well of by friends and neighbours, or from a sense of dislike at not being thought a feeling person. Not to feel distress would be contrary to all human feeling. Just as not to feel shame and disgrace and not to defer to others and not to have a sense of right and wrong are contrary to all human feeling. This feeling of distress (at the suffering of others) is the first sign of Humanity. This feeling of shame and disgrace is the first sign of justice. This feeling of deference to others is the first sign of propriety. This sense of right and wrong is the first sign of wisdom. Men have these four innate feelings just as they have four limbs. To possess these four things, and to protest that one is incapable of fulfilling them, is to deprive oneself. To protest that the ruler is incapable of doing so is to deprive him. Since all have these four capacities within themselves, they should know how to develop and to fulfil them. They are like a fire about to burst into flame, or a spring about to gush forth from the ground. If, in fact, a ruler can fully realize them, he has all that is needed to protect the entire world. But if he does not realize them fully, he lacks what is needed to serve even his own parents."

(2A.6)

6.2

Mencius said, "All men have things they cannot tolerate, and if what makes this so can be fully developed in the things they can tolerate, the result is Humanity. All men have things they will not do, and if what makes this so can be fully developed in the things they will do, then Justice results. If a man can fully exploit the thing in his mind which makes him not wish to harm others, then Humanity will result in overwhelming measure. If a man can fully exploit the thing in his mind which makes him reluctant to break through or jump over (other people's) walls, Justice will ensue in overwhelming measure. If a man can fully exploit the reluctance he feels in the use of the salutation *ju* and *erh*[1] wherever he goes he will act justly. When a knight says something which he should not have said, and by doing so gains his end, or when by failing to say something he should have said similarly gains his end, this is only in principle the same as 'breaking through other people's walls.'"

(7B.31)

6.3

Mencius said, "Of all seeds, the five grains are the best. But if they do not come to fruit, then the *t'i* and *pai* are better.[2] With Humanity it is the same. It is a question of its coming to fruit—nothing more."

(6A.19)

6.4

Mencius said, "It is by what he guards in his thoughts that the True Gentleman differs from other men. He guards Humanity and propriety in his thoughts. The man of Humanity loves others. The man of propriety respects others. He who loves others is in turn loved by others. He who respects others is in turn respected by others. Suppose someone treats us badly. The True Gentleman will look for the reason within himself, feeling that he must have failed in Humanity or propriety, and will ask himself how such a thing could in fact have happened to him. If after examination he finds that he has acted Humanely and with propriety, and the bad treatment continues, he will look within himself again, feeling that he must have failed to do his best. But if on examination he finds that he has done his best, and the bad treatment continues, he will say, 'This person, after all, is an utter reprobate; I will have done with him. If he behaves like this, how does he differ from an animal? Why should I be put out by an animal?'

"Therefore the True Gentleman spends a lifetime of careful thought, but not a day in worrying. There are things to which he does give careful thought. 'Shun,' he says, 'was a man. I too am a man. But Shun became an examplar to the whole world, an example that has been passed down to us who come after, while I, as it were, am still a mere villager.' This is a matter about which he might take careful thought—taking careful thought only that he might be like Shun. As to those things about which the True Gentleman worries—they do not exist. What is contrary to Humanity he would not be. What is contrary to propriety he would not do. As to 'spending the day worrying,' the True Gentleman simply does not worry."

(4B.28)

---

[1]Pronouns of a direct and less direct form of address. The first is informal and intimate, but would be *gauche* if used to a superior. The latter indicates deference and would be comic if used, for example, to a child.

[2]Said to be wild, as opposed to cultivated, grain plants, with a very low yield. The "five grains" are the edible crops of the farmer: rice, millet of two kinds, wheat, and pulse.

6.5

Mencius said, "Is the arrow-maker any less Humane than the armourer because his main concern is that his arrows should do the utmost damage, while the armourer's concern is that the least damage might be done? Is the shaman more Humane than the coffin-maker (because the shaman is interested in the patient's recovery, while the coffin-maker is interested in his death)? And, too, in the matter of the choice of the doctrine one follows, one cannot be too careful.

"Confucius said, 'It is Humanity that adorns a village. What can be said of the wisdom of him who chooses to live where Humanity is not? Humanity is the patent of honour bestowed by Heaven, the house of security where man should dwell. Since none can prevent us being Humane, not to be Humane is folly. Not to be Humane, not to be wise, is to lack a sense of propriety and to lack a sense of Justice. Such a person is the bondservant of others. To be a servant, and to be ashamed of one's servitude, is like the bow-maker being ashamed of his bows, and the arrow-maker of his arrows. Rather than be ashamed of such servitude it were better to be Humane. To be Humane is like engaging in archery. The archer adjusts his person before shooting. Having shot and failed to hit the bull's eye, he does not rail against those who have shot better. He seeks the remedy in himself."

(2A.7)

6.6

Mencius said, "If one is Humane then glory results, but if one is not Humane then disgrace results. For a man to fear disgrace, and yet to continue contrary to Humanity, is like fearing the damp and continuing to live in a low-lying place. Rather than fear disgrace, it were better to ennoble virtue, and to accord honour to the knights who exemplify it.[3] When worthy men are in positions of authority, the competent carry out their duties. At such times as the state is in repose, its policies and laws can be made clear to all. Even a major state will stand in fear of such a state. In the *Book of Songs* it says:

> Before the days of cloud and rain came
> I took the mulberry roots
> And wove them into a window and door,
> You people down below!
> Who dares insult me now?

Confucius said, 'How well the author of this song knew the Way! Who dares to impugn the man who governs his House and State well?' But today, at such times as the state is in repose, its officers abandon themselves to pleasure and indolent ease. They are merely seeking catastrophe for themselves. Catastrophe or happiness are invariably self-sought. The *Book of Songs* says:

[3]It was King Hui of Liang who "feared disgrace" and sought for "honour."

Think always of being the fit recipient of the Charge.
Seek for yourself its many blessings.

and the *T'ai Chia* says:

When catastrophe is of Heaven's making
We may still escape.
When Catastrophe is of our own making
We will not survive.

The *Songs* and the *Book of Documents* are here referring to this.

(2A.4)

6.7

Mencius said, "A Paramount Prince was one who, pretending to Humanity, resorted to force. Such a one had need of the rule of a major state. A True King is one who, practicing Humanity, resorts only to virtue. Such a one has no need of a major state. T'ang the Successful had a state of only seventy miles square, and King Wen a state of only a hundred miles square. They were True Kings. Allegiance which is gained by the use of force is not an allegiance of the heart—it is the allegiance which comes from imposing upon weakness. Allegiance which is gained by the exercise of virtue is true allegiance. It is the response of joy felt deeply in the heart. Such was the allegiance that Confucius gained from his seventy followers. The *Book of Songs* says:

From the West, from the East,
From the North and from the South,
There was no thought of not rendering allegiance.

The *Songs* here refer to the allegiance of the heart."

(2A.3)

6.8

Mencius said, "When a minister is not up to remonstrating with his prince, then it is not enough to find fault with his government. It is only a great man who can rectify error in the prince's mind. If the prince is a man of Humanity, then nothing in his state but will be Humane. If the prince is a man of Justice, then nothing in his state but will be Just. If the prince is a man of rectitude, then nothing in his state but will be upright. Once the prince is corrected, the good government of the kingdom is assured."

(4A.21)

6.9

If the prince is a man of Humanity then nothing in his state but will be Humane.

If the prince is a man of Justice, then nothing in his state but will be Just.

(4B.5)

6.10

Mencius said, "The Three Dynasties[4] gained the Empire by Humanity and lost it by Inhumanity. States rise and fall, and are held and are lost for the same reason. If the Son of Heaven is Inhumane he will lose his Empire. If the Feudatory are Inhumane they will surrender their altars.[5] If ministers and Great Officers are Inhumane they will forfeit their family shrines. If knights and commoners are Inhumane they will not keep their four limbs intact. If a man abhors death and destruction, yet delights in the Inhumane, it is as though he were revolted by drunkenness, yet allowed himself to be urged to drink more wine."

(4A.3)

6.11

Mencius said, "Humanity extinguishes Inhumanity just as water extinguishes fire. Men of Humanity today are like a cup of water used to extinguish a wagon-load of burning kindling, which, when it fails to extinguish such a fire, is said to show that water is ineffectual against fire. But the Inhumane are in a more serious plight than they (the Humane). The Inhumane are, after all, headed in the end for destruction."

(6A.18)

FAMILIAL DUTY

To the man of Justice and Humanity, "the duty from which all others spring" is his duty towards his parents. Hsiao, "filial piety," the son owes to his father, and t'i "the duty of the younger brother," the brother owes to his older brother. Familial duty derives from the ancient religion where the ever present ancestors stored up the virtus *of the line, and to whom worship was offered, and whose help was invoked for the fortunes of the family. This was later extended to "serving the parents while they are still living." And hence was developed the Confucian teaching of filial duty. In later Confucianism hsiao becomes almost a metaphysical principle, but in Mencius' time it still lies within the realm of precept.*

The Mohists developed this idea even further. The duty we owe to parents, they argued, we owe in equal measure to all mankind. Thus, incongruously perhaps, Confucians and Mohists saw an antithesis between "familial duty" and "universal love," though both argued that the one led eventually to the other.[6] [Translator's Note]

---

[4]I.e., of Hsia, Shang, and Chou. The House of Chou, though *de jure* still rulers, had "lost" their Mandate in the eighth century under King Yu and King Li (see 4.11).

[5]That is, the altars of the soul and crops, the proprietorship of which was the patent of feudal tenure.

[6]See 6.34: "The Humane include all within their affections."

6.12

Mencius said, "Humanity attains its finest flower in the service of parents. Justice attains its finest flower in obedience to older brothers. Wisdom its finest flower in the realization of these two things and consistently adhering to them. Ritual attains its finest flower in the formulation of these two things into a disciplined pattern. Joy has its finest flower in the pleasure that is derived from these two things. In pleasure they grow, and growing they are irrepressible. And being irrepressible all unknowingly the feet take up the measure and the hands begin the dance."

(4A.27)

6.13

Mencius said, "Of all my duties, which is the greatest? My duty to my own parents! Of all that is held in trust by me which is the greatest? The preservation of my body! I have heard of those who, having kept their bodies inviolate, could serve their parents, but not of those who, failing to do so, still served their parents. Whichever duty I fail to perform, it must not be my duty to my parents, for that is the duty from which all others spring. Whichever trust I fail to fulfil, it must not be that of keeping my body inviolate, for that is the trust from which all others arise.

"When Tseng Tzu was providing for his father, Tseng Hsi, he invariably served wine and meat. On removing the dishes at the end of a meal he would ask his father to whom the remainder should be given. If asked if there was any more, he always answered yes. When Master Tseng in his turn was being provided for by his son Tseng Yüan, Tseng Yüan too served wine and meat, but on removing the dishes at the end of the meal he did not ask his father to whom the remainder should be given, and, if asked if there was any more, he always said no. This was because he intended to serve anything left over again the next day. Tseng Yüan's duty to his aged father was what might be called 'ministering to the mouth and body' (the outer shell of observance), while that of Tseng Tzu to his father was what might be called 'ministering to the heart' (an observance of sincerity).[7]

"It is familial duty as exemplified by Tseng Tzu that has my approval."

(4A.20)

6.14

The Way lies close at hand, yet men seek for it afar. Duty is not hard, yet men seek it in the most difficult things. If each man individually were to treat his own kin as properly they should be treated, and respected his elders with the respect that is due to them, the whole world would be at peace.

(4A.12)

---

[7]Or, as we should say, the "letter of the law" in contrast to the "spirit of the law."

6.15

Mencius said, "A True Gentleman loves all living creatures, but does not treat all with Humanity. He treats all human beings with Humanity, but does not treat them all with familial affection.

"He who feels the love of family towards his own kin will feel Humanity for all men. He who feels Humanity for all men will be kind to all living creatures."[8]

(7A.45)

6.16

Mencius said, "Three things delight the True Prince, but being sovereign of the universe is not one of them. His first delight is that his parents are still living and that his brothers give no occasion for anxiety. His second delight is that he can look at Heaven unabashed and face his fellow men without a blush. His third delight is to gain the allegiance of the world's most talented men, and to instruct and train them. These are his three delights, but being sovereign of the universe is not one of them."

(7A.20)

6.17

Mencius said, "The support of parents during their lifetime does not by itself meet the requirements of the supreme duty; these are only met in full when parents have been properly interred."

(4B.13)

6.18

Mencius said, "There are three contraventions of the rules of filial piety, and of these the greatest is to have no progeny. It was for this reason that Shun married, even at the cost of failing to inform his parents. The True Gentleman would regard the reasons which prompted Shun to marry as cancelling out his obligation to inform his parents first."

(4A.26)

MAN'S NATURE AND HIS FATE

Man's nature, hsing *(about which several theories were held in Mencius' day), was to Mencius innately good, and this was attested by the universality of a sense of kinship and of right and wrong. It is in this that man differs from other living creatures. But the* hsing *can "be hacked away at" and atrophy and disappear if not "nurtured" aright. Nurturing the* hsing *consists in "guarding the mind" (ts'un hsin), for the mind is the repository of "Humanity" and "Justice." It is the*

---

[8]In the Mencian system, *ai*, "love" is contained within *jen*, "Humanity," and *jen* is contained within *ch'in*, "family love." *Ch'in* and *jen* take priority over *ai*. In the Mician system *ai* is supreme, and *chien ai*, "universal love," takes priority over *jen* and *ch'in*.

hsing and hsin *that determine what we are. It is our* ming, *"fate," that governs our fortunes and determines our lease on life.* Ming *was originally a patent to a fief-holder, given by the Son of Heaven, as heaven's deputy, to a feudatory. In extended usage it is our "lot in life"—the fate ordained by Heaven. While a man can "guard his mind" and determine his conduct, he cannot determine his fate, which is in Heaven's hands.*

Though all men are innately good, the realization of that good comes with self-cultivation and self-knowledge. [Translator's Note]

6.19

The difference between a man and an animal is slight. The common man disregards it altogether, but the True Gentleman guards the distinction most carefully. Shun understood all living things, but saw clearly the relationships that exist uniquely among human beings. These relationships proceed from Humanity and Justice. It is not because of these relationships that we proceed towards Humanity and Justice.

(4B.19)

6.20

Mencius said, "Bull Mountain was once beautifully wooded. But, because it was close to a large city, its trees all fell to the axe. What of its beauty then? However, as the days passed things grew, and with the rains and the dews it was not without greenery. Then came the cattle and goats to graze. That is why, today, it has that scoured-like appearance. On seeing it now, people imagine that nothing ever grew there. But this is surely not the true nature of a mountain? And so, too, with human beings. Can it be that any man's mind naturally lacks Humanity and Justice? If he loses his sense of the good, then he loses it as the mountain lost its trees. It has been hacked away at—day after day—what of its beauty then?

"However, as the days pass he grows, and, as with all men, in the still air of the early hours his sense of right and wrong is at work. If it is barely perceptible, it is because his actions during the day have disturbed or destroyed it. Being disturbed and turned upside down the 'night airs' can barely sustain it. If this happens he is not far removed from the animals. Seeing a man so close to an animal, people cannot imagine that once his nature was different—but this is surely not the true nature of the man? Indeed, if nurtured aright, anything will grow, but if not nurtured aright anything will wither away. Confucius said, 'Hold fast to it, and you preserve it; let it go and you destroy it; it may come and go at any time no one knows its whereabouts.' Confucius was speaking of nothing less than the mind."

(6A.8)

6.21

Mencius said, "I am fond of fish, but, too, I am fond of bear's paws. If I cannot have both, then I prefer bear's paws. I care about life, but, too, I care about Justice. If I cannot have both, then I choose Justice. I care about life, but then there are things I care about more than life. For that reason I will not seek life improperly. I do not like death, but then there are things I dislike more than death. For that reason there are some contingencies from which I will not escape.

"If men are taught to desire life above all else, then they will seize it by all means in their power. If they are taught to hate death above all else, then they will avoid all contingencies by which they might meet it. There are times when one might save one's life, but only by means that are wrong. There are times when death can be avoided, but only by means that are improper. Having desires above life itself and having dislikes greater than death itself is a type of mind that all men possess—it is not only confined to the worthy. What distinguishes the worthy is that he ensures that he does not lose it.

"Even though it be a matter of life or death to him, a traveller will refuse a basket of rice or a dish of soup if offered in an insulting manner. But food that has been trampled upon, not even a beggar will think fit to eat. And yet a man will accept emoluments of ten thousand *chung* regardless of the claims of propriety and Justice. And what does he gain by that? Elegant palaces and houses, wives and concubines to wait on him, and the allegiance of the poor among his acquaintance! I was previously speaking of matters affecting life and death, where even there under certain conditions one will not accept relief, but this is a matter of palaces and houses, of wives and concubines, and of time-serving friends. Should we not stop such things? This is what I mean by 'losing the mind with which we originally were endowed.'"

(6A.10)

6.22

Mencius said, "To the hungry all food is sweet; to the thirsty all water is sweet. Such cannot judge when food and drink is as it should be. Their hunger and thirst blunt their palate. And it is not surely only the mouth and belly that are affected by hunger and thirst; they affect the minds of men. If, though he suffers from hunger and thirst, a man can remain unaffected in his mind, it need occasion him no regret that, in this, he is not like other men."[9]

(7A.27)

6.23

Mencius said, "In the nurturing of the mind, there is no better method than that of cutting down the number of desires. A man who has few desires, though he may have things in his mind which he should not have, will have but few of them. A man who has many desires, though he may have things in his mind which he should have, will have but few of them."

(7B.35)

[9]That he is, so to say, a freak.

6.24

Mencius said, "It is the man who has stretched his mind to the full who fully understands man's true nature. And understanding his true nature, he understands Heaven. To guard one's mind and to nourish one's true nature is to serve Heaven. Do not be in two minds about premature death or a ripe old age. Cultivate yourself and await the outcome. In this way you will attain to your allotted span."

(7A.1)

6.25

Mencius said, "It is of their essential nature for the mouth to be concerned with taste, for the eye with colour, for the ear with sound, for the nose with smell, and for the four limbs to seek rest and repose. But in these functions, there is, too, the element of Heaven's purposes. The True Gentleman does not call this element 'essential nature.'

"Humanity is concerned with father and son, Justice with prince and subject, the Rites with host and guest, wisdom with worthy men, and being a Sage with the Way of Heaven. These are Heaven's purposes, but, too, there is in them an element of the 'essential nature.' The True Gentlemen does not call this element 'Heaven's purpose.'"

(7B.24)

6.26

Mencius said, "Nothing, but is preordained. We should accept obediently our rightful lot. Therefore he who understands Heaven's ordinances does not walk below high walls, but when he dies in the full discharge of his principles he has fulfilled the lot that Heaven has ordained for him. He who dies, however, in a felon's chains cannot be said to have fulfilled the lot that Heaven ordained for him."

(7A.2)

6.27

Mencius said, " 'Seek and we find; let go and we lose.' Seeking is only of value in finding, when what is sought lies with us to seek. But there is a principle in seeking. When what we are to find is already preordained then seeking itself is of no value. What is sought is beyond our control."

(7A.3)

6.28

Mencius said, "The functions of the body are the endowments of Heaven. But it is only a Sage who can properly manipulate them."

(7A.38)

6.29

Mencius said, "A man cares about all parts of his body without discrimination, and so he nurtures all parts equally. There is not a square inch of skin that he does not care about, and so he tends all of his skin equally. His decision as to what is most effective for himself comes from within himself. The human body has parts which are large and parts which are small. He does not treat one to the detriment of the rest. But he who gives preferential treatment to the lesser parts of the body becomes a lesser man. He who gives preferential treatment to the great parts becomes a greater man.

"Suppose a wood-lot owner neglected the timber trees and looked after the undergrowth; he would be a very poor wood-lot operator. A doctor who treated one finger and neglected the back and shoulders would be a very befuddled physician. Men despise one who lives only to eat and drink, because he develops the lesser functions of his body and neglects the greater. If he wishes not to neglect the greater, should he not regard his mouth and belly as a 'single square inch of skin?'"

(6A.14)

6.30

Determination is like digging a well; if water is not struck after digging for nine fathoms, one might as well abandon the well.[10]

(7A.29)

6.31

Mencius said, "If a man love others, and his love is not reciprocated let him think about his own feelings for Humanity. If a man govern others, and they fail to respond, let him think about his own wisdom. If a man extend courtesies to others, and is not in turn treated with courtesy, let him think about his own sense of reverence. If a man pursue a course, and his way is impeded, let him seek the remedy in himself. With these things correct within himself, the whole world will turn to him. The *Book of Songs* says,

'Think always of being the fit recipient of the Charge
Seek for yourself its many blessings.'"

(4A.4)

6.32

Mencius said, "Anyone who really wishes to grow a small tree like the *t'ung* or *szu* tree learns how to tend it. But in the matter of one's own person, there are those who do not learn how to tend it, not so much because they have a greater love for a tree than for themselves, but because of a heedlessness that is very deep-seated."

(6A.13)

6.33

Mencius said, "Suppose a man has a little finger which is crooked, and which he cannot straighten out. He feels no pain; neither does it affect his

[10]I.e., there is no virtue in setting one's sights upon the unattainable (c.f. 6.27).

work. He will, even so, go as far as Ch'u or Ch'in if there were someone there who could set it straight again. Why? Because it makes him different from other men.[11] If a man's little finger makes him different from others, he knows enough to feel embarrassed about it. If a man's mind makes him different from other men and he does not know enough to feel embarrassed about it, then that is what I call 'being unaware of things of like kind.'"

(6A.12)

6.34

Mencius said, "The wise take all knowledge for their province, but are most concerned about important things. The Humane include all within their affections, but are most concerned with affection for the worthy. Yao and Shun in their wisdom did not know everything—they were concerned with things of the first priority. The Humanity of Yao and Shun was not impartially displayed to all men—they were concerned most with affection for the worthy. Those who are meticulous about the light mourning worn for distant relatives, but neglect the deep mourning for close relatives, who gulp and guzzle at meals yet ask questions about the propriety of biting meat with the teeth—these are examples of not being concerned with the important things."

(7A.46)

6.35

Mencius said, "A Humane word does not affect men so profoundly as a Humane reputation. Good government does not affect them so profoundly as gaining their allegiance by good teaching. Good government the people respect, but good teaching the people love. By good government one may elicit the people's wealth, but by good teaching one elicits their hearts."

(7A.14)

6.36

Mencius said, "Most people do things without knowing what they do, and go on doing them without any thought as to what they are doing. They do this all their lives without ever understanding the Way."

(7A.5)

6.37

A man cannot be shameless. Shamelessness is the shame of having no sense of shame.

(7A.6)

6.38

Mencius said, "All things are complete within ourselves. There is no joy that exceeds that of the discovery, upon self-examination, that we have acted

[11]I.e., a freak.

with integrity. And we are never closer to achieving Humanity than when we seek to act, constrained by the principle of reciprocity."

(7A.4)

6.39

Mencius said, "Humanity is the mind of man. Justice, the path he follows. If by closing the way he fails to follow it, then he loses his mind and has no way of retrieving it. How sad this is! If a fowl or a dog stray we know how to find them again, but if the mind strays we have no such recourse. The whole purport of learning is nothing more than this: to regain the mind that has strayed."

(6A.11)

6.40

Mencius said, "The True Gentleman pursues knowledge profoundly according to the Way, wishing to appropriate it for himself. Having appropriated it, he abides with it in perfect assurance. Abiding with it in assurance, he stores it deeply, and storing it deeply he draws from it whichever way he moves, as though he were encountering a spring. For this reason the True Gentleman wishes to appropriate knowledge for himself."[12]

(4B.14)

6.41

Mencius said, "Those men who have the wisdom of virtue, and many-sided knowledge, will often be found to have discovered it in personal distress. Like the orphaned servant or the concubine's son, they take careful thought as though in imminent danger, and anticipate trouble with profound care. That is why they succeed."

(7A.18)

6.42

Mencius said, "The abilities men have which are not acquired by study are part of their endowment of good. The knowledge men have which is not acquired by deep thought is part of their endowment of good. Every baby in his mother's arms knows about love for his parents. When they grow up, they know about the respect they must pay to their elder brothers. The love for parents is Humanity. The respect for elders is Justice. It is nothing more than this, and it is so all over the world."

(7A.15)

---

[12]This does not, I confess, make very much sense. There is reason to suppose that the text is corrupt.

18

The Laws of Manu, Chapters 2–6*

The holy text known as The Laws of Manu *has served as an enormously influential social document for Hindus. It draws together and restates many of the long-standing traditions of social life in India. Among the concerns addressed in the document are the roles of the castes and the status of women.*

2. GENERAL PATTERN OF THE SOCIAL ORDER

87. The student, the householder, the hermit, and the ascetic, these (constitute) four separate orders, which all spring from (the order of) householders.

88. But all (or) even (any of) these orders, assumed successively in accordance with the Institutes (of the sacred law), lead the *brāhmin* who acts by the preceding (rules) to the highest state.

89. And in accordance with the precepts of the Veda and of the traditional texts, the housekeeper [householder] is declared to be superior to all of them [the other three orders]; for he supports the other three.

90. As all rivers, both great and small, find a resting place in the ocean, even so men of all orders find protection with householders.

91. By twice-born men belonging to (any of) these four orders, the tenfold law must be ever carefully obeyed.

92. Contentment, forgiveness, self-control, abstention from unrighteously appropriating anything, (obedience to the rules of) purification, coercion of the organs [control of the senses], wisdom, knowledge (of the supreme Self), truthfulness, and abstention from anger (form) the tenfold law.

(VI.87–92)

63. Abstention from injuring (creatures), veracity, abstention from unlawfully appropriating (the goods of others), purity, and control of the organs, Manu has declared to be the summary of the law for the four castes.

(X.63)

1. Let the three twice-born castes, discharging their (prescribed) duties,

*Sarvepalli Radhakrishnan and Charles A. Moore, eds., *A Sourcebook in Indian Philosophy*. Copyright © 1957, © renewed 1985 by Princeton University Press. Pages 175–192 reprinted by permission.

study (the Veda); but among them the *brāhmin* (alone) shall teach it, not the other two; that is an established rule.

2. The *brāhmin* must know the means of subsistence (prescribed) by law for all, instruct the others, and himself live according to (the law).

3. On account of his pre-eminence, on account of the superiority of his origin, on account of his observance of (particular) restrictive rules, and on account of his particular sanctification, the *brāhmin* is the lord of (all) castes.

4. The *brāhmin*, the *kṣatriya*, and the *vaiśya* castes are the twice-born ones, but the fourth, the *śūdra*, has one birth only; there is no fifth (caste).

(x.1–4)

31. But for the sake of the prosperity of the worlds, he [the Lord] caused the *brāhmin*, the *kṣatriya*, the *vaiśya*, and the *śūdra* to proceed from his mouth, his arms, his thighs, and his feet.[1]   (I.31)

87. But in order to protect this universe He, the most resplendent one, assigned separate (duties and) occupations to those who sprang from his mouth, arms, thighs, and feet.   (I.87)

45. All those tribes in this world, which are excluded from the (community of) those born from the mouth, the arms, the thighs, and the feet (of *Brahman*), are called Dasyus, whether they speak the language of the Mlekkhas [*Mlecchas*] (barbarians) or that of the Āryans.   (x.45)

41. (A King) who knows the sacred law, must inquire into the laws of castes, of districts, of guilds, and of families, and (thus) settle the peculiar law of each.

42. For men who follow their particular occupations and abide by their particular duty, become dear to people, though they may live at a distance.

46. What may have been practised by the virtuous, by such twice-born men as are devoted to the law, that he shall establish as law, if it be not opposed to the (customs of) countries, families, and castes.   (VIII.41–2, 46)

5. In all castes those (children) only which are begotten in the direct order on wedded wives, equal (in caste and married as) virgins, are to be considered as belonging to the same caste (as their fathers).[2]   (x.5)

24. By adultery (committed by persons) of (different) castes, by marriages with women who ought not to be married, and by the neglect of the

---

[1]See *R. Veda* x.90.

[2]The text, x.6ff., contains elaborate and detailed treatment of many combinations of castes, assigning names and occupations to all such mixed castes, and describing the status of present and later generations of descendants.

duties and occupations (prescribed) to each, are produced (sons who owe their origin) to a confusion of the castes.   (x.24)

352. Men who commit adultery with the wives of others, the king shall cause to be marked by punishments which cause terror, and afterwards banish.

353. For by (adultery) is caused a mixture of the castes among men; thence (follows) sin, which cuts up even the roots and causes the destruction of everything.   (VIII.352–3)

3. THE FOUR ORDERS (OR *ĀŚRAMAS*) AND THEIR DUTIES

87. The student, the householder, the hermit, and the ascetic, these (constitute) four separate orders, . . .   (VI.87[Repeated])

(A) THE STUDENT

165. An Āryan must study the whole Veda together with the Rahasyas [Upaniṣads], performing at the same time various kinds of austerities and the vows prescribed by the rules (of the Veda).   (II.165)

36. In the eighth year after conception, one should perform the initiation (*upanāyana*) of a *brāhmin*, in the eleventh [year] after conception (that) of a *kṣatriya*, but in the twelfth that of a *vaiśya*.   (II.36)

68. Thus has been described the rule for the initiation of the twice-born, which indicates a (new) birth, and sanctified; learn (now) to what duties they must afterwards apply themselves.

69. Having performed the (rite of) initiation, the teacher must first instruct the (pupil) in (the rules of) personal purification, of conduct, of the fire-worship [fire sacrifice], and of the twilight [morning and evening] devotions.   (II.68–9)

108. Let an Āryan who has been initiated, (daily) offer fuel in the sacred fire, beg food, sleep on the ground and do what is beneficial to his teacher, until (he performs the ceremony of) *Samāvartana* [the rite of returning home] (on returning home).   (II.108)

173. The (student) who has been initiated must be instructed in the performance of the vows [acts of discipline, *vrata*], and gradually learn the Veda, observing the prescribed rules.   (II.173)

175. . . . a student who resides with his teacher must observe the following restrictive rules, duly controlling all his organs, in order to increase his spiritual merit.

176. Every day, having bathed, and being purified, he must offer libations

of water to the gods, sages and manes, worship (the images of) the gods, and place fuel on (the sacred fire).

177. Let him abstain from honey, meat, perfumes, garlands, substances (used for) flavouring (food), women, all substances turned acid, and from doing injury to living creatures.

178. From anointing (his body), applying collyrium to his eyes, from the use of shoes and of an umbrella (or parasol), from (sensual) desire, anger, covetousness, dancing, singing, and playing (musical instruments),

179. From gambling, idle disputes, backbiting, and lying, from looking at and touching women, and from hurting others.

180. Let him always sleep alone, . . .

182. Let him fetch a pot full of water, flowers, cowdung, earth, and *Kuśa* grass, as much as may be required (by his teacher), and daily go to beg food.

(II.175–80, 182)

188. He who performs the vow (of studentship) shall constantly subsist on alms, (but) not eat the food of one (person only);[3] the subsistence of a student on begged food is declared to be equal (in merit) to fasting.   (II.188)

199. Let him not pronounce the mere name of his teacher (without adding an honorific title) behind his back even, and let him not mimic his gait, speech, and deportment.

201. By censuring (his teacher), though justly, he will become (in his next birth) an ass, by falsely defaming him, a dog; he who lives on his teacher's substance, will become a worm, and he who is envious (of his merit), a (larger) insect.   (II.199, 201)

225. The teacher, the father, the mother, and an elder brother must not be treated with disrespect, especially by a *brāhmin*, though one be grievously offended (by them).

226. The teacher is the image of *Brahman*, the father the image of Prajāpati (the lord of created beings), the mother the image of the earth, and an (elder) brother the image of oneself.   (II.225–6)

233. By honouring his mother he gains this (nether) world, by honouring his father the middle sphere, but by obedience to his teacher the world of *Brahman*.

234. All duties have been fulfilled by him who honours those three; but to him who honours them not, all rites remain fruitless.

237. By (honouring) these three all that ought to be done by man, is accomplished; that is clearly the highest duty, every other (act) is a subordinate duty.   (II.233–4, 237)

---

[3]That is, he will not beg always from the same house.

145. The teacher is ten times more venerable than a sub-teacher, the father a hundred times more than the teacher, but the mother a thousand times more than the father.

146. Of him who gives natural birth and him who gives (the knowledge of) the Veda, the giver of the Veda is the more venerable father; for the birth for the sake of the Veda (ensures) eternal (rewards) both in this (life) and after death.

148. But that birth which a teacher acquainted with the whole Veda, in accordance with the law, procures for him through the Sāvitrī, is real, exempt from age and death.   (II.145–6, 148)

1. The vow (of studying) the three Vedas under a teacher must be kept for thirty-six years, or for half that time, or for a quarter, or until the (student) has perfectly learnt them.   (III.1)

(B) HOUSEHOLDER

77. As all living creatures subsist by receiving support from air, even so (the members of) all orders subsist by receiving support from the householder.

78. Because men of the three (other) orders are daily supported by the householder with (gifts of) sacred knowledge and food, therefore (the order of) householders is the most excellent order.   (III.77–8)

89. And in accordance with the precepts of the Veda and of the traditional texts, the housekeeper [householder] is declared to be superior to all of them [the other three orders]; for he supports the other three.

90. As all rivers, both great and small, find a resting-place in the ocean, even so men of all orders find protection with householders.

                                                   (VI.89–90 [Repeated])

2. (A student) who has studied in due order the three Vedas, or two, or even one only, without breaking the (rules of) studentship, shall enter the order of householders.

4. Having bathed, with the permission of his teacher, and performed according to the rule the rite on returning home, a twice-born man shall marry a wife of equal caste who is endowed with auspicious (bodily) marks.   (III.2, 4)

12. For the first marriage of twice-born men (wives) of equal caste are recommended; but for those who through desire proceed (to marry again) the following females, (chosen) according to the (direct) order (of the castes), are most approved.

13. It is declared that a *śūdra* woman alone (can be) the wife of a *śūdra*, she and one of his own caste (the wives) of a *vaiśya*, those two and one of his own caste (the wives) of a *kṣatriya*, those three and one of his own caste (the wives) of a *brāhmin*.   (III.12–13)

75. Let (every man) in this (second order, at least) daily apply himself to the private recitation of the Veda, and also to the performance of the offering to the gods; for he who is diligent in the performance of sacrifices, supports both the movable and the immovable creation.   (III.75)

1. Having dwelt with a teacher during the fourth part[4] of (a man's) life, a *brāhmin* shall live during the second quarter (of his existence) in his house, after he has wedded a wife.

2. A *brāhmin* must seek a means of subsistence which either causes no, or at least little pain (to others), and live (by that) except in times of distress.

3. For the purpose of gaining bare subsistence, let him accumulate property by (following those) irreproachable occupations (which are prescribed for) his (caste), without (unduly) fatiguing his body.

11. Let him never, for the sake of subsistence, follow the ways of the world; let him live the pure, straightforward, honest life of a *brāhmin*.

12. He who desires happiness must strive after a perfectly contented disposition and control himself; for happiness has contentment for its root, the root of unhappiness is the contrary (disposition).

15. Whether he be rich or even in distress, let him not seek wealth through pursuits to which men cleave, nor by forbidden occupations, nor (let him accept presents) from any (giver whosoever he may be).

16. Let him not, out of desire (for enjoyments), attach himself to any sensual pleasures, and let him carefully obviate an excessive attachment to them, by (reflecting on their worthlessness in) his heart.

17. Let him avoid all (means of acquiring) wealth which impede the study of the Veda; (let him maintain himself) anyhow, but study, because that (devotion to the Veda-study secures) the realisation of his aims.

18. Let him walk here (on earth), bringing his dress, speech, and thoughts to a conformity with his age, his occupation, his wealth, his sacred learning, and his race.

19. Let him daily pore over those Institutes of science which soon give increase of wisdom, those which teach the acquisition of wealth, those which are beneficial (for other worldly concerns), and likewise over the *Nigamas* which explain the Veda.   (IV.1–3, 11–12, 15–19)

21. Let him never, if he is able (to perform them), neglect the sacrifices to the sages, to the gods, to the *bhūtas* [elementary forces], to men, and to the manes.   (IV.21)

169. (Living) according to the (preceding) rules, he must never neglect the five (great) sacrifices, and, having taken a wife, he must dwell in (his own) house during the second period of his life.   (V.169)

(C) THE FOREST-DWELLER

1. A twice-born *snātaka*,[5] who has thus lived according to the law in the

---

[4]The first quarter.
[5]One who has completed his studentship.

order of householders, may, taking a firm resolution and keeping his organs in subjection, dwell in the forest, duly (observing the rules given below).

2. When a householder sees his (skin) wrinkled, and (his hair) white, and the sons of his sons, then he may resort to the forest.

3. Abandoning all food raised by cultivation, and all his belongings, he may depart into the forest, either committing his wife to his sons, or accompanied by her.

4. Taking with him the sacred fire and the implements required for domestic (sacrifices), he may go forth from the village into the forest and reside there, duly controlling his senses.

5. Let him offer those five great sacrifices according to the rule, with various kinds of pure food fit for ascetics, or with herbs, roots, and fruit.

8. Let him be always industrious in privately reciting the Veda; let him be patient in hardships, friendly (towards all), of collected mind, ever liberal, and never a receiver of gifts, and compassionate towards all living creatures.

26. Making no effort (to procure) things that give pleasure, chaste, sleeping on the ground, not caring for any shelter, dwelling at the roots of trees.

27. From *brāhmins* (who live as) ascetics, let him receive alms, (barely sufficient) to support life, or from other householders of the twice-born (castes) who reside in the forest.

28. Or (the hermit) who dwells in the forest may bring (food) from a village, receiving it either in a hollow dish (of leaves), in (his naked) hand, or in a broken earthen dish, and may eat eight mouthfuls.

29. These and other observances must a *brāhmin* who dwells in the forest diligently practise, and in order to attain complete (union with) the (supreme) Self, (he must study) the various sacred texts contained in the Upaniṣads,

30. (As well as those rites and texts) which have been practised and studied by the sages (*ṛṣis*) and by *brāhmin* householders, in order to increase their knowledge (of *Brahman*), and their austerity, and in order to sanctify their bodies;

31. Or let him walk, fully determined and going straight on, in a northeasterly direction, subsisting on water and air, until his body sinks to rest.

32. A *brāhmin*, having got rid of his body by one of those modes practised by the great sages, is exalted in the world of *Brahman*, free from sorrow and fear.   (VI.1–5, 8, 26–32)

(D) THE WANDERING ASCETIC

33. . . . having thus passed the third part of (a man's natural term of) life in the forest, he may live as an ascetic during the fourth part of his existence, after abandoning all attachment to worldly objects.

34. He who after passing from order to order, after offering sacrifices and subduing his senses, becomes, tired with (giving) alms and offerings of food, an ascetic, gains bliss after death.

36. Having studied the Vedas in accordance with the rule, having begat sons according to the sacred law, and having offered sacrifices according to his ability, he may direct his mind to (the attainment of) final liberation.

37. A twice-born man who seeks final liberation, without having studied the Vedas, without having begotten sons, and without having offered sacrifices, sinks downwards.

38. Having performed the *Isti*,[6] sacred to the Lord of creatures (Prajāpati), where (he gives) all his property as a sacrificial fee, having reposited the sacred fires in himself, a *brāhmin* may depart from his house (as an ascetic).

41. Departing from his house fully provided with the means of purification, let him wander about absolutely silent, and caring nothing for enjoyments that may be offered (to him).

42. Let him always wander alone, without any companion, in order to attain (final liberation), fully understanding that the solitary (man, who) neither forsakes nor is forsaken, gains his end.

43. He shall neither possess a fire, nor a dwelling, he may go to a village for his food, (he shall be) indifferent to everything, firm of purpose, meditating (and) concentrating his mind on *Brahman*.

45. Let him not desire to die, let him not desire to live; let him wait for (his appointed) time, as a servant (waits) for the payment of his wages.

49. Delighting in what refers to the Self, sitting (in the postures prescribed by the Yoga), independent (of external help), entirely abstaining from sensual enjoyments, with himself for his only companion, he shall live in this world, desiring the bliss (of final liberation).

65. By deep meditation let him recognise the subtle nature of the supreme Self, and its presence in all organisms, . . .

73. Let him recognise by the practise of meditation the progress of the individual soul through beings of various kinds, (a progress) hard to understand for unregenerate men.

74. He who possesses the true insight (into the nature of the world), is not fettered by his deeds; but he who is destitute of that insight, is drawn into the circle of births and deaths.

75. By not injuring any creatures, by detaching the senses (from objects of enjoyment), by the rites prescribed in the Veda, and by rigorously practising austerities, (men) gain that state (even) in this (world).

80. When by the disposition (of his heart) he becomes indifferent to all objects, he obtains eternal happiness both in this world and after death.

81. He who has in this manner gradually given up all attachments and is freed from all the pairs (of opposites), reposes in *Brahman* alone.

83. Let him constantly recite (those texts of) the Veda which refer to the sacrifice, (those) referring to the deities, and (those) which treat of the Self and are contained in the concluding portion of the Veda (Vedānta).

85. A twice-born man who becomes an ascetic, after the successive performance of the above-mentioned acts, shakes off sin here below and reaches the highest *Brahman*.

(IV.33–4, 36–8, 41–3, 45, 49, 65, 73–5, 80–81, 83, 85)

[6]A sacrifice.

4. DUTIES OF MEMBERS OF THE FOUR CASTES[7]

(A) *BRĀHMIN* (PRIEST OR TEACHER)

97. It is better (to discharge) one's own (appointed) duty incompletely than to perform completely that of another; for he who lives according to the law of another (caste) is instantly excluded from his own.   (x.97)

74. *Brāhmins* who are intent on the means (of gaining union with) *Brahman* and firm in (discharging) their duties, shall live by duly performing the following six acts (which are enumerated) in their (proper) order.

75. Teaching, studying, sacrificing[8] for himself, sacrificing for others, making gifts and receiving them are the six acts (prescribed) for a *brāhmin*.

76. But among the six acts (ordained) for him three are his means of subsistence, (viz.,) sacrificing[8] for others, teaching, and accepting gifts from pure men.   (x.74–6)

77. (Passing) from the *brāhmin* to the *kṣatriya*, three acts (incumbent on the former) are forbidden, (viz.,) teaching, sacrificing[8] for others, and, thirdly, the acceptance of gifts.

78. The same are likewise forbidden to a *vaiśya*, that is a settled rule; for Manu, the lord of creatures (Prajāpati), has not prescribed them for (men of) those two (castes).

79. To carry arms for striking and for throwing (is prescribed) for *kṣatriyas* as a means of subsistence; to trade, (to rear) cattle, and agriculture for *vaiśya;* but their duties are liberality, the study of the Veda, and the performance of sacrifices.

80. Among the several occupations the most commendable are, teaching the Veda for a *brāhmin,* protecting (the people) for a *kṣatriya,* and trade for a *vaiśya.*

81. But a *brāhmin* unable to subsist by his peculiar occupations just mentioned, may live according to the law applicable to *kṣatriyas;* for the latter is next to him in rank.

82. If it be asked, "How shall it be, if he cannot maintain himself by either (of these occupations?" the answer is), he may adopt a *vaiśya's* mode of life, employing himself in agriculture and rearing cattle.

83. But a *brāhmin,* or a *kṣatriya,* living by a *vaiśya's* mode of subsistence, shall carefully avoid (the pursuit of) agriculture, (which causes) injury to many beings and depends on others.

85. But he who, through a want of means of subsistence, gives up the strictness with respect to his duties, may sell, in order to increase his wealth, the commodities sold by *vaiśya,* making (however) the (following) exceptions.

[7]See also previous references to status and duties of a *brāhmin.*
[8]That is, performing sacrifices.

92. By (selling) flesh, salt, and lac a *brāhmin* at once becomes an out-caste; by selling milk he becomes (equal to) a *śūdra* in three days.

93. But by willingly selling in this world other (forbidden) commodities, a *brāhmin* assumes after seven nights the character of a *vaiśya*.

95. A *kṣatriya* who has fallen into distress, may subsist by all these (means); but he must never arrogantly adopt the mode of life (prescribed for his) betters.

98. A *vaiśya* who is unable to subsist by his own duties, may even maintain himself by a *śūdra*'s mode of life, avoiding (however) acts forbidden (to him), and he should give it up, when he is able (to do so).

99. But a *śūdra*, being unable to find service with the twice-born and threatened with the loss of his sons and wife (through hunger), may maintain himself by handicrafts.

101. A *brāhmin* who is distressed through a want of means of subsistence and pines (with hunger), (but) unwilling to adopt a *vaiśya*'s mode of life and resolved to follow his own (prescribed) path, may act in the following manner.

102. A *brāhmin* who has fallen into distress may accept (gifts) from anybody; for according to the law it is not possible (to assert) that anything pure can be sullied.

103. By teaching, by sacrificing for, and by accepting gifts from despicable (men) *brāhmins* (in distress) commit not sin; for they (are as pure) as fire and water.

104. He who, when in danger of losing his life, accepts food from any person whatsoever, is no more tainted by sin than the sky by mud.

(x.77–83, 85, 92–3, 95, 98–9, 101–4)

(B) *KṢATRIYA* (KING OR PRINCE OR WARRIOR)

1. I will declare the duties of kings, (and) show how a king should conduct himself, . . . and how (he can obtain) highest success.

2. A *kṣatriya* who has received according to the rule the sacrament prescribed by the Veda, must duly protect this whole (world).

3. For, when these creatures, being without a king, through fear dispersed in all directions, the Lord created a king for the protection of this whole (creation),

8. Even an infant king must not be despised, (from an idea) that he is a (mere) mortal; for he is a great deity in human form.

13. Let no (man), therefore, transgress that law which the king decrees with respect to his favourites, nor (his orders) which inflict pain on those in disfavour.

14. For the (king's) sake the Lord formerly created his own son, Punishment, the protector of all creatures, (an incarnation of) the law, formed of *Brahman's* glory.

18. Punishment alone governs all created beings, punishment alone protects them, punishment watches over them while they sleep; the wise declare punishment (to be identical with) the law.

19. If (punishment) is properly inflicted after (due) consideration, it makes all people happy; but inflicted without consideration, it destroys everything.

20. If the king did not, without tiring, inflict punishment on those worthy to be punished, the stronger would roast the weaker, like fish on a spit;

22. The whole world is kept in order by punishment, for a guiltless man is hard to find; through fear of punishment the whole world yields the enjoyments (which it owes).

24. All castes would be corrupted (by intermixture), all barriers would be broken through, and all men would rage (against each other) in consequence of mistakes with respect to punishment.

26. They declare that king to be a just inflicter of punishment, who is truthful, who acts after due consideration, who is wise, and who knows (the respective value of) virtue, pleasure, and wealth.

35. The king has been created (to be) the protector of the castes and orders, who, all according to their rank, discharge their several duties.

87. A king who, while he protects his people, is defied by (foes), be they equal in strength, or stronger, or weaker, must not shrink from battle, remembering the duty of *ksatriyas*.

88. Not to turn back in battle, to protect the people, to honour the *brāhmins,* is the best means for a king to secure happiness.

89. Those kings who, seeking to slay each other in battle, fight with the utmost exertion and do not turn back, go to heaven.

99. Let him strive to gain what he has not yet gained; what he has gained let him carefully preserve; let him augment what he preserves, and what he has augmented let him bestow on worthy men.

100. Let him know that these are the four means for securing the aims of human (existence); let him, without ever tiring, properly employ them.

144. The highest duty of a *ksatriya* is to protect his subjects, for the king who enjoys the rewards, just mentioned, is bound to (discharge that) duty.

198. He should (however) try to conquer his foes by conciliation, by (well-applied) gifts, and by creating dissension, used either separately or conjointly, never by fighting, (if it can be avoided).

199. For when two (princes) fight, victory and defeat in the battle are, as experience teaches, uncertain; let him therefore avoid an engagement.

205. All undertakings (in) this (world) depend both on the ordering of fate and on human exertion; but among these two (the ways of) fate are unfathomable; in the case of man's work action is possible.

(VII.1–3, 8, 13–14, 18–20, 22, 24, 26, 35, 87–89
99–100, 144, 198–9, 205)

410. (The king) should order a *vaiśya* to trade, to lend money, to cultivate the land, or to tend cattle, and a *śūdra* to serve the twice born castes.

418. (The king) should carefully compel *vaiśyas* and *śūdras* to perform the work (prescribed) for them; for if these two (castes) swerved from their duties, they would throw this (whole) world into confusion.

420. A king who thus brings to a conclusion all the legal business enumerated above, and removes all sin, reaches the highest state (of bliss).

(VIII.410, 418, 420)

(C) *VAIŚYA* (TRADESMAN)

326. After a *vaiśya* has received the sacraments and has taken a wife, he shall be always attentive to the business whereby he may subsist and to (that of) tending cattle.

327. For when the Lord of creatures (Prajāpati) created cattle, he made them over to the *vaiśya;* to the *brāhmin* and to the king he entrusted all created beings.

328. A *vaiśya* must never (conceive this) wish, "I will not keep cattle"; and if a *vaiśya* is willing (to keep them), they must never be kept by (men of) other (castes).

329. (A *vaiśya*) must know the respective value of gems, of pearls, of coral, of metals, of (cloth) made of thread, of perfumes, and of condiments.

330. He must be acquainted with the (manner of) sowing of seeds, and of the good and bad qualities of fields, and he must perfectly know all measures and weights.

331. Moreover, the excellence and defects of commodities, the advantages and disadvantages of (different) countries, the (probable) profit and loss on merchandise, and the means of properly rearing cattle.

332. He must be acquainted with the (proper) wages of servants, with the various languages of men, with the manner of keeping goods, and (the rules of) purchase and sale.

333. Let him exert himself to the utmost in order to increase his property in a righteous manner, and let him zealously give food to all created beings.

(IX.326–33)

(D) *ŚŪDRAS* (WORKERS)

334. . . . to serve *brāhmins* (who are) learned in the Vedas, householders, and famous (for virtue) is the highest duty of a *śūdra*, which leads to beatitude.

335. (A *śūdra* who is) pure, the servant of his betters, gentle in his speech, and free from pride, and always seeks a refuge with *brāhmins,* attains (in his next life) a higher caste.   (IX.334–5)

413. But a *śūdra*, whether bought or unbought, he may compel to do servile work; for he was created by the Self-existent (*Svayambhū*) to be the slave of a *brāhmin*.

414. A *śūdra*, though emancipated by his master, is not released from servitude; since that is innate in him, who can set him free from it?

(VIII.413–14)

121. If a *śūdra*, (unable to subsist by serving *brāhmins*), seeks a livelihood, he may serve *kṣatriyas*, or he may also seek to maintain himself by

attending on a wealthy *vaiśya*.

122. But let a (*śūdra*) serve *brāhmins,* either for the sake of heaven, or with a view to both (this life and the next); for he who is called the servant of a *brāhmin* thereby gains all his ends.

123. The service of *brāhmins* alone is declared (to be) an excellent occupation for a *śūdra*; for whatever else besides this he may perform will bear him no fruit.

126. A *śūdra* cannot commit an offence, causing loss of caste, and he is not worthy to receive the sacraments; he has no right to (fulfill) the sacred law (of the Āryans, yet) there is no prohibition against (his fulfilling certain portions of) the law.

127. (*Śūdras*) who are desirous to gain merit, and know (their) duty, commit no sin, but gain praise, if they imitate the practice of virtuous men without reciting sacred texts.

128. The more a (*śūdra*), keeping himself free from envy, imitates the behaviour of the virtuous, the more he gains, without being censured, (exaltation in) this world and the next.   (x.121–3, 126–8)

5. STATUS AND DUTIES OF WOMEN

55. Women must be honoured and adorned by their fathers, brothers, husbands, and brothers-in-law, who desire (their own) welfare.

56. Where women are honoured, there the gods are pleased; but where they are not honoured, no sacred rite yields rewards.

57. Where the female relations live in grief, the family soon wholly perishes; but that family where they are not unhappy ever prospers.

58. The houses on which female relations, not being duly honoured, pronounce a curse, perish completely, as if destroyed by magic.

59. Hence men who seek (their own) welfare, should always honour women on holidays and festivals with (gifts of) ornaments, clothes, and (dainty) food.

60. In that family, where the husband is pleased with his wife and the wife with her husband, happiness will assuredly be lasting.   (iii.55–60)

2. Day and night women must be kept in dependence by the males (of) their (families), and, if they attach themselves to sensual enjoyments, they must be kept under one's control.

3. Her father protects (her) in childhood, her husband protects (her) in youth, and her sons protect (her) in old age; a woman is never fit for independence.

4. Reprehensible is the father who gives not (his daughter in marriage) at the proper time; reprehensible is the husband who approaches not (his wife in due season), and reprehensible is the son who does not protect his mother after her husband has died.

6. Considering that the highest duty of all castes, even weak husbands (must) strive to guard their wives.

7. He who carefully guards his wife, preserves (the purity of) his offspring, virtuous conduct, his family, himself, and his (means of acquiring) merit.

18. For women no (sacramental) rite (is performed) with sacred texts, thus the law is settled; women (who are) destitute of strength and destitute of (the knowledge of) Vedic texts, (are as impure as) falsehood (itself), that is a fixed rule.

45. He only is a perfect man who consists (of three persons united), his wife, himself, and his offspring; thus (says the Veda), and (learned) *brāhmins* propound this (maxim) likewise, "The husband is declared to be one with the wife."   (IX.2–4, 6–7, 18, 45)

67. The nuptial ceremony is stated to be the Vedic sacrament for women (and to be equal to the initiation), serving the husband (equivalent to) the residence in (the house of the) teacher, and the household duties (the same) as the (daily) worship of the sacred fire.   (II.67)

147. By a girl, by a young woman, or even by an aged one, nothing must be done independently, even in her own house.

148. In childhood a female must be subject to her father, in youth to her husband, when her lord is dead to her sons; a woman must never be independent.

149. She must not seek to separate herself from her father, husband, or sons; by leaving them she would make both (her own and her husband's) families contemptible.

150. She must always be cheerful, clever in (the management of her) household affairs, careful in cleaning her utensils, and economical in expenditure.

151. Him to whom her father may give her, or her brother with her father's permission, she shall obey as long as he lives, and when he is dead, she must not insult (his memory).

152. For the sake of procuring good fortune to (brides), the recitation of benedictory texts, and the sacrifice to the Lord of creatures (Prajāpati) are used at weddings; (but) the betrothal (by the father or guardian) is the cause of (the husband's) dominion (over his wife).

153. The husband who wedded her with sacred texts, always gives happiness to his wife, both in season and out of season, in this world and in the next.

154. Though destitute of virtue, or seeking pleasure (elsewhere), or devoid of good qualities, (yet) a husband must be constantly worshipped as a god by a faithful wife.

155. No sacrifice, no vow, no fast must be performed by women apart (from their husbands); if a wife obeys her husband, she will for that (reason alone) be exalted in heaven.

156. A faithful wife, who desires to dwell (after death) with her husband, must never do anything that might displease him who took her hand, whether he be alive or dead.

157. At her pleasure let her emaciate her body by (living on) pure flowers, roots, and fruit; but she must never even mention the name of another man after her husband has died.

160. A virtuous wife who after the death of her husband constantly remains chaste, reaches heaven, though she have no son, just like those chaste men.

164. By violating her duty towards her husband, a wife is disgraced in this world, (after death) she enters the womb of a jackal, and is tormented by diseases (the punishment of) her sin.

165. She who, controlling her thoughts, words, and deeds, never slights her lord, resides (after death) with her husband (in heaven), and is called a virtuous (wife).

167. A twice-born man, versed in the sacred law, shall burn a wife of equal caste who conducts herself thus and dies before him, with (the sacred fires used for) the *Agnihotra*,[9] and with the sacrificial implements.

168. Having thus, at the funeral, given the sacred fires to his wife who dies before him, he may marry again, and again kindle (the fires).

(v.147–57, 160, 164–5, 167–8)

6. THE GAINING OF SUPREME BLISS

102. In whatever order (a man) who knows the true meaning of the Veda-science may dwell, he becomes even while abiding in this world, fit for the union with *Brahman*.   (XII.102)

83. Studying the Veda, (practising) austerities, (the acquisition of true) knowledge, the subjugation of the organs, abstention from doing injury, and serving the *Guru* [preceptor] are the best means for attaining supreme bliss.

84. (If you ask) whether among all these virtuous actions, (performed) here below, (there be) one which has been declared more efficacious (than the rest) for securing supreme happiness to man,

85. (The answer is that) the knowledge of the Self is stated to be the most excellent among all of them; for that is the first of all sciences, because immortality is gained through that.   (XII.83–5)

91. He who sacrifices to the Self (alone), equally recognising the Self in all created beings, and all created beings in the Self, becomes (independent like) an autocrat and self-luminous.

125. He who thus recognises the Self through the Self in all created beings, becomes equal (-minded) towards all, and enters the highest state, *Brahman*.

126. A twice-born man who recites these Institutes, revealed by Manu, will be always virtuous in conduct, and will reach whatever condition he desires.   (XII.91, 125–6)

[9]A fire sacrifice.

19

Stivers, et al.

"AIDS Protection—For Whom?" from *Christian Ethics: A Case Method Approach**

This selection is from a contemporary Christian textbook and gives a practical application of religious ethics. The textbook presents an actual case involving medical patients with AIDS and then applies Christian ethical principles. This case also illustrates the strains that the complicated modern world often puts on long-standing religious principles.

The urgency in the nurse's voice rang in Sarah Cochran's ears as she hurried down the university clinic hallway to the central foyer. As the only medic on duty in the emergency room, she had been called to attend to someone who had fallen on the stairs.

Sarah entered the foyer and pushed through the crowd of onlookers to find a young man lying on the floor. He was bleeding profusely from what appeared to be a deep gash on his forehead. He seemed to have fainted and was slowly reviving. Sarah lifted his hand to take his pulse. Because he was dressed in street clothes, she was startled to find he wore a hospital I.D. bracelet. She asked softly, "Are you a patient here?"

The young man looked up at Sarah and saw the sea of faces surrounding them. The young man nodded. "What are you being treated for?" asked Sarah. He hesitated only a moment, then said, "You need to take body fluid precautions. I'm an AIDS patient."

There was an audible gasp as the crowd backed away. Sarah's most immediate reactions were of anger at the crowd and of compassion for the distress she saw in the man's eyes. She then realized her next thoughts were for her own safety. It was with real discomfort that she reached for the plastic gloves in her case before she began to apply pressure to the wound and wipe away some of the blood.

The patient, Donald Hughes, was taken to the emergency room. Sarah had some concern that the cut would scar his face. She consulted the plastic surgeon on duty to ask if he needed to suture the wound. Following a brief examination, the physician indicated the cut was "not deep enough to require two layers of suturing." Sarah then proceeded to suture and bandage the lacer-

*This case was written by Alice Frazer Evans. Copyright © The Case Study Institute. The names and places in this case have been disguised to protect the privacy of the individuals involved. From Robert L. Stivers, *et al.*, eds., *Christian Ethics* (Maryknoll, New York: Orbis Books, 1989).

ation herself. In the course of her conversation with Donald Hughes, Sarah learned that he was an outpatient being treated for an AIDS-related infection. He had come into the infirmary to get an intravenous injection of antibiotics and to have routine blood samples taken. He suggested that being in too great a hurry to get to a class and not sitting long enough after the blood work precipitated his fainting. He must have hit his head on the stair railing as he fell.

The following day Sarah learned from Janice Adams, an infirmary staff nurse, that Dr. Donald Hughes was an assistant professor in the university. His illness was not far advanced. Beyond the medical staff who worked with him directly, Jan thought that very few people outside of his immediate family had known of his illness. After the accident in the hallway this would certainly no longer be the case. Jan also expressed concern for Hughes's teaching position. "You and I know that there is absolutely no way Dr. Hughes can infect any of his students through casual contact in the classroom, but 'hyper' parents will probably bring pressure on the university. He has enough grief without losing his job."

Sarah also learned from one of the orderlies that leaders of the union to which over one hundred of the clinic's technical and clerical employees belonged were "hopping mad." No one had told the workers who cleaned up the blood on the stairs that the patient had AIDS, so no precautions were taken. One of the women had badly chapped hands, and there was a possibility that she had been infected. The orderly cited an article that had been in the paper only two days before. The article was clear that most cases of AIDS were contracted through sexual intercourse and sharing of needles by intravenous drug users. But there were now documented cases of lab technicians and other hospital workers who had been infected with HIV (human immunodeficiency virus, the virus that causes AIDS) through their work because of "needlesticks" and other open skin lacerations.

These conversations and others Sarah had during the day increased her unhappiness with the way the clinic administration handled identification of PWAs (Persons with AIDS). As a physician's assistant, Sarah was involved in primary care of emergency patients who came into the clinic. She was fully aware that she didn't have the same kind of "clout" the physicians did. Nevertheless, Sarah made an appointment to speak with Tom Anderson, the chief administrator of the university clinic.

As she voiced her strong concern for the safety of the hospital staff, Sarah could hear the agitation in her own voice. "What if Dr. Hughes had been unconscious? What if he had chosen not to tell me? The burden shouldn't be on him to announce his condition to the world." She concluded by urging that some form of notification for bodily fluid precautions be placed on charts and wrist bands of patients with active cases of AIDS.

Sarah was assured by Mr. Anderson that all necessary precautions were being taken. A manual, available to all employees, had clear guidelines for dealing with AIDS patients. In addition, it was the clinic's policy to put the information in the "in-patient" charts for those personnel who came directly and regularly into contact with the patient. In response to Sarah's challenge on this point, he acknowledged his awareness that some members of the staff refused to place this information on the charts. He reminded her that whether intended or not, charts and bracelets were open to public view. Because of the ignorance and irrational reactions of the general public, confidentiality was even more important in AIDS cases. "We have other AIDS patients besides Dr. Hughes. For all these patients the right to privacy comes first. I realize that the emergency room protocol has not previously been one of automatically wearing protective gloves for all cases, but perhaps you personally should take this precaution. True health care professionals take these kinds of risks every day and put the welfare of the patient first. That's what the Hippocratic oath is all about."

During lunch Sarah visited with Rebecca Andrews, a young physician who had recently joined the staff. Rebecca spoke carefully but with strong conviction: "I don't agree with Tom Anderson. Historically the risk went with the territory, and many physicians died from diseases they contracted from their patients. This includes 15 percent of the physicians who treated tuberculosis patients in the early 1900s. AIDS is unique. It is uniformly fatal. During my internship, I watched emaciated AIDS patients in severe pain, with no control of their minds and bodies. For two years I had nightmares about dying like this.

"I overheard your conversation with the plastic surgeon and Hughes. In spite of assurances from the Center for Disease Control [CDC] of minimal risk, there are surgeons who resist operating on an AIDS patient unless it's an extreme emergency. First, we're dealing with a terminal patient. Second, no matter how well a surgeon is protected, when there's a lot of blood, there's an increase in the risk of infection through nicked gloves, errant suture needles, and spurting blood. I disagree with the American Medical Association's directive on AIDS. It says, and I quote, 'When an epidemic prevails, a physician must continue his labors without regard to the risk to his own health.' I say, no. There are limits to professional responsibility."

A week passed. In spite of Sarah's meeting with Tom Anderson and growing dissent by the union officials, no announcements on AIDS policies were made by the administration. Sarah called the union steward and volunteered to attend a union meeting and to express her concerns. The steward's reception seemed cool; he told Sarah that he would contact her if he thought this would help their grievance against the university's handling of infectious diseases. After she hung up the phone, Sarah had the uneasy feeling that as part of the professional staff, she was perceived as one of the "enemy." She wouldn't hold her breath for that call.

Sarah also spoke with several of the nurses and physicians in the clinic, some of whom had become close friends during her two years on the staff. She was surprised that their reactions to her press for identifying patients who necessitated body fluid precautions were so mixed. Some were angry—"These people are dying in a horrible way. Don't add to their agony by going out and tatooing their foreheads!"

Others seemed to be wrestling with the issues as much as Sarah. Carol Simmons, a nurse in the emergency department, took a strong position in support of identifying AIDS patients within the university clinic. "I have to admit that I know physicians who have refused to help AIDS patients, but this isn't the case with anyone on our staff. There are hospitals that refuse to identify AIDS patients out of fear of patients losing their insurance. And others where terminal patients are evicted as soon as their insurance runs out. Again, that hasn't been the case here within our university system. We are considered a 'liberal' university, with basic commitments to the 'common good.' But is it always in the common good to protect the rights of individuals?

"In our greater metropolitan area there are over two hundred documented cases of AIDS. Five years from now there will be over two thousand. These are people already infected, and we have no way of preventing the progress of the disease. Our present community health care facilities aren't able to care for patients now, and the number of cases doubles every year. The specialized care needed for AIDS patients—disinfecting procedures, slower, more careful handling, expensive trial drugs, counseling for patients and family—will dramatically affect medical costs in the future. I'm convinced this care is more costly and time-consuming when it is covert. We're hiding our heads in the sand. Until institutions openly acknowledge *and* support AIDS patients, the archaic denial of this vicious disease is going to continue. The university clinic is in a unique position to take a stand on this."

Though Carol was clearly supporting her position, Sarah was conscious of her own reservations about public declaration of PWAs or of individuals who had been exposed to the HIV but might never fully develop AIDS. She knew of a family whose baby had been given a blood transfusion shortly after birth, before the present intensive blood screening had begun. They were recently notified that Tim's blood now tested HIV positive. Though he had no trace of AIDS, and there was a chance he would never contract the disease, the parents felt they couldn't tell friends or family members or even the family physician. They were afraid even grandparents would stop hugging and holding the baby, though there was no chance he would infect them.

If the information was in Tim's medical history, he could never be insured. Suppose Tim did develop AIDS. Sarah knew that often hospital costs for an AIDS patient exceeded $150,000, and families are faced with bankruptcy. Sarah was acutely aware of the loneliness, depression, fear, and helplessness of these families. She was also aware that some states were considering legislation to make it a felony not to reveal HIV positive results. This was directed toward adults who deliberately withheld information from sexual partners or when donating blood, but the legislation could have much broader implications. Maybe Will Jackson was on the right track, after all.

Will, an intern on the staff, took a position quite different from Carol Simmons. "As I see it, one of the main problems is that the American public is just not ready to deal with knowing who has AIDS. Rather than listen to the facts about infection and respond rationally to PWAs, we fire them from their jobs, evict them from their apartments, make them eat from paper plates, and even keep them *and* their children out of public schools. AIDS is so associated with homosexuals and intravenous drug users—both seen by most people in terms of voluntary choice—that the basic tendency is to blame PWAs for having brought this onto themselves. I'm convinced that beyond ignorance, the source of our violent reaction is fear, not only fear of death but fear of our own sexuality. Until the public gets beyond that point, we must keep the AIDS records strictly confidential. As medical professionals we have to continue to take the risks and assume the primary responsibility for our own health."

Sarah was impressed with Will's sincerity and his analysis, but not with his conclusion. Assuming primary responsibility implied that the staff assumed all the precautions. The Center for Disease Control in Atlanta had published a guide warning that "any time contact with blood or other body fluids of any patient is anticipated," health care workers should take precautions. "Contact with blood" involved a significant number of patients seen in the emergency room. In a recent publication the CDC not only recommended wearing disposable gloves but also stated that "masks and protective eyewear or face shields should be worn" during procedures that would expose the health care worker's mouth, nose, and eyes to blood or other body fluids. This approach was totally alien to Sarah's training and her deep sense of compassion for others. If the emergency room moved to adopt radical precautions, she could just imagine the anxiety of injured children or even adults greeted by masks and goggles! Not only would patients be alienated, but such obvious precautions by hospital personnel could only add to the public hysteria about contracting AIDS. She was convinced that many of the staff would resist these suggestions.

It wasn't possible to know for sure which patients were infected, but the chance of infection of staff was significantly reduced if they could identify the ambulatory patients who definitely required body fluid precautions. She was still convinced that there was some way that confidentiality could be preserved without medical personnel having to take greater risks than necessary.

Several other friends were sympathetic, urging Sarah to continue to press the administration—"The institution should care as much about us as it does about its patients."

With encouragement from her friends, coupled with her own frustration with no response, Sarah decided to write a letter to the university board of directors responsible for administering the clinic. She was struck, however, by the fact that not a single one of her supporters was willing to cosign the letter. In her letter Sarah related the incident of emergency care of the AIDS patient. She acknowledged that there was established protocol for identifying patients with AIDS on the medical charts. However, once the infirmary accepts such a patient, "it is by extension committing all departments to caring for them."

Sarah's letter continued: "I was asked by three clinical staff members if the patient had promptly identified himself as having AIDS, implying that the onus was on him to inform me. I believe this line of question directs attention away from the central issue: the burden of identification should not rest solely with the patient. The clinic must assume primary responsibility for implementing a system that identifies ambulatory patients with this risk factor. The patient himself told me how embarrassing it was for him to state publicly that he has AIDS."

In the letter Sarah then made two specific proposals:

1. A special wrist bracelet identifying the patient's blood/secretion precaution by either a color or code differentiation. All staff would be informed of the code.
2. A list of ambulatory patients with blood/secretion precautions. The list could be kept in an accessible yet private area in the emergency department. This is the most likely department to have a patient brought in under emergency conditions without benefit of a chart.

Sarah concluded the letter with a number of other suggestions, including the need to post AIDS protocols clearly in the nursing stations with information about how to disinfect contaminated instruments and how to dispose of contaminated paper products.

Though Sarah received a brief acknowledgement of receipt of her letter, she received no further word from the administration. Two weeks later there were notices that union and clinic administrators were meeting to discuss the union demands. Officials later announced that there would be mandatory training sessions on infectious diseases in addition to the short-term workshops for employees initiated shortly after the Hughes incident. However, no mention was made of patient identification for body fluid precautions.

Sarah Cochran felt determined to get some kind of response from the administration. Her sister had always joked that her determination doubled when she was confronted by a stone wall. Maybe the present policy was right, and a patient's confidentiality should be protected at all costs. It seemed pretty clear that was the direction the university was going to take. Then where did the legitimate rights of caregivers begin? Sarah was convinced that the issues needed at least to be openly discussed. She glanced down and saw the newspaper articles in which the union's grievances had been aired. Sarah picked up a copy of her unanswered letter to the board, wondering if the publicity which would come if she released it to the media would bring in fresh air or completely destroy the possibility of future changes. She also glanced at the wastebasket. Maybe she had taken her concerns as far as she could.

Commentary
AIDS Protection—For Whom?

All the subjects in this case seem to recognize that a tension exists between the interests of health care workers and those of PWAs (Persons with AIDS, the term preferred by PWAs). The PWA has a right to confidentiality, which is especially important given the hysteria and prejudice surrounding AIDS.

Health care workers have a right to be protected as thoroughly as possible from contracting this deadly disease. A public policy effective in stemming the rising tide of AIDS cases requires that both sets of rights be protected. If the confidentiality of PWAs is not respected, persons at risk will be much less motivated to seek testing that will identify them and help prevent inadvertent spread of AIDS. If health care workers are not protected it will become more difficult to recruit workers willing to treat PWAs and possibly any patients. Health care in general could be greatly affected.

SCRIPTURAL AND THEOLOGICAL RESOURCES

What scriptural and theological teachings are relevant for issues involving AIDS? We have some scriptural analogies, especially around treatment of leprosy, which was a relatively common, degenerative, deadly, and communicable disease. In the Old Testament, the Mosaic law refers to leprosy extensively (e.g., Lev. 13–14). Lepers were largely excluded from the community and forced to live apart. They were obliged to cry "unclean" as a warning to anyone who approached them (Lev. 13). They were often the victims of abuse; their lives were blighted by their disease. This is especially tragic to note since primitive diagnostic skills often resulted in the priests, who were charged with diagnosis, confusing leprosy and many nonserious, noncommunicable diseases. In general, the Old Testament treatment of leprosy was designed to protect the community at the expense of the afflicted individual.

In the New Testament we find Jesus active in healing lepers, whom he allowed to approach him in defiance of law and custom. He usually healed through the laying on of hands, and made no exception for lepers, even though this contact contained a risk of contamination (Mark 1:40–44). Jesus presented his healing miracles as a sign of the love of God available to all, and as a call to his followers to imitate him in communicating God's love to all through similar outreach.

All followers of Jesus should recognize the shared mission of embodying God's love to all, especially those most in need. This mission mandates a pastoral attitude toward those suffering from communicable disease, despite the risks. Though we are to minister to the needy in spite of the risks, this does not prohibit the use of precautions. In fact, we have an obligation to use all available precautions. Jesus calls us to love our neighbor as ourselves, and love of self requires that we safeguard our health while we minister to the neighbor. If we did not, we threaten our ability to love other needy neighbors in the future.

The need to extend ourselves in love to neighbors in need does not mean that the needs of the patient with communicable disease take precedence over the need to protect the entire community of neighbors, whom we are also called to love as ourselves. Biblical teachings do not solve the dilemma of choosing between the needs of the afflicted individual and the well-being of the community, but only give us criteria which set the limits on our decisions. Biblical teachings, for example, could not justify a doctor's decision to refuse to treat all PWAs. Similarly, there is no Christian warrant for PWAs to protect their confidentiality and rights by refusing to inform a fiancé, spouse, sexual partner, or medical worker who could be infected by contact with them. Neither action is compatible with Christian love.

The real problems in this case revolve around public policy making, not around personal moral decisions. Public policy questions are often the more difficult aspect of AIDS. Although many personal decisions around AIDS entail great suffering, it is somewhat easier to decide what the moral action should be, if not to carry it out, than it is in public policy questions. Many personal decisions—telling a fiancé that one is HIV positive, deciding not to fire or expel employees or students who have AIDS, deciding to get tested because one is a member of a high risk group—seem to require more courage and suffering from us than seems possible to endure. In this case the cost of personal decisions around AIDS is very high. Dr. Hughes has risked his future to protect Sarah and others from danger in handling his blood. Sarah herself was willing to put herself on the line in writing the university board when none of her co-workers were willing to go public with their concerns. She risked not only the disapproval of her employers on the job, but the uncomfortable notoriety which can accompany such stands. However painful to ourselves and others, we cannot morally destroy lives either by allowing others to be infected or by rejecting and discriminating against PWAs who are not a threat to others.

Public policy, on the other hand, must deal with the problem of how to treat those who are not acting in morally responsible ways. Should we force members of high risk groups to be tested? Should we compel health workers to treat PWAs? Should we forbid discrimination against PWAs by employers, hospitals, insurance companies, landlords, and morticians? In making such decisions we must balance as best we can the interests and needs of all.

There are no simple formulas. Attempts to protect at all costs the needs of the majority—a kind of utilitarianism—can backfire in two ways. If the limitations and suffering in the situation are not distributed, but attributed to only one individual group, then we have unjust scapegoating of the minority, which in turn endangers the majority. For future situations could find groups within the present majority selected as scapegoats. On the other hand, insistence on the rights of the individual needy, here PWAs, can lead to the misuse of rights in ways that spread the disease and engender backlash against the infected minority.

RESPONSIBILITY FOR PROTECTING THE COMMON GOOD

Sarah is concerned that the responsibility for precautions against the spread of the AIDS epidemic not be placed solely on PWAs. Dr. Donald Hughes should not have had to announce publicly that he had AIDS, because of the serious effects this would have on his life: the probable loss of employment, and possible loss of housing and friends. Sarah is also concerned because Dr. Hughes could have been unconscious from his fall and therefore unable to give the warning. These are legitimate concerns; she wants to protect both PWAs and health care workers: The real issue is how this is best done.

Sarah wants body fluid precaution notices placed on charts and on wrist bracelets for all inpatients and outpatients to protect all hospital personnel. Such notices would not only cover PWAs, but other types of illness communicated through body fluids as well, for example, hepatitis, which claimed the lives of two hundred hospital workers last year in the United States.

There are a number of possible problems with her suggestions. First, there is the very real probability that the wearing of such identification bracelets, especially for outpatients, would increase acts of discrimination and abuse against PWAs as the community came to identify the bracelet with the rising numbers of PWAs. (Hepatitis is usually treated on an inpatient basis.) The fear and hatred around AIDS in the United States, which seems to be far worse than in other parts of the world where AIDS is not so identified with homosexuality, might find ready targets in outpatients. This in turn would almost certainly result in a refusal of PWAs to wear the identification.

In addition, the nature of AIDS itself works against the adequacy of such a system. AIDS may take five to ten years, perhaps even longer, to develop in exposed persons. This means that there are many exposed persons who do not know they carry the disease, and yet are capable of passing it on. Any person who enters the emergency room may carry the AIDS virus, not just those who have been tested HIV positive.

Sarah's suggestion in itself might not have prevented the spread of infection in the very case which gave rise to it. For the persons who were not protected by Dr. Hughes's warning—the housekeeping staff—would not necessarily know that the blood on the stairs came from a person wearing body fluid precaution identification. Housekeeping is not generally done until the patient and medical staff have moved away from the scene of an incident.

The hospital's decision seems to be an adoption of general procedures which will, if followed, reduce risk to health workers. If precautions in handling body fluids become routine and are taken with all patients, then workers will be protected not only from already diagnosed PWAs, but also from as yet undiagnosed AIDS carriers. The greatest obstacle to such a policy is compliance. It takes a great deal of effort to make the donning of masks, gloves, and other precautions routine, even when we know the risks. The effort might be compared to convincing people to stop smoking or begin wearing seatbelts. We know that quitting smoking and wearing seatbelts greatly reduce the chances of early death. But we also know that the dangers of smoking this one cigarette, or driving on this one errand without seatbelts, are relatively low. We take our chances. If we knew which cigarette would begin lung cancer, or which trip would involve us in an accident, we would be sure to use precautions. But we don't, just as health workers don't know which patients have AIDS.

This difficulty of making caution routine seems to be a major reason for preferring identification of PWAs over making body fluids precautions routine.

The role of habit in the moral life is greatly undervalued. If we are consistently to act lovingly and responsibly toward all, we must make many kinds of action habitual. This is what we mean when we speak of character formation as a moral task of humans. For the most part we form our character through first discerning responsible reactions and then over time making them habitual.

Another problem with Sarah's suggestion is that it assumes that PWAs are a small minority. This is true in most areas of the country now. But in some major metropolitan areas AIDS cases already represent a significant percentage of the ill, and the projected increases in cases are likely to make that a common occurrence. As that happens, "special" precautions with identified patients would become more and more routine anyway. Understanding AIDS cases as minority, as an unusual occurrence, is a major problem in coming to grips with this disease not only in the United States, but in the world as a whole. It is estimated that between a million and a million and a half people in the United States have been exposed to the virus—that is, have antitoxins present in their bodies. The vast majority of those exposed will contract the disease (some scientists insist that all will), and, barring some unexpected new cure, everyone who contracts the disease dies from it. In some African nations whole villages and even regions are decimated by the disease, which is spread in Africa predominantly through heterosexual sex and childbirth. Predictions are that as many as one-third of the populations of Uganda and Zaire will die from AIDS in the next decade or so.

AIDS is a worldwide threat which will be around for the long haul. We need to take our heads out of the sand and institute international cooperative procedures and structures to succor the dying and protect the still healthy. In the United States we need to stop blaming homosexuals for the disease as if by pinning the blame on them we become safe from the ravages of AIDS.

Sarah had two objections to the hospital's response. First, she felt the hospital was refusing to accept any institutional responsibility for the protection of its workers, but was instead making them responsible as individuals for their protection. Second, she objected to routine donning of protective equipment as an intrusion between health care providers and patients. She feels that such protection distances care providers from patients and prevents patient trust in care providers.

It would certainly be wrong for the hospital merely to adopt guidelines which throw total responsibility on the workers. But if the hospital administrators were not only to provide workshops for employees in all areas of the hospital to explain necessary precautions, but also provide the needed equipment, post guidelines, and monitor compliance with the guidelines, this would indicate their willingness to share responsibility with workers. If all supervisors were charged with enforcing the use of protective equipment, if all training programs for new employees included instructions about the precautions, then the precautions could quickly become routine. In an earlier age of medicine before antisepsis was fully accepted, frequent washing of hands by doctors was regarded as annoying, unnecessary, and insulting to patients. But it did become routine, and within a generation maternal mortality rates in hospitals plummeted to a fraction of their earlier rate.

As for such precautions as gloves and masks intruding between care providers and patients, this may be so. Jesus himself in the healing of lepers eschewed precautions and the strictures of the law. But even Jesus sometimes changed his mind when he became convinced that his intentions could be carried out in a better way (Mark 7:24–30). Our actions must not only be lovingly intended, but they must appear loving if we are effectively to mediate God's love to our neighbor. Because patients are not accustomed to them and do not understand the need for them, gloves and masks could easily be resented. This problem, however, is not insurmountable. Patients accept the need for such precautions in all types of surgical procedures already. In some ways gloves and masks could free care providers to be *more* compassionate with patients, to reach out to touch them or hold their hand during feared or painful procedures, with less fear of contracting anything from or transmitting anything to patients. It is not as if hospitals were disease-free before AIDS. Hospitals have always been one of the highest disease-producing environments both for patients and workers. Such garb could lower risks for both, and would in time become routine.

AIDS AS A SPECIAL CASE

In some ways AIDS is a special case among diseases. There are other fatal diseases, but they are either fatal only sometimes or are not communicable except genetically. As an always fatal communicable disease without a cure, AIDS stands alone. The fear it engenders is enhanced by its connections with sexuality. In the United States, unlike many other countries, the most common method of contracting AIDS has been homosexual sexual activity, although shared needles among drug users now account for over a quarter of the cases, with birth, heterosexual contact, laboratory accidents, and blood transfusions all accounting for small percentages. Ours is a homophobic community; we fear homosexuality and often shun and discriminate against homosexuals, as Will Jackson pointed out in the case. We also fear and have disdain for drug users. The public understands the vast majority of PWAs to belong to two groups considered dangerously deviant, and therefore treats them as pariahs. Many respond to the threat of AIDS not with reasonable precautions, but irrationally, by blaming all PWAs for their situation and assuming they are enemies of society.

There are no grounds for such a response. Any of us have run the risk of contracting AIDS if we have had unprotected sexual contact with either sex, have received a blood transfusion, handled human blood without protection, shared a syringe with anyone, or been born of a parent who did any of these. Anyone can turn out to have been born of an infected parent, had sex with a spouse who had other sexual partners before us, or handled contaminated blood with exposed skin lacerations. We can choose to abstain from intravenous drug use and homosexuality, but we have little or no control over the many other ways that AIDS can be contracted.

One of the reasons that such strong fears and hysteria prevail around AIDS is that we are socialized to see ourselves as being in control of our lives, and to demand such control as normal. We are strongly attracted to the idea that we control our own fate. This attitude is largely a product of the phenomenal economic and scientific success our society has experienced. Our ability to control our world and to conquer many of the destructive illnesses and natural disasters which have victimized societies of the past has created the illusion that we are invulnerable, or at least on the verge of being invulnerable. AIDS is also more threatening to large segments of our population because it is a disease that attacks the young, often in the prime of life.

There are some very positive aspects to our attitude that we control our fate. People *should* realize that they have responsibility for their lives, that they irresponsibly raise the risk of serious medical problems when they smoke, fail to exercise, or eat poorly balanced or high cholesterol diets. We do control many of the behaviors which influence our health. We need to accept such responsibility in many different areas of our lives.

But we are not ultimately in control of our lives, even of our health. So that while my guilt feelings at being a smoker may be appropriate, it would be wrong to assume that all lung cancer patients are responsible for their illness. Some have never smoked, others were put at risk by smog or conditions of their work, or by an inherited predisposition. We often do not make this distinction. We move from the assumption of individual responsibility and control to blaming those who are unfortunate enough to be needy and suffering.

We do this because we are uncomfortable acknowledging our lack of ultimate control. Such an acknowledgment means that we are constantly at risk, in danger, vulnerable. In the past, Christian theology understood the assumption that we are in control of our lives as atheism, a failure to acknowledge that God controls all. Many theologians and ethicists today deny that God causes things like AIDS and cancer or other evils, and would rather say that when we insist that we are in control, we deny the reality of our finitude. This has implications for our relationship with God, for if we believe we can prevent ourselves from being needy, from falling victim to suffering and disaster, we do not need God, and cut ourselves off from God who offers us solace and strength. This same process which leads us to cut ourselves off from God leads to cutting ourselves off from others, and thus we sever ties that bind the human community together. We especially cut ourselves off from those who suffer and cultivate an ignorance about them. For they represent a special threat to our desire to believe in our own omnipotence: if these are innocent and are nevertheless afflicted, why not us? It is this desire to protect our own sense of safety that makes us shun the diseased, the raped, the poor, and other sufferers. We *want* to believe they are to blame. This is not only un-Christian, but is it an ultimately ineffective strategy, for we are not in full control of our lives. Suffering and death fall on the just and the unjust.

In making effective public policy around AIDS, we must all claim some responsibility for stopping the spread of the disease and supporting the needs of those who have contracted it. In order to do that we must understand AIDS as another in a long series of epidemics which have arisen in history to scourge humanity: bubonic plague, tuberculosis, smallpox, and venereal disease, to name just a few. The danger of AIDS is a part of the human condition which we all share. Only when we accept the danger can we accept the responsibility. To do this is both a practical need and a moral challenge. Rising to meet this challenge will demand both courage and solidarity. We can hope that science can come up with treatments and ultimately a cure, but there is no guarantee of that. Even if there were some certainty that a cure existed in the future, there would be no excuse to ignore the challenge which AIDS represents today.

The practice of Christian ethics is not only about choosing action which promotes the coming of God's reign, but about making ourselves into moral persons modeled on Jesus Christ, persons who in some ways embody that reign. We are called to model the hope, the love, the justice, and the community that God intends for us. Part of that task is making responsible action habitual. Another part is acquiring the habit of understanding ourselves as part of the human community, sharing its dangers and successes, its temptations and failings. The temptation to evade responsibility by blaming those we regard as sinners has a long history in the annals of Christianity and other religions. Committing ourselves to follow Jesus does not make us righteous, as opposed to others who are sinners. Rather it calls us to root out of ourselves this temptation to understand ourselves as other than sinners.

CONCLUSION

Sarah Cochran's insistence both that the hospital take responsibility for protecting workers from AIDS, and that such responsibility should not be left to PWAs like Donald Hughes, is well grounded. Whether her suggestions for chart coding and coded wrist identification for inpatients and outpatients are the most effective ways both to protect workers and meet the needs of PWAs is not clear. Whatever the final decision, and that decision may well be a combination of her suggestions and the hospital's guidelines, that decision should involve a sharing of responsibility by all involved. Everyone is potentially vulnerable to AIDS; therefore the task of preventing its spread belongs to all. We cannot expect that our employer, or our government, or any other institution, can or should relieve us of the responsibility to protect ourselves or our neighbors. Nor can we expect that our own actions can make us invulnerable to AIDS. We have no source of total immunity.

It often happens that it is only when we come to accept that we are all endangered by a common threat that we can come together in solidarity. This is what has happened in many areas of the homosexual community in the cities of our nation. Countless individuals in the homosexual community, transformed by their witness of the devastation caused by AIDS in that community, have committed their lives to practical and pastoral work for AIDS patients, and in that work have found profound community. It is tragic that so often we only find such solidarity in the face of disaster. But regardless of our feelings about homosexuality or the homosexual community, such examples of solidarity should be understood as a model for all of us of what the Christian community is called to be. We are not called to avoid the evil of death and suffering, but to struggle against it in solidarity with the suffering.

PART **VI**

RELIGIOUS COMMUNITY

The Western Wall and Dome of the Rock Mosque, Jerusalem.
(Photo by J. T. Carmody)

INTRODUCTION

Religious experience has its private, individualistic aspects, but it also has its communal aspects. People experience their gods together, in their rituals. Individuals receive from their communities their traditions, the images and categories in which they tend to anticipate and express their experiences. So it is misleading to set the individual against the community: individuals have both started communities and reformed them, while communities have guided most ordinary members throughout their religious lives.

The role of communities in the formation and sustenance of mythology and ritual is even clearer. Myths are community property, and the vast majority of rituals have in mind not individuals but groups. Much the same communitarian context holds for doctrine and ethics. What religious teachers teach is the traditional belief of their community. What ethicists propose as ideal behavior is what their community has long revered or is likely to require in the future. Just as communities are necessary to acculturate children, so also do they continue to form their members throughout the life cycle. Traditional people arise from their gods together, exist together before their gods, and sustain one another's hopes to please their gods at death.

In this part we focus on four traditions' sense of religious community. The first selection, from the documents of Vatican II, the ecumenical council (1962–1965) that transformed modern Catholicism, treats of the Christian community—the church. This topic occasioned much debate in the council because it focused very clearly on Pope John XXIII's charge in convening the bishops from around the world: to bring the church up to date.

The bishops tried to fulfill this charge in various ways. Especially significant were their documents on the role of the church in the modern world and on religious liberty. The church ought to embrace the modern world and enter into dialogue with it. It ought to endorse the principle that all people have the right to worship as they choose, without suffering discrimination. In their study of the church itself, the bishops' most notable achievement was to shift the imagery by which Christians ought to understand their communal life. Whereas previous Catholic theology had presented a juridical imagery, stressing the rights of the leaders to command and the duties of the followers to obey, the ecumenical council approved imagery that was both more biblical and more pastoral. Underscoring the notion that members of the church constitute the people of God, the document from which we quote explains the Christian significance of this notion—how it orients believers to think about their salvation. More broadly, the council urged both clergy and laity to take to heart the warm, hopeful implications of "the people of God," reforming pastoral care to bring out the deep joy that Christian faith ought to nourish.

The second selection comes from Judaism. Before World War II, Jews of Eastern Europe continued to live much as their ancestors had done for centuries. Their lives were structured by the Torah, and their common acceptance of this discipline made them a tightly knit community. Certainly their differences from their Gentile neighbors (which their fidelity to talmudic law heightened) also helped to fashion their sense of community as Jews, but the acceptance of talmudic discipline was more central and positive.

The selection, from a book that collects memories of Jews who lived in East Europe *shtetls* (small villages) before nazism and World War II, stresses the intense sociability of traditional Jewish life. Very little in the existence of the *shtetl* was solitary or individualistic. Certainly people were individuals with different talents and temperaments. But households flowed back and forth, talk babbled night and day, gossip and charity created a dozen different connections on every street. The three treasures of traditional Jewish life were Torah, marriage, and good deeds. Torah—divine instruction—gave the community its basic map of reality. Marriage and family life were the context for all religion (Judaism never sponsored a celibate clergy). And good deeds were the fundamental expression of neighborliness—of the fact that all Jews needed one another, belonged together. When traditional Jews prayed, it was in the plural. The needs of the community came before the needs of the individual. When a Jew was born or died, other Jews were present to welcome or bid farewell. And through all the intermediary stages, family members, friends, and acquaintances reached into one's life and claimed large shares of one's attention, affection, and gratitude. So Jewish religious existence was thoroughly social, as most other traditional religious existences have been.

The third example of religious sociability comes from the autobiography of Mohandas (Mahatma) Gandhi, the Hindu holy man who did more than anyone else to free India from British control after World War II. Gandhi took inspiration from several sources, including the Christian New Testament, but as he developed his distinctive style of political and religious leadership he came more and more to resemble a traditional Hindu holy man. One of his strongest convictions was that representing the justice of Indians' demands for self-rule nonviolently could bring about a decent, worthy liberation.

To achieve so lofty a motivation and tactics, it was necessary to train people in *satyagraha*, the force of truth. Gandhi realized that such training could not be accomplished overnight and that his movement required a solid core of disciples who had appropriated *satyagraha* through much prayer, discussion, and practice. So he decided to form a religious community that would provide the atmosphere needed for such an appropriation. Indian culture had a familiar term for such a venture: the *ashram*, or Hindu religious community, was a common sight. Gurus would gather disciples around them, convinced that only when they could shape the disciples' full lives would they then mature and flower. The chapters from Gandhi's autobiography that we include give the flavor of the movement that the Mahatma was leading as well as an indication of what sort of community he hoped to create.

In the case of Gandhi's ashram, the mutual support that believers might give one another was obvious. Gandhi was marching against the tide of Indian as well as British assumptions. Neither side was committed to nonviolence as he was, so he hoped that his little community would become a bastion of countercultural conviction. With fellow believers on their left and right, those of immature conviction might stiffen their upper lips and square their shoulders.

The fourth selection is from the Qur'an, which is central to Muslim life. Throughout, the Qur'an assumes that Muslims form a community. The basis of their solidarity is their belief in Allah. All who make the profession of faith ("There is no Allah but Allah, and Muhammad is Allah's Prophet") belong to "the house of Islam." Muslims are those who submit to Allah, bowing low in prayer, opening their hearts to the divine will. In the *surahs* (chapters) from the Qur'an that we present to illustrate the Muslim sense of community, we find the voice of Allah rallying believers to confidence. Their God stands by them. The conduct that fidelity to Allah requires is clear and strict, but eminently noble. We find in these surahs the assumptions and assurances that have undergirded Islam since the seventh century. What Muslims share has been dictated by God. How they are to act and think, imagine and feel, flows from the revelation given them through the Prophet. Their solidarity is no flimsy ethnic tradition or worldly advantage. Ideally, it is their common conviction that nothing is more sublime than fidelity to God.

Large religious communities such as the Islamic *ummah* and the Catholic Church function as props to believers' convictions. When large numbers of people are saying the same prayers, receiving the same sacraments, trying to live up to the same ethical principles, obeying the same teachers, the whole enterprise seems reasonable, possible. Left alone, most people slacken. They need the support and pressure of their peers to persevere. Only the rare, strong spirits can trek off to the desert by themselves. Thus, the success or failure of religious traditions depends in good measure on the quality of the communal life that they inspire. If people find themselves in the midst of a warm, congenial, reasonable community, they find it relatively easy to enjoy their religious identity, to be proud of being Catholics, or Jews, or Hindus or Muslims.

The Jewish version of this truism about the need for peer support is clear from the description of *shtetl* life that we present. If anything, the *shtetl* could be oppressive, leaving individuals too little space in which to unlimber and breathe. But Jews had learned through centuries of opposition that their only strength lay in solidarity. Within their own precincts they might disagree, bicker, even attack one another (verbally), but when it came to threats from outside, they had to pull together. If they did not, they were extremely vulnerable to the whims of an often antagonistic Gentile majority.

In times of peace, most religious communities have realized that sociability itself is a blessing. Simply by being together, enjoying one another's company, most groups have felt favored. Indeed, at such times most groups have felt that their God was in their midst.

20

*Vatican II's Constitution on the Church, Chapter 2: "The People of God"**

This reading is from documents issued by the Roman Catholic Church after Vatican II, the momentous ecumenical council of 1962–65. Pope John XXIII convened this world-wide council of bishops in the hope of bringing the Church more fully into modern times so that it might better serve its faithful. This selection contains some of the ideas the council had to improve the Church's self-image.

THE PEOPLE OF GOD[27]

9. At all times and among every people, God has given welcome to whosoever fears Him and does what is right (cf. Acts 10:35). It has pleased God, however, to make men holy and save them not merely as individuals without any mutual bonds, but by making them into a single people, a people which acknowledges Him in truth and serves Him in holiness. He therefore chose the race of Israel as a people unto Himself. With it He set up a covenant. Step by step He taught this people by manifesting in its history both Himself and the decree of His will, and by making it holy unto Himself. All these things, however, were done by way of preparation and as a figure of that new and perfect covenant which was to be ratified in Christ, and of that more luminous revelation which was to be given through God's very Word made flesh.

"Behold the days shall come, saith the Lord, and I will make a new covenant with the house of Israel, and with the house of Judah. . . . I will give my law in their bowels, and I will write it in their heart: and I will be their God, and they shall be my people. . . . For all shall know me, from the least of them even to the greatest, saith the Lord" (Jer. 31:31–34). Christ instituted this new covenant, that is to say, the new testament, in His blood (cf. 1 Cor.

---

[27] Completing the study of the biblical images and designations in the second half of Chap. 1, the Constitution devotes an entire chapter to the description of the Church as the "new People of God." This title, solidly founded in Scripture, met a profound desire of the Council to put greater emphasis on the human and communal side of the Church, rather than on the institutional and hierarchical aspects which have sometimes been overstressed in the past for polemical reasons. While everything said about the people of God as a whole is applicable to the laity, it should not be forgotten that the term "People of God" refers to the total community of the Church, including the pastors as well as the other faithful.

*From *The Documents of Vatican II: In a New and Definitive Translation with Commentaries and Notes.* Walter M. Abbott, S.J., General Editor. Copyright © 1966 by The America Press, Inc. Reprinted by permission of the publisher, Crossroad/Continuum.

11:25), by calling together a people made up of Jew and Gentile, making them one, not according to the flesh but in the Spirit.

This was to be the new People of God. For, those who believe in Christ, who are reborn not from a perishable but from an imperishable seed through the Word of the living God (cf. 1 Pet. 1:23), not from the flesh but from water and the Holy Spirit (cf. Jn. 3:5–6), are finally established as "a chosen race, a royal priesthood, a holy nation, a purchased people. . . . You who in times past were not a people, but are now the people of God" (1 Pet. 2:9–10).

That messianic people has for its head Christ, "who was delivered up for our sins, and rose again for our justification" (Rom. 4:25), and who now, having won a name which is above all names, reigns in glory in heaven.[28] The heritage of this people are the dignity and freedom of the sons of God, in whose hearts the Holy Spirit dwells as in His temple. Its law is the new commandment to love as Christ loved us (cf. Jn. 13:34). Its goal is the kingdom of God, which has been begun by God Himself on earth, and which is to be further extended until it is brought to perfection by Him at the end of time. Then Christ our life (cf. Col. 3:4), will appear, and "creation itself also will be delivered from its slavery to corruption into the freedom of the glory of the sons of God" (Rom. 8:21).

So it is that this messianic people, although it does not actually include all men, and may more than once look like a small flock, is nonetheless a lasting and sure seed of unity, hope, and salvation for the whole human race. Established by Christ as a fellowship of life, charity, and truth, it is also used by Him as an instrument for the redemption of all, and is sent forth into the whole world as the light of the world and the salt of the earth (cf. Mt. 5:13–16).

Israel according to the flesh, which wandered as an exile in the desert, was already called the Church of God (2 Esd. 13:1; cf. Num. 20:4; Dt. 23:1 ff). Likewise the new Israel which, while going forward in this present world, goes in search of a future and abiding city (cf. Heb. 13:14) is also called the Church of Christ (cf. Mt. 16:18). For He has bought it for Himself with His blood (cf. Acts 20:28), has filled it with His Spirit, and provided it with those means which befit it as a visible and social unity. God has gathered together as one all those who in faith look upon Jesus as the author of salvation and the source of unity and peace, and has established them as the Church, that for each and all she may be the visible sacrament of this saving unity.[29]

While she transcends all limits of time and of race, the Church is destined to extend to all regions of the earth and so to enter into the history of mankind. Moving forward through trial and tribulation, the Church is strengthened by the power of God's grace promised to her by the Lord, so that in the

---

[28] This paragraph, one of the most beautiful in the entire Constitution, touches on a number of characteristic themes of Vatican II: the universal expansiveness of the Church, its role as a sacrament of unity, its weakness and dependence upon God's help during its earthly pilgrimage, and its ardent hope for the final fulfillment of God's kingdom.

[29] *Cf. St. Cyprian., "Epist.," 69, 6: PL 3, 1142 (Hartel, III B, p. 754): "inseparabile unitatis sacramentum" ["the unbreakable sacrament of unity"].*

weakness of the flesh she may not waver from perfect fidelity, but remain a bride worthy of her Lord; that moved by the Holy Spirit she may never cease to renew herself, until through the cross she arrives at the light which knows no setting.

10. Christ the Lord, High Priest taken from among men (cf. Heb. 5:1–5), "made a kingdom and priests to God his Father" (Apoc. 1:6; cf. 5:9–10) out of this new people.[30] The baptized, by regeneration and the anointing of the Holy Spirit, are consecrated into a spiritual house and a holy priesthood. Thus through all those works befitting Christian men they can offer spiritual sacrifices and proclaim the power of Him who has called them out of darkness into His marvelous light (cf. 1 Pet. 2:4–10). Therefore all the disciples of Christ, persevering in prayer and praising God (cf. Acts 2:42–47), should present themselves as a living sacrifice, holy and pleasing to God (cf. Rom. 12:1). Everywhere on earth they must bear witness to Christ and give an answer to those who seek an account of that hope of eternal life which is in them (cf. 1 Pet. 3:15).

Though they differ from one another in essence and not only in degree, the common priesthood of the faithful and the ministerial or hierarchical priesthood are nonetheless interrelated. Each of them in its own special way is a participation in the one priesthood of Christ.[31] The ministerial priest, by the sacred power he enjoys, molds and rules the priestly people. Acting in the person of Christ, he brings about the Eucharistic Sacrifice, and offers it to God in the name of all the people. For their part, the faithful join in the offering of the Eucharist by virtue of their royal priesthood.[32] They likewise exercise that priesthood by receiving the sacraments, by prayer and thanksgiving, by the witness of a holy life, and by self-denial and active charity.

11. It is through the sacraments[33] and the exercise of the virtues that the sacred nature and organic structure of the priestly community is brought

---

[30] Art. 10–13 form a unit in which the Church is considered as reflecting in itself the triple office of Christ as priest, prophet, and king. This the Church does by its threefold function of worship (ministry), witness, and communal life. The present paragraph deals particularly with the priestly office. The common priesthood of all the baptized provides the basis for, and requires for its completion, the ministerial priesthood of the ordained clergy.

[31] *Cf. Pius XII, allocution "Magnificate Dominum," Nov. 2, 1954: AAS 46 (1954), p. 669; Pius XII, encyclical "Mediator Dei," Nov. 20, 1947: AAS 59 (1947), p. 555.*

[32] *Cf. Pius XI, encyclical "Miserentissimus Redemptor," May 8, 1928: AAS 20 (1928), pp. 171 f.; Pius XII, allocution "Vous nous avez," Sept. 22, 1956: AAS 48 (1956) p. 714.*

[33] Amplifying Art. 10, the Council goes on to show that the priestly function of the Church is exercised in various ways in the administration and reception of the sacraments. Three of these (baptism, confirmation, and holy orders) make their recipients sharers in various degrees in the priestly office of Christ, thus qualifying them to receive or administer the other sacraments. The sacraments are here envisaged not as the actions of individuals but in their relation to the entire Church, whose life they articulate. They constitute public, communal worship, and the grace which flows from them serves to build up the life of the whole Church.

into operation. Incorporated into the Church through baptism, the faithful are consecrated by the baptismal character to the exercise of the cult of the Christian religion. Reborn as sons of God, they must confess before men the faith which they have received from God through the Church.[34] Bound more intimately to the Church by the sacrament of confirmation, they are endowed by the Holy Spirit with special strength. Hence they are more strictly obliged to spread and defend the faith both by word and by deed as true witnesses of Christ.[35]

Taking part in the Eucharistic Sacrifice, which is the fount and apex of the whole Christian life, they offer the divine Victim to God, and offer themselves along with It.[36] Thus, both by the act of oblation and through holy Communion, all perform their proper part in this liturgical service, not, indeed, all in the same way but each in that way which is appropriate to himself. Strengthened anew at the holy table by the Body of Christ, they manifest in a practical way that unity of God's People which is suitably signified and wonderously brought about by this most awesome sacrament.

Those who approach the sacrament of penance obtain pardon from the mercy of God for offenses committed against Him. They are at the same time reconciled with the Church, which they have wounded by their sins, and which by charity, example, and prayer seeks their conversion. By the sacred anointing of the sick and the prayer of her priests, the whole Church commends those who are ill to the suffering and glorified Lord, asking that He may lighten their suffering and save them (cf. Jas. 5:14–16). She exhorts them, moreover, to contribute to the welfare of the whole People of God by associating themselves freely with the passion and death of Christ (cf. Rom. 8:17; Col. 1:24; 2 Tim. 2:11–12; 1 Pet. 4:13). Those of the faithful who are consecrated by holy orders are appointed to feed the Church in Christ's name with the Word and the grace of God.

Finally, Christian spouses, in virtue of the sacrament of matrimony, signify and partake of the mystery of that unity and fruitful love which exists between Christ and His Church (cf. Eph. 5:32). The spouses thereby help each other to attain to holiness in their married life and by the rearing and education of their children. And so, in their state and way of life, they have their own special gift among the People of God (cf. 1 Cor. 7:7).[37]

For from the wedlock of Christians there comes the family, in which new citizens of human society are born. By the grace of the Holy Spirit received in baptism these are made children of God, thus perpetuating the People of God through the centuries. The family is, so to speak, the domestic Church. In it

---

[34] *Cf. St. Thomas, "Summa Theol.," 3, q. 63, a. 2.*

[35] *Cf. St. Cyril of Jerusalem, "Catech," 17, De Spiritu Sancto, II, 35–7: PG 33, 1009–12; Nic. Cabasilas, "De vita in Christo," bk. III, De utilitate chrismatis: PG 150, 569–80; and St. Thomas, "Summa Theol." 3, q. 65, a. 3 and q. 72, a. 1 and 5.*

[36] *Cf. Pius XII, encyclical "Mediator Dei," Nov. 20, 1947; AAS 39 (1947) especially pp. 552 f.*

[37] *I Cor 7:7 "Everyone has his own particular gift ["idion charisma"] from God, some one thing and some another." Cf. St. Augustine, "De dono persev.," 14, 37: PL 45, 1015 f.: "It is not just continence that is a gift of God—so also is the chastity of the married."*

parents should, by their word and example, be the first preachers of the faith to their children. They should encourage them in the vocation which is proper to each of them, fostering with special care any religious vocation.

Fortified by so many and such powerful means of salvation, all the faithful, whatever their condition or state, are called by the Lord, each in his own way, to that perfect holiness whereby the Father Himself is perfect.

12. The holy People of God shares also in Christ's prophetic office.[38] It spreads abroad a living witness to Him, especially by means of a life of faith and charity and by offering to God a sacrifice of praise, the tribute of lips which give honor to His name (cf. Heb. 13:15). The body of the faithful as a whole, anointed as they are by the Holy One (cf. Jn. 2:20, 27), cannot err in matters of belief. Thanks to a supernatural sense of the faith which characterizes the People as a whole, it manifests this unerring quality when, "from the bishops down to the last member of the laity,"[39] it shows universal agreement in matters of faith and morals.[40]

For, by this sense of faith which is aroused and sustained by the Spirit of truth, God's People accepts not the word of men but the very Word of God (cf. 1 Th. 2:13). It clings without fail to the faith once delivered to the saints (cf. Jude 3), penetrates it more deeply by accurate insights, and applies it more thoroughly to life. All this it does under the lead of a sacred teaching authority to which it loyally defers.

It is not only through the sacraments and Church ministries that the same Holy Spirit sanctifies and leads the People of God and enriches it with virtues. Allotting His gifts "to everyone according as he will" (1 Cor. 12:11), He distributes special graces among the faithful of every rank. By these gifts He makes them fit and ready to undertake the various tasks or offices advantageous for the renewal and upbuilding of the Church, according to the words of the Apostle: "The manifestation of the Spirit is given to everyone for profit" (1 Cor. 12:7). These charismatic gifts, whether they be the most outstanding or the more simple and widely diffused, are to be received with thanksgiving and consolation, for they are exceedingly suitable and useful for the needs of the Church.[41]

---

[38] The entire People of God, just as it shares in Christ's prietly office, shares in his role as prophet, bearing witness to the gospel.

[39] Cf. *St. Augustine, "De praed. sanct.," 14, 27: PL 44, 980.*

[40] The idea that the "sense of the faithful," imprinted on their hearts by the Holy Spirit, cannot err, was a favorite theme of Cardinal Newman, who foresaw its importance for the theology of the laity, which was in its infancy in his day. The fact that the faithful as a whole bear witness to the gospel does not make superfluous the teaching of the hierarchy. To them it falls to shepherd the whole flock by clear, authoritative doctrine.

[41] To guard against a common misunderstanding, the Constitution makes it clear that charisms should not necessarily be identified with extraordinary and spectacular phenomena, which are by their very nature rare. The whole question of charisms is well treated by Karl Rahner in his book *The Dynamic Element in the Church* (New York: Herder and Herder, 1964).

Still, extraordinary gifts are not to be rashly sought after, nor are the fruits of apostolic labor to be presumptuously expected from them. In any case, judgment as to their genuineness and proper use belongs to those who preside over the Church, and to whose special competence it belongs, not indeed to extinguish the Spirit, but to test all things and hold fast to that which is good (cf. 1 Th. 5:12, 19–21).

13. All men are called to belong to the new People of God.[42] Wherefore this People, while remaining one and unique, is to be spread throughout the whole world and must exist in all ages, so that the purpose of God's will may be fulfilled. In the beginning God made human nature one. After His children were scattered, He decreed that they should at length be unified again (cf. Jn. 11:52). It was for this reason that God sent His Son, whom He appointed heir of all things (cf. Heb. 1:2), that He might be Teacher, King, and Priest of all, the Head of the new and universal people of the sons of God. For this God finally sent His Son's Spirit as Lord and Lifegiver. He it is who, on behalf of the whole Church and each and every one of those who believe, is the principle of their coming together and remaining together in the teaching of the apostles and in fellowship, in the breaking of bread and in prayers (cf. Acts 2:42, Greek text).

It follows that among all the nations of earth there is but one People of God, which takes its citizens from every race, making them citizens of a kingdom which is of a heavenly and not an earthly nature. For all the faithful scattered throughout the world are in communion with each other in the Holy Spirit, so that "he who occupies the See of Rome knows the people of India are his members."[43] Since the kingdom of Christ is not of this world (cf. Jn. 18:36), the Church or People of God takes nothing away from the temporal welfare of any people by establishing that kingdom. Rather does she foster and take to herself, insofar as they are good, the ability, resources, and customs of each people. Taking them to herself she purifies, strengthens, and ennobles them. The Church in this is mindful that she must harvest with that King to whom the nations were given for an inheritance (cf. Ps. 2:8) and into whose city they bring gifts and presents (cf. Ps. 71[72]:10; Is. 60:4–7; Apoc. 21:24). This characteristic of universality which adorns the People of God is a gift from the Lord Himself. By reason of it, the Catholic Church strives energetically and constantly to bring all humanity with all its riches back to Christ its Head in the unity of His Spirit.[44]

---

[42] Thirdly, the People of God is considered in its relationship to Christ as King. In this regard it is a fellowship of life. Reflecting the universal Lordship of Christ, the Church spontaneously tends to spread everywhere, thereby bringing men of every nation into intimate spiritual union with one another. Since the Church's unity is vital and organic, it does not impose rigid uniformity, but rather thrives on a variety of gifts and functions.

[43] Cf. St. John Chrysostom, "In Io.," Hom. 65, 1: PG 59, 361.

[44] Cf. St. Irenaeus, "Adv. haer.," III, 16, 6; III, 22, 1–3: PG 7, 925 C–926 A and 955 C–958 A (Harvey, 2, 87 f. and 120–3; Sagnard, pp. 290–2 and 372 ff.).

In virtue of this catholicity each individual part of the Church contributes through its special gifts to the good of the other parts and of the whole Church. Thus through the common sharing of gifts and through the common effort to attain fullness in unity, the whole and each of the parts receive increase. Not only, then, is the People of God made up of different peoples but even in its inner structure it is composed of various ranks. This diversity among its members arises either by reason of their duties, as is the case with those who exercise the sacred ministry for the good of their brethren, or by reason of their situation and way of life, as is the case with those many who enter the religious state and, tending toward holiness by a narrower path, stimulate their brethren by their example.

Moreover, within the Church particular Churches hold a rightful place. These Churches retain their own traditions without in any way lessening the primacy of the Chair of Peter. This Chair presides over the whole assembly of charity[45] and protects legitimate differences, while at the same time it sees that such differences do not hinder unity but rather contribute toward it. Finally, between all the parts of the Church there remains a bond of close communion with respect to spiritual riches, apostolic workers, and temporal resources. For the members of the People of God are called to share these goods, and to each of the Churches the words of the Apostle apply: "According to the gift that each has received, administer it to one another as good stewards of the manifold grace of God" (1 Pet. 4:10).

All men are called to be part of this catholic unity of the People of God, a unity which is harbinger of the universal peace it promotes. And there belong to it or are related to it in various ways, the Catholic faithful as well as all who believe in Christ, and indeed the whole of mankind. For all men are called to salvation by the grace of God.[46]

14. This sacred Synod turns its attention first to the Catholic faithful. Basing itself upon sacred Scripture and tradition, it teaches that the Church, now sojourning on earth as an exile, is necessary for salvation.[47] For Christ, made present to us in His Body, which is the Church, is the one Mediator and the unique Way of salvation. In explicit terms He Himself affirmed the necessity of faith and baptism (cf. Mk. 16:16; Jn. 3:5) and thereby affirmed also the necessity of the Church, for through baptism as through a door men enter the Church. Whosoever, therefore, knowing that the Catholic Church was made

---

[45] Cf. St. Ignatius of Antioch, "Ad Rom.," Praef.: ed. Funk, I, p. 252.

[46] The Constitution now passes on to consider in the last section of this Chapter the various ways in which men can be united or linked with the people of God.

[47] To indicate the importance of union with the Church, the Council first reiterates the traditional Catholic teaching on the necessity of the Church for salvation. This necessity is a double one arising both from the positive precept of Christ that men should enter the Church and from the efficacy of the Church's means of grace (especially her proclamation of the faith and her administration of the sacrament of baptism) for imparting and sustaining an authentically Christian life.

necessary by God through Jesus Christ, would refuse to enter her or to remain in her could not be saved.

They are fully incorporated into the society of the Church who, possessing the Spirit of Christ, accept her entire system and all the means of salvation given to her, and through union with her visible structure are joined to Christ, who rules her through the Supreme Pontiff and the bishops.[48] This joining is effected by the bonds of professed faith, of the sacraments, of ecclesiastical government, and of communion. He is not saved, however, who, though he is part of the body of the Church, does not persevere in charity. He remains indeed in the bosom of the Church, but, as it were, only in a "bodily" manner and not "in his heart."[49] All the sons of the Church should remember that their exalted status is to be attributed not to their own merit but to the special grace of Christ. If they fail moreover to respond to that grace in thought, word, and deed, not only will they not be saved but they will be the more severely judged.[50]

Catechumens who, moved by the Holy Spirit, seek with explicit intention to be incorporated into the Church are by that very intention joined to her. With love and solicitude Mother Church already embraces them as her own.

15. The Church recognizes[51] that in many ways she is linked with those who, being baptized, are honored with the name of Christian, though they do not profess the faith in its entirety or do not preserve unity of communion with the successor of Peter.[52] For there are many who honor sacred Scripture, taking it as a norm of belief and of action, and who show a true religious zeal. They lovingly believe in God the Father Almighty and in Christ, Son of God and Savior.[53] They are consecrated by baptism, through which they are united with

---

[48] The Council here makes it clear that only Catholic Christians are fully incorporated in the Church. But for full incorporation it is not sufficient to be externally a Catholic; one must also be animated by the Spirit of Christ. Where charity is absent, a bond of union essential to salvation is lacking.

[49] Cf. St. Augustine, "Bapt. c. Donat.," V, 28, 39: PL 43, 197: "It is certainly clear that when we speak of 'within' and 'without' with regard to the Church, our consideration must be directed to what is in the heart, not to what is in the body." See also in the same work, III, 19, 26: PL 43, 152; V, 18, 24: PL 43, 189; and the same author's "In Jo.," tr. 61, 2: PL 35, 1800, as well as many texts in other of his works.

[50] Cf. Lk. 12:48: "Much will be expected from the one who has been given much." Also Mt. 5:19–20; 7:21–2; 25:41–6; Jas. 2:14.

[51] This paragraph gives a concise summary of the ways in which those Christians who do not have full visible union with the Catholic Church may nevertheless be linked to the Church by salutary bonds. The Decree on Ecumenism treats this point more fully especially in Art. 3, which details the various elements of the Church that can subsist outside the visible boundaries of Catholicism. By treating the relationship of the other Christians to the Catholic Church under the heading of the "People of God" rather than that of the "Mystical Body" (treated in Chap. I), the Constitution is able to avoid various subtle and controverted questions concerning "degrees of membership" which have been much discussed since the time of *Mystici Corporis*.

[52] Cf. Leo XIII, apostolic epistle "*Praeclara gratulationis*," June 20, 1894: Acta Sanctae Sedis, 26 (1893–4), p. 707.

[53] Cf. Leo XIII, encyclical "*Satis Cognitum*," June 29, 1896: Acta Sanctae Sedis, 28 (1895–6), p. 738; Leo XII, encyclical "*Caritatis studium*," July 25, 1898; Acta Sanctae Sedis, 31 (1898–9), p. 11; and the radio message of Pius XIII, "*Nell'abla*," Dec. 24, 1941: AAS 34 (1942), p. 21.

Christ. They also recognize and receive other sacraments within their own Churches or ecclesial communities. Many of them rejoice in the episcopate, celebrate the Holy Eucharist, and cultivate devotion toward the Virgin Mother of God.[54] They also share with us in prayer and other spiritual benefits.

Likewise, we can say that in some real way they are joined with us in the Holy Spirit, for to them also He gives His gifts and graces, and is thereby operative among them with His sanctifying power. Some indeed He has strengthened to the extent of the shedding of their blood. In all of Christ's disciples the Spirit arouses the desire to be peacefully united; in the manner determined by Christ, as one flock under one shepherd, and He prompts them to pursue this goal.[55] Mother Church never ceases to pray, hope, and work that they may gain this blessing. She exhorts her sons to purify and renew themselves so that the sign of Christ may shine more brightly over the face of the Church.

16. Finally, those who have not yet received the gospel[56] are related in various ways to the People of God.[57] In the first place there is the people to whom the covenants and the promises were given and from whom Christ was born according to the flesh (cf. Rom. 9:4–5). On account of their fathers, this people remains most dear to God, for God does not repent of the gifts He makes nor of the calls He issues (cf. Rom. 11:28–29).

But the plan of salvation also includes those who acknowledge the Creator. In the first place among these there are the Moslems, who, professing to hold the faith of Abraham, along with us adore the one and merciful God, who on the last day will judge mankind. Nor is God Himself far distant from those who in shadows and images seek the unknown God, for it is He who gives to all men life and breath and every other gift (cf. Acts 17:25–28), and who as Savior wills that all men be saved (cf. 1 Tim. 2:4).

Those also can attain to everlasting salvation who through no fault of their own do not know the gospel of Christ or His Church, yet sincerely seek God and, moved by grace, strive by their deeds to do His will as it is known to them[58] through the dictates of conscience.[59] Nor does divine Providence deny

---

[54] Cf. Pius XI, encyclical "Rerum Orientalium," Sept. 8, 1928: AAS 20 (1928), p. 287; Pius XII, encyclical "Orientalis Ecclesiae," Apr. 9, 1944: AAS 36 (1944), p. 137.

[55] Cf. instruction of the Holy Office, Dec. 20, 1949: AAS 42 (1950), p. 142.

[56] Extending the range of its view beyond the Christian fold, the Council now touches on the relationship of non-Christian communities to the Church, thus preparing the way for the Declaration on the Relationship of the Church to Non-Christian Religions. Special mention is here made of the Jews and Mohammedans because of the biblical basis of their respective faiths.

[57] Cf. St Thomas, "Summa Theol.," 3, q. 8, a. 3, ad 1.

[58] The Council is careful to add that men unacquainted with the biblical revelation, and even those who have not arrived at explicit faith in God, may by the grace of Christ attain salvation if they sincerely follow the lights God gives them. In a footnote, the Council makes reference to the important 1949 letter of the Holy Office to Archbishop (now Cardinal) Cushing of Boston, which lucidly explained how according to Catholic doctrine it can be possible for non-Catholics to attain salvation through the grace of God.

[59] Cf. letter of the Holy Office to the Archbishop of Boston: Denz. 3869-72.

the help necessary for salvation to those who, without blame on their part, have not yet arrived at an explicit knowledge of God, but who strive to live a good life, thanks to His grace. Whatever goodness or truth is found is for the gospel.[60] She regards such qualities as given by Him among them as looked upon by the Church as a preparation that enlightens all men so that they may finally have life.

But rather often men, deceived by the Evil One, have become caught up in futile reasoning and have exchanged the truth of God for a lie, serving the creature rather than the Creator (cf. Rom. 1:21,25). Or some there are who, living and dying in a world without God, are subject to utter hopelessness. Consequently, to promote the glory of God and procure the salvation of all such men, and mindful of the command of the Lord, "Preach the gospel to every creature" (Mk. 16:16), the Church painstakingly fosters her missionary work.

17. Just as the Son was sent by the Father, so He too sent the apostles (cf. Jn. 20:21), saying: "Go, therefore, and make disciples of all nations, baptizing them in the name of the Father and of the Son and of the Holy Spirit, teaching them to observe all that I have commanded you; and behold, I am with you all days even unto the consummation of the world" (Mt. 28:18–20).

The Church has received from the apostles as a task to be discharged even to the ends of the earth this solemn mandate of Christ to proclaim the saving truth (cf. Acts 1:8).[61] Hence she makes the words of the Apostle her own: "Woe to me, if I do not preach the gospel" (1 Cor. 9:16), and continues unceasingly to send heralds of the gospel until such time as the infant churches are fully established and can themselves carry on the work of evangelizing. For the Church is compelled by the Holy Spirit to do her part towards the full realization of the will of God, who has established Christ as the source of salvation for the whole world.[62] By the proclamation of the gospel, she prepares her hearers to receive and profess the faith, disposes them for baptism, snatches them from the slavery of error, and incorporates them into Christ so that through charity they may grow up into full maturity in Christ.

Through her work, whatever good is in the minds and hearts of men, whatever good lies latent in the religious practices and cultures of diverse peoples, is not only saved from destruction but is also healed, ennobled, and perfected unto the glory of God, the confusion of the devil, and the happiness of man. The obligation of spreading the faith is imposed on every disciple of

---

[60] Cf. Eusebius of Caesarea, "Praeparatio evangelica," 1, 1: PG 21, 28 AB.

[61] The concluding lines of the preceding paragraph lead naturally to a consideration of the missionary mandate of the Church, which brings this important chapter to a dynamic conclusion.

[62] As in the Gospels, so here the missionary mandate of the Church is closely related to the doctrine of the Trinity, the heart of the Church's faith. The respective roles of hierarchy and laity in the missions, here briefly intimated, will be more fully spelled out in the Decree on the Church's Missionary Activity.

Christ, according to his ability.[63] Though all the faithful can baptize, the priest alone can complete the building up of the Body in the Eucharistic Sacrifice. Thus are fulfilled the Words of God, spoken through His prophet: "From the rising of the sun even to the going down, my name is great among the Gentiles, and in every place there is sacrifice, and there is offered to my name a clean oblation" (Mal. 1:11).[64] In this way the Church simultaneously prays and labors in order that the entire world may become the People of God, the Body of the Lord, and the Temple of the Holy Spirit, and that in Christ, the Head of all, there may be rendered to the Creator and Father of the Universe all honor and glory.

[63] Cf. Benedict XV, apostolic epistle "Maximum illud": AAS 11 (1919), p. 440 and especially pp. 451 ff.; Pius XI, encyclical "Rerum Ecclesiae": AAS 18 (1926), pp. 68–70; Pius XII, encyclical "Fidei donum," Apr. 21, 1957: AAS 49 (1957), pp. 236–7.

[64] Cf. the "Didache," 14: ed. Funk, I, p. 32; St. Justin, "Dial.," 41: PG 6, 564; St Irenaeus, "Adv. haer.," IV, 17, 5: PG 7, 1023 (Harvey, 2, pp. 199f.); and the Council of Trent, Session 22, Chap. 1: Denz. 939 (1742).

21

Mark Zborowski and Elizabeth Herzog,
Life Is With People*

Life Is With People is a collection of memories of Jews who lived in the small villages [shtetls] of Eastern Europe before the Nazis and World War II all but destroyed their way of life. Many of these memories stress the deep importance that sociability played in the villages. The intense neighborliness depicted illustrates the traditional belief that Jews need to live among other Jews in order to survive.

The shtetl dispenses social justice by means of systematic benefactions in which the real motive power is informal, although an elaborate series of organizations exists and functions. In the whole machinery of community functioning the same combination is evident: the basic motive power is informal and operates largely without regard to—sometimes in spite of—the formal apparatus.

The formal apparatus is complex and variegated, exhibiting different forms at different times and places. For the outsider a detailed picture of it may be confusing. For a member of the shtetl this confusion does not exist—partly because each is habituated to his own forms but chiefly because the informal mechanisms are constant, and paramount. Moreover, regardless of local and temporal variations in specific form, the underlying relationship of shtetl autonomy to official government power is also constant.

As an "island" culture, a minority embedded in and subordinate to a majority group, the shtetl functions always within a conditioning element. In certain areas and in certain situations it is absolutely influenced by the "ocean" culture, as an island is coast-carved, storm-tossed and occasionally inundated by the surrounding waters. At any time its general climate is affected by them. Yet to a large extent it leads a life of its own.

The two groups, minority and majority, recognize different values, follow different customs, and to some extent have been subject to different laws. In Eastern Europe there have always been special decrees aimed specifically at the Jews, to enforce certain observances or more often to restrict movement or residence and to prohibit certain activities. In this they are not unique, for throughout Eastern Europe and especially in Russia there have been many instances of legislation particularly affecting special groups. Gypsies, for example, were prohibited from living in or even entering large cities in Russia. No other group in the region, however, has been the target of so much discrimi-

*Reprinted from *Life Is With People* by Mark Zborowski and Elizabeth Herzog. By permission of International Universities Press, Inc. Copyright 1952 by International Universities Press.

natory legislation. The type of proscription under which they have lived is generally familiar, as is the fact that it has varied in different countries and at different times—for example, that they have been subject to more official prohibitions in Russia, and more informal interference in Poland. Where they might live, where they might go, what they might do for a living have been stringently limited, with major and much-discussed effects on their habits, behavior and attitudes, and on the stereotypes generally held about them. That legal edict has on occasion been compounded by officially condoned massacre has intensified the traits characteristic of the "island" culture.

Officially the functions of the shtetl community have been confined to religious, educational and welfare activities—those described in official parlance as "cultural." Even these have been subject to fluctuating outside influence and control, as when attendance at government schools and edicts requiring all to learn the official language have been enforced, or as in the appointment of a local government rabbi. Fluctuations have been due not only to the institution of new regulations but also to the varying enforcement of old ones. The constant need to adjust to sudden stipulations or to the revival of previously ignored ones has resulted in a high degree of adaptability and a corresponding adjustment to instability and insecurity.

In practice, a large measure of local autonomy has been granted to the shtetl. The government retains active jurisdiction in matters of criminal law. It levies taxes, exacts military service, punishes offenders against the law of the land, and issues special edicts. The whole area of local civil control, however, is left largely to the community.

The local representatives of the national government are always present, as are the police who enforce their rulings and are responsible for maintaining orderly behavior. Even though the Jews may constitute a majority of the local population, there is no question about the power and authority of the national majority. For the most part, however, in immediate day-by-day affairs, the shtetl is self-governing within limits that can be dismissed from the foreground of consciousness during certain periods.

The center of its self-governing authority, as of all shtetl authority and activity, is the synagogue, and in this capacity it serves as the House of Assembly. If there is a central community administration and council, it centers about the main synagogue of the shtetl. This was true of the community council, the *kahal*, which functioned for a period before the middle of the nineteenth century. It was true also to a great extent of the Polish *kehila*. In the larger cities, however, the kehila became an arena for conflicts between political parties as well as between the traditionalists and the "progressives."

The synagogue as House of Assembly is the town hall of the shtetl. Here community business is conducted, whether in the main central shul for the whole shtetl, or in a smaller shul in connection with welfare activities of that one congregation. All important announcements are made in the synagogue, from new decrees of the local or national government to announcements of a marriage, a birth, a death, involving some member of the congregation. No clear-cut distinction is made between religious and secular functions, since for the shtetl Judaism is not a religion but a way of life.

Adult males participate in the community activities, and among the most important meetings are those at which officers and delegates are elected. The actual mechanics of election vary widely, but a constant feature is the campaigning inseparable from all elections, the forming of factions, the influencing of the humble members by the *shtot balebatim*, the city bosses. These are of course men of the Eastern Wall, the ones who dominate all aspects of shtetl activity.

The meetings are not notable for parliamentary procedure. On the contrary, there is little order and more talking than listening. Any event calling for group action or consensus is the occasion for debate, dispute, disagreement and exhaustive weighings of the pro and the con. It is taken for granted that there will be differences of opinion and much taking of sides.

Majority rule is followed but not accepted. The minority may concede momentary victory but the issue is not considered settled. There is a tendency to believe, we were right, and it was mere accident that we were out-voted—the wrong people stayed at home. Dissent is most forcibly expressed by walking out of a meeting or by ostentatious absence from it.

Disagreement is characteristically associated with ideas rather than with individuals. There is no blind following of a leader on the theory that he is right and we will support him whatever he says. On the contrary, the leader's dictum is always subject to analysis and criticism. "Every Jew has his own Shulkhan Arukh," they say, meaning his own interpretation of the Law. They follow, not an individual, but their own version of the point of view he is currently expressing.

Neither do they obey orders blindly. Even the humblest man in the shtetl resents being told to do something that goes against his reason and judgment. He feels that it is not his duty to obey blindly, but to appraise the reasons for any act. Under compulsion he will obey within certain limits, but such compliance is strictly under duress and without acceptance.

The synagogue is the place where any individual is privileged to voice complaint or grievance against the community administration, or any of its officers and representatives. Just before the reading of the Torah a person who wishes to protest will stand up before the congregation, strike the stand on which the scrolls are to be placed, and cry out, "I forbid the reading!" It takes a strong spirit to stand forth in this way, for he may be shouted down or shoved aside. Members of the congregation will pound the reading racks before them, calling for silence. Others will register their support of the plaintiff, also by thumping on the wooden racks and shouting, "Keep quiet, let him talk!" The objectors will shout back, "Silence in the Holy Place!" with still more pounding on the racks. The little boys in the congregation join in with a will, yelling and thumping, with no clear notion what it is all about but with keen appreciation of the chance to make a fine noise and not be scolded for it. Startled by the sudden outbreak, the women upstairs will climb on their benches to peer down through the high, small windows, while here and there in the shouting group below an unperturbed few quietly go on with their prayers.

The women also have the right of interruption, and if one is too weak to pound hard enough for attention, she may demand that the sexton, the shammes, do it for her.

Within the area of shtetl autonomy the highest legal authority is the rabbi, who is also the highest religious and scholastic authority. He is the judge, and the law by which he judges is that set down in the sacred writings. Those who come before him are judged, not by the law of the land but by the law of the Promised Land, the sacred Law.

Shul and court are merged, within the area of autonomy, not only by virtue of the authority vested by the Chosen People in their Rov, their rabbi, but also with the express sanction of the official government. In his office or court, the *bes din*, the Rov judges strictly legal matters such as money disputes, strictly religious matters such as the ritual status of a meat pot on which three drops of milk were splashed, and matters like divorce which are considered to belong to both the religious and the legal spheres. The folk who appear before him may come as citizens to a court of law, as members of a congregation to their leader, or as both.

If the shtetl is large the Rov will have an assistant, called the judge or dayan, who will help him in both his religious and his legal duties. If it is very small, there may be only a dayan. Or again, a town may boast several rabbis with several assistants.

In a dispute, if other means have failed, the complainant will call the defendant to the rabbi, *rufn tsum Rov*, where the case will be decided. If the defendant refuses to go, there is no way to force him aside from the pressure of public opinion, but there are few instances of refusal to answer such a call. Some cases could be taken either to the rabbi or to the official court—for example, inheritance problems or failure to fulfill partnership contracts. In such cases the first choice is usually the Rov.

Certain kinds of wage dispute are examples of a strictly legal case that nevertheless could be handled only in the bes din, since it would not have legal status in the police court. The Law rules that a man must be paid enough to live, and therefore if he has six children he requires more than if he is newly married with no children. If the employer is too poor to pay him, that is another problem. These are legal tangles that the Rov puzzles over, between ruling on the breaking of a marriage contract and the case of a chicken with a lump on its gizzard.

The rabbi's decision will be enforced only by the pressure of public opinion. A salient feature of the civil machinery is the lack of enforcing power for the functions that are delegated to the shtetl. There are no police to implement the verdict of the rabbi or the decisions of other officials. Enforcement is solely by the combined authority of God and of man. As long as belief in the Almighty is effective, the Holy Books are the Law and the rabbi's interpretation of the Law carries weight. As long as concern about what people think is strong, the popularly accepted arbiter keeps his authority—and such concern is extremely strong in the shtetl.

It is taken for granted that the rabbi's judgments are not backed up by physical force. Words should rule, for they are the weapon of reason and all human behavior should be reasonable. The punishments decreed by the rabbi are most often imposed donations to charity, or penalties such as reading certain prayers and psalms, or fasting. Occasionally he will recommend a certain number of lashes. Since there is no mechanism of enforcement, it is left to the culprit to ask the shammes to administer them, or, if that official is unavailable, to persuade some friend to put the ruling into effect.

More severe is the penalty of boycott or ostracism and public shaming, for offense and penalty will be announced in the synagogue: "Do not buy of this man," or "Do not speak to him," during a specified period. Another familiar penalty is prohibition from being called to the reading of the Torah—one man who committed an act against the interest of the community was punished by "not being called to Torah for a whole year."

The most extreme form of punishment is almost never inflicted and operates more as a threat, or even as a remote fear, than as a fact. This is excommunication, *kheyrem*, the ultimate form of ostracism and isolation, complete rejection by man and by God. Few have witnessed the ceremony but it is referred to with horror as extremely sinister, taking place in darkness while black candles are being burned. The horror may be aroused more by the significance than by the actual practices. Threat of excommunication is the proverbial ultimate in menace—"even if you ask me under threat of kheyrem," a person may say, "I couldn't do what you ask."

The Rov's authority is not absolute in the sense that his verdict cannot be questioned nor appealed. No authority is absolute in that sense for the shtetl. If one questions the correctness of the decision rendered at the bes din, he may go to another rabbi; but the verdict of the first will be respected until another authority upsets it. One can also take his case to the government court, if it falls within that jurisdiction. That verdict will be final and enforced, and there can be no going to the rabbi once it has been delivered. Moreover, one comes under criticism for going to "their" courts unless it is absolutely necessary. "They considered it a sacrilege to seek advice from the civic authorities, and preferred by far to get their help from their own rabbi. To him they would bring disputes of all kinds, usually with each point of view represented by one speaker, and the rabbi would make a decision."

Not only can the decision be appealed, but one is free to choose among the local rabbis the one to whom he will take his case, that is to select his own judge. He is also free, before going to any rabbi, to "call to men," *rufn tsu mentshen*; that is, to submit the case to one or more arbiters, whose decision shall be binding. They will of course be chosen from among the "beautiful [the most prestigious] Jews."

Because the bes din belongs to the shtetl, cases will always be taken there if possible, and it is chiefly the criminal cases that get to the government courts. This suits the government well enough. If localities will handle strictly local affairs, so much the better.

Legal duties are, of course, only one part of the rabbi's functions. He is also a teacher, and an intimate personal adviser to his congregation. Moreover, these religious leaders often command the respect and affection of the peasants. "The prosteh yidn and the peasants considered my grandfather a holy man, in fact they used to call him Holy Rabbi. They were superstitious; if my grandfather walked in the fields and it rained the next day, they said he had blessed the fields and had caused it to rain. And the Gentiles always came to him for advice, they never went to court. He was a very wonderful person and the peasants were extremely loyal to him. Once in a big storm, he harnessed his horse and went to shul because he had to say evening prayers. When he didn't come back for several hours my grandmother became very worried so she went to the peasant and asked him to look for my grandfather. It didn't take five minutes and in that big storm the whole town of Gentiles was out looking for Holy Rabbi. They found him in shul studying with some men. He had completely forgotten what time it was."

The importance of the rabbi to the shtetl is tremendous, especially since he is appointed for life and serves as the center for community activities of all kinds. When a position falls vacant, usually through death, the new Rov is selected by the important men of the synagogue, after endless debate and investigation. On no subject is factionalism more lively, and even aside from appointments, the relative merits of different rabbis furnish matter for endless arguments that on occasion become open and sustained hostilities.

In some regions, in addition to the rabbi chosen by the people, there will be one appointed by the government. This "crown rabbi" is likely to be completely ignored by the pious, seldom referred to for advice or judgment, and usually disliked. Nevertheless, if the government appoints him, it is obligatory for the community to support him. Unlike their "own" rabbis, the "state rabbi" receives an outright salary, instead of living by some other occupation or having his stipend conveyed to him in some indirect manner that would maintain the convention of "not using Torah as an axe." He must be paid by the congregation, although it has no voice in appointing him. His functions are chiefly official: serving as a means of communication between the community and the government and issuing certificates of birth, marriage or death.

Welfare activities are supported chiefly, though not wholly, by more or less voluntary donations and contributions. The remainder of the community expenses are defrayed by taxes levied on religious objects and services—yeast, candles, the mikva, matsos, and meat. The meat tax is much the most important as source of revenue and also as economic burden. Jews can eat only animals or fowl killed by the licensed slaughterer according to the correct procedure. The kosher meat he sells is invariably and heavily taxed. It is not quite a temptation but it is a trial for the poor to see the peasants buying meat for less than half what they must pay.

The shtetl citizen carries a dual tax burden. The local taxes must be paid. In addition, the demands of the national government are high and there is no escaping the tax collector. "Everyone in the shtetl hated the tax collector. . . . If you didn't have any money to pay your taxes, he took away your candlesticks, your pillows or your samovar."

Although the burden on the taxed is severe, the return to the community employees is proverbially less than they can live on. Most of them have a guaranteed minimum which is eked out by supplements or bonuses from the more prosperous men. The Rov receives no official salary, although usually some device is found to remunerate him. The *gaboyim*, the board or council, are paid only in status and prestige, and in many ways the honor costs them dear. Regular payments are usually given, however, to the cantor, the ritual slaughterer, the shammes, the teacher of the Talmud Toyreh, and the mikva attendants, male and female.

The ritual slaughterer, the *shokhet*, fares well since he provides the main community revenue through his occupation. He is apt to be a man of learning and status and may combine with his calling the duties of *mohel*, who performs the circumcision ritual. The other paid employees, however, sorely need the supplements slipped to them by the prosperous members of the congregation. This need, added to the fact that public servants are appointed by the board or council, further enhances the power of these "shul bosses" who are also "city bosses."

The appointed officers, whose duties involve the highest level of religious activities, are known as the Holy Tools, *kley kodesh*. These implements of God's Law include the rabbi, the cantor, and the shokhet.

Through its complicated network of organized group action and individual activity, the shtetl deals with crises and continuing needs, directed always by the leaders who take initiative in civil, charitable, educational, and religious affairs. In reviewing the organizations and their activities, it becomes evident that the system by which community problems are handled provides for certain kinds of situations, while for others there is a conspicuous lack of existing mechanisms.

There is systematic provision for meeting needs connected with problems and crises of the individual life cycle—the continuing needs of food, shelter, clothing, the critical needs of birth, marriage, illness, death, and education. Analogous mechanisms are lacking, however, to deal with situations that might be described as "Acts of God," such as fires, floods, pogroms, which are frequent enough to be part of normal expectation. These arise from the external environment, over which the community is felt to lack control. The strictly human needs are systematically provided for, and when they occur steps are taken to meet them directly. The catastrophe that is visited from without, however, is met indirectly, by means designed to influence the source of the trouble rather than to control its overt manifestation.

Fires are frequent enough so that they are a constant and recognized source of danger. The closeness of the dwellings and their flimsy construction increase the possibility of the flame's spreading, once it has begun. However, responsibility for a volunteer fire brigade—if there is one—is left to the government. Effort is concentrated primarily on rescuing those in danger, salvaging household goods, and fleeing the flame, rather than on putting out or checking the fire. Later, when one is homeless, other members of the community will give relief and will help to rebuild the ruins. But the shtetl is unprepared to control the situation from the outset.

If an epidemic strikes the shtetl, prayers are of course offered up. Other steps consist chiefly in marrying off two orphans or cripples, so that God will be mollified by the good deeds of his worshipers. That is, one tries to placate or alleviate, rather than to control. "Whenever there was an epidemic in the shtetl they used to blame it on the people's sins. They tried to find the guilty ones and would expose them to the public. The Rov would pin up leaflets wherever people could see them saying that the reason why our children are dying is because the people are not pious enough: they don't go to shul; they don't keep kosher too well; and because the women don't go to the mikva. . . . Another method for getting rid of an epidemic, was to get two orphans if possible and to marry them off on the cemetery. This was done as a mitsva for God to show Him the good deeds the people are doing and by pleasing Him thus He would call back the plague."

In this sense pogroms are treated also as acts of God. There is usually no defense organization. If organized resistance is attempted by the prosteh or by young people who have broken away from traditional attitudes, it is criticized by the very orthodox as "un-Jewish." One pleads with God for help and mercy. Perhaps one sends a delegation to the leader of the attacking group. But to fight back is the exception rather than the rule.

This passivity cannot be attributed simply to fear of death. There are too many instances of Jews who have accepted avoidable death rather than to violate the Sabbath. There are instances also like that of the shokhet, the ritual slaughterer, "a big husky man, strong as a horse," who allowed himself to be killed when he might have escaped by killing an unarmed assailant in a pogrom. "The funny part about it is that the shokhet is accustomed to killing and seeing blood shed. He even says a blessing over it, but yet he couldn't kill a man."

Within the area where the community has autonomy and exercises control, the shtetl is run by the men who know and the men who give. Their leadership, like their earthly honor and their heavenly merits, must constantly be validated. If they want to preserve their status they must respond to any appeal of their fellows. The rabbi's house should always be open, the sheyneh layt have no right to refuse a call, whether it be to attend a wedding, mediate a dispute, or obtain permission for nearby soldiers to go to the synagogue on Passover. The burden of high status is suggested by a familiar phrase used to describe someone who enjoys a lazy, luxurious life: "He lives like God in

Odessa." In Odessa, "the Paris of Russia" and "a city of heretics," people very seldom mention God's name. "They don't bother Him, they seldom stifle Him with requests and complaints." Therefore, "His life is easy there."

Like everyone in the shtetl, the leaders live always under the watchful eyes of "people," mentshen. Nobody is exempt from criticism, and the sheyneh yidn the least of all. The familiar exclamation, "What can you expect of a prosteh?" gives to the common people a certain latitude. The nogid, however, is constantly subject to approval or disapproval. The people give him deference and honor, but they claim a right to know "how did he earn it?" If they dare not criticize him to his face they do it behind his back. If he is not living up to his position, "God will punish him," they say wisely, or "there will come a day—" His behavior is constantly tested and examined, and any fault may undermine his prestige. No authority and no position is ever absolute and final; it must be validated continually and visibly.

If one sins, however, it is worse to do it openly than secretly. "Un-Jewish" behavior is despised and condemned, but public violation of prescribed standards adds to the offense, because in that case one influences others. Smoking on Sabbath in a privy is bad enough but smoking at the open window is a crime against the community. A sin that is unknown to the shtetl is regarded as a sin against God, who will take care of it, but overt violation is a crime against the people, and people will retaliate. Atheists were beaten by pious Jews, not because they ate on the Day of Atonement, but because they ate in public where they were seen by worshipers going to or from the synagogue.

To sin publicly is a crime, but to insist on privacy if you are not sinning is a serious misdemeanor. Again, the lives of the sheyneh layt especially must be open to all. One of the worst things you can say of a man is, "he keeps it for himself" or "he hides it from others," whether "it" is money or wisdom, clothing or news.

Locked doors, isolation, avoidance of community control, arouse suspicion. "You know, so-and-so locks his doors" is a comment which implies that "so-and-so" has something to hide. Locks are against thieves and outsiders, but not against "home people," *heymisheh mentshen*, who are free to come in whenever they like at any time of the day. "To come in for a glass of tea" means to find out how your neighbor lives, what he is doing, what kind of household he has. Sipping the tea through a lump of sugar, you will tell him, "I don't want to interfere with your business, it's no concern of mine, but—" and this will serve as preface to a long series of helpful comments about your neighbor's way of bringing up children or of cooking a Sabbath fish. In the besmedresh everyone will hear that so-and-so spoke to his wife unbecomingly, or was reading a Russian newspaper, or gave a substantial loan to his poor relative to start a new business. The matchmaker does not wait until the father comes to him, but will remind him that "it is already time" for him to think about finding a son-in-law.

The authority of "mentshen," of people, is as compelling as the official power of the Rov and perhaps more so. "What will people say," is the constant reminder of parents to children, husband to wife, friend to friend, partner to business partner. Added to all the other pressures for conforming with usage and religious prescription is the powerful inducement, "because of people." "People will laugh," "people will talk," "we will be ashamed before people," "we will be unable to show our face to people." The wife of the impoverished nogid keeps several pots of water boiling—"people should think" she still has plenty of food to cook. An ignoramus sits with an open book before him on the Sabbath—people should think that he too is studying.

"What does one not do for people?" they ask. There are husbands who go into debt "over the head" in order to buy their wives a fur coat or jewels, or send them "to the country" for a summer outing. People "kill themselves" in order to give an expensive wedding and invite more guests than they can afford so that "people shall see." For the most part, however, such efforts are futile, for "people see everything, they know everything, one cannot hide from people."

It is proverbial that "there are no secrets in the shtetl," and the shtetl itself jokes about the need of everyone to know all about everyone else's affairs. "If you want to know what goes on at my home," they say, "ask my neighbor." It is a joking point rather than a sore point, because basically the shtetl wants no secrets. One tries to hide his private lacks and weaknesses, but the great urge is to share and to communicate. There is no need to veil inquisitiveness behind a discreet pretense of "minding one's own business," for it is normal, natural and right to mind everyone's business. Withdrawal is felt as attack, whether physical or psychological, and isolation is intolerable. "Life is with people."

Whenever possible one "goes a little bit among people," the men to shul, the women to gossip with their neighbors. You dart into the house next door to relay the latest tidbit, and perhaps to borrow an onion. The door is never locked and nobody stops to knock. In the evening, you "sit a little bit" on the *prisbeh*, the low embankment that protects the base of the house, and "look at the people." Everywhere people cluster to talk, at home, in the market place, on the street. Everyone wants to pick up the latest news, the newest gossip. Everyone is interested in "what people say" about war, about the nogid's latest transactions, about the pregnancy of the rabbi's wife, about the illness of the melamed's youngest son.

News is never kept for oneself. It is immediately passed to the neighbors, spread from the Eastern Wall to the beggar at the door, and exaggerated in transit until it comes back unrecognizable. Whether the event is personal or general, it must be shared. When death strikes, the bereaved widow is more likely to rush out into the street crying, "He is dead," than to fling herself on the body of her husband. When a new regulation is announced, "circles of people," *reydlakh*, gather in the market place, talking, speculating, debating.

The freedom to observe and to pass judgment on one's fellows, the need to communicate and share events and emotions, is inseparable from a strong feeling that individuals are responsible to and for each other. Collective responsibility is imposed by outside pressures on a minority group, but these pressures combine with and re-enforce the basic tenets of religious faith. The Covenant solemnized on Mount Sinai is with all Jews and with each Jew. Since it involves them individually and collectively, the punishment inflicted on any Jew may be for his personal misdeed or for an act of the group; and calamity to the group may be for collective behavior or for an individual sin. Again and again in the books studied from early childhood until old age, it is repeated, "All Jews are responsible each for the other."

If a member of the community fails in his obligations, if he "jumps the fence," and is "a sinner in Israel," the whole community may suffer from his misbehavior. God is just and does not punish without reason. An epidemic in the community, an unfavorable edict of the government, a pogrom, are the direct consequences of wrongdoing. Nobody is free from sin—"a man is only a man," "*a mentsh iz nur a mentsh*," therefore every member of the community has to be watched and controlled, lest the whole community suffer.

Just as the sins of the individual are borne also by his family and community, so the benefactions of the baal zkhus add to the welfare of "his own." Zkhus ovos, the merits of the ancestors, are invoked when one appeals to God for help, and may mean not only direct biological ancestors but also the patriarchs Abraham, Isaac and Jacob. In a family crisis one reminds God of the pious and outstanding scholars in his lineage, but the same scholars will be invoked by the community in a group crisis. The baal zkhus becomes a representative in heaven, entitled on the basis of his earthly deeds to ask of God favors for his family or community. Pious Jews will "go on the graves," that is, write specific requests and leave them on the grave of the baal zkhus, expecting him to use his influence in their behalf. The family invokes the zkhus of its ancestors, the Hassidim rely upon the zkhus of their Rebbeh, and the whole community counts upon the zkhus of its sheyneh layt.

Under the Covenant, people are interdependent, not only because the acts of one affect the fate of all, but also because each needs the others. The underprivileged depend on the privileged to help them with instruction, advice, services, material assistance. The privileged depend on the underprivileged in order to validate themselves as "real Jews," since the position of privilege is validated only through the sharing of values with those who lack them. This interdependence is evident not only in connection with charitable activities but in every aspect of human relations, personal as well as communal. The husband needs the wife for her domestic and economic services and for aid in fulfilling the mitsvos. The wife needs the husband for guidance, for performance of domestic ritual, and for final admission to Olam Habo, the world to come. Parents and children are similarly dependent on each other for fulfillment of earthly needs and of the holy Law.

Within this community where each person is linked and identified with the group and all its members, the individual is never lost. He is merged but not submerged. In the shtetl crowd, each person has his own face, and his own voice. "Nearly everyone in the shtetl was a separate character—a 'type' all for himself." Each one has a name, a nickname, a specialty or at least a distinctive trait. One is a student, the other a specialist in military strategy because years ago he was a soldier in the Russian army. The cantor is an authority on music, but he may be challenged by the tailor who considers himself a better expert, *meyvn*. The shtetl accepts everyone's specialty and everyone feels free to challenge the connoisseurship of anyone else. It is a good day for the congregation when three or four "experts" begin a "hot" discussion in the shul, during the interval between the afternoon and evening prayers. Everyone can join in and offer a few "clever words." No one admits defeat, everyone is right even if the others do not agree. Faces are red, hands fly in excited gestures—if they are not busy twisting somebody's button or lapel—all talk together, each wanting to "outshout" his opponent. Suddenly the shammes hits the table with the palm of his hand and the argument is over—it is time to pray.

The community, a whole made up of many closely welded parts, is felt as an extension of the family. "My shtetl" means all the Jews who live in it and the bond persists even when members meet in distant lands. Each shtetl has its known characteristics, suggested in the many nicknames designating members of other towns. Often the names are hostile or derogatory, for "my shtetl" is always best and the one that differs is to that extent inferior. People from Belz are called "Belzer jelly" because the fervent Hassidim of that shtetl shake when they pray like "jellied fish gravy." The women of Yanov are referred to scornfully as "Yanov mares," in honor of the royal stables at Yanov, and the name survived longer than the royalty. The inhabitants of Glowno are named for *teyglakh*, the small pellets of dough boiled in honey because "Glowno folks speak as if they have teyglakh in their mouths."

Despite local pride and prejudice, the region or country is also felt as a wider community. The people who apply derisory nicknames to inhabitants of a neighboring shtetl will feel a sense of kinship with them as compared to outlanders, and will join them in the cultivation of unflattering regional stereotypes. A "Litvak," a "Galitsianer," a Hungarian, a Ukrainian, is "outlandish" everywhere but in his own province. The long caftan and the fur hat of the Hungarian Jew are at odds with the custom of Lithuania, and the man who wears them will be viewed askance. In Poland the shorter coat will offend and its wearer will be given the scornful appellation, "der Daytsh," the German. The Polish Jew recoils from the "Litvak's cold rationalistic mind," and the Lithuanian in turn scorns the Polish Hassid for his "fanatical" devotion to the Rebbeh. At the same time, all the East European Jews feel closer to each other than to those from West Europe who are known as Daytshen.

Beyond the regional or national boundaries, there is still a strong sense of responsible identification with Klal Isroel, "the all of Israel." The folk of the shtetl regard a sense of collective responsibility as another mark of the Jew. "Praying three times a day does not make you a Jew. You have to be a Jew for the world. That means you have to do something for other people as well." Especially, one has to take care of other Jews. "A Jew is always concerned with the troubles of all other Jews . . . he is very conscious of the fact that his personal lot is dependent on the way other Jews live and are treated."

It is a standing joke, enjoyed as much by them as by others, that when Eastern European Jews meet they will always try to establish some bond of relationship or residence—and that it is assumed they will usually succeed. First they find out whether the stranger is Jewish, then comes the question of country, then of province; next the shtetl. The ultimate tendency is to find common relatives. Once these data are established they feel secure. "Among Jews one is never lost."

The transient who is a member of Klal Isroel is accepted by the community as a guest who has claims to hospitality. If he wishes to move in and settle, however, he does well to establish ties with someone who belongs. If the stranger has relatives in the shtetl all is well for then "he is from our own." He can buy a seat in the synagogue and become part of the community organism. "Real strangers," however, are "something different," especially if they come from a region marked by different clothes and customs. Anyone who imports foreign ways is viewed with mistrust. The Talmud itself instructs the pious, "separate not yourself from the community," and again, "a man should never depart from established practice; behold, when Moses ascended above he did not eat, and when the ministering angels descended to earth they partook of food."

To leave the great community of Klal Isroel, that is to renounce the faith of the fathers, is the ultimate sin, just as excommunication is the ultimate punishment. It is one of the three sins that not even mortal peril can excuse. It is a social as well as a religious offense, since withdrawal is always felt as a hostile act.

When people die they remain part of the community, which includes the world to come. The dead are invoked for aid in times of distress, remembered in times of joy. A bride goes to the grave of her dead relatives to beg their presence at her wedding. When a person leaves the faith, however, he is pronounced dead forever. Funeral rites are held for him, his relatives solemnize a ritual mourning for his loss for an hour—a token ceremony. After that, mention of him or of his name is banned.

The most frequent reason for formally leaving the faith is marriage with someone who is not Jewish. To drift away from complete orthodoxy is of course very different from actually embracing another religion. To have one's child marry a goy means shame as well as pain and grief. One cannot "show one's face to people." Something must be wrong with parents to whom this happens, they have failed to make their children into "real Jews," God is punishing them. The person who sins is committing a crime against his parents, his community and his God.

Every possible pressure is brought to avert such a catastrophe. Rabbi, friends, relatives exhort the renegade to reconsider before it is too late. If all fails, the convert, the *meshumed*, is dead to the group. Yet nothing is final, no relationship is irrevocably broken. He can always repent and return. If he does not, then his children may—and sometimes do. Even if they do not, they will still be somehow vaguely regarded as Jewish. A "real Jew" is known by his

"Jewish heart," his "Jewish head," his scrupulous fulfillment of all the mitsvos. But there is also a saying, "a Jew always remains a Jew." If you are born of Jewish parents, if you have any Jewish blood in you, then you have some bond with Klal Isroel.

The shtetl folk feel themselves united not only by bonds of blood, belief and usage, but also by their common burden and reward. In accepting the Covenant the Jews accepted the tremendous *ol fun Yiddishkayt*, "yoke of Jewishness." The burden is the complement to the rewards of belonging to the Chosen People, celebrated in one of the most popular Hassidic songs, sung at the Tsaddik's court to the accompaniment of dancing and often quoted as an expression of pride and joy:

> Whatever else we are, we are
> But Jews we are!
> Whatever else we study, we study
> But Torah we study.

Beyond the Jewish community—the immediate community of the shtetl and the world-wide community of Klal Isroel—lie the others, those who are not Jewish, the goyim. They too are part of the divine plan, but there is always lehavdl, the difference.

Recognition of the difference carries no denial of temporal and worldly jurisdiction. On the contrary, according to talmudic principle, the law of the land where one resides is the law one must obey, except where it would require change of faith. One must fulfill zealously all the duties of a citizen. One must also pray for the welfare of the rulers who govern one's country, even if they rule harshly, for authority is given by God according to His will.

Because of differences in laws and language, customs and values, it is generally assumed that the dominant group does not fully understand "Yiddishkayt." Experience has shown, however, that they do understand money, and bribery has come to be a routine part of dealings with their official representatives. In this respect the shtetl merely accepts the prevailing pattern of Eastern Europe where the "good official" is the one who can be bribed. Jews and non-Jews alike assume that "policemen expect to be bribed." Efforts are made to meet their expectations by the individual involved or—if he is helpless—by the community, which draws together to present a solid front against the outsider. An incident involving a boy who had lost one parent and therefore was considered an orphan, illustrates not only the expectations of the official outsider but also the coexistence of unity and conflict within the group and the assumptions about social justice.

"There was a little boy my age who lived in the shtetl. He was an orphan. . . . Just his father was dead and his mother wasn't a strong woman and she couldn't take care of him very well. They were very poor and I remember how that boy used to walk around in those cold winter nights with torn boots. So he comes to the market on one of these busy days and he goes over to one of the stands where a man is selling these heavy boots that we used to wear in the shtetl. They were called *shtivl*. The man has a small shack which he calls a store and he has dozens of boots hanging from the wall and over the doorway. So the orphan stole a pair of boots. All of a sudden the storekeeper rushes out of the store into the market and starts yelling 'a *ganef*, a *ganef*,' 'a thief, a thief!' And people start rushing from all sides and the policeman comes and naturally they find the orphan boy who stole the pair of shoes, and the boy doesn't deny it. They return the pair of boots and the policeman is ready to take the boy to jail.

"All the Jews stand around and the women weep and cry, 'What are we going to do, how can we let the police take away a Jewish boy. . . . And he is an orphan, what will happen to his mother? We have to do something about it,' and so on. So one fat market woman, who is selling some sort of beygl, picks up one of her dozen skirts—you know, they wore two or three skirts, one on top of the other to keep warm, and the money was kept in a pocket sown into the last skirt so nobody should steal it. She takes out some money and offers it to the storekeeper and so on until a collection is taken up and about $2.00 is collected. The policeman puts his hand in the back and the money is slipped into his hand and he lets the boy go. This the policeman always expected. Whenever he is called in to an affair like that he knows that he will be bribed to let the 'criminal' go.

"When the policeman goes away, then the real fireworks begin. The people start yelling that if the community took care of the boy, he wouldn't have to steal a pair of shoes. But the rich people are all too busy giving money to those who don't really need it instead of taking care of the orphans and the widows. So a committee goes up to speak to the big shots in the community. And the gabai begins to apologize that he didn't know that the widow was so poor and if somebody had only told him he would have seen to it that she and her family had enough to eat and to wear. And from that incident, the boy was always decked out in good clothes, and they always had food in the house. Now, I think, that could only happen in the shtetl."

When communication with members of the official government is necessary, the shtetl needs people who can talk with them, who know their language, their ways, their preferences, and who if possible have special channels and contacts. The need is frequent enough that there is a special term for this sort of intermediary, who is called the *shtadlan*.

The pattern of the intermediary is well developed in the shtetl. The matchmaker is the middleman for marriage. The Tsaddik is the intermediary of the Hassidim in dealing with God—unlike the rabbi, the interpreter of God's law to laymen who for the most part address Him directly. In crises, however, they call on the baal zkhus, who is in effect a heavenly shtadlan. The cantor is also a sort of intermediary, in fact he is referred to as "delegate of the group" in whose name he addresses God. When one needs assistance, one tries to send an intermediary rather than to go and appeal in person.

For official business there are two kinds of intermediary, the professional who is paid for his services and the one who intercedes as a service to the community. The one who is paid in money commands little esteem, for it is well known that his methods are shady and his profits abundant. He is the *makher*, the "fixer." The intermediary who donates his services commands honor, koved. When he operates on an impressive scale he is a shtadlan, literally "one who exerts himself" in behalf of others. To be a shtadlan on a big scale requires outstanding ability and position, and such a man's efforts greatly enhance his prestige. The local intermediary may not be referred to as a shtadlan, but his services are similar, and similarly rewarded.

To be a successful shtadlan one must understand and to some extent conform with "their" ways, so that a certain amount of "un-Jewish" behavior may be forgiven the one who exercises this office.

Both understanding and flexibility were required of a nogid who, during a wave of pogroms, was delegated to persuade the Chief of Police to have his men protect the Jewish stores in the community. The nogid, who was on friendly terms with the officer, invited him to dinner in a private dining room of the local café. Although normally strict in his observance of the dietary laws, on this occasion he did not hesitate to eat nonkosher food, since the lives and livelihood of many were at stake.

After a full and merry meal the subject was broached, and as delicately as possible the nogid offered a bribe for protecting Jewish property from violence—that is, for performance of normal police duties. The officer regretfully explained that this time he could do nothing—he had "orders from the top." The nogid did not argue but, embracing his guest, flung him gently upon a couch that was next to the table and forced the money into his pocket.

No more was said on the subject. The meal over, farewells were casual and cordial. Next day a cordon of police surrounded the Jewish stores and homes, and throughout the duration of that particular pogrom they were safe.

In selecting a representative for matters of moment to the community it is important to choose a man who will command respect and recognition. When a delegate is sent out to raise funds, it is always an honored individual, one whom it would be hard to refuse. He is invited in, asked to sit down, given a glass of tea, and treated with deferential hospitality. "To such a man it is difficult to say no."

If the community wants to plead for mercy against a formidable edict or to beg the leader of a bloody gang to stop a pogrom, the rabbi or one of the most illustrious of the sheyneh layt will be selected. The obligation of their status demands that they seize this dangerous opportunity to serve. In the days of pogroms in the Ukraine, when "Jewish blood was flowing in the streets," rabbis, negidim, learned men, had no right to stay at home hiding in cellars or attics when people called for their services. "They would walk right into the lion's den," saying their prayers on the way, accepting with resignation the jeers of drunken peasants. They would offer ransom for the shtetl, would bargain for the life of their community, and often would be killed on the spot. To do this was part of the ol and part of the honor of being a "real Jew."

When the weak appeal to the strong, the appeal is to mercy rather than to justice. Claims on justice are reserved for one's peers, or else for those who are assumed to be reasonable. One would say to the rabbi, "where is the justice?" but not to a government official from whom one has no right to expect it. In addressing such a man one begs for mercy, and to ask with tears and outcries is part of the pattern.

God is all powerful, but He is also a reasonable being, therefore one may ask Him both for mercy and for justice. Those two attributes, *rakhmones* and *yoysher*, are the two aspects of God which the Chosen People regularly invoke. One asks Him in justice to fulfill His promises under the Covenant, and one begs Him in mercy to forgive the transgressions of imperfect mortals.

The worshiper in the shtetl appeals to divine compassion because he is convinced that the trials visited upon him represent just punishment for some transgression, and only by invoking God's pity may he expect relief. Admitting that he deserves what is inflicted upon him, he asks for pardon. This appeal to the compassion of God is expressed, for example, in the daily prayers:

> With abounding love hast Thou loved us, Oh Lord, our God, with great and exceeding pity hast Thou pitied us. Oh our Father, our King, for our father's sake, who trusted in Thee, and whom Thou didst teach the statutes of Life, be also gracious unto us and teach us. Oh our Father, merciful Father, ever compassionate, have mercy upon us. . . . Oh Thou who art merciful and gracious, I have sinned before Thee. Oh Lord, full of mercy, have mercy upon me and receive my supplications.

In order to be pardoned by God, however, one must repent. Hence the emphasis of *tshuva*, remorse or repentance. Every day in his prayers, and especially on Yom Kippur, the Day of Atonement, the Jew repents of conscious or unconscious failures to fulfill the pact. Not only may one have sinned without realizing it; in addition, since each is responsible for the errors of all, it is right to confess and repent the evil that other Jews have done. The "Confession of Sins" on the Day of Atonement contains about fifty specified sins for which each member of the community implores God's pardon. It is a routine confession recited with tears and moans by all members of the community, men, women, and children.

There are times, however, when the punishment seems to exceed the magnitude of the sin, and then the Jew will appeal to the justice of God. The Torah itself furnishes examples of such an appeal, occasionally even a kind of challenge to God's justice. The patriarch Abraham, pleading for the inhabitants of Sodom, cries out: "Shall not the Judge of all the earth do justly?"

According to a traditional Hassidic song, the great Rabbi Levi-Yitschok of Berditchev went so far as to start a "law suit" against the Almighty:

Good morning to You, Lord of the Universe
I, Levi-Yitschok, son of Sarah, of Berditchev,
Have come to You in a law-suit
On behalf of Your people Israel.
What have You against Your people Israel?
And why do You oppress Your people Israel?
. . . . .

And I, Levi-Yitschok, son of Sarah, of Berditchev, say:
. . . I will not stir from here!
An end there must be to this—it must all stop!

Rabbi Levi-Yitschok based his appeal on his right to question God's justice—the right implied by a pact in which God and Israel are the contracting parties, each with duties and privileges. There is implied also a belief that God is a responsible, reasoning power with whom you can argue—provided you have lived up to your side of the bargain.

This faith in ultimate justice triumphs over temporal tests, holding that always in the long run there will be retribution for evil and reward for virtue. After centuries of suffering, permitted by the Almighty because of their sins, the Chosen People will reach the Promised Land. Whoever has abused them, it is pointed out, has enjoyed immediate gain and ultimate ruin. Cases are cited: Babylon, Greece, Rome, the Russian Czars, Poland. All enjoyed their moment of triumph and now all are gone.

22

Mohandas K. Gandhi
from *An Autobiography: The Story of My Experiments with Truth*, Chapters 17–22*

This reading is from the autobiography of the Indian political leader Mahatma Gandhi. Gandhi was a Hindu holy man who utilized spiritual ideals to free India from British rule. While the popular view was that violence would be the key to liberation, he held that non-violence and belief in the truth of the cause would result in an independent India. To try to change popular sentiment he established a core religious community, or ashram, of disciples who might subsequently win over the masses through prayer, discussion, practice, and good example.

XVII
COMPANIONS

Brajkishorebabu and Rajendrababu were a matchless pair. Their devotion made it impossible for me to take a single step without their help. Their disciples, or their companions—Shambhubabu, Anugrahababu, Dharanibabu, Ramnavmibabu and other vakils—were always with us. Vindhyababu and Janak-dharibabu also came and helped us now and then. All these were Biharis. Their principal work was to take down the ryots' statements.

Professor Kripalani could not but cast in his lot with us. Though a Sindhi he was more Bihari than a born Bihari. I have seen only a few workers capable of merging themselves in the province of their adoption. Kripalani is one of those few. He made it impossible for anyone to feel that he belonged to a different province. He was my gatekeeper in chief. For the time being he made it the end and aim of his life to save me from *darshan* [blessing]-seekers. He warded off people, calling to his aid now his unfailing humour, now his non-violent threats. At nightfall he would take up his occupation of a teacher and regale his companions with his historical studies and observations, and quicken any timid visitor into bravery.

Maulana Mazharul Haq had registered his name on the standing list of helpers whom I might count upon whenever necessary, and he made a point of looking in once or twice a month. The pomp and splendour in which he then lived was in sharp contrast to his simple life of today. The way in which

*From Mohandas K. Gandhi, *An Autobiography: The Story of My Experiments with Truth* (Boston, Beacon Press, 1957).

he associated with us made us feel that he was one of us, though his fashionable habit gave a stranger a different impression.

As I gained more experience of Bihar, I became convinced that work of a permanent nature was impossible without proper village education. The ryots' ignorance was pathetic. They either allowed their children to roam about, or made them toil on indigo plantations from morning to night for a couple of coppers a day. In those days a male labourer's wage did not exceed ten pice, a female's did not exceed six, and a child's three. He who succeeded in earning four annas a day was considered most fortunate.

In consultation with my companions I decided to open primary schools in six villages. One of our conditions with the villagers was that they should provide the teachers with board and lodging while we would see to the other expenses. The village folk had hardly any cash in their hands, but they could well afford to provide foodstuffs. Indeed they had already expressed their readiness to contribute grain and other raw materials.

From where to get the teachers was a great problem. It was difficult to find local teachers who would work for a bare allowance or without remuneration. My idea was never to entrust children to commonplace teachers. Their literary qualification was not so essential as their moral fiber.

So I issued a public appeal for voluntary teachers. It received a ready response. Sjt. Gangadharrao Deshpande sent Babasaheb Soman and Pundalik. Shrimati Avantikabai Gokhale came from Bombay and Mrs. Anandibai Vaishampayan from Poona. I sent to the Ashram for Chhotalal, Surendranath and my son Devdas. About this time Mahadev Desai and Narahari Parikh with their wives cast in their lot with me. Kasturbai was also summoned for the work. This was a fairly strong contingent. Shrimati Avantikabai and Shrimati Anandibai were educated enough, but Shrimati Durga Desai and Shrimati Manibehn Parikh had nothing more than a bare knowledge of Gujarati, and Kasturbai not even that. How were these ladies to instruct the children in Hindi?

I explained to them that they were expected to teach the children not grammar and the three R's so much as cleanliness and good manners. I further explained that even as regards letters there was not so great a difference between Gujarati, Hindi and Marathi as they imagined, and in the primary classes, at any rate, the teaching of the rudiments of the alphabet and numerals was not a difficult matter. The result was that the classes taken by these ladies were found to be most successful. The experience inspired them with confidence and interest in their work. Avantikabai's became a model school. She threw herself heart and soul into her work. She brought her exceptional gifts to bear on it. Through these ladies we could, to some extent, reach the village women.

But I did not want to stop at providing for primary education. The villages were insanitary, the lanes full of filth, the wells surrounded by mud and stink and the courtyards unbearably untidy. The elder people badly needed education in cleanliness. They were all suffering from various skin diseases. So it was decided to do as much sanitary work as possible and to penetrate every department of their lives.

Doctors were needed for this work. I requested the Servants of India Society to lend us the services of the late Dr. Dev. We had been great friends, and he readily offered his services for six months. The teachers—men and women—had all to work under him.

All of them had express instructions not to concern themselves with grievances against planters or with politics. People who had any complaints to make were to be referred to me. No one was to venture out of his beat. The friends carried out these instructions with wonderful fidelity. I do not remember a single occasion of indiscipline.

XVIII
PENETRATING THE VILLAGES

As far as was possible we placed each school in charge of one man and one woman. These volunteers had to look after medical relief and sanitation. The womenfolk had to be approached through women.

Medical relief was a very simple affair. Castor oil, quinine and sulphur ointment were the only drugs provided to the volunteers. If the patient showed a furred tongue or complained of constipation, castor oil was administered, in case of fever quinine was given after an opening dose of castor oil, and the sulphur ointment was applied in case of boils and itch after thoroughly washing the affected parts. No patient was permitted to take home any medicine. Wherever there was some complication Dr. Dev was consulted. Dr. Dev used to visit each centre on certain fixed days in the week.

Quite a number of people availed themselves of this simple relief. This plan of work will not seem strange when it is remembered that the prevailing ailments were few and amenable to simple treatment, by no means requiring expert help. As for the people the arrangement answered excellently.

Sanitation was a difficult affair. The people were not prepared to do anything themselves. Even the field labourers were not ready to do their own scavenging. But Dr. Dev was not a man easily to lose heart. He and the volunteers concentrated their energies on making a village ideally clean. They swept the roads and the courtyards, cleaned out the wells, filled up the pools near by, and lovingly persuaded the villagers to raise volunteers from amongst themselves. In some villages they shamed people into taking up the work, and in others the people were so enthusiastic that they even prepared roads to enable my car to go from place to place. These sweet experiences were not unmixed with bitter ones of people's apathy. I remember some villagers frankly expressing their dislike for this work.

It may not be out of place here to narrate an experience that I have described before now at many meetings. Bhitiharva was a small village in which was one of our schools. I happened to visit a smaller village in its vicinity and found some of the women dressed very dirtily. So I told my wife to ask them why they did not wash their clothes. She spoke to them. One of the women took her into her hut and said: 'Look now, there is no box or cupboard here containing other clothes. The *sari* I am wearing is the only one I have. How am I to wash it? Tell Mahatmaji to get me another *sari*, and I shall then promise to bathe and put on clean clothes every day.'

This cottage was not an exception, but a type to be found in many Indian villages. In countless cottages in India people live without any furniture, and without a change of clothes, merely with a rag to cover their shame.

One more experience I will note. In Champaran there is no lack of bamboo and grass. The school hut they had put up at Bhitiharva was made of these materials. Someone—possibly some of the neighbouring planters' men—set fire to it one night. It was not thought advisable to build another hut of bamboo and grass. The school was in charge of Sjt. Soman and Kasturbai. Sjt. Soman decided to build a *pukka* house, and thanks to his infectious labour, many co-operated with him, and a brick house was soon made ready. There was no fear now of this building being burnt down.

Thus the volunteers with their schools, sanitation work and medical relief gained the confidence and respect of the village folk, and were able to bring good influence to bear upon them.

But I must confess with regret that my hope of putting this constructive work on a permanent footing was not fulfilled. The volunteers had come for temporary periods, I could not secure any more from outside, and permanent honorary workers from Bihar were not available. As soon as my work in Champaran was finished, work outside, which had been preparing in the meantime, drew me away. The few months' work in Champaran, however, took such deep root that its influence in one form or another is to be observed there even today.

XIX
WHEN A GOVERNOR IS GOOD

Whilst on the one hand social service work of the kind I have described in the foregoing chapters was being carried out, on the other the work of recording statements of the ryots' grievances was progressing apace. Thousands of such statements were taken, and they could not but have their effect. The ever growing number of ryots coming to make their statements increased the planters' wrath, and they moved heaven and earth to counteract my inquiry.

One day I received a letter from the Bihar Government to the following effect: 'Your inquiry has been sufficiently prolonged; should you not now bring it to an end and leave Bihar?' The letter was couched in polite language, but its meaning was obvious.

I wrote in reply that the inquiry was bound to be prolonged, and unless and until it resulted in bringing relief to the people, I had no intention of leaving Bihar. I pointed out that it was open to Government to terminate my inquiry by accepting the ryots' grievances as genuine and redressing them, or by recognizing that the ryots had made out a *prima facie* case for an official inquiry which should be immediately instituted.

Sir Edward Gait, the Lieutenant Governor, asked me to see him, expressed his willingness to appoint an inquiry and invited me to be a member of the Committee. I ascertained the names of the other members, and after consultation with my co-workers agreed to serve on the Committee, on condition that I should be free to confer with my co-workers during the progress of the inquiry, that Government should recognize that, by being a member of the Committee, I did not cease to be the ryots' advocate, and that in case the result of the inquiry failed to give me satisfaction, I should be free to guide and advise the ryots as to what line of action they should take.

Sir Edward Gait accepted the condition as just and proper and announced the inquiry. The late Sir Frank Sly was appointed Chairman of the Committee.

The Committee found in favour of the ryots, and recommended that the planters should refund a portion of the exactions made by them which the Committee had found to be unlawful, and that the *tinkathia* [rent] system should be abolished by law.

Sir Edward Gait had a large share in getting the Committee to make a unanimous report and in getting the agrarian bill passed in accordance with the Committee's recommendations. Had he not adopted a firm attitude, and had he not brought all his tact to bear on the subject, the report would not have been unanimous, and the Agrarian Act would not have been passed. The planters wielded extraordinary power. They offered strenuous opposition to the bill in spite of the report, but Sir Edwin Gait remained firm up to the last and fully carried out the recommendations of the Committee.

The *tinkathia* system which had been in existence for about a century was thus abolished, and with it the planters' *raj* [rule] came to an end. The ryots, who had all along remained crushed, now somewhat came to their own, and the superstition that the stain of indigo could never be washed out was exploded.

It was my desire to continue the constructive work for some years, to establish more schools and to penetrate the villages more effectively. The ground had been prepared, but it did not please God, as often before, to allow my plans to be fulfilled. Fate decided otherwise and drove me to take up work elsewhere.

XX
IN TOUCH WITH LABOUR

Whilst I was yet winding up my work on the Committee, I received a letter from Sjts. Mohanlal Pandya and Shankarlal Parikh telling me of the failure of crops in the Kheda district, and asking me to guide the peasants, who were unable to pay the assessment. I had not the inclination, the ability or the courage to advise without an inquiry on the spot.

At the same time there came a letter from Shrimati Anasuyabai about the condition of labour in Ahmedabad. Wages were low, the labourers had long been agitating for an increment, and I had a desire to guide them if I could. But I had not the confidence to direct even this comparatively small affair from that long distance. So I seized the first opportunity to go to Ahmedabad. I had hoped that I should be able to finish both these matters quickly and get back to Champaran to supervise the constructive work that had been inaugurated there.

But things did not move as swiftly as I had wished, and I was unable to return to Champaran, with the result that the schools closed down one by one. My co-workers and I had built many castles in the air, but they all vanished for the time being.

One of these was cow protection work in Champaran, besides rural sanitation and education. I had seen, in the course of my travels, that cow protection and Hindi propaganda had become the exclusive concern of the Marwadis. A Marwadi friend had sheltered me in his *dharmashala* [study room] whilst at Bettiah. Other Marwadis of the place had interested me in their *goshala* (dairy). My ideas about cow protection had been definitely formed then, and my conception of the work was the same as it is today. Cow protection, in my opinion, included cattle-breeding, improvement of the stock, humane treatment of bullocks, formation of model dairies, etc. The Marwadi friends had promised full co-operation in this work, but as I could not fix myself up in Champaran, the scheme could not be carried out.

The *goshala* in Bettiah is still there, but it has not become a model dairy, the Champaran bullock is still made to work beyond his capacity, and the so-called Hindu still cruelly belabours the poor animal and disgraces his religion.

That this work should have remained unrealized has been, to me, a continual regret, and whenever I go to Champaran and hear the gentle reproaches of the Marwadi and Birhari friends, I recall with a heavy sigh all those plans which I had to drop so abruptly.

The educational work in one way or another is going on in many places. But the cow protection work had not taken firm root, and has not, therefore, progressed in the direction intended.

Whilst the Kheda peasants' question was still being discussed, I had already taken up the question of the millhands in Ahmedabad.

I was in a most delicate situation. The mill-hands' case was strong. Shrimati Anasuyabai had to battle against her own brother, Sjt. Ambalal Sarabhai, who led the fray on behalf of the mill-owners. My relations with them were friendly, and that made fighting with them the more difficult. I held consultations with them, and requested them to refer the dispute to arbitration, but they refused to recognize the principle of arbitration.

I had therefore to advise the labourers to go on strike. Before I did so, I came in very close contact with them and their leaders, and explained to them the conditions of a successful strike:

1. never to resort to violence
2. never to molest blacklegs
3. never to depend upon alms, and
4. to remain firm, no matter how long the strike continued, and to earn bread, during the strike, by any other honest labour.

The leaders of the strike understood and accepted the conditions, and the labourers pledged themselves at a general meeting not to resume work until either their terms were accepted or the mill-owners agreed to refer the dispute to arbitration.

It was during this strike that I came to know intimately Sjts. Vallabhbhai Patel and Shankarlal Banker. Shrimati Anasuyabai I knew well before this.

We had daily meetings of the strikers under the shade of a tree on the bank of the Sabarmati. They attended the meeting in their thousands, and I reminded them in my speeches of their pledge and of the duty to maintain peace and self-respect. They daily paraded the streets of the city in peaceful procession, carrying their banner bearing the inscription *'Ek Tek'* (keep the pledge).

The strike went on for twenty-one days. During the continuance of the strike I consulted the mill-owners from time to time and entreated them to do justice to the labourers. 'We have our pledge too,' they used to say. 'Our relations with the labourers are those of parents and children. . . . How can we brook the interference of a third party? Where is the room for arbitration?'

XXI
A PEEP INTO THE ASHRAM

Before I proceed to describe the progress of the labour dispute it is essential to have a peep into the Ashram. All the while I was in Champaran the Ashram was never out of my mind, and occasionally I paid it flying visits.

At that time the Ashram was in Kochrab, a small village near Ahmedabad. Plague broke out in this village, and I saw evident danger to the safety of the Ashram children. It was impossible to keep ourselves immune from the effects of the surrounding insanitation, however scrupulously we might observe the rules of cleanliness within the Ashram walls. We were not then equal either to getting the Kochrab people to observe these rules nor to serving the village otherwise.

Our ideal was to have the Ashram at a safe distance both from town and village, and yet at a manageable distance from either. And we were determined, some day, to settle on ground of our own.

The plague, I felt, was sufficient notice to quit Kochrab. Sjt. Punjabhai Hirachand, a merchant in Ahmedabad, had come in close contact with the Ashram, and used to serve us in a number of matters in a pure and selfless spirit. He had a wide experience of things in Ahmedabad, and he volunteered to procure us suitable land. I went about with him north and south of

Kochrab in search of land, and then suggested to him to find out a piece of land three or four miles to the north. He hit upon the present site. Its vicinity to the Sabarmati Central Jail was for me a special attraction. As jail-going was understood to be the normal lot of Satyagrahis [those committed to using the force of truth], I liked this position. And I knew that the sites selected for jails have generally clean surroundings.

In about eight days the sale was executed. There was no building on the land and no tree. But its situation on the bank of the river and its solitude were great advantages.

We decided to start by living under canvas, and having a tin shed for a kitchen, till permanent houses were built.

The Ashram had been slowly growing. We were now over forty souls, men, women and children, having our meals at a common kitchen. The whole conception about the removal was mine, the execution was as usual left to Maganlal.

Our difficulties, before we had permanent living accommodation, were great. The rains were impending, and provisions had to be got from the city four miles away. The ground, which had been a waste, was infested with snakes, and it was no small risk to live with little children under such conditions. The general rule was not to kill the snakes, though I confess none of us had shed the fear of these reptiles, nor have we even now.

The rule of not killing venomous reptiles has been practised for the most part at Phœnix, Tolstoy Farm and Sabarmati. At each of these places we had to settle on waste lands. We have had, however, no loss of life occasioned by snake-bite. I see, with the eye of faith, in this circumstance the hand of the God of Mercy. Let no one cavil at this, saying that God can never be partial, and that He has no time to meddle with the humdrum affairs of men. I have no other language to express the fact of the matter, to describe this uniform experience of mine. Human language can but imperfectly describe God's ways. I am sensible of the fact that they are indescribable and inscrutable. But if mortal man will dare to describe them, he has no better medium than his own inarticulate speech. Even if it be a superstition to believe that complete immunity from harm for twenty-five years in spite of a fairly regular practice of non-killing is not a fortuitous accident but a grace of God, I should still hug that superstition.

During the strike of the mill-hands in Ahmedabad the foundation of the Ashram weaving shed was being laid. For the principal activity of the Ashram was then weaving. Spinning had not so far been possible for us.

XXII
THE FAST

For the first two weeks the mill-hands exhibited great courage and self-restraint and daily held monster meetings. On these occasions I used to remind them of their pledge, and they would shout back to me the assurance that they would rather die than break their word.

But at last they began to show signs of flagging. Just as physical weakness in men manifests itself in irascibility, their attitude towards the blacklegs became more and more menacing as the strike seemed to weaken, and I began to fear an outbreak of rowdyism on their part. The attendance at their daily meetings also began to dwindle by degrees, and despondency and despair were writ large on the faces of those who did attend. Finally the information was brought to me that the strikers had begun to totter. I felt deeply troubled and set to thinking furiously as to what my duty was in the circumstances. I had had experience of a gigantic strike in South Africa, but the situation that confronted me here was different. The mill-hands had taken the pledge at my suggestion. They had repeated it before me day after day, and the very idea that they might now go back upon it was to me inconceivable. Was it pride or was it my love for the labourers and my passionate regard for truth that was at the back of this feeling—who can say?

One morning—it was at a mill-hands' meeting—while I was still groping and unable to see my way clearly, the light came to me. Unbidden and all by themselves the words came to my lips: 'Unless the strikers rally,' I declared to the meeting, 'and continue the strike till a settlement is reached, or till they leave the mills altogether, I will not touch any food.'

The labourers were thunderstruck. Tears began to course down Anasuyabehn's cheeks. The labourers broke out, 'Not you but we shall fast. It would be monstrous if you were to fast. Please forgive us for our lapse, we will now remain faithful to our pledge to the end.'

'There is no need for you to fast,' I replied. 'It would be enough if you could remain true to your pledge. As you know we are without funds, and we do not want to continue our strike by living on public charity. You should therefore try to eke out a bare existence by some kind of labour, so that you may be able to remain unconcerned, no matter how long the strike may continue. As for my fast, it will be broken only after the strike is settled.'

In the meantime Vallabhbhai was trying to find some employment for the strikers under the Municipality, but there was not much hope of success there. Maganlal Gandhi suggested that, as we needed sand for filling the foundation of our weaving school in the Ashram, a number of them might be employed for that purpose. The labourers welcomed the proposal. Anasuyabehn led the way with a basket on her head and soon an endless stream of labourers carrying baskets of sand on their heads could be seen issuing out of the hollow of the river-bed. It was a sight worth seeing. The labourers felt themselves infused with a new strength, and it became difficult to cope with the task of paying out wages to them.

My fast was not free from a grave defect. For as I have already mentioned in a previous chapter, I enjoyed very close and cordial relations with the mill-owners, and my fast could not but affect their decision. As a Satyagrahi I knew that I might not fast against them, but ought to leave them free to be influenced by the mill-hands' strike alone. My fast was undertaken not on account of lapse of the mill-owners, but on account of that of the labourers in which, as their representative, I felt I had a share. With the mill-owners, I could only plead; to fast against them would amount to coercion. Yet in spite of my knowledge that my fast was bound to put pressure upon them, as in fact it did, I felt I could not help it. The duty to undertake it seemed to me to be clear.

I tried to set the mill-owners at ease. 'There is not the slightest necessity for you to withdraw from your position,' I said to them. But they received my words coldly and even flung keen, delicate bits of sarcasm at me, as indeed they had a perfect right to do.

The principal man at the back of the mill-owners' unbending attitude towards the strike was Sheth Ambalal. His resolute will and transparent sincerity were wonderful and captured my heart. It was a pleasure to be pitched against him. The strain produced by my fast upon the opposition, of which he was the head, cut me, therefore, to the quick. And then, Sarladevi, his wife, was attached to me with the affection of a blood-sister, and I could not bear to see her anguish on account of my action.

Anasuyabehn and a number of other friends and labourers shared the fast with me on the first day. But after some difficulty I was able to dissuade them from continuing it further.

The net result of it was that an atmosphere of good-will was created all round. The hearts of the mill-owners were touched, and they set about discovering some means for a settlement. Anasuyabehn's house became the venue of their discussions. Sjt. Anandshankar Dhruva intervened and was in the end appointed arbitrator, and the strike was called off after I had fasted only for three days. The mill-owners commemorated the event by distributing sweets among the labourers, and thus a settlement was reached after 21 days' strike.

At the meeting held to celebrate the settlement, both the mill-owners and the Commissioner were present. The advice which the latter gave to the mill-hands on this occasion was: 'You should always act as Mr. Gandhi advises you.' Almost immediately after these events I had to engage in a tussle with this very gentleman. But circumstances were changed, and he had changed with the circumstances. He then set about warning the Patidars of Kheda against following my advice!

I must not close this chapter without noting here an incident, as amusing as it was pathetic. It happened in connection with the distribution of sweets. The mill-owners had ordered a very large quantity, and it was a problem how to distribute it among the thousands of labourers. It was decided that it would be the fittest thing to distribute it in the open, beneath the very tree under which the pledge had been taken, especially as it would have been extremely inconvenient to assemble them all together in any other place.

I had taken it for granted that the men who had observed strict discipline for full 21 days would without any difficulty be able to remain standing in an orderly manner while the sweets were being distributed, and not make an impatient scramble for them. But when it came to the test, all the methods that were tried for making the distribution failed. Again and again their ranks would break into confusion after distribution had proceeded for a couple of minutes. The leaders of the mill-hands tried their best to restore order, but in vain. The confusion, the crush and the scramble at last became so great that quite an amount of the sweets was spoiled by being trampled under foot, and the attempt to distribute them in the open had finally to be given up. With difficulty we succeeded in taking away the remaining sweets to Sheth Ambalal's bungalow in Mirzapur. Sweets were distributed comfortably the next day within the compound of that bungalow.

The comic side of this incident is obvious, but the pathetic side bears mention. Subsequent inquiry revealed the fact that the beggar population of Ahmedabad, having got scent of the fact that sweets were to be distributed under the *Ek-Tek* tree, had gone there in large numbers, and it was their hungry scramble for the sweets that had created all the confusion and disorder.

The grinding poverty and starvation with which our country is afflicted is such that it drives more and more men every year into the ranks of the beggars, whose desperate struggle for bread renders them insensible to all feelings of decency and self-respect. And our philanthropists, instead of providing work for them and insisting on their working for bread, give them alms.

23

The Glorious Qur'an, Surah 23: "The Believers" and Surah 24: "Light"*

The ideas set forth in this reading are from the Qur'an, which is central to Muslim life. These particular teachings concern ideas essential to the Muslim sense of community. They are based on the Muslim's relationship with Allah, which is centered on fidelity to Allah. The fidelity serves as the basis of Muslim life.

THE BELIEVERS

REVEALED AT MECCA

In the name of Allah, the Beneficent, the Merciful.

1. Successful indeed are the believers
2. Who are humble in their prayers,
3. And who shun vain conversation,
4. And who are payers of the poor-due;
5. And who guard their modesty—
6. Save from their wives or the (slaves) that their right hands possess, for then they are not blameworthy,
7. But whoso craveth beyond that, such are transgressors—
8. And who are shepherds of their pledge and their covenant,
9. And who pay heed to their prayers.
10. These are the heirs
11. Who will inherit Paradise. There they will abide.
12. Verily We created man from a product of wet earth;
13. Then placed him as a drop (of seed) in a safe lodging;
14. Then fashioned We the drop a clot, then fashioned We the clot a little lump, then fashioned We the little lump bones, then clothed the bones with flesh, and then produced it as another creation. So blessed be Allah, the Best of Creators!
15. Then lo! after that ye surely die.
16. Then lo! on the Day of Resurrection ye are raised (again).
17. And We have created above you seven paths, and We are never unmindful of creation.

*Mohammed Marmaduke Pickthall, trans., *The Meaning of The Glorious Koran* (New York: The New American Library, 1963). Reprinted with permission of George Allen & Unwin, Ltd.

18. And We send down from the sky water in measure, and We give it lodging in the earth, and lo! We are able to withdraw it.

19. Then We produce for you therewith gardens of date-palms and grapes, wherein is much fruit for you and whereof ye eat;

20. And a tree that springeth forth from Mount Sinai that groweth oil and relish for the eaters.

21. And lo! in the cattle there is verily a lesson for you. We give you to drink of that which is in their bellies, and many uses have ye in them, and of them do ye eat;

22. And on them and on the ship we are carried.

23. And We verily sent Noah unto his folk, and he said: O my people! Serve Allah. Ye have no other god save Him. Will ye not ward off (evil)?

24. But the chieftains of his folk, who disbelieved, said: This is only a mortal like you who would make himself superior to you. Had Allah willed, He surely could have sent down angels. We heard not of this in the case of our fathers of old.

25. He is only a man in whom is a madness, so watch him for a while.

26. He said: My Lord! Help me because they deny me.

27. Then We inspired in him, saying: Make the ship under Our eyes and Our inspiration. Then, when Our command cometh and the oven gusheth water, introduce therein of every (kind) two spouses, and thy household save him thereof against whom the Word hath already gone forth. And plead not with Me on behalf of those who have done wrong. Lo! they will be drowned.

28. And when thou art on board the ship, thou and whoso is with thee, then say: Praise be to Allah Who hath saved us from the wrongdoing folk!

29. And say: My Lord! Cause me to land at a blessed landing-place, for Thou art best of all who bring to land.

30. Lo! herein verily are portents, for lo! We are ever putting (mankind) to the test.

31. Then, after them, We brought forth another generation;

32. And We sent among them a messenger of their own, saying: Serve Allah. Ye have no other god save Him. Will ye not ward off (evil)?

33. And the chieftains of his folk, who disbelieved and denied the meeting of the Hereafter, and whom We had made soft in the life of the world, said: This is only a mortal like you, who eateth of that whereof ye eat and drinketh of that ye drink.

34. If ye were to obey a mortal like yourselves, ye surely would be losers.

35. Doth he promise you that you, when ye are dead and have become dust and bones, will (again) be brought forth?

36. Begone, begone, with that which ye are promised!

37. There is naught but our life of the world; we die and we live, and we shall not be raised (again).

38. He is only a man who hath invented a lie about Allah. We are not going to put faith in him.

39. He said: My Lord! Help me because they deny me.

40. HE said: In a little while they surely will become repentant.

41. So the (Awful) Cry overtook them rightfully, and We made them like a wreckage (that a torrent hurleth). A far removal for wrongdoing folk!

42. Then after them We brought forth other generations.

43. No nation can outstrip its term, nor yet postpone it.

44. Then We sent our messengers one after another. Whenever its messenger came unto a nation they denied him; so We caused them to follow one another (to disaster) and We made them bywords. A far removal for folk who believe not!

45. Then We sent Moses and his brother Aaron with Our tokens and a clear warrant

46. Unto Pharaoh and his chiefs, but they scorned (them) and they were despotic folk.

47. And they said: Shall we put faith in two mortals like ourselves, and whose folk are servile unto us?

48. So they denied them, and became of those who were destroyed.

49. And We verily gave Moses the Scripture, that haply they might go aright.

50. And We made the son of Mary and his mother a portent, and We gave them refuge on a height, a place of flocks and water-springs.

51. O ye messengers! Eat of the good things, and do right. Lo! I am Aware of what ye do.

52. And lo! this your religion is one religion and I am your Lord, so keep your duty unto Me.

53. But they (mankind) have broken their religion among them into sects, each sect rejoicing in its tenets.

54. So leave them in their error till a time.

55. Think they that in the wealth and sons wherewith We provide them

56. We hasten unto them with good things? Nay, but they perceive not.

57. Lo! those who go in awe for fear of their Lord,

58. And those who believe in the revelations of their Lord,

59. And those who ascribe not partners unto their Lord,

60. And those who give that which they give with hearts afraid because they are about to return unto their Lord,

61. These race for the good things, and they shall win them in the race.

62. And We task not any soul beyond its scope, and with Us is a Record which speaketh the truth, and they will not be wronged.

63. Nay, but their hearts are in ignorance of this (Qur'ân), and they have other works, besides, which they are doing;

64. Till when We grasp their luxurious ones with the punishment, behold! they supplicate.

65. Supplicate not this day! Assuredly ye will not be helped by Us.

66. My revelations were recited unto you, but ye used to turn back on your heels,

67. In scorn thereof. Nightly did ye rave together.

68. Have they not pondered the Word, or hath that come unto them which came not unto their fathers of old?

69. Or know they not their messenger, and so reject him?

70. Or say they: There is a madness in him? Nay, but he bringeth them the Truth; and most of them are haters of the Truth.

71. And if the Truth had followed their desires, verily the heavens and the earth and whosoever is therein had been corrupted. Nay, We have brought them their Reminder, but from their Reminder they now turn away.

72. Or dost thou ask of them (O Muhammad) any tribute? But the bounty of thy Lord is better, for He is best of all who make provision.

73. And lo! thou summonest them indeed unto a right path.

74. And lo! those who believe not in the Hereafter are indeed astray from the path.

75. Though We had mercy on them and relieved them of the harm afflicting them, they still would wander blindly on in their contumacy.

76. Already have We grasped them with punishment, but they humble not themselves unto their Lord, nor do they pray,

77. Until, when We open for them the gate of extreme punishment, behold! they are aghast thereat.

78. He it is Who hath created for you ears and eyes and hearts. Small thanks give ye!

79. And He it is Who hath sown you broadcast in the earth, and unto Him ye will be gathered.

80. And He it is Who giveth life and causeth death, and His is the difference of night and day. Have ye then no sense?

81. Nay, but they say the like of that which said the men of old;

82. They say: When we are dead and have become (mere) dust and bones, shall we then, forsooth, be raised again?

83. We were already promised this, we and our forefathers. Lo! this is naught but fables of the men of old.

84. Say: Unto Whom (belongeth) the earth and whosoever is therein, if ye have knowledge?

85. They will say: Unto Allah. Say: Will ye not then remember?

86. Say: Who is Lord of the seven heavens, and Lord of the Tremendous Throne?

87. They will say: Unto Allah (all that belongeth). Say: Will ye not then keep duty (unto Him)?

88. Say: In Whose hand is the dominion over all things and He protecteth, while against Him there is no protection, if ye have knowledge?

89. They will say: Unto Allah (all that belongeth). Say: How then are ye bewitched?

90. Nay, but We have brought them the Truth, and lo! they are liars.

91. Allah hath not chosen any son, nor is there any God along with Him; else would each God have assuredly championed that which he created, and some of them would assuredly have overcome others. Glorified be Allah above all that they allege.

92. Knower of the invisible and the visible! and exalted be He over all that they ascribe as partners (unto Him)!

93. Say: My Lord! If they shouldst show me that which they are promised,

94. My Lord! then set me not among the wrongdoing folk.

95. And verily We are Able to show thee that which We have promised them.

96. Repel evil with that which is better. We are best Aware of that which they allege.

97. And say: My Lord! I seek refuge in Thee from suggestions of the evil ones,

98. And I seek refuge in Thee, my Lord, lest they be present with me,

99. Until, when death cometh unto one of them, he saith: My Lord! Send me back,

100. That I may do right in that which I have left behind! But nay! It is but a word that he speaketh; and behind them is a barrier until the day when they are raised.

101. And when the trumpet is blown there will be no kinship among them that day, nor will they ask of one another.

102. Then those whose scales are heavy, they are the successful.

103. And those whose scales are light are those who lose their souls, in hell abiding.

104. The fire burneth their faces, and they are glum therein.

105. (It will be said): Were not My revelations recited unto you, and then ye used to deny them?

106. They will say: Our Lord! Our evil fortune conquered us, and we were erring folk.

107. Our Lord! Oh, bring us forth from hence! If we return (to evil) then indeed we shall be wrong-doers.

108. He saith: Begone therein, and speak not unto Me.

109. Lo! there was a party of My slaves who said: Our Lord! We believe, therefor forgive us and have mercy on us for Thou art best of all who show mercy;

110. But ye chose them from a laughing-stock until they caused you to forget remembrance of Me, while ye laughed at them.

111. Lo! I have rewarded them this day forasmuch as they were steadfast: and they verily are the triumphant.

112. He will say: How long tarried ye in the earth, counting by years?

113. They will say: We tarried but a day or part of a day. Ask of those who keep count!

114. He will say: Ye tarried but a little if ye only knew.

115. Deemed ye then that We had created you for naught, and that ye would not be returned unto Us?

116. Now Allah be exalted, the True King! There is no God save Him, the Lord of the Throne of Grace.

117. He who crieth unto any other god along with Allah hath no proof thereof. His reckoning is only with his Lord. Lo! disbelievers will not be successful.

118. And (O Muhammad) say: My Lord! Forgive and have mercy, for Thou art best of all who show mercy.

Sûrah XXIV

An-Nûr, "Light," takes its name from vv. 35–40, descriptive of the Light of God as it should shine in the homes of believers, the greater part of the Sûrah being legislation for the purifying of home life. All its verses were revealed at Al-Madînah. Tradition says that vv. 11–20 relate to the slanderers of Ayeshah in connection with an incident which occurred in the fifth year of the Hijrah when the Prophet was returning from the campaign against the Banî'l-Mustaliq, Ayeshah, having been left behind on a march, and found and brought back by a young soldier who let her mount his camel and himself led the camel. A weaker tradition places the revelation of vv. 1–10 as late as the ninth year of the Hijrah.

The period of revelation is the fifth and sixth years of the Hijrah.

LIGHT

REVEALED AT AL-MADÎNAH

In the name of Allah, the Beneficent, the Merciful.

1. (Here is) a Sûrah which We have revealed and enjoined, and wherein We have revealed plain tokens, that haply we may take heed.

2. The adulterer and the adulteress, scourge ye each one of them (with) a hundred stripes. And let not pity for the twain withhold you from obedience to Allah, if ye believe in Allah and the Last Day. And let a party of believers witness their punishment.

3. The adulterer shall not marry save an adulteress or an idolatress, and the adulteress none shall marry save an adulterer or an idolater. All that is forbidden unto believers.

4. And those who accuse honourable women but being not four witnesses, scourge them (with) eighty stripes and never (afterward) accept their testimony—They indeed are evil-doers—

5. Save those who afterward repent and make amends. (For such) lo! Allah is Forgiving, Merciful.

6. As for those who accuse their wives but have no witnesses except themselves: let the testimony of one of them be four testimonies, (swearing) by Allah that he is of those who speak the truth;

7. And yet a fifth, invoking the curse of Allah on him if he is of those who lie.

8. And it shall avert the punishment from her if she bear witness before Allah four times that the thing he saith is indeed false.

9. And a fifth (time) that the wrath of Allah be upon her if he speaketh truth.

10. And had it not been for the grace of Allah and His mercy unto you, and that Allah is Clement, Wise (ye had been undone).

11. Lo! they who spread the slander are a gang among you. Deem it not a bad thing for you; nay, it is good for you. Unto every man of them (will be paid) that which he hath earned of the sin; and as for him among them who had the greater share therein, his will be an awful doom.

12. Why did not the believers, men and women, when ye heard it, think good of their own folk, and say: It is a manifest untruth?

13. Why did they not produce four witnesses? Since they produce not witnesses, they verily are liars in the sight of Allah.

14. Had it not been for the grace of Allah and His mercy unto you in the world and the Hereafter an awful doom had overtaken you for that whereof ye murmured.

15. When ye welcomed it with your tongues, and uttered with your mouths that whereof ye had no knowledge, ye counted it a trifle. In the sight of Allah it is very great.

16. Wherefor, when ye heard it, said ye not: It is not for us to speak of this. Glory be to Thee (O Allah); This is awful calumny.

17. Allah admonisheth you that ye repeat not the like thereof ever, if ye are (in truth) believers.

18. And He expoundeth unto you His revelations. Allah is Knower, Wise.

19. Lo! those who love that slander should be spread concerning those who believe, theirs will be a painful punishment in the world and the Hereafter. Allah knoweth. Ye know not.

20. Had it not been for the grace of Allah and His mercy unto you, and that Allah is Clement, Merciful, (ye had been undone).

21. O ye who believe! Follow not the footsteps of the devil. Unto whomsoever followeth the footsteps of the devil, lo! he commandeth filthiness and wrong. Had it not been for the grace of Allah and His mercy unto you, not one of you would ever have grown pure. But Allah causeth whom He will to grow. And Allah is Hearer, Knower.

22. And let not those who possess dignity and ease among you swear not to give to the near of kin and to the needy, and to fugitives for the cause of Allah.[1] Let them forgive and show indulgence. Yearn ye not that Allah may forgive you? Allah is Forgiving, Merciful.

23. Lo! as for those who traduce virtuous, believing women (who are) careless, cursed are they in the world and the Hereafter. Theirs will be an awful doom.

24. On the day when their tongues and their hands and their feet testify against them as to what they used to do,

---

[1]Tradition says that Abû Bakr, when he heard that a kinsman of his own whom he had supported had been among the slanderers of his daughter Ayeshah, swore no longer to support him, and that this verse was revealed on that occasion.

25. On that day Allah will pay them their just due, and they will know that Allah, He is the Manifest Truth.

26. Vile women are for vile men, and vile men for vile women. Good women are for good men, and good men for good women; such are innocent of that which people say: For them is pardon and a bountiful provision.

27. O ye who believe! Enter not houses other than your own without first announcing your presence and invoking peace upon the folk thereof. That is better for you, that ye may be heedful.

28. And if ye find no one therein, still enter not until permission hath been given. And if it be said unto you: Go away again, then go away, for it is purer for you. Allah knoweth what ye do.

29. (It is) no sin for you to enter uninhabited houses wherein is comfort for you. Allah knoweth what ye proclaim and what ye hide.

30. Tell the believing men to lower their gaze and be modest. That is purer for them. Lo! Allah is Aware of what they do.

31. And tell the believing women to lower their gaze and be modest, and to display of their adornment only that which is apparent, and to draw their veils over their bosoms, and not to reveal their adornment save to their own husbands or fathers or husbands' fathers, or their sons or their husbands' sons, or their brothers or their brothers' sons or sisters' sons, or their women, or their slaves, or male attendants who lack vigour, or children who know naught of women's nakedness. And let them not stamp their feet so as to reveal what they hide of their adornment. And turn unto Allah together, O believers, in order that ye may succeed.

32. And marry such of you as are solitary and the pious of your slaves and maid-servants. If they be poor, Allah will enrich them of His bounty. Allah is of ample means, Aware.

33. And let those who cannot find a match keep chaste till Allah give them independence by His grace. And such of your slaves as seek a writing (of emancipation), write it for them if ye are aware of aught of good in them, and bestow upon them of the wealth of Allah which He hath bestowed upon you. Force not your slave-girls to whoredom that ye may seek enjoyment of the life of the world, if they would preserve their chastity. And if one force them, then (unto them), after their compulsion, Lo! Allah will be Forgiving, Merciful.

34. And verily We have sent down for you revelations that make plain, and the example of those who passed away before you. An admonition unto those who ward off (evil).

35. Allah is the Light of the heavens and the earth. The similitude of His light is as a niche wherein is a lamp. The lamp is in a glass. The glass is as it were a shining star. (This lamp is) kindled from a blessed tree, an olive neither of the East nor of the West, whose oil would almost glow forth (of itself) though no fire touched it. Light upon light, Allah guideth unto His light whom He will. And Allah speaketh to mankind in allegories, for Allah is Knower of all things.

36. (This lamp is found) in houses which Allah hath allowed to be exalted and that His name shall be remembered therein. Therein do offer praise to Him at morn and evening.

37. Men whom neither merchandise nor sale beguileth from remembrance of Allah and constancy in prayer and paying to the poor their due; who fear a day when hearts and eyeballs will be overturned;

38. That Allah may reward them with the best of what they did, and increase reward for them of His bounty. Allah giveth blessings without stint to whom He will.

39. As for those who disbelieve, their deeds are as a mirage in a desert. The thirsty one supposeth it to be water till he cometh unto it and findeth it naught, and findeth, in the place thereof, Allah, Who payeth him his due; and Allah is swift at reckoning.

40. Or as darkness on a vast, abysmal sea. There covereth him a wave, above which is a wave, above which is a cloud. Layer upon layer of darkness. When he holdeth out his hand he scarce can see it. And he for whom Allah hath not appointed light, for him there is no light.

41. Hast thou not seen that Allah, He it is Whom all who are in the heavens and the earth praise, and the birds in their flight? Of each He knoweth verily the worship and the praise; and Allah is Aware of what they do.

42. And unto Allah belongeth the sovereignty of the heavens and the earth, and unto Allah is the journeying.

43. Hast thou not seen how Allah wafteth the clouds, then gathereth them, then maketh them layers, and thou seest the rain come forth from between them; He sendeth down from the heaven mountains wherein is hail, and smiteth therewith whom He will, and averteth it from whom He will. The flashing of His lightning all but snatcheth away the sight.

44. Allah causeth the revolution of the day and the night. Lo! herein is indeed a lesson for those who see.

45. Allah hath created every animal of water. Of them is (a kind) that goeth upon its belly and (a kind) that goeth upon two legs and (a kind) that goeth upon four. Allah createth what He will. Lo! Allah is Able to do all things.

46. Verily We have sent down revelations and explained them. Allah guideth whom He will unto a straight path.

47. And they say: We believe in Allah and the messenger, and we obey; then after that a faction of them turn away. Such are not believers.

48. And when they appeal unto Allah and His messenger to judge between them, lo! a faction of them are averse;

49. But if right had been with them they would have come unto him willingly.

50. Is there in their hearts a disease, or have they doubts, or fear they lest Allah and His messenger should wrong them in judgement? Nay, but such are evil-doers.

51. The saying of (all true) believers when they appeal unto Allah and His messenger to judge between them is only that they say: We hear and we obey. And such are the successful.

52. He who obeyeth Allah and His messenger, and feareth Allah, and keepeth duty (unto Him): such indeed are the victorious.

53. They swear by Allah solemnly that, if thou order them, they will go forth. Say: Swear not; known obedience (is better). Lo! Allah is Informed of what ye do.

54. Say: Obey Allah and obey the messenger. But if ye turn away, then (it is) for him (to do) only that wherewith he hath been charged and for you (to do) only what wherewith ye have been charged. If ye obey him, ye will go aright. But the messenger hath no other charge than to convey (the message), plainly.

55. Allah hath promised such of you as believe and do good works that He will surely make them to succeed (the present rulers) in the earth even as He caused those who were before them to succeed (others); and that He will surely establish for them their religion which He hath approved for them, and will give them in exchange safety after their fear. They serve Me. They ascribe no thing as partner unto Me. Those who disbelieve henceforth, they are the miscreants.

56. Establish worship and pay the poor-due and obey the messenger, that haply ye may find mercy.

57. Think not that the disbelievers can escape in the land. Fire will be their home—a hapless journey's end!

58. O ye who believe! Let your slaves, and those of you who have not come to puberty, ask leave of you at three times (before they come into your presence): Before the prayer of dawn, and when ye lay aside your raiment for the heat of noon, and after the prayer of night.[2] Three times of privacy for you. It is no sin for them or for you at other times, when some of you go round attendant upon others (if they come into your presence without leave). Thus Allah maketh clear the revelations for you. Allah is Knower, Wise.

59. And when the children among you come to puberty then let them ask leave even as those before them used to ask it. Thus Allah maketh clear His revelations for you. Allah is Knower, Wise.

60. As for women past child-bearing, who have no hope of marriage, it is no sin for them if they discard their (outer) clothing in such a way as not to show adornment. But to refrain is better for them. Allah is Hearer, Knower.

61. No blame is there upon the blind nor any blame upon the lame nor any blame upon the sick nor on yourselves if ye eat from your houses, or the houses of your fathers, or the houses of your mothers, or the houses of your brothers, or the houses of your sisters, or the houses of your fathers' brothers, or the houses of your fathers' sisters, or the houses of your mothers' brothers, or the houses of your mothers' sisters, or (from that) whereof ye hold the keys, or (from the house) of a friend. No sin shall it be for you whether ye eat together or apart. But when ye enter houses, salute one another with a greeting from Allah, blessed and sweet. Thus Allah maketh clear His revelations for you, that haply ye may understand.

[2]The prayer to be offered when the night has fully come.

62. They only are the true believers who believe in Allah and His messenger and, when they are with him on some common errand, go not away until they have asked leave of him. Lo! those who ask leave of thee, those are they who believe in Allah and His messenger. So, if they ask thy leave for some affair of theirs, give leave to whom thou wilt of them, and ask for them forgiveness of Allah. Lo! Allah is Forgiving, Merciful.

63. Make not the calling of the messenger among you as your calling one of another. Allah knoweth those of you who steal away, hiding themselves. And let those who conspire to evade orders beware lest grief or painful punishment befall them.

64. Lo! verily unto Allah belongeth whatsoever is in the heavens and the earth. He knoweth your condition. And (He knoweth) the Day when they are returned unto Him so that He may inform them of what they did. Allah is Knower of all things.

PART VII

RECENT RELIGIOUS MOVEMENTS

Ancient Standing Stones (Megaliths), Callenish, Scotland.
(Photo by J. T. Carmody)

INTRODUCTION

New communities form around new experiences and ideas. As they form, they create new myths, rituals, doctrines, and ethical attitudes. Usually they do not make these out of whole cloth. Rather, they patch together bits from the past and bits that seem new—the product of recent trials or blessings. In this part we consider four movements that have brought some novelty onto the religious scene.

The first movement we sample is the new witchcraft, also known as the new Goddess religion. Women dominate this movement, but it also attracts some men. The movement is pagan in that it repudiates the established biblical traditions, Christian and Jewish. Witches tend to give several reasons for such a repudiation. First, the established religions have been patriarchal and suppressed women. Second, they have suppressed reverence for nature (contributing to the current ecological crisis). Third, they have distorted people's sense of their own bodies, including especially their sexuality. And fourth, they have located divinity apart from the natural world and human experience, usually depicting God as a stern lawgiver.

Representatives of the biblical traditions can certainly question these judgments, but adherents of the new Goddess religion are more interested in positive programs for bringing people joy, peace, healing, and self-affirmation. Harkening back to pre-Christian traditions in Europe (many of them associated with Celtic religion), the new witch Starhawk (Miriam Simos) has developed imaginative rituals for communing with the natural elements, centering the self, and celebrating the divinity of the physical world. Regardless of how one evaluates such rituals, they suggest much that the traditional Western religions must do if they are to bring their beliefs abreast of current ecology and psychology.

The second selection describes the situation in Iran after the revolution that brought the Ayatollah Khomeini to power. V. S. Naipaul, a distinguished novelist and journalist, traveled throughout Iran and other Muslim countries, trying to gauge the temper of the increasingly prominent fundamentalists. Naipaul is critical of the fundamentalist mentality. His education in England was modern and secular, offering little space for religious fundamentalism. In previous books based on journeys in India (his family's home two generations earlier), he had tried to come to grips with traditional religion but found it more harmful than helpful. In India it seemed to him part of a system condemning millions of people to poverty and great suffering. His experience in Iran was different, but no more supportive of traditional religion. So Naipaul not only reports on the recent movement of Muslim fundamentalists to power, he also represents the now centuries-old movement of Western intellectuals away from traditional religion.

The third selection represents liberation theology. This movement has been strongest in Latin America, but it has also developed Asian and African currents. In the first world (the United States and Western Europe) many theologians have sponsored a cognate "political theology." Although most of the liberation theologians have been Christians, other religions seem on the verge of developing analogous schools. Throughout, the accent falls on making religion a force for freeing people from their oppressions, whether these are political, economic, or ideological. The liberation theologies also have racial and sexual as well as class aspects. But in all cases they raise up a cry for justice. This third selection comes from a representative book, Gustavo Gutierrez's *We Drink from Our Own Wells.* Gutierrez is examining the spirituality that poverty brings into focus. Overall, his book is a powerful argument that unless Christianity (and, by implication, any other religion) labors mightily to improve the situation of the poor and oppressed, it is unworthy of its God. Gutierrez has suffered considerable opposition from Catholic church authorities for his criticism of past church thought and practice that helped to enslave the poor, but most liberation theologians consider him a hero as well as a prophetic spokesperson for what the Christian gospel ought to inspire.

The fourth selection, from Elie Wiesel's novel *Night,* indicates some of the experience that underlies recent concern with the Holocaust. The Holocaust was the slaughter of six million Jews, and millions of other opponents of the Nazis, in the German concentration camps of World War II. Trying to gain perspective on the Holocaust has become a major preoccupation of recent Jewish theology, and also of many Christian theologians. The naked evil of an Auschwitz or Dachau raises profound questions about the justice of God and the anti-Semitism of Christianity. It impinges on estimates of Zionism and the modern state of Israel. It has become a major feature of Jewish literature and art, as well as Jewish religion, since the 1950s. Wiesel's novel has played a genetic role in such reflection. As virtually no other piece of Holocaust literature, it presents the harrowing experience of a survivor of the camps and shows the havoc wreaked on his faith. Wiesel has continued to bear witness to the implications of the Holocaust, and in 1986 he received the Nobel Prize for Peace.

Many things have changed in the generations since World War II, including the rise of fundamentalism. Numerous analysts link this rise to the kind of despair that threatened Wiesel. On a popular level, for the masses, the prospect of a world without divinity or colorful religious rituals to sustain a sense of meaning or hope has proven so repugnant that tens of millions have been willing to take leaps of faith. Christians, Muslims, Jews, Hindus, and others have dotted the globe with movements that insist that culture make sense, be rooted in sacredness. Terrible as many of the political consequences of such fundamentalism have been, one can sympathize with the fears and pains underlying it.

The new witches tend to show considerable sympathy for fear and pain but to think that fundamentalism is misguided. The problem will not be solved by a will-to-power that tries to impose old creeds. As the witches see it, the problem is our not having made peace with nature and our own bodies, for both of which death is as natural as life. Revealed religion, especially on the western models, tends to dichotomize reality into life and death, goodness and evil, truth and falsity. In reality (as nature presents it) things are more mixed.

Indeed, perhaps the first characteristic of natural reality is that all things flow together. Life is a continuum, a stream, an ecological whole. One has to enter it but not get swept away, love it but remain detached. Above all, one must not fear it—not think it or oneself wicked, especially regarding one's body. Male and female, body and spirit, individual and communal, human beings do best when they admit the flux of experience and go with it. When they find their own place in it and are able to tap their natural sources of (psychic) power, they feel better about themselves and so are able to be better for other people—less destructive, more cooperative, in general healthier.

The Goddess religion focuses many of these aspirations on a feminine divinity, adding a rich stratum of religious feminism. Other so-called New Age movements take a different focus, but they agree that people should be more natural, more open to the powers latent in their psyches, less fearful, aggressive, and conflicted. This view clashes at many points with traditional religions, especially as fundamentalists interpret them, but it can also find much in the history of established religions to buttress its argument. Religion has always been concerned with healing, and healing has always sought wholeness. Healing for the body as well as the spirit has meant seeking harmony: with nature, within the self, for the community, with divinity. Full healing has always implied political and economic liberation. Even the problem of evil does not separate traditional religions from New Age movements on all counts. Traditional religions attribute evil to ignorance or sin, and they claim that their programs—rituals, myths, creeds, ethics—are the best way to keep evil at bay. Indeed, traditional Christianity claims that the grace of God makes it possible to love even one's enemies, and that it takes one into the very life of God, who is pure love.

Secular intellectuals, whether in academic life or government, tend to agree with Naipaul (and the Wiesel of *Night*) in rejecting the core of the religious position, old or new. They tend to hold back from considering the mysteriousness of human existence a warrant for confessing faith in God or surrendering themselves to an evolution that they intuit has finally to be benign. When they think about ultimate matters, they tend to experience darkness. The best they can say, the most honest report they can make, is that they don't know how or whether the world makes sense. Often they have also to say that they do not find the data encouraging—but that now and then, on a beautiful day or with an innocent child, they would like to be hopeful.

24

Starhawk

"Witchcraft as Goddess Religion" from *The Spiral Dance**

Beliefs of the new witchcraft, or the new Goddess religion, appear in this sample of writings by Starhawk, a contemporary witch. The movement repudiates more traditional and established religions, citing their suppression of women and lack of reverence for the forces of nature. As this reading indicates, the new witchcraft emphasizes self-affirmation, healing, and joy rather than negative qualities.

BETWEEN THE WORLDS

The moon is full. We meet on a hilltop that looks out over the bay. Below us, lights spread out like a field of jewels, and faraway skyscrapers pierce the swirling fog like the spires of fairytale towers. The night is enchanted.

Our candles have been blown out, and our makeshift altar cannot stand up under the force of the wind, as it sings through the branches of tall eucalyptus. We hold up our arms and let it hurl against our faces. We are exhilarated, hair and eyes streaming. The tools are unimportant; we have all we need to make magic: our bodies, our breath, our voices, each other.

The circle has been cast. The invocations begin:

> All-dewy, sky-sailing pregnant moon,
> Who shines for all.
> Who flows through all . . .
> Aradia, Diana, Cybele, Mah . . .
>
> Sailor of the last sea,
> Guardian of the gate,
> Ever-dying, ever-living radiance . . .
> Dionysus, Osiris, Pan, Arthur, Hu . . .

The moon clears the treetops and shines on the circle. We huddle closer for warmth. A woman moves into the center of the circle. We begin to chant her name:

Excerpt from The Spiral Dance by Starhawk. Copyright © 1979 by Miriam Simos. Reprinted by permission of HarperCollins Publishers.

"Diana . . . "
"Dee-ah-nah . . . "
"Aaaah . . . "
The chant builds, spiraling upward. Voices merge into one endlessly modulated harmony. The circle is enveloped in a cone of light.
Then, in a breath—silence.
"You are Goddess," we say to Diane, and kiss her as she steps back into the outer ring. She is smiling.
She remembers who she is.

One by one, we will step into the center of the circle. We will hear our names chanted, feel the cone rise around us. We will receive the gift, and remember:
"I am Goddess. You are God, Goddess. All that lives, breathes, loves, sings in the unending harmony of beings is divine."
In the circle, we will take hands and dance under the moon.

"To disbelieve in witchcraft is the greatest of all heresies."
                                        Malleus Maleficarum (1486)

On every full moon, rituals such as the one described above take place on hilltops, beaches, in open fields and in ordinary houses. Writers, teachers, nurses, computer programmers, artists, lawyers, poets, plumbers, and auto mechanics—women and men from many backgrounds come together to celebrate the mysteries of the Triple Goddess of birth, love, and death, and of her Consort, the Hunter, who is Lord of the Dance of life. The religion they practice is called *Witchcraft*.

Witchcraft is a word that frightens many people and confuses many others. In the popular imagination, Witches are ugly old hags riding broomsticks, or evil Satanists performing obscene rites. Modern Witches are thought to be members of a kooky cult, primarily concerned with cursing enemies by jabbing wax images with pins, and lacking the depth, the dignity and seriousness of purpose of a true religion.

But Witchcraft is a religion, perhaps the oldest religion extant in the West. Its origins go back before Christianity, Judaism, Islam—before Buddhism and Hinduism, as well, and it is very different from all the so-called great religions. The Old Religion, as we call it, is closer in spirit to Native American traditions or to the shamanism of the Arctic. It is not based on dogma or a set of beliefs, nor on scriptures or a sacred book revealed by a great man. Witchcraft takes its teachings from nature, and reads inspiration in the movements of the sun, moon, and stars, the flight of birds, the slow growth of trees, and the cycles of the seasons.

According to our legends, Witchcraft began more than 35 thousand years ago, when the temperature of Europe began to drop and the great sheets of ice crept slowly south in their last advance. Across the rich tundra, teeming with animal life, small groups of hunters followed the free-running reindeer and the thundering bison. They were armed with only the most primitive of weapons, but some among the clans were gifted, could "call" the herds to a cliffside or a pit, where a few beasts, in willing sacrifice, would let themselves be trapped. These gifted shamans could attune themselves to the spirits of the herds, and in so doing they became aware of the pulsating rhythm that infuses all life, the dance of the double spiral, of whirling into being, and whirling out again. They did not phrase this insight intellectually, but in images: the Mother Goddess, the birthgiver, who brings into existence all life; and the Horned God, hunter and hunted, who eternally passes through the gates of death that new life may go on.

Male shamans dressed in skins and horns in identification with the God and the herds; but female priestesses presided naked, embodying the fertility of the Goddess.[1] Life and death were a continuous stream; the dead were buried as if sleeping in a womb, surrounded by their tools and ornaments, so that they might awaken to a new life.[2] In the caves of the Alps, skulls of the great bears were mounted in niches, where they pronounced oracles that guided the clans to game.[3] In lowland pools, reindeer does, their bellies filled with stones that embodied the souls of deer, were submerged in the waters of the Mother's womb, so that victims of the hunt would be reborn.[4]

In the East—Siberia and the Ukraine—the Goddess was Lady of the Mammoths; She was carved from stone in great swelling curves that embodied her gifts of abundance.[5] In the West, in the great cave temples of southern France and Spain, her rites were performed deep in the secret wombs of the

[1] The female figure is almost always shown naked in Paleolithic art. Examples include: The bas-reliefs of Laussel, Dordogne, France—see Johannes Maringer and Hans-George Bandi, *Art in the Ice Age* (New York: Frederick A. Praeger, 1953), pp. 84–85 for photograph; nude figures in La Magdaleine and Angles-Sur-Anglin, Dordogne, France, described by Philip Van Doren Stern in *Prehistoric Europe: From Stone Age Man to the Early Greeks* (New York: W. W. Norton, 1969) p. 162; engraved figures in the underground sanctuary of Pech-Merle, France, described by Stern, pp. 174–175; and the Aurignacian sculptured "fat Venuses" such as that of Willendorf, shown by Maringer and Bandi on p. 28 and Lespugue, see Maringer and Bandi, p. 29.

Examples of male "sorcerers" are found painted in the cave of Le Trois Freres, Dordogne, France, (Stern, p. 115) and the chamois-headed figures of Abu Mege, Teyjat, France, (Stern, p. 166) among many other examples.

References are given for the purpose of indicating descriptions and illustrations of archaeological and anthropological finds that corroborate Craft oral traditions. The interpretations given here of the meanings of finds and customs illustrate Craft traditions of our history, and are by no means meant to be taken as academically accepted or proven. If scholars agree on anything, it is that they don't know what many of these figures meant, or how they were used.

[2] See descriptions of La Ferassie, Dordogne, France in Stern, pp. 85, 95; also La Barma Grande, France in Grahame Clark and Stuart Piggott, *Prehistoric Societies* (London: Hutchinson & Co., 1967) pp. 77–79, and Grimaldi, Calabria, Italy, in Clark and Piggott, pp. 77–79.

[3] As at Drachenloch, Switzerland, described by Stern, p. 89.

[4] At Meindorf and Stellmoor, Germany; see Alberto C. Blanc, "Some Evidence for the Ideologies of Early Man," in Sherwood L. Washburn, ed., *The Social Life of Early Man* (Chicago, Aldine Publications, 1961), p. 124.

[5] Finds of the Mammoth Goddess near the Desna River in the Ukraine are described by Joseph Campbell, *The Masks of God: Primitive Mythology* (New York: Viking Press, 1959) p. 327.

earth, where the great polar forces were painted as bison and horses, superimposed, emerging from the cave walls like spirits out of a dream.[6]

The spiral dance was seen also in the sky: in the moon, who monthly dies and is reborn; in the sun, whose waxing light brings summer's warmth and whose waning brings the chill of winter. Records of the moon's passing were scratched on bone,[7] and the Goddess was shown holding the bison horn, which is also the crescent moon.[8]

The ice retreated. Some clans followed the bison and the reindeer into the far north. Some passed over the Alaskan land bridge to the Americas. Those who remained in Europe turned to fishing and gathering wild plants and shell-fish. Dogs guarded their campsites, and new tools were refined. Those who had the inner power learned that it increased when they worked together. As isolated settlements grew into villages, shamans and priestesses linked forces and shared knowledge. The first covens were formed. Deeply attuned to plant and animal life, they tamed where once they had hunted, and they bred sheep, goats, cows, and pigs from their wild cousins. Seeds were no longer only gathered; they were planted, to grow where they were set. The Hunter became Lord of the Grain, sacrificed when it is cut in autumn, buried in the womb of the Goddess and reborn in the spring. The Lady of the Wild Things became the Barley Mother, and the cycles of moon and sun marked the times for sowing and reaping and letting out to pasture.

Villages grew into the first towns and cities. The Goddess was painted on the plastered walls of shrines, giving birth to the Divine Child—her consort, son, and seed.[9]

In the lands once covered with ice, a new power was discovered, a force that runs like springs of water through the earth Herself. Barefoot priestesses traced out "ley" lines on the new grass. It was found that certain stones increase the flow of power. They were set at the proper points in great marching rows and circles that mark the cycles of time. The year became a great wheel divided into eight parts: the solstices and equinoxes and the cross-quarter days between, when great feasts were held and fires lit. With each ritual, with each ray of the sun and beam of the moon that struck the stones at the times of power, the force increased. They became great reservoirs of subtle energy, gateways between the worlds of the seen and the unseen. Within the circles,

---

[6] Annette Laming, *Lascaux,* trans. by Eleanor Frances Armstrong (Harmondsworth, Middlesex: Penguin Books, 1959); André Leroi-Gourhan, "The Evolution of Paleolithic Art," in *Scientific American,* Vol. 218, No. 17, 1958, pp. 58–68.

[7] Gerald S. Hawkins, *Beyond Stonehenge* (New York, Harper & Row, 1973), see descriptions of engraved mammoth tusks (15,000 B.C.) from Gontzi in the Ukraine, Russia, pp. 236–237; red ochre markings at Abri de las Vinas, Spain (8000–6000 B.C.), pp. 232–233; and wall paintings at Canchal de Mahoma, Spain (7000 B.C.), pp. 230–231.

[8] Laussel, Dordogne, France: see Maringer and Bandi, pp. 84–85.

[9] James Mellaart, *Catal Hüyük, a Neolithic Town in Anatolia* (New York: McGraw-Hill, 1967).

beside the menhirs and dolmens and passage graves, priestesses could probe the secrets of time, and the hidden structure of the cosmos. Mathematics, astronomy, poetry, music, medicine, and the understanding of the workings of the human mind developed side by side with the lore of the deeper mysteries.[10]

But in other lands, cultures developed that devoted themselves to the arts of war. Wave after wave of invasion swept over Europe from the Bronze Age on. Warrior gods drove the Goddess peoples out from the fertile lowlands and fine temples, into the hills and high mountains where they became known as the Sidhe, the Picts or Pixies, the Fair Folk or Faeries.[11] The mythological cycle of Goddess and Consort, Mother and Divine Child, which had held sway for 30 thousand years, was changed to conform to the values of the conquering patriarchies. In Greece, the Goddess, in her many guises, "married" the new gods—the result was the Olympian Pantheon. In the British Isles, the victorious Celts adopted many features of the Old Religion, incorporating them into the Druidic mysteries.

The Faeries, breeding cattle in the stony hills and living in turf-covered, round huts, preserved the Old Religion. Clan mothers, called "Queen of Elphame," which means Elfland, led the covens, together with the priest, the Sacred King, who embodied the dying God, and underwent a ritualized mock death at the end of his term of office. They celebrated the eight feasts of the Wheel with wild processions on horseback, singing, chanting, and the lighting of ritual fires. The invading people often joined in; there was mingling and intermarriage, and many rural families were said to have "Faery blood." The Colleges of the Druids, and the Poetic Colleges of Ireland and Wales, preserved many of the old mysteries.

Christianity, at first, brought little change. Peasants saw in the story of Christ only a new version of their own ancient tales of the Mother Goddess and her Divine Child who is sacrificed and reborn. Country priests often led the dance at the Sabbats, or great festivals.[12] The covens, who preserved the knowledge of the subtle forces, were called *Wicca* or *Wicce,* from the Anglo-Saxon root word meaning "to bend or shape." They were those who could shape the unseen to their will. Healers, teachers, poets, and midwives, they were central figures in every community.

Persecution began slowly. The twelfth and thirteenth centuries saw a revival of aspects of the Old Religion by the troubadours, who wrote love poems to the Goddess under the guise of living noble ladies of their times. The magnificent cathedrals were built in honor of Mary, who had taken over many of the aspects of the ancient Goddess. Witchcraft was declared a heretical act, and in 1324 an Irish coven led by Dame Alice Kyteler was tried by the Bishop of

---

[10] Alexander Thom, "Megaliths and Mathematics," *Antiquity,* 1966, *40,* 121–8.
[11] Margaret A. Murray, *The Witch-Cult in Western Europe* (Oxford, England: Oxford University Press, 1971), pp. 238–246.
[12] Murray, p. 49.

Ossory for worshipping a non-Christian god. Dame Kyteler was saved by her rank, but her followers were burned.

Wars, Crusades, plagues, and peasant revolts raged over Europe in the next centuries. Joan of Arc, the "Maid of Orleans," led the armies of France to victory, but was burned as a Witch by the English. "Maiden" is a term of high respect in Witchcraft, and it has been suggested that the French peasantry loved Joan so greatly because she was, in truth, a leader of the Old Religion.[13] The stability of the medieval Church was shaken, and the feudal system began to break down. The Christian world was swept by messianic movements and religious revolts, and the Church could no longer calmly tolerate rivals.

In 1484, the Papal Bull of Innocent VIII unleashed the power of the Inquisition against the Old Religion. With the publication of the *Malleus Malleficarum*, "The Hammer of the Witches," by the Dominicans Kramer and Sprenger in 1486, the groundwork was laid for a reign of terror that was to hold all of Europe in its grip until well into the eighteenth century. The persecution was most strongly directed against women: Of an estimated 9 million Witches executed, 80 percent were women, including children and young girls, who were believed to inherit the "evil" from their mothers. The asceticism of early Christianity, which turned its back on the world of the flesh, had degenerated, in some quarters of the Church, into hatred of those who brought that flesh into being. Misogyny, the hatred of women, had become a strong element in medieval Christianity. Women, who menstruate and give birth, were identified with sexuality and therefore with evil. "All witchcraft stems from carnal lust, which is in women insatiable," stated the *Malleus Maleficarum*.

The terror was indescribable. Once denounced, by anyone from a spiteful neighbor to a fretful child, a suspected Witch was arrested suddenly, without warning, and not allowed to return home again. She* was considered guilty until proven innocent. Common practice was to strip the suspect naked, shave her completely in hopes of finding the Devil's "marks," which might be moles or freckles. Often the accused were pricked all over their bodies with long, sharp needles; spots the Devil had touched were said to feel no pain. In England, "legal torture" was not allowed, but suspects were deprived of sleep and subjected to slow starvation, before hanging. On the continent, every imaginable atrocity was practiced—the rack, the thumbscrew, "boots" that broke the bones in the legs, vicious beatings—the full roster of the Inquisition's horrors. The accused were tortured until they signed confessions prepared by the Inquisitors, until they admitted to consorting with Satan, to dark and obscene practices that were never part of true Witchcraft. Most cruelly, they were tortured until they named others, until a full coven quota of thirteen were taken. Confession earned a merciful death: strangulation before the stake. Recalcitrant suspects, who maintained their innocence, were burned alive.

---

[13] Murray, pp. 270–276.

*Generically, Witches are female—this usage is meant to include males, not to exclude them.

Witch hunters and informers were paid for convictions, and many found it a profitable career. The rising male medical establishment welcomed the chance to stamp out midwives and village herbalists, their major economic competitors. For others, the Witch trials offered opportunities to rid themselves of "uppity women" and disliked neighbors. Witches themselves say that few of those tried during the Burning Times actually belonged to covens or were members of the Craft. The victims were the elderly, the senile, the mentally ill, women whose looks weren't pleasing or who suffered from some handicap, village beauties who bruised the wrong egos by rejecting advances, or who had roused lust in a celibate priest or married man. Homosexuals and freethinkers were caught in the same net. At times, hundreds of victims were put to death in a day. In the Bishopric of Trier, in Germany, two villages were left with only a single female inhabitant apiece after the trials of 1585.

The Witches and Faeries who could do so, escaped to lands where the Inquisition did not reach. Some may have come to America. It is possible that a genuine coven was meeting in the woods of Salem before the trials, which actually marked the end of active persecution in this country. Some scholars believe that the family of Samuel and John Quincy Adams were members of the megalithic "Dragon" cult, which kept alive the knowledge of the power of the stone circles.[14] Certainly, the independent spirit of Witchcraft is very much akin to many of the ideals of the "Founding Fathers": for example, freedom of speech and worship, decentralized government, and the rights of the individual rather than the divine right of kings.

In America, as in Europe, the Craft went underground, and became the most secret of religions. Traditions were passed down only to those who could be trusted absolutely, usually to members of the same family. Communications between covens were severed; no longer could they meet on the Great Festivals to share knowledge and exchange the results of spells or rituals. Parts of the tradition became lost or forgotten. Yet somehow, in secret, in silence, over glowing coals, behind closed shutters, encoded as fairytales and folksongs, or hidden in subconscious memories, the seed was passed on.

After the persecutions ended, in the eighteenth century, came the age of disbelief. Memory of the true Craft had faded; the hideous stereotypes that remained seemed ludicrous, laughable, or tragic. Only in this century have Witches been able to "come out of the broom closet," so to speak, and counter the imagery of evil with truth. The word "Witch" carries so many negative connotations that many people wonder why we use the word at all. Yet to reclaim the word "Witch" is to reclaim our right, as women, to be powerful; as men, to know the feminine within as divine. To be a Witch is to identify with 9 million victims of bigotry and hatred and to take responsibility for shaping a world in which prejudice claims no more victims. A Witch is a "shaper,"

[14] Andrew E. Rothovius, "The Adams Family and the Grail Tradition: The Untold Story of the Dragon Persecution," *East-West* 1977, 7 (5), 24–30; Andrew E. Rothovius, "The Dragon Tradition in the New World," *East-West* 1977, 7 (8), 43–54.

a creator who bends the unseen into form, and so becomes one of the Wise, one whose life is infused with magic.

Witchcraft has always been a religion of poetry, not theology. The myths, legends, and teachings are recognized as metaphors for "That-Which-Cannot-Be-Told," the absolute reality our limited minds can never completely know. The mysteries of the absolute can never be explained—only felt or intuited. Symbols and ritual acts are used to trigger altered states of awareness, in which insights that go beyond words are revealed. When we speak of "the secrets that cannot be told," we do not mean merely that rules prevent us from speaking freely. We mean that the inner knowledge literally *cannot* be expressed in words. It can only be conveyed by experience, and no one can legislate what insight another person may draw from any given experience. For example, after the ritual described at the opening of this chapter, one woman said, "As we were chanting, I felt that we blended together and became one voice; I sensed the oneness of everybody." Another woman said, "I became aware of how different the chant sounded for each of us, of how unique each person is." A man said simply, "I felt love." To a Witch, all of these statements are equally true and valid. They are no more contradictory than the statements, "Your eyes are as bright as stars" and "Your eyes are as blue as the sea."

The primary symbol for "That-Which-Cannot-Be-Told" is the Goddess. The Goddess has infinite aspects and thousands of names—She is the reality behind many metaphors. She *is* reality, the manifest deity, omnipresent in all of life, in each of us. The Goddess is not separate from the world—She *is* the world, and all things in it: moon, sun, earth, star, stone, seed, flowing river, wind, wave, leaf and branch, bud and blossom, fang and claw, woman and man. In Witchcraft, flesh and spirit are one.

As we have seen, Goddess religion is unimaginably old, but contemporary Witchcraft could just as accurately be called the New Religion. The Craft, today, is undergoing more than a revival, it is experiencing a renaissance, a re-creation. Women are spurring this renewal, and actively reawakening the Goddess, the image of "the legitimacy and beneficence of female power."[15]

Since the decline of the Goddess religions, women have lacked religious models and spiritual systems that speak to female needs and experience. Male images of divinity characterize both western and eastern Religions. Regardless of how abstract the underlying concept of God may be, the symbols, avatars, preachers, prophets, gurus, and Buddhas are overwhelmingly male. Women are not encouraged to explore their own strengths and realizations; they are taught to submit to male authority, to identify masculine perceptions as their spiritual ideals, to deny their bodies and sexuality, to fit their insights into a male mold.

[15] Carol P. Christ, "Why Women Need The Goddess" in Carol P. Christ and Judith Plaskow, *Womanspirit Rising: A Feminist Reader in Religion* (San Francisco: Harper & Row, 1979), p. 278.

Mary Daly, author of *Beyond God The Father*, points out that the model of the universe in which a male God rules the cosmos from outside serves to legitimize male control of social institutions. "The symbol of the Father God, spawned in the human imagination and sustained as plausible by patriarchy, has in turn rendered service to this type of society by making its mechanisms for the oppression of women appear right and fitting."[16] The unconscious model continues to shape the perceptions even of those who have consciously rejected religious teachings. The details of one dogma are rejected, but the underlying structure of belief is imbibed at so deep a level it is rarely questioned. Instead, a new dogma, a parallel structure, replaces the old. For example, many people have rejected the "revealed truth" of Christianity without ever questioning the underlying concept that truth is a set of beliefs revealed through the agency of a "Great Man," possessed of powers or intelligence beyond the ordinary human scope. Christ, as the "Great Man," may be replaced by Buddha, Freud, Marx, Jung, Werner Erhard, or the Maharaj Ji in their theology, but truth is always seen as coming from someone else, as only knowable secondhand. As feminist scholar Carol Christ points out, "Symbol systems cannot simply be rejected, they must be replaced. Where there is no replacement, the mind will revert to familiar structures at times of crisis, bafflement, or defeat."[17]

The symbolism of the Goddess is not a parallel structure to the symbolism of God the Father. The Goddess does not rule the world; She *is* the world. Manifest in each of us, She can be known internally by every individual, in all her magnificent diversity. She does not legitimize the rule of either sex by the other and lends no authority to rulers of temporal hierarchies. In Witchcraft, each of us must reveal our own truth. Deity is seen in our own forms, whether female or male, because the Goddess has her male aspect. Sexuality is a sacrament. Religion is a matter of relinking, with the divine within and with her outer manifestations in all of the human and natural worlds.

The symbol of the Goddess is *poemagogic*, a term coined by Anton Ehrenzweig to "describe its special function of inducing and symbolizing the ego's creativity."[18] It has a dreamlike, "slippery" quality. One aspect slips into another: She is constantly changing form and changing face. Her images do not define or pin down a set of attributes; they spark inspiration, creation, fertility of mind and spirit: "One thing becomes another/In the Mother . . . In the Mother . . . " (ritual chant for the Winter Solstice).

The importance of the Goddess symbol for women cannot be overstressed. The image of the Goddess inspires women to see ourselves as divine, our bodies as sacred, the changing phases of our lives as holy, our aggression as healthy, our anger as purifying, and our power to nurture and create, but also to limit and destroy when necessary, as the very force that sustains all life.

---

[16] Mary Daly, *Beyond God the Father* (Boston: Beacon Press, 1973), p. 13.

[17] Christ, p. 275.

[18] Anton Ehrenzweig, *The Hidden Order of Art* (London: Paladin, 1967), p. 190.

Through the Goddess, we can discover our strength, enlighten our minds, own our bodies, and celebrate our emotions. We can move beyond narrow, constricting roles and become whole.

The Goddess is also important for men. The oppression of men in Father God-ruled patriarchy is perhaps less obvious but no less tragic than that of women. Men are encouraged to identify with a model no human being can successfully emulate: to be minirulers of narrow universes. They are internally split, into a "spiritual" self that is supposed to conquer their baser animal and emotional natures. They are at war with themselves: in the West, to "conquer" sin; in the East, to "conquer" desire or ego. Few escape from these wars undamaged. Men lose touch with their feelings and their bodies, becoming the "successful male zombies" described by Herb Goldberg in *The Hazards of Being Male*: "Oppressed by the cultural pressures that have denied him his feelings, by the mythology of the woman and the distorted and self-destructive way he sees and relates to her, by the urgency for him to 'act like a man,' which blocks his ability to respond to his inner promptings both emotionally and physiologically, and by a generalized self-hate that causes him to feel comfortable only when he is functioning well in harness, not when he lives for joy and personal growth."[19]

Because women give birth to males, nurture them at the breast, and in our culture are primarily responsible for their care as children, "every male brought up in a traditional home develops an intense early identification with his mother and therefore carries within him a strong feminine imprint."[20] The symbol of the Goddess allows men to experience and integrate the feminine side of their nature, which is often felt to be the deepest and most sensitive aspect of self. The Goddess does not exclude the male; She contains him, as a pregnant woman contains a male child. Her own male aspect embodies both the solar light of the intellect and wild, untamed animal energy.

Our relationship to the earth and the other species that share it has also been conditioned by our religious models. The image of God as outside of nature has given us a rationale for our own destruction of the natural order, and justified our plunder of the earth's resources. We have attempted to "conquer" nature as we have tried to conquer sin. Only as the results of pollution and ecological destruction become severe enough to threaten even urban humanity's adaptability have we come to recognize the importance of ecological balance and the interdependence of all life. The model of the Goddess, who is immanent in nature, fosters respect for the sacredness of all living things. Witchcraft can be seen as a religion of ecology. Its goal is harmony with nature, so that life may not just survive, but thrive.

The rise of Goddess religion makes some politically oriented feminists uneasy. They fear it will sidetrack energy away from direct action to bring about social change. But in areas as deeply rooted as the relations between the

---

[19] Herb Goldberg, *The Hazards of Being Male* (New York: Signet, 1977), p. 4.
[20] Goldberg, p. 39.

sexes, true social change can only come about when the myths and symbols of our culture are themselves changed. The symbol of the Goddess conveys the spiritual power both to challenge systems of oppression and to create new, life-oriented cultures.

Modern Witchcraft is a rich kaleidoscope of traditions and orientations. Covens, the small, closely knit groups that form the congregations of Witch-craft, are autonomous; there is no central authority that determines liturgy or rites. Some covens follow practices that have been handed down in an un-broken line since before the Burning Times. Others derive their rituals from leaders of modern revivals of the Craft—the two whose followers are most widespread are Gerald Gardner and Alex Sanders, both British. Feminist covens are probably the fastest-growing arm of the Craft. Many are Dianic: a sect of Witchcraft that gives far more prominence to the female principle than the male. Other covens are openly eclectic, creating their own traditions from many sources. My own covens are based on the Faery Tradition, which goes back to the Little People of Stone Age Britain, but we believe in creating our own rituals, which reflect our needs and insights of today.

The myths underlying philosophy and "thealogy" (a word coined by reli-gious scholar Naomi Goldenburg from "thea," the Greek word for Goddess) in this book are based on the Faery Tradition. Other Witches may disagree with details, but the overall values and attitudes expressed are common to all of the Craft. Much of the Faery material is still held secret, so many of the rituals, chants and invocations come from our creative tradition. In Witch-craft, a chant is not necessarily better because it is older. The Goddess is con-tinually revealing Herself, and each of us is potentially capable of writing our own liturgy.

In spite of diversity, there are ethics and values that are common to all tra-ditions of Witchcraft. They are based on the concept of the Goddess as imma-nent in the world and in all forms of life, including human beings.

Theologians familiar with Judeo-Christian concepts sometimes have trou-ble understanding how a religion such as Witchcraft can develop a system of ethics and a concept of justice. If there is no split between spirit and nature, no concept of sin, no covenant or commandments against which one can sin, how can people be ethical? By what standards can they judge their actions, when the external judge is removed from his place as ruler of the cosmos? And if the Goddess is immanent in the world, why work for change or strive toward an ideal? Why not bask in the perfection of divinity?

Love for life in all its forms is the basic ethic of Witchcraft. Witches are bound to honor and respect all living things, and to serve the life force. While the Craft recognizes that life feeds on life and that we must kill in order to sur-vive, life is never taken needlessly, never squandered or wasted. Serving the life force means working to preserve the diversity of natural life, to prevent the poisoning of the environment and the destruction of species.

The world is the manifestation of the Goddess, but nothing in that con-cept need foster passivity. Many Eastern religions encourage quietism not because they believe the divine is truly immanent, but because they believe She/He is not. For them, the world is Maya, Illusion, masking the perfection of the Divine Reality. What happens in such a world is not really important; it is only a shadow play obscuring the Infinite Light. In Witchcraft, however, what happens in the world is vitally important. The Goddess is immanent, but She needs human help to realize her fullest beauty. The harmonious balance of plant/animal/human/divine awareness is not automatic; it must constantly be renewed, and this is the true function of craft rituals. Inner work, spiritual work, is most effective when it proceeds hand in hand with outer work. Meditation on the balance of nature might be considered a spiritual act in Witchcraft, but not as much as would cleaning up garbage left at a campsite or marching to protest an unsafe nuclear plant.

Witches do not see justice as administered by some external authority, based on a written code or set of rules imposed from without. Instead, justice is an inner sense that each act brings about consequences that must be faced responsibly. The Craft does not foster guilt, the stern, admonishing, self-hating inner voice that cripples action. Instead, it demands responsibility. "What you send, returns three times over" is the saying—an amplified version of "Do unto others as you would have them do unto you." For example, a Witch does not steal, not because of an admonition in a sacred book, but because the threefold harm far outweighs any small material gain. Stealing diminishes the thief's self-respect and sense of honor; it is an admission that one is incapable of providing honestly for one's own needs and desires. Stealing creates a climate of suspicion and fear, in which even thieves have to live. And, because we are all linked in the same social fabric, those who steal also pay higher prices for groceries, insurance, taxes. Witchcraft strongly imbues the view that all things are interdependent and interrelated and therefore mutually responsible. An act that harms anyone harms us all.

Honor is a guiding principle in the Craft. This is not a "macho" need to take offense at imagined slights against one's virility—it is an inner sense of pride and self-respect. The Goddess is honored in oneself, and in others. Women, who embody the Goddess, are respected, not placed on pedestals or etherealized but valued for all their human qualities. The self, one's individuality and unique way of being in the world, is highly valued. The Goddess, like nature, loves diversity. Oneness is attained not through losing the self, but through realizing it fully. "Honor the Goddess in yourself, celebrate your self, and you will see that Self is everywhere."

In Witchcraft, "All acts of love and pleasure are My rituals." Sexuality, as a direct expression of the life force, is seen as numinous and sacred. It can be expressed freely, so long as the guiding principle is love. Marriage is a deep commitment, a magical, spiritual, and psychic bond. But it is only one possibility out of many for loving, sexual expression.

Misuse of sexuality, however, is heinous. Rape, for example, is an intolerable crime because it dishonors the life force by turning sexuality to the expression of violence and hostility instead of love. A woman has the sacred right to control her own body, as does a man. No one has the right to force or coerce another.

Life is valued in Witchcraft, and it is approached with an attitude of joy and wonder, as well as a sense of humor. Life is seen as the gift of the Goddess. If suffering exists, it is not our task to reconcile ourselves to it, but to work for change.

Magic, the art of sensing and shaping the subtle, unseen forces that flow through the world, of awakening deeper levels of consciousness beyond the rational, is an element common to all traditions of Witchcraft. Craft rituals are magical rites: they stimulate an awareness of the hidden side of reality, and awaken long-forgotten powers of the human mind.

The magical element in Witchcraft is disconcerting to many people. Much of this book is devoted to a deep exploration of the real meaning of magic, but here I would like to speak to the fear I have heard expressed that Witchcraft and occultism are in some way a revival of Nazism. There does seem to be evidence that Hitler and other Nazis were occultists—that is, they may have practiced some of the same techniques as others who seek to expand the horizons of the minds. Magic, like chemistry, is a set of techniques that can be put to the service of any philosophy. The rise of the Third Reich played on the civilized Germans' disillusionment with rationalism and tapped a deep longing to recover modes of experience Western culture had too long ignored. It is as if we had been trained, since infancy, never to use our left arms: The muscles have partly atrophied, but they cry out to be used. But Hitler perverted this longing and twisted it into cruelty and horror. The Nazis were not Goddess worshippers; they denigrated women, relegating them to the position of breeding animals whose role was to produce more Aryan warriors. They were the perfect patriarchy, the ultimate warrior cult—not servants of the life force. Witchcraft has no ideal of a "superman" to be created at the expense of inferior races. In the Craft, all people are already seen as manifest gods, and differences in color, race, and customs are welcomed as signs of the myriad beauty of the Goddess. To equate Witches with Nazis because neither are Judeo-Christian and both share magical elements is like saying that swans are really scorpions because neither are horses and both have tails.

Witchcraft is not a religion of masses—of any sort. Its structure is cellular, based on covens, small groups of up to thirteen members that allow for both communal sharing and individual independence. "Solitaries," Witches who prefer to worship alone, are the exception. Covens are autonomous, free to use whatever rituals, chants and invocations they prefer. There is no set prayer book or liturgy.

Elements may change, but Craft rituals inevitably follow the same underlying patterns. The techniques of magic, which has been termed by occultist Dion Fortune "the art of changing consciousness at will," are used to create states of ecstasy, of union with the divine. They may also be used to achieve material results, such as healings, since in the Craft there is no split between spirit and matter.

Each ritual begins with the creation of a sacred space, the "casting of a circle," which establishes a temple in the heart of the forest or the center of a covener's living room. Goddess and God are then invoked or awakened within each participant and are considered to be physically present within the circle and the bodies of the worshippers. Power, the subtle force that shapes reality, is raised through chanting or dancing and may be directed through a symbol or visualization. With the raising of the cone of power comes ecstasy, which may then lead to a trance state in which visions are seen and insights gained. Food and drink are shared, and coveners "earth the power" and relax, enjoying a time of socializing. At the end, the powers invoked are dismissed, the circle is opened, and a formal return to ordinary consciousness is made.

Entrance to a coven is through an initiation, a ritual experience in which teachings are transmitted and personal growth takes place. Every initiate is considered a priestess or priest; Witchcraft is a religion of clergy.

This book is structured around those elements that I feel are constants among all the varied traditions of the Craft. Interest in Witchcraft is growing rapidly. Colleges and universities are beginning to feature courses in the Craft in their religious studies departments. Women in ever greater numbers are turning to the Goddess. There is a desperate need for material that will intelligently explain Witchcraft to non-Witches in enough depth so that both the practices and philosophy can be understood. Because entrance to a coven is a slow and delicate process, there are many more people who want to practice the Craft than there are covens to accommodate them. So this book also contains exercises and practical suggestions that can lead to a personal Craft practice. A person blessed with imagination and a moderate amount of daring could also use it as a manual to start her or his own coven. It is not, however, meant to be followed slavishly; it is more like a basic musical score, on which you can improvise.

Mother Goddess is reawakening, and we can begin to recover our primal birthright, the sheer, intoxicating joy of being alive. We can open new eyes and see that there is nothing to be saved *from*, no struggle of life *against* the universe, no God outside the world to be feared and obeyed; only the Goddess, the Mother, the turning spiral that whirls us in and out of existence, whose winking eye is the pulse of being—birth, death, rebirth—whose laughter bubbles and courses through all things and who is found only through love: love of trees, of stones, of sky and clouds, of scented blossoms and thundering waves; of all that runs and flies and swims and crawls on her face; through love of ourselves; life-dissolving world-creating orgasmic love of each other; each of us unique and natural as a snowflake, each of us our own star, her Child, her lover, her beloved, her Self.

25

V. S. Naipaul
"The Holy City" from *Among the Believers**

This reading is from a critical appraisal of the Islamic fundamentalist movement (and by extension, all fundamentalism) by the Western writer V. S. Naipaul. The full source book is a harrowing account of a visit to Iran and other Muslim countries after the rise of the Ayatollah Khomeini. It illustrates the trend of Western intellectuals to shun religious fundamentalism.

Behzad and I went to Qom by car. It was past noon when we got back to the hotel, and the hotel taxi drivers, idle though they were, didn't want to make the long desert trip. Only one man offered—he was the man who had made me listen to the Koranic readings on his car radio one evening—and he asked for seventy dollars. Behzad said it was too much; he knew someone who would do it for less.

We waited a long time for Behzad's driver, and then we found that between our negotiations on the telephone and his arrival at the hotel his charges had gone up. He was a small, knotty man, and he said he wasn't a Muslim. He didn't mean that. He meant only that he wasn't a Shia or a Persian. He was a "tribesman," a Lur, from Luristan in the west.

Qom had a famous shrine, the tomb of the sister of the Eighth Shia Imam; for a thousand years it had been a place of pilgrimage. It also had a number of theological schools. Khomeini had taught and lectured at Qom; and on his return to Iran after the fall of the Shah he had made Qom his headquarters. He was surrounded there by ayatollahs, people of distinction in their own right, and it was one of these attendant figures, Ayatollah Khalkhalli, whom I was hoping to see.

Khomeini received and preached and blessed; Khalkhalli hanged. He was Khomeini's hanging judge. It was Khalkhalli who had conducted many of those swift Islamic trials that had ended in executions, with official before-and-after photographs: men shown before they were killed, and then shown dead, naked on the sliding mortuary slabs.

Khalkhalli had recently been giving interviews, emphasizing his activities as judge, and a story in Tehran was that he had fallen out of favour and was trying through these interviews to keep his reputation alive. He told the

Tehran Times that he had "probably" sentenced four hundred people to death in Tehran. "On some nights, he said, bodies of thirty or more people would be sent out in trucks from the prison. He claimed he had also signed the death warrants of a large number of people in Khuzistan Province." Khuzistan was the Arab province in the southwest, where the oil was.

He told another paper that there had been a plot—worked out in the South Korean embassy—to rescue Hoveida, the Shah's prime minister, and other important people from the Tehran jail. As soon as he, Khalkhalli, had heard of this plot he had decided—to deal a blow to the CIA and Zionism—to bring forward the cases. "I reviewed all their cases in one night and had them face the firing squad." He told the *Tehran Times* how Hoveida had died. The first bullet hit Hoveida in the neck; it didn't kill him. Hoveida was then ordered by his executioner—a priest—to hold his head up; the second bullet hit him in the head and killed him.

"Would this man see me?" I had asked an agency correspondent, when we were talking about Khalkhalli.

"He would *love* to see you."

And Behzad thought it could be arranged. Behzad said he would telephone Khalkhalli's secretary when we got to Qom.

The telephone, the secretary: the modern apparatus seemed strange. But Khalkhalli saw himself as a man of the age. "He said"—this was from the *Tehran Times* —"the religious leaders were trying to enforce the rule of the Holy Prophet Mohammed in Iran. During the days of the Prophet swords were used to fight, now they have been replaced by Phantom aircraft." Phantoms: not American, not the products of a foreign science, but as international as swords, part of the stock of the great world bazaar, and rendered Islamic by purchase.

There was a confusion of this sort in Behzad's mind as well, though Behzad was not religious, was a communist, and had been kept away from religion by his communist father. Behzad's father had been imprisoned during the Shah's time, and Behzad had inherited his father's dream of a "true" revolution. Such a revolution hadn't come to Iran; but Behzad, employing all the dialectic he had learnt, was forcing himself to see, in the religious fervour of Khomeini's revolution, the outline of what could be said to be true. And as we drove south through Tehran—at first like a bazaar, and then increasingly like a settlement in a polluted desert—it was the city of proletarian revolt that he was anxious to show me.

Low brick buildings were the colour of dust; walls looked unfinished; bright interiors seemed as impermanent as their paint. Tehran, in the flat land to the south, had been added and added to by people coming in from the countryside, and clusters of traditional square clay-brick houses with flat roofs were like villages.

We passed a great factory shed. Some kind of beige fur had adhered to the walls below every window. Behzad told me it was a cloth factory and had been a centre of the revolution. The army had gone in, and many workers had been killed.

After the oil refinery, puffing out flame from its chimney, we were in the true desert. There were no trees now, and the views were immense: mounds, hills, little ranges. The road climbed, dipped into wide valleys. Hills and mounds were smooth, and sometimes, from a distance and from certain angles, there was the faintest tinge of green on the brown, from tufts of grass and weeds, which were then seen to be really quite widely scattered.

From the top of a hill we saw, to the left, the salt lake marked on the map. It looked small and white, as though it was about to cake into salt; and the white had a fringe of pale green. Behzad said that sometimes it all looked blue. Many bodies had been dumped there by the Shah's secret police, from helicopters. And the lake was bigger than it looked. It was a desolation when we began to pass it; the green water that fringed the white was very far away. The land after that became more broken. Hills were less rounded, their outlines sharper against the sky.

It was desert, but the road was busy; and occasionally there were roadside shacks where soft drinks or melons could be had. Behzad thought we should drink or eat something before we got to Qom; in Qom, where they were strict about the Ramadan fasting, there would be nothing to eat or drink before sunset.

We stopped at a bus-and-truck halt, with a big rough café in Mediterranean colours and a watermelon stall on a platform beside the road. The watermelon man, seated at his stall below a thin cotton awning that gave almost no shade, was sleeping on his arms.

We woke him up and bought a melon, and he lent a knife and forks. Behzad halved the melon and cut up the flesh, and we all three—the driver joining us without being asked—squatted round the melon, eating as it were from the same dish. Behzad, I could see, liked the moment of serving and sharing. It could be said that it was a Muslim moment; it was the kind of sharing Muslims practised—and the driver had joined us as a matter of course. But the driver was a worker; Behzad was sharing food with someone of the people, and he was imposing his own ritual on this moment in the desert.

Two saplings had been planted on the platform. One was barked and dead; the other was half dead. Between them lay an old, sunburnt, ill-looking woman in black, an inexplicable bit of human debris an hour away from Tehran. Scraps of newspaper from the stall blew about in the sand and caught against the trunks of the trees. Across the road a lorry idled, its exhaust smoking; and traffic went by all the time.

We squatted in the sand and ate. The driver spat out the watermelon seeds onto the road. I did as the driver did; and Behzad—but more reverentially—did likewise. Abruptly, stabbing his fork into the melon, saying nothing, the square-headed little Lur jumped off the platform. He was finished; he had had enough of the melon. He walked across the dingy desert yard to the café to look for a lavatory, and Behzad's moment was over.

I had imagined that Qom, a holy city, would have been built on hills: it would have been full of cliff walls and shadows and narrow lanes cut into the rock, with cells or caves where pious men meditated. It was set flat in the desert, and the approach to it was like the approach to any other desert town: shacks, gas stations. The road grew neater; shacks gave way to houses. A garden bloomed on a traffic roundabout—Persian gardens had this abrupt, enclosed, oasislike quality. A dome gleamed in the distance between minarets. It was the dome of the famous shrine.

Behzad said, "That dome is made of gold."

It had been gilded in the last century. But the city we began to enter had been enriched by oil; and it seemed like a reconstructed bazaar city, characterless except for the gold dome and its minarets.

Behzad said, "How shall I introduce you? Correspondent? Khalkhalli likes correspondents."

"That isn't how I want to talk to him, though. I really just want to chat with him. I want to understand how he became what he is."

"I'll say you are a writer. Where shall I say you come from?"

That was a problem. England would be truest, but would be misleading. Trinidad would be mystifying, and equally misleading. South America was a possibility, but the associations were wrong.

"Can you say I am from the Americas? Would that make sense in Persian?"

Behzad said, "I will say that you come from America, but you are not an American."

We made for the dome and stopped in a parking area outside the shrine. It was midafternoon, and hotter in the town than in the desert; the gilded dome looked hot. The Lur driver, in spite of our sacramental watermelon feast, was mumbling about food. Ramadan or not, he wanted to take the car and go out of Qom to look for something to eat; and he wanted to know what our plans were.

Across the road, near the watermelon stall at the gateway to the shrine, there was a glass-walled telephone booth of German design. Behzad went to telephone Khalkhalli's secretary.

The high wall of the shrine was aerosolled and painted with slogans in Persian. There were two in English—*WE WANT REPUBLIC, KHOMEINI IS OUR LEADER*—and they must have been meant for the foreign television cameras. The second slogan was a direct translation of *Khomeini e Imam* [leader], but as a translation it was incomplete, suggesting only (with the help of the first slogan) a transfer of loyalty from the Shah to Khomeini, not stating the divine authority of the leader or the access to heaven that he gave. In Iran, where for eleven hundred years they had been waiting for the return of the Twelfth Imam, *Imam* was a loaded word; and especially here at Qom, where the sister of the Eighth Imam was buried. Access to heaven, rejection of nondivine rule, was the purpose of the "republic" proclaimed here.

Behzad, opening the door of the telephone booth, the telephone in his hand, waved me over.

When I went to him he said, "The secretary says that Khalkhalli is pray-ing. He will see you at nine this evening, after he has broken his fast."

It was 3:30. We had told the driver we would be only three or four hours in Qom.

Behzad said, "What do you want me to tell the secretary?"

"Tell him we'll come."

Then we went to break the bad news to the impatient Lur—or the good news: he was charging by the hour. He said something that Behzad didn't translate. And he drove off to look for food, leaving Behzad and me to think of ways of spending five and a half hours in the torpid, baking city, where nothing could be eaten or drunk for the next five hours.

The shops opposite the shrine sold souvenirs—plates with Khomeini's face, cheap earthenware vases—and sweets: flat, round cakes, brown, soft, very sweet-looking, breaking up at the edges. Food could be sold to travellers dur-ing Ramadan, Behzad said; but it wasn't worth the trouble. Not many people were about. A crippled old woman, a pilgrim no doubt, was wheeling herself slowly past the shops. We surprised a plump boy in a booth taking a nibble at a brown cake, part of his stock; but he judged us harmless and smiled (though a couple of people had been whipped some days before for eating).

The souvenir shops also sold little clay tablets stamped with Arabic letter-ing. The clay was from the Arabian cities of Mecca and Medina (good business for somebody over there); so that the faithful, bowing down in prayer and resting their foreheads on these tablets, touched sacred soil. High on the shrine wall, in glazed blue-and-white tiles, there was, as I supposed, a Koranic quotation. Behzad couldn't translate it; it was in Arabic, which he couldn't read.

Arabia! Its presence in Iran shouldn't have surprised me, but it did. Because with one corner of my mind I approached Iran through classical his-tory and felt awe for its antiquity—the conqueror of Egypt, the rival of Greece, undefeated by Rome; and with another corner of my mind I approached it through India, where, at least in the northwest, the idea of Persia is still an idea of the highest civilization—as much as France used to be for the rest of Europe—in its language, its poetry, its carpets, its food. In Kashmir, *Farsi khanna,* Persian food, is the supreme cuisine; and of the *chenar,* the trans-planted plane tree or sycamore of Persia (so prominent in both Persian and Indian Mogul painting) it is even said that its shade is medicinal. In Qom these ideas had to be discarded. Here they looked to spartan Arabia as to the fount.

Behzad suggested that we should visit the shrine. If anyone asked, I was to say I was a Muslim. I said I wouldn't be able to carry it off. I wouldn't know how to behave. Was it with the right foot that one entered a mosque, and with the left the lavatory? Or was it the other way round? Was it the Sunnis who, during their ablutions, let the water run down their arms to their fingers? Did the Shias, contrariwise, run the water down from their hands to their elbows? And what were the gestures of obeisance or reverence? There were too many traps. Even if I followed Behzad and did what he did, it wouldn't look convincing.

Behzad said, "You wouldn't be able to follow me. I don't know what to do, either. I don't go to mosques."

But we could go into the courtyard, and to do that we didn't have to take off our shoes. The courtyard was wide and very bright. At one side was a clock tower, with an austere modern clock that had no numerals. On the other side was the entrance to the shrine. It was high and recessed and it glittered as with silver, like a silver cave, like a silver-vaulted dome cut down the middle. But what looked like silver was only glass, thousands of pieces catching light at different angles. And here at last were the pilgrims, sunburnt peasants, whole families, who had come from far. They camped in the open cells along the courtyard wall (each cell the burial place of a famous or royal person), and they were of various racial types: an older Persia, a confusion of tribal and transcontinental movements.

One Mongoloid group was Turkoman, Behzad said. I hardly knew the word. In the 1824 English novel *Hajji Baba* (which I had bought at the hotel in a pirated offset of the Oxford World's Classics edition), there were Turkoman bandits. I had once, in a London sale room, seen a seventeenth-century Indian drawing of a yoked Turkoman prisoner, his hands shackled to a block of wood at the back of his neck. So the Turkomans were men of Central Asia who were once feared. How they fitted into Persian history I didn't know; and their past of war and banditry seemed far from these depressed campers at the shrine. Small, sunburnt, ragged, they were like debris at the edge of a civilization that had itself for a long time been on the edge of the world.

Near the mosque was the two-story yellow brick building where Khomeini had taught and lectured. It was neutral, nondescript; and nothing was going on there now. Behzad and I walked in the bazaar. For most of the stall-keepers it was siesta time. In one bread stall, stacked high with flat perforated rounds of sweet bread, the man was stretched out on a shelf or counter on the side wall and seemed to be using part of his stock as a pillow. Behzad bought a paper. It was very hot; there was little to see; Qom's life remained hidden. We began to look for shade, for a place to sit and wait.

We came upon a small hotel. It was cramped inside, but newly furnished. The two men seated behind the desk pretended not to see us, and we sat in the little front lounge; nobody else was there. After some minutes one of the men from the desk came and told us to leave. The hotel was closed for Ramadan; that was why, he added disarmingly, he and his friend hadn't stood up when we came in.

We went out again into the light and dust, past the souvenir shops again, with the brown cakes and the tablets of Arabian clay; and were permitted to sit in the empty café opposite the *KHOMEINI IS OUR LEADER* slogan. It was a big place, roughly designed and furnished, but the pillars were clad with marble.

There was nothing to drink—a bottled "cola" drink seemed only full of chemical danger—and the place was warm with the raw smell of cooking mutton. But the shade was refreshing; and the relaxed exhaustion that presently came to me, while Behzad read his Persian paper, helped the minutes by.

At the table in the far corner, near the serving counter, there was a family group, as I thought: father, two boys, and a little girl in a long black dress and veil. So small, I thought, and already veiled. But she was active; she talked all the time and was encouraged by the others, who seemed to find everything she said funny. From time to time the man smiled at me, as though inviting me to admire. Shrieking at one stage, the girl ran up the steps to the upper gallery, shrieked some more up there, encouraging fresh laughter downstairs. She came down again, showed the others what she had brought down. She turned—and for the first time we could see her face—and she came to Behzad and me.

She wasn't a girl. She was very small, about four feet, very old, and possibly mad. She showed us what she had brought down from upstairs: a plate of white rice with a little lozenge of brown-black mutton. Was she pleased with what she had been given, or was she complaining? Behzad didn't say. He listened while she spoke, but he said nothing to her. Then she went out.

I said to Behzad, "I thought they were a family. I thought they owned the place."

Behzad said, "Oh, no. They're not a family. They're workers."

We went out ourselves, to telephone Khalkhalli's secretary again to see whether the appointment couldn't be brought forward. It was about half past five, and a little cooler. There were more people in the street. Our driver had come back; he hadn't found anything to eat.

Behzad telephoned. Then, coming out of the booth, he got into conversation with two bearded young men who were in mullah's costume. I hadn't seen them approach; I had been looking at Behzad.

I had so far seen mullahs only on television, in black and white, and mainly heads and turbans. The formality of the costume in real life was a surprise to me. It made the two men stand out in the street: black turbans, white collarless tunics, long, lapel-less, two-button gowns in pale green or pale blue, and the thin black cotton cloaks that were like the gowns of scholars and fellows at Oxford and Cambridge and St. Andrews in Scotland. Here, without a doubt, was the origin of the cleric's garb of those universities, in medieval times centres of religious learning, as Qom still was.

The costume, perhaps always theatrical, a mark of quality, also gave physical dignity and stature, as I saw when Behzad brought the young men over. They were really quite small men, and younger than their beards suggested.

Behzad said, "You wanted to meet students."

We had talked about it in the car but hadn't known how to go about it.

Behzad added, "Khalkhalli's secretary says we can come at eight."

I felt sure we could have gone at any time, and had been kept waiting only for the sake of Khalkhalli's dignity.

The two young men were from Pakistan. They wanted to know who I was, and when Behzad told them that I came from America but was not American, they seemed satisfied; and when Behzad further told them that I was anxious to learn about Islam, they were immediately friendly. They said they had some books in English in their hostel that I would find useful. We should go there first, and then we would go to the college to meet students from many countries.

Behzad arranged us in the car. He sat me next to the Lur driver, who was a little awed by the turbans and gowns and beards; Behzad himself sat with the Pakistanis. They directed the driver to an unexpectedly pleasant residential street. But they couldn't find the books they wanted to give me, and so we went on, not to the college, but to an administrative building opposite the college.

And there, in the entrance, we were checked by authority: a middle-aged man, dressed like the students but with a black woollen cap instead of a turban. He was not as easily satisfied as the students had been by Behzad's explanation. He was, in fact, full of suspicion.

"He is from America?"

Behzad and the students, all now committed to their story, said, "But he's not American."

The man in the woollen cap said, "He doesn't have to talk to students. He can talk to me. I speak English."

He, too, was from Pakistan. He was thin, with the pinched face of Mr. Jinnah, the founder of that state. His cheeks were sunken, his lips parched and whitish from his fast.

He said, "Here we publish books and magazines. They will give you all the information you require."

He spoke in Persian or Urdu to one of the students, and the student went off and came back with a magazine. It was *The Message of Peace,* Volume One, Number One.

So this was where they churned it out, the rage about the devils of the Western democracies, the hagiographies of the Shia Imams. This was where they read Schumacher and Toynbee and used their words—about technology and ecology—to lash the West.

I said to the man with the woollen cap, "But I know your magazine."

He was thrown off balance. He looked disbelieving.

"I've been reading Volume One, Number Two. The one with the article about Islamic urban planning."

He didn't seem to understand.

"I bought it in Tehran."

Grimly, he beckoned us in. And we went up to his office after taking off our shoes. The terrazzo steps were wide, the corridors were wide; the rooms were spacious, with carpet tiling.

The man in the woollen cap—the director, as I now took him to be—sat behind his new steel desk. One of the students sat on his left. Behzad and I and the other student sat in a line on chairs against the far wall, facing the desk. And, as formally as we were seated, we began.

The student on the director's left said that Islam was the only thing that made humans human. He spoke with tenderness and conviction; and to understand what he meant it was necessary to try to understand how, for him, a world without the Prophet and revelation would be a world of chaos.

The director picked at his nose, and seemed to approve. On his desk there were rubber stamps, a new globe, a stapler, a telephone of new design. On the shelves there were box files, the *Oxford English Dictionary,* and a Persian-English dictionary.

There were fourteen thousand theological students in Qom, they told me. (And yet, arriving at the worst time of the day, we had found the streets empty.) The shortest period of study was six years.

"Six years!"

The director smiled at my exclamation. "Six is nothing. Fifteen, twenty, thirty years some people can study for."

What did they study in all that time? This wasn't a place of research and new learning. They were men of faith. What was there in the subject that called for so much study? Well, there was Arabic itself; there was grammar in all its branches; there was logic and rhetoric; there was jurisprudence, Islamic jurisprudence being one course of study and the principles of jurisprudence being another; there was Islamic philosophy; there were the Islamic sciences—biographies, genealogies, "correlations," traditions about the Prophet and his close companions.

I had expected something more casual, more personal: the teacher a holy man, the student a disciple. I hadn't expected this organization of learning or this hint of antique classical methods. I began to understand that the years of study were necessary. Faith still absolutely bounded the world here. And, as in medieval Europe, there was no end to theological scholarship.

One of the great teachers at Qom, a man who still lectured and led prayers five times a day, had produced (or produced materials for) a twenty-five-volume commentary on a well-known work about the Shia idea of the Imam. Seven of those volumes had been published. A whole corps of scholars—no doubt collating their lecture notes: the medieval method of book transmission—were at work on the remaining eighteen. Khomeini himself, famous for his lectures on jurisprudence and Islamic philosophy, had produced eighteen volumes on various topics.

That ordered life of prayer and lecture, commentary and reinterpretation, had almost perished towards the end of the Shah's time. Khomeini had been banished; the security forces had occupied Qom; and even the Pakistani students had been harassed by the secret police.

The student sitting on the director's left said, his voice falling, "If there had been no revolution here, Islam would have been wiped out."

The students both came from priestly families in country towns in the Punjab, and had always known that they were meant to be mullahs. They were doing only eight years in Qom. They were taking the two-year Arabic course, with logic and rhetoric (rhetoric being no more than the classical way of laying out an argument); but they weren't doing literature. History was no part of their study, but they were free to read it privately. It was for Islamic philosophy that they had come to Qom. In no other university was the subject gone into so thoroughly; and their attendance at Qom, Khomeini's place, and Marashi's, and Shariatmadari's (all great teaching ayatollahs), would make them respected among Shias when they got back to Pakistan.

The student on Behzad's left said, in Behzad's translation, "I compare this place to Berkeley or Yale."

I said to Behzad, "That's a strange thing for him to say."

Behzad said, "He didn't say Berkeley and Yale. I said it, to make it clearer to you."

The three Pakistanis, the director and the students, talked among themselves, and the student at the director's desk lifted the telephone and began to dial.

Behzad said, "They want you to meet their teacher. Ayatollah Shirazi. He's telephoning him now to get an appointment."

With the child's part of my mind I was again amazed, in this world of medieval schoolmen I had walked into, at this telephoning of ayatollahs, great men, for appointments. And I was nervous of meeting Shirazi—as I would have been at the sudden prospect (assuming such a thing possible) of a disputation with Peter Abelard or John of Salisbury or even some lesser medieval learned man. I knew nothing of Shirazi's discipline; I wouldn't know what to say to him.

The student who was telephoning put the modern receiver down. His shyness and reverence were replaced by elation. He said, "Ayatollah Shirazi will see you at seven o'clock. As soon as I told him about you he agreed to meet you."

The director's face lit up for the first time, as though Shirazi's readiness to receive me had at last made it all right for me to be in his own office, talking to guileless students. He had been picking his nose constantly, in a way that made me feel that the Ramadan fasting that had dried and whitened his lips was also affecting his nostrils and irritating him. Now he relaxed; he wanted to show me over the building. We all stood up; the formal interview was over.

I tried to find out, as we left the room, about the fees and expenses of students. But I couldn't get a straight reply; and it was Behzad who told me directly, with an indication that I was to press no further, that it was the religious foundation at Qom that paid for the students, however long they stayed.

In a room across the wide corridor a calligrapher was at work, writing out a Koran. He was in his forties, in trousers and shirt, and he was sitting at a sloping desk. His hand was steady, unfree, without swash or elegance; but he was pleased to let us watch him plod on, dipping his broadnibbed pen in the black ink. His face bore the marks of old stress; but he was at peace now, doing his new-found scribe's work in his safe modern cell.

The director showed photographs of a meeting of Muslim university heads that had taken place in Qom two years before. And again, though it oughtn't to have been surprising, it was: this evidence of the existence of the sub-world, or the parallel world, of medieval learning in its Islamic guise, still intact in the late twentieth century. The rector of Al-Azhar University in Cairo, the director said, had been so impressed by what he had seen in Qom that he had declared that Qom students would be accepted without any down-grading by Al-Azhar.

We walked down the steps. Against one wall there were stacks of the cen-tre's publications—not only *The Message of Peace*, but also two new paperback books in Persian. One was an account of the Prophet's daughter, Fatima, who had married the Prophet's cousin, Ali, the Shia hero; this book was called *The Woman of Islam*. The other book or booklet, with a sepia-coloured cover, was written, the director said, by an Iranian who had spent an apparently shattering year in England. This book was called *The West Is Sick*.

Shirazi's house was in a blank-walled dirt lane in another part of the town. The lane sloped down from both sides to a shallow central trough, but this trough was only full of dust.

We knocked at a closed door set in the wall; and children in the lane mocked the Pakistanis, threatening them with the anger of Shirazi when they got inside. It seemed a traditional form of play, a licenced mockery that in no way mocked belief: the "clerk," the religious student in his student's costume, a recognized butt, as he perhaps had been in the European Middle Ages. It was a difficult moment for the Pakistanis, though, trying to shoo away the children, keep their dignity, preserve their courtesy to Behzad and myself, and prepare for the grave reception ahead.

The door opened. We entered a vestibule, took off shoes, went up car-peted steps to a gallery which ran right around a sunken paved courtyard to the left, with fig trees, all covered by a high white awning which cooled light and colour, so that, abruptly, after the dust and warmth of the lane, the mid-summer desert climate seemed benign, perfect for men.

I would have liked to pause, to consider the shaded courtyard with the fig trees. But wonder almost at once turned to shock: there was a barefooted man just a few feet ahead in the carpeted gallery with an Israeli-made submachine gun: Shirazi's bodyguard. He stayed in the gallery. We turned into the car-peted, empty room on the right and sat down in silence beside an electric fan, to wait. The Pakistani students smiled, at once expectant and encouraging.

"He is coming," Behzad said. "Stand."

We all stood up. Ceremony assists an entrance, and Shirazi's entrance was impressive, regal. He was a big man, with a full, fleshy face; his beard, as neatly trimmed as his moustache, made it hard to guess his age. His two-button gown was pale fawn; his black cloak was of the thinnest cotton.

The students appeared to fall forward before him—a flurry of black cloaks and turbans. He, allowing his hand to be kissed, appeared to give them his benediction. And then we all sat down. He said nothing; he seemed only to smile. The student said nothing.

I said, "It is very good of you to see me. Your students here have spoken of you as a man of great learning."

Behzad translated what I had said, and Shirazi began to speak slowly, melodiously, with an intonation that was new to me. He spoke for a long time, but Behzad's translation was brief.

"It was good of them to say what they said. It is good of you to say what you said."

Shirazi spoke some more.

Bahzad translated: "Education cannot begin too soon. I would like children to be brought as babies to school. There is a tape recorder in the human brain. Hitler had that idea." And Behzad added on his own, "He wants to know what your religion is."

"What can I say?"

"You must tell me."

I said, "I am a seeker."

Shirazi, his face calm, his large eyes smiling, assessing, spoke at length. His enunciation was clear, deliberate, full of rhythm. His full-lipped mouth opened wide, his clean teeth showed.

Behzad said, "He wants to know what you were before you became a seeker. You must have been born into some kind of belief."

It was of the Pakistani students that I was nervous. They had been told—with some truth, but more for the sake of simplicity—that I came from America but was not an American. For them to hear now that my ancestry was Hindu would, I thought, be unsettling to them; the Hindu-Muslim antagonisms of the Indo-Pakistani subcontinent went deep. They would feel fooled; and they had been so welcoming, so open. They had arranged this meeting with their great teacher, and even now never took their gaze—beatific rather than obedient or even awed—off Shirazi.

I said to Behzed, "Can you tell him I never had any belief? Tell him I was born far away in the Americas, and wasn't brought up to any faith."

"You can't tell him that. Say you are a Christian."

"Tell him that."

And as soon as Behzad began to talk, I regretted what I had asked him to say. Shirazi hadn't been taken in by my equivocations; he knew that something was wrong. And I decided that I would never again on my Islamic journey, out of nervousness or a wish to simplify, complicate matters for myself like this, and consequently falsify people's response to me. Strain apart, it would have been more interesting now—it would have served my purpose better—to get Shirazi's response to me as a man without religion, and as a man of an idolatrous-mystical-animistic background.

Shirazi spoke in his special rhythmic way, the mullah's way, as Behzad told me later, his accent and intonation more Arabic than Persian. He made "Islam" into "Ess-lam"; and "Allah" became a word of three syllables, with a round, open-mouthed pronunciation: "Oll-lor-huh."

He asked, "What kind of Christian are you?"

I thought. "Protestant."

"Then you are closer to the truth."

"Why?"

"Catholics are inflexible."

He didn't mean that. He was only giving a Shia twist to Christian divisions. The Shias, with their own line of succession to the Prophet disregarded by other Muslims, see themselves as an embattled minority.

And conversation after that was as hard as I had feared. I asked whether history—the history of Islamic civilization—was something he had studied. He misunderstood; he thought I was asking a question about Muslim theology, and he said of course he knew Islamic history: when the Prophet first gave the message the people of his village didn't want it, and so he had to go to the next village. And always—whether I attempted to get him to talk about the scientific needs of Muslim countries, or about his ideas for Iran after the revolution—we slid down his theology to the confusion of his certainties. With true Islam, science would flourish: the Prophet said that people should go out and learn. With true Islam, there was freedom (he meant the freedom to be Islamic and Shia, to be divinely ruled); and everything came with freedom (this idea of freedom quite separate from the first).

There was a long pause.

I said, "You look serene."

He said, "I thank you for that." He didn't return the compliment.

I wanted to be released.

I said to Behzad, "Tell him I feel I am taking up too much of his time."

Shirazi said, with his smile, "I am free until I break my fast."

It was only 7:30. I said, just to keep the conversation going, "Ask him when he is going to break his fast."

Behzad said, "I can't ask him that. You're forgetting. I am a Muslim. I am supposed to know these things."

Someone else came in, a holy man in a white turban, a Turkoman, pale from his Ramadan seclusion, not as sunburnt or as meagre as the Turkoman pilgrim families camped in the courtyard of the shrine. With him was a very pale little girl. Shirazi was warm and welcoming. We stood up, to take our leave. The students fell again before Shirazi and kissed his hand. Shirazi smiled, and he continued to smile as—our own audience over—the little girl rushed to kiss his hand.

The awning over the courtyard and the fig trees had been taken down. The light was now golden; shadows were no longer hard. Our shoes waited for us at the bottom of the steps; and in the small room off the vestibule the barefooted bodyguard with the submachine gun was bending down to play with another child.

Outside, in the dirt lane, where dust was like part of the golden evening, the Pakistani students turned bright faces on me, and one of them said, "How did you like him?"

For them the meeting had gone well. They asked Behzad and me to dine with them, to break the fast together and eat the simple food of students. But that invitation (as the qualification about the simple food of students showed) was only a courtesy, their way of breaking off, of seeing us into the car and picking up again the routine of their Ramadan evening that we had interrupted.

The lane and the street at the end of it were full of busy, black-cloaked figures: it was like an old print of an Oxford street scene. But here the clerical costumes were not borrowed; here they belonged and still had meaning; here the Islamic Middle Ages still lived, and the high organization of its learning, which had dazzled men from the Dark Ages of Europe.

And there was more than old Oxford in the streets. This desert town— with its blank walls that concealed sunken courtyards, its straight pavements lined with trees, its enclosed, thick-planted garden squares—was the pattern for small towns I had seen far away in Spanish America, from Yucatan in southeast Mexico to the pampa of Argentina. Spain had been the vehicle: conquered by the Arabs between 710 and 720 A.D., just eighty years after Persia, and incorporated into the great medieval Muslim world, the great universal civilization of the time. Spain, before it had spread to the Americas, had rejected that Muslim world, and gained vigour and its own fanaticism from that rejection. But here in Iran, five hundred years on, that world still existed, with vague ideas of its former greatness, but ignorant (as the article about Islamic urban planning in *The Message of Peace* showed) of the contributions it had once made, and of the remote continent whose fate it had indirectly influenced.

The Pakistani students had given our Lur driver directions. As we drove to Ayatollah Khalkhalli's, Komeini's hanging judge, Behzad said, "You know why I couldn't tell Shirazi you hadn't been brought up in any religion? He was trying to find out whether you were a communist. If I had told him that you had no religion, he would have thought you were a communist. And that would have been bad for you."

Khalkhalli's house was the last in a dead end, a newish road with young trees on the pavement. It was near sunset; the desert sky was full of colour. There were men with guns about, and we stopped a house or two away. Behzad went and talked to somebody and then called me. The house was new, of concrete, not big, and it was set back from the pavement, with a little paved area in front.

In the verandah or gallery we were given a body search by a short, thickly built young man in a tight blue jersey, who ran or slapped rough hands down our legs; and then we went into a small, carpeted room. There were about six or eight people there, among them an African couple, sitting erect and still on the floor. The man wore a dark-grey suit and was hard to place; but from the costume of the woman I judged them to be Somalis, people from the north-eastern horn of Africa.

I wasn't expecting this crowd—in fact, a little court. I had been hoping for a more intimate conversation with a man who, as I thought, had fallen from power and might be feeling neglected.

A hanging judge, a figure of revolutionary terror, dealing out Islamic justice to young and old, men and women: but the bearded little fellow, about five feet tall, who, preceded by a reverential petitioner, presently came out of an inner room—and was the man himself—was plump and jolly, with eyes merry behind his glasses.

He moved with stiff, inelastic little steps. He was fair-skinned, with a white skull cap, no turban or clerical cloak or gown; and he looked a bit of a mess, with a crumpled long-tailed tunic or shirt, brown-striped, covering a couple of cotton garments at the top and hanging out over slack white trousers.

This disorder of clothes—in one who, given Shirazi's physical presence, might have assumed Shirazi's high clerical style—was perhaps something Khalkhalli cultivated or was known for: the Iranians in the room began to smile as soon as he appeared. The African man fixed glittering eyes of awe on him, and Khalkhalli was tender with him, giving him an individual greeting. After tenderness with the African, Khalkhalli was rough with Behzad and me. The change in his manner was abrupt, willful, a piece of acting: it was the clown wishing to show his other side. It didn't disturb me; it told me that my presence in the room, another stranger who had come from far, was flattering to him.

He said, "I am busy. I have no time for interviews. Why didn't you telephone?"

Behzad said, "We telephoned twice."

Khalkhalli didn't reply. He took another petitioner to the inner room with him.

Behzad said, "He's making up his mind."

But I knew that he had already made up his mind, that the idea of the interview was too much for him to resist. When he came out—and before he led in someone else to his room—he said, with the same unconvincing roughness, "Write out your questions."

It was another piece of picked-up style, but it was hard for me. I had been hoping to get him to talk about his life; I would have liked to enter his mind, to see the world as he saw it. But I had been hoping for conversation; I couldn't say what questions I wanted to put to him until he had begun to talk. Still, I had to do as he asked: the Iranians and the Africans were waiting to see me carry out his instructions. How could I get this hanging judge to show a little more than his official side? How could I get this half-clown, with his medieval learning, to illuminate his passion?

I could think of nothing extraordinary; I decided to be direct. On a sheet of hotel paper, which I had brought with me, I wrote: *Where were you born? What made you decide to take up religious studies? What did your father do? Where did you study? Where did you first preach? How did you become an ayatollah? What was your happiest day?*

He was pleased, when he finally came out, to see Behzad with the list of questions, and he sat cross-legged directly in front of us. Our knees almost touched. He answered simply at first. He was born in Azerbaijan. His father was a very religious man. His father was a farmer.

I asked, "Did you help your father?"

"I was a shepherd when I was a boy." And then he began to clown. Raising his voice, making a gesture, he said, "Right now I know how to cut off a sheep's head." And the Iranians in the room—including some of his bodyguards—rocked with laughter. "I did every kind of job. Even selling. I know everything."

But how did the shepherd boy become a mullah?

"I studied for thirty-five years."

That was all. He could be prodded into no narrative, no story of struggle or rise. He had simply lived; experience wasn't something he had reflected on. And, vain as he was ("I am very clever, very intelligent"), the questions about his past didn't interest him. He wanted more to talk about his present power, or his closeness to power; and that was what, ignoring the remainder of the written questions, he began to do.

He said, "I was taught by Ayatollah Khomeini, you know. And I was the teacher of the son of Ayatollah Khomeini." He thumped me on the shoulder and added archly, to the amusement of the Iranians, "So I cannot say I am *very* close to Ayatollah Khomeini."

His mouth opened wide, stayed open, and soon he appeared to be choking with laughter, showing me his gums, his tongue, his gullet. When he recovered he said, with a short, swift wave of his right hand, "The mullahs are going to rule now. We are going to have ten thousand years of the Islamic republic. The Marxists will go on with their Lenin. We will go on in the way of Khomeini."

He went silent. Crossing his legs neatly below him, fixing me with his eyes, becoming grave, appearing to look up at me through his glasses, he said, in the silence he had created, "I killed Hoveida, you know."

The straightness of his face was part of the joke for the Iranians. They—squatting on the carpet—threw themselves about with laughter.

It was what was closest to him, his work as revolutionary judge. He had given many interviews about his sentencing of the Shah's prime minister; and he wanted to tell the story again.

I said, "You killed him yourself?"

Behzad said, "No, he only gave the order. Hoveida was killed by the son of a famous ayatollah."

"But I have the gun," Khalkhalli said, as though it was the next-best thing.

Again the Iranians rolled about the carpet with laughter. And even the African, never taking his glittering eyes off Khalkhalli, began to smile.

Behzad said, "A Revolutionary Guard gave him the gun."

I said, "Do you have it on you?"

Khalkhalli said, "I have it in the next room."

So at the very end he had forced me, in that room full of laughter, to be his straight man.

It was fast-breaking time now, no time to dally, time for all visitors to leave, except the Africans. For some minutes young men had been placing food on the verandah floor. Khalkhalli, dismissing us, appeared to forget us. Even before we had put our shoes on and got to the gate, he and the African couple were sitting down to dinner. It was a big dinner; the clown ate seriously.

And at last our Lur driver could eat, and Behzad could repeat the sacramental moment of food-sharing with him. We drove back to the centre of the town, near the shrine, and they ate in the café where we had waited earlier in the afternoon, in a smell of cooking mutton.

They ate rice, mutton, and flat Persian bread. It was all that the café offered. I left them together, bought some nuts and dried fruit from a stall, and walked along the river, among families camping and eating on the river embankment in the dark. Across the road from the embankment electric lights shone on melons and other fruit in stalls: a refreshing night scene, after the glare and colourlessness of the day.

When I was walking back to the café, and was on the other side of the river, I passed an illuminated shoeshop. It had a big colour photograph of Khomeini. I stopped to consider his unreliable face again: the creased forehead, the eyebrows, the hard eyes, the sensual lips. In the light of the shop I looked at the handful of nuts and *kishmish* raisins I was about to put in my mouth. It contained a drawing pin. Without that pause in front of Khomeini's picture, I would have done damage to my mouth in ways I preferred not to think of; and my own unbeliever's day in Khomeini's holy city of Qom would have ended with a nasty surprise.

The highway to Tehran was busy. There was a moon, but the lights of cars and buses killed the view. It was only in snatches that the desert and the moonlight and the outlines of hills could be seen. Behzad was tired; he dozed off. When he awakened he asked the driver to put on the car radio for the news.

The news was bad for Behzad. *Ayandegan*, the newspaper of the left, the paper Behzad read and had told me about, had been closed down by the Islamic prosecutor in Tehran. The paper was charged with publishing "diversionary ideologies and beliefs among the revolutionary Muslims of Iran"; with attempting "to create dissent among the various Muslim groups of Iran"—a reference to the racial and non-Shia minorities; with falsifying its circulation figures; with sending out incomplete copies of the paper to some parts of the country, in order to save newsprint "for publishing material aimed at dividing the nation." The assets of the paper had been handed over to the Foundation for the Deprived; and Revolutionary Guards had occupied its offices.

Behzad—in spite of Shirazi and Khalkhalli—still claimed the revolution as his own, seeing in one popular movement the possibility and even the beginnings of another. The revolution, though, had now turned against him. But revolutionaries have to be patient; and Behzad had learnt patience from his revolutionary father. The loss of the paper was serious—it would have been shattering to me, if the cause had been mine—but Behzad bore his disappointment well.

He didn't go back to sleep. From time to time, as we drove through the moonlit desert, he went abstracted. We passed the white salt lake on the right, where he had said bodies had been dumped by the Shah's secret police; the cemetery, on the left, where martyrs of the revolution had been buried, which we would have visited if we had returned in daylight; and then Tehran Refinery on the right, puffs of flame leaping from its tall chimney—Iran making money while it slept.

About midnight we got back to the hotel. And it was at the hotel gate that the Lur slapped on the extra charges that he must have been meditating for hours. He charged for both distance and time; he charged for late hours; he was in the end more expensive than the hotel taxi we had turned down. But it had been a harder day than he had bargained for; he had been denied the lunch he badly wanted; I had studied, with growing tenderness, the back of his square little head for so long; his passion for his rice and mutton, when eating time had at last come for him, had been so winning; the lean and knobby face that he turned to me to ask for more was so appealing, in the dim saloon light of the car; he was so completely Behzad's ideal of the good and gentle worker; that I paid without demur.

26

Gustavo Gutierrez

"The Song of the Poor" from
We Drink from Our Own Wells:
The Spiritual Journey of a People*

Gustavo Gutierrez is a leading proponent of Latin American liberation theology, a movement that holds that religion should work to free the world's poor from poverty and oppression, through political activity. His insistence that past actions of the Catholic Church have contributed to the system that enslaves the poor, and that Christianity must change if it is to be worthy of God, have brought him both praise and vilification.

What we are confronted with, then, is a foreign land, a passage through a desert; testing and discernment. But in this same land, from which God is not in fact absent, the seeds of a new spirituality can germinate. This spirituality gives rise to new songs to the Lord, songs filled with an authentic joy because it is spirituality that is nourished by the hope of a people familiar with the suffering caused by poverty and contempt.

The present experience of Latin American Christians is one that has been given profound expression in the psalms. Trusting as he does in the Lord who is "a stronghold for the oppressed" (Ps. 9:9), the psalmist is able to proclaim:

> I will give thanks to the Lord with my whole heart;
>   I will tell of all thy wonderful deeds.
> I will be glad and exult in thee,
>   I will sing praise to thy name, O Most High
>   [Ps. 9:1–2].

Because he is sure that the Lord "loves righteousness and justice" (Ps. 33:5), the psalmist can sing:

> Rejoice in the Lord, O you righteous!
>   Praise befits the upright.
> Praise the Lord with the lyre,
>   make melody to him with the harp of ten strings!
> Sing to him a new song,
>   play skillfully on the strings, with loud shouts
>   [Ps. 33:1–3].

*From Gustavo Gutierrez, *We Drink from Our Own Wells: The Spiritual Journey of a People,* Matthew O'Connell, trans. (Maryknoll, New York: Orbis Books, 1984).

We are living in a favorable time, a *kairos*, in which the Lord says: "Behold, I stand at the door and knock; if any one hears my voice and opens the door, I will come in to him and eat with him, and he with me" (Rev. 3:20). Not a violent entrance but a quiet knock that calls for an attitude of welcome and active watchfulness, of confidence and courage. Indifference, the privileges they have gained, and fear of the new make many persons spiritually deaf; as a result, the Lord passes by without stopping at their houses. But there are also many in our countries and in these times who hear the Lord's call and try to open the doors of their lives. We are living in a special period of God's saving action, a time when a new route is being carved out for the following of Jesus.

A FAVORABLE TIME

Our increasingly clear awareness of the harsh situation in Latin America and the sufferings of the poor must not make us overlook the fact that the harshness and suffering are not what is truly new in the present age. What is new is not wretchedness and repression and premature death, for these, unfortunately, are ancient realities in these countries. What is new is that the people are beginning to grasp the causes of their situation of injustice and are seeking to release themselves from it. Likewise new and important is the role which faith in the God who liberates is playing in the process.

It can therefore be said without any fear of exaggeration that we are experiencing today an exceptional time in the history of Latin America and the life of the church. Of this situation we may say with Paul: "Now is the favorable time; this is the day of salvation" (2 Cor. 6:2, JB). Such a vision of things does not make the journey of the poor less difficult nor does it gloss over the obstacles they encounter in their efforts to defend their most elementary rights. The demanding, cruel reality of wretchedness, exploitation, hostility, and death—our daily experience—will not allow us to forget it. There is question here, then, not of a facile optimism but rather of a deep trust in the historical power of the poor and, above all, a firm hope in the Lord.

These attitudes do not automatically ensure a better future; but as they draw nourishment from a present that is full of possibilities, they in turn nourish the present with promises. So true is this that if we do not respond to the demands of the present, because we do not know in advance whither we may be led, we are simply refusing to hear the call of Jesus Christ. We are refusing to open to him when he knocks on the door and invites us to sup with him.

We are today experiencing a *time of solidarity* in Latin America. Throughout its length and breadth there is a growing movement of solidarity in defense of human rights and, in particular, the rights of the poor. This has been true of Nicaragua, El Salvador, Guatemala, and Bolivia; it is true also of those who have been exiled or have disappeared in Haiti, Uruguay, Chile, Argentina, Paraguay, and other countries. More than this, at the base level and the local level there has been a proliferation of groups and organizations dedicated to solidarity among and with the dispossessed. The ease with which the popular sectors move from the local scene to the Latin American scene is impressive. This is the first flowering at the continental level of what José María Arguedas used to call "the fellowship of the wretched." The anonymous heroes involved in these efforts are countless, and the generosity poured out in them is beyond measure.

Recent events in European history have made the word "solidarity" fashionable. In the Latin American experience, however, for many years now the word has been used among the poor of the continent for the action that follows upon their new awareness of their situation of exploitation and marginalization, as well as of the role they must play in the building of a new and different society. For Christians this action is an efficacious act of charity, of love for neighbor and love for God in the poor. Christians thus realize that the question is not simply one of personal attitudes. The issue is the solidarity of the entire ecclesial community—the church—with movements of the poor in defense of their rights. This accounts for the rise of many groups whose purpose is not simply to practice solidarity themselves but also to help the church as a whole to bear witness to, and to live up to, its proclamation of the reign of God.

The present is also a *time of prayer*. Anyone who is in contact with base-level ecclesial communities can attest that there is a great deal of intense and hope-filled prayer going on in Latin America today. Yet the forecaster of doom and failure, those of the type whom at the beginning of the Second Vatican Council John XXIII spoke of as "prophets of gloom," have been claiming that the life of prayer is vanishing from Latin America.

Latin Americans at the base level have a completely different experience. Nor am I speaking only of those great moments that are milestones in the journey of a people with its advances and retreats. At such moments the communities have given evidence of great creativity and depth in the matter of prayer. But when I speak of the wealth and intensity of prayer I have in mind also, and above all, the daily practice of humble prayer in numberless localities. Nowhere in the Latin American church is more fervent and joyous prayer to be found amid daily suffering and struggle than in the Christian communities among the poor. It is our acts of gratitude and hope in the Lord that make us free (Gal. 5:1).

For many, then (I am indeed not unaware of the failures of some in this area), a growing maturity in their solidarity with the commitment to liberation has, by a dialectical process, brought with it a new emphasis on prayer as a fundamental dimension of Christian life. The result has been a mighty development of prayer in popular Christian groups. I know how difficult it is to measure such things, but daily experience, and even the result in writings (this among a people for whom oral expression is the dominant kind), are proof that prayer is widespread and creative.

It is, then, a time of solidarity and a time of prayer—but also, and in a sense synthesizing those two, a *time of martyrdom* as well. There are many who have devoted their lives, to the point of suffering death, in order to bear witness to the presence of the poor in the Latin American world and to the preferential love that God has for them. Nor has the bloodletting ceased as yet. The first manifestations of this unparalleled and astonishing situation (after all, when many of the persecutors and murderers come out into the open, they claim to be Christians) go back to about 1968. We are perhaps still too close historically to these events to be able to gauge their full significance.

What did the contemporaries of the early martyrs think about the events of their time? Perhaps the complexity of the factors in any historical situation, their own closeness to the events, and even their lack of personal courage prevented them from seeing the significance of occurrences that today seem so clearly to have been heroic testimonies to faith in the Lord. It is a fact that a consensus with regard to what is happening before our eyes is always more difficult to reach; this is because present events, unlike those of the past, are not situated in a world that we regard as idyllic and that we envelop in golden legends. Present events form part of our own universe and demand of the individual a personal decision, a rejection of every kind of complicity with executioners, a straightforward solidarity, an uncompromising denunciation of evil, a prayer of commitment.

But the poor are not fooled; they see the truth and speak out when others remain silent. They see in the surrender of these lives a profound and radical testimony of faith; they observe that in a continent where the powerful spread death in order to protect their privileges, such a testimony to God often brings the murder of the witness; and they draw nourishment from the hope that sustains these lives and these deaths. According to the very earliest Christian tradition the blood of martyrs gives life to the ecclesial community, the assembly of the disciples of Jesus Christ. This is what is happening today in Latin America. Fidelity unto death is a wellspring of life. It signals a new, demanding, and fruitful course in the following of Jesus.

The new way is, of course, not entirely new. The present-day Latin American experience of martyrdom bids us all turn back to one of the major sources of all spirituality: the blood-stained experience of the early Christian community, which was so weak in the face of the imperial power of that day.

I have spoken of questions and crises. These two terms, however, do not adequately cover the total reality of the following of Jesus in present-day Latin America; in fact, they are not even most representative of that following. They simply represent a road that must be traveled and a price that must be paid for the sake of what is fundamental: *the recognition of the time of salvation* in which these countries are now living. A little earlier I cited Psalm 42. But, despite the words I quoted, the psalmist's prayer is not turned nostalgically to the past, for such nostalgia would mean attachment to our own feelings rather than to God. The psalmist in fact goes on to say:

> Why are you cast down, O my soul,
>   and why are you disquieted within me?

> Hope in God; for I shall again praise him,
>   my help and my God. . . .
> Oh send out thy light and thy truth;
>   let them lead me,
> let them bring me to thy holy hill
>   and to thy dwelling!
> Then I will go to the altar of God,
>   to God my exceeding joy;
> and I will praise thee with the lyre,
>   O God, my God [Ps. 42:11; 43:3–4].

The "I shall again give him praise" is already a present reality. The Latin American church is passing through an unparalleled period of its history. The concrete and efficacious commitment of so many Christians to the poorest and most disinherited, as well as the serious difficulties they encounter in their commitment to solidarity, are leaving a profound mark on the history of Latin America. The attitude of those who believe they can continue to rely on the support of the church for maintaining their privileges is changing, but so is the attitude of those who were beginning to look upon the church as an institution belonging to the past. We are not now in the evening of the history of the church but are beginning the new day of an opportunity for evangelization that we never had before.

To some all this may smack of facile and naive optimism. True enough, the exhaustion produced by an unending situation of wretchedness; the tensions caused by the resistance men and women must engage in if they are to win out in their commitment to liberation; the depression felt at the abiding attitude of suspicion that greets every effort at effective solidarity with an exploited people; the resistance experienced within the people of God itself—these facts do not permit an easy optimism or allow us to forget the marginalization, the suffering, the deaths. At the same time, however, we must be aware of the change that has taken place. When all is said and done, despite—or thanks to—the immense price that is being paid, the present situation is nourishing new life, revealing new paths to be followed, and providing reason for profound joy.

The spendthrift generosity (sometimes accompanied by the giver's own blood, as I have pointed out) that has been shown in Latin America in recent years is making its nations fruitful and is confronting the ecclesial community with a demanding, but at the same time, most promising moment in its history. In the faces and hands of the dispossessed the Lord is knocking, and knocking loudly, on the community's door. By feeding the hope of the poor (that is what Archbishop Romero accepted as his pastoral mission) the church will be accepting the banquet to which the Lord of the kingdom invites us. Two paragraphs above, I mentioned "an opportunity for evangelization." The question is, Do we know how to make use of that opportunity?

Solidarity, prayer, and martyrdom add up to a time of salvation and judgment, a time of grace and stern demand—a time, above all, of hope.

TOWARD A NEW SPIRITUALITY

The period that Latin America is now living through is filled with questions and varied perspectives, with impasses and new pathways, with suffering and hope. For this reason it is also becoming the crucible in which a new and different way of following Jesus is being developed. "Different" means proper to Latin America and shaped by the real experiences of the Latin American countries.

In these countries the pain that is felt at the wretchedness of the poor and the atrocities to which they are subjected, but also the love of God that burns especially in those who have given their lives out of love for their brothers and sisters, have become a fire that consumes—and fuses—the disparate elements of our Latin American reality and our Latin American history. From this action—which is only apparently destructive, inasmuch as in it a basically creative work is also being accomplished—there is emerging the "gold refined by fire" (Rev. 3:18) of a new spirituality. If we reject what is presently occurring and if we are not even willing to be thus consumed, along with our weapons and our baggage, we remain bogged down in what is secondary and anecdotal and perhaps even in the deformity and perversity that marks what is happening in Latin America today. We prefer a selfish inertia to constancy, illusion to hope, the honor of worldly trappings to a profound fidelity to the church, fads to the truly new, authoritarianism to moral authority and service, a tranquilizing past to a challenging present. In short, we prefer mammon to the God of Jesus Christ.

HISTORICAL MOVEMENTS AND THE FOLLOWING OF JESUS

Every great spirituality is connected with the great historical movement of the age in which it was formulated. This linkage is not to be understood in the sense of mechanical dependence, but the following of Jesus is something that penetrates deeply into the course of human history. This is true, for example, of the mendicant spirituality that was born at a time when, despite apparent good health, the first germs of a crisis for Christianity were incubating. The new spiritual way was closely linked to those movements of the poor that represented a social and evangelical reaction to the wealth and power that the church had attained at that time. The time of the pontificate of Innocent III (1198–1216) showed clearly the heights that the political power and affluence of the church had reached. Without attention to the historical context in which Francis of Assisi and Dominic Guzmán developed their apostolate and bore their evangelical witness, it is impossible to understand either the full significance of the mendicant orders or the reception and resistance they encountered.

The same holds true for Ignatius of Loyola. His spirituality had for its context the transition to the so-called modern age. The broadening of the known world by geographical discoveries, the assertion of human reason that found expression in the birth of experimental science, the extension of the scope of human subjectivity in religious matters as evidenced by the Protestant Reformation—these were converging phenomena that led to a new way of understanding the role of human freedom. It was not a mere coincidence that freedom, a freedom directed to the service of God and others, should be a central theme in Ignatian spirituality.

Examples might be multiplied (John of the Cross and Teresa of Avila and their relationship to the reform within the Catholic Church, and many others). They would only confirm what I have already said: the concrete forms of the following of Jesus are connected with the great historical movements of an age.

A grasp of that constant enables us to understand what is happening before our eyes today in Latin America. Perhaps we lack the perspective required for realizing what is happening, inasmuch as the immediacy of events makes impossible the distance needed. The events are there, nonetheless, and we have begun to experience the change. The breakthrough of the poor to which I referred at the beginning of part 1 is finding expression in the consciousness of the identity and the organization of the oppressed and marginalized of Latin America. In the future, Latin American society will be judged, and transformed, in terms of the poor. These are the ones who in this foreign land of death that is Latin America seek what G. García Márquez, in his beautiful address upon receiving the Nobel Prize, called the utopia of life: "Faced with oppression, pillage, and abandonment, our response is life. . . . It is a new and splendid utopia of life, where no one can decide for others how they will die, where love will be certain and happiness possible, and where those condemned to a hundred years of solitary confinement find, finally and forever, a second chance on this earth."

In search of this utopia, an entire people—with all its traditional values and the wealth of its recent experience—has taken to the path of building a world in which persons are more important than things and in which all can live with dignity, a society that respects human freedom when it is in the service of a genuine common good, and exercises no kind of coercion, from whatever source.

All this we call the historical process of liberation, and with its ideas and its impetuosity it is sweeping all Latin America. The process is only beginning. It is not advancing triumphantly and without obstacles to the applause of the entire world; it is not reaching into all the corners of the Latin American landscape or all the nooks and crannies of the lives of those who live there. Nonetheless we are in the presence of a coherent and dynamic movement that is bringing out what is best and most promising in the peoples of Latin America.

Nor is the movement principally a movement within the church; it is rather something that is happening in the history of the Latin American peoples as a whole. For that very reason, however, the movement involves, and is reflected in, the church. The movement is a far-reaching one that is leaving its inescapable mark on the world in which the church lives and in which it must be a sacrament of salvation and a community of witnesses to the life of the risen Christ.

The struggles of the poor for liberation represent an assertion of their right to life. The poverty that the poor suffer means death: a premature and unjust death. It is on the basis of this affirmation of life that the poor of Latin America are trying to live their faith, recognize the love of God, and proclaim their hope. Within these struggles, with their many forms and phases, an oppressed and believing people is increasingly creating a way of Christian life, a spirituality. Latin American Christians will thus cease to be consumers of spiritualities that are doubtless valid but that nonetheless reflect other experiences and other goals, for they are carving out their own way of being faithful both to the Lord and to the experiences of the poorest.

This historical movement, with its focus in the process of liberation, is truly the terrain on which a people's spiritual experience is located as it affirms its right to life. This is the soil in which its response to the gift of faith in the God of life is taking root. The poverty that brings death to the poor is no longer a motive for resignation to the conditions of present existence, nor does it discourage Latin American Christians in their aspirations. The historical experience of liberation that they are now beginning to have is showing them, or reminding them of, something down deep in themselves: that God wants them to live.

A reading in the light of faith, then, gives us to understand that the breakthrough of the poor in Latin American society and the Latin American church is in the final analysis a breakthrough of God in our lives. This breakthrough is the point of departure and also the axis of the new spirituality. It therefore points out to us the way that leads to the God of Jesus Christ.

CHOOSE LIFE AND YOU SHALL LIVE (DEUT. 30:19)

It may seem somewhat reckless to speak of a spirituality taking shape amid the Latin American poor, but that is precisely what is happening as I see it. Perhaps some are surprised because they think of the struggle for liberation as taking place in the social and political sphere, and thus in an area that had nothing to do with the spiritual. Clearly, everything depends here on what one understands by "spiritual." I shall have occasion further on to define this term more closely; for the moment, let me say that the process of liberation is a global one and that it affects every dimension of the human. Moreover, the poverty in which the vast majority of Latin Americans live is not simply a "social problem"; it is a human situation that issues a profound challenge to the Christian conscience.

Surprise may also come from the idea that the subject of the experience that is giving rise to a spirituality is an entire people, and not an individual who stands apart and is to some extent isolated, at least initially. This is another point I must discuss more fully. What is happening among us today represents a departure from the beaten path; it also forces us to realize that the following of Jesus is not along a private route but is part of a collective enterprise. In this way we recover the biblical understanding of people's journey in search of God.

The spirituality being born in Latin America is the spirituality of the church of the poor, to which Pope John XXIII called all of us, the spirituality of an ecclesial community that is trying to make effective its solidarity with the poorest of this world. It is a collective, ecclesial spirituality that, without losing anything of its universal perspective, is stamped with the religious outlook of an exploited and believing people. The journey is one undertaken by the entire people of God. It leaves behind it a land of oppression and, without illusions but with constancy, seeks its way in the midst of a desert. It is a "new" spirituality because the love of the Lord who urges us to reject inertia and inspires us to creativity is itself always new.

In this following of Jesus the central drama is played out in the dialectic of *death followed by life*. In this dialectic and in the victory of the risen Jesus, the God of our hope is revealed. This is a profound and strictly paschal spirituality. It bears in mind all the things that exploit and marginalize the poor, and it draws its nourishment from the victory against the "death out of due time" (as Bartolomé de Las Casas put it) that that situation entails. It embodies the conviction that life, not death, has the final word. The following of Jesus feeds upon the witness given by the resurrection, which means the death of death, and upon the liberating efforts of the poor to assert their unquestionable right to life.

The relationship between an oppressive system and the God who liberates, between death that seems to have the upper hand and the God of life, adumbrates a way of following Jesus and being his disciples under the conditions now prevailing in Latin America. Jesus is not to be sought among the dead: he is alive (Luke 24:5). To seek him among the living is to choose life, as the Book of Deuteronomy says. This choice is the basis of a spiritual experience that is pointing the way to a new path in the following of Jesus in Latin America.

MAKING OUR OWN THE SPIRITUAL EXPERIENCE OF THE PEOPLE

For many Latin American Christians at the present time the possibility of following Jesus depends on their ability to make their own the spiritual experience of the poor. This requires of them a deep-going conversion; they are being asked to make their own the experience that the poor have of God and of God's will that every human being have life.

In the past, Christians, formed in one or another spiritual school—missionaries, for example—may have felt that it was for them to communicate their own experiences to the people and to point out to the people the path of a suitable Christian life. Today, however, they are called upon to turn that past attitude around. The "evangelizing potential" that Puebla (no. 1147) recognizes in the poor and oppressed points implicitly to one source of that power and ability to proclaim the Christian message. That source is precisely the spiritual experience to which the revelation of God's preference for "mere children" (cf. Matt. 11:25) gives rise. It is this encounter with the Lord that the Christians I am speaking of must make their own.

The need is not simply to recognize that the experience of the people raises questions and challenges for the spirituality of these Christians. That may have been the case for a time. Many of those bound by religious vows, for example, have felt challenged by the real poverty of the dispossessed and marginalized. They asked themselves what meaning their own promise of living a poor life had in the face of such a situation. The questions were legitimate ones and showed a sensitivity entirely deserving of respect. At present, however, the situation is a more inclusive one and reaches deeper. We are no longer faced with isolated questions, however penetrating. Something more systematic is making its appearance; its parts resist separation: they form an organic whole. In this framework the religious vows are recovering their full meaning.

This new reality invites Christians to leave the familiar world they have long inhabited, and leads many of them to reread their own spiritual tradition. Above all, it is a question of making our own the world of the poor and their manner of living out their relationship with the Lord and taking over the historical practice of Jesus. Otherwise we shall be traveling a road that simply parallels that taken by oppressed believers. Then we shall have to try to build bridges that connect these different roads: bridges of commitment to the exploited, friendly relationships with some of them, celebration of the Eucharist with them, and so on. All these would be meritorious efforts no doubt, but they are inadequate because such connections do not change the fact that the roads are only parallel. At the present time, the spiritual experience of the poor is too radical and too comprehensive in scope to merit only that kind of attention. That is why I have spoken here of making that experience our own. That is the issue. Any other response will be a halfway response.

For those who are located within a particular spiritual tradition, entry into the experience of the poor means taking that tradition with them. A rich variety has marked the ways in which throughout its history the Christian community has undertaken the following of Jesus; these ways represent experiences that we cannot simply leave behind. Advantage must rather be taken of that tradition in order to enrich the contemporary spiritual experience of the poor. The refusal thus to enrich the poor would betray a kind of avarice in the area of spirituality. Furthermore, such avarice turns against the distrustful owners: their spiritual riches spoil and lose their value when kept "under the mattress." It is appropriate here to recall the parable of the buried talents.

The faith and hope in the God of life that provide a shelter in the situation of death and struggle for life in which the poor and oppressed of Latin America are now living—they are the well from which we must drink if we want to be faithful to Jesus. This is the water of which Archbishop Oscar Romero had drunk when he said he had been converted to Christ by his own people. Once this change had taken place, he could not but view his following of Jesus as closely bound up with the life (and death) of the Salvadoran people whose sufferings and hopes we all carry in our hearts. His spiritual life abandoned the ways of individualism and began instead to draw its nourishment from the experiences of an entire people. This is why he could say two weeks before he was murdered:

> My life has been threatened many times. I have to confess that, as a Christian, I don't believe in death without resurrection. If they kill me, *I will rise again in the Salvadoran people.* I'm not boasting, or saying this out of pride, but rather as humbly as I can.

We all have the same vocation: to rise to life with the people in its spirituality. This implies a death to the alleged "spiritual ways" that individualisms of one or another kind create but that in fact lead only to an impasse. It also supposes a birth into new ways of being disciples of Jesus, the risen Christ. The newness draws its strength from the Bible and from the best in the history of spirituality and in this respect is profoundly traditional. Such is the experience of the poor of Latin America. Theirs is an authentic spiritual experience, an encounter with the Lord who points out a road for them to follow.

I intend to sketch some markings of this itinerary. But first it is necessary to examine what can be called the "dimensions" of a full spirituality—dimensions that are also those of the spiritual path that is being opened up in Latin America.

27

Elie Wiesel
Night*

A major effort of recent Jewish theology has been an attempt to gain perspective on the Holocaust. The horror and evil of that slaughter have caused many to ask basic questions about the justice of God. Elie Wiesel, a Holocaust survivor, has contributed much to this effort through novels based on his personal experiences. This reading is from his book Night. *It suggests the devastating effect the Holocaust had on his faith.*

The cherished objects we had brought with us thus far were left behind in the train, and with them, at last, our illusions.

Every two yards or so an SS man held his tommy gun trained on us. Hand in hand we followed the crowd.

An SS noncommissioned officer came to meet us, a truncheon in his hand. He gave the order:

"Men to the left! Women to the right!"

Eight words spoken quietly, indifferently, without emotion. Eight short, simple words. Yet that was the moment when I parted from my mother. I had not had time to think, but already I felt the pressure of my father's hand: we were alone. For a part of a second I glimpsed my mother and my sisters moving away to the right. Tzipora held Mother's hand. I saw them disappear into the distance; my mother was stroking my sister's fair hair, as though to protect her, while I walked on with my father and the other men. And I did not know that in that place, at that moment, I was parting from my mother and Tzipora forever. I went on walking. My father held onto my hand.

Behind me, an old man fell to the ground. Near him was an SS man, putting his revolver back in its holster.

My hand shifted on my father's arm. I had one thought—not to lose him. Not to be left alone.

The SS officers gave the order:

"Form fives!"

Commotion. At all costs we must keep together.

"Here, kid, how old are you?"

It was one of the prisoners who asked me this. I could not see his face, but his voice was tense and weary.

"I'm not quite fifteen yet."

"No. Eighteen."

"But I'm not," I said. "Fifteen."

"Fool. Listen to what *I* say."

Then he questioned my father, who replied:

"Fifty."

The other grew more furious than ever.

"No, not fifty. Forty. Do you understand? Eighteen and forty."

He disappeared into the night shadows. A second man came up, spitting oaths at us.

"What have you come here for, you sons of bitches? What are you doing here, eh?"

Someone dared to answer him.

"What do you think? Do you suppose we've come here for our own pleasure? Do you think we asked to come?"

A little more, and the man would have killed him.

"You shut your trap, you filthy swine, or I'll squash you right now! You'd have done better to have hanged yourselves where you were than to come here. Didn't you know what was in store for you at Auschwitz? Haven't you heard about it? In 1944?"

No, we had not heard. No one had told us. He could not believe his ears. His tone of voice became increasingly brutal.

"Do you see that chimney over there? See it? Do you see those flames? (Yes, we did see the flames.) Over there—that's where you're going to be taken. That's your grave, over there. Haven't you realized it yet? You dumb bastards, don't you understand anything? You're going to be burned. Frizzled away. Turned into ashes."

He was growing hysterical in his fury. We stayed motionless, petrified. Surely it was all a nightmare? An unimaginable nightmare?

I heard murmurs around me.

"We've got to do something. We can't let ourselves be killed. We can't go like beasts to the slaughter. We've got to revolt."

There were a few sturdy young fellows among us. They had knives on them, and they tried to incite the others to throw themselves on the armed guards.

One of the young men cried:

"Let the world learn of the existence of Auschwitz. Let everybody hear about it, while they can still escape. . . ."

But the older ones begged their children not to do anything foolish:

"You must never lose faith, even when the sword hangs over your head. That's the teaching of our sages. . . ."

The wind of revolt died down. We continued our march toward the square. In the middle stood the notorious Dr. Mengele (a typical SS officer: a cruel face, but not devoid of intelligence, and wearing a monocle); a conductor's baton in his hand, he was standing among the other officers. The baton moved unremittingly, sometimes to the right, sometimes to the left.

I was already in front of him:

"How old are you?" he asked, in an attempt at a paternal tone of voice.

"Eighteen." My voice was shaking.

"Are you in good health?"

"Yes."

"What's your occupation?"

Should I say that I was a student?

"Farmer," I heard myself say.

This conversation cannot have lasted more than a few seconds. It had seemed like an eternity to me.

The baton moved to the left. I took half a step forward. I wanted to see first where they were sending my father. If he went to the right, I would go after him.

The baton once again pointed to the left for him too. A weight was lifted from my heart.

We did not yet know which was the better side, right or left; which road led to prison and which to the crematory. But for the moment I was happy; I was near my father. Our procession continued to move slowly forward.

Another prisoner came up to us:

"Satisfied?"

Yes," someone replied.

"Poor devils, you're going to the crematory."

He seemed to be telling the truth. Not far from us, flames were leaping up from a ditch, gigantic flames. They were burning something. A lorry drew up at the pit and delivered its load—little children. Babies! Yes, I saw it—saw it with my own eyes . . . those children in the flames. (Is it surprising that I could not sleep after that? Sleep had fled from my eyes.)

So this was where we were going. A little farther on was another and larger ditch for adults.

I pinched my face. Was I still alive? Was I awake? I could not believe it. How could it be possible for them to burn people, children, and for the world to keep silent? No, none of this could be true. It was a nightmare. . . . Soon I should wake with a start, my heart pounding, and find myself back in the bedroom of my childhood, among my books. . . .

My father's voice drew me from my thoughts: "It's a shame . . . a shame that you couldn't have gone with your mother. . . . I saw several boys of your age going with their mothers. . . . "

His voice was terribly sad. I realized that he did not want to see what they were going to do to me. He did not want to see the burning of his only son.

My forehead was bathed in cold sweat. But I told him that I did not believe that they could burn people in our age, that humanity would never tolerate it. . . .

"Humanity? Humanity is not concerned with us. Today anything is allowed. Anything is possible, even these crematories. . . ."

His voice was choking.

"Father," I said, "if that is so, I don't want to wait here. I'm going to run to the electric wire. That would be better than slow agony in the flames."

He did not answer. He was weeping. His body was shaken convulsively. Around us, everyone was weeping. Someone began to recite the Kaddish, the prayer for the dead. I do not know if it has ever happened before, in the long history of the Jews, that people have ever recited the prayer for the dead for themselves.

"*Yitgadal veyitkadach shmé raba.* . . . May His Name be blessed and magnified. . . ." whispered my father.

For the first time, I felt revolt rise up in me. Why should I bless His name? The Eternal, Lord of the Universe, the All-Powerful and Terrible, was silent. What had I to thank Him for?

We continued our march. We were gradually drawing closer to the ditch, from which an infernal heat was rising. Still twenty steps to go. If I wanted to bring about my own death, this was the moment. Our line had now only fifteen paces to cover. I bit my lips so that my father would not hear my teeth chattering. Ten steps still. Eight. Seven. We marched slowly on, as though following a hearse at our own funeral. Four steps more. Three steps. There it was now, right in front of us, the pit and its flames. I gathered all that was left of my strength, so that I could break from the ranks and throw myself upon the barbed wire. In the depths of my heart, I bade farewell to my father, to the whole universe; and, in spite of myself, the words formed themselves and issued in a whisper from my lips: *Yitgadal veyitkadach shmé raba.* . . . May His name be blessed and magnified. . . . My heart was bursting. The moment had come. I was face to face with the Angel of Death. . . .

No. Two steps from the pit we were ordered to turn to the left and made to go into a barracks.

I pressed my father's hand. He said:

"Do you remember Madame Schächter, in the train?"

Never shall I forget that night, the first night in camp, which has turned my life into one long night, seven times cursed and seven times sealed. Never shall I forget that smoke. Never shall I forget the little faces of the children, whose bodies I saw turned into wreaths of smoke beneath a silent blue sky.

Never shall I forget those flames which consumed my faith forever.

Never shall I forget that nocturnal silence which deprived me, for all eternity, of the desire to live. Never shall I forget those moments which murdered my God and my soul and turned my dreams to dust. Never shall I forget these things, even if I am condemned to live as long as God Himself. Never.

The barracks we had been made to go into was very long. In the roof were some blue-tinged skylights. The ante-chamber of Hell must look like this. So many crazed men, so many cries, so much bestial brutality!

There were dozens of prisoners to receive us, truncheons in their hands, striking out anywhere, at anyone, without reason. Orders:

"Strip! Fast! *Los!* Keep only your belts and shoes in your hands. . . ."

We had to throw our clothes at one end of the barracks. There was already a great heap there. New suits and old, torn coats, rags. For us, this was the true equality: nakedness. Shivering with the cold.

Some SS officers moved about in the room, looking for strong men. If they were so keen on strength, perhaps one should try and pass oneself off as sturdy? My father thought the reverse. It was better not to draw attention to oneself. Our fate would then be the same as the others. (Later, we were to learn that he was right. Those who were selected that day were enlisted in the *Sonder-Kommando*, the unit which worked in the crematories. Bela Katz—son of a big tradesman from our town—had arrived at Birkenau with the first transport, a week before us. When he heard of our arrival, he managed to get word to us that, having been chosen for his strength, he had himself put his father's body into the crematory oven.)

Blows continued to rain down.

"To the barber!"

Belt and shoes in hand, I let myself be dragged off to the barbers. They took our hair off with clippers, and shaved off all the hair on our bodies. The same thought buzzed all the time in my head—not to be separated from my father.

Freed from the hands of the barbers, we began to wander in the crowd, meeting friends and acquaintances. These meetings filled us with joy—yes, joy—"Thank God! You're still alive!"

But others were crying. They used all their remaining strength in weeping. Why had they let themselves be brought here? Why couldn't they have died in their beds? Sobs choked their voices.

Suddenly, someone threw his arms round my neck in an embrace: Yechiel, brother of the rabbi of Sighet. He was sobbing bitterly. I thought he was weeping with joy at still being alive.

"Don't cry, Yechiel," I said. "Don't waste your tears. . . ."

"Not cry? We're on the threshold of death. . . . Soon we shall have crossed over. . . . Don't you understand? How could I not cry?"

Through the blue-tinged skylights I could see the darkness gradually fading. I had ceased to feel fear. And then I was overcome by an inhuman weariness.

Those absent no longer touched even the surface of our memories. We still spoke of them—"Who knows what may have become of them?"—but we had little concern for their fate. We were incapable of thinking of anything at all. Our senses were blunted; everything was blurred as in a fog. It was no longer possible to grasp anything. The instincts of self-preservation, of self-defense, of pride, had all deserted us. In one ultimate moment of lucidity it seemed to me that we were damned souls wandering in the half-world, souls condemned to wander through space till the generations of man came to an end, seeking their redemption, seeking oblivion—without hope of finding it.

Toward five o'clock in the morning, we were driven out of the barracks. The Kapos beat us once more, but I had ceased to feel any pain from their blows. An icy wind enveloped us. We were naked, our shoes and belts in our hands. The command: "Run!" And we ran. After a few minutes of racing, a new barracks.

A barrel of petrol at the entrance. Disinfection. Everyone was soaked in it. Then a hot shower. At high speed. As we came out from the water, we were driven outside. More running. Another barracks, the store. Very long tables. Mountains of prison clothes. On we ran. As we passed, trousers, tunic, shirt, and socks were thrown to us.

Within a few seconds, we had ceased to be men. If the situation had not been tragic, we should have roared with laughter. Such outfits! Meir Katz, a giant, had a child's trousers, and Stern, a thin little chap, a tunic which completely swamped him. We immediately began the necessary exchanges.

I glanced at my father. How he had changed! His eyes had grown dim. I would have liked to speak to him, but I did not know what to say.

The night was gone. The morning star was shining in the sky. I too had become a completely different person. The student of the Talmud, the child that I was, had been consumed in the flames. There remained only a shape that looked like me. A dark flame had entered into my soul and devoured it.

So much had happened within such a few hours that I had lost all sense of time. When had we left our houses? And the ghetto? And the train? Was it only a week? One night—*one single night*?

How long had we been standing like this in the icy wind? An hour? Simply an hour? Sixty minutes?

Surely it was a dream.

Not far from us there were some prisoners at work. Some were digging holes, others carrying sand. None of them so much as glanced at us. We were so many dried-up trees in the heart of a desert. Behind me, some people were talking. I had not the slightest desire to listen to what they were saying, to know who was talking or what they were talking about. No one dared to raise his voice, though there was no supervisor near us. People whispered. Perhaps it was because of the thick smoke which poisoned the air and took one by the throat. . . .

We were made to go into a new barracks, in the "gypsies' camp." In ranks of five.

"And now stay where you are!"

There was no floor. A roof and four walls. Our feet sank into the mud.

Another spell of waiting began. I went to sleep standing up. I dreamed of a bed, of my mother's caress. And I woke up: I was standing, my feet in the mud. Some people collapsed and lay where they were. Others cried:

"Are you mad? We've been told to stay standing. Do you want to bring trouble on us all?"

As if all the trouble in the world had not descended already upon our heads! Gradually, we all sat down in the mud. But we had to jump up constantly, every time a Kapo came in to see if anybody had a pair of new shoes. If so, they had to be given up to him. It was no use opposing this: blows rained down and in the final reckoning you had lost your shoes anyway.

I had new shoes myself. But as they were coated with a thick layer of mud, no one had noticed them. I thanked God, in an improvised prayer, for having created mud in His infinite and wonderful universe.

Suddenly the silence grew oppressive. An SS officer had come in and, with him, the odor of the Angel of Death. We stared fixedly at his fleshy lips. From the middle of the barracks, he harangued us:

"You're in a concentration camp. At Auschwitz. . . ."

A pause. He observed the effect his words had produced. His face has stayed in my memory to this day. A tall man, about thirty, with crime inscribed upon his brow and in the pupils of his eyes. He looked us over as if we were a pack of leprous dogs hanging onto our lives.

"Remember this," he went on. "Remember it forever, Engrave it into you minds. You are at Auschwitz. And Auschwitz is not a convalescent home. It's a concentration camp. Here, you have got to work. If not, you will go straight to the furnace. To the crematory. Work or the crematory—the choice is in your hands."

We had already lived through so much that night, we thought nothing could frighten us any more. But his clipped words made us tremble. Here the word "furnace" was not a word empty of meaning: it floated on the air, mingling with the smoke. It was perhaps the only word which did have any real meaning here. He left the barracks. Kapos appeared, crying:

"All skilled workers—locksmiths, electricians, watchmakers—one step forward!"

The rest of us were made to go to another barracks, a stone one this time. With permission to sit down. A gypsy deportee was in charge of us.

My father was suddenly seized with colic. He got up and went toward the gypsy, asking politely, in German:

"Excuse me, can you tell me where the lavatories are?"

The gypsy looked him up and down slowly, from head to foot. As if he wanted to convince himself that this man addressing him was really a creature of flesh and bone, a living being with a body and a belly. Then, as if he had suddenly woken up from a heavy doze, he dealt my father such a clout that he fell to the ground, crawling back to his place on all fours.

I did not move. What had happened to me? My father had just been struck, before my very eyes, and I had not flickered an eyelid. I had looked on and said nothing. Yesterday, I should have sunk my nails into the criminal's flesh. Had I changed so much, then? So quickly? Now remorse began to gnaw at me. I thought only: I shall never forgive them for that. My father must have guessed my feelings. He whispered in my ear, "It doesn't hurt." His cheek still bore the red mark of the man's hand.

"Everyone outside!"

Ten gypsies had come and joined our supervisor. Whips and truncheons cracked round me. My feet were running without my being aware of it. I tried to hide from the blows behind the others. The spring sunshine.

"Form fives!"

The prisoners whom I had noticed in the morning were working at the side. There was no guard near them, only the shadow of the chimney. . . . Dazed by the sunshine and by my reverie, I felt someone tugging at my sleeve. It was my father. "Come on, my boy."

We marched on. Doors opened and closed again. On we went between the electric wires. At each step, a white placard with a death's head on it stared us in the face. A caption: "Warning. Danger of death." Mockery: was there a single place here where you were not in danger of death?

The gypsies stopped near another barracks. They were replaced by SS, who surrounded us. Revolvers, machine guns, police dogs.

The march had lasted half an hour. Looking around me, I noticed that the barbed wires were behind us. We had left the camp.

It was a beautiful April day. The fragrance of spring was in the air. The sun was setting in the west.

But we had been marching for only a few moments when we saw the barbed wire of another camp. An iron door with this inscription over it:

"Work is liberty!"

Auschwitz.

First impression: this was better than Birkenau. There were two-storied buildings of concrete instead of wooden barracks. There were little gardens here and there. We were led to one of these prison blocks. Seated on the ground by the entrance, we began another session of waiting. Every now and then, some one was made to go in. These were the showers, a compulsory formality at the entrance to all these camps. Even if you were simply passing from one to the other several times a day, you still had to go through the baths every time.

After coming out from the hot water, we stayed shivering in the night air. Our clothes had been left behind in the other block, and we had been promised other outfits.

Toward midnight, we were told to run.

"Faster," shouted our guards. "The faster you run, the sooner you can go to bed."

After a few minutes of this mad race we arrived in front of another block. The prisoner in charge was waiting for us. He was a young Pole, who smiled at us. He began to talk to us, and, despite our weariness, we listened patiently.

"Comrades, you're in the concentration camp of Auschwitz. There's a long road of suffering ahead of you. But don't lose courage. You've already escaped the gravest danger: selection. So now, muster your strength, and don't lose heart. We shall all see the day of liberation. Have faith in life. Above all else, have faith. Drive out despair, and you will keep death away from yourselves. Hell is not for eternity. And now, a prayer—or rather, a piece of advice: let there be comradeship among you. We are all brothers, and we are all suffering the same fate. The same smoke floats over all our heads. Help one another. It is the only way to survive. Enough said. You're tired. Listen.

You're in Block 17. I am responsible for keeping order here. Anyone with a complaint against anyone else can come and see me. That's all. You can go to bed. Two people to a bunk. Good night." The first human words.

No sooner had we climbed into the bunks than we fell into a deep sleep.

The next morning, the "veteran" prisoners treated us without brutality. We went to the wash place. We were given new clothes. We were brought black coffee.

We left the block at about ten o'clock, so that it could be cleaned. Outside the sunshine warmed us. Our morale was much improved. We were feeling the benefit of a night's sleep. Friends met each other, exchanged a few sentences. We talked of everything, except those who had disappeared. The general opinion was that the war was about to end.

At about noon they brought us soup: a plate of thick soup for each person. Tormented though I was by hunger, I refused to touch it. I was still the spoiled child I had always been. My father swallowed my ration.

In the shade of the block, we then had a little siesta. He must have been lying, that SS officer in the muddy barracks. Auschwitz was in fact a rest home. . . .

In the afternoon we were made to line up. Three prisoners brought a table and some medical instruments. With the left sleeve rolled up, each person passed in front of the table. The three "veterans," with needles in their hands, engraved a number on our left arms. I became A-7713. After that I had no other name.

At dusk, roll call. The working units came back. Near the door, the band was playing military marches. Tens of thousands of prisoners stood in rows while the SS checked their numbers.

After roll call, the prisoners from all the blocks scattered to look for friends, relatives, and neighbors who had arrived in the last convoy.

Days passed. In the morning, black coffee. At noon, soup. (By the third day I was eating any kind of soup hungrily.) At six p.m., roll call. Then bread and something. At nine o'clock, bed.

We had already been eight days at Auschwitz. It was during roll call. We were not expecting anything except the sound of the bell which would announce the end of roll call. I suddenly heard someone passing between the rows asking, "Which of you is Wiesel of Sighet?"

The man looking for us was a bespectacled little fellow with a wrinkled, wizened face. My father answered him.

"I'm Wiesel of Sighet."

The little man looked at him for a long while, with his eyes narrowed.

"You don't recognize me—you don't recognize me. I'm a relative of yours. Stein. Have you forgotten me already? Stein! Stein of Antwerp. Reizel's husband. Your wife was Reizel's aunt. She often used to write to us . . . and such letters!"

My father had not recognized him. He must scarcely have known him,

since my father was always up to his neck in the affairs of the Jewish community, and much less well versed in family matters. He was always elsewhere, lost
in his thoughts. (Once a cousin came to see us at Sighet. She had been staying
with us and eating at our table for over a fortnight before my father noticed
her presence for the first time.) No, he could not have remembered Stein. As
for me, I recognized him at once. I had known his wife Reizel before she left
for Belgium.

He said, "I was deported in 1942. I heard that a transport had come in
from your region, and I came to find you. I thought perhaps you might have
news of Reizel, and my little boys. They stayed behind in Antwerp. . . ."

I knew nothing about them. Since 1940, my mother had not had a single
letter from them. But I lied.

"Yes, my mother's had news from your family. Reizel is very well. The
children too. . . ."

He wept with joy. He would have liked to stay longer, to learn more
details, to drink in the good news, but an SS came up, and he had to go, calling to us that he would be back the next day.

The bell gave us the signal to disperse. We went to get our evening meal
of bread and margarine. I was dreadfully hungry and swallowed my ration on
the spot.

My father said, "You don't want to eat it all at once. Tomorrow's another
day. . . ."

And seeing that his advice had come too late and that there was nothing
left of my ration, he did not even begin his own.

"Personally, I'm not hungry," he said.

We stayed at Auschwitz for three weeks. We had nothing to do. We slept a
great deal in the afternoon and at night.

The only worry was to avoid moves, to stay here as long as possible. It
was not difficult; it was simply a matter of never putting oneself down as a
skilled worker. Laborers were being kept till the end.

At the beginning of the third week, the prisoner in charge of our block
was deprived of his office, being considered too humane. Our new head was
savage, and his assistants were real monsters. The good days were over. We began
to wonder if it would not be better to let oneself be chosen for the next move.

Stein, our relation from Antwerp, continued to visit us, and from time to
time he would bring a half ration of bread.

"Here, this is for you, Eliezer."

Every time he came, there would be tears running down his face, con-
gealing there, freezing. He would often say to my father:

"Take care of your son. He's very weak and dried up. Look after him well,
to avoid the selection. Eat! It doesn't matter what or when. Eat everything
you can. The weak don't hang about for long here. . . ."

And he was so thin himself, so dried up, so weak. . . .

"The only thing that keeps me alive," he used to say, "is that Reizel and
the children are still alive. If it wasn't for them, I couldn't keep going."

He came toward us one evening, his face radiant.

"A transport's just come in from Antwerp. I'm going to see them tomorrow. They'll be sure to have news."

He went off.

We were not to see him again. He had had news. Real news.

In the evening, lying on our beds, we would try to sing some of the Hasidic melodies, and Akiba Drumer would break our hearts with his deep, solemn voice.

Some talked of God, of his mysterious ways, of the sins of the Jewish people, and of their future deliverance. But I had ceased to pray. How I sympathized with Job! I did not deny God's existence, but I doubted His absolute justice.

Akiba Drumer said: "God is testing us. He wants to find out whether we can dominate our base instincts and kill the Satan within us. We have no right to despair. And if he punishes us relentlessly, it's a sign that He loves us all the more."

Hersch Genud, well versed in the cabbala, spoke of the end of the world and the coming of Messiah.

Only occasionally during these conversations did the thought occur to me: "Where is my mother at this moment? And Tzipora . . . ?"

"Your mother is still a young woman," said my father on one occasion. "She must be in a labor camp. And Tzipora's a big girl now, isn't she? She must be in a camp, too."

How we should have liked to believe it. We pretended, for what if the other one should still be believing it?

All the skilled workers had already been sent to other camps. There were only about a hundred of us ordinary laborers left.

"It's your turn today," said the secretary of the block. "You're going with the next transport."

At ten o'clock we were given our daily ration of bread. We were surrounded by about ten SS. On the door the plaque: "*Work is liberty.*" We were counted. And then, there we were, right out in the country on the sunny road. In the sky a few little white clouds.

We walked slowly. The guards were in no hurry. We were glad of this. As we went through the villages, many of the Germans stared at us without surprise. They had probably already seen quite a few of these processions.

On the way, we met some young German girls. The guards began to tease them. The girls giggled, pleased. They let themselves be kissed and tickled, exploding with laughter. They were all laughing and joking and shouting blandishments at one another for a good part of the way. During this time, at least we did not have to endure either shouts or blows from the rifle butt.

At the end of four hours, we reached our new camp: Buna. The iron gate closed behind us.

PART **VIII**

FAITH AND
RELIGION

Prayer Tower, Oral Roberts University, Tulsa.
(Photo by J. T. Carmody)

INTRODUCTION

In this part we deal with faith: the act or disposition by which people accept God, the tenets of their religion, and their group's way of life. We also suggest how influential interpreters of religion have thought about what religion is—about what people are doing when they accept God or follow the tenets of their faith. Naturally, there have been numerous and differing views about both faith and the nature of religion. As soon as human beings began to analyze their religious behavior, they began to apply their particular convictions and prejudices. Nonetheless, our selections are representative.

The first issue that we study is whether modern people can responsibly believe in God. Is it possible, in good conscience, to overlook or outweigh the data that tell against the providence of a good God? What is one to say about the character of ultimate reality in light of all the suffering in the world, all the evil? Albert Camus (1913–1960), one of the most influential of the existentialists who came to prominence after World War II, pursued the question of the ethics of belief in brilliant essays and novels. He was no village atheist. His passion was to find meaning in a world apparently full of strong threats to meaning. For Camus, human beings found themselves in an absurd situation. They seemed to crave meaning, sense, fulfillment, in every pore of their being, yet reality seemed designed always to frustrate them. Reaching back to Greek mythology, Camus presented Sisyphus as the archetypal modern personality. Sisyphus was condemned to roll a rock up a hill, only to find that each time, just as it neared the top, the rock would roll back to the bottom again. In the novel from which we draw, *The Plague,* Camus presents the different approaches to calamity taken by an atheistic doctor and a good but traditional priest. The death of innocent children puts the sharpest possible edge on the question of faith in God. The doctor is Camus's modern hero: the person who keeps doing what is right, admirable, in the service of humankind, even though he or she believes in no God who might finally reward such behavior.

The second selection, from the writings of William James (1842–1910), takes a different approach to religion. James is one of the most famous of America's creative philosophers. His school, known as pragmatism, opposed the idealism that was dominant in the last quarter of the nineteenth century. Idealism made the intellectual content of a proposition the key to its significance. James and other Americans, such as John Dewey, were more interested in experience and results. To their minds, truth appeared not just in clear ideas but also, and more fully, in practice. A good idea showed its goodness by producing good effects. James had a long interest in religion, and his book *The Varieties of Religious Experience* was a pioneering effort to make a place for the mystical and supernatural aspects of human existence. When he stepped back to think about how religion functioned in human culture, his pragmatism led him to stress the ways that religion helps people to cope with things they do not understand. James opposed rationalists who ruled that religion dealt only with feelings, subjectivity, the irrational. Looking at how people used their religious convictions and practices, he found that religion could be a profound help in coping with a world that never granted human beings full understanding, and so James gave religion an objective, rational weight. This did not mean that James accepted traditional Christian views of God. He did not. But it did mean that he granted religious people the right to use their faith, inasmuch as they found that it strengthened them or eased their way through difficult times.

A third aspect of the question of faith that interested many intellectuals in the late nineteenth and early twentieth centuries was the relation between science and religion. Albert Einstein (1879–1955), the greatest physicist since Newton, struggled with this question. In his later years, when ethical issues arising from the development of the atomic bomb were much on his mind, he became convinced that science and religion are more complementary than antagonistic. Science deals with facts, objective relationships in the physical world. Religion deals with values, choices that go beyond the matter of simple physical facts. If each sticks to its proper zone there should be little conflict. In taking such a position, Einstein was being more positive toward religion than many of his fellow scientists would have been. Like James's rationalist, many modern scientists have considered religion completely irrational—no more objective or probative than poetry or private emotion. Since the time of Einstein, science itself has become more complicated, more intuitive, less rationalistic. This has led many thinkers to suspect that science, art, and religion can often be grappling with similar questions, only using different data and methods of analysis. The world remains mysterious, even after brilliant developments in astronomy, physics, and biology. Einstein reminds us that many exceptionally creative people have chafed under artificial disjunctions among the different ways of studying reality and have longed to give the wonderful character of reality its full due.

The last selection comes from a famous work by Rudolf Otto (1869–1937), *The Idea of the Holy.* Otto was a German professor who did pioneering studies in the phenomenology of religion. He helped to found the discipline known in the United States as the history of religions. In analyzing the idea of the holy, Otto was seeking to determine the components of the human experience of sacredness. What goes into the encounter with the holy, the divine, the ultimate and really real? Across historical periods and cultures many different human beings have reported such encounters. Almost always they have claimed that their lives were changed profoundly. Otto found that the holy is a mystery that induces fear yet is enormously attractive. It makes one's hair stand on end because it seems all-powerful and of blazing purity. On the other hand, it is the most beautiful, alluring thing that one has ever met. So, typically, the person who has a numinous experience (an encounter with the divine or holy) is torn. Part of the person wants to run away, but another part wants to stay, abide, never leave what has been so fascinating. In our selection, Otto focuses on the third part of the experience, the sense that one is dealing with a mystery. A mystery is more than a puzzle. We shall never solve a mystery. It is a fullness of light and being, a surplus of significance and value. It may be precisely that for which our souls have been made.

These four selections are far from exhausting the question of faith or the nature of religion. All the selections in this reader bear on this question, because people's religious experiences, myths, rituals, doctrines, ethical stances, convictions about religious community, and efforts to find new ways to deal with ultimate issues are all relevant. Nonetheless, hearing from four influential writers who could not leave the question of faith alone should remind us that literature, philosophy, science, and psychology are never far from religious questions. Always, the mystery at the core of human existence colors what people do. So, always, there is the chance to propose a dialogue.

28

Albert Camus

Excerpt from *The Plague**

Albert Camus (1913–1960) was one of the best-known of the "existentialists," thinkers who emphasized the individual and the freedom over the universe that he or she can have. In the novel from which this reading is taken, The Plague, *Camus offers the contrasting characters of a traditional priest and an atheistic doctor forced to grapple with the question of faith in God when facing the seemingly senseless deaths caused by a horrible outbreak of disease.*

Toward the close of October Castel's anti-plague serum was tried for the first time. Practically speaking, it was Rieux's last card. If it failed, the doctor was convinced the whole town would be at the mercy of the epidemic, which would either continue its ravages for an unpredictable period or perhaps die out abruptly of its own accord.

The day before Castel called on Rieux, M. Othon's son had fallen ill and all the family had to go into quarantine. Thus the mother, who had only recently come out of it, found herself isolated once again. In deference to the official regulations the magistrate had promptly sent for Dr. Rieux the moment he saw symptoms of the disease in his little boy. Mother and father were standing at the bedside when Rieux entered the room. The boy was in the phase of extreme prostration and submitted without a whimper to the doctor's examination. When Rieux raised his eyes he saw the magistrate's gaze intent on him, and, behind, the mother's pale face. She was holding a handkerchief to her mouth, and her big, dilated eyes followed each of the doctor's movements.

"He has it, I suppose?" the magistrate asked in a toneless voice.

"Yes." Rieux gazed down at the child again.

The mother's eyes widened yet more, but she still said nothing. M. Othon, too, kept silent for a while before saying in an even lower tone:

"Well, doctor, we must do as we are told to do."

Rieux avoided looking at Mme Othon, who was still holding her handkerchief to her mouth.

"It needn't take long," he said rather awkwardly, "if you'll let me use your phone."

The magistrate said he would take him to the telephone. But before going, the doctor turned toward Mme Othon.

"I regret very much indeed, but I'm afraid you'll have to get your things ready. You know how it is."

Mme Othon seemed disconcerted. She was staring at the floor.

Then, "I understand," she murmured, slowly nodding her head. "I'll set about it at once."

Before leaving, Rieux on a sudden impulse asked the Othons if there wasn't anything they'd like him to do for them. The mother gazed at him in silence. And now the magistrate averted his eyes.

"No," he said, then swallowed hard. "But—save my son."

In the early days a mere formality, quarantine had now been reorganized by Rieux and Rambert on very strict lines. In particular they insisted on having members of the family of a patient kept apart. If, unawares, one of them had been infected, the risks of an extension of the infection must not be multiplied. Rieux explained this to the magistrate, who signified his approval of the procedure. Nevertheless, he and his wife exchanged a glance that made it clear to Rieux how keenly they both felt the separation thus imposed on them. Mme Othon and her little girl could be given rooms in the quarantine hospital under Rambert's charge. For the magistrate, however, no accommodation was available except in an isolation camp the authorities were now installing in the municipal stadium, using tents supplied by the highway department. When Rieux apologized for the poor accommodation, M. Othon replied that there was one rule for all alike, and it was only proper to abide by it.

The boy was taken to the auxiliary hospital and put in a ward of ten beds which had formerly been a classroom. After some twenty hours Rieux became convinced that the case was hopeless. The infection was steadily spreading, and the boy's body putting up no resistance. Tiny, half-formed, but acutely painful buboes were clogging the joints of the child's puny limbs. Obviously it was a losing fight.

Under the circumstances Rieux had no qualms about testing Castel's serum on the boy. That night, after dinner, they performed the inoculation, a lengthy process, without getting the slightest reaction. At daybreak on the following day they gathered round the bed to observe the effects of this test inoculation on which so much hung.

The child had come out of his extreme prostration and was tossing about convulsively on the bed. From four in the morning Dr. Castel and Tarrou had been keeping watch and noting, stage by stage, the progress and remissions of the malady. Tarrou's bulky form was slightly drooping at the head of the bed, while at its foot, with Rieux standing beside him, Castel was seated, reading, with every appearance of calm, an old leather-bound book. One by one, as the light increased in the former classroom, the others arrived. Paneloux, the first to come, leaned against the wall on the opposite side of the bed to Tarrou. His face was drawn with grief, and the accumulated weariness of many weeks, during which he had never spared himself, had deeply seamed his somewhat prominent forehead. Grand came next. It was seven o'clock, and he apologized for being out of breath; he could only stay a moment, but wanted to know if any definite results had been observed. Without speaking, Rieux pointed to the child. His eyes shut, his teeth clenched, his features frozen in an agonized grimace, he was rolling his head from side to side on the bolster. When there was just light enough to make out the half-obliterated figures of an equation chalked on a blackboard that still hung on the wall at the far end of the room, Rambert entered. Posting himself at the foot of the next bed, he took a package of cigarettes from his pocket. But after his first glance at the child's face he put it back.

From his chair Castel looked at Rieux over his spectacles.

"Any news of his father?"

"No," said Rieux. "He's in the isolation camp."

The doctor's hands were gripping the rail of the bed, his eyes fixed on the small tortured body. Suddenly it stiffened, and seemed to give a little at the waist, as slowly the arms and legs spread out X-wise. From the body, naked under an army blanket, rose a smell of damp wool and stale sweat. The boy had gritted his teeth again. Then very gradually he relaxed, bringing his arms and legs back toward the center of the bed, still without speaking or opening his eyes, and his breathing seemed to quicken. Rieux looked at Tarrou, who hastily lowered his eyes.

They had already seen children die—for many months now death had shown no favoritism—but they had never yet watched a child's agony minute by minute, as they had now been doing since daybreak. Needless to say, the pain inflicted on these innocent victims had always seemed to them to be what in fact it was: an abominable thing. But hitherto they had felt its abomination in, so to speak, an abstract way; they had never had to witness over so long a period the death-throes of an innocent child.

And just then the body had a sudden spasm, as if something had bitten him in the stomach, and uttered a long, shrill wail. For moments that seemed endless he stayed in a queer, contorted position, his body racked by convulsive tremors; it was as if his frail frame were bending before the fierce breath of the plague, breaking under the reiterated gusts of fever. Then the storm-wind passed, there came a lull, and he relaxed a little; the fever seemed to recede, leaving him gasping for breath on a dank, pestilential shore, lost in a languor that already looked like death. When for the third time the fiery wave broke on him, lifting him a little, the child curled himself up and shrank away to the edge of the bed, as if in terror of the flames advancing on him, licking his limbs. A moment later, after tossing his head wildly to and fro, he flung off the blanket. From between the inflamed eyelids big tears welled up and trickled down the sunken, leaden-hued cheeks. When the spasm had passed, utterly exhausted, tensing his thin legs and arms, on which, within forty-eight hours, the flesh had wasted to the bone, the child lay flat, racked on the tumbled bed, in a grotesque parody of crucifixion.

Bending, Tarrou gently stroked with his big paw the small face stained with tears and sweat. Castel had closed his book a few moments before, and his eyes were now fixed on the child. He began to speak, but had to give a cough before continuing, because his voice rang out so harshly.

"There wasn't any remission this morning, was there, Rieux?"

Rieux shook his head, adding, however, that the child was putting up more resistance than one would have expected. Paneloux, who was slumped against the wall, said in a low voice:

"So if he is to die, he will have suffered longer."

Light was increasing in the ward. The occupants of the other nine beds were tossing about and groaning, but in tones that seemed deliberately subdued. Only one, at the far end of the ward, was screaming, or rather uttering little exclamations at regular intervals, which seemed to convey surprise more than pain. Indeed, one had the impression that even for the sufferers the frantic terror of the early phase had passed, and there was a sort of mournful resignation in their present attitude toward the disease. Only the child went on fighting with all his little might. Now and then Rieux took his pulse—less because this served any purpose than as an escape from his utter helplessness—and when he closed his eyes, he seemed to feel its tumult mingling with the fever of his own blood. And then, at one with the tortured child, he struggled to sustain him with all the remaining strength of his own body. But, linked for a few moments, the rhythms of their heartbeats soon fell apart, the child escaped him, and again he knew his impotence. Then he released the small, thin wrist and moved back to his place.

The light on the whitewashed walls was changing from pink to yellow. The first waves of another day of heat were beating on the windows. They hardly heard Grand saying he would come back as he turned to go. All were waiting. The child, his eyes still closed, seemed to grow a little calmer. His clawlike fingers were feebly plucking at the sides of the bed. Then they rose, scratched at the blanket over his knees, and suddenly he doubled up his limbs, bringing his thighs above his stomach, and remained quite still. For the first time he opened his eyes and gazed at Rieux, who was standing immediately in front of him. In the small face, rigid as a mask of grayish clay, slowly the lips parted and from them rose a long, incessant scream, hardly varying with his respiration, and filling the ward with a fierce, indignant protest, so little childish that it seemed like a collective voice issuing from all the sufferers there. Rieux clenched his jaws, Tarrou looked away. Rambert went and stood beside Castel, who closed the book lying on his knees. Paneloux gazed down at the small mouth, fouled with the sores of the plague and pouring out the angry death-cry that has sounded through the ages of mankind. He sank on his knees, and all present found it natural to hear him say in a voice hoarse but clearly audible across that nameless, never ending wail:

"My God, spare this child!"

But the wail continued without cease and the other sufferers began to grow restless. The patient at the far end of the ward, whose little broken cries had gone on without a break, now quickened their tempo so that they flowed together in one unbroken cry, while the others' groans grew louder. A gust of sobs swept through the room, drowning Paneloux's prayer, and Rieux, who was still tightly gripping the rail of the bed, shut his eyes, dazed with exhaustion and disgust.

When he opened them again, Tarrou was at his side.

"I must go," Rieux said. "I can't bear to hear them any longer."

But then, suddenly, the other sufferers fell silent. And now the doctor grew aware that the child's wail, after weakening more and more, had fluttered out into silence. Around him the groans began again, but more faintly, like a far echo of the fight that now was over. For it was over. Castel had moved round to the other side of the bed and said the end had come. His mouth still gaping, but silent now, the child was lying among the tumbled blankets, a small, shrunken form, with the tears still wet on his cheeks.

Paneloux went up to the bed and made the sign of benediction. Then gathering up his cassock, he walked out by the passage between the beds.

"Will you have to start it all over again?" Tarrou asked Castel.

The old doctor nodded slowly, with a twisted smile.

"Perhaps. After all, he put up a surprisingly long resistance."

Rieux was already on his way out, walking so quickly and with such a strange look on his face that Paneloux put out an arm to check him when he was about to pass him in the doorway.

"Come, doctor," he began.

Rieux swung round on him fiercely.

"Ah! That child, anyhow, was innocent, and you know it as well as I do!"

He strode on, brushing past Paneloux, and walked across the school playground. Sitting on a wooden bench under the dingy, stunted trees, he wiped off the sweat that was beginning to run into his eyes. He felt like shouting imprecations—anything to loosen the stranglehold lashing his heart with steel. Heat was flooding down between the branches of the fig trees. A white haze, spreading rapidly over the blue of the morning sky, made the air yet more stifling. Rieux lay back wearily on the bench. Gazing up at the ragged branches, the shimmering sky, he slowly got back his breath and fought down his fatigue.

He heard a voice behind him. "Why was there that anger in your voice just now? What we'd been seeing was as unbearable to me as it was to you."

Rieux turned toward Paneloux.

"I know. I'm sorry. But weariness is a kind of madness. And there are times when the only feeling I have is one of mad revolt."

"I understand," Paneloux said in a low voice. "That sort of thing is revolting because it passes our human understanding. But perhaps we should love what we cannot understand."

Rieux straightened up slowly. He gazed at Paneloux, summoning to his gaze all the strength and fervor he could muster against his weariness. Then he shook his head.

"No, Father. I've a very different idea of love. And until my dying day I shall refuse to love a scheme of things in which children are put to torture."

A shade of disquietude crossed the priest's face. "Ah, doctor," he said sadly, "I've just realized what is meant by 'grace.'"

Rieux had sunk back again on the bench. His lassitude had returned and from its depths he spoke, more gently:

"It's something I haven't got; that I know. But I'd rather not discuss that with you. We're working side by side for something that unites us—beyond blasphemy and prayers. And it's the only thing that matters."

Paneloux sat down beside Rieux. It was obvious that he was deeply moved.

"Yes, yes," he said, "you, too, are working for man's salvation."

Rieux tried to smile.

"Salvation's much too big a word for me. I don't aim so high. I'm concerned with man's health; and for me his health comes first."

Paneloux seemed to hesitate. "Doctor—" he began, then fell silent. Down his face, too, sweat was trickling. Murmuring: "Good-by for the present," he rose. His eyes were moist. When he turned to go, Rieux, who had seemed lost in thought, suddenly rose and took a step toward him.

"Again, please forgive me. I can promise there won't be another outburst of that kind."

Paneloux held out his hand, saying regretfully:

"And yet—I haven't convinced you!"

"What does it matter? What I hate is death and disease, as you well know. And whether you wish it or not, we're allies, facing them and fighting them together." Rieux was still holding Paneloux's hand. "So you see"—but he refrained from meeting the priest's eyes—"God Himself can't part us now."

29

William James

"Pragmatism and Religion" from *Pragmatism and Other Essays**

The prominent American philosopher William James (1842–1910) offers a unique view of religion and faith in his essay "Pragmatism and Religion." While he did not personally accept traditional Christian views of God, he acknowledged that they were helpful to the faithful. The pragmatic James found that faith in God could be a great comfort to people trying to function in a world where they could never reach a full understanding of life.

At the close of the last lecture I reminded you of the first one, in which I had opposed tough-mindedness to tender-mindedness and recommended pragmatism as their mediator. Tough-mindedness positively rejects tender-mindedness's hypothesis of an eternal perfect edition of the universe coexisting with our finite experience.

On pragmatic principles we can not reject any hypothesis if consequences useful to life flow from it. Universal conceptions, as things to take account of, may be as real for pragmatism as particular sensations are. They have, indeed, no meaning and no reality if they have no use. But if they have any use they have that amount of meaning. And the meaning will be true if the use squares well with life's other uses.

Well, the use of the Absolute is proved by the whole course of men's religious history. The eternal arms are then beneath. Remember Vivekananda's use of the Atman—not indeed a scientific use, for we can make no particular deductions from it. It is emotional and spiritual altogether.

It is always best to discuss things by the help of concrete examples. Let me read therefore some of those verses entitled "To You" by Walt Whitman— "You" of course meaning the reader or hearer of the poem whosoever he or she may be.

> Whoever you are, now I place my hand upon you that you
>   be my poem;
> I whisper with my lips close to your ear,
> I have loved many men and women and men, but I love none
>   better than you.

O I have been dilatory and dumb;
I should have made my way to you long ago;
I should have blabbed nothing but you, I should have chanted
    nothing but you.

I will leave all and come and make the hymns of you;
None have understood you, but I understand you;
None have done justice to you—you have not done justice to
    yourself;
None but have found you imperfect—I only find no
    imperfection in you.
O I could sing such glories and grandeurs about you;
You have not known what you are—you have slumbered upon
    yourself all your life;
What you have done returns already in mockeries.

But the mockeries are not you;
Underneath them and within them, I see you lurk
I pursue you where none else has pursued you.
Silence, the desk, the flippant expression, the night, the
    accustomed routine, if these conceal you from others,
    or from yourself, they do not conceal you from me;
The shaved face, the unsteady eye, the impure complexion,
    if these balk others, they do not balk me;
The pert apparel, the deformed attitude, drunkenness, greed,
    premature death, all these I part aside.

There is no endowment in man or woman that is not tallied
    in you;
There is no virtue, no beauty, in man or woman, but as good
    is in you;
No pluck nor endurance in others, but as good is in you;
No pleasure waiting for others, but an equal pleasure waits
    for you.

Whoever you are! claim your own at any hazard!
These shows of the east and west are tame, compared with
    you;
These immense meadows—these interminable rivers—you are
    immense and interminable as they;
You are he or she who is master or mistress over them,
Master or mistress in your own right over Nature, elements,
    pain, passion, dissolution.

The hobbles fall from your ankles—you find an unfailing
    sufficiency;
Old or young, male or female, rude, low, rejected by the rest
    whatever you are promulges itself;
Through birth, life, death, burial, the means are provided,
    nothing is scanted;
Through angers, losses, ambition, ignorance, ennui, what you
    are picks its way.

Verily a fine and moving poem, in any case, but there are two ways of taking it, both useful.

One is the monistic way, the mystical way of pure cosmic emotion. The glories and grandeurs, they are yours absolutely, even in the midst of your defacements. Whatever may happen to you, whatever you may appear to be, inwardly you are safe. Look back, *lie* back, on your true principle of being! This is the famous way of quietism, of indifferentism. Its enemies compare it to a spiritual opium. Yet pragmatism must respect this way, for it has massive historic vindication.

But pragmatism sees another way to be respected also, the pluralistic way of interpreting the poem. The you so glorified, to which the hymn is sung, may mean your better possibilities phenomenally taken, or the specific redemptive effects even of your failures, upon yourself or others. It may mean your loyalty to the possibilities of others whom you admire and love so that you are willing to accept your own poor life, for it is that glory's partner. You can at least appreciate, applaud, furnish the audience, of so brave a total world. Forget the low in yourself, then, think only of the high. Identify your life therewith; then, through angers, losses, ignorance, ennui, whatever you thus make yourself, whatever you thus most deeply are, picks its way.

In either way of taking the poem, it encourages fidelity to ourselves. Both ways satisfy; both sanctify the human flux. Both paint the portrait of the *you* on a gold background. But the background of the first way is the static One, while in the second way it means possibles in the plural, genuine possibles, and it has all the restlessness of that conception.

Noble enough is either way of reading the poem; but plainly the pluralistic way agrees with the pragmatic temper best, for it immediately suggests an infinitely larger number of the details of future experience to our mind. It sets definite activities in us at work. Altho this second way seems prosaic and earth-born in comparison with the first way, yet no one can accuse it of tough-mindedness in any brutal sense of the term. Yet if, as pragmatists, you should positively set up the second way *against* the first way, you would very likely be misunderstood. You would be accused of denying nobler conceptions, and of being an ally of tough-mindedness in the worst sense.

You remember the letter from a member of this audience from which I read some extracts at our previous meeting. Let me read you an additional extract now. It shows a vagueness in realizing the alternatives before us which I think is very widespread.

"I believe," writes my friend and correspondent, "in pluralism; I believe that in our search for truth we leap from one floating cake of ice to another, on an infinite sea, and that by each of our acts we make new truths possible and old ones impossible; I believe that each man is responsible for making the universe better, and that if he does not do this it will be in so far left undone.

"Yet at the same time I am willing to endure that my children should be incurably sick and suffering (as they are not) and I myself stupid and yet with brains enough to see my stupidity, only on one condition, namely, that through the construction, in imagination and by reasoning, of a *rational unity of all things,*

I can conceive my acts and my thoughts and my troubles as *supplemented by all the other phenomena of the world, and as forming—when thus supplemented—a scheme which I approve and adopt as my own;* and for my part I refuse to be persuaded that we can not look beyond the obvious pluralism of the naturalist and pragmatist to a logical unity in which they take no interest or stock."

Such a fine expression of personal faith warms the heart of the hearer. But how much does it clear his philosophic head? Does the writer consistently favor the monistic, or the pluralistic, interpretation of the world's poem? His troubles become atoned for *when thus supplemented,* he says, supplemented, that is, by all the remedies that *the other phenomena* may supply. Obviously here the writer faces forward into the particulars of experience, which he interprets in a pluralistic-melioristic way.

But he believes himself to face backward. He speaks of what he calls the rational *unity* of things, when all the while he really means their possible empirical *unification.* He supposes at the same time that the pragmatist, because he criticizes rationalism's abstract One, is cut off from the consolation of believing in the saving possibilities of the concrete many. He fails in short to distinguish between taking the world's perfection as a necessary principle, and taking it only as a possible *terminus ad quem* [goal].

I regard the writer of the letter as a genuine pragmatist but as a pragmatist *sans le savoir* [without knowing it]. He appears to me as one of that numerous class of philosophic amateurs whom I spoke of in my first lecture, as wishing to have all the good things going, without being too careful as to how they agree or disagree. "Rational unity of all things" is so inspiring a formula, that he brandishes it off-hand, and abstractly accuses pluralism of conflicting with it (for the bare names do conflict), although concretely he means by it just the pragmatistically unified and ameliorated world. Most of us remain in this essential vagueness, and it is well that we should, but in the interest of clearheadedness it is well that some of us should go farther, so I will try now to focus a little more discriminatingly on this particular religious point.

Is then this *you of yous,* this absolutely real world, this unity that yields the moral inspiration and has the religious value, to be taken monistically or pluralistically? Is it *ante rem* [before the fact] or *in rebus* [in the matter itself]? Is it a principle or an end, an absolute or an ultimate, a first or a last? Does it make you look forward or lie back? It is certainly worth while not to clump the two things together, for if discriminated, they have decidedly diverse meanings for life.

Please observe that the whole dilemma revolves pragmatically about the notion of the world's possibilities. Intellectually, rationalism invokes its absolute principle of unity, as a ground of possibility for the many facts. Emotionally, it sees it as a container and limiter of possibilities, a guarantee that the upshot shall be good. Taken in this way, the absolute makes all good things certain, and all bad things impossible (in the eternal, namely), and may be said to transmute the entire category of possibility into categories more secure. One sees at this point that the great religious differences lies between the men who insist that the world *must and shall be,* and those who are contented with believing that the world *may be,* saved. The whole clash of rationalistic and empiricist religion is thus over the validity of possibility. It is necessary therefore to begin by focusing upon that word. What may the word "possible" definitely mean? To unreflecting men it means a sort of third estate of being, less real than existence, more real than non-existence, a twilight realm, a hybrid status, a limbo into which and out of which realities ever and anon are made to pass.

Such a conception is of course too vague and nondescript to satisfy us. Here, as elsewhere, the only way to extract a term's meaning is to use the pragmatic method on it. When you say that a thing is possible, what difference does it make? It makes at least this difference, that if any one calls it impossible you can contradict him, if any one calls it actual you can contradict *him,* and if any one calls it necessary you can contradict him too.

But these privileges of contradiction don't amount to much. When you say a thing is possible, does not that make some farther difference in terms of actual fact?

It makes at least this negative difference, that if the statement be true, it follows that *there is nothing extant capable of preventing* the possible thing. The absence of real grounds of interference may thus be said to make things *not impossible,* possible therefore in the *bare* or *abstract* sense.

But most possibles are not bare, they are concretely grounded, or well-grounded, as we say. What does this mean pragmatically? It means not only that there are no preventive conditions present, but that some of the conditions of production of the possible thing actually are here. Thus a concretely possible chicken means: (1) that the idea of chicken contains no essential self-contradiction; (2) that no boys, skunks, or other enemies are about; and (3) that at least an actual egg exists. Possible chicken means actual egg—plus actual sitting hen, or incubator, or what not. As the actual conditions approach completeness the chicken becomes a better-and-better-grounded possibility. When the conditions are entirely complete, it ceases to be a possibility, and turns into an actual fact.

Let us apply this notion to the salvation of the world. What does it pragmatically mean to say that this is possible? It means that some of the conditions of the world's deliverance do actually exist. The more of them there are existent, the fewer preventing conditions you can find, the better-grounded is the salvation's possibility, the more *probable* does the fact of the deliverance become.

So much for our preliminary look at possibility.

Now it would contradict the very spirit of life to say that our minds must be indifferent and neutral in questions like that of the world's salvation. Any one who pretends to be neutral writes himself down here as a fool and a sham. We all do wish to minimize the insecurity of the universe, we are and ought to be unhappy when we regard it as exposed to every enemy and open to every life-destroying draft. Nevertheless there are unhappy men who think the salvation of the world impossible. Theirs is the doctrine known as pessimism.

Optimism in turn would be the doctrine that thinks the world's salvation inevitable.

Midway between the two there stands what may be called the doctrine of meliorism, though it has hitherto figured less as a doctrine than as an attitude in human affairs. Optimism has always been the regnant *doctrine* in European philosophy. Pessimism was only recently introduced by Schopenhauer and counts few systematic defenders as yet. Meliorism treats salvation as neither necessary nor impossible. It treats it as a possibility, which becomes more and more of a probability the more numerous the actual conditions of salvation become.

It is clear that pragmatism must incline towards meliorism. Some conditions of the world's salvation are actually extant, and she can not possibly close her eyes to this fact: and should the residual conditions come, salvation would become an accomplished reality. Naturally the terms I use here are exceedingly summary. You may interpret the word "salvation" in any way you like, and make it as diffuse and distributive, or as climacteric and integral a phenomenon as you please.

Take, for example, any one of us in this room with the ideals which he cherishes and is willing to live and work for. Every such ideal realized will be one moment in the world's salvation. But these particular ideals are not bare abstract possibilities. They are grounded, they are *live* possibilities, for we are their live champions and pledges, and if the complementary conditions come and add themselves, our ideals will become actual things. What now are the complementary conditions? They are first such a mixture of things as will in the fullness of time give us a chance, a gap that we can spring into, and, finally, *our act*.

Does our act then *create* the world's salvation so far as it makes room for itself, so far as it leaps into the gap? Does it create, not the whole world's salvation of course, but just so much of this as itself covers of the world's extent?

Here I take the bull by the horns, and in spite of the whole crew of rationalists and monists, of whatever brand they be, I ask *why not*? Our acts, our turning-places, where we seem to ourselves to make ourselves and grow, are the parts of the world to which we are closest, the parts of which our knowledge is the most intimate and complete. Why should we not take them at their face value? Why may they not be the actual turning-places and growing-places which they seem to be, of the world—why not the workshop of being, where we catch fact in the making, so that nowhere may the world grow in any other kind of way than this?

Irrational! we are told. How can new being come in local spots and patches which add themselves or stay away at random, independently of the rest? There must be a reason for our acts, and where in the last resort can any reason be looked for save in the material pressure or the logical compulsion of the total nature of the world? There can be but one real agent of growth, or seeming growth, anywhere, and that agent is the integral world itself. It may grow all-over, if growth there be, but that single parts should grow *per se* is irrational.

But if one talks of rationality—and of reasons for things, and insists that they can't just come in spots, what *kind* of a reason can there ultimately be why anything should come at all? Talk of logic and necessity and categories and the absolute and the contents of the whole philosophical machine-shop as you will, the only *real* reason I can think of why anything should ever come is that *some one wishes it to be here*. It is *demanded*—demanded, it may be, to give relief to no matter how small a fraction of the world's mass. This is *living reason,* and compared with it material causes and logical necessities are spectral things.

In short the only fully rational world would be the world of wishing-caps, the world of telepathy, where every desire is fulfilled instanter, without having to consider or placate surrounding or intermediate powers. This is the Absolute's own world. He calls upon the phenomenal world to be, and it *is,* exactly as he calls for it, no other condition being required. In our world, the wishes of the individual are only one condition. Other individuals are there with other wishes and they must be propitiated first. So Being grows under all sorts of resistances in this world of the many, and, from compromise to compromise, only gets organized gradually into what may be called secondarily rational shape. We approach the wishing-cap type of organization only in a few departments of life. We want water and we turn a faucet. We want a kodak-picture and we press a button. We want information and we telephone. We want to travel and we buy a ticket. In these and similar cases, we hardly need to do more than the wishing—the world is rationally organized to do the rest.

But this talk of rationality is a parenthesis and a digression. What we were discussing was the idea of a world growing not integrally but piecemeal by the contributions of its several parts. Take the hypothesis seriously and as a live one. Suppose that the world's author put the case to you before creation, saying: "I am going to make a world not certain to be saved, a world the perfection of which shall be conditional merely, the condition being that each several agent does its own 'level best.' I offer you the chance of taking part in such a world. Its safety, you see, is unwarranted. It is a real adventure, with real danger, yet it may win through. It is a social scheme of co-operative work genuinely to be done. Will you join the procession? Will you trust yourself and trust the other agents enough to face the risk?"

Should you in all seriousness, if participation in such a world were proposed to you, feel bound to reject it as not safe enough? Would you say that, rather than be part and parcel of so fundamentally pluralistic and irrational a universe, you preferred to relapse into the slumber of nonentity from which you had been momentarily aroused by the tempter's voice?

Of course if you are normally constituted, you would do nothing of the sort. There is a healthy-minded buoyancy in most of us which such a universe would exactly fit. We would therefore accept the offer—"Top! und schlag auf schlag!" ["Right on! and blow to blow!"] It would be just like the world we practically live in; and loyalty to our old nurse Nature would forbid us to say no. The world proposed would seem "rational" to us in the most living way.

Most of us, I say, would therefore welcome the proposition and add our *fiat* to the *fiat* of the creator. Yet perhaps some would not, for there are morbid minds in every human collection, and to them the prospect of a universe with only a fighting chance of safety would probably make no appeal. There are moments of discouragement in us all, when we are sick of self and tired of vainly striving. Our own life breaks down, and we fall into the attitude of the prodigal son. We mistrust the chances of things. We want a universe where we can just give up, fall on our father's neck, and be absorbed into the absolute life as a drop of water melts into the river or the sea.

The peace and rest, the security desiderated at such moments is security against the bewildering accidents of so much finite experience. Nirvana means safety from this everlasting round of adventures of which the world of sense consists. The Hindoo and the Buddhist, for this is essentially their attitude, are simply afraid, afraid of more experience, afraid of life.

And to men of this complexion, religious monism comes with its consoling words: "All is needed and essential—even you with your sick soul and heart. All are one with God, and with God all is well. The everlasting arms are beneath, whether in the world of finite appearance you seem to fail or to succeed." There can be no doubt that when men are reduced to their last sick extremity absolutism is the only saving scheme. Pluralistic moralism simply makes their teeth chatter, it refrigerates the very heart within their breast.

So we see concretely two types of religion in sharp contrast. Using our old terms of comparison, we may say that the absolutistic scheme appeals to the tender-minded while the pluralistic scheme appeals to the tough. Many persons would refuse to call the pluralistic scheme religious at all. They would call it moralistic, and would apply the word religious to the monistic scheme alone. Religion in the sense of self-surrender, and moralism in the sense of self-sufficingness, have been pitted against each other as incompatibles frequently enough in the history of human thought.

We stand here before the final question of philosophy. I said in my fourth lecture that I believed the monistic-pluralistic alternative to be the deepest and most pregnant question that our minds can frame. Can it be that the disjunction is a final one? that only one side can be true? Are a pluralism and monism genuine incompatibles? So that, if the world were really pluralistically constituted, if it really existed distributively and were made up of a lot of eaches, it could only be saved piecemeal and *de facto* as the result of their behavior, and its epic history in no wise short-circuited by some essential oneness in which the severalness were already "taken up" beforehand and eternally "overcome"? If this were so, we should have to choose one philosophy or the other. We could not say "yes, yes" to both alternatives. There would have to be a "no" in our relations with the possible. We should confess an ultimate disappointment: we could not remain healthy-minded and sick-minded in one indivisible act.

Of course as human beings we can be healthy minds on one day and sick souls on the next; and as amateur dabblers in philosophy we may perhaps be allowed to call ourselves monistic pluralists, or free-will determinists, or whatever else may occur to us of a reconciling kind. But as philosophers aiming at clearness and consistency, and feeling the pragmatistic need of squaring truth with truth, the question is forced upon us of frankly adopting either the tender or the robustious type of thought. In particular *this* query has always come home to me: May not the claims of tender-mindedness go too far? May not the notion of a world already saved *in toto* anyhow, be too saccharine to stand? May not religious optimism be too idyllic? Must *all* be saved? Is *no* price to be paid in the work of salvation? Is the last word sweet? Is all "yes, yes" in the universe? Doesn't the fact of "no" stand at the very core of life? Doesn't the very "seriousness" that we attribute to life mean that ineluctable no's and losses form a part of it, that there are genuine sacrifices somewhere, and that something permanently drastic and bitter always remains at the bottom of its cup?

I can not speak officially as a pragmatist here; all I can say is that my own pragmatism offers no objection to my taking sides with this more moralistic view, and giving up the claim of total reconciliation. The possibility of this is involved in the pragmatistic willingness to treat pluralism as a serious hypothesis. In the end it is our faith and not our logic that decides such questions, and I deny the right of any pretended logic to veto my own faith. I find myself willing to take the universe to be really dangerous and adventurous, without therefore backing out and crying "no play." I am willing to think that the prodigal-son attitude, open to us as it is in many vicissitudes, is not the right and final attitude towards the whole of life. I am willing that there should be real losses and real losers, and no total preservation of all that is. I can believe in the ideal as an ultimate, not as an origin, and as an extract, not the whole. When the cup is poured off, the dregs are left behind for ever, but the possibility of what is poured off is sweet enough to accept.

As a matter of fact countless human imaginations live in this moralistic and epic kind of a universe, and find its disseminated and strung-along successes sufficient for their rational needs. There is a finely translated epigram in the Greek anthology which admirably expresses this state of mind, this acceptance of loss as unatoned for, even though the lost element might be one's self:

> A shipwrecked sailor, buried on this coast,
>   Bids you set sail.
> Full many a gallant bark, when we were lost,
>   Weathered the gale.

Those puritans who answered "yes" to the question: Are you willing to be damned for God's glory? were in this objective and magnanimous condition of mind. The way of escape from evil on this system is *not* by getting it "aufgehoben," or preserved in the whole as an element essential but "overcome." *It is by dropping it out altogether, throwing it overboard and getting beyond it, helping to make a universe that shall forget its very place and name.*

It is then perfectly possible to accept sincerely a drastic kind of a universe from which the element of "seriousness" is not to be expelled. Whoso does so is, it seems to me, a genuine pragmatist. He is willing to live on a scheme of uncertified possibilities which he trusts; willing to pay with his own person, if need be, for the realization of the ideals which he frames.

What now actually *are* the other forces which he trusts to co-operate with him, in a universe of such a type? They are at least his fellow men, in the stage of being which our actual universe has reached. But are there not superhuman forces also, such as religious men of the pluralistic type we have been considering have always believed in? Their words may have sounded monistic when they said "there is no God but God;" but the original polytheism of mankind has only imperfectly and vaguely sublimated itself into monotheism, and monotheism itself, so far as it was religious and not a scheme of classroom instruction for the metaphysicians, has always viewed God as but one helper, *primus inter pares* [first among equals] in the midst of all the shapers of the great world's fate.

I fear that my previous lectures, confined as they have been to human and humanistic aspects, may have left the impression on many of you that pragmatism means methodically to leave the superhuman out. I have shown small respect indeed for the Absolute, and I have until this moment spoken of no other superhuman hypothesis but that. But I trust that you see sufficiently that the Absolute has nothing but its superhumanness in common with the theistic God. On pragmatistic principles, if the hypothesis of God works satisfactorily in the widest sense of the word, it is true. Now whatever its residual difficulties may be, experience shows that it certainly does work, and that the problem is to build it out and determine it so that it will combine satisfactorily with all the other working truths. I can not start upon a whole theology at the end of this last lecture; but when I tell you that I have written a book on men's religious experience, which on the whole has been regarded as making for the reality of God, you will perhaps exempt my own pragmatism from the charge of being an atheistic system. I firmly disbelieve, myself, that our human experience is the highest form of experience extant in the universe. I believe rather that we stand in much the same relation to the whole of the universe as our canine and feline pets do to the whole of human life. They inhabit our drawing-rooms and libraries. They take part in scenes of whose significance they have no inkling. They are merely tangent to curves of history the beginnings and ends and forms of which pass wholly beyond their ken. So we are tangent to the wider life of things. But, just as many of the dog's and cat's ideals coincide with our ideals, and the dogs and cats have daily living proof of the fact, so we may well believe, on the proofs that religious experience affords, that higher powers exist and are at work to save the world on ideal lines similar to our own.

You see that pragmatism can be called religious, if you allow that religion can be pluralistic or merely melioristic in type. But whether you will finally put up with that type of religion or not is a question that only you yourself can decide. Pragmatism has to postpone dogmatic answer, for we do not yet know certainly which type of religion is going to work best in the long run. The various overbeliefs of men, their several faith-ventures, are in fact what are needed to bring the evidence in. You will probably make your own ventures severally. If radically tough, the hurly-burly of the sensible facts of nature will be enough for you, and you will need no religion at all. If radically tender, you will take up with the more monistic form of religion: the pluralistic form, with its reliance on possibilities that are not necessities, will not seem to afford you security enough.

But if you are neither tough nor tender in an extreme and radical sense, but mixed as most of us are, it may seem to you that the type of pluralistic and moralistic religion that I have offered is as good a religious synthesis as you are likely to find. Between the two extremes of crude naturalism on the one hand and transcendental absolutism on the other, you may find that what I take the liberty of calling the pragmatistic or melioristic type of theism is exactly what you require.

30

Albert Einstein

"Science and Religion" from *Out of My Later Years**

The author of the following reading, the great physicist Albert Einstein (1879–1955), had a unique perspective for examining the relationship between religion and science. He confounded many of his fellows scientists by finding the two areas more complementary than antagonistic. These reflections came at a time in his life when he was wrestling with ethical questions, such as those arising from the development of the atomic bomb.

I

During the last century, and part of the one before, it was widely held that there was an unreconcilable conflict between knowledge and belief. The opinion prevailed among advanced minds that it was time that beliefs should be replaced increasingly by knowledge; belief that did not itself rest on knowledge was superstition, and as such had to be opposed. According to this conception, the sole function of education was to open the way to thinking and knowing, and the school, as the outstanding organ for the people's education, must serve that end exclusively.

One will probably find but rarely, if at all, the rationalistic standpoint expressed in such crass form; for any sensible man would see at once how one-sided is such a statement of the position. But it is just as well to state a thesis starkly and nakedly, if one wants to clear up one's mind as to its nature.

It is true that convictions can best be supported with experience and clear thinking. On this point one must agree unreservedly with the extreme rationalist. The weak point of his conception is, however, this, that those convictions which are necessary and determinant for our conduct and judgments, cannot be found solely along this solid scientific way.

For the scientific method can teach us nothing else beyond how facts are related to, and conditioned by, each other. The aspiration toward such objective knowledge belongs to the highest of which man is capable, and you will certainly not suspect me of wishing to belittle the achievements and the heroic efforts of man in this sphere. Yet it is equally clear that knowledge of what *is*

* Albert Einstein, *Out of My Later Years* (New York: The Citadel Press).

does not open the door directly to what *should be*. One can have the clearest and most complete knowledge of what *is*, and yet not be able to deduct from that what should be the *goal* of our human aspirations. Objective knowledge provides us with powerful instruments for the achievements of certain ends, but the ultimate goal itself and the longing to reach it must come from another source. And it is hardly necessary to argue for the view that our existence and our activity acquire meaning only by the setting up of such a goal and of corresponding values. The knowledge of truth as such is wonderful, but it is so little capable of acting as a guide that it cannot prove even the justification and the value of the aspiration towards that very knowledge of truth. Here we face, therefore, the limits of the purely rational conception of our existence.

But it must not be assumed that intelligent thinking can play no part in the formation of the goal and of ethical judgments. When someone realizes that for the achievement of an end certain means would be useful, the means itself becomes thereby an end. Intelligence makes clear to us the interrelation of means and ends. But mere thinking cannot give us a sense of the ultimate and fundamental ends. To make clear these fundamental ends and valuations, and to set them fast in the emotional life of the individual, seems to me precisely the most important function which religion has to perform in the social life of man. And if one asks whence derives the authority of such fundamental ends, since they cannot be stated and justified merely by reason, one can only answer: they exist in a healthy society as powerful traditions, which act upon the conduct and aspirations and judgments of the individuals; they are there, that is, as something living, without its being necessary to find justification for their existence. They come into being not through demonstration but through revelation, through the medium of powerful personalities. One must not attempt to justify them, but rather to sense their nature simply and clearly.

The highest principles for our aspirations and judgments are given to us in the Jewish-Christian religious tradition. It is a very high goal which, with our weak powers, we can reach only very inadequately, but which gives a sure foundation to our aspirations and valuations. If one were to take that goal out of its religious form and look merely at its purely human side, one might state it perhaps thus: free and responsible development of the individual, so that he may place his powers freely and gladly in the service of all mankind.

There is no room in this for the divinization of a nation, of a class, let alone of an individual. Are we not all children of one father, as it is said in religious language? Indeed, even the divinization of humanity, as an abstract totality, would not be in the spirit of that ideal. It is only to the individual that a soul is given. And the high destiny of the individual is to serve rather than to rule, or to impose himself in any other way.

If one looks at the substance rather than at the form, then one can take these words as expressing also the fundamental democratic position. The true democrat can worship his nation as little as can the man who is religious, in our sense of the term.

What, then, in all this, is the function of education and of the school? They should help the young person to grow up in such a spirit that these fundamental principles should be to him as the air which he breathes. Teaching alone cannot do that.

If one holds these high principles clearly before one's eyes, and compares them with the life and spirit of our times, then it appears glaringly that civilized mankind finds itself at present in grave danger. In the totalitarian states it is the rulers themselves who strive actually to destroy that spirit of humanity. In less threatened parts it is nationalism and intolerance, as well as the oppression of the individuals by economic means, which threaten to choke these most precious traditions.

A realization of how great is the danger is spreading, however, among thinking people, and there is much search for means with which to meet the danger—means in the field of national and international politics, of legislation, of organization in general. Such efforts are, no doubt, greatly needed. Yet the ancients know something which we seem to have forgotten. All means prove but a blunt instrument, if they have not behind them a living spirit. But if the longing for the achievement of the goal is powerfully alive within us, then shall we not lack the strength to find the means for reaching the goal and for translating it into deeds.

II

It would not be difficult to come to an agreement as to what we understand by science. Science is the century-old endeavor to bring together by means of systematic thought the perceptible phenomena of this world into as thoroughgoing an association as possible. To put it boldly, it is the attempt at the posterior reconstruction of existence by the process of conceptualization. But when asking myself what religion is I cannot think of the answer so easily. And even after finding an answer which may satisfy me at this particular moment I still remain convinced that I can never under any circumstances bring together, even to a slight extent, all those who have given this question serious consideration.

At first, then, instead of asking what religion is I should prefer to ask what characterizes the aspirations of a person who gives me the impression of being religious: A person who is religiously enlightened appears to me to be one who has, to the best of his ability, liberated himself from the fetters of his selfish desires and is preoccupied with thoughts, feelings, and aspirations to which he clings because of their super-personal value. It seems to me that what is important is the force of this super-personal content and the depth of the conviction concerning its overpowering meaningfulness, regardless of whether any attempt is made to unite this content with a divine Being, for otherwise it would not be possible to count Buddha and Spinoza as religious personalities. Accordingly, a religious person is devout in the sense that he has no doubt of the significance and loftiness of those super-personal objects and goals which neither require nor are capable of rational foundation. They exist with the same necessity and matter-of-factness as he himself. In this sense religion is the age-old endeavor of mankind to become clearly and completely conscious of these values and goals and constantly to strengthen and extend their effect. If one conceives of religion and science according to these definitions then a conflict between them appears impossible. For science can only ascertain what *is*, but not what *should be*, and outside of its domain value judgments of all kinds remain necessary. Religion, on the other hand, deals only with evaluations of human thought and action: it cannot justifiably speak of facts and relationships between facts. According to this interpretation the well-known conflicts between religion and science in the past must all be ascribed to a misapprehension of the situation which has been described.

For example, a conflict arises when a religious community insists on the absolute truthfulness of all statements recorded in the Bible. This means an intervention on the part of religion into the sphere of science; this is where the struggle of the Church against the doctrines of Galileo and Darwin belongs. On the other hand, representatives of science have often made an attempt to arrive at fundamental judgments with respect to values and ends on the basis of scientific method, and in this way have set themselves in opposition to religion. These conflicts have all sprung from fatal errors.

Now, even though the realms of religion and science in themselves are clearly marked off from each other, nevertheless there exist between the two strong reciprocal relationships and dependencies. Though religion may be that which determines the goal, it has, nevertheless, learned from science, in the broadest sense, what means will contribute to the attainment of the goals it has set up. But science can only be created by those who are thoroughly imbued with the aspiration towards truth and understanding. This source of feeling, however, springs from the sphere of religion. To this there also belongs the faith in the possibility that the regulations valid for the world of existence are rational, that is, comprehensible to reason. I cannot conceive of a genuine scientist without that profound faith. The situation may be expressed by an image: Science without religion is lame, religion without science is blind.

Though I have asserted above that in truth a legitimate conflict between religion and science cannot exist I must nevertheless qualify this assertion once again on an essential point, with reference to the actual content of historical religions. This qualification has to do with the concept of God. During the youthful period of mankind's spiritual evolution human fantasy created gods in man's own image, who, by the operations of their will were supposed to determine, or at any rate to influence the phenomenal world. Man sought to alter the disposition of these gods in his own favor by means of magic and prayer. The idea of God in the religions taught at present is a sublimation of that old conception of the gods. Its anthropomorphic character is shown, for instance, by the fact that men appeal to the Divine Being in prayers and plead for the fulfilment of their wishes.

Nobody, certainly, will deny that the idea of the existence of an omnipotent, just and omnibeneficent personal God is able to accord man solace, help, and guidance; also, by virtue of its simplicity it is accessible to the most undeveloped mind. But, on the other hand, there are decisive weaknesses attached to this idea in itself, which have been painfully felt since the beginning of history. That is, if this being is omnipotent then every occurrence, including every human action, every human thought, and every human feeling and aspiration is also His work; how is it possible to think of holding men responsible for their deeds and thoughts before such an almighty Being? In giving out punishment and rewards He would to a certain extent be passing judgment on Himself. How can this be combined with the goodness and righteousness ascribed to Him?

The main source of the present-day conflicts between the spheres of religion and of science lies in this concept of a personal God. It is the aim of science to establish general rules which determine the reciprocal connection of objects and events in time and space. For these rules, or laws of nature, absolutely general validity is required—not proven. It is mainly a program, and faith in the possibility of its accomplishment in principle is only founded on partial successes. But hardly anyone could be found who would deny these partial successes and ascribe them to human self-deception. The fact that on the basis of such laws we are able to predict the temporal behavior of phenomena in certain domains with great precision and certainty is deeply embedded in the consciousness of the modern man, even though he may have grasped very little of the contents of those laws. He need only consider that planetary courses within the solar system may be calculated in advance with great exactitude on the basis of a limited number of simple laws. In a similar way, though not with the same precision, it is possible to calculate in advance the mode of operation of an electric motor, a transmission system, or of a wireless apparatus, even when dealing with a novel development.

To be sure, when the number of factors coming into play in a phenomenological complex is too large scientific method in most cases fails us. One need only think of the weather, in which case prediction even for a few days ahead is impossible. Nevertheless no one doubts that we are confronted with a causal connection whose causal components are in the main known to us. Occurrences in this domain are beyond the reach of exact prediction because of the variety of factors in operation, not because of any lack of order in nature.

We have penetrated far less deeply into the regularities obtaining within the realm of living things, but deeply enough nevertheless to sense at least the rule of fixed necessity. One need only think of the systematic order in heredity, and in the effect of poisons, as for instance alcohol, on the behavior of organic beings. What is still lacking here is a grasp of connections of profound generality, but not a knowledge of order in itself.

The more a man is imbued with the ordered regularity of all events the firmer becomes his conviction that there is no room left by the side of this ordered regularity for causes of a different nature. For him neither the rule of human nor the rule of divine will exists as an independent cause of natural events. To be sure, the doctrine of a personal God interfering with natural events could never be *refuted,* in the real sense, by science, for this doctrine can always take refuge in those domains in which scientific knowledge has not yet been able to set foot.

But I am persuaded that such behavior on the part of the representatives of religion would not only be unworthy but also fatal. For a doctrine which is able to maintain itself not in clear light but only in the dark, will of necessity lose its effect on mankind, with incalculable harm to human progress. In their struggle for the ethical good, teachers of religion must have the stature to give up the doctrine of a personal God, that is, give up that source of fear and hope which in the past placed such vast power in the hands of priests. In their labors they will have to avail themselves of those forces which are capable of cultivating the Good, the True, and the Beautiful in humanity itself. This is, to be sure, a more difficult but an incomparably more worthy task.[1] After religious teachers accomplish the defining process indicated they will surely recognize with joy that true religion has been ennobled and made more profound by scientific knowledge.

If it is one of the goals of religion to liberate mankind as far as possible from the bondage of egocentric cravings, desires, and fears, scientific reasoning can aid religion in yet another sense. Although it is true that it is the goal of science to discover rules which permit the association and foretelling of facts, this is not its only aim. It also seeks to reduce the connections discovered to the smallest possible number of mutually independent conceptual elements. It is in this striving after the rational unification of the manifold that it encounters its greatest successes, even though it is precisely this attempt which causes it to run the greatest risk of falling a prey to illusions. But whoever has undergone the intense experience of successful advances made in this domain, is moved by profound reverence for the rationality made manifest in existence. By way of the understanding he achieves a far-reaching emancipation from the shackles of personal hopes and desires, and thereby attains that humble attitude of mind towards the grandeur of reason incarnate in existence, and which, in its profoundest depths, is inaccessible to man. This attitude, however, appears to me to be religious, in the highest sense of the word. And so it seems to me that science not only purifies the religious impulse of the dross of its anthropomorphism but also contributes to a religious spiritualization of our understanding of life.

The further the spiritual evolution of mankind advances, the more certain it seems to me that the path to genuine religiosity does not lie through the fear of life, and the fear of death, and blind faith, but through striving after rational knowledge. In this sense I believe that the priest must become a teacher if he wishes to do justice to his lofty educational mission.

---

[1] This thought is convincingly presented in Herbert Samuel's book, *Belief and Action.*

31

Rudolf Otto

"The Analysis of 'Mysterium'" from *The Idea of the Holy**

The Idea of the Holy, the book from which the last reading comes, is considered the classical description of what it is like to meet God or ultimate reality. The author, Rudolf Otto, was a German university professor whose views shaped all scholars of the world religions during the middle half of the twentieth century. In the selection, Otto explains the part of the experience of meeting God that brings home the otherness, the truly awesome holiness, of the force responsible for creation.

> *Ein begriffener Gott ist kein Gott.*
> 'A God comprehended is no God.' (TERSTEEGEN.)

We gave to the object to which the numinous consciousness is directed the name *mysterium tremendum,* and we then set ourselves first to determine the meaning of the adjective *tremendum*—which we found to be itself only justified by analogy—because it is more easily analysed than the substantive idea *mysterium*. We have now to turn to this, and try, as best we may, by hint and suggestion, to get to a clearer apprehension of what it implies.

4. *The 'Wholly Other'*

   It might be thought that the adjective itself gives an explanation of the substantive; but this is not so. It is not merely analytical; it is a synthetic attribute to it; i.e. *tremendum* adds something not necessarily inherent in *mysterium*. It is true that the reactions in consciousness that correspond to the one readily and spontaneously overflow into those that correspond to the other; in fact, anyone sensitive to the use of words would commonly feel that the idea of 'mystery' (*mysterium*) is so closely bound up with its synthetic qualifying attribute 'aweful' (*tremendum*) that one can hardly say the former without catching an echo of the latter, 'mystery' almost of itself becoming 'aweful mystery' to us. But the passage from the one idea to the other need not by any means be always so easy. The elements of meaning implied in 'awefulness' and 'mysteriousness' are in themselves definitely different. The latter may so far preponderate in the religious consciousness, may stand out so vividly, that in comparison with it the former almost sinks out of sight; a case which again

* Reprinted from *The Idea of the Holy* by Rudolf Otto, translated by John W. Harvey (2nd ed 1950) by permission of Oxford University Press.

could be clearly exemplified from some forms of mysticism. Occasionally, on the other hand, the reverse happens, and the *tremendum* may in turn occupy the mind without the *mysterium*.

This latter, then, needs special consideration on its own account. We need an expression for the mental reaction peculiar to it; and here, too, only one word seems appropriate, though, as it is strictly applicable only to a 'natural' state of mind, it has here meaning only by analogy: it is the word 'stupor'. *Stupor* is plainly a different thing from *tremor*; it signifies blank wonder, an astonishment that strikes us dumb, amazement absolute.[1] Taken, indeed, in its purely natural sense, *mysterium* would first mean merely a secret or a mystery in the sense of that which is alien to us, uncomprehended and unexplained; and so far *mysterium* is itself merely an ideogram, an analogical notion taken from the natural sphere, illustrating, but incapable of exhaustively rendering, our real meaning. Taken in the religious sense, that which is 'mysterious' is— to give it perhaps the most striking expression—the 'wholly other' (θατερον, *anyad, alienum*), that which is quite beyond the sphere of the usual, the intelligible, and the familiar, which therefore falls quite outside the limits of the 'canny', and is contrasted with it, filling the mind with blank wonder and astonishment.

This is already to be observed on the lowest and earliest level of the religion of primitive man, where the numinous consciousness is but an inchoate stirring of the feelings. What is really characteristic of this state is *not*—as the theory of Animism would have us believe—that men are here concerned with curious entities, called 'souls' or 'spirits', which happen to be invisible. Representations of spirits and similar conceptions are rather one and all early modes of 'rationalizing' a precedent experience, to which they are subsidiary. They are attempts in some way or other, it little matters how, to guess the riddle it propounds, and their effect is at the same time always to weaken and deaden the experience itself. They are the source from which springs, not religion, but the rationalization of religion, which often ends by constructing such a massive structure of theory and such a plausible fabric of interpretation, that the 'mystery' is frankly excluded.[2] Both imaginative 'myth', when developed into a system, and intellectualist Scholasticism, when worked out to its completion, are methods by which the fundamental fact of religious experience is, as it were, simply rolled out so thin and flat as to be finally eliminated altogether.

[1] Compare also *obstupefacere*. Still more exact equivalents are the Greek θαμβος and θαμβειν. The sound θ α μ β (*thamb*) excellently depticts this state of mind of blank, staring wonder. And the difference between the moments of *stupor* and *tremor* is very finely suggested by the passage, Mark x. 32 (cf. *infra*, p. 158). On the other hand, what was said above of the facility and rapidity with which the two moments merge and blend is also markedly true of θαμβος, which then becomes a classical term for the (ennobled) awe of the numinous in general. So Mark xvi. 5 is rightly translated by Luther 'und sie entsetzten sich', and by the English Authorized Version 'and they were affrighted'.

[2] A spirit or soul that has been conceived and comprehended no longer prompts to 'shuddering', as is proved by Spiritualism. But it thereby ceases to be of interest for the psychology of religion.

Even on the lowest level of religious development the essential characteristic is therefore to be sought elsewhere than in the appearance of 'spirit' representations. It lies rather, we repeat, in a peculiar 'moment' of consciousness, to wit, the *stupor* before something 'wholly other', whether such an other be named 'spirit' or 'daemon' or 'deva', or be left without any name. Nor does it make any difference in this respect whether, to interpret and preserve their apprehension of this 'other', men coin original imagery of their own or adapt imaginations drawn from the world of legend, the fabrications of fancy apart from and prior to any stirrings of daemonic dread.

In accordance with laws of which we shall have to speak again later, this feeling or consciousness of the 'wholly other' will attach itself to, or sometimes be indirectly aroused by means of, objects which are already puzzling upon the 'natural' plane, or are of a surprising or astounding character; such as extraordinary phenomena or astonishing occurrences or things in inanimate nature, in the animal world, or among men. But here once more we are dealing with a case of association between things specifically different—the 'numinous' and the 'natural' moments of consciousness—and not merely with the gradual enhancement of one of them—the 'natural'—till it becomes the other. As in the case of 'natural fear' and 'daemonic dread' already considered, so here the transition from natural to daemonic amazement is not a mere matter of degree. But it is only with the latter that the complementary expression *mysterium* perfectly harmonizes, as will be felt perhaps more clearly in the case of the adjectival form 'mysterious'. No one says, strictly and in earnest, of a piece of clockwork that is beyond his grasp, or of a science that he cannot understand: 'That is "mysterious" to me.'

It might be objected that the mysterious is something which is and remains absolutely and invariably beyond our understanding, whereas that which merely eludes our understanding for a time but is perfectly intelligible in principle should be called, not a 'mystery', but merely a 'problem'. But this is by no means an adequate account of the matter. The truly 'mysterious' object is beyond our apprehension and comprehension, not because our knowledge has certain irremovable limits, but because in it we come upon something inherently 'wholly other', whose kind and character are incommensurable with our own, and before which we therefore recoil in a wonder that strikes us chill and numb.[3]

This may be made still clearer by a consideration of that degraded offshoot and travesty of the genuine 'numinous' dread or awe, the fear of ghosts. Let us try to analyse this experience. We have already specified the peculiar

---

[3] In *Confessions*, ii. 9. I, Augustine very strikingly suggests this stiffening, benumbing element of the 'wholly other' and its contrast to the rational aspect of the numen; the *dissimile* and the *simile*:

'Quid est illud, quod interlucet mihi et percutit cor meum sine laesione? Et inhorresco et inardesco. *Inhorresco*, in quantum dissimilis ei sum. Inardesco, in quantum similis ei sum.'

('What is that which gleams through me and smites my heart without wounding it? I am both a-shudder and a-glow. A-shudder, in so far as I am unlike it, a-glow in so far as I am like it.')

feeling-element of 'dread' aroused by the ghost as that of 'grue', grisly hor-ror.[4] Now this 'grue' obviously contributes something to the attraction which ghost-stories exercise, in so far, namely, as the relaxation of tension ensuing upon our release from it relieves the mind in a pleasant and agreeable way. So far, however, it is not really the ghost itself that gives us pleasure, but the fact that we are rid of it. But obviously this is quite insufficient to explain the ensnaring attraction of the ghost-story. The ghost's real attraction rather con-sists in this, that of itself and in an uncommon degree it entices the imagina-tion, awakening strong interest and curiosity; it is the weird thing itself that allures the fancy. But it does this, not because it is 'something long and white' (as someone once defined a ghost), nor yet through any of the positive and conceptual attributes which fancies about ghosts have invented, but because it is a thing that 'doesn't really exist at all', the 'wholly other', something which has no place in our scheme of reality but belongs to an absolutely different one, and which at the same time arouses an irrepressible interest in the mind.

But that which is perceptibly true in the fear of ghosts, which is, after all, only a caricature of the genuine thing, is in a far stronger sense true of the 'daemonic' experience itself, of which the fear of ghosts is a mere off-shoot. And while, following this main line of development, this element in the numi-nous consciousness, the feeling of the 'wholly other', is heightened and clarified, its higher modes of manifestation come into being, which set the numinous object in contrast not only to everything wonted and familiar (i.e. in the end, to nature in general), thereby turning it into the 'supernatural', but finally to the world itself, and thereby exalt it to the 'supramundane', that which is above the whole world-order.

In mysticism we have in the 'beyond' ($\epsilon\pi\epsilon\kappa\epsilon\iota\nu\alpha$) again the strongest stressing and over-stressing of those non-rational elements which are already inherent in all religion. Mysticism continues to its extreme point this contrast-ing of the numinous object (the numen), as the 'wholly other', with ordinary experience. Not content with contrasting it with all that is of nature or this world, mysticism concludes by constrasting it with Being itself and all that 'is', and finally actually calls it 'that which is nothing'. By this 'nothing' is meant not only that of which nothing can be predicated, but that which is absolutely and intrinsically other than and opposite of everything that is and can be thought. But while exaggerating to the point of paradox this *negation* and contrast—the only means open to conceptual thought to apprehend the *mys-terium*—mysticism at the same time retains the *positive quality* of the 'wholly other' as a very living factor in its over-brimming religious emotion.

But what is true of the strange 'nothingness' of our mystics holds good equally of the *sūnyam* and the *sūnyatā*, the 'void' and 'emptiness' of the Buddhist mystics. This aspiration for the 'void' and for becoming void, no less than the aspiration of our western mystics for 'nothing' and for becoming nothing, must seem a kind of lunacy to anyone who has no inner sympathy for

[4] *gruseln, gräsen.*

the esoteric language and ideograms of mysticism, and lacks the matrix from which these come necessarily to birth. To such an one Buddhism itself will be simply a morbid sort of pessimism. But in fact the 'void' of the eastern, like the 'nothing' of the western, mystic is a numinous ideogram of the 'wholly other'.

These terms 'supernatural' and 'transcendent'[5] give the appearance of positive attributes, and, as applied to the mysterious, they appear to divest the *mysterium* of its originally negative meaning and to turn it into an affirmation. On the side of conceptual thought this is nothing more than appearance, for it is obvious that the two terms in question are merely negative and exclusive attributes with reference to 'nature' and the world or cosmos respectively. But on the side of the feeling-content it is otherwise; that *is* in very truth positive in the highest degree, though here too, as before, it cannot be rendered explicit in conceptual terms. It is through this positive feeling-content that the concepts of the 'transcendent' and 'supernatural' become forthwith designations for a unique 'wholly other' reality and quality, something of whose special character we can *feel*, without being able to give it clear conceptual expression.

---

[5] Literally, supramundane: *überweltlich.*

CONCLUSION

THE CHALLENGE OF RELIGION

We have seen the range of religion. The selection has been partial but sufficient to indicate how consistently throughout history—recorded and unrecorded—men and women have sought the sacred, the truly real, something they might worship. No aspect of traditional culture has stood apart from this search. The impetus to anchor the meaningfulness of the human venture in sacredness has reached into every nook and cranny. It has touched adolescents setting out to find their way through life. It has emerged in the desires of young people marrying. It has adorned the use of power, and the suffering of the weak. The elderly have hoped that their accumulation of experience might consecrate them in wisdom. The dying have hoped that they might find a good reception in a state beyond the ravages of time. And parents gazing on their newborn, humanity's way of defeating death, have prayed that this child would have a good life, a life rooted in genuine values, real sacredness.

People in Asia have reacted to the fragility and promise of human existence in ways like these, as have people in Africa. Traditional Europeans have created myths and rituals to shape their lives toward sacredness, and so have traditional Native Americans. Wherever one travels in studying religion, whatever the locale or epoch, one finds human beings sensing that their lives do not explain themselves and so have to be tied to something Other. The Other to whom Muslims have recurred is Allah. Traditional Chinese have recurred to the Tao or the Buddha. In India beloved deities such as Krishna and Devi have given the Other a congenial face. In Christian cultures Jesus, crucified yet risen, has been the sacred countenance. Jews have walked toward sacredness, secure meaning, by following the Torah. Buddhists have followed the Dharma. Even modern agnostics have shown the inevitability of religion, turning to it when their concerns about meaninglessness moved them to lash out at old, imperfect ways of construing the good life.

The challenge of religion is to face up to the equation between being fully human and searching for secure meaning and value. If one skims off their cream, the many different traditions agree in saying that one cannot be fully human apart from struggling to outwit finitude, ignorance, death, and evil.

Quixotic as such a struggle may be, it burns in every person willing to honor the hunger of the mind to know, the thirst of the heart to love. The more one knows, the more one realizes how much there is to know—how infinitely the universe stretches. The more one loves, the more one realizes how distant is a fully adequate, truly pure love—a love that would be everything one's heart desires. To be sure, there is a paradox in this pursuit of knowing and loving. At an unspecified yet definite point in the process one realizes that one has to stop striving to know, stop desiring to love. That is the point at which the task becomes unknowing, the call sounds to abandon one's ambitions.

The challenge of the religions changes, therefore. It does not keep singing the same note, keep traveling the same path. It may begin simply enough, straightforwardly enough, but as one matures it becomes paradoxical. What is truly living and what is truly dying start to exchange places. Buddha, giving up the royal life of the palace, steps out of death and begins to live. Lao Tzu, thinking about his isolation, thinks that everyone else is clear, he alone is cloudy. The prophet who stutters as a child becomes the most eloquent spokesperson for God. The man condemned as a criminal becomes the new Adam. Will we persevere when the paradoxes start to make their presence felt? Are we willing to lose our lives in order to gain them? What will we give in exchange for our souls, the selves we would like to be on Judgment Day? The religions challenge us with such questions.

Nor does religion end its challenges with paradox. Beyond paradox lies complete abnegation. The threshold between the illuminative phase, when we realize the privileged place of metaphor and the permanence of mystery, and the unitive phase, when we are like Confucius at seventy, so at one with the Way that we want nothing it does not command, is a dark night of the soul. There we have to lose even the securities of paradox. There all of our cleverness becomes nothing, all of our treasures become straw. Thomas Aquinas looked at the many volumes he had written and counted them all straw. Not only had he grown weary of human words, he had also emerged from the darkness and begun to enjoy the light. One glimpse of divinity unveiled, one taste of the divine love not diluted to human measure, and his earthly work was consummated.

These are mystical accents, but we could also cast the challenge of religion in mythological, ritualistic, doctrinal, ethical, and social terms. The mythological challenge is to find our own master story, our own narrative that stands up to the full range of human experience, making it not just bearable but beautiful. The ritualistic challenge is to find our own ceremonies so we can celebrate the pathos and splendor of children born of women as well as our ancestors did. Qoheleth (*Ecclesiastes*) says that there is a time to rejoice and a time to mourn. Traditional peoples knew how to sing joyful songs to the Lord, and they knew how to weep and keen. Do we do this well today? Have we created ceremonies, liturgies, that raise us up to the heavens in joy, or have we settled for fun? How should we read the evidence of our drug addiction, suicide, divorce, child abuse, depression? If we read it honestly, we may admit that traditional religion has much to teach us.

Traditional religion is far from perfect, of course, and if we read its evidence honestly we may also see that religion is different from the sacred, that traditions are not identical with God. The Muslim community (*ummah*) is different from Allah. The church is not the Father of Jesus Christ. There is no equality in the covenant between the Lord and Israel that does not come solely from the Lord. So to say that religion is a worthy challenger is not to say that religion has captured God. Zen Buddhists say that one may have to slay the Buddha so as not to make a hindrance of him. Taoists follow Lao Tzu in repeating that the Way that can be named is not the real Way. The sacred is mediated through very imperfect men, women, institutions, rituals, doctrines. Always one must look through and beyond the containers, toward the light and love that are never contained.

But this too is part of the challenge of religion. Only the callow let themselves off by blaming the church, or the synagogue, or their parents, or their clergy, or their teachers for their disillusionment with religion, or their lives, or their selves. The Bible says, in various ways, that we should not put our trust in princes. The religions know, in various ways, that the self is the most fragile reed. And through such saying, such knowing, the religions ask us to judge them severely but kindly, and to judge ourselves the same way.

Nobody knows, so nobody can pontificate. Everyone falls, fails, sins, so everyone needs forgiveness and should be able to grant it. The challenge of religion is to get below the money and banking, the kissing and telling, the boasting and being down in the dumps. Below all this stuff, material or psychic, something solid, worthy, astringent remains: owning up to the mysteriousness of our human condition, saying yes to the inevitability of our wanting and not getting, our failing and yet hearing a word of encouragement, a call never to give up. Saint Teresa said, "Let nothing disturb you." That is a great consolation, but it is also a great challenge. How can we let nothing disturb us? How can we become so unimportant in our own eyes, let go of so much pain and ego?

A great help is stressing the irony, the humor, the satire that runs through so much religious literature. Lao Tzu's rival for Taoist honors, Chuang Tzu, is a master at deflating pomposity. The Bible brims with shrewd realism, knowing how regularly people delude themselves. If we can hear these voices with good cheer, half the battle is won. We begin to laugh at ourselves and to pity all who suffer from foolishness. We begin to answer the challenge of religion, surrendering our pretense at self-sufficiency, asking the very darkness of the mystery to be our strength.

THE CONSOLATION OF RELIGION

Can the darkness of the mystery be our strength? The religions are unanimous in answering yes. They think that the darkness is really light too bright for us to see. They believe that help, God, is more intimate to us than we are to ourselves. The Hindu Upanishads say that whatever ultimate reality is, we are. The Buddhist philosophers say that all reality is intrinsically enlightened. For

Muslims, Allah is as near as the pulse at our throats. For Christian philosophers, we would not seek God if we had not already found God.

We begin, ignorantly, thinking that the problem is to prove the existence of God. The saints end by thinking that the problem is to explain the existence of the world. The world has no reason to be. At any moment it could fall back into nothingness. Only God or nirvana explains itself. So the wonder is where the world came from, why God chose to create.

The parallel to this wonder in the moral order is why God puts up with evil humanity. What makes the deity, the Tao, so patient? As they struggle with this question, the rabbis and mullahs, the monks and gurus, tend to glimpse a divine goodness. Only the ultimate can explain why it tolerates the limited, the disfigured. Only God can explain the divine mercy. Israel did not deserve the covenant. Only the swearing of the Lord, and his promising not to repent, kept the chosen people chosen. Nothing in human nature explained the obedience of Jesus, all the way to the cross. The foolishness of God is wiser than men. The love of God is more than that a nursing mother feels for her child. The great compassion that Buddhists find in their saints reflects the deepest secrets of the universe. The great humaneness that Confucians treasure reflects how the ancients decoded the world.

These may be mere opinions, sentiments, words—or they may be the highest wisdom. "Taste and see," the sages challenge us. Put the tradition to the test. If it does not sustain you, throw it on the dung heap. No genuine wisdom is afraid of being tested. Any gurus who have won their stripes rest their case on experience. Do you want to live superficially? That's easy. Masters of superficiality are a dime a dozen. Do you want to live deeply? That's hard. The sages do not accept candidates easily.

At many Zen monasteries, one had to knock at the door again and again to gain admittance. Only those who persevered were considered serious. There was no sense in wasting time on people who were not serious. It was hard enough to gain enlightenment when one was wholehearted. The western equivalent might be the biblical injunction not to throw pearls before swine. One of the hardest tasks of the churches has been to preach the gospel compassionately without diluting it. Is is better to err on the side of laxity and ease, or is the first obligation to keep faith with the cross?

The consolation in these questions is that they show how human even the holiest masters have been. Not even they, the people lifted to the heights, the paragons of virtue, could substitute for God. At their peak, they knew most clearly that they were only unprofitable servants. The more enlightened they became, the more dazzled they were by the light that they could not master. The light mastered them. The priority was always with God. If the light chose not to shine, or God chose not to be gracious, their venture would be a shambles.

Has the light shone? Can one still claim that the darkness has not comprehended it? Does grace still abound over sin? Is the Tao still moving the ten thousand things? One can think so if one accepts the humanity of the sages of the past and the reality of their contemporary successors. There are still mystics who claim to have been seared by God's love and whose lives make their claim credible. There are still rabbis who dance with the Torah and cry for joy at God's goodness. The wisdom of the Buddha, his enigmatic smile, endures in East Asia, lives still among Tibetan refugees. The Muslim mystical tradition, going back to the Persian poet Rumi, still identifies with the reed of God, mourning its separation from the riverbank, singing constantly for love.

The problems that living religious traditions arose to solve remain as pressing as they ever were. What might turn human beings from violence to peace? What is the way to true happiness? Is death the finale, and if so can life be meaningful? Why do the innocent children still suffer, even after Auschwitz? Why is so much of life boring, tedious, having to put up with fools and knaves? Should one hie off to a monastery, or is working with the poor the way? Is money a blessing from heaven, or the root of all evil? What keeps sex from becoming sordid? How can the sexes get along? On and on they go, the difficult questions. The only way not to go mad, it seems, is to disregard the mind, that the heart might make it stable.

The consolation of religion is an affair of the heart. Spontaneously, it seems, most peoples have considered the heart the best symbol of the whole person, body and soul, mind and emotion. A woman racked with sobs is heartbroken. A man who has lost heart can fight no more. Let not your hearts be troubled, Jesus said before he departed. I will give you a new heart, of flesh, the Lord told Israel through the prophet. We must feel compunction if we are to have a change of heart. Merely knowing the definition of compunction will not convert us. We have to love our God, our Way, with whole mind, heart, soul, and strength. And we can. Because other people have done it, it must be possible. Because the people who wrote the scriptures knew about purity of heart, it must have existed. As long as wisdom and consolation are possible, as long as they have existed, we can keep going. We don't have to reach our goal. It is enough to know it is possible.

So wisdom and consolation both boil down to keeping going. If we listen for the Way in the morning, we too may die in the evening content. If we praise brother sun and sister moon, the elements may send us off kindly. Like the smoke rising from the sacred pipe, we can send our spirits ahead. Right now the best of us can be there. And there we may find those who have gone ahead of us. There we may be bound to the mystery forevermore.